Contracts

Contracts

Problems, Cases and Materials

Walter W. Miller, Jr.
Professor of Law
Boston University School of Law

Carolina Academic Press
Durham, North Carolina

ISBN 0-89089-842-1
LCCN 99-65647

Carolina Academic Press
700 Kent Street
Durham, North Carolina 27701
Telephone (919) 489-7486
Fax (919) 493-5668
E-mail: cap@cap-press.com
www.cap-press.com

Printed in the United States of America.

For Anne

Contents

Table of Cases

Preface

No one writes a book alone. Among those who helped me with it are David Goodearl J.D. '00, Barbara Van Gorder J.D. '98, Raisha Vaidya J.D. '98, and Mark Weiss J.D. '98 L.L.M. '99. I am very grateful to them. Thanks also to my secretaries, Ken Westhassel and Nick Stenzel.

Most first year books in law school are casebooks. Cases, in law school unlike business school, really mean court opinions. Thus, most books are made up almost exclusively of the opinions of judges deciding controversies brought before them. This book is different. It combines cases with problems and its purpose is not only to have you read and learn from cases, but also to use cases to solve problems which are made part of your study.

This book is intended exclusively for a one term course. It is my belief that no book can be designed for both a one and two term course. Of necessity the amount of material that can be covered in one term is less. Therefore, either much of the material in a two term course book is superfluous to begin with or as is more likely is important to developing a theme but must be dropped when the course is one term.

The value of a book designed as a one term book is that material is balanced so that nothing need be cut out. The course instructor need not make the hard calls of what to skip and what to keep or, where the writer provides such a guide, follow the recommendation of someone else of what is important and what is less important. The book itself is designed for a one semester course.

Thirty years teaching contracts has convinced me that there is nothing very mysterious about it. Like most good law it is 90% or more common sense. It grew out of people making agreements so that they could rely on someone doing something in the future. The law grew up to fulfill the expectations of the people agreeing. While some areas are complex, none are so deep, or dense or intricate as to be incomprehensible. It is the intent of this book to smooth the path of the law and make it if not a broad highway to understanding at least a passable way to knowledge so that after a semester the student who is diligent will have a solid, basic comprehension of a most vital area of the law—Contracts.

Introduction

This book is made up of six parts. Each part is designed to be covered in approximately two weeks. The first part may take somewhat longer, perhaps an extra week. The intent of the structure is that the instructor will finish the material in twelve to thirteen weeks allowing a final week for review. Depending on available time, more time may obviously be spent on particular areas as the course progresses.

The first part concerns what a contract is and what the word, contract, means. It also distinguishes between contracts that are enforceable and agreements or promises that are not. The second part discusses the manner of offer and acceptance as the primary way in which contractual liability is assumed. The third section concerns itself with interpreting the contract. How do we determine what terms should be in the contract and how do we know what those terms mean. The fourth section concerns conditions. The word condition is used in two senses. First, it refers to an event which has the effect of bringing the contract into existence. Second, it refers to an event which determines the obligation of a party to perform a duty created by the contract. The fifth section is concerned with escaping liability. Assuming someone has entered a contract, what are the grounds for escaping liability under it. The sixth section covers third parties. Two people can make a contract for the benefit of a third person. Furthermore, one or both of the two people who made the contract and, if it is made for the benefit of a third person, the third person can assign his/her rights and/or obligations to someone else. This final part is a crucial area of contracts, so much so that at the January 1997 Association of American Law Schools (AALS) conference, the section on Contracts was devoted solely to third party rights.

No single part of the book is devoted to remedies. The author believes a remedial stance is necessary in the development of any course (on the grounds that it is pointless to be right or have a right if you don't have a remedy; or as the Chief Justice of a state Supreme Court once put it to me: "It's not whose right or wrong; its who can prove his/her case.") Nevertheless, in a one semester course, an entire section devoted to remedy is a luxury which must be passed by. Instead, remedies will be interspersed in text and in both note and paraphrased cases. Also remedies questions will not always be excised from principal cases being used to illustrate other points.

Each part of the book contains problems, cases, questions. Cases should be read for their own value and also used to solve problems. Each part, therefore, and often some sub parts begin with problems. Read the problem, then the cases and text following it, and attempt to solve it. As you progress in the book, problems will depend for their solution not only on the material following them but also on cases and text preceding them.

Consider the book an introduction to a field which will be of vital importance throughout your law school careers and your practice. An understanding of many fields of law depends on an understanding of Contracts. Similarly, many fields have developed from Contracts and draw their governing principles from it. For example, the field of Negotiable Instruments (checks, promissory notes, drafts) depends on Contract law. When you write a check it is a three party instrument. You have a contract with your bank which says that it will pay checks drawn on that bank if you have money in your account to cover them. When you write a check to someone's order and give it to her, you are making a contract with her (the payee) that if your bank doesn't pay it, you will. The first contract is created when you open your account with the bank and sign the forms they slide across the desk to you — signature sample etc. The second one is created by force of law without your having any necessary intention to create it; the Negotiable Instruments Law of the Uniform Commercial Code (U.C.C.) section 3-413 or 3-414, depending on which version of Article 3 of the U.C.C. you consult, creates the liability. The U.C.C. was revised only a few years ago and not all states have the same version. However, you may look it up in the library in your state's version of the U.C.C. Another related field is domestic relations — marriage contracts and divorce agreements are common today. Corporate law depends on contract: the By-laws and Articles of Incorporation of a corporation are the contract among the creators of the corporation and between the creators and the state where the corporation is incorporated. A constitution for the founding of a nation or even a private society is a contract — see Locke's *Social Contract* or Hobbes' *Leviathan*. The Bible refers to the covenants (contracts) made between God and His people. Western Civilization depends on Contract for its survival. It is the way in which people depend on one another to do things that they would not ordinarily be required to do.

As you work your way through the book, read the text, problems and cases *not* as something to be memorized and given back to the professor at the end of the course. It is not enough to glean the principles and rules of law from the text, problems and cases and repeat those at term's end. Rather, read to learn the underlying principles of the law and how those principles are developed and expressed in particular rules of law and most importantly how to apply them. Thus, the text introduces you to particular ideas — principles, rules.

The problem gives you a fact pattern much as you will get in practice. The cases show you how issues, controversies (problems) similar to that in the problem you are working on were solved. Learn how the cases develop and apply principles and rules and then apply them to the problem or problems given to you in the book. In short — don't memorize what you read, analyze it. That is, take it apart. Don't just learn what happened — which you don't need to remember — learn how and why it happened. The how and why give you the rules and principles of the law. Then apply what you learned to the problems.

How do you "brief" cases? Remember — you are reading cases to learn the basics of law which you will then apply to other situations. You are also reading cases so that you can participate in class discussions about them. Therefore, you brief them; you make outlines to which you can refer to quickly refresh your recollection of what was in them and why they are important. How do you brief a case?

- **Facts** — these are the essential facts of the case; the story line; what happened.

- **Issue** — this is the basic question or questions which the court is trying to answer and is *the* most important thing to spot.

- **Decision** — what did the court do? Did it reverse a lower court? Did it reverse the lower court and send the case back for another trial on all the issues or on just some of the issues? In other words did the lower court decide the case correctly on all but one or two issues or must it all be tried over again?

- **Holding**—the legal result the court reaches by applying rules and principles of law to the facts of the case. A holding may be stated as "We hold for the defendant because the Statute of Frauds requires a writing in this case and there was none."
- **Rationale**—Why the court reached the result it did. This is second in importance to the issue only because the reasons are meaningless if you do not know what it is the court is trying to resolve.

Notice how the parts interact. Facts—What happened? From the facts arises the issue—What are we trying to decide? In deciding the issue the court applies rules of law to the facts and comes up with a Decision—what to do with this case. The Holding—the legal rule of law, the summary statement of the result of applying rules to facts. Rationale—why did the court apply certain rules and principles to the facts and in applying them why did they result in a particular decision and holding.

In addition to briefing cases, you should look up any unclear terms or words in a reference book, like Black's Law Dictionary. Like any foreign language, the only way to truly understand the concepts of Contracts (and any other topic of law) is to understand the language. As a starting point you should know that a promis*or* is one who makes a promise; a promis*ee* is one to whom it is made. An oblig*or* owes an obligation to someone; an oblig*ee* is someone to whom it is owed. An offer*or* is someone who makes an offer to someone else; and offer*ee* is the one to whom the offer is made.

Once you have done all of the above you are ready to participate in class discussions. Many second and third years and even some 1Ls during their second term do not brief cases. It is hard work and it often seems easier to just remember what happened or pull a brief out of some cram book that has outlined it for you. If you do this, you are impairing your education right at the start. The real key to lawyering is not genius but sweat. Genius helps but it is useless if not trained. If you brief at the start, if you force yourself to summarize and condense and organize what a court is doing and saying and learn for yourself why the court has reached the conclusion it has, then as your careers develop your eye will move quickly not only through cases but through treatises, text discussions, computer read-outs and print-outs. Applying the law to new situations will become second nature if you take the time in the first months of your careers to do the hard work of learning how lawyers reason their way to conclusions.

The final step is to take the ideas, the rules, the principles you have gleaned from the cases and use them to solve problems. There often is no easy answer or sure answer. You read what courts have done in similar situations and why they have done it and then attempt to answer a problem someone brings to you. The better you do your job the easier it will be to predict the probable outcome and the better counselor you will be and become.

Many students like to outline the course as they go along. Some wait until the end. Some never outline. Some students work in groups. Some work alone. These are personal preferences. But whatever you do—work! The first rule in the lawyer's canon of ethics is the duty to be prepared. That is true here also. Prepare. Also be Present in class. Finally, Participate in class discussions. Ask questions—in class, after class—from your professor, from your friends. Take an active part. It's your education and your life.

Contracts

Part I

Intent to Be Bound

Introduction

What is a contract? There are many definitions. Black's Law Dictionary defines it as "A promissory agreement between two or more persons that creates, modifies, or destroys a legal relation." It also defines it as "An agreement upon sufficient consideration to do or not to do a particular thing." The Restatement of Contracts 2nd, defines it as follows: "A contract is a promise or set of promises for the breach of which the law gives a remedy, or the performance of which the law in some way recognizes as a duty." The Uniform Commercial Code [U.C.C.] in section 1-201(11) states: " 'Contract' means the total legal obligation which results from the parties' agreement as affected by this Act and any other applicable rules of law." Section 1-201(3) defines "agreement" as: "the bargain of the parties in fact as found in their language or by implication from other circumstances including course of dealing or usage of trade or course of performance as provided in this Act (Sections 1-205, 2-208, and 2-207). Whether an agreement has legal consequences is determined by the provisions of this Act, if applicable; otherwise by the law of contracts (Section 1-103)." The U.C.C. is law in 49 states but covers only limited transactions. The contract defined in 1-201 refers to contracts for the sale of goods and some intangibles, and to contracts for security interests in goods and some intangibles. It does not, for example, cover contracts for the sale of real property or for personal services including such complex services as constructing buildings or performing brain surgery. Black's and the Restatement have no force of law at all except where their definitions are adopted by the courts as a statement of their rule of law. The Restatement has grown increasingly popular with courts in recent decades.

Notice that in all of the definitions the future is important. Black's and the Restatement refer to "promise," a key element in contract, and not just any promise but one that gives rise to a legal relation, one for whose breach the law gives a remedy. This element of the future is key also in the U.C.C. because "bargain" refers to the future. One person bargains with another; one of them agrees to do something in the future in exchange for the other person either doing something now or agreeing to also do something in the future. In a sense Contract is the effort to control the future, to be able to rely on other people doing something in the future. In this way, Contract is essential for advancement of business, personal and professional relationships. If it were impossible to rely on what people say, then soon all commerce and relationships would deteriorate to the most primitive and immediate results. Contract, therefore, is a promise or series of promises binding on a person and requiring some action (or some refraining from action) at a future time.

Not all promises are binding. Not all promises lead to contracts. Not all promises lead to a remedy at law. The test the law implies, to determine whether or not a promise is binding, whether or not it is a contract, whether or not it is part of a contract, and as a result may lead to an action at law for a remedy if it is broken, is intent. Did the person who made the statement intend to be bound to it. Was it really a promise or just an assurance. A physician says to a patient prior to an operation: "Don't worry. You'll be just fine." The patient, despite the doctor's best efforts, dies or ends up more seriously ill or debilitated than before the surgery. Has the doctor made a contract which the law should enforce or is he/she just trying to calm the patient. A used car salesman says: "That's the best car you'll ever buy." Is that a promise? Should the buyer be able to sue the seller if it's not the "best" car he or she will ever buy? An employer, asked by his employee who supervises traveling sales personnel whether he has a job for the next year, only says to the employee: "I am busy right now. Get your people out on the road. You'll be O.K." Did he make a promise of a job to the employee? Did he intend to? Will the law find an intent? Thus, step one is intent. What did the person saying the words intend? Intent is not always easy to find. Furthermore what a person seems to intend may be more important than what he or she actually intended. Beyond this, not all promises that a person actually or seemingly intends will necessarily be enforced. The law puts limits on what promises it will require a person to live by.

Thus, the definitions in Black's, the Restatement and the U.C.C. gradually come into focus. A contract is a promissory agreement that creates a legal relation. In other words some promissory agreements will not lead to "legal" relationships and hence will not have legal consequences. The U.C.C. distinguishes between "agreement" and "contract" for just this reason. A "contract" is the legal obligation that arises out of the agreement which is the bargain. Presumably, not every agreement leads to a legal obligation. The Restatement speaks of promises, the breach of which results in a legal remedy or performance of which satisfies a legal duty. Legal remedies result from a failure to perform (breach) a legal duty. (This statement of duty and breach are two sides of the same coin. If you have a legal duty to perform a promise, failing to do so results in breach which can lead to a legal remedy). All of these definitions imply that not all promises have to be kept. Breaking some leads to no results at all. Breaking others leads to a remedy which the law will enforce.

Not every promise made with intent that it be kept results in a legal relationship with legal consequences. In addition to asking if a promise was intended, the law also inquires as to whether one of three basic tests for enforceability has been met. The oldest test, which is no longer in effect in all jurisdictions, is the seal. If a person writes down a promise and seals it, then the law will enforce it. Thus, if I say to someone "I'll give you title to and possession of my Contracts book next Monday" or even if I write this down, and in both cases intend this as a promise, I probably cannot be sued by the person to whom I said it or for whom I wrote it. But in some jurisdictions, if I write this down and sign and seal it, I can be held liable for this promise. I have created a legal liability for myself.

The second and most important test is what is called consideration. Did I bargain with someone for some benefit in exchange for what I was turning over to him. If I said, "I promise to give you title to and possession of my Contracts book next Monday if you promise to pay me $25 for it" and you say "O.K." then because you have promised me a benefit which I sought in exchange for my book, I have entered a legal relation with you and am liable to you if I do not deliver the book to you on Monday. The third way to create legal liability is fairly new to the law and not yet in much use. This is promissory estoppel. If I promise you my book and the promise is neither under seal nor part of a bargain, if you reasonably rely on my promise and suffer some loss because of that reliance, I may be liable to you for your loss.

Thus, one looks for intent to be bound by a promise. That is step one. If intent is there, then the next step is to find one of the formal requirements for enforcement — seal, consideration or reliance. If one is found, then a legal relationship has developed. Put another way, the person breaking such a promise can be sued for the breach.

What then is the remedy for breaking a contract? Only rarely will a court order the breaching party to perform his promise. If a court does so order and the party still refuses to perform it, the court may put the breaching party in jail until he does. But this is rare. More than likely the injured party — the one not breaking the contract — will have to sue the breaching party for damages, i.e. money, a sum of money which will be the equivalent to the performance the injured party would have received from the breaching party if he had not breached. This is called the injured party's expectancy interest — what he expected to get out of the contract. Of course, the injured party expected to obtain the breaching party's promised performance not money. But in theory of law the injured party can take and use the money to obtain an equivalent performance from someone else. This expectancy interest is available for promises under seal and those supported by consideration. In most jurisdictions, if a promisor breaches a promise supported only by reliance, then the remedy is not expectancy but reliance damages. Reliance is not measured by what the injured party hoped to get out of the contract, his expectancy, but rather by what he or she spent "out of pocket" in reliance on the promise. For example if I promised to sell you my Contracts book for $25 and you promised to pay $25 for it and I broke my promise, you would get expectancy. If a similar book available at all times at the book store would cost you $40, and if I could foresee that you would have to pay $15 more for the book, you would receive $15 damages. In theory, you could then take the $25 you planned to pay me plus the $15 and buy the other book. If, however, you had not made a promise to me to buy the book but had reasonably relied on my promise to sell it to you for $25 and I sold it to someone else, you would not have a right to $15 damages. You would only have a right to any money you spent in reliance on the promise or any loss you suffered in reliance on it. Because the books were always available at the bookstore you suffered no loss relying on my promise. But what if someone else had offered to sell you a book for $30 and you turned him down because you relied on my promise and planned to buy my book for $25. How much would your loss be in this case?

Before there is a remedy, however, there must be a breach of a promise the performance of which was a legal duty. To determine whether such a promise exists, we must first look to intent. That is the subject of our next section.

Read through the following problem. Ask yourself what you would look for or want to find if you were representing the movie studio or actor. Do not try to resolve the issues now but keep them in the back of your mind until you finish working on Part I of these materials. Then try to work it out. In the meantime re-read it as you are going through the Part I materials.

Problem to Part I

Alex Hunter is a prominent movie star. He appears often in "action" type films. For most of his films he has contracted only after consulting with his agent, Ms. Holly Smart. Ms. Smart sets the terms with a studio representative, they put them in a writing which is then signed by Hunter and a studio representative. Occasionally Hunter discusses a possible role in a film with the proposed movie's director or producer and agrees to do it, leaving it to Smart to work out details later.

When he was a young unknown actor, with only a few successful roles to his credit, he agreed to do a role in a war film, "Company," which later won an academy award. At the time he agreed, he was unemployed and was standing on a studio set where he was watching the film being made. The producer walked up to him and said "Hunter, I want you to be Captain Swift (a leading role)." Hunter said "O.K." Smart and the studio making the film later agreed on specific terms, such as Hunter's fee, the time it would be made etc. and Hunter and the studio signed a writing reflecting these terms. Hunter went on to win an academy award for his role.

On several later occasions during the last 10 years Hunter would say to a producer or director "I'd like that role." The producer or director, if he wanted Hunter, would say "O.K. I'll call Holly and work out the details." Most often Smart finds a proposed film that she thinks would have a good role for Hunter, reads the script, and recommends it to Hunter. If he agrees that it is a role he wants, Smart then works out all the details with the producer or director if the producer or director wants Hunter. Usually, Hunter (though sometimes Smart acting for Hunter) then signs a writing with the studio reflecting these terms. Sometimes there is no writing.

Last spring at a studio party both Hunter and the producer to whom he spoke agreed that Hunter said to the producer, "I hear you're going to be making a Vietnam war film based on Billy Jones' book 'Never-ending Apocalypse.'" The producer said, "You're right." After some small talk about the book, the producer then said, "I've been thinking that you're just the man for the role of Captain Lee Peters."

Peters, in the book, is an American pilot who was captured by the North Vietnamese Army when his plane was shot down and who after his release, suffered and came through severe post-traumatic-stress-syndrome to become a successful test pilot for a large American aircraft manufacturer. The book is about equally divided into three parts—Peters' career as a fighter-bomber pilot, his captivity when he questions United States policy but refuses to cooperate with the North Vietnamese Army captors who want him to make anti-war statements on film, and his problems with and conquest of post-traumatic-stress-syndrome to live a heroic life as a test pilot. At the end of the book, Peters dies in a fiery crash because he stayed with a malfunctioning plane in order to give his observer in the plane time to parachute to safety.

According to Hunter, the following conversation occurred. Hunter said: "It sounds like a great role. Do you have a script yet?" The producer answered, "No, but we plan to follow the book. We'll pay you what we did on the last film you did for us and we'll give you script approval and approval on who directs it." Hunter then said, "How about Phil Jones, or maybe Frank Topola for director? I've worked with both of them and I like them." The producer then said. "I've already talked with Phil and he said he wants you for the role." Hunter then said, "O.K. Send the script over to Holly as soon as you have it and if she OKs it it's a deal."

According to the producer, after he told Hunter that he wanted Hunter for the film, Hunter said, "I'd like to do it. Is there a lot of action in it?" The producer then said, We're focusing more on Peters' post war problems but we're going to work the action sequences in to explain them. We'll be following the general plan or sequence of the book" Hunter then said: "What about pay, script and director?" The producer said, "It's going to be a big budget film and we want to start soon. We don't have a script yet but I've talked to Phil Jones and he thinks you're great for the role." Hunter then said, "O.K. I'll do it. Pay me what you did for the last film and get the script over as soon as possible." The producer said, "We can count on you? We've got to start promotion early on this one." Hunter said, "It's a deal."

Both Hunter and the producer agree that last week the producer sent the script to Smart. Smart read it and told Hunter that it was not for him. Peters was depicted as a burned out case, a tragic figure who failed to cope with, let alone conquer, his post-traumatic-stress-syndrome, and whose death resulted from that failure.

They both further agree that Hunter called the producer on the telephone and said: "I'm not doing 'Never-ending Apocalypse.' It's not my kind of film." The producer said, "Wait a minute. We've got a contract. All the promotions start in a few weeks. Everyone else is lined up. We start shooting within a month. There's a lot of money tied up in this." Hunter and the producer discussed the script. Hunter maintained that it was not the story in the book. The producer said that it generally followed the book, had action sequences and generally emphasized Peters' post Vietnam War problems. Hunter pointed out that Peters was a very different character in the book from that in the script. Hunter asked if a director had been hired. The producer said Francis Crimins. Hunter said, "I'm supposed to have a first refusal on any film I make." The producer said, "Look. We agreed last spring that you'd do the film." Hunter said, "There's no contract and there's not going to be one," and hung up.

Further conversations proved useless and the studio which the producer represented sued Hunter for damages for breach of contract and in the alternative for damages based on promissory estoppel. Hunter responded through his lawyers that there never was a contract nor was there any breach of a promise by him on which the producer or the studio could have reasonable relied.

Assume that the above problem was given to you as a new associate in a law firm. Read it carefully. Then read the cases, text and other problems in Part I. As you go through the materials in each of the sections in Part I discover if you can answer the questions below. As you answer the questions, be sure to identify what facts in the problem are relevant to each of the questions.

- Based first on Hunter's version and then on the producer's version of the conversations between them, do you think there is a contract?
- Is there a promise, even if not embodied in a bargain, whose enforceability Hunter should be estopped to deny because of the studio's reliance on it?
- Does it matter that there is no writing?
- If there is an enforceable promise, what would be the studio's remedy?

A. How Do We Know that Someone Intends to Be Bound?

The law looks to words and circumstances to determine intent. The setting is often as important as the sentences; the way something is said or done as much as what it is that is said or done.

Intent to be bound to an obligation or promise is not always easy to find. In the first case a person went to a physician for surgery on a finger. The patient needed the surgery for both cosmetic and practical reasons. Because of an earlier injury the finger was stiff and in the words of the court "had a slight deformity on the distal tip." The court found that the injury did not hinder the plaintiff in her schooling as a court reporter. Three months after the initial consultation, the doctor agreed to perform surgery and did so. After the surgery, plaintiff went to a physical therapist recommended by the doctor. In the course of the therapy the therapist fractured the finger. The patient then went back to the doctor who treated the finger and recommended further therapy after the fracture had healed. Plaintiff did not seek further therapy. The finger became stiff and in the words of the opinion "was not very useful." Plaintiff sued the doctor for negligence in applying a cast to her finger after surgery, negligent referral of a physical therapist, and breach of an express contract to heal her finger. The doctor was granted summary judgment on all three counts by the trial court. The plaintiff appealed only the granting of summary judgment in the express contract portion of the action. [Normally trials conclude with a verdict, either from the jury or by the judge if the jury has been waived. However, judges are empowered to dismiss a particular claim (or claims) of an ongoing case through granting a motion of summary judgment. Judges only grant summary judgment when no dispute of material fact exists. The rational behind summary judgment is efficiency. If there is no disputed material fact, then there is no reason for the case to be in court.]

Note: All the cases and footnotes have been edited. If you wish to read the full version, locate the relevant volume and page in the library using the citation with the case.

Van Zee, v. Witzke

445 N.W.2d 34

Supreme Court of South Dakota., 1989.

MORGAN, Justice.

As a result of complications after surgery on one of her fingers, Sylvia Van Zee (Van Zee) brought negligence and breach of contract actions against Dr. D.J. Witzke (Dr. Witzke). Summary judgment was entered in favor of Dr. Witzke on all of Van Zee's claims. Van Zee appeals only the adverse summary judgment on her breach of contract cause of action. We affirm.

ISSUE

DID THE TRIAL COURT PROPERLY GRANT SUMMARY JUDGMENT FOR DR. WITZKE ON VAN ZEE'S CLAIM FOR BREACH OF AN EXPRESS CONTRACT TO HEAL?

DECISION

The standard of review of the grant or denial of a summary judgment is well established: In reviewing a grant or a denial of summary judgment, we must determine whether the moving party demonstrated the absence of any genuine issue of material fact and showed entitlement to judgment on the merits as a matter of law. The evidence must be viewed most favorably to the nonmoving party and reasonable doubts should be resolved against the moving party. The nonmoving party, however, must present specific facts showing that a genuine, material issue for trial exists. Our task on appeal is to determine only whether a genuine issue of material fact exists and whether the law was correctly applied. If there exists any basis which supports the ruling of the trial court, affirmance of a summary judgment is proper.

Van Zee argues that the trial court erred in granting Dr. Witzke summary judgment because a genuine issue of material fact is present concerning the existence of an express contract to heal her finger. We disagree.

A physician or surgeon normally undertakes only to exercise the skill and care common to the profession. However, a doctor may, although he seldom does, contract to cure a patient, or to accomplish a particular result, in which case the doctor may be liable for breach of contract when he does not succeed. In the absence of such an express agreement, the doctor does not warrant or insure either a correct diagnosis or a successful course of treatment, and the doctor will not be liable for an honest mistake of judgment, where the proper course is open to reasonable doubt. W. Prosser & W. Keeton, The Law of Torts§ 32 (5th ed. 1984) (footnotes omitted).

"The existence of a valid express contract is a question of law to be determined by a court, not a jury." Mid-America Marketing Corp. v. Dakota, Etc., 289 N.W.2d 797, 799 (S.D.1980). In determining whether a physician has entered into an express contract to heal, courts have been careful to distinguish between a doctor's promise of a particular result from mere generalized statements that the result of the treatment will be good. As the Supreme Court of Michigan observed long ago: A doctor and his patient, of course, have the same general liberty to contract with respect to their relationship as other parties entering into [a] consensual relationship with one another, and a breach thereof will give rise to a cause of action. It is proper to note, with respect to the contracts of physicians, that certain qualitative differences should be observed, since the doctor's therapeutic reassurance that his patient will be all right, not to worry, must not be converted into a binding promise by the disappointed or quarrelsome.

In this instance, Dr. Witzke's office notes indicated that he discussed all of the risks, alternatives and imponderables of surgery with Van Zee. During his deposition he explained that this included an increased risk of infection and delayed healing due to previous scarring, free tendon grafts, highly motivated post-operative physical therapy and the possibility of a useless or lost finger. According to Van Zee, Dr. Witzke, "never said there were any risks."

Dr. Witzke testified that he told Van Zee during her initial consultation that he would only consider doing the surgery if she felt that the functional disability was so great that she could not continue court reporting school. Van Zee testified that she delayed having surgery after the initial consultation in order to arrange financing for the operation. Van Zee's mother, who ultimately financed the surgery, was opposed to the operation and wanted Van Zee to obtain a guarantee from the doctor that the finger would be all right. Van Zee herself testified that she told her mother that no doctor would do that. Nevertheless, Van Zee stated that she did ask Dr. Witzke for a guarantee. According to Van Zee, Dr. Witzke, "took my hand and he looked at it and he said I can tell you right now no matter what it won't be any worse than it is right now," and assured her that, "there would be no problem at all." According to Dr. Witzke, he told her, "[t]here are no absolute guarantees."

Viewing the claimed statements as detailed by Van Zee in a light most favorable to her, we agree that they fail the clear proof of an express contract upon which to ground liability. Van Zee's sole proof of any express agreement by Dr. Witzke to heal her finger is limited to the statement made by him in response to her request for a guarantee. In Karriman v. Orthopedic Clinic, 516 P.2d 534 (Okla.1973), the Supreme Court of Oklahoma reviewed a back patient's suit against his orthopedic surgeons for breach of an express guarantee to heal. As in this case, the guarantee was premised on statements by one of the surgeons that the patient would not be, and could not possibly be, worse off after surgery. The Oklahoma high court found the evidence insufficient to show that a special contract of warranty was entered into between the patient and the doctors.

We are in accord with the conclusion of the Oklahoma court and find Dr. Witzke's statement that Van Zee's finger would not be worse off after surgery insufficient as a matter of law to constitute an express contract to heal the finger. The statement falls into the category of statements constituting mere therapeutic reassurances of a good result. Accordingly, we find no error by the trial court in granting Dr. Witzke summary judgment on Van Zee's cause of action for breach of an express contract to heal.

Affirmed.

[Note: Questions of fact and law pervade most cases. It is essential early on to identify them. Later on you will learn that the interpretation of the meaning of a contract as well its very existence is most often a question of law.]

Questions

1. The court said that their task was to discover whether a "genuine issue of material fact exists and whether the law was correctly applied?" What might have been an issue of material fact that the plaintiff thought should have been tried to a jury?"

2. What did the court conclude about the existence of a "genuine issue of material fact?" Why?

3. If the existence of a valid express contract is a question of law to be decided by the court, what is there for a jury to decide?

4. What did the doctor agree to do, if not to cure the patient? Where do you find this in the opinion?

Hawkins v. McGee, 84 N.H. 14, 146 A. 641 (New Hampshire, 1929). Plaintiff's hand had suffered a severe burn. The doctor operated to graft skin from plaintiff's chest to the hand. The doctor disputed making any contract with the plaintiff to cure the hand. There was evidence that the doctor in response to a question about how long plaintiff would be in the hospital said, "Three or four days, not over four." The doctor added that the plaintiff would be able to "go back to work with a good hand" a few days after going home. The doctor also was alleged to have said prior to Hawkins agreeing to the operation, "I will guarantee to make the hand a hundred per cent perfect or a one hundred per cent perfect hand." Defendant argued that there was no question of fact to be decided by the jury because even if the doctor said both things, "no reasonable man would understand that they were used with the intention of entering 'into any contractual relation whatever.'" The court found the first statement not indicative of any intent to be bound to a promise but the latter if spoken could lead to liability. The court also found that the doctor solicited plaintiff for the operation because he wanted experience in skin grafting.

What is the difference between the *Van Zee* and *Hawkins* cases? Why did Hawkins win and Van Zee not only lose but never get a chance to go to a jury? Why did the court treat the two statements differently? If the doctor couldn't be held legally liable for his statement about three or four days, what was he doing when he said it? Lying? Why would the reluctance of Hawkins to be operated on and the doctor's solicitation be relevant to determine whether the words of guarantee meant the doctor intended to be bound to a contractual obligation? Once again, if the words don't lead to legal liability, what was the doctor doing?

Note on Language

When a child falls down on the sidewalk and starts to cry, mother or dad almost always says something like: "Be a big girl (or boy.) Big boys (or girls) don't cry. Here, let me look at it. Where does it hurt?" Parent looks at skinned knee or elbow. "That'll be fine. Don't cry. How would you like an ice cream cone?" Why don't the words "That'll be fine" lead to a binding promise, on which might be based contractual liability. How are these words similar to "You'll be out of the hospital in three or four days" or "There won't be any problem at all." Do you think the child believes the parent? Does the patient believe the doctor? What about the used car dealer who says: "You won't find a better deal anywhere" or

"I give you my word, we have the best deals" or "I promise you, you won't do better than Slick Sam's deal"? Could any of these be the basis of a suit? Is there a difference between a patient, a child, a used car dealer? Are there any differences in the words used and the circumstances under which they are used? The examples are endless. What about the politician who says: "I promise to lower taxes" or as one said "Read my lips; no new taxes." How many promises for social justice, better schools, health care reform, stopping crime, improving schools etc. have you heard in your lifetime? the past decade? the past year? How many have you believed? Is there an "intent to be bound" here by the parent, the politician, the used car dealer, the doctor? What is the intent of these "promises?" What is being promised?

As we go through the cases and problems, you will discover many grounds for not enforcing promises and many more for enforcing them. Right now we focus on intent. How do language and circumstances help us to find the intent to be bound?

Note on Enforceability

What good is a promise if it can't be enforced? Sometimes enforceability is a test used to determine if a contractual promise, an intent to be bound, exists. It is not a good test because enforceability and contractual liability are two different concepts. But they are related. Assume that Drs. Witzke and McGee are both liable; that is, they both made promises that the courts found were made with an intent to be legally bound. What would the law require either defendant to do? The answer at English common law and in American Law is: Pay money. Both doctors would be sued, as they were, and would be found liable. First a jury would decide their liability and the amount they should pay. The jury would do this under the direction of and following instructions from the court. The court would then render judgment based on the verdict. If the judge thought the amount of money the jury said the defendant should pay was too high, the judge could tell the plaintiff if he doesn't agree to take a smaller sum the judge would order a new trial. In some jurisdictions the judge can tell the defendant to accept a higher award if the judge thought the jury award was too low or in the alternative allow the plaintiff a new trial. In many cases, these new trials will be on the issue of "damages" (also called "money damages") alone. At other times, the judge may disagree with the verdict. Although the judge cannot reverse a jury's decision and give judgment for the other party unless the judge is convinced that under the facts there is only one possible conclusion and the jury did not find it (known as judgment non obstante veredicto or judgment n.o.v.), a judge can always order a new trial if the judge is satisfied that the verdict is "against the weight of the evidence." The ordering of a new trial and judgment n.o.v. are a judge's way of reversing the jury's determination after the verdict. Of course, the losing party can appeal.

The other possible remedy is specific performance. In English and American law this remedy is available only if there is "no adequate remedy at law." What this means is if money will not reasonably compensate you for your loss because someone broke a contract with you, you *may* (not will) be able to get specific performance. Why would Hawkins and Van Zee not be likely to want specific performance from Drs. Witzke and McGee? Specific performance is likely where something is unique. For example, if you contracted with X to buy the pace car for the Indianapolis 500 race, after the race was over, and X broke the contract and refused to deliver it you would probably get specific performance. There is only one such car. No amount of money would enable you to buy another from someone else. There aren't any.

How much money should someone get when a contract is broken? The rule is threefold: expectancy, if it can be measured; reliance if expectancy cannot be measured or where granting expectancy is considered excessive, as in promissory estoppel cases (see *infra*); or restitution. Expectancy is meant to give you the equivalent of what you were promised. What did Van Zee and Hawkins allege that they were promised? How do you give them money equivalent to a working hand or finger? Reliance is the amount of money you put out to fulfill your end of the contract. Restitution is what you have given the other person which it would be unjust for him to keep.

Problem on Damages

Tyson Bruiser, a famous boxer, and Dr. Fixit contract to repair Bruiser's injured right hand. Dr. Fixit guarantees to make Bruiser's hand "as good as new" for his upcoming multi-million dollar boxing fight. Unfortunately for Bruiser, Dr. Fixit confuses his patients and performs the wrong surgery. Bruiser decides to sue Fixit for breach of contract, negligence and medical malpractice. Bruiser's expenses relating to his fiasco with Dr. Fixit include:

(1) $5,000,000 lost wages from upcoming fights.

(2) $500 initial consultant fee with Dr. Fixit.

(3) $10,000 doctors fees.

(4) $5,000 hospital fees.

(5) $100 taxi ride to the hospital the morning of the operation.

(6) $1,000 to hire a personal trainer to rehabilitate the hand.

(7) $300,000 canceled video game deal.

(8) $5,000 down deposit with Dr. Fixit one month prior to the operation.

How much damages will Bruiser be awarded if he can collect expectancy damages? What are his restitution damages? Reliance? Why should a plaintiff not receive both expectancy and reliance damages?

We will return to the subject of damages later in the course.

Problem on Advertising and Intent to Be Bound

You see the following advertisement in the newspaper. "Greatest deals in town. We will not be undersold. Verge of bankruptcy sale. Lowest prices. Best selection." Has the ad really said anything? Read the following case. It is over 100 years old. Some things never change. Although we will consider advertisements under "Offer and Acceptance" in the next chapter, ask yourself here what the court looked to in order to determine the liability of the defendants. Put another way, how did the court determine that the words were used in the advertisement with an intent to be bound.

Carlill v. Carbolic Smoke Ball Company

(1 Q.B. 256) 1893

APPEAL from a decision of Hawkins, J.

The defendants, who were the proprietors and vendors for a medical preparation called "The Carbolic Smoke Ball," inserted in the *Pall Mall Gazette* of November 13, 1891, and in other newspapers, the following advertisement; "100*l*. reward will be paid by the Carbolic Smoke Ball Company to any person who contracts the increasing epidemic influenza, colds, or any disease caused by taking cold, after having used the ball three times daily for two weeks according to the printed directions supplied with each ball. 1000*l*. is deposited with the Alliance Bank, Regent Street, shewing our sincerity in the matter.

"During the last epidemic of influenza many thousand carbolic smoke balls were sold as preventives against this disease, and in no ascertained case was the disease contracted by those using the carbolic smoke ball.

"One carbolic smoke ball will last a family several months, making it the cheapest remedy in the world at the price, 10*s*., post free. The ball can be refilled at a cost of 5*s*. Address, Carbolic Smoke Ball Company, 27, Princes Street, Hanover Square, London."

The plaintiff, on the faith of this advertisement, bought one of the balls at the chemist's, and used it as directed, three times a day, from November 20, 1891, to January 17, 1892, when she was attacked by influenza. Hawkins, J., held that she was entitled to recover the 100*l*. The defendants appealed.

Finlay, Q.C., and *T. Terrell,* for the defendants.

The facts show that there was no binding contract between the parties. The case is not like *Williams v. Carwardine,* where the money was to become payable on the performance of certain acts by the plaintiff; here the plaintiff could not by any act of her own establish a claim, for, to establish her right to the money, it was necessary that she should be attacked by influenza — an event over which she had no control. The words express an intention, but do not amount to a promise. The advertisement is too vague to be the basis of a contract; there is no limit as to time, and no means of checking the use of the ball. Anyone who had influenza might come forward and depose that he had used the ball for a fortnight, and it would be impossible to disprove it. *Guthing v. Lynn* supports the view that the terms are too vague to make a contract; there being no limit as to time, a person might claim who took the influenza ten years after using the remedy.

Dickens, Q.C., and *W.B. Allen,* for the plaintiff.

The advertisement clearly was an offer by the defendants; it was published that it might be read and acted on, and they cannot be heard to say that it was an empty boast, which they were under no obligation to fulfill. The offer was duly accepted. An advertisement was addressed to all the public — as soon as a person does the act mentioned, there is a contract with him. It is urged that the terms are too vague and uncertain to make a contract; but, as regards parties, there is no more uncertainty than in all other cases of this description. As to the want of restriction as to time, there are several possible constructions of the terms; they may mean that, after you have used it for a fortnight, you will be safe so long as you go on using it, or that you will be safe during the prevalence of the epidemic. Or the true view may be that a fortnight's use will make a person safe for a reasonable time.

Finlay, Q.C., in reply. There is no binding contract.

As to the want of limitation as to time, it is conceded that the defendants cannot have meant to contract without some limit, and three limitations have been suggested. The limitation "during the prevalence of the epidemic" is inadmissible, for the advertisement applies to colds as well as influenza. The limitation "during use" is excluded by the language "after having used." The third is, "within a reasonable time," and that is probably what was intended; but it cannot be deduced from the words; so the fair result is that there was no legal contract at all.

Lindley, L.J. [The Lord Justice stated the facts, and proceeded:-]

The first observation I will make is that we are not dealing with any inference of fact. We are dealing with an express promise to pay 100*l.* in certain events. Read the advertisement how you will, and twist it about as you will, here is a distinct promise expressed in language which is perfectly unmistakable "100*l.* reward will be paid by the Carbolic Smoke Ball Company to any person who contracts the influenza after having used the ball three times daily for two weeks according to the printed directions supplied with each ball."

We must first consider whether this was intended to be a promise at all, or whether it was a mere puff which meant nothing. Was it a mere puff? My answer to that question is No, and I base my answer upon this passage: "1000*l.* is deposited with the Alliance Bank, showing our sincerity in the matter." Now, for what was that money deposited or that statement made except to negative the suggestion that this was a mere puff and meant nothing at all? The deposit is called in aid by the advertiser as proof of his sincerity in the matter—that is, the sincerity of his promise to pay this 100*l.* in the event which he has specified. I say this for the purpose of giving point to the observation that we are not inferring a promise; there is the promise, as plain as words can make it.

We find here all the elements which are necessary to form a binding contract enforceable in point of law, subject to two observations. First of all it is said that this advertisement is so vague that you cannot really construe it as a promise-that the vagueness of the language shows that a legal promise was never intended or contemplated. The language is vague and uncertain in some respects, and particularly in this, that the 100*l.* is to be paid to any person who contracts the increasing epidemic after having used the balls three times daily for two weeks. It is said, When are they to be used? According to the language of the advertisement no time is fixed, and, construing the offer most strongly against the person who has made it, one might infer that any time was meant. I do not think that was meant, and to hold the contrary would be pushing too far, the doctrine of taking language most strongly against the person using it. I do not think that business people or reasonable people would understand the words as meaning that if you took a smoke ball and used it three times daily for two weeks you were to be guaranteed against influenza for the rest of your life, and I think it would be pushing the language of the advertisement too far to construe it as meaning that. But if it does not mean that, what does it mean? It is for the defendants to show what it does mean; and it strikes me that there are two, and possibly three, reasonable constructions to be put on this advertisement, any one of which will answer the purpose of the plaintiff. Possibly it may be limited to persons catching the "increasing epidemic" (that is, the then prevailing epidemic), or any colds or diseases caused by taking cold, during the prevalence of the increasing epidemic. That is one suggestion; but it does not commend itself to me. Another suggested meaning is that you are warranted free from catching this epidemic, or colds or other diseases caused by taking cold, whilst you are using this remedy after using it for two weeks. If that is the meaning, the plaintiff is right, for she used the remedy for two weeks and went on using it till she got the epidemic. Another meaning, and the one which I rather prefer, is that the reward is offered to any person who contracts the epidemic or other disease within a reasonable time after having used the smoke ball. Then it is asked, What is a reasonable time? It has been suggested that there is no standard of reasonableness for a germ to develop. I do not feel pressed. It strikes me that a reasonable time may be ascertained in a business sense and in a sense satisfactory to a lawyer, find out from a chemist what the ingredients are; find out from a skilled physician how long the effect of such ingredients on the system could be reasonably expected to endure so as to protect a person from an epidemic or cold, and in that way you will get a standard to be laid before a jury, or a judge without a jury, by which they might exercise their judgment as to what a reasonable time would be. It strikes me, I confess, that the true construction of this advertisement is that 100*l.* will be paid to anybody who uses this smoke ball three times daily for two weeks according to the printed directions, and who gets the influenza or cold or other diseases caused by taking cold within a reasonable time after so using it; and if that is the true construction, it is enough for the plaintiff.

It appears to me, therefore, that the defendants must perform their promise, and if they have been so unwary as to expose themselves to a great many actions, so much the worse for them.

BOWEN, L.J. I am of the same opinion. We were asked to say that this document was a contract too vague to be enforced.

The main point seems to be that the vagueness of the document shows that no contract whatever was intended. It seems to me that in order to arrive at a right conclusion we must read this advertisement in its plain meaning, as the public would understand it. It was intended unquestionably to have some effect, and I think the effect which it was intended to have, was to make people use the smoke ball, because the suggestions and allegations which it contains are directed immediately to the use of the smoke ball as distinct from the purchase of it. The intention was that the circulation of the smoke ball should be promoted, and that the use of it should be increased.

It is said: "How long is this protection to endure? Is it to go on for ever, or for what limit of time?" I think the immunity is to last during the use of the ball. That is the way in which I should naturally read it, and it seems to me that the subsequent language of the advertisement supports that construction. It says: "During the last epidemic of influenza many thousand carbolic smoke balls were sold, and in no ascertained case was the disease contracted by those using" (not "who had used") "the carbolic smoke ball," and it concludes with saying that one smoke ball will last a family several months (which imports that it is to be efficacious while it is being used), and that the ball can be refilled at a cost of 5s. I, therefore, have myself no hesitation in saying that I think, on the construction of this advertisement, the protection was to endure during the time that the carbolic smoke ball was being used. My brother, the Lord Justice who preceded me, thinks that the contract would be sufficiently definite if you were to read it in the sense that the protection was to be warranted during a reasonable period after use. I have some difficulty myself on that point; but it is not necessary for me to consider it further, because the disease here was contracted during the use of the carbolic smoke ball.

Was it intended that the 100*l*. should, if the conditions were fulfilled, be paid? The advertisement says that 1000*l*. is lodged at the bank for the purpose. Therefore, it cannot be said that the statement that 100*l*. would be paid was intended to be a mere puff.

[Affirmed.]

Questions

1. Re-read the language of the advertisement. What parts of it seem to be intended to be relied upon?

2. Under the court's interpretation of this language as a promise to which the defendant should be legally held, how many lawsuits might the defendant have to defend? How many judgments pay? Could the 1000*l* on deposit be said to be a limit of liability?

3. What about cigarette companies which used to advertise that their smoke was cool and refreshing on the throat; that the 100 mm cigarettes made it even better; that the longer the smoke was filtered the less tar and nicotine it had? How did such ads differ from the Carbolic Smoke ball ad? What did the cigarette companies not say? What could you imply they were saying from their ads?

4. What is the relationship between vagueness of language and intent?

5. Should it matter that defendant was not addressing itself to any one person or definable group but to the 'whole world?'

6. What should the Carbolic Smoke Ball Co. have done to make an effective advertisement that would not lead to liability? Are paragraphs two and three satisfactory as they are written?

7. Is there a general principle that you might recommend to advertisers to create an effective commercial for which they will not be liable?

Embry v. McKittrick, 105 S.W. 777 (St. Louis Court of Appeals, 1907). In the *Carlill* case we saw how language was used to find intent to be bound. Finlay for the defendant kept saying it was too vague. The court found a way to employ reasonableness to make the terms effective. The court also found intent to be bound. But did defendants really intend to be bound? Did they really think that they were undertaking a legal liability. Finlay certainly did his best to say they didn't. What if Finlay and Terrell had just come out and said: "Look, I don't care how you read it; we didn't mean it. Now sue us for fraud if you want and we'll return the 10s you paid for the ball. After all, we didn't cause you to catch the flu by using the ball. We just cheated you out of 10s. But don't sue us on a contract where you are making us pay 100*l* because you caught the flu. We never intended to keep this promise and a moment's reflection among business people will show you that. After all, how could we pay thousands of people. We never would have intended to do that. So if it's intent to be bound you want, we never intended to be legally bound." [A shilling then was worth about 25 cents (U.S.) and a pound (*l*) was worth 20 shillings or $5.00.] Assume that Finlay and Terell are believed. The defendants never intended to be bound. Before you answer, read the excerpts from *Embry* and re-read Lindley's and Bowen's opinions on reasonableness.

In *Embry,* a store manager in charge of traveling sales personnel, had a one year contract with his employer. The year expired on December 15, 1903. The manager said that on several occasions before the 15th he had approached the employer but been "put off" twice when he asked for a renewal of his contract for another year. On December 23rd he again approached the manager and said he wanted "an understanding or contract" because if he could have none he wanted to go elsewhere before January 1st. The employer asked how things were going (it then being the height of the season getting sales personnel out) and Embry said that he was very busy. McKittrick then said, according to Embry, "Go ahead, you're all right. Get your men out, and don't let that worry you." Embry worked until February 15, thinking he had a contract, when he was given notice that on March 1st his services would be discontinued. McKittrick had a different version of the conversation. The trial judge instructed the jury that it was necessary "in order to return a verdict for appellant (Embry), not only to find that the conversation occurred as appellant swore but that both parties intended by such conversation to contract with each other. . . ." The appellate court opinion begins here.

GOODE, J.

Judicial opinion and elementary treatises abound in statements of the rule that to constitute a contract there must be a meeting of the minds of the parties, and both must agree to the same thing in the same sense. Generally speaking, this may be true; but it is not literally or universally true. That is to say, the inner intention of parties to a conversation subsequently alleged to create a contract cannot either make a contract of what transpired, or prevent one from arising, if the words used were sufficient to constitute a contract. In so far as their intention is an influential element, it is only such intention as the words or acts of the parties indicate; not one secretly cherished which is inconsistent with those words or acts. The rule is thus stated by a text-writer, and many decisions are cited in support of his text: "The primary object of construction in contract law is to discover the intention of the parties. This intention in express contracts is, in the first instance, embodied in the words which the parties have used and is to be deduced therefrom." In Brewington v. Mesker, 51 Mo. App. 348, 356, it is said that the meeting of minds, which is essential to the formation of a contract, is not determined by the secret intention of the parties, but by their expressed intention, which may be wholly at variance with the former. In Smith v. Hughes, L.R. 6 Q. B. 695, 607, it was said: "If, whatever a man's real intention may be, he so conducts himself that a reasonable man would believe that he was assenting to the terms proposed by the other party, and that other party upon that belief enters into the contract with him, the man thus conducting himself would be equally bound as if he had intended to agree to the other party's terms." And that doctrine was adopted in Phillip v. Gallant, 62 N.Y. 256. In 9 Cyc. 245, we find the following text: "The law imputes to a person an intention corresponding to the reasonable meaning of his words and acts. It judges his intention by his outward expressions and excludes all questions in regard to his unexpressed intention. If his words or acts, judged by a reasonable standard, manifest an intention to agree in regard to the matter in question, that agreement is established, and it is immaterial what may be the real, but unexpressed, state of his mind on the subject." Even more pointed was the language of Baron Bramwell in Brown v. Hare, 3 Hurlst. & N.: "Intention is immaterial till it manifests itself in an act. If a man intends to buy, and says so to the intended seller, and he intends to sell, and says so to the intended buyer, there is a contract of sale; and so there should be if neither had the intention." In view of those authorities, we hold that, though McKittrick may not have intended to employ Embry by what transpired between them according to the latter's testimony, yet if what McKittrick said would have been taken by a reasonable man to be an employment, and Embry so understood it, it constituted a valid contract of employment for the ensuing year.

The next question is whether or not the language used was of that character, namely, was such that Embry, as a reasonable man, might consider he was re-employed for the ensuing year on the previous terms, and act accordingly. McKittrick said: "Go ahead you are all right. Get your men out and do not let that worry you." We think no reasonable man would construe that answer to Embry's demand, that he be employed for another year, otherwise than as an assent to the demands and that Embry had the right to rely on it as an assent.

[Reversed and remanded]

Questions

1. How important was the date Embry went to see McKittrick?
2. How important was it that Embry was getting the sales personnel out on the road?
3. What if Embry had gone to see McKittrick on September 23, 1903 with the same demand and McKittrick had responded the same as on December 23rd? Different result?

In *E.I. Du Pont De Nemours & Co. v. Claiborne-Reno Co., 64 F.2d 224 (8th Cir. 1933)* Du Pont, the plaintiff, defending against a counterclaim brought by Claiborne-Reno, tried to claim that a statement made in a letter was not one on which it should be held to be bound. The court disagreed. In another portion of the opinion, not reproduced here, the court found for Du Pont on another issue.

SANBORN, Circuit Judge.

The parties will be referred to in this opinion as the Du Pont Company and the Reno Company.

The Du Pont Company brought suit against the Reno Company for $5,989.88, part of which was for goods sold and delivered, and part for a balance due upon a promissory note. The Reno Company admitted this indebtedness, but set up a counterclaim for $350,000 damages for breach of contract. The case was tried to a jury, which returned a verdict in favor of the Reno Company for $41,588.12. From the judgment entered upon the verdict, the Du Pont Company has appealed.

The Reno Company had been, from the 23d day of October, 1924, until the 1st day of December, 1930, the sole distributor in the state of Iowa of certain products manufactured only by the Du Pont Company, and intended mainly for the finishing, refinishing, and polishing of automobiles. These products were referred to as Duco. The original contract between the parties, which was made in 1924, had been several times renewed, with slight variations, prior to October 1, 1927. On that date a contract substantially similar to those which preceded it was entered into. It was in the form of a letter prepared by the Du Pont Company and accepted by the Reno Company. [It is set forth only in part below.]

"September 1, 1927.

Claiborne-Reno Co., 1023 Locust St., Des Moines, Iowa. 'Gentlemen: This will confirm our agreement whereby you will act as sole distributor of our Spray Duco, Spray Thinner, Blue Diamond Undercoats and Rubbing Compounds to automobile refinishing shops and furniture refinishing shops in the following territory, with the exception of such shops as we may find it necessary to serve direct because of their connection with manufacturing or industrial consumers of Duco materials.

Entire State of Iowa.

It is understood and agreed that this contract is entered into upon the following conditions: 'That it is our intention and desire to continue under this agreement so long as your services, in our judgment, prove satisfactory.'"

On October 17, 1930, the Du Pont Company gave notice to the Reno Company of the termination of the contract effective the December 1st following, and it was this termination by the Du Pont Company which the Reno Company asserts constituted a breach of the contract.

With some of the contentions of the Du Pont Company we cannot agree. It is urged that the language of the contract does not indicate a promise by the Du Pont Company to remain bound until dissatisfied with the services of the Reno Company; that all that is expressed is a mere desire and intention to continue the contract while satisfied. The mere expression of an intention or desire is not a promise. An intention is but the purpose a man forms in his own mind; a promise is an express undertaking, or agreement to carry the purpose into effect.

No special form of words, however, is necessary to create a promise. All that is necessary is that a fair interpretation of the words used shall make it appear that a promise was intended.

It is undoubtedly true, as argued by counsel, that neither express words of covenant, nor any particular technical words, nor any special form of words, is necessary in order to charge a party with covenant.

The common or ordinary meaning of language will be applied to the words of a contract in the absence of anything to show that they were used in a different sense.

The writing must be construed as a whole, and all its provisions read together.

If possible, a court will give effect to all parts of an instrument, and a construction which gives a reasonable meaning to all its provisions will be preferred to one which leaves a portion of the writing useless or inexplicable.

A construction which renders the contract valid and its performance possible will be preferred to one which renders it void and its performance impossible or meaningless.

The language of a contract will be construed most strongly against the party preparing it. Sternberg v. Drainage Dist. No. 17 of Miss. County, Ark. (C. C. A. 8) 44 F.(2d) 560, 562.

Contracts are ordinarily to be performed by business men, and should be given the interpretation which would be placed upon them by the business world. Where one corporation presents to another corporation a form of agreement reciting, "It is understood and agreed that this contract is entered into upon the following conditions: That it is our intention and desire to continue under this agreement so long as your services, in our judgment, prove satisfactory," we have no doubt that such language would ordinarily be understood to mean a promise to continue until dissatisfied.

[Reversed and remanded]

Question

1. Does the last paragraph of the Du Pont opinion reproduced above remind you of any language in the *Carlill* or *Embry* cases?

So far we have considered contracts alleged to exist between just two people and contracts which might exist between a single person (Carbolic Smoke Ball) and an unknown number of people (the users of the smoke balls). In the case below (*Robbins*) we consider contracts between an employer and the representative of its employees (the union), between employer and employee associations representing more than one employer/ee, and between employer and union to be bound by such an association agreement. We also consider the right of a pension group, which was never a party to any of these contracts, to sue the employer for contributions despite the denial by the employer of any intent to ever be bound. In 1975 employer and union reached agreement which expired on April 1, 1976. The employer then made repeated promises to be bound by whatever agreements were reached by a multiunion labor organization and a multiemployer organization. Lynch later said he never intended to be bound by such agreements. A pension group, which was to have received contributions from employer based on the collective bargaining agreement to which employer denied ever intending to be bound, later sued the employer on the promise made to the union which the employer said he never intended to keep. Read the case and questions. Contracts appear everywhere.

Robbins, v. Lynch
836 F.2d 330
Court of Appeals, Seventh Circuit, 1988.

EASTERBROOK, Circuit Judge.

Lynch Truck Service signed the national master collective bargaining agreement with the Teamsters in 1975, when it entered the business. The agreement expired on April 1, 1976; Lynch executed on April 2 a promise to be bound by any agreement thereafter concluded by the multiemployer and multiunion bargaining associations. Once agreement was reached, Lynch adhered to its terms. That agreement expired April 1, 1979. Following its practice, Lynch sent the local union on March 29, 1979, a promise to adhere to the next national agreement: Want To Inform You We Are Willing To Pay What Ever The International And The Truckers Agree On For The New Contract Which Is Due 4-1-79. We Would Like To Continue [sic] To Operate. If It Is O.K. With The Union And We Will Sign The New Contract. Please Send Us A Letter To That Effect. The local did not reply, and Lynch never signed the agreement. But until the end of 1981, Lynch paid the wages called for by the 1979-82 agreement, made pension and welfare contributions per the agreement, negotiated and settled grievances under the terms of the agreement, and rendered to the local union the dues withheld from the pay of its members. On January 5, 1982, Lynch sent the local this letter: Pursuant to Article 39 of the National Master Freight Agreement and Article 63 of the Local Agreement which was [sic] previously entered into, please be advised that Lynch Truck Service desires to cancel and terminate the Agreement and you are hereby notified accordingly.

The health and welfare trust funded under the agreement kept Lynch's employees on the rolls through the end of March 1982; the pension trust credited Lynch's employees with work through the end of March. The trustees of these two funds filed this suit to recover the sums provided by the agreement and the damages authorized by statute for noncompliance. The funds initially requested roughly $10,000, but during discovery they learned that Lynch concealed the identities of some employees from the funds during 1979-82 and had paid nothing on their account. The funds ultimately received a judgment for more than $125,000.

Lynch's principal defense is that it never signed the 1979-82 agreement. So much is undisputed. It is also undisputed that Lynch promised in March 1979 to adhere to the agreement and gave signs of doing so. It paid the union scale, turned over dues under a checkoff system, negotiated grievances, and paid (some) pension and welfare contributions. It later invoked the termination clause of the agreement. Employers may adopt a collective bargaining agreement by a course of conduct. Gariup v. Birchler Ceiling & Interior Co., 777 F.2d 370 (7th Cir.1985). Lynch did so.

The district court granted summary judgment to the funds, and Lynch protests that this is improper because it denies intending to be bound by the agreement. This disputed issue of fact calls for a trial, Lynch insists. But only a "material" dispute staves off summary judgment, and Lynch's undisclosed intent is not material. References in cases to the importance of "intent to be bound" are misleading if taken literally. As so frequently in law, "intent" is a conclusion rather than a fact. A signatory to a contract is bound by its ordinary meaning even if he gave it an idiosyncratic one; private intent counts only if it is conveyed to the other party and shared. You can't escape contractual obligation by signing with your fingers crossed behind your back, even if that clearly shows your intent not to be bound. This sense of "intent" denotes agreement between the parties and is not a license to allow undisclosed intent to dominate. Even statutes, widely said to follow the "intent of the legislature", draw meaning only from visible indicators such as their structure, the nature of the problem at hand, and public statements (as in committee reports). Private intent is irrelevant. See Oliver Wendell Holmes, The Theory of Legal Interpretation, 12 Harv.L.Rev. 417

(1899), reprinted in Collected Legal Papers 203 (1920). So it is here. Lynch may have had a private intent, but the signs visible to the union all pointed to Lynch's acceptance of the collective bargaining agreement. Lynch is bound by its terms.

Albert L. Lynch, Jr., the proprietor of Lynch Trucking Service during the years in question, filed an affidavit contending [in part] that Lynch "would not have complied with the demands of the Union if they had been properly informed of the facts". The only "facts" to which this could refer are the absence of the signed agreement and the threat to strike. Neither is material. The local union's reference to a signed agreement must have come after March 29, 1979, probably substantially afterward (the affidavit does not supply a date). By then Lynch was bound, under the approach of Gariup. The threat to strike is unexceptional. Unions frequently decline to work unless the employer adheres to a collective bargaining agreement. The threat of "no agreement, no work" hardly makes adherence to the agreement involuntary, as Lynch supposes. This is the threat, express or implied, of every contractual negotiation. (E.g., "Unless you pay my price, I won't sell you my iron ore.")

AFFIRMED.

Questions

1. What is a "'material dispute' that staves off summary judgment?"

2. What were the "signs visible to the union" that showed that Lynch had accepted the collective bargaining agreement, that its promise was not just talk but meant to be relied and acted upon? What did Lynch mean to establish by the defense that it never signed the 1979-82 agreement?

3. What was Lynch trying to establish when it said the union threatened to strike? What did the court mean "The threat to strike is unexceptional.... The threat of 'no agreement, no work' hardly makes adherence to the agreement involuntary, as Lynch supposes."

Empro Manufacturing Co., Inc., v. Ball-Co Manufacturing, Inc.

870 F.2d 423
Court of Appeals, Seventh Circuit, 1989.

EASTERBROOK, Circuit Judge.

We have a pattern common in commercial life. Two firms reach concord on the general terms of their transaction. They sign a document, captioned "agreement in principle" or "letter of intent", memorializing these terms but anticipating further negotiations and decisions—an appraisal of the assets, the clearing of a title, the list is endless. One of these terms proves divisive, and the deal collapses. The party that perceives itself the loser then claims that the preliminary document has legal force independent of the definitive contract. Ours is such a dispute.

Ball-Co Manufacturing, a maker of specialty valve components, floated its assets on the market. Empro Manufacturing showed interest. After some preliminary negotiations, Empro sent Ball-Co a three-page "letter of intent" to purchase the assets of Ball-Co and S.B. Leasing, a partnership holding title to the land under Ball-Co's plant. Empro proposed a price of $2.4 million, with $650,000 to be paid on closing and a 10-year promissory note for the remainder, the note to be secured by the "inventory and equipment of Ballco." The letter stated "[t]he general terms and conditions of such proposal (which will be subject to and incorporated in a formal, definitive Asset Purchase Agreement signed by both parties)". Just in case Ball-Co might suppose that Empro had committed itself to buy the assets, paragraph four of the letter stated that "Empro's purchase shall be subject to the satisfaction of certain conditions precedent to closing including, but not limited to" the definitive Asset Purchase Agreement and, among five other conditions, "[t]he approval of the shareholders and board of directors of Empro".

Although Empro left itself escape hatches, as things turned out Ball-Co was the one who balked. The parties signed the letter of intent in November 1987 and negotiated through March 1988 about many terms. Security for the note proved to be the sticking point. Ball-Co wanted a security interest in the land under the plant; Empro refused to yield.

When Empro learned that Ball-Co was negotiating with someone else, it filed this diversity suit. Contending that the letter of intent obliges Ball-Co to sell only to it, Empro asked for a temporary restraining order. The district judge set the case for a prompt hearing and, after getting a look at the letter of intent, dismissed the complaint. Relying on Interway, Inc. v. Alagna, 85 Ill.App.3d 1094, 41 Ill.Dec. 117, 407 N.E.2d 615 (1st Dist.1980), the district judge concluded that the statement, appearing twice in the letter, that the agreement is "subject to" the execution of a definitive contract meant that the letter has no independent force.

Empro insists on appeal that the binding effect of a document depends on the parties' intent, which means that the case may not be dismissed— for Empro says that the parties intended to be bound, a factual issue. Empro treats "intent to be bound" as a matter of the parties' states of mind, but if intent were wholly subjective there would be no parol evidence rule, no contract case could be decided without a jury trial, and no one could know the effect of a commercial transaction until years after the documents were inked. That would be a devastating blow to business. Contract law gives effect to the parties' wishes, but they must express these openly. Put differently, "intent" in contract law is objective rather than subjective— a point Interway makes by holding that as a matter of law parties who make their pact "subject to" a later definitive agreement have manifested an (objective) intent not to be bound, which under the parol evidence rule becomes the definitive intent even if one party later says that the true intent was different. As the Supreme Court of Illinois said in Schek v. Chicago Transit Authority, 42 Ill.2d 362, 364, 247 N.E.2d 886, 888 (1969), "intent must be determined solely from the language used when no ambiguity in its terms exists". Parties may decide for themselves whether the results of preliminary negotiations bind them, but they do this through their words.

Because letters of intent are written without the care that will be lavished on the definitive agreement, it may be a bit much to put dispositive weight on "subject to" in every case, and we do not read Interway as giving these the status of magic words. They might have been used carelessly, and if the full agreement showed that the formal contract was to be nothing but a memorial of an agreement already reached, the letter of intent would be enforceable. Conversely, Empro cannot claim comfort from the fact that the letter of intent does not contain a flat disclaimer, such as one pronouncing that the letter creates no obligations at all. The text and structure of the letter—the objective manifestations of intent—might show that the parties agreed to bind themselves to some extent immediately.

A canvass of the terms of the letter Empro sent does not assist it, however. "Subject to" a definitive agreement appears twice. The letter also recites, twice, that it contains the "general terms and conditions", implying that each side retained the right to make (and stand on) additional demands. Empro insulated itself from binding effect by listing, among the conditions to which the deal was "subject", the "approval of the shareholders and board of directors of Empro". The board could veto a deal negotiated by the firm's agents for a reason such as the belief that Ball-Co had been offered too much (otherwise the officers, not the board, would be the firm's final decision makers, yet state law vests major decisions in the board). The shareholders could decline to give their assent for any reason (such as distrust of new business ventures) and could not even be required to look at the documents, let alone consider the merits of the deal. Empro even took care to require the return of its $5,000 in earnest money "without set off, in the event this transaction is not closed", although the seller usually gets to keep the earnest money if the buyer changes its mind. So Empro made clear that it was free to walk.

Neither the text nor the structure of the letter suggests that it was to be a one-sided commitment, an option in Empro's favor binding only Ball-Co. From the beginning Ball-Co assumed that it could negotiate terms in addition to, or different from, those in the letter of intent. The cover letter from Ball-Co's lawyer returning the signed letter of intent to Empro stated that the "terms and conditions are generally acceptable" but that "some clarifications are needed in Paragraph 3(c) (last sentence)", the provision concerning Ball-Co's security interest. "Some clarifications are needed" is an ominous noise in a negotiation, foreboding many a stalemate. Although we do not know what "clarifications" counsel had in mind, the specifics are not important. It is enough that even on signing the letter of intent Ball-Co proposed to change the bargain, conduct consistent with the purport of the letter's text and structure.

The shoals that wrecked this deal are common hazards in business negotiations. Letters of intent and agreements in principle often, and here, do no more than set the stage for negotiations on details. Sometimes the details can be ironed out; sometimes they can't. Illinois, allows parties to approach agreement in stages, without fear that by reaching a preliminary understanding they have bargained away their privilege to disagree on the specifics. Approaching agreement by stages is a valuable method of doing business. So long as Illinois preserves the availability of this device, a federal court in a diversity case must send the disappointed party home empty-handed. Empro claims that it is entitled at least to recover its "reliance expenditures", but the only expenditures it has identified are those normally associated with pre-contractual efforts: its complaint mentions the expenses "in negotiating with defendants, in investigating and reviewing defendants' business, and in preparing to acquire defendants' business." Outlays of this sort cannot bind the other side any more than paying an expert to tell you whether the painting at the auction is a genuine Rembrandt compels the auctioneer to accept your bid.

AFFIRMED.

Questions.

1. Paragraphs 2, 6 and 7 outline the problems with making the signed letter one in which either or both of the parties intended to be bound to do something. What were some of these factors?

2. At the end of paragraph 3 there is a reference to "security for the note" and "security interest in the land under the plant." Why did Ball-Co want the security interest? What is a "note?" It is the same usually as "promissory note."

3. Line 5 of paragraph 5 refers to the parol evidence rule. What is this rule? Although we will study it in depth later, a basic understanding of it is helpful now.

4. Paragraph 6 speaks of the care which will be lavished on the finished agreement. What is the significance of this "care" as opposed to the "letter of intent" we have here? Note, however, that the lack of care might result in an "intent to be bound," legally bound, whereas in the finished agreement it might indicate an intent not to be bound. If the words "subject to" were used carelessly there might be an intent to be bound. Why? If they were used carefully, there might be an intent not to be bound. Why?

5. Paragraph 6 also speaks of a *memorial* of an agreement already reached." (Emphasis supplied.) What is such a memorial? What is the significance of something being a memorial? What is another word for this? Again in paragraph 6 we have "definitive agreement," "full agreement," "formal contract," "memorial of an agreement already reached," and "letter of intent." What is the difference among these terms? How do they relate to each other? How do they relate to the concept "parol evidence" in paragraph 4?

6. Intent is objective, according to paragraph 5. What is the difference between objective and subjective?

7. Were there "open terms" in *Empro*? What was the "open term" in *Carlill* and how did the court resolve the dilemma?

B. Not All Intents Are Enforced

Problems

1. Joe says to Mary: Let's go to the prom. Both are high school juniors. Mary says yes. She really means it. He really means it. One or the other changes his/her mind and says: "I'm not going." Enforce the promise(s)? See *Fischer, infra.*

2. Employer makes agreement with Union Representative to pay union employees $25 per hour. Both parties do not intend to keep agreement because Employer cannot afford it but put agreement in writing to satisfy national organization whose rules say that all member unions must reach agreements with wages equal to or greater than national organization guidelines (which are $25 per hour.) Employer pays employees $15 per hour. Prospective employee who has worked in different state takes job with employer because prospective employee received $25 in other state and knew that all agreements were

similar. Prospective Employee sues Employer for breach of contract for not paying $25 per hour in accordance with agreement between Employer and Union. See *N.Y. Trust, infra.*

3. A is trapped by fire in building and falls unconscious. B, who is with A, is unable to drag or carry A from building. B runs outside and tells C who hurries inside with B to find and help A. B, who is exhausted, says he cannot go on but tells C where A is. C, at great risk to himself, finds A and carries A out. C, whose clothes are torn and smoke-damaged, is hospitalized for smoke inhalation. C has no medical insurance. A and B visit C at hospital and express their thanks. Both A and B tell C how grateful they are and both promise to pay C's hospital bills and buy C new clothes. When C later asks them for money, both A and B say: "Look, what you did was very nice and you're a really nice person to do it but the fire department would have gotten me out. You really shouldn't try to gouge money out of grateful people." Does C have a cause of action? Would it matter if C had bought new clothes before asking them for money? See *Harrington, Goldstick,* and *Webb, infra.*

4. Smith is a lifelong member of a social organization. During an illness, many members of the organization came to visit Smith who expressed gratitude by saying, "You know that library we've always wanted to have. Well, when I get out of here and am doing things again I'm giving $25,000 to the organization so we can have one." After recovery, Smith refused to give the money. Does the organization have a cause of action against Smith?

Fischer v. Union Trust Co.

138 Mich. 612, 101 N.W. 852
Supreme Court of Michigan, 1904.

[The father of the plaintiff, who was not well, wanted to do something to help care for her. Therefore, he gave her a deed to some real estate which he owned. The deed contained the promise of the grantor—the father—to pay two mortgages which were on the property when they came due. The father handed the deed to the daughter saying that it was a "nice present" for her. One of her brothers then gave her a dollar which she gave to her father. Later, an effort was made on her behalf to enforce the promise.]

GRANT, J. (after stating the facts).

The facts and circumstances of the delivery of the deed are not in dispute. Counsel differ only in the conclusion to be drawn from them. We think that the conceded facts show a delivery. After the deed was signed and acknowledged, the grantor made manual delivery of it to the grantee. She took it and handed it to her brother, evidently to be kept by him for her. The grantor reserved no control over it, and retained no right to withdraw or cancel it. He never attempted to. Under those circumstances the delivery was complete.

The meritorious question in the case is: Was the claimant in position to enforce the executory contract in the deed against her father while living, and to enforce it against his estate now that he is dead, or to recover damages at law for nonperformance? To say that the one dollar was the real, or such valuable consideration as would of itself sustain a deed of land worth several thousand dollars, is not in accord with reason or common sense. The passing of the dollar by the brother to his sister, and by her to her father, was treated rather as a joke than as any actual consideration. The real and only consideration for the deed and the agreement, therein contained, to pay the mortgages, was the grantor's love and affection for his unfortunate daughter, and his parental desire to provide for her support after he was dead. The consideration was meritorious, but is not sufficient to compel the performance of a purely executory contract. The deed was a gift, and the gift was consummated by its execution and delivery. The title to the land, subject to the mortgages, passed as against all except the grantor's creditors. The gift was expressly made subject to the mortgages, and coupled with it was a promise to pay them. This promise has no additional force because it is contained in the deed. It has no other or greater force than would a promise by him to pay mortgages upon her own land, or to pay her $8,000 in money, or his promise to her evidenced by a promissory note for a like amount, and given for the same purpose and the same consideration. 'The doctrine of meritorious consideration originates in the distinction between the three classes of consideration on which promises may be based, viz., valuable consideration, the performance of a moral duty, and mere voluntary bounty. The first of these classes alone entitles the promisee to enforce his claim against an unwilling promisor; the third is for all legal purposes a mere nullity until actual performance of the promise. The second, or intermediate class, is termed meritorious, and is confined to three duties of charity, of payment of creditors, and of maintaining a wife and children; and under this last head are included provisions made for persons, not being children of the party promising, but in relation to whom he has manifested an intention to stand in loco parentis in reference to the parental duty of making provision for a child. Considerations of this imperfect class are not distinguished at law from mere voluntary bounty, but are to a modified extent recognized in equity. And the doctrine with respect to them is that, although a promise made without a valuable consideration cannot be enforced against the promisor, or against any one in whose favor he has altered his intention, yet if an intended gift on meritorious consideration be imperfectly executed, and if the intention remains unaltered at the death of the donor, there is an equity to enforce it, in favor of his intention, against persons claiming by operation of law without an equally meritorious claim.' Adams' Eq. (8th Ed.) 98.

So, where the contract of conveyance is fully executed, the grantee may maintain a suit in equity to correct the description in the deed. Hutsell v. Crewse, 138 Mo. 1, 39 S. W. 449. In that case the father deeded to his minor child the land for the same purpose as did Mr. Fischer in this case. He had also deeded certain other lands to his other children. His wife died, after which he remarried. After his death, suit was brought against the widow and her children to reform the deed. The basis of the decision is that the contract was executed, the title had passed, and the land was susceptible of identification aliunde.

If the promise made by Mr. Fischer to his daughter to pay these incumbrances had been omitted from the deed, clearly he would have been under no obligation as to her to pay them, although the mortgagee could enforce his (Fischer's) primary liability. In such case the gift would have been only that of the equity of redemption. If Mr. Fischer had voluntarily paid the mortgages, he would then simply have carried out his nonenforceable contract and have completed his gift, as, perhaps, he then intended to do. For some reason, perhaps a good one, he chose not to pay them. A void promise is no more effective than no promise, and the void promise in the deed had no more effect than if it had been omitted therefrom. If it is void for one purpose, it is void for all, and cannot be made available, either directly or indirectly. Only performance of the promise can be of any avail to the claimant.

A gift of personality can be consummated only by an unconditional delivery of the thing. A gift of realty can be consummated only by the execution and delivery of a deed. If either is encumbered, the donor gives only what he had to give. He cannot give the interest of a third party in the property. However clear may be the intention of the donor to pay the encumbrances and thus give the entire property, he can accomplish this only by actually paying them. Neither his promise without a valuable consideration, nor his intention as evidence by such promise, is of any avail to the donee.

Other interesting questions are raised, but they become immaterial in view of the conclusion we have reached.

Judgment is reversed, and new trial ordered. The other Justices concurred.

Questions

1. The court distinguishes three kinds of consideration. Although we will take up the doctrine of valuable consideration in Part D, it is useful to consider meritorious consideration and voluntary bounty. How do the last two differ from each other, according to the court? A valuable consideration, or simply "consideration" as it is generally known, is one in which a benefit comes to the promisor or a detriment is suffered by the promisee in exchange for the promise made by the promisor. Why does the promise made by the father in this case not fit the bargained for exchange theory of benefit and detriment?

2. What do you think was the theory of the case in suing on the father's promise because it was embodied in a deed? What is a deed? What happened when the father gave the daughter the deed?

3. What was the role of the dollar in this case? What role did the father and/or brother presumably hope it would have?

4. If meritorious consideration was insufficient to enforce the father's promise, what was its role in *Hutsell v. Crewse*, cited and discussed in *Fischer?*

5. The dollar did not have the role the brother and father presumably hoped it would. The plaintiff apparently hoped that the father, by embedding the promise in the deed, had made it enforceable as a form of meritorious consideration. What is the difference between *Fischer* and *Hutsell?* What does "correct the description in the deed" mean?

Note on Meritorious Consideration, Voluntary Bounty and Nominal Consideration.

Meritorious consideration, as the case points out, was no consideration at all for enforcing the father's promise. Distinguishing meritorious from valuable consideration can be difficult. What if the father wanted to make a gift to the daughter but also wanted a book which the daughter had which was a first edition and worth much more than a dollar but much less than the value of the land? What if before giving her the deed he had said: "If you give me the book, I'll give you the land and pay the mortgages?" What if she had said "yes"? Would it have mattered if he had said "If you give me a dollar, I'll give you the land and pay the mortgages"? What if the book was only worth a dollar on the market but had an inscription in it from father's great grandfather and father wanted the book? Meritorious is where you have someone who is a natural object of your love, affection and care and you promise them something. Voluntary bounty is where you promise something to one is not the natural object of your love etc. Valuable consideration is where you want something from the other person and make a bargain for it. Like all definitions, be wary of this one. Also, reserve final judgment on promises of gift until you have studied promissory estoppel. Promissory estoppel did not exist at the time of the *Fischer* case, or at least was not recognized by the courts. When you reach promissory estoppel, reflect on the *Fischer* case and ask if the doctrine might have affected the outcome.

Meritorious consideration and voluntary bounty also blur into nominal consideration. This is because as in the *Fischer* case they often go together. Nominal is something that is not of value. The consideration for the father's gift was the love of his daughter and his love for her. The dollar had no significance; it was merely nominal. Yet, today, we still see people who wish to have a dollar exchanged to show their sincerity in promising. Again, as we will see later, if people exchange promises that is enough. If only one promises and receives in exchange no promise or other benefit from the promisee, and if the promisor has not sought a detriment to be suffered by the promisee, a dollar will not make the promise binding. Still, people do it. It does no harm so long as there is something else to make the promise binding. That something else is what we look at in the next three sections.

New York Trust Co. v. Island Oil and Transport Corporation, 34 F.2d 655 (2nd Cir. 1929). This case is very relevant to today's world of multi-national corporations and governmental restrictions and preferences in the international community. Mexican law required that only Mexican corporations could own and operate oil-bearing lands within 50 miles of the coast. To avoid this restriction, the officers and directors of a non-Mexican corporation which wished to operate such lands set up a number of Mexican corporations staffed with Mexican officers. The non-Mexican corporation (known as the parent corporation) owned all the stock in the Mexican corporations (known as subsidiary corporations), with the exception of the shares required to be owned by the Mexican directors. Mexican law also required all books of account to be kept in Spanish and while this was done the business was operated by the non-Mexican corporation out of New York or Tampico. The books showed a number of transactions between the subsidiaries and the parent, including "a very large indebtedness for oil, which the parent had not paid." The stock of the subsidiaries having ended up in the hands of third persons, who now owned the subsidiaries, a suit by one of the subsidiaries against the parent was begun based on the books of account showing the indebtedness from parent to subsidiaries. Learned Hand, one of the most famous appellate judges of the 20th century wrote the opinion, quoted in part below.

L. Hand, Circuit Judge.

We have very recently considered the liability of a parent company to third persons for acts, formally those of a subsidiary, and we held that the question turned upon whether the parent acted directly in the transaction, through its own officers, or only through its indirect power retained by virtue of its ownership of the subsidiary's shares. Costan v. Manila Electric Co., 24 F. (2d) 383; Kingston Dry Dock Co. v. Lake Champlain Transportation Co., 31 F. (2d) 265. If this were such a situation, so that those decisions applied, we should be content to rest upon them without further comment. It is not; the parent's liability to a third person depends on quite different considerations from that to a subsidiary; the second is a question of intent, like that in any other contract. Having for one reason or another adopted the form of independent companies for the conduct of their enterprises, each with a jural personality of its own, the associates could create whatever rights between themselves they wished, provided they gave the necessary expression to their intent.

However, the form of utterance chosen is never final; it is always possible to show that the parties did not intend to perform what they said they would, as, for example, that the transaction was a joke; or that it arose in relations between the members of a family which forbade it. It is quite true that contracts depend upon the meaning which the law imputes to the utterances, not upon what the parties actually intended; but, in ascertaining what meaning to impute, the circumstances in which the words are used is always relevant and usually indispensable. The standard is what a normally constituted person would have understood them to mean, when used in their actual setting. In the case at bar it is abundantly clear that no such person, making the records here in question in such a background, would have supposed that they represented actual sales of oil; that is, commercial transactions. They were made for quite other purposes, formally to conform with, and, if one chooses, to evade, the Mexican law. They were a sham, which nobody did, and nobody advised could, understand as intended to be more. Perhaps for this reason they were a fraud on the Mexican government, an effort to keep the pretense of compliance with its own notions of what was essential to its national safety, while the parties went their way at their own pleasure. While this is perhaps not directly proved, it is certainly not improbable, and, since we think it makes no difference in the result, we shall assume as much arguendo.

The question then becomes whether legal obligations shall be attached to utterances which would otherwise not create them, because they were part of a plan to deceive third persons. We are to distinguish between such a situation and one in which the person deceived has acted in reliance upon the truth of the utterances, and bases his rights upon them, for here we are only concerned with the existence of obligations between parties equally implicated. We cannot see why their common fault should so change the relations between them. Indeed, if we were asked to intervene between them, and give relief based upon the sham transaction, we might refuse; 'in pari delicto potior est conditio possidentis.' Here we must raise an obligation where none would otherwise exist, because by hypothesis both were concerned in a fraud upon a third. As compensation, this would be fruitless; as punishment, it would be capricious; as law, it would create an obligation ex turpi causa.

The law in Vermont appears to be otherwise (Conner v. Carpenter, 28 Vt. 237; Grand Isle v. Kinney, 70 Vt. 381, 41 A. 130); but there are other cases to the contrary, though it is only fair to say that they do not seem directly to have faced the issue (Kelly v. Sayle, 15 Dom.L.R. 776 (Can.); Lavalleur v. Hahn, 152 Iowa, 649, 132 N.W. 877, 39 L.R.A.(N.S.) 24). Professor Wigmore (section 2406) appears to support the Vermont rule, and this would ordinarily be to our minds conclusive; but for the reasons given we cannot in this instance yield even to the great weight of his authority.

Decree affirmed.

In re H. Hicks and Son, Inc., 82 F.2d 277 (2nd Cir., 1936). This case is similar to *Island Oil* in that a "joke" is involved. One person, Mrs. Downs, held substantially all of the shares of two corporations and as such effectively controlled both of them. One of the corporations leased space in a building to the other corporation. From time to time the lessor corporation "forgave" or waived the rent of the lessee. In a suit by the lessor against the lessee for an alleged debt owed by the lessee, the court refused to allow the claim in a bankruptcy proceeding where the lessor was competing with other creditors for a share of the assets of the lessee who was bankrupt.

L. HAND, Circuit Judge.

The referee, finding that there was adequate formal evidence to establish both debts, and believing that two corporations might contract with each other though their shares were held in common, allowed the claim; he could not see that the debts had been legally discharged. The judge expunged the claim, because the lessor had 'waived' the debt by its constant equivocation. We should find some difficulty in concluding, if the debts had ever come into being at all, that they had been discharged. Nevertheless, it appears to us that the lease and the loan did not create any obligation at the outset; that they were mere forms, intended never to become binding on the companies, and for that reason never contracts. It is well settled that whatever the formal documentary evidence, the parties to a legal transaction may always show that they understand a purported contract not to bind them; it may, for example, be a joke, or a disguise to deceive others. New York Trust Co. v. Island Oil & Transport Corporation, 34 F.(2d) 655 (C.C.A. 2). It is no objection that such an understanding contradicts the writing; a writing is conclusive only so far as the parties intend it to be the authoritative memorial of the transaction. Whatever the presumptions, their actual understanding may also be shown except in so far as expressly or implicitly they have agreed that the writing alone shall control. While it is true that an intent to make a contract is not necessary to the creation of a contract and that parties who exchange promises will find themselves bound, whatever they may have thought, nevertheless they will not be bound if they agree that their words, however coercive in form, shall not bind them.

A contract between two companies all of whose shares are held by a single shareholder, in a fundamental sense cannot create an obligation, for an obligation implies a power in one person to control, to coerce, the will of another, and there is only one will concerned. Here, for example, Mrs. Downs could not in the nature of things compel herself to make these payments if her purpose to pay them should change. When we say therefore that two companies so controlled may make a contract, no meaning can be attached to it but this, that the interests of others may intervene in such a way as to measure the companies' interests just as though they had created obligations between themselves. This is such a situation because the lessor, or more properly Mrs. Downs in the mask of the lessor, is asking for a dividend competition with other creditors. Contracts resulted upon their execution if she then meant to bind the companies quoad the creditors of both; but if she did not, and only meant to use the evidence of the contracts as her subsequent needs might dictate, they always remained mere forms as of necessity they had to be between the companies themselves.

Therefore it may not be immediately relevant that the bankrupt was forgiven the rent or that its amount was changed; that does not prove that the contracts had not been intended to stand against the interests of creditors. But playing fast and loose after the rights of creditors came in prospect, was quite different. In November, 1932, and steadily thereafter there were repeated evidences that the contracts were not then at least intended as claims against other creditors; not only does this follow from the books but from Mrs. Downs's deliberate declarations, sworn and unsworn. She only meant to hold them in reserve, using or suppressing them as she found convenient; such an intent would negative any obligation, at least if it went back to the time of execution. Thus the last question is whether the evidence is enough to carry back that intent to that time. Most of it related to later transactions, all indeed except the shuffling back and forth of the debt of 1926. But we see no reason to cut the web in halves; we find a continuous and consistent practice, looking one way, indicating that the putative obligations created were only phantoms, evoked or laid at rest at the whim of this lady to satisfy her momentary interest. The reasonable conclusion is that her intent never changed; at no time did she mean her corporate puppets to engage in transactions which would later handicap her absolute freedom of action.

Order affirmed.

Harrington v. Taylor, 36 S.E.2d 227 (Sup. Ct. N.C., 1945). This very short case is reprinted in full. How does it differ from *Fischer*? How is it similar? Does it have anything in common with *New York Trust* and *Hicks*? Why are all of these cases grouped under a section entitled "Not all Intents are Enforced"? What is the nature of the intent in *Fischer* and *Harrington*? Is it subjective, objective, both, neither? [Review *Embry v. McKittrick, infra,* for the two types of intent.] What about the intent in *New York Trust* and *Hicks*? In none of these four cases is there a recovery by the promisee. Why?

PER CURIAM.

The plaintiff in this case sought to recover of the defendant upon a promise made by him under the following peculiar circumstances:

The defendant had assaulted his wife, who took refuge in plaintiff's house. The next day the defendant gained access to the house and began another assault upon his wife. The defendant's wife knocked him down with an axe, and was on the point of cutting his head open or decapitating him while he was laying on the floor, and the plaintiff intervened, caught the axe as it was descending, and the blow intended for defendant fell upon her hand, mutilating it badly, but saving defendant's life.

Subsequently, defendant orally promised to pay the plaintiff her damages; but, after paying a small sum, failed to pay anything more. So, substantially, states the complaint. The defendant demurred to the complaint as not stating a cause of action, and the demurrer was sustained. Plaintiff appealed.

The question presented is whether there was a consideration recognized by our law as sufficient to support the promise. The Court is of the opinion that, however much the defendant should be impelled by common gratitude to alleviate the plaintiff's misfortune, a humanitarian act of this kind, voluntarily performed, is not such consideration as would entitle her to recover at law.

The judgment sustaining the demurrer is

Affirmed.

Question

1. The Court found plaintiff's sacrifice to save defendant's life to be a "humanitarian act." How could plaintiff have received the consideration she needed for an enforceable contract to result? Would it have been possible for plaintiff to have received this consideration before she had thrust herself at the axe?

Problems on Recovery for Services Rendered

In considering the following problems, ask whether each is closer to *Fischer, supra, Webb, infra, New York Trust, supra, Harrington, supra, Hicks, supra* or *Goldstick, infra*.

1. Dr. Jones treats a patient whom the doctor finds unconscious by the roadside as the result of an accident. The doctor stays with the patient, goes to the hospital and remains with him until he is conscious and out of danger. The doctor's actions save the person's life. The doctor later sends the patient a bill for $2,000, a reasonable sum in terms of the doctor's time and effort. The patient refuses to pay the bill. If you represent the doctor what case(s) do you rely on? If you represent the patient?

2. Assume that Dr. Jones is the patient's wife. Both were riding in the car in which patient was injured. Dr. Jones was uninjured. Any change in result?

3. Assume that a priest/rabbi/minister happens by and renders assistance. Later the priest/rabbi/minister sends a bill for services rendered (of both a spiritual and material nature). What result?

4. Assume a good samaritan who is neither a doctor, a wife, a priest/rabbi/minister, but just a passerby renders aid. He later sends a bill. What result?

5. Is there any way to be sure in each of the above cases? What is it we are trying to find out? What factual question are we seeking to answer? What motivational question?

6. Next door neighbor mows my lawn while I am away and sends me a bill for $250, a reasonable sum. I had never asked to have it mowed and planned to do it myself on my return. Can neighbor collect?

7. Yachtsperson, seeing my boat listing at the pier where I have moored it goes aboard without my knowledge and consent, bails it out and fixes a hole

which had been driven through the planking by an underwater pier support. The next day when I discover what he has done, out of gratitude I say: "Thanks. I'll be glad to pay you for your help. What do I owe you?" It turns out that yachtsperson is investment banker who rates his time at a minimum of $1,000 per hour. Because he put 10 hours in to fix my boat he wants $10,000. Do I owe him this? What if I had said nothing. Would I owe him nothing? A repair person would have charged no more than $1,500 to fix the boat.

8. Assume in #1 that patient is a son or daughter of a wealthy person who is then sued by Dr. Jones. Assume that wealthy person after learning of the doctor's services had promised to pay for them. What result?

9. Assume in #1 that patient is unrelated to a wealthy person who learns of doctor's services and promises to pay bill. The wealthy person later changes his/her mind. Now, what result?

What is the intent in the next case? Why isn't it enforced? Is it because it can't be enforced? In *Carlill* the court found a way to enforce a rather vague advertisement. That was over a hundred years ago. The U.C.C. finds a way to come up with a price, as the court in *Goldstick* mentions. Then why isn't something enforced here?

Goldstick v. ICM Realty
788 F.2d 456
Court of Appeals, 7th Circuit, 1985

POSNER, Circuit Judge.

The plaintiffs, former law partners named Goldstick and Smith, brought this diversity suit for breach of contract against John Kusmiersky, U.S. Managers Realty, Inc., and ICM Realty, seeking payment of a legal fee for getting real estate taxes reduced on a large apartment complex owned by ICM, leased by Kusmiersky, and managed by U.S. Managers. ICM moved for summary judgment, which was granted. After settling with Kusmiersky and U.S. Managers, Goldstick and Smith appealed the judgment for ICM.

In 1969 ICM bought an apartment complex in Rolling Meadows, Illinois, from Walter Kassuba, to whom ICM leased back the land and sold the improvements. He went broke, however, and in 1975 ICM leased the land to Kusmiersky, a "work-out specialist," who also bought the improvements. In a separate agreement ICM promised to advance Kusmiersky $1.5 million to operate the property and pay past-due real estate taxes, hoping that this advance would enable him to resuscitate the property so that ICM could recover its investment in the land. Kusmiersky retained the plaintiffs under a contingent-fee arrangement to seek a reduction in the past-due taxes. ICM approved this arrangement and by 1977 the plaintiffs had succeeded in getting them reduced by some $870,000. The plaintiffs billed Kusmiersky $290,000 for their legal services. The bill was never paid, though neither its reasonableness nor its conformity to the terms of the contingent-fee contract has ever been questioned.

The property continued to decline, and Kusmiersky and ICM entered into negotiations to transfer Kusmiersky's interest to Ted Netzky, who agreed to invest fresh capital in the property. Netzky refused to close the deal, however, unless ICM agreed to pay the remaining past-due real estate taxes and the plaintiffs released their claim for legal fees. In an effort to obtain this release Kusmiersky offered the plaintiffs a reduced fee of $250,000, payable over 10 years with interest at 7 percent per annum. Goldstick (for the plaintiffs) refused the offer. ICM drafted a release for the plaintiffs to sign which stated that the $250,000 would be paid over time but only out of the profits of the property; if there were none, the fee would not be paid. Goldstick refused to sign the release until Kusmiersky assured him that ICM was honorable and that something would be worked out, which Goldstick took to mean that he and Smith would receive the $250,000, over time but with interest, regardless of whether the property showed a profit. The plaintiffs signed the release and the deal with Netzky closed. Goldstick and Smith continued to negotiate with Kusmiersky and ICM over the terms of payment of their fee, but no agreement was reached, for ICM held steadfastly to the position that the payment of the fee would have to be out of the profits, if any, of the property. There were no profits, and eventually Goldstick and Smith demanded payment of the full $290,000 and when that was refused brought this suit.

We come to the negotiations with Netzky, upon which the plaintiffs' theories are founded. One theory is that the plaintiffs had a contract with ICM to be paid $250,000 in exchange for a release of their claim, but we agree with the district judge that they did not. When Kusmiersky offered to pay $250,000 over 10 years (and with no payment of principal in the early years, just interest at 7 percent), Goldstick turned him down; so there was no contract, express or implied. Later Kusmiersky assured Goldstick that something would be worked out. But just what that "something" was is hopelessly vague. Even if Goldstick could reasonably have understood Kusmiersky to mean that the obligation would be unconditional—and maybe he could, as we shall see—there would still be the question of the period over which the money was to be paid. When Kusmiersky spoke to Goldstick about working something out, it was after Goldstick had refused to accept payment conditioned on the property's turning a profit. We cannot know whether, faced with ICM's proposal to make payment conditional in this way, Goldstick would gladly have embraced Kusmiersky's previous offer, for payment over 10 years; or whether he would have accepted payment over this period only if the fee was restored to its original level of $290,000; or whether he would have insisted on much more if it was to be paid over 10 years—bearing in mind that at a discount rate of 10 percent per annum (for example), $290,000 paid in equal annual installments over 10 years is worth only $178,000 today, and $250,000 is worth only $154,000. It would be impossible to fix within reasonable bounds the present value of the contract that Goldstick and Kusmiersky made, if Kusmiersky's reference to working something out is treated as an offer and Goldstick's thereafter signing the release as an acceptance. An offer must be more definite to create an enforceable contract.

Although the Uniform Commercial Code has made inroads into the common law principle that a contract that does not fix a price is unenforceable, see UCC § 2-305, it has done so in order to make contracts for the sale of goods at whatever the market price is on the day when the goods are delivered enforceable, and in such a case the court has an objective basis for determining the contract price.

That is not the case here and anyway this contract is not governed by the Code. The common law principle that a contract cannot be enforced if its terms are indefinite (see Farnsworth, Contracts § 3.27 (1982)) retains a core of vitality. If people want the courts to enforce their contracts they have to take the time to fix the terms with reasonable definiteness so that the courts are not put to an undue burden of figuring out what the parties would have agreed to had they completed their negotiations. The parties have the comparative advantage over the court in deciding on what terms a voluntary transaction is value-maximizing; that is a premise of a free-enterprise system.

This is not to say that enforcement should be denied if the parties by inadvertence failed to specify some peripheral term. Such omissions both are the unavoidable consequence of the limitations of human foresight and can be repaired by the courts without undue difficulty. But in this case essential terms were missing: the contract price, the period over which that price would be paid, the interest rate, and the repayment profile (e.g., equal annual installments or a balloon payment at the end?). We are talking about a possible difference in present value of at least $136,000 (more, if the proper discount rate would have been even more than 10 percent, which is entirely possible)—the difference between $290,000, Goldstick's demand, and $154,000, the present value at a 10 percent discount rate of Kusmiersky's offer (ignoring interest and the balloon feature of the offer, which would tend to offset each other). The difference is too high a fraction of the value of the "contract" to allow a court to conclude that a contract was made and to enforce the contract.

The last string on the plaintiffs' bow is restitution. Assume that if Kusmiersky had broken his contract with the plaintiffs before Netzky came on the scene, they would have had no recourse against ICM because ICM had paid Kusmiersky for the benefits they had conferred; still, by the time Netzky came into the picture, everything had changed. Kusmiersky was on his way out and ICM was on the verge of abandoning the property. Netzky appeared as a possible savior but attached two conditions to putting new capital into the property: that the back taxes be paid by ICM and that the plaintiffs release their claim. The back taxes were lower as a result of the plaintiffs' efforts, and while it is true that ICM had paid Kusmiersky to pay off the taxes he had not done so. They loomed as an obligation of ICM—an obligation less onerous as a result of the plaintiffs' efforts than it otherwise would have been. In addition, by executing the release the plaintiffs conferred a benefit on ICM by making it possible to close the deal with Netzky.

A person who confers benefits gratuitously—officiously—obtains no legal claim for compensation. If Goldstick had appeared at a meeting of ICM's shareholders and serenaded them with his violin, and the shareholders had listened raptly, still Goldstick would have no claim of restitution against ICM for benefits conferred; he would have had to negotiate a contract with ICM in advance. But when a businessman confers benefits in circumstances where payment is normal and any inference of altruism can be rejected, a claim for restitution, or "quasi-contract," arises. That describes this case—or so a reasonable jury could find. By executing the release the plaintiffs conferred a benefit on ICM. The release allowed the deal with Netzky to go through, which gave ICM hope (though later dashed) of recovering its investment in Rolling Meadows. This is not the kind of benefit that one businessman or professional renders another without expectation of payment.

A second benefit was conferred but its legal significance is different. As a result of Kusmiersky's departure from the scene without paying the back taxes, by the time of the negotiations with Netzky it was clear that the plaintiffs' legal work had conferred substantial benefits on ICM by reducing the amount of money it would have to pay in back taxes in order to get Netzky to put in additional capital. In this way too the plaintiffs facilitated the transaction, a transaction that conferred benefits on ICM ex ante though not ex post. But they cannot recover these benefits on a theory of restitution. The reason is the original contract that the plaintiffs signed with Kusmiersky to do the legal work that resulted in the reduction of the taxes that were past due. If the contract was authorized or ratified by ICM as Kusmiersky's principal, it defined the plaintiffs' rights against ICM and they cannot rewrite the contract by suing for restitution rather than breach of contract.

If on the other hand the contract was just between the plaintiffs and Kusmiersky, the plaintiffs cannot bring ICM in through the back door by pointing out that their contractual performance conferred benefits on ICM. To illustrate, if you do work pursuant to a contract with X, you don't expect that Y, a non-party, will pay you if X defaults, merely because Y was benefited by your work; and expectation of payment is an essential element of a claim for restitution. For the doctrine of restitution does not make altruism a paying proposition. As its synonym "contract implied in law" brings out, it allows damages to be recovered in settings where (unlike our example of the unsolicited serenade) the parties would have agreed that there was a contractual obligation had the point occurred to them. If Kusmiersky was merely a tenant of ICM and not an agent, ICM would not have expected to have to make good on a claim by the plaintiffs arising from the performance of their contract with him; and this, as the Illinois cases make abundantly clear, defeats a claim of restitution for the benefits conferred on ICM by that performance.

The district judge emphasized another point: that under a functional definition of ownership ICM was not the owner of the Rolling Meadows property, so much control had it given up to Kusmiersky and intended to give up to his successor, Netzky, and therefore it was not liable under Illinois law for payment of back taxes on the property. We do not understand the significance of this point. Whether under Illinois law ICM had to pay the back taxes or Netzky would have had to pay them has no economic significance. Someone had to pay them—that, or the property would have to be abandoned. Netzky was unwilling to pay them. So ICM's choice was either to pay them or abandon the property and with it all hope of recouping its investment. Since it wasn't prepared to abandon the property it had to pay the back taxes, as a matter of economics if not law; and this being so it derived a real benefit from the fact that the taxes were lower thanks to the efforts of Goldstick and Smith. It just is not the kind of benefit for which compensation can be obtained under the law of restitution.

But concerning the separate benefit that the plaintiffs conferred on ICM by releasing their contract claims against it and thereby enabling the deal with Netzky to go through, the plaintiffs may be entitled to restitution, for they would expect to be paid for the release, and paid by ICM, the beneficiary. So far as liability is concerned, it makes no difference (it could make a difference with respect to damages) whether Goldstick and Smith could have slapped a lien on the property to enforce the payment of their legal fee by Kusmiersky. Netzky refused—it

doesn't matter why—to go through with a deal that ICM very much wanted unless ICM procured a release of the lawyers' claim, and by executing that release
Goldstick and Smith conferred a benefit on ICM for which they are entitled to be
compensated. Of course it is possible that the only compensation they sought
and received was contingent on the property's yielding a profit; if so, though they
are entitled to compensation, that compensation would be zero. But that is an
issue in hot dispute, and a jury could find that Goldstick and Smith never accepted an offer of contingent payment.

If the plaintiffs conferred a benefit for which they reasonably expected to be
compensated, and not on a contingent basis either, the next question is the "reasonable worth" of the benefit. It might seem to be zero, since in fact ICM never made
a profit from the deal with Netzky. But that is to take an incorrect, ex post perspec-
tive. A lottery ticket is not worth zero when it is bought, merely because it later
turns out not to be the winning ticket. The question is what ICM would have paid
for the release to close the deal with Netzky—what the release was worth to it at
the time that it obtained it from Goldstick and Smith. That will be an issue for trial.

Other grounds presented by the defendants for upholding the district judge's
decision are unpersuasive. To summarize, we agree with the district judge that
the plaintiffs have no claim for breach of an express contract made at the time of
the deal with Netzky. They may however have claims for promissory estoppel,
restitution, and breach of a contract made by Kusmiersky but authorized or ratified by ICM. We do not say they do. We hold only that they have raised genuine
issues of material fact which preclude summary judgment for the defendants.

[Reversed and remanded.]

Note on Quasi-contracts

In Goldstick, a new idea, restitution, appears. This is also called quasi-contract. The word "quasi" (as if) is used because contract depends on the intent of
the parties. In quasi-contact (as if-contract) recovery from someone is not based
on that person's intent to be bound to a contract, but rather on the receipt of
benefits which it would be unjust to allow the recipient to keep without paying
for them. The person is made to pay "as if" he had promised to pay for them, intended to pay for them and expressed that intent, even though he had never expressed any such intention.

The following excerpt from *Lirtzman v. Fuqua Industries Inc.*, 677 F.2d 548
(7th Cir., 1982) further discusses what a quasi- contract is (and is not).

"A quasi-contract is not a contract at all, but a duty thrust under certain
conditions upon one party to reimburse another party in order to avoid
the first party's unjust enrichment. (G)enerally, in order to recover on a
quasi-contractual claim, the plaintiff must show that the defendant was
unjustly enriched at the plaintiff's expense, and that the circumstances
were such that in good conscience the defendant should make restitution.
Because quasi-contractual obligations rest upon equitable considerations,
they do not arise when it would not be unfair for the recipient to keep
the benefit without having to pay for it. Thus, to make out his case, it is
not enough for the plaintiff to prove merely that he has conferred an ad-

vantage upon the defendant, but he must demonstrate that retention of the benefit without compensating the one who conferred it is unjustified. Thus, in situations involving personal services, it has been variously stated that a duty to pay will not be recognized where it is clear that the benefit was conferred gratuitously or officiously, or that the question of payment was left to the unfettered discretion of the recipient. Nor is compensation mandated where the services were rendered simply in order to gain a business advantage. And the courts have reached the same conclusion where the plaintiff did not contemplate a personal fee, or the defendant could not reasonably have supposed that he did. Nor, we add, can an uncommunicated expectation of remuneration serve the plaintiff's purpose where the defendant had no cause to believe that such was the fact."

In the next case, *Webb v. McGowin*, there is a receipt of benefits followed by a promise. Once again, as in *Fischer*, we have a promise of a gift. Do you see why? In Webb the promise was made after the benefit had been received; the promise did not induce the benefit. First the benefit was received; then the promise was made. The benefit in such a case cannot be a valuable consideration for the promise. To be a valuable consideration for the promise, the promise must be made not just because of a benefit, but because the party making the promise wants to receive the benefit, bargains for the benefit, and makes the promise to induce the other party to confer the benefit. Nevertheless, in *Webb* the plaintiff recovered. If the reasoning seems tortured at times, it is. The concurring opinion goes along with the judgment but dissociates itself from the reasoning. The Restatement of Contracts, in its often cryptic way, has endeavored to reach the problem of distinguishing gifts for which the recipient ought not be expected to pay, and services which the recipient did not bargain for but which benefited her and for which payment ought to be made. Both *Webb* and *Goldstick* deal with this. *Goldstick* is the newer case and is more straightforward in saying — if you receive a benefit for which the grantor would normally expect payment, you *may* be liable. *Webb* depends on an *ex post facto* promise for its result. We will consider this subject again when we come to the case of *Wood v. Lucy, Lady Duff Gordon*.

Webb v. McGowin

168 So. 196, 27 Ala.App. 82
Court of Appeals of Alabama, 1935

BRICKEN, Presiding Judge.

The complaint as amended averred in substance: (1) That on August 3, 1925, appellant saved J. Greeley McGowin, appellee's testator, from death or grievous bodily harm; (2) that in doing so appellant sustained bodily injury crippling him for life; (3) that in consideration of the services rendered and the injuries received by appellant, McGowin agreed to care for him the remainder of appellant's life, the amount to be paid being $15 every two weeks; (4) that McGowin complied with this agreement until he died on January 1, 1934, and the payments were kept up to January 27, 1934, after which they were discontinued.

The action was for the unpaid installments accruing after January 27, 1934, to the time of the suit.

The principal grounds of demurrer to the original and amended complaint are: (1) It states no cause of action; (2) its averments show the contract was without consideration; (3) it fails to allege that McGowin had, at or before the services were rendered, agreed to pay appellant for them; (4) the contract declared on is void under the statute of frauds.

1. The averments of the complaint show that appellant saved McGowin from death or grievous bodily harm. This was a material benefit to him of infinitely more value than any financial aid he could have received. Receiving this benefit, McGowin became morally bound to compensate appellant for the services rendered. Recognizing his moral obligation, he expressly agreed to pay appellant as alleged in the complaint and complied with this agreement up to the time of his death; a period of more than 8 years.

Had McGowin been accidentally poisoned and a physician, without his knowledge or request, had administered an antidote, thus saving his life, a subsequent promise by McGowin to pay the physician would have been valid. Likewise, McGowin's agreement as disclosed by the complaint to compensate appellant for saving him from death or grievous bodily injury is valid and enforceable.

Where the promisee cares for, improves, and preserves the property of the promisor, though done without his request, it is sufficient consideration for the promisor's subsequent agreement to pay for the service, because of the material benefit received.

In Boothe v. Fitzpatrick, 36 Vt. 681, the court held that a promise by defendant to pay for the past keeping of a bull which had escaped from defendant's premises and been cared for by plaintiff was valid, although there was no previous request, because the subsequent promise obviated that objection; it being equivalent to a previous request. On the same principle, had the promisee saved the promisor's life or his body from grievous harm, his subsequent promise to pay for the services rendered would have been valid. Such service would have been far more material than caring for his bull. Any holding that saving a man from death or grievous bodily harm is not a material benefit sufficient to uphold a subsequent promise to pay for the service, necessarily rests on the assumption that saving life and preservation of the body from harm have only a sentimental value. The converse of this is true. Life and preservation of the body have material, pecuniary values, measurable in dollars and cents. Because of this, physicians practice their profession charging for services rendered in saving life and curing the body of its ills, and surgeons perform operations. The same is true as to the law of negligence, authorizing the assessment of damages in personal injury cases based upon the extent of the injuries, earnings, and life expectancies of those injured.

In the business of life insurance, the value of a man's life is measured in dollars and cents according to his expectancy, the soundness of his body, and his ability to pay premiums. The same is true as to health and accident insurance.

It follows that if, as alleged in the complaint, appellant saved J. Greeley McGowin from death or grievous bodily harm, and McGowin subsequently agreed to pay him for the service rendered, it became a valid and enforceable contract.

2. It is well settled that a moral obligation is a sufficient consideration to support a subsequent promise to pay where the promisor has received a material

benefit, although there was no original duty or liability resting on the promisor. State ex rel. Bayer v. Funk, 105 Or. 134, 199 P. 592, 209 P. 113, 25 A.L.R. 625, 634. In the case of State ex rel. Bayer v. Funk, supra, the court held that a moral obligation is a sufficient consideration to support an executory promise where the promisor has received an actual pecuniary or material benefit for which he subsequently expressly promised to pay.

The case at bar is clearly distinguishable from that class of cases where the consideration is a mere moral obligation or conscientious duty unconnected with receipt by promisor of benefits of a material or pecuniary nature. Park Falls State Bank v. Fordyce, supra. Here the promisor received a material benefit constituting a valid consideration for his promise.

3. Some authorities hold that, for a moral obligation to support a subsequent promise to pay, there must have existed a prior legal or equitable obligation, which for some reason had become unenforceable, but for which the promisor was still morally bound. This rule, however, is subject to qualification in those cases where the promisor, having received a material benefit from the promisee, is morally bound to compensate him for the services rendered and in consideration of this obligation promises to pay. In such cases the subsequent promise to pay is an affirmance or ratification of the services rendered carrying with it the presumption that a previous request for the service was made.

Under the decisions above cited, McGowin's express promise to pay appellant for the services rendered was an affirmance or ratification of what appellant had done raising the presumption that the services had been rendered at McGowin's request.

4. The averments of the complaint show that in saving McGowin from death or grievous bodily harm, appellant was crippled for life. This was part of the consideration of the contract declared on. McGowin was benefited. Appellant was injured. Benefit to the promisor or injury to the promisee is a sufficient legal consideration for the promisor's agreement to pay.

5. Under the averments of the complaint the services rendered by appellant were not gratuitous. The agreement of McGowin to pay and the acceptance of payment by appellant conclusively shows the contrary.

6. The contract declared on was not void under the statute of frauds (Code 1923, § 8034). The demurrer on this ground was not well taken.

The cases of Shaw v. Boyd, 1 Stew. & P. 83, and Duncan v. Hall, 9 Ala. 128, are not in conflict with the principles here announced. In those cases the lands were owned by the United States at the time the alleged improvements were made, for which subsequent purchasers from the government agreed to pay. These subsequent purchasers were not the owners of the lands at the time the improvements were made. Consequently, they could not have been made for their benefit.

From what has been said, we are of the opinion that the court below erred in the ruling complained of; that is to say, in sustaining the demurrer, and for this error the case is reversed and remanded.

Reversed and remanded.

SAMFORD, Judge (concurring).

The questions involved in this case are not free from doubt, and perhaps the strict letter of the rule, as stated by judges, though not always in accord, would bar a recovery by plaintiff, but following the principle announced by Chief Justice Marshall in Hoffman v. Porter, Fed.Cas. No. 6,577, 2 Brock. 156, 159, where he says, "I do not think that law ought to be separated from justice, where it is at most doubtful," I concur in the conclusions reached by the court.

Questions

1. What is the significance of *Shaw v. Boyd* and *Duncan v. Hall* cited on the last page of *Webb*?

2. Notice in #3 of *Webb* that a previous request is mentioned as being presumed where a benefit was received. This presumption is known as a legal fiction. If a request had been made, how would that change the case? How might a request have been made?

Note on Statute of Frauds

The Statute of Frauds is mentioned in *Webb*. First passed in 1677 in England it was a statute that required certain promises to be in a writing signed by the person against whom they are to be enforced, in order for that enforcement to be successful. A promise would not be sufficient over the objection of the party alleged to have made it unless it was written. Three of the more common promises that must be in writing in almost all states are:

1. Promises to sell land.

2. Promises to sell or buy goods for a price of $500 or more.

3. Promises to perform personal services for a period of over one year. This includes everything from teaching someone to play the violin to constructing a 1,500' tall skyscraper with a revolving restaurant on the top. If no time is specified for the performance of the services, then if they could have been completed in less than a year, even if in fact they took longer, the promise need not be in writing.

There are some other promises relating to marriage and suretyship for which the original statute required a writting. The statute, however, is needlessly complex and to a great extent superseded by later statutory enactments.

The Statute of Frauds will not enter the picture if the promise does not involve an aforementioned topic. For example, an oral promise to sell a book for $20 need not be in writing. However, a contract to teach someone piano for thirteen months must be in writing. If the thirteen month contract was not in writing and the student sued the teacher for breach the teacher can escape liability through asserting the Statute of Frauds defense. Is there any change of result if you were told the contract was for eleven months of teaching? We will later see in Part V that the defense of the Statute of Frauds is raised constantly for land, goods and personal services.

There are ways around the Statute. One is "part performance." If an alleged contract has been partly performed, some jurisdictions allow this performance as a substitute for a writing—the performance indicates the likelihood of a contract as much as a signed writing would. Another way is to allege that the promise is not part of an express or formal contract, but is a promise to be enforced by promissory estoppel. We will consider this later in Part E. A third way is to hope that the person against whom the action is brought and who has not signed a writing will forget to plead the Statute. In some jurisdictions the Statute of Frauds is an affirmative defense that if not pleaded is waived.

Concluding note to part B: Go over the Problems at the start of this Part B. Have the cases helped you resolve any of them? What about the movie star problem at the start of Part I? Any light on his problems yet?

C. Enforcement by Seal

The seal is one of the oldest devices for making promises enforceable. In Section 95 of the Restatement of Contracts (Second) [hereinafter referred to as "Restatement"] a promise is considered binding without consideration if: (1) it is written and sealed; (2) delivered within a document; and (3) both the promisor and promisee can be identified from the document when the writing is delivered. Despite statutory enactments in many states reducing the seal to little or no legal force, it was once a very important device for making promises enforceable. As you noticed in Part B, consideration keeps popping up as the way to make a promise enforceable. In *Fischer* even though the promise was made under the most sincere conditions, it was not enforced. In *Webb* the court practically did handstands to make a particular result occur. What if those promises had been under seal? At common law, and in some states today, that alone would make them enforceable. In theory, a seal like a bargained for valuable consideration, makes a person stop and think: Do I really mean this; do I really want to be bound to do this? It is often called a "cautionary" function.

The sealing of a document at one time was an elaborate ceremony involving melting wax next to a person's signature and then impressing on the hot wax that person's seal. By the time you were done melting and impressing, you at least in theory knew that you were involved in something serious. My single experience with sealing something occurred many years ago when I was a student at Oxford. A friend passing through asked me to insure a package of clothes and books and mail it to his address in Belgium. I agreed only to learn that the British postal authorities required that all insured packages leaving the country had to be sealed "with a distinctive seal." I told the postmaster I had no such seal unless I used my class ring. He said not to risk damaging it but to go next door and buy a child's metal ring for sixpence (about 10 cents at the time) at a general merchandise store, and a candle, and bring it back with some matches. I asked if a child's ring whose design was no doubt duplicated by several dozen others even in that store was "distinctive" and wouldn't the seals break before reaching Belgium. He told me the ring would be distinctive enough and yes the seals would probably break even before leaving the post office. But so long as they were intact when I gave him the package it was O.K. Standing in the corner of that post office, melting wax over the corners of a package where the paper came together and then impressing my distinctive seal from a ring I had bought 10 minutes before for sixpense left an indelible impression on my mind. I never forgot it. It was also a grass roots lesson in legal fictions. Even though the seals would break, they had to be applied. It was similar to the experience I had when applying for an International Driver's License and noticing that the application said "I state that I have read and agree to abide by the Rules of the Road a copy of which I have read." I said to the administrator, "I just got the Rules two minutes ago. I haven't had time to read them." She said: "But you do intend to read them, don't you sir?" I said "yes" and signed the form.

In time the letters L.S. printed or written next to a person's name took the place of the seal. (Locus Sigilli) — "Place of the Seal". Soon, documents were printed with L.S. already printed on them. No one took any notice but they were considered sealed documents. All the cautionary effects were gone. In time many legislatures abolished the seal's legal effect. In some states, however, it survives. Where it does not act as a substitute for consideration, it often extends the Statute of Limitations, the time after an event (such as a contract breach) during which an injured party may bring suit.

Thomason v. Bescher

176 N.C. 622, 97 S.E. 654
Supreme Court of North Carolina, 1918.

ACTION to enforce specific performance of a contract to sell timber, tried before *Long, J.*, and a jury, at July Term, 1918, of Randolph.

There were facts in evidence tending to show that on 18 June, 1919, J.C. and W.M. Bescher, two tenants in common in a tract of land, entered into a written contract, under seal, giving plaintiff Thomason the option to purchase the timber thereon, at $6,000, within sixty days, or by 18 August, 1917, the said contract being in terms as follows:

"Know all men by these presents, that in consideration of the sum of one dollar to us in hand paid by C.E. Thomason, of Davidson County, N.C., the receipt of which is hereby acknowledged, we, J.C. and W.M. Bescher, do hereby contract and agree with said C.E. Thomason to sell and convey unto said C.E. Thomason and his heirs and assigns all that certain tract or parcel of timber and roads over land, with sawmill sites, situate, lying and being in Concord Township, Randolph County, adjoining the lands of B.M. Pierce and others, and known as the John S. Bescher place, and containing 715 acres, more or less, and that we will execute and deliver to said C.E. Thomason and his heirs and assigns, at his or their requests, on or before 18 August 1917, a good and sufficient deed for the said timber and roads and mill sites with full covenants and warranty, provided and upon condition, nevertheless, that the said C.E. Thomason, his heirs and assigns, pay us or our representatives or assigns the sum of $6,000 in cash, or equivalent, it is understood and agreed that the said sale is to be made at the option of the said C.E. Thomason or his heirs or assigns, to be exercised on or before 18 August, 1917.

"And it is further understood and agreed that if the said C.E. Thomason and his heirs and assigns shall not demand of us the deed herein provided for and tender payment as herein provided for and on or before said 18 August, 1917, then this agreement is to be null and void, and we are to be at liberty to dispose of the timber to any other person or to use it as we may desire in the same manner as if this contract had never been made; but otherwise this contract is to remain in full force and effect.

"And to the true and faithful performance of this agreement we do hereby bind myself and my heirs, executors, administrators and assigns.

"Witness our hands and seals, this 18 June, 1917. All oldfield pine is hereby excepted, all other included."

Coplaintiff J.F. Curry having acquired one-half interest in said contract prior to institution of suit. That prior to 23 June, 1917, plaintiff Thomason, then holding the contract, notified one of the defendants that he would take the timber, etc.... That plaintiff tendered the purchase price on 7 August, 1917, and had always been ready and willing to pay it. There was denial of obligation on the part of defendants, with evidence tending to show that before any acceptance or notice thereof defendants had, in writing, notified plaintiffs that they elected to terminate the contract.

On issues submitted, the jury rendered the following verdict:

1. At the time of execution of the option on 18 June, 1917, and as a consideration therefor, did the plaintiff C.E. Thomason pay the one dollar to the defendants, as recited in the said option? Answer: "No."

2. Did the plaintiffs thereafter notify the defendants, or either of them, and prior to 23 June, 1917, that they would take the timber, roads and mill sites, under the terms of the said option set up in the complaint and would be down the following week to pay the price and take the deed therefor? Answer: "Yes."

3. Were the plaintiffs at all times able and willing to pay the purchase price of $6,000 for the property, as recited in the option, in event deed was made therefor? Answer: "Yes."

4. Did the defendants on 23 June, 1917, serve the plaintiffs with the following notice: "This is to notify you that the option given you on your timber, Randolph County, on Monday, the 18th of June, is withdrawn and we will not convey the timber according to its terms"? Answer: "Yes."

Judgment on verdict for plaintiff, and defendant excepted and appealed.

HOKE, J.

It is the accepted principle of the common law that instruments under seal require no consideration to support them. Whether this should rest on the position that a seal conclusively imports a consideration or that the solemnity of the act imports such reflection and care that a consideration is regarded as unnecessary, such instruments are held to be binding agreements enforceable in all actions before the common-law courts.

Speaking to the question in *Harrell v. Watson*, 63 N.C., 454, *Pearson, C.J.*, said: "A bond needs no consideration. The solemn act of sealing and delivering is a deed—a thing done which by the rule of the common law, has full force and effect without any consideration. *Nudum pactum* applies only to simple contracts."

A similar position is stated with approval in Prof. Mordecai's Lectures, at p. 931, and Dr. Minor in his *Institutes*, pt. 1, vol. 3, p. 139, says: "In all contracts under seal a valuable consideration is always presumed, from the solemnity of the instrument, as a matter of public policy and for the sake of peace, and presumed conclusively, no proof to the contrary being admitted either in law or equity so far as the parties themselves are concerned."

While there is much diversity of opinion on the subject, we think it the better position and sustained by the weight of authority that the principle should prevail in reference to these unilateral contracts or options when, as in this case, they take the form of solemn written covenants under seal, and its proper application is to render them binding agreements, irrevocable within the time designated, and that the stipulations may be enforced and made effective by appropriate remedies when such time is reasonable and there is nothing oppressive and unconscionable in the terms or the principal contract.

In *Watkins v. Robertson*, 105 Va., 269, the question is directly presented, and in a convincing and learned opinion by *Judge Cardwell* the conclusion of the Court on the subject is announced to the effect: "That an option under seal for the sale of shares in a joint stock company is a binding offer from which the promisor cannot recede during the time stipulated for in the option, and if accepted during that time constitutes a contract the specific performance of which a court of equity will compel. The option is in the nature of a continuing offer to sell, and, being under seal, must be regarded as made upon sufficient consideration, and no proof to the contrary will be received at law of in equity."

In *Willard v. Tayloe*, 75 U.S., 557, *Associate Justice Field*, delivering the opinion, it was held, among other things: "A covenant in a lease giving to the lessee a right or option to purchase the premises leased at any time during the term is in the nature of a continuing offer to sell. The offer thus made, if under seal, is regarded as made upon sufficient consideration, and therefore one from which the lessor is not at liberty to recede." And the position is approved by other courts of the highest authority and by writers of established repute.

Questions

1. Notice what it is that the contract calls for: "on or before 18 August...C.E. Thomason pay us $6,000 in cash." In the section on Offer and Acceptance (Part II) we will learn that when a person makes an offer the person receiving the offer must do exactly what the offer states to create a contract. Here the Beschers agreed to convey the timber if Thomason would give them the $6,000 cash before August 18th. Thomason didn't do that. Instead he promised to take it sometime prior to June 23rd. This is not an acceptance sufficient to create a contract because the offeror had not required a promise but rather cash. On June 23, Beschers attempted to withdraw the option before Thomason could tender the cash. On August 7th the cash was tendered.

2. The big question here is was the promise of the Beschers to keep the offer of the timber open until August 18th, an enforceable promise. There was no consideration to keep it open. What if there had been no seal and the dollar had been paid? What if there had been neither a seal nor a dollar? The key point to remember here is what we have already learned—a promise is usually unenforceable unless there is consideration, a seal or some reliance which causes a loss to the promisee. What is the promise here? To whom was it made? By whom? What is the option here? Whose option?

United States Trust Co. of N.Y. v. Preston, 34 N.Y.S. 2d 646 (A.D., 1942) outlines the history of the seal in New York State to 1942. "It is contended by plaintiff (1) that as the liability is founded on a sealed instrument, defendant is

estopped to attack the instrument for lack of consideration, and (2) that the facts
affirmatively establish consideration precisely coextensive with the obligation.

At the time the instrument in suit was executed, section 342 of the Civil
Practice Act (Laws 1920, c. 925) provided: 'A seal upon an executory instrument
is only presumptive evidence of a sufficient consideration, which may be rebutted
as if the instrument was not sealed.' Since this statute was effective when the
bond was executed, the instrument under seal could not be invalidated for lack
of consideration. Cochran v. Taylor, 273 N.Y. 172, 7 N.E.2d 89. A party to a
sealed instrument, executed and delivered before the amendment of the statute in
1935, is estopped from asserting want of consideration. In Cochran v. Taylor,
supra, the Court, in passing upon the significance of a seal upon a contract made
before the statutory change effected by the Laws of 1935, said (Rippey, J.), 273
N.Y. at page 179, 7 N.E.2d at page 91:

'Williston points out (section 217) that, long before the action of assumpsit was
developed, a promise under seal but without consideration was binding and that
it was binding by its own force by the common law (section 109). It is agreed
upon substantially universal authority that a statement of consideration in a
sealed instrument is unnecessary. Thomason v. Bescher, 176 N.C. 622, 97 S.E.
654. It is also frequently stated by the courts that a sealed instrument carries
with it a presumption that it is given for a valid consideration without the necessity of a recital of the consideration therein and that the party signing and sealing
is estopped to assert lack of consideration. [Cases cited.]'

In 1935, Section 342 was amended, Laws of 1935, ch. 708, so as to provide
that a seal upon a written instrument thereafter executed should not be received
as conclusive or presumptive evidence of a sufficient consideration. In 1941 the
Legislature enacted a new Section 342 declaring that 'Except as otherwise expressly provided by statute, the presence or absence of a seal upon a written instrument hereafter executed shall be without legal effect.' These statutory
changes, occurring after the execution of the agreement here, have no bearing
upon the relationship between the parties to this controversy. The liability being
founded on a sealed instrument made prior to the amendment of 1935, defendant is estopped to attack it for lack of consideration."

Dixon v. Betten, 277 N.E.2D 355 (Ill. App,. 1971) "It has been long established
in Illinois that, '(I)n the absence of statutory enactments to the contrary, it is necessary in actions upon contracts to allege a consideration, except in the case of
contracts under seal, bills of exchange, and negotiable promissory notes, all of
which by intendment of law import a consideration, and a failure to state a consideration or a statement of an insufficient consideration may be taken advantage
of by demurrer'. Schwerdt v. Schwerdt, 141 Ill.App. 386, aff'd. 235 Ill. 386, 85
N.E. 613 (1908)."

McGowan v. Beach, 86 S.E.2d 763 (N.C., 1955). "The instrument in this action
purports to be under seal and wholly in the handwriting of the executant thereof,
and the plaintiff offered evidence to the effect that the entire instrument was in
the handwriting of W. H. McGowan. Moreover, the defendant does not attack
the sufficiency of the evidence to support the answer of the jury to the first issue,
except by motion to nonsuit. However, in his brief, the only argument in support
of this motion is to the effect that the plaintiff offered no proof that the word
'seal' was written after the name of the maker at the time he executed the instru-

ment and, if so, that he adopted it as his seal. There is no contention on the part of the defendant that if the maker of the instrument wrote the word 'seal' after his name at the time he executed the instrument and adopted it as his seal that the defendant would be entitled to a nonsuit. We think that where an instrument is wholly in the handwriting of the maker, it would be strange indeed for him to go to the trouble of writing the word 'seal' after his name unless it was his intention to adopt it as his seal, and such intention will be presumed. In fact, our Court has held that a seal appearing upon an instrument, opposite the name of the maker, in the place where the seal belongs, will in the absence of proof that the maker intended otherwise, be valid as a seal. And this Court said in Jefferson Standard Life Insurance Co. v. Morehead, 209 N.C. 174, 183 S.E. 606, 607, that '... in any event, the maker would have the burden of overcoming the presumption arising from the presence of a seal.' Furthermore, the defendant admits in his brief that in the trial below, 'no questions were asked about the seal, and no evidence offered tending to show its presence or adoption.'

It is said in 12 Am.Jur., Contracts under Seal, section 74, page 567: 'At common law a promise under seal, but without any consideration, is binding because no consideration is required in such a case or, as is sometimes said, because the seal imports, or gives rise to a presumption of, consideration. It has been said that the solemnity of a sealed instrument imports consideration or, to speak more accurately, estops a covenantor from denying a consideration except for fraud,' citing Thomason v. Bescher, 176 N.C. 622, 97 S.E. 654, 655, 2 A.L.R. 626.

Hoke, J. (later Chief Justice), in speaking for the Court in the last cited case, said: 'It is the accepted principle of the common law that instruments under seal require no consideration to support them. Whether this should rest on the position that a seal conclusively imports a consideration, or that the solemnity of the act imports such reflection and care that a consideration is regarded as unnecessary, such instruments are held to be binding agreements enforceable in all actions before the common-law courts.'

Pearson, C. J., in considering this question in Harrell v. Watson, 63 N.C. 454, said: 'A bond needs no consideration. The solemn act of sealing and delivering is a deed, a thing done, which, by the rule of the common law, has full force and effect, without any consideration. Nudum pactum applies only to simple contracts.'

Whether we construe the instrument under consideration to be a nonnegotiable note, a due bill, or merely an acknowledgment by W. H. McGowan of a debt to his wife in the sum of $15,000, the fact that it was executed under seal, which in the absence of proof to the contrary, imports a consideration, the instrument is sufficient as an acknowledgment of such debt.

In the trial below we find

No error."

Read *Hopkins v. Griffin* carefully. Note that it is a modern case and that without the seal Hopkins would have been subject to suit by the Spruills for the money they paid for the allegedly invalid partnership interest, or would have had to prove that he had given consideration for his interest. Because of the seal none of this was necessary. Note in the last half dozen or so paragraphs of the case that there are ways to overcome the import and effect of a seal — fraud, for example. What if someone forged another person's name and/or seal to a document? Note that the court overruled a case which stated that equity will disregard the presumption of consideration which a seal imports.

Hopkins v. Griffin
241 Va. 307, 402 S.E.2d 11
Supreme Court of Virginia, 1991.

WHITING, Justice.

In this declaratory judgment case, the principal issue is whether one party to a contract under seal must show that the other parties' promises were supported by consideration.

On August 28, 1975, Edward McAllister Hopkins and Russell L. Leonard, two real estate agents, together with five other persons, formed a partnership known as Mid-City Properties for the purpose of developing a shopping center in Chesterfield County. Each of the original partners held an equal interest, which was 14.2857% of the whole. R. Garland Dodd, J.W. Sanderson, H. Lee Griffin, Plato G. Eliades, and Dorothy Branch now own the original interests of the seven partners.

Paragraph four of the original partnership agreement provided that the seven partners were equally responsible for capital contributions and losses and that they would share profits and losses equally. Paragraph nine of the partnership agreement gave the partners a 60-day preemptive right to purchase the interest of a deceased or withdrawing partner at its pro rata share of the fair market value of the partnership real estate as of the date of the withdrawing partner's death or notice of election to withdraw.

On September 23, 1977, paragraph four was amended to vest Hopkins and Leonard with additional five percent interests in the partnership income and net assets on distribution, but subjected them to an additional five percent of the partnership losses. The amendment, however, provided that although the owners would continue to contribute the needed capital in equal shares, those contributions would be credited in accordance with the following adjusted partnership interests: 17.857142% each for Hopkins and Leonard, and 12.857142% each for the remaining five partners. Just above the seven partners' signatures was the following language: "IN WITNESS WHEREOF, the parties have hereunto set their hands and seals."

On November 15, 1978, Leonard sold "12.857142% of his total interest of 17.857142%" to Eliades, and the following month he sold "the final five percent (5%) of his interest in said partnership" to Hopkins. The sale to Hopkins recited that the partners agreed that Hopkins "is now a partner to the extent of a total of 22.857142%." On November 26, 1979, Hopkins sold to Griffin "his regular share of 12.857142% of his total interest of 22.857142%, thereby retaining the special 10% interest." These three sales were reflected in amendments to the partnership agreement, each of which was signed under seal by all partners.

On January 6, 1981, Hopkins signed an agreement transferring his two "(5) percent non-funding interest[s]" to Elbert Jay Spruill and Patricia Smith Spruill (collectively Spruill). Before signing the agreement, Hopkins met with the remaining partners and advised them of his desire to sell his "ten percent interest." According to Hopkins, one partner moved that "they purchase that ten percent and I don't think it was ever voted on, but they decided they weren't interested in purchasing it." Hopkins also testified that when he advised Eliades that he had an offer for the share and a deposit, Eliades told him to "take it and run."

On the other hand, the only partners who testified contended that the two five percent interests of Hopkins and Leonard were invalid because Hopkins and Leonard had not performed the work that was the consideration for issuance of those interests. Upon the partnership's refusal to recognize that Hopkins had a 10% partnership interest, Spruill brought this declaratory judgment suit against the partners and Hopkins, seeking to establish the validity of Hopkins' 10% interest and its sale to Spruill, or, if either be invalid, to obtain a money judgment against Hopkins for the amounts paid for his alleged partnership interest.

After hearing evidence and argument, the trial court held that there was no consideration for the agreement to vest the two additional five percent interests in Hopkins and Leonard and, therefore, that Hopkins had nothing he could sell to Spruill. The court further held that, even if Hopkins had acquired the two five percent partnership interests, he had not validly transferred those interests to Spruill because he had not first offered the remaining partners their preemptive rights to purchase those interests. The court reserved decision on the issue whether the owner of this 10% interest was obligated to share in certain capital contributions. Spruill and Hopkins appeal the court's adverse interlocutory decree.

First, we consider the contention that there was no consideration for issuance of the two five percent interests to Hopkins and Leonard. Because the contract is under seal, we need not decide whether there was an actual consideration for the transfer. We do not accept the partners' premise that "in equity" a court always can inquire into the question of consideration even if the contract is under seal. "In a contract under seal, a valuable consideration is presumed from the solemnity of the instrument, as a matter of public policy and for the sake of peace, and presumed conclusively, no proof to the contrary being admitted either at law or in equity so far as the parties themselves are concerned." Watkins v. Robertson, 105 Va. 269, 279, 54 S.E. 33, 36 (1906) (citation omitted; emphasis in original). We cited Watkins and relied upon this principle in the equity suits of Mitchell v. Wayave, 185 Va. 679, 688, 40 S.E.2d 284, 288 (1946), and Parker v. Murphy, 152 Va. 173, 191, 146 S.E. 254, 260 (1929).

Norris v. Barbour, 188 Va. 723, 51 S.E.2d 334 (1949), did not modify Watkins, as contended by the partners. In Norris, we permitted a widow to show a lack of consideration for her husband's execution of a bond under seal that would have reduced her distributive rights in her husband's estate by obligating her husband's estate to pay a sum of money to fund a trust to support his brothers and sisters. Id. at 741, 51 S.E.2d at 341. We cited and reaffirmed Watkins and its progeny, but noted that the rule did not apply in Norris because the widow was not a party to the bond and the bond was a fraud on her distributive rights in her deceased husband's estate. Id. at 737, 740-41, 51 S.E.2d at 339-40, 341. Similarly, in Cooper v. Gregory, 191 Va. 24, 31, 60 S.E.2d 50, 53 (1950), litigants who were neither parties to a sealed instrument, nor their successors in title, were permitted to show a lack of consideration.

The partners rely upon Branch v. Richmond Cold Storage, 146 Va. 680, 693-94, 132 S.E. 848, 852 (1926). There, we said that "a seal imports consideration at common law but...equity will in proper cases disregard this presumption." Branch cited no Virginia authority to support the statement, and we have never cited Branch for this proposition. Indeed, after Branch, we decided Norris, Mitchell, Parker, and Wilson v. Butt, 168 Va. 259, 269, 190 S.E. 260, 264 (1937), applying the contrary principle. Accordingly, to the extent that Branch is at variance with Watkins and its progeny, it is expressly overruled.

Although Griffin, Eliades, and Branch were not parties to the instrument creating the two five percent interests, they claim as successors in title to parties who were bound by the instrument. Therefore, they are subject to its terms. Selden v. Williams, 108 Va. 542, 550, 62 S.E. 380, 382 (1908) (assignee of judgment subject to all defenses judgment debtor could make against assignor).

Finally, the partners argue that even if Hopkins had a 10% partnership interest, his sale to Spruill was not valid because the evidence does not indicate that he offered the partners their 60-day preemptive right to purchase the stock. However, any tender of that right would have been a vain act because the partners denied that Hopkins had a 10% partnership interest. Under these circumstances Hopkins was not obliged to offer them the right to purchase his 10% interest because "[t]he law does not require one to do a vain thing." Reiber v. James M. Duncan, Jr., & Assocs., 206 Va. 657, 662, 145 S.E.2d 157, 161 (1965) (purchaser not required to tender payment after owner advised he would not consummate sale).

Accordingly, we will reverse the interlocutory decree of the trial court. We will also remand the case for entry of a declaratory judgment in conformity with this opinion and for the necessary further proceedings.

Reversed and remanded.

Conclusion: The seal is an old device. It is often overlooked. Do not do so. The word "seal" written after someone's name, or a simple L.S. can change the whole complexion of a case.

D. Enforcement by Bargain — Consideration: The Heart of Contract

The seal is not much in use today as a means of making a promise enforceable. Consideration, however, is alive and well. What this is and what it means in Contract formation is the subject of this section. Consider the following problems and how you would solve them as you read the cases and text that follow.

Problems on Consideration

1. Daughter says to Mother. "I'm glad you've decided to quit smoking. I'm going to clean my room every day to show how much I appreciate it.

2. Mother says to Sister: "I'd really like to have you come and visit more often. I've fixed up the guest room for you." Sister comes to visit and says "This is really nice. I'll come more often." She doesn't come again.

3. Father says to Son who lives in another state: "Your mother and I are getting old. We really miss you and your wife. If you come and live here with us, I'll set you up in the my business and if it works out you can have a half interest in it when I retire. We have a big house here and there's plenty of room for all of us. If your mother and I decide to retire in Florida, you can have the house too. I'd really like to have you here." Son and his wife comes to live with his parents. Neither he and his wife nor his father and mother are happy with the arrangement. Father says to Son: "This isn't working out. You'd better go back." Son says: "Go back to what? You owe me a half interest in the business. Why don't you and Mom go to Florida. We're happy here."

4. Businessman says to friend: "We've both made a lot of money over the years in our separate businesses. Why don't we form a partnership? That way if we combine what we have we can do even better." Businessman includes the details of how they would share expenses, profits etc. Friend says: "O.K". Businessman then says: "I don't think this is such a good idea. I'm not going through with it."

Note on Consideration

Consideration is a bargained for benefit or detriment. Note that for a contract to be formed in the cases that follow the person to whom an offer is made must respond by acting or promising to act in the way spelled out in the offer. If I say to you: "I'll take $1,000 cash for my old car, if you bring me the cash today" and you say "O.K." there may not be a contract. However, if I say: "I want to sell my old car; I'll sell it to you for $1,000" and you say "O.K." we probably have a contract. What is the difference?

In the first instance the $1,000 is the consideration for my promise to sell the car. No contract is formed until you bring me the cash. My offer to you is a promise to sell you the car if you bring me the cash. I am not looking for you to promise me anything. If you want the car, bring the cash.

In the second instance the simple promise to pay $1,000 at some future date is the consideration for the promise to sell the car. What I am really saying is "I promise to sell you my old car for $1,000 if you promise to pay me $1,000 for it." When you say "O.K." you are saying "I promise to pay you $1,000 for it."

In Part II, we will consider offer and acceptance in depth; how an offer is made, when and how an offer can be revoked; what is necessary for an acceptance. Here, it is necessary to discuss offer only because offer and acceptance are tied up with consideration. Every offer seeks a consideration. To make the offer into a binding promise to do or not do something, the offeree (the one to whom the offer is directed) must do what the offer seeks: either perform or refrain from performing an act, or promise to perform or not perform the act sought by the offer. By definition an offer is a communication which can be accepted and with the acceptance a contract is formed. Every offer seeks something—an act or a promise. By performing the act or making the promise, a contract is formed which means that the offer is converted into a promise, an obligation to do or not do something.

If a promise is sought by the offeror (the person making the offer) and the promise is made by the offeree, a bilateral contract is formed. It is called bilateral because there are two binding promises made, one on each side, by each person, the offeror and the offeree. The second example above is an example of a bilateral contract since I am promising to sell you my car after you promise to pay me $1,000.

If an act is sought by the offeror and the act is performed, a unilateral contract is formed. That is because there is one binding promise made, the offeror's. Notice the offeror did not seek a promise from the offeree; the offeror sought an action and once it was performed the single promise embedded in the offer became binding. The first example above is an example of an unilateral contract. The $1,000 cash payment (action) binds the offeror to his promise to sell the car.

It is often said that consideration is based on benefit or detriment moving from one person to another. This is only part of the story. It is also a question of seeking something. There is an element of motivation involved. I either want $1,000 or your promise to pay $1,000 for my car. My motive is not to give you the car. It is to have you confer a benefit on me and correspondingly suffer a detriment in that you will be $1,000 poorer. If I wrote "I promise to sell my car to X for $1,000" and signed and sealed the document, as seen in the last section, that promise would be binding in some states. No consideration is needed. The promise could be enforced. Even though you have given me nothing in return at the time I sign and seal the document, neither the money nor a promise, the seal makes my promise enforceable. Take away the seal and there is nothing to support the promise. Therefore, it is unenforceable.

As you read *Hamer v. Sidway* ask yourself what distinguishes it from *Fischer* and *Hopkins*. Was the uncle really trying to enter into a contract? The court thought so. Why?.

Hamer v. Sidway
124 N.Y. 538, 27 N.E. 256
Court of Appeals of New York, 1891.

PARKER, J.,

The question which provoked the most discussion by counsel on this appeal, and which lies at the foundation of plaintiff's asserted right of recovery, is whether by virtue of a contract defendant's testator, William E. Story, became indebted to his nephew, William E. Story, 2d, on his twenty-first birthday in the sum of $5,000. The trial court found as a fact that 'on the 20th day of March, 1869,...William E. Story agreed to and with William E. Story, 2d, that if he would refrain from drinking liquor using tobacco, swearing, and playing cards or billiards for money until he should become twenty-one years of age, then he, the said William E. Story, would at that time pay him, the said William E. Story, 2d, the sum of $5,000 for such refraining, to which the said William E. Story, 2d, agreed,' and that he 'in all things fully performed his part of said agreement.' The defendant contends that the contract was without consideration to support it, and therefore invalid. He asserts that the promisee, by refraining from the use of liquor and tobacco, was not harmed, but benefited; that that which he did was best for him to do, independently of his uncle's promise,—and insists that it follows that, unless the promisor was benefited, the contract was without consideration,—a contention which, if well founded, would seem to leave open for controversy in many cases whether that which the promisee did or omitted to do was in fact of such benefit to him as to leave no consideration to support the enforcement of the promisor's agreement. Such a rule could not be tolerated, and is without foundation in the law. The exchequer chamber in 1875 defined 'consideration' as follows: 'A valuable consideration, in the sense of the law, may consist either in some right, interest, profit, or benefit accruing to the one party, or some forbearance, detriment, loss, or responsibility given, suffered, or undertaken by the other.' Courts 'will not ask whether the thing which forms the consideration does in fact benefit the promisee or a third party, or is of any substantial value to any one. It is enough that something is promised, done, forborne, or suffered by the party to whom the promise is made as consideration for the promise made to him.' Anson, Cont. 63. 'In general a waiver of any legal right at the request of another party is a sufficient consideration for a promise.' Pars. Cont..'Any damage, or suspension, or forbearance of a right will be sufficient to sustain a promise.' 2 Kent, Comm. (12th Ed.). Pollock in his work on Contracts, (page 166,) after citing the definition given by the exchequer chamber, already quoted, says: 'The second branch of this judicial description is really the most important one. 'Consideration' means not so much that one party is profiting as that the other abandons some legal right in the present, or limits his legal freedom of action in the future, as an inducement for the promise of the first.' Now, applying this rule to the facts before us, the promisee used tobacco, occasionally drank liquor, and he had a legal right to do so. That right he abandoned for a period of years upon the strength of the promise of the testator that for such forbearance he would give him $5,000. We need not speculate on the effort which may have been required to give up the use of those stimulants. It is sufficient that he restricted his lawful freedom of action within certain prescribed limits upon the faith of his uncle's agreement, and now, having fully performed the conditions imposed, it is of no moment whether such performance actually proved a benefit to the promisor, and the court will not inquire into it; but, were it a proper subject of inquiry, we see nothing in this record that would permit a determination that the uncle was not benefited in a legal sense. Few cases have been found which may be said to be precisely in point, but such as have been, support the position we have taken. In Shadwell v. Shadwell, 9 C. B. (N. S.) 159, an uncle wrote to his nephew as follows: 'My dear Lancey: I am so glad to hear of your intended marriage with Ellen Nicholl, and, as I promised to assist you at starting, I am happy to tell you that I will pay you 150 pounds yearly during my life and until your annual income derived from your profession of a chancery barrister shall amount to 600 guineas, of which your own admission will be the only evidence that I shall receive or require. Your affectionate uncle, CHARLES SHADWELL.' It was held that the promise was binding, and made upon good consideration. In Lakota v. Newton, (an unreported case in the superior court of Worcester, Mass.,) the complaint averred defendant's promise that 'if you [meaning the plaintiff] will leave off drinking for a year I will give you $100,' plaintiff's assent thereto, performance of the condition by him, and demanded judgment therefor. Defendant demurred, on the ground, among others, that the plaintiff's declaration did not allege a valid and sufficient consideration for the agreement of the defendant. The demurrer was overruled. In Talbott v. Stemmons, 12 S. W. Rep. 297, (a Kentucky case, not yet officially reported,) the step-grandmother of the plaintiff made with him the following agreement: 'I do promise and bind myself to give my grandson Albert R. Talbott $500 at my death if he will never take another chew of tobacco or smoke another cigar during my life, from this date up to my death; and if he breaks this pledge he is to refund double the amount to his mother.' The executor of Mrs. Stemmons demurred to the complaint on the ground that the agreement was not based on a sufficient consideration. The demurrer was sustained, and an appeal taken therefrom to the court of appeals, where the decision of the court below was reversed. In the opinion of the court it is said that 'the right to use and enjoy the use of tobacco was a right that belonged to the plaintiff, and not forbidden by law. The abandonment of its use may have saved him money, or contributed to his health; nevertheless, the surrender of that right caused the promise, and, having the right to contract with reference to the subjectmatter, the abandonment of the use was a sufficient consideration to uphold the promise.' Abstinence from the use of intoxicating liquors was held to furnish a good consideration for a promissory note in Lindell v. Rokes, 60 Mo. 249. The cases cited by the defendant on this question are not in point. In Mallory v. Gillett, 21 N. Y. 412; Belknap v. Bender, 74 N. Y. 446; and Berry v. Brown, 107 N. Y. 659, 14 N. E. Rep. 289,—the promise was in contravention of that provision of the statute of frauds which declares void all promises to answer for the debts of third persons unless reduced to writing. In Beaumont v. Reeve, Shir. Lead. Cas. 7, and Porterfield v. Butler, 47 Miss. 165, the question was whether a moral obligation furnishes sufficient consideration to uphold a subsequent express promise. In Duvoll v. Wilson, 9 Barb. 487, and Wilbur v. Warren, 104 N. Y. 192, 10 N. E. Rep. 263, the proposition involved was whether an executory covenant against incumbrances in a deed given in consideration of natural love and affection could be enforced. In Vanderbilt v. Schreyer, 91 N. Y. 392, the plaintiff contracted with defendant to build a house, agreeing to accept in part payment therefor a specific bond and mortgage. Afterwards he refused to finish his contract unless the defendant would guaranty its payment, which was done. It was held that the guaranty could not be enforced for want of consideration; for in building the house the plaintiff only did that which he had contracted to do. And in Robinson v. Jewett, 116 N. Y. 40, 22 N. E. Rep. 224, the court simply held that 'the performance of an act which the party is under a legal obligation to perform cannot constitute a consideration for a new contract.' It will be observed that the agreement which we have been considering was within the condemnation of the statute of frauds, because not to be performed within a year, and not in writing. But this defense the promisor could waive, and his letter and oral statements subsequent to the date of final performance on the part of the promisee must be held to amount to a waiver. Were it otherwise, the statute could not now be invoked in aid of the defendant. It does not appear on the face of the complaint that the agreement is one prohibited by the statute of frauds, and therefore such defense could not be made available unless set up in the answer. Porter v. Wormser, 94 N. Y. 431, 450. This was not done.

The order appealed from should be reversed, and the judgment of the special term affirmed, with costs payable out of the estate. All concur.

Questions

1. In *Fischer* a dollar changed hands. Here nothing changed hands. Why is there a contract here and not in *Fischer*?

2. Would it matter if the uncle's promise took place at a family gathering? What if the uncle had said at a party: "Willie, drinking, smoking, card playing and billiards lead to bad things. You ought to give them up at least until you're

21." At age 21 nephew writes to uncle and says "I've followed your advice and I feel great for it" Uncle writes back: "You're a good boy Willie and to show you how much I appreciate it I'm going to send you a check for $5,000." Uncle never pays the money and is sued by nephew. Would nephew win?

3. Why is the case of *Shadwell v. Shadwell* cited as authority by the court not a good example of consideration? Why is it closer to *Fischer* than the facts in *Hamer*?

4. Was the uncle seeking a promise or an action? Notice that the court says "William E. Story agreed to and with William E. Story the 2d" and also says that the uncle made his offer "to which the said William E. Story 2d agreed." Read that whole passage again at the start of the case. As you will learn in the section on offer and acceptance, offers normally can be revoked before they are accepted. In this case it was not. So it really does not matter. If it were a bilateral contract and if nephew first stopped and then took up smoking before reaching 21, would nephew be in breach of contract? Would uncle have any remedy? How would it be possible to measure damages? Why would a court be unlikely to order nephew to not smoke? If it were an offer to enter into a unilateral contract, when would the contract come into being? What is it the uncle wants?

5. If the uncle wanted a promise not to smoke from his nephew in exchange for his (the uncle's) promise to pay nephew $5,000 on nephew's 21st birthday, what would be the consideration for the uncle's promise, the nephew's promise not to smoke or the nephew's actually not smoking?

Nat Nal Service Stations, Inc. v. Wolf, 304 N.Y. 332, 107 N.E.2d 473 (Court of Appeals of New York, 1952). This case concerned a gasoline station owner (plaintiff) who sued on the basis of an alleged agreement with the defendants for the purchase of gasoline from Standard Oil Company. According to the plaintiff, if plaintiff placed orders for gasoline through defendants, defendants would pay to plaintiffs whatever discount Standard gave to defendants. The complaint stated in part: "...the defendants promised...that so long as plaintiff purchased from the Standard Oil Company...its requirements for gasoline at its place of business through the defendants and the defendants accepted the same, the defendants would pay to the plaintiff...the discount allowed to defendants by... Standard Oil Company." The defendants in their answer denied each and every allegation quoted above and also pleaded that the oral agreement which plaintiff alleged was "by its terms...not to be performed within one year from the making thereof." Under New York law, the Statute of Frauds, as it related to the need for a writing based on when the contract was to be performed, "has been so construed as to apply only to agreements which by their terms do not admit of performance within one year from the time of their making and if performance be possible within one year, however unlikely or improbable that may be, the agreement does not come within the proscription of the statute." The court found that (1) the agreement alleged "by its terms did not of necessity extend beyond one year from the time of its making" and (2) "that neither party obligated itself to do anything." The court went on to say "We are confronted with an alleged contract by the terms of which neither party was bound to do anything at any time and consequently there is nothing in its terms to bring it within the Statute of Frauds."

Questions

1. If neither party was bound to do anything at any time was there consideration? Was there a contract?

2. Plaintiff bought over 900,000 gallons of gasoline through defendants and wanted the discount which amounted to at least one cent a gallon. Although the lower courts granted summary judgment to defendants and hence denied this right the Court of Appeals reversed. It said in part: "Here, neither party has, nor is it possible for them under the terms of the alleged agreement, to furnish consideration through performance which will bind the other party for a period beyond the offering and acceptance of a particular order." What is the court saying here? Was there an agreement or agreements between plaintiff and defendants? What was the consideration for it (them)? What was (were) the agreement(s)?

Petroleum Refractionating Corp. v. Kendrick Oil Co.

65 F.2D 997
Court of Appeals, 10th Circuit, 1933.

PHILLIPS, Circuit Judge.

The Petroleum Corporation brought this action against the Kendrick Company to recover damages for breach of contract. After setting out the jurisdictional facts, the amended petition alleged that on January 15, 1932, the Kendrick Company gave an order to the Petroleum Corporation, the material portions of which read as follows:

'January 15th, 1932.

'To Petroleum Refractionating Company, Tulsa, Oklahoma.

Ship to Metropolitan Utilities District, Gas Plant, 20th & Center Streets,

Omaha, Nebraska. * * *

Shipping date, February, March, April and May.

Cars—1,500,000 gallons, 10% more or less.

Commodity—35-37 straight run gas oil, meeting Metropolitan Utilities

District specifications.

Price—45 cents barrel.

F. O. B.—Pampa, Texas.

Terms—1-10. * * *

Seller may cancel any unshipped portion of this order on five days' notice, if for any reason, he should discontinue making this grade of oil. * * *'

That the Petroleum Corporation accepted such order and delivered thereunder 62,601 gallons of such oil; that on February 16, 1932, the Kendrick Company notified the Petroleum Corporation that it would not accept further deliveries under such order for the reason that the grade of oil being shipped was not of the standard stipulated in the order; that after notice to the Kendrick Company, and on February 21, 1932, the Petroleum Corporation resold the portion of the oil remaining undelivered under such contract at 25 cents a barrel. It sought damages for the difference between the contract price and the resale price of such oil.

The Kendrick Company demurred to the petition on the ground that it did not state facts sufficient to constitute a cause of action. The trial court held that there was no consideration for the promise of the Kendrick Company to purchase, and sustained the demurrer. The Petroleum Corporation elected to stand on its amended petition, and the trial court entered judgment for the Kendrick Company. This is an appeal therefrom.

Counsel for the Petroleum Corporation contend that the promise of the Kendrick Company to purchase was supported by the agreement of the Petroleum Corporation either to sell, which would be a benefit to the Kendrick Company, or, in the alternative, to discontinue making such grade of oil, which would be a detriment to the Petroleum Corporation. On the other hand, counsel for the Kendrick Company contend that whether the Petroleum Corporation should sell and deliver the oil was conditioned only by the will or wish of the Petroleum Corporation.

A benefit to the promisor or a detriment to the promisee is a sufficient consideration for a contract.

The detriment need not be real; it need not involve actual loss to the promisee. The word, as used in the definition, means legal detriment as distinguished from detriment in fact. It is the giving up by the promisee of a legal right; the refraining from doing what he has the legal right to do, or the doing of what he has the legal right not to do.

And where there is a detriment to the promisee, there need be no benefit to the promisor.

Under the terms of the contract, the Petroleum Corporation agreed either to sell and deliver the oil or to discontinue making the grade of oil contracted for, and to give five days' notice of cancellation of the contract.

Since alternative courses were open to the Petroleum Corporation, the contract was without consideration on its part, if any one of the courses standing alone would have been an insufficient consideration. Restatement, Contracts, § 79; Williston on Contracts, § 104, p. 219.

The question then is, Would a discontinuance by the Petroleum Corporation to manufacture the grade of oil contracted for result in such a detriment to it as would constitute a consideration for the promise of the Kendrick Company to purchase?

The giving up by the seller of the right to sell to others such goods as he should manufacture during a specified period has been held a sufficient consideration for the promise of the buyer to purchase such goods, although the seller was not obligated to manufacture any goods whatever.

The giving of a preferential right to purchase personal property, in the event the owner should conclude to sell it, has been held a sufficient consideration for the promise of another to purchase, although there was no obligation on the part of the owner to sell.

In City of Marshall v. Kalman, 153 Minn. 320, 190 N. W. 597, Kalman agreed to purchase all the street improvement certificates which the city should issue during a specified period, at par plus accrued interest. It was urged that the contract was without consideration on the part of the city because it was not obligated to issue any certificates. The court held that, although the city had not agreed to issue any certificates, it had restricted its freedom to sell to others any certificates which it might issue, and that such restriction was a valid consideration for the promise of Kalman to purchase.

Should the Petroleum Corporation, under the alternative provision of the contract, discontinue to manufacture the grade of oil specified in the contract, it would refrain from doing that which it had the right to do; and it would thereby give up a legal right—the right to continue to make the grade of oil specified.

It follows that, under the principles above stated, the discontinuance by the Petroleum Corporation to manufacture the grade of oil specified in the contract would constitute a detriment to it, and the promise so to do would be a sufficient consideration for the promise of the Kendrick Company to purchase.

The judgment is reversed with instructions to overrule the demurrer.

Questions

1. What if seller discontinues making the grade of oil for one day? one month? one year? one hour? Would this continue to be consideration? In *Hamer* the uncle was bargaining for something, wasn't he? In *Nat Nal* was there a bargain, something being sought? Is it fair to say that it is likely that buyer couldn't care less whether seller makes a grade of oil or not, or is that fair? What if buyer really didn't care? Would that make something not a consideration because the buyer was not really seeking it? Or is consideration like intent—if something is objectively true it is true? Who sent the communication here that contained the cancellation clause? Should that even matter? Is it enough if the appearance of a bargain exists? But if that is true, why wasn't it true for *Fischer*?

2. Assume that the cancellation clause did not refer to discontinuing making a grade of oil but ended with the words "on five days' notice." Would that be consideration? One day? What if the clause made no reference to notice or discontinuing making the grade of oil?

3. What is a "demurrer?" If the court is reversing and overruling the demurrer, who demurred to what in the trial court and with what result?

4. What measure of damages is being sought by plaintiff? How will that compensate plaintiff? Given that compensation is the purpose of money damages, why couldn't plaintiff simply sue for 45 cents a barrel without reselling anything? Could plaintiff sue for 20 cents a barrel without reselling anything? The Uniform Commercial Code, not then in effect, would allow four possible means for determining damages here. (1) Plaintiff makes a reasonable contract to sell the goods to someone else at a reasonable price within a reasonable time after plaintiff learns of defendant's breach and charges the difference to the defendant. (2) Plaintiff proves what the market price for the oil is at the time for delivery and without selling any oil to anyone, sues for the difference between market and contract. (3) Plaintiff proves that there is

no market for the goods—that is, plaintiff cannot sell them to anyone for any price—and sues defendant for the contract price—here 45 cents a barrel. (4) Plaintiff proves that there is an unlimited supply of oil and a limited number of buyers and that plaintiff should not have to use options (1) or (2) because that does not compensate plaintiff; plaintiff could have sold other oil to other buyers and made a profit on that oil as well as the profit from defendant if defendant had not broken the contract. As an example of number (4), suppose that the oil cost 15 cents a barrel to manufacture and that defendant refused to take 100,000 barrels called for by the contract. If plaintiff sells the 100,000 barrels to another buyer (B) for 25 cents per barrel, plaintiff makes 10 cents per barrel on that oil or $10,000. If plaintiff then sues defendant for the difference between the contract price and the price paid by B, plaintiff receives 20 cents per barrel from defendant or $20,000 to make up the difference between the contract price of 45 cents per barrel and the resale to B at 25 cents per barrel. Plaintiff makes a total profit of $30,000. BUT does this really compensate plaintiff? If defendant had not breached and had bought the oil for 45 cents per barrel, plaintiff would have made a profit of $30,000 on that transaction. Then plaintiff could have sold another 100,000 barrels to B for 25 cents per barrel for a profit of 10 cents per barrel or $10,000 for a total profit of $40,000. Why might it be easier for the nonbreaching party to use method # 1 or # 2 than # 4? Why might it be easier today, than before the age of computers, to figure out cost and profit per barrel and so make # 4 an easier option? Remember that # 4 is a fairly recent innovation to the law. See Uniform Commercial Code sections 2-706, 2-708, 2-709 and their comments.

Embola v. Tuppela

127 Wash. 285, 220 P. 789
Supreme Court of Washington, 1923.

PEMBERTON, J.

John Tuppela joined the gold seekers' rush to Alaska, and after remaining there a number of years prospecting was adjudged insane, and committed to an asylum in Portland, Or. Upon his release, after a confinement of about four years, he found that his mining properties in Alaska had been sold by his guardian. In May of 1918 Tuppela, destitute and without work, met respondent at Astoria, Or. They had been close friends for a period of about 30 years. Respondent advanced money for his support, and in September brought him to Seattle to the home of Herman Lindstrom, a brother-in-law of respondent. Tuppela had requested a number of people to advance money for an undertaking to recover his mining property in Alaska, but found no one who was willing to do so. The estimated value of this mining property was about $500,000. In the month of September Tuppela made the following statement to respondent: 'You have already let me have $270. If you will give me $50 more so I can go to Alaska and get my property back, I will pay you ten thousand dollars when I win my property.'

Respondent accepted this offer, and immediately advanced the sum of $50. In January, 1921, after extended litigation, Tuppela recovered his property. Tuppela, remembering his agreement with respondent, requested Mr. Cobb, his trustee, to pay the full amount, and upon his refusal so to do this action was instituted to collect the same.

The answer of the appellant denies the contract, and alleges that, if it were made, it is unconscionable, not supported by adequate consideration, procured through fraud, and is usurious. The appellant also alleges that the amount advanced did not exceed $100, and he has paid $150 into the registry of the court for the benefit of respondent.

The court found in favor of the respondent, and from the judgment entered this appeal is taken.

It is contended by appellant that the amount advanced is a loan, and therefore usurious, and that the sum of $300 is not an adequate consideration to support a promise to repay $10,000. It is the contention of respondent that the money advanced was not a loan, but an investment; that the transaction was in the nature of a grubstake contract, which has been upheld by this court.

This is not a case wherein respondent advanced money to carry on prospecting. The money was advanced to enable appellant to recover his mining property. Appellant had already been advised by an attorney that he could not recover this property. The risk of losing the money advanced was as great in this case as if the same had been advanced under a grubstake contract. Where the principal sum advanced is to be repaid only on some contingency that may never take place, the sum so advanced is considered an investment, and not a loan, and the transaction is not usurious. 'To constitute usury it is essential that the principal sum loaned shall be repayable at all events and not put in hazard absolutely. If it is payable only on some contingency then the transaction is not usurious....' 27 R. C. L. § 21, p. 220.

The fact that the money advanced was not to be returned until appellant won his property, a contingency at that time unlikely to occur, supports the finding that the consideration was not inadequate. To the contention that the contract was procured through fraud the testimony shows that appellant voluntarily offered to pay the $10,000, and at the time was of sound and disposing mind, and considered that the contract was fair and to his advantage.

The trial court having found that there was no fraud, and that the contract was not unconscionable, we should uphold these findings unless the evidence preponderates against them. We are satisfied that the evidence supports the findings.

The judgment is affirmed.

Questions

1. Was the $270 part of the consideration for the promise of $10,000?

2. What is an "advance" as used in the case? A gift? A loan? Is it used in different ways in paragraphs one and two?

3. If the $270 had originally been a loan, at the time Tuppela asked respondent for $50, was Tuppela treating it as something else? An investment? What is an investment? Assume that Tuppela never received his property in Alaska. Assume further that respondent sues Tuppela for $270 plus interest and $50 plus interest. Using the court's reasoning is respondent likely to win either or both actions?

4. If I say to you, "if you will lend me 25 cents today, I promise to repay you $20 tomorrow," is this court likely to uphold this as a valid contract? Why or why not?

5. It is five minutes before five P.M. and you have just received a message that a job you want for the summer has become available but you must call back the prospective employer before 5:00 P.M. You rush to the pay phone and find someone else about to use it. You say, "If you let me use the phone right now, I'll pay you $20." S/he hands you the phone. Contract? You then find you don't have a quarter. You say to the person, "I'll pay you $25 if you'll give me a quarter." The person gives you a quarter. Do you owe $25? Does it matter if the phone doesn't work? What if it doesn't work because the quarter is bent? What if it works but the line is busy and when it finally isn't it is 5:02 P.M. and all you get is an answering machine which says, "If this call is about any job offer, all offers expired at 5:00 P.M." Do you owe $20? $25? $45? Why? Does this differ from the example in # 4? How would the court characterize this relationship? Gift, loan, investment, something else?

6. Jones owns a coin—a silver dollar from before 1900. It is still legal tender and is worth $1.00 if you wish to exchange it for a federal reserve note (a paper dollar) at any bank. The silver in the coin makes it worth $17.50 and because the coin is old a collector might pay between $25 and $50 for it. Jones agrees to sell the coin to Smith for $50. Consideration? Contract?

7. Smith owns a paper dollar like the kind we use daily in vending machines. It is in no way different from other paper dollars of its type. Smith agrees to sell the paper dollar to Jones for ten paper dollars. The courts are very unlikely to uphold this exchange. Their grounds are likely to be a lack of or an "insufficiency" of as opposed to an "inadequacy" of consideration, as discussed in the note case following. Why would the courts uphold a contract as being supported by consideration in # 6 but not in this case?

In *Browning v. Johnson, 70 Wash. 2d 145, 422 P.2d 314 (Wash., 1967),* Browning, an osteopath, entered a contract for the sale of Browning's practice to Johnson. Both parties and their lawyers thought that the contract was valid and enforceable. Later Browning wanted to cancel this contract and agreed to pay Johnson $40,000 if Johnson would enter a new contract whose purpose would be canceling the old. Both parties entered such a new contract. Later Browning wanted to avoid paying the $40,000 on the ground that the original contract for purchase and sale of the practice was invalid and unenforceable and thus when Johnson canceled it he did not give Browning anything of value in exchange for Browning's promise to pay $40,000. The trial court concluded that the canceled contract for the sale of Browning's practice was lacking in mutuality and was too indefinite. It, nevertheless, concluded that canceling this "contract" was a sufficient consideration for the promise of the $40,000 by Browning. The appellate court agreed.

"Courts are loath to inquire into the 'adequacy' of consideration, that is, into the comparative value of the promises and acts exchanged. As we said in Rogich v. Dressel, 45 Wash.2d 829, 843, 278 P.2d 367 (1954): (W)e must apply the rule followed in this state that parties who are competent to contract will not be relieved from a bad bargain they make unless the consideration is so inadequate as to be constructively fraudulent * * *. But 'adequacy' of consideration, into which courts seldom inquire, is to be distinguished from the legal 'sufficiency' of any particular consideration. The latter phrase is concerned not with comparative value but with that which will support a promise. '(A)nything which fulfils the requirements of consideration will support a promise whatever may be the comparative value of the consideration, and of the thing promised.' 1 Williston, Contracts § 115, cited in Puget Mill Co. v. Kerry, 183 Wash. 542, 558, 49 P.2d 57, 64, 100 A.L.R. 1220 (1935). (T)he relative values of a promise and the consideration for it, do not affect the sufficiency of consideration.' Restatement, Contracts § 81 (1932). This distinction is sometimes lost sight of. In the instant case, Browning bargained for Johnson's act of giving up the contract of sale. The issue is whether the law regards Johnson's act of giving up that contract as legally 'sufficient' consideration to support Browning's promise to pay him for such an act. The trial court concluded that giving up the contract of sale was 'adequate' consideration for Browning's promise.

Whether there exists something which will support a promise and which therefore may be called legally sufficient consideration is obviously prior to the question of whether that consideration is adequate when compared to the value of the promise given in exchange for it. Therefore, whether the trial court meant (1) that giving up the contract of sale was a bargained-for act legally sufficient to support Browning's promise, or (2) that giving up the contract of sale was sufficient consideration, and moreover, consideration not so inadequate as to be constructively fraudulent is not important. We hold that Browning's promise was supported by sufficient consideration and there is nothing in this case which induces us, under the Rogich formulation, to consider the relative values of the things exchanged.

This is a unilateral contract. See Cook v. Johnson, 37 Wash.2d 19, 221 P.2d 525 (1950). A unilateral contract is one in which a promise is given in exchange for an act or forbearance. Here, Browning gave Johnson a promise to pay $40,000 in exchange for Johnson's act of giving up the contract of sale. Sufficiency of consideration in unilateral contracts is discussed by Professor Williston in his treatise, Contracts § 102 (3d ed. 1957). There he indicates that the requirement of sufficient consideration to support a promise is met by a detriment incurred by the promisee (Johnson) or a benefit received by the promisor (Browning) at the request of the promisor. 'That a detriment suffered by the promisee at the promisor's request and as the price for the promise is sufficient, though the promisor is not benefited, is well settled.' Williston, supra. This has been the law in Washington for over 50 years. The question then becomes the nature of a detriment. Detriment is defined by Williston as the giving up of 'something which immediately prior thereto the promisee was privileged to retain, or doing or refraining from doing something which he was then privileged not to do, or not to refrain from doing.' Williston, supra, § 102A. We have already had occasion to quote this definition with approval. We have employed the definition for many years, see, where we said: Indeed there is a consideration if the promisee, in return for the promise, does anything legal which he is not bound to do, or refrains from doing anything which he has a right to do, whether there is any actual loss or detriment to him or actual benefit to the promisor or not. Citing 9 Cyc. 311 et seq.

The problem presented by this case is not a new one. Over a century ago, in England, Brooks obtained a certain document from Haigh believing that it was a guarantee, and promised to pay a certain sum of money in consideration of

Haigh's giving it up. The guarantee proved to be unenforceable. Haigh sued Brooks for the money promised. The court said: (T)he plaintiffs were induced by the defendant's promise to part with something which they might have kept, and the defendant obtained what he desired by means of that promise. Both being free and able to judge for themselves, how can the defendant be justified in breaking this promise, by discovering afterwards that the thing in consideration of which he gave it did not possess that value which he supposed to belong to it? It cannot be ascertained that that value was what he most regarded. He may have had other objects and motives; and of their weight he was the only judge. Haigh v. Brooks, 10 A. & E. 309, 320 (1839). Similarly here, of Browning's objects and motives, he was the only judge.

The judgment is affirmed."

Question

1. If we follow the reasoning in *Browning* to its logical conclusion regarding detriment, especially if we use the rational of *Haigh v. Brooks*, what does that do to the example of bargaining for one paper dollar by promising ten paper dollars? Does this mean that the courts finally will not enforce some bargains where they can find no semblance of benefit or detriment of any kind?

In the next case we look for a promise in the provisions of a contract which does not have promissory words as such. Lady Duff Gordon promised Wood an exclusive right to market her designs. Wood did not promise to do anything. Thus, there is no consideration for Lady Duff Gordon's promise. Put another way, there is not mutuality of obligation. Lady Duff Gordon got nothing in exchange for her promise; Wood did not do anything nor did he promise to do anything. So reasoned the Appellate Division and three out of seven judges of the Court of Appeals of New York. Four judges, however, reasoned otherwise.

Wood v. Lucy, Lady Duff-Gordon
222 N.Y. 88, 118 N.E. 214
Court of Appeals of New York, 1917.

CARDOZO, J.

The defendant styles herself 'a creator of fashions.' Her favor helps a sale. Manufacturers of dresses, millinery, and like articles are glad to pay for a certificate of her approval. The things which she designs, fabrics, parasols, and what not, have a new value in the public mind when issued in her name. She employed the plaintiff to help her to turn this vogue into money. He was to have the exclusive right, subject always to her approval, to place her indorsements on the designs of others. He was also to have the exclusive right to place her own designs on sale, or to license others to market them. In return she was to have one-half of 'all profits and revenues' derived from any contracts he might make. The exclusive right was to last at least one year from April 1, 1915, and thereafter from year to year unless terminated by notice of 90 days. The plaintiff says that he kept the contract on his part, and that the defendant broke it. She placed her indorsement on fabrics, dresses, and millinery without his knowledge, and withheld the profits. He sues her for the damages, and the case comes here on demurrer.

The agreement of employment is signed by both parties. It has a wealth of recitals. The defendant insists, however, that it lacks the elements of a contract. She says that the plaintiff does not bind himself to anything. It is true that he does not promise in so many words that he will use reasonable efforts to place the defendant's indorsements and market her designs. We think, however, that such a promise is fairly to be implied. The law has outgrown its primitive stage of formalism when the precise word was the sovereign talisman, and every slip was fatal. It takes a broader view today. A promise may be lacking, and yet the whole writing may be 'instinct with an obligation,' imperfectly expressed. If that is so, there is a contract.

The implication of a promise here finds support in many circumstances. The defendant gave an exclusive privilege. She was to have no right for at least a year to place her own indorsements or market her own designs except through the agency of the plaintiff. The acceptance of the exclusive agency was an assumption of its duties. We are not to suppose that one party was to be placed at the mercy of the other. Many other terms of the agreement point the same way. We are told at the outset by way of recital that: 'The said Otis F. Wood possesses a business organization adapted to the placing of such indorsements as the said Lucy, Lady Duff-Gordon, has approved.'

The implication is that the plaintiff's business organization will be used for the purpose for which it is adapted. But the terms of the defendant's compensation are even more significant. Her sole compensation for the grant of an exclusive agency is to be one-half of all the profits resulting from the plaintiff's efforts. Unless he gave his efforts, she could never get anything. Without an implied promise, the transaction cannot have such business 'efficacy, as both parties must have intended that at all events it should have.' Bowen, L. J., in the Moorcock, 14 P. D. 64, 68. But the contract does not stop there. The plaintiff goes on to promise that he will account monthly for all moneys received by him, and that he will take out all such patents and copyrights and trade-marks as may in his judgment be necessary to protect the rights and articles affected by the agreement. It is true, of course, as the Appellate Division has said, that if he was under no duty to try to market designs or to place certificates of indorsement, his promise to account for profits or take out copyrights would be valueless. But in determining the intention of the parties the promise has a value. It helps to enforce the conclusion that the plaintiff had some duties. His promise to pay the defendant one-half of the profits and revenues resulting from the exclusive agency and to render accounts monthly was a promise to use reasonable efforts to bring profits and revenues into existence. For this conclusion the authorities are ample.

The judgment of the Appellate Division should be reversed, and the order of the Special Term affirmed, with costs in the Appellate Division and in this court.

Questions

1. Assume that the contract between Lady Duff Gordon and Wood had said "If Wood successfully markets 10 of Lady Duff Gordon's designs in the next six months, he will have an exclusive agency for the year following the marketing of the 10th design." The rest of the contract is as in the case. Assume further that "successfully markets" is sufficiently defined so as not to fail for indefiniteness. Wood performs as requested. Would the court still find that Wood had assumed an obligation to use best efforts? Would this still be a bi-

lateral contract requiring mutuality of obligation for Lady Duff Gordon's promise to be enforceable?

2. Use the facts as in the case and also as modified in # 1 above. Notice that it is Wood suing Lady Duff Gordon. Same result if Lady Duff Gordon had sued Wood?

3. The implied promise is not so radical a departure as might seem at first. See the note below.

Note on Implied Promises

In Wood v Lady Duff Gordon the court found an implied promise in a contract with a "wealth of recitals" (paragraph 2 sentence 2). Implying an obligation to do something is very old, even if no express promise is made. At early common law the action of quantum meruit (how much is it worth) arose. It still exists today. You will encounter it throughout the course. Quantum meruit is a first cousin to quasi contact and to some extent both have been co-opted by the implied promise in the more formally expressed relationship. Quantum meruit refers to the obligation a person (P) incurs without expressly promising anything where (P) requests a service from someone (S) under circumstances indicating that the person performing it (S) expects or normally would expect to be paid. If I say to a lawn mowing service (L), please come over here and mow my lawn, I should know that because that is their business they expect to be paid. Therefore, a promise by me is implied to pay the reasonable value of L's services. This may or may not be L's usual rate. If L charges more than most I may pay less that L's usual rate. If L charges less than most, I may pay more than L's usual rate. The key point is a promise by me is implied even though I expressly promise nothing. In the *Wood* case, Wood is probably suing for lost profits because Lady Duff Gordon placed her own designs. In other words, he is suing for what he would have made, his expectancy (what he expected to make), if she had used him exclusively to market her designs. Assume for the moment that the Appellate Division rationale had won in the Court of Appeals and Wood had no contract. He could still have sued for damages for the designs he had placed on the grounds that she had requested him to place them and he has a right to the reasonable value of his services in so doing. He would not, however, receive one half of the profits called for in the unenforceable contract. He would only receive the value of what he had performed at her request. Just as quasi contract protects someone by imposing an obligation where no one has expressly requested anything, quantum meruit imposes an obligation where a request has been made, but the details of an express contract do not exist. Quasi contract is rare. Quantum meruit is not. It is the second strand to the bow. If the express contract fails, some recovery is still possible. Where a promise can be implied in an express contractual setting, however, the injured party (Wood here) will not only recover on a theory that the wrongdoer (breaching party) requested something and ought to pay for what (s)he got, but will also recover on the expectancy of the whole express contract. Wood will receive not just the reasonable value of the services he performed in placing designs, he will receive the full amount as damages that he could have made had Lady Duff Gordon lived up to her promise and allowed him to place all of her designs. As courts more readily imply promises, quantum meruit becomes less important. Where the express contract fails, however, or is unenforceable on grounds such as Statute of Frauds, quantum meruit has a very important place. Some courts, in situations where the contract is valid and enforceable, will allow the non-breaching party to choose to sue on the contract or in quantum meruit. Some will not. Some will give the choice but limit the damages to no more than what the damages suit on the contract would bring. Watch for quantum meruit situations in future cases. Consider past cases.

E. Enforcement of a Promise Even When There Is No Seal and No Consideration: Promissory Estoppel and the Nature of Reliance

Note on Enforcement of Promises

Not every promise is enforceable. The most commonly enforceable promises are those based on bargain. In theory this is because people would not go through the trouble of the give and take, the exchange of suggestions and inquiries, the expression of a desire to obtain something and the willingness to provide something in return, unless they took the promise seriously. In other words, if I get something for my promise, something that I have sought and asked for, then I ought to realize that the other person expects me to keep my promise — after all he/she paid for it. In reality, not every "bargain" is a bargain. Not every benefit or detriment is sought. Did Kendrick Oil Co. really bargain for Petroleum Refractionating Co. to either deliver a certain grade of oil or stop making it? Isn't it more likely that Petroleum Refractionating wanted an out and told Kendrick Oil that only if they made an offer in these terms, where Kendrick Oil was bargaining for itself to receive a benefit or Petroleum Refractionating to suffer a detriment, would Petroleum Refractionating make a contract with it at all? Wasn't it good lawyering on Petroleum Refractionating's part to have Kendrick Oil make the offer as if and in the form of Kendrick Oil's wanting Petroleum Refractionating to give up producing oil if it wasn't going to deliver to Kendrick Oil. Notice the different result if instead of Kendrick Oil seeming to bargain for Petroleum Refractionating to give up production Petroleum Refractionating had promised: "I promise to deliver the oil to you or in the alternative I won't deliver it to you." That is not a promise containing a consideration because both alternatives must provide consideration. If Petroleum Refractionating had promised "I promise to deliver or in the alternative give up producing that grade of oil" the result should be as in the case but a court would find giving up production a detriment more easily if the other party was seemingly seeking it.

Form of a bargain is enough for a legal contract. Courts will enforce agreements if a person can be seen as objectively seeking a detriment or benefit, even if subjectively he/she couldn't care less. Note the parallel with intent — the objective vs. the subjective. Only if clearly both parties intended a joke, or if one did and the other knew it, and if no third person relied, will the objective be overcome by the subjective intent of the parties. As we will see in Part III Section D "standardized contracts" people often today sign writings purporting to be the contract, the bargain, the promise(s) of the parties which the law then presumes to be the final expression of the "bargain" of the parties. There may have been no "bargaining" at all prior to signing the writing, but if the writing expresses a consideration, an exchange, a bargain, the law presumes that the party signing has read it and agrees that this is his/her bargain, contract or promise. While it is also possible that extensive bargaining took place prior to the parties signing the writing, the writing is likely to control any conflicts between it and what one of the parties says was agreed. A person signing a writing presumably reads what she is signing and would not sign it if she did not understand and agree to what was written. This is another fiction, just like the fiction of Kendrick Oil seeking and bargaining for Petroleum Refractionating to give up producing a grade of oil. But just as Kendrick Oil was found to have received a bargained for consideration because it went through the form of a bargain, so too will the person who signs a standardized, printed form of a contract be found to have intended this "writing" to be the final embodiment of all that was bargained for previously, including any terms in the writing neither discussed nor intended to be part of the "bargain." So ingrained is the notion that the written terms control, that people, including judges, often refer to the writing, where there is one, as the contract. The writing is never the contract. The writing may, and most often is, presumed to embody the contract which is the promissory intent of the parties, but the writing is never the contract.

Another type of promise which is enforceable, where the seal is still recognized, is the promise under seal. Like consideration, there is fiction here too. Just as a real bargain has deteriorated into the form of a bargain, and just as a writing is presumed to embody the intent or bargain even if it is a printed form that a salesperson fills in moments before the customer signs it, so also the seal deteriorated from the melted wax image onto which a person impressed his own personal, specially designed seal to the simple L.S. printed after the line for a person's signature. Because the seal no longer acted to alert people to the seriousness of what they were doing (once you have had burned wax on your fingers you remember what you're doing), many states abolished it. Today, many writings have the legend in capital letters just below or above the signature line to the effect: I HAVE READ THIS ENTIRE CONTRACT, FRONT AND BACK, AND UNDERSTAND IT AND AGREE TO ABIDE BY ALL ITS TERMS AND FURTHER AGREE THAT IT REPRESENTS THE ENTIRE AGREEMENT. I FURTHER AGREE THAT NO ORAL REPRESENTATION MADE BY ANY PERSON IS A PART OF THIS CONTRACT. Like the L.S. this legend might as well be in Latin. It is there, however, because courts have begun to look behind the fictions and realize that the bargains are not always found in the writings and also that what appear to be bargains are not. In Britain and the United States, from time to time the necessity for consideration has been called into question and its abolition suggested. Such attempts have failed. At one time, in the United States, a uniform law was proposed that would make any written promise enforceable if the writing said that the signer intended it to be enforceable. Only one state adopted the law and that state later dropped it. For the most part, as we will see later, if the form is followed, the courts will usually enforce the "bargain" of the parties.

A third means for enforcement of promises is what is known as "promissory estoppel." The origin of this doctrine is discussed in part in the dissent in the *Al-*

legheny case. It was a means to make promises of gifts to charities enforceable when the promises were not under seal and when they expressed no consideration. Thus, a promise of a gift became enforceable the same as if it had been bargained for or had been made under seal.

The term estoppel comes from the French and is an old doctrine. Estoppel in pais, or as it is also known equitable estoppel, refers to the fact that a person may not say something which refers to a present fact or do something on which another person might reasonable rely and later deny the truth of the statement or the efficacy of the action. For example, if someone says to me "Is that your signature as drawer of this check?" and I say "Yes" and the person who asked me reasonably relies on what I said and takes the check from someone and the signature is later a forgery, I may be "stopped" ("estopped") from denying that it is my signature. If I operate a business and allow someone to wear the uniform of a driver and allow him or her to drive the business van, I may be stopped ("estopped") from denying that this person is my employee for whom I am responsible if he/she causes harm, an accident with the van.

Promissory estoppel differs from *equitable* estoppel in that a person makes a statement or promise referring to the future rather than the present on which someone relies. According to Section 90 of the Restatement a promisor can be estopped from denying any promise or statement if: (1) the promisor should have reasonably believed his statement would induce a response by the promisee or other party; (2) the promisor's statement did result in a response or action by the promisee; and (3) injustice is avoided through the enforcement of the promise. Significantly, the promise is enforced through the person's reliance upon it, not by consideration or by a seal. The promisor is thus liable for what he/she promised. At the earliest use of this doctrine, when it was principally employed to enforce the non-bargained for non-sealed promises made to charities, the exact thing promised or damages based on the failure to perform what was promised was required of the promisor. Early on, it was said that promissory estoppel was a substitute for consideration and the breaching party was liable to the promisee for the promisee's expectancy. For example, if someone promised a charity a gift of $25,000 and failed to give it, the promisor could be sued for $25,000. The idea behind this was that charities depend on gifts and rely on them to survive. As promissory estoppel moved into other areas (the cases we examine in this section include charity, legal fees, franchise, land improvement, employment) the doctrine came under stricter scrutiny. Expectancy was no longer the rule. Rather, reliance was the key. In charity cases reliance was presumed; in other situations it had to be proved. Furthermore, once reliance was proved damages were measured not by what the promisee expected to receive as a result of the promise but the degree to which the promisee was damaged by the reliance on the promise. If nephew said to uncle: "I'm going to college next year. I sure would like a car to take with me" and uncle said to nephew: "I'll give you $25,000" and nephew bought a car for $15,000, in most states the most nephew could get from uncle would be $15,000 damages, the amount he relied, not $25,000 the amount promised. The reasonableness of the reliance, whether or not the promisor had reason to believe anyone would rely on the promise, whether or not a promise had been made—all of these became issues. Some of them we will explore.

This section in Part I is very significant. Do not isolate it or pigeonhole it. Keep it in mind with other forms of contract liability. People will not ask you whether or not there is a promissory estoppel. They won't know what it is. People want a remedy. So you ask: is there a contract? A bargain? A seal? Is what was said or written definite enough to be enforced. If there is no formal bargain or seal or if it is indefinite, will quantum meruit give a remedy? Did someone at least request something for which payment should be made? If that isn't there what about quasi contract? Will the law impose a liability even where the rock bottom basic of a request was not present? If no bargain, seal, request, or basis for quasi contract can be found, was there at least a promise? Did someone rely on it? Reasonably rely? Did the promisor have reason to think someone would rely? If all else fails, promissory estoppel may give a remedy.

Allegheny College v. National Chautaugua County Bank of Jamestown

246 N.Y. 369, 159 N.E. 173
Court of Appeals of New York, 1927.

CARDOZO, C. J.

The plaintiff, Allegheny College, is an institution of liberal learning at Meadville, Pa. In June, 1921, a 'drive' was in progress to secure for it an additional endowment of $1,250,000. An appeal to contribute to this fund was made to Mary Yates Johnston, of Jamestown, New York. In response thereto, she signed and delivered on June 15, 1921, the following writing:

'Estate Pledge, Allegheny College Second Century Endowment.

'Jamestown, N. Y., June 15, 1921. In consideration of my interest in Christian education, and in consideration of others subscribing, I hereby subscribe and will pay to the order of the treasurer of Allegheny College, Meadville, Pennsylvania, the sum of five thousand dollars; $5,000. This obligation shall become due thirty days after my death, and I hereby instruct my executor, or administrator, to pay the same out of my estate. This pledge shall bear interest at the rate of ___ per cent. per annum, payable annually, from ___ till paid. The proceeds of this obligation shall be added to the Endowment of said Institution, or expended in accordance with instructions on reverse side of this pledge. Name: Mary Yates Johnston, Address: 306 East 6th Street, Jamestown, N. Y. Dayton E. McClain, Witness, T. R. Courtis, Witness, To authentic signature.'

On the reverse side of the writing is the following indorsement: 'In loving memory this gift shall be known as the Mary Yates Johnston memorial fund, the proceeds from which shall be used to educate students preparing for the ministry, either in the United States or in the Foreign Field. This pledge shall be valid only on the condition that the provisions of my will, now extant, shall be first met. Mary Yates Johnston.'

The subscription was not payable by its terms until 30 days after the death of the promisor. The sum of $1,000 was paid, however, upon account in December, 1923, while the promisor was alive. The college set the money aside to be held as a scholarship fund for the benefit of students preparing for the ministry. Later, in July, 1924, the promisor gave notice to the college that she repudiated the promise. Upon the expiration of 30 days following her death, this action was brought against the executor of her will to recover the unpaid balance.

The law of charitable subscriptions has been a prolific source of controversy in this state and elsewhere. We have held that a promise of that order is unenforceable like any other if made without consideration. On the other hand, though professing to apply to such subscriptions the general law of contract, we have found consideration present where the general law of contract, at least as then declared, would have said that it was absent.

A classic form of statement identifies consideration with detriment to the promisee sustained by virtue of the promise. Hamer v. Sidway, 124 N. Y. 538, 27 N. E. 256. So compendious a formula is little more than a half truth. There is need of many a supplementary gloss before the outline can be so filled in as to depict the classic doctrine. 'The promise and the consideration must purport to be the motive each for the other, in whole or at least in part. It is not enough that the promise induces the detriment or that the detriment induces the promise if the other half is wanting.' Walton Water Co. v. Village of Walton, 238 N. Y. 46, 51, 143 N. E. 786. If A promises B to make him a gift, consideration may be lacking, though B has renounced other opportunities for betterment in the faith that the promise will be kept.

The half truths of one generation tend at times to perpetuate themselves in the law as the whole truth of another, when constant repetition brings it about that qualifications, taken once for granted, are disregarded or forgotten. The doctrine of consideration has not escaped the common lot. As far back as 1881, Judge Holmes in his lectures on the common law (page 292), separated the detriment, which is merely a consequence of the promise from the detriment, which is in truth the motive or inducement, and yet added that the courts 'have gone far in obliterating this distinction.' The tendency toward effacement has not lessened with the years. On the contrary, there has grown up of recent days a doctrine that a substitute for consideration or an exception to its ordinary requirements can be found in what is styled 'a promissory estoppel.' Williston, Contracts, ss 139, 116. Whether the exception has made its way in this state to such an extent as to permit us to say that the general law of consideration has been modified accordingly, we do not now attempt to say. Cases such as Siegel v. Spear & Co., 234 N. Y. 479, 138 N. E. 414, and De Cicco v. Schweizer, 221 N. Y. 431, 117 N. E. 807, may be signposts on the road. Certain, at least, it is that we have adopted the doctrine of promissory estoppel as the equivalent of consideration in connection with our law of charitable subscriptions. So long as those decisions stand, the question is not merely whether the enforcement of a charitable subscription can be squared with the doctrine of consideration in all its ancient rigor. The question may also be whether it can be squared with the doctrine of consideration as qualified by the doctrine of promissory estoppel.

We have said that the cases in this state have recognized this exception, if exception it is thought to be. Thus, in Barnes v. Perine, 12 N. Y. 18, the subscription was made without request, express or implied, that the church do anything on the faith of it. Later, the church did incur expense to the knowledge of the promisor, and in the reasonable belief that the promise would be kept. We held the promise binding, though consideration there was none except upon the theory of a promissory estoppel. In Presbyterian Society v. Beach, 74 N. Y. 72, a situation substantially the same became the basis for a like ruling. So in Roberts v. Cobb, 103 N. Y. 600, 9 N. E. 500, and Keuka College v. Ray, 167 N. Y. 96, 60 N. E. 325, the moulds of consideration as fixed by the old doctrine were subjected to a like expansion. Very likely, conceptions of public policy have shaped, more or less subconsciously, the rulings thus made. Judges have been affected by the thought that 'defenses of that character' are 'breaches of faith towards the public, and especially towards those engaged in the same enterprise, and an unwarrantable disappointment of the reasonable expectations of those interested.' W. F. Allen, J., in Barnes v. Perine, supra, p. 24. The result speaks for itself irrespective of the motive. Decisions which have stood so long, and which are supported by so many considerations of public policy and reason, will not be overruled to save the symmetry of a concept which itself came into our law, not so much from any reasoned conviction of its justice, as from historical accidents of practice and procedure. The concept survives as one of the distinctive features of our legal system. We have no thought to suggest that it is obsolete or on the way to be abandoned. As in the case of other concepts, however, the pressure of exceptions has led to irregularities of form.

It is in this background of precedent that we are to view the problem now before us. The background helps to an understanding of the implications inherent in subscription and acceptance. This is so though we may find in the end that without recourse to the innovation of promissory estoppel the transaction can be fitted within the mould of consideration as established by tradition.

The promisor wished to have a memorial to perpetuate her name. She imposed a condition that the 'gift' should 'be known as the Mary Yates Johnston Memorial Fund.' The moment that the college accepted $1,000 as a payment on account, there was an assumption of a duty to do whatever acts were customary or reasonably necessary to maintain the memorial fairly and justly in the spirit of its creation. The college could not accept the money and hold itself free thereafter from personal responsibility to give effect to the condition. More is involved in the receipt of such a fund than a mere acceptance of money to be held to a corporate use. The purpose of the founder would be unfairly thwarted or at least inadequately served if the college failed to communicate to the world, or in any event to applicants for the scholarship, the title of the memorial. By implication it undertook, when it accepted a portion of the 'gift,' that in its circulars of information and in other customary ways when making announcement of this scholarship, it would couple with the announcement the name of the donor. The donor was not at liberty to gain the benefit of such an undertaking upon the payment of a part and disappoint the expectation that there would be payment of the residue. If the college had stated after receiving $1,000 upon account of the subscription, that it would apply the money to the prescribed use, but that in its circulars of information and when responding to prospective applicants it would deal with the fund as an anonymous donation, there is little doubt that the subscriber would have been at liberty to treat this statement as the repudiation of a duty impliedly assumed, a repudiation justifying a refusal to make payments in the future. Obligation in such circumstances is correlative and mutual. A case much in point is New Jersey Hospital v. Wright, 95 N. J. Law, 462, 464, 113 A. 144, where a subscription for the maintenance of a bed in a hospital was held to be enforceable by virtue of an implied promise by the hospital that the bed should be maintained in the name of the subscriber. A parallel situation might arise upon the endowment of a chair or a fellowship in a university by the aid of annual payments with the condition that it should commemorate the name of the founder or that of a member of his family. The university would fail to live up to the fair meaning of its promise if it were to publish in its circulars of information and elsewhere the existence of a chair or a fellowship in the prescribed subject, and omit the benefactor's name. A duty to act in ways beneficial to the promisor and beyond the application of the fund to the mere uses of the trust would be cast upon the promisee by the acceptance of the money. We do not need to measure the extent either of benefit to the promisor or of detriment to the promisee implicit in this duty. 'If a person chooses to make an extravagant promise for an inadequate consideration, it is his own affair.' 8 Holdsworth, History of English Law, p. 17. It was long ago said that 'when a thing is to be done by the plaintiff, be it never so small, this is a sufficient consideration to ground an action.' Sturlyn v. Albany, 1587, Cro. Eliz. 67, quoted by Holdsworth, supra. The longing for posthumous remembrance is an emotion not so weak as to justify us in saying that its gratification is a negligible good.

We think the duty assumed by the plaintiff to perpetuate the name of the founder of the memorial is sufficient in itself to give validity to the subscription within the rules that define consideration for a promise of that order. When the promisee subjected itself to such a duty at the implied request of the promisor, the result was the creation of a bilateral agreement. There was a promise on the one side and on the other a return promise, made, it is true, by implication, but expressing an obligation that had been exacted as a condition of the payment. A bilateral agreement may exist though one of the mutual promises be a promise 'implied in fact,' an inference from conduct as opposed to an inference from words. Williston, Contracts, ss 90, 22a. We think the fair inference to be drawn from the acceptance of a payment on account of the subscription is a promise by the college to do what may be necessary on its part to make the scholarship effective. The plan conceived by the subscriber will be mutilated and distorted unless the sum to be accepted is adequate to the end in view. Moreover, the time to affix her name to the memorial will not arrive until the entire fund has been collected. The college may thus thwart the purpose of the payment on account if at liberty to reject a tender of the residue. It is no answer to say that a duty would then arise to make restitution of the money. If such a duty may be imposed, the only reason for its existence must be that there is then a failure of 'consideration.' To say that there is a failure of consideration is to concede that a consideration has been promised, since otherwise it could not fail. No doubt there are times and situations in which limitations laid upon a promisee in connection with the use of what is paid by a subscriber lack the quality of a consideration, and are to be classed merely as conditions. Williston, Contracts, § 112; Page, Contracts, § 523. 'It is often difficult to determine whether words of condition in a promise indicate a request for consideration or state a mere condition in a gratuitous promise. An aid, though not a conclusive test in determining which construction of the promise is more reasonable is an inquiry whether the happening of the condition will be a benefit to the promisor. If so, it is a fair inference that the happening was requested as a consideration.' Williston, supra, § 112. Such must be the meaning of this transaction unless we are prepared to hold that the college may keep the payment on account, and thereafter nullify the scholarship which is to preserve the memory of the subscriber. The fair implication to be gathered from the whole transaction is assent to the condition and the assumption of a duty to go forward with performance. The subscriber does not say: I hand you $1,000, and you may make up your mind later, after my death, whether you will undertake to commemorate my name. What she says in effect is this: I hand you $1,000, and if you are unwilling to commemorate me, the time to speak is now.

The conclusion thus reached makes it needless to consider whether, aside from the feature of a memorial, a promissory estoppel may result from the assumption of a duty to apply the fund, so far as already paid, to special purposes not mandatory under the provisions of the college charter (the support and education of students preparing for the ministry)—an assumption induced by the belief that other payments sufficient in amount to make the scholarship effective would be added to the fund thereafter upon the death of the subscriber.

The judgment of the Appellate Division and that of the Trial Term should be reversed, and judgment ordered for the plaintiff as prayed for in the complaint, with costs in all courts.

KELLOGG, J. (dissenting).

The Chief Judge finds in the expression, 'In loving memory this gift shall be known as the Mary Yates Johnston Memorial Fund,' an offer on the part of Mary Yates Johnston to contract with Allegheny College. The expression makes no such appeal to me. Allegheny College was not requested to perform any act through which the sum offered might bear the title by which the offeror states that it shall be known. The sum offered was termed a 'gift' by the offeror. Consequently, I can see no reason why we should strain ourselves to make it, not a gift, but a trade. Moreover, since the donor specified that the gift was made, 'In consideration of my interest in Christian education, and in consideration of others subscribing,' considerations not adequate in law, I can see no excuse for asserting that it was otherwise made in consideration of an act or promise on the part of the donee, constituting a sufficient quid pro quo to convert the gift into a contract obligation. To me the words used merely expressed an expectation or wish on the part of the donor and failed to exact the return of an adequate consideration. But if an offer indeed was present, then clearly it was an offer to enter into a unilateral contract. The offeror was to be bound provided the offeree performed such acts as might be necessary to make the gift offered become known under the proposed name. This is evidently the thought of the Chief Judge, for he says: 'She imposed a condition that the 'gift' should be known as the Mary Yates Johnston Memorial Fund.' In other words, she proposed to exchange her offer of a donation in return for acts to be performed. Even so, there was never any acceptance of the offer, and therefore no contract, for the acts requested have never been performed. The gift has never been made known as demanded. Indeed, the requested acts, under the very terms of the assumed offer, could never have been performed at a time to convert the offer into a promise. This is so for the reason that the donation was not to take effect until after the death of the donor, and by her death her offer was withdrawn. Williston on Contracts, § 62. Clearly, although a promise of the college to make the gift known, as requested, may be implied, that promise was not the acceptance of an offer which gave rise to a contract. The donor stipulated for acts, not promises. 'In order to make a bargain it is necessary that the acceptor shall give in return for the offer or the promise exactly the consideration which the offeror requests. If an act is requested, that very act and no other must be given. If a promise is requested, that promise must be made absolutely and unqualifiedly.' Williston on Contracts, § 73. 'It does not follow that an offer becomes a promise because it is accepted; it may be, and frequently is, conditional, and then it does not become a promise until the conditions are satisfied; and in case of offers for a consideration, the performance of the consideration is always deemed a condition.' Langdell, Summary of the Law of Contracts, § 4.

It seems clear to me that there was here no offer, no acceptance of an offer, and no contract. Neither do I agree with the Chief Judge that this court 'found consideration present where the general law of contract, at least as then declared, would have said that it was absent' in the cases of Barnes v. Perine, 12 N. Y. 18, Presbyterian Society v. Beach, 74 N. Y. 72, and Keuka College v. Ray, 167 N. Y. 96, 60 N. E. 325. In the Keuka College Case an offer to contract, in consideration of the performance of certain acts by the offeree, was converted into a promise by the actual performance of those acts. This form of contract has been known to the law from time immemorial (Langdell, § 46), and for at least a century longer than the other type, a bilateral contract (Williston, § 13). It may be that the basis of the decisions in Barnes v. Perine and Presbyterian Society v. Beach, supra, was the same as in the Keuka College Case. See Presbyterian Church of Albany v. Cooper, 112 N. Y. 517, 20 N. E. 352, 3 L. R. A. 468, 8 Am. St. Rep. 767. However, even if the basis of the decisions be a so-called 'promissory estoppel,' nevertheless they initiated no new doctrine. A so-called 'promissory estoppel,' although not so termed, was held sufficient by Lord Mansfield and his fellow judges as far back as the year 1765. Pillans v. Van Mierop, 3 Burr. 1663. Such a doctrine may be an anomaly; it is not a novelty. Therefore I can see no ground for the suggestion that the ancient rule which makes consideration necessary to the formation of every contract is in danger of effacement through any decisions of this court. To me that is a cause for gratulation rather than regret. However, the discussion may be beside the mark, for I do not understand that the holding about to be made in this case is other than a holding that consideration was given to convert the offer into a promise. With that result I cannot agree and, accordingly, must dissent.

KELLOGG, J., dissents in opinion, in which ANDREWS, J., concurs.

Judgment accordingly.

Questions

1. Consider what Cardozo means when he writes of "the symmetry of a concept which itself came into our law, not so much from any reasoned conviction of its justice, as from historical accidents of practice and procedure."

2. Did Cardozo base his holding on the theory of promissory estoppel, unilateral contract or bilateral contract? How did he do it? Why did he do it?

3. What is the meaning of the quotation which Cardozo uses: "If a person chooses to make an extravagant promise for an inadequate consideration, it is his own affair?"

4. What is the "implied in fact" promise to which Cardozo refers?

5. The dissenter speaks of the phrase "[i]n consideration of my interest in Christian education and in consideration of others subscribing" as not being considerations adequate in law. Why are they inadequate?

6. How does the dissenter conclude that "[t]he donor stipulated for acts, not promises?"

7. What is the meaning of the statement: "It does not follow that an offer becomes a promise because it is accepted; it may be, and frequently is, conditional, and then it does not become a promise until the conditions are satisfied...?"

8. The dissenter notes that Cardozo talked a lot about promissory estoppel and then decided the case on the basis of contract. Why do you suppose Cardozo did this? Merely to tangle the thinking of future generations of students, or perhaps instruct them? If the case is not decided on promissory estoppel grounds, what is the value of all the discussion of it?

Goldstick v. ICM Realty, 188 F.2d 456, (1985)
[Refer back to principal case in part B. for facts.]

"The plaintiffs have two other strings to their bow. The first is promissory estoppel. If an unambiguous promise is made in circumstances calculated to induce reliance, and it does so, the promisee if hurt as a result can recover damages. Netzky, when he said he wouldn't close the deal unless the plaintiffs released their claim for the legal fee, unwittingly armed the plaintiffs with a weapon to use in trying to collect the fee. It was two-edged, because if through their intransigence the plaintiffs killed the deal, Kusmiersky and ICM might abandon the property and with it any incentive to pay the plaintiffs without putting them to the expense and uncertainty of litigation. But it was a weapon, and one that Kusmiersky, acting for ICM (for there is no question that in these negotiations Kusmiersky was ICM's agent), induced the plaintiffs to surrender by promising to work things out. Made in the context of Goldstick's refusal to make his and Smith's fee doubly contingent (it had been contingent on their getting the back taxes reduced, and now ICM wanted to make it contingent on the property's showing profits), this promise could be understood (or so a reasonable jury conceivably might find) as a waiver of the condition that the property turn a profit. Although much was left in doubt—in particular the payment period—it is a question for a jury whether Kusmiersky made a promise that estops his principal, ICM, to deny that it was assuring Goldstick that the plaintiffs' fee would be paid by ICM even if the property never showed a profit.

The part of the district judge's opinion in which he rejected the plaintiffs' argument for promissory estoppel is very brief and essentially all it says is that the promise was ambiguous because the question whether payment would be contingent on the property's turning a profit was left unresolved. However, a jury could find that Goldstick reasonably understood Kusmiersky's statement that something would be worked out to mean that ICM would not insist on conditioning payment on profit. If so, Kusmiersky could be understood to be promising to do better than his previous offer of $250,000 over 10 years with interest at 7 percent but no principal the first few years. How much better is unclear, but that is not critical. If the minimum value of a promise is unambiguous, that should be enough to work an estoppel to the extent of that value, though no more.

Although to our knowledge the precise issue has not arisen before, we find nothing in principle or in the cases to exclude recovery on a theory of promissory estoppel when the promise is unambiguous on the downside but not the upside. In Yardley there was no promise, period. In Levitt Homes Inc. v. Old Farm Homeowner's Ass'n, 111 Ill.App.3d 300, 314-15, 67 Ill.Dec. 155, 165, 444 N.E.2d 194, 204 (1982), the alleged promise was only a statement of intentions, and there was a written disclaimer of any promises. In Ziese v. Ramada Inns, Inc., 463 F.2d 1058, 1060 (7th Cir.1972), we implied that if the defendant had told the plaintiff "Quit worrying, you've got a deal," there would have been (much as in this case) a promissory estoppel. The evidence held to create a triable issue in Swansea Concrete Products, Inc. v. Distler, 126 Ill.App.3d 927, 933, 81 Ill.Dec. 688, 692-93, 467 N.E.2d 388, 392- 93 (1984), was of a promise no more definite than what the jury could find had been the minimum promise in this case, while evidence of a less definite promise was held to create a triable issue in Bank Computer Network Corp. v. Continental Illinois Nat'l Bank & Trust Co., 110 Ill.App.3d 492, 497-99, 66 Ill.Dec. 160, 165-66, 442 N.E.2d 586, 591-92 (1982).

The fact that Goldstick rejected Kusmiersky's offer does not show that he did not rely on it. He may have regarded it as a floor, once the possibility of its being only contingent was dispelled by the assurance (if that is what it was) that something would be worked out. Thus reassured, he may have been sufficiently encouraged to execute the release that Kusmiersky and ICM needed to complete the deal with Netzky, even though he hoped to get a better settlement than Kusmiersky had offered. At least this is sufficiently plausible to create a triable issue of reliance as well as of the existence of a promise.

Should the plaintiffs prevail on this theory, it will become necessary to consider the proper measure of damages. As a matter of strict logic one might suppose that since the promise was not accepted, the plaintiffs, even if they succeeded in establishing a promissory estoppel, would not necessarily be able to recover the value of the promise—the $250,000 discounted to present value. It would seem they would have to show their actual damages: what they gave up when they signed the release in reliance on Kusmiersky's promise. Maybe they gave up little. Maybe in the end they would have signed the release without any promises, knowing that if they did not the Netzky deal might fall through and with it all prospects for recovering their fee without a lawsuit. Or maybe as ICM argues the plaintiffs were more optimistic about the prospects of the property's showing a profit than they have let on in this lawsuit.

Consistently with our leanings, the Restatement of Contracts implies, if somewhat unclearly, that the value of the promise is the presumptive measure of damages for promissory estoppel, to be rejected only if awarding so much would be inequitable. See comment d to section 90. That would not be inequitable here when we recall that no one has ever questioned the reasonableness of the plaintiffs' original—and higher—legal fee. But we need not decide whether this is the correct approach under the law of Illinois. The issue may wash out on remand; anyway we would want the district judge's views before deciding a difficult question of state law."

[Reversed and remanded]

Question

1. What is the measure of damages for promissory estoppel according to the case? Do courts in the following cases agree?

Hoffman v. Red Owl Stores, Inc.

26 Wis.2d 683, 133 N.W.2d 267

Supreme Court of Wisconsin, 1965.

Action by Joseph Hoffman (hereinafter 'Hoffman') and wife, plaintiffs, against defendants Red Owl Stores, Inc. (hereinafter 'Red Owl') and Edward Lukowitz.

The complaint alleged that Lukowitz, as agent for Red Owl, represented to and agreed with plaintiffs that Red Owl would build a store building in Chilton and stock it with merchandise for Hoffman to operate in return for which plaintiffs were to put up and invest a total sum of $18,000; that in reliance upon the above mentioned agreement and representations plaintiffs sold their bakery building and business and their grocery store and business; also in reliance on the agreement and representations Hoffman purchased the building site in Chilton and rented a residence for himself and his family in Chilton; plaintiffs' actions in reliance on the representations and agreement disrupted their personal and business life; plaintiffs lost substantial amounts of income and expended large sums of money as expenses. Plaintiffs demanded recovery of damages for the breach of defendants' representations and agreements.

CURRIE, Chief Justice.

The instant appeal and cross-appeal present these questions:

(1) Whether this court should recognize causes of action grounded on promissory estoppel as exemplified by sec. 90 of Restatement, 1 Contracts?

(2) Do the facts in this case make out a cause of action for promissory estoppel?

(3) Are the jury's findings with respect to damages sustained by the evidence?

Recognition of a Cause of Action Grounded on Promissory Estoppel

Sec. 90 of Restatement, 1 Contracts, provides (at p. 110): 'A promise which the promisor should reasonably expect to induce action or forbearance of a definite and substantial character on the part of the promisee and which does induce such action of forbearance is binding if injustice can be avoided only by enforcement of the promise.'

Many courts of other jurisdictions have seen fit over the years to adopt the principle of promissory estoppel, and the tendency in that direction continues. As Mr. Justice McFADDIN, speaking in behalf of the Arkansas court, well stated, that the development of the law of promissory estoppel 'is an attempt by the courts to keep remedies abreast of increased moral consciousness of honesty and fair representations in all business dealings.' Peoples National Bank of Little Rock v. Linebarger Construction Company (1951), 219 Ark. 11, 17, 240 S.W.2d 12, 16.

The Restatement avoids use of the term 'promissory estoppel,' and there has been criticism of it as an inaccurate term. See 1A Corbin, Contracts, p. 232, et seq., sec. 204. On the other hand, Williston advocated the use of this term or something equivalent. 1 Williston, Contracts (1st ed.), p. 308, sec. 139. Use of the word 'estoppel' to describe a doctrine upon which a party to a lawsuit may obtain affirmative relief offends the traditional concept that estoppel merely serves as a shield and cannot serve as a sword to create a cause of action. See Utschig v. McClone (1962), 16 Wis.2d 506, 509, 114 N.W.2d 854. 'Attractive nuisance' is also a much criticized term. See concurring opinion, Flamingo v. City of Waukesha (1952), 262 Wis. 219, 227, 55 N.W.2d 24. However, the latter term is still in almost universal use by the courts because of the lack of the better substitute. The same is also true of the wide use of the term 'promissory estoppel.' We have employed its use in this opinion not only because of its extensive use by other courts but also since a more accurate equivalent has not been devised.

Because we deem the doctrine of promissory estoppel, as stated in sec. 90 of Restatement, 1 Contracts, is one which supplies a needed tool which courts may employ in a proper case to prevent injustice, we endorse and adopt it.

Applicability of Doctrine to Facts of this Case

The record here discloses a number of promises and assurances given to Hoffman by Lukowitz in behalf of Red Owl upon which plaintiffs relied and acted upon to their detriment.

Foremost were the promises that for the sum of $18,000 Red Owl would establish Hoffman in a store. After Hoffman had sold his grocery store and paid the $1,000 on the Chilton lot, the $18,000 figure was changed to $24,100. Then in November, 1961, Hoffman was assured that if the $24,100 figure were increased by $2,000 the deal would go through. Hoffman was induced to sell his grocery store fixtures and inventory in June, 1961, on the promise that he would be in his new store by fall. In November, plaintiffs sold their bakery building on the urging of defendants and on the assurance that this was the last step necessary to have the deal with Red Owl go through.

We determine that there was ample evidence to sustain the answers of the jury to the questions of the verdict with respect to the promissory representations made by Red Owl, Hoffman's reliance thereon in the exercise of ordinary care, and his fulfillment of the conditions required of him by the terms of the negotiations had with Red Owl.

There remains for consideration the question of law raised by defendants that agreement was never reached on essential factors necessary to establish a contract between Hoffman and Red Owl. Among these were the size, cost, design, and layout of the store building; and the terms of the lease with respect to rent, maintenance, renewal, and purchase options. This poses the question of whether the promise necessary to sustain a cause of action for promissory estoppel must embrace all essential details of a proposed transaction between promisor and promisee so as to be the equivalent of an offer that would result in a binding contract between the parties if the promisee were to accept the same.

Originally the doctrine of promissory estoppel was invoked as a substitute for consideration rendering a gratuitous promise enforceable as a contract. See

Williston, Contracts (1st ed.), p. 307, sec. 139. In other words, the acts of reliance by the promisee to his detriment provided a substitute for consideration. If
promissory estoppel were to be limited to only those situations where the
promise giving rise to the cause of action must be so definite with respect to all
details that a contract would result were the promise supported by consideration,
then the defendants' instant promises to Hoffman would not meet this test.
However, sec. 90 of Restatement, 1 Contracts, does not impose the requirement
that the promise giving rise to the cause of action must be so comprehensive in
scope as to meet the requirements of an offer that would ripen into a contract if
accepted by the promisee. Rather the conditions imposed are:

(1) Was the promise one which the promisor should reasonably expect to in-
    duce action or forbearance of a definite and substantial character on the
    part of the promisee?

(2) Did the promise induce such action or forbearance?

(3) Can injustice be avoided only by enforcement of the promise? [2]

We deem it would be a mistake to regard an action grounded on promissory
estoppel as the equivalent of a breach of contract action. As Dean Boyer points
out, it is desirable that fluidity in the application of the concept be maintained.
98 University of Pennsylvania Law Review (1950), 459, at page 497. While the
first two of the above listed three requirements of promissory estoppel present issues of fact which ordinarily will be resolved by a jury, the third requirement,
that the remedy can only be invoked where necessary to avoid injustice, is one
that involves a policy decision by the court. Such a policy decision necessarily
embraces an element of discretion.

We conclude that injustice would result here if plaintiffs were not granted
some relief because of the failure of defendants to keep their promises which induced plaintiffs to act to their detriment.

Where damages are awarded in promissory estoppel instead of specifically
enforcing the promisor's promise, they should be only such as in the opinion of
the court are necessary to prevent injustice. Mechanical or rule of thumb approaches to the damage problem should be avoided. In discussing remedies to be
applied by courts in promissory estoppel we quote the following views of writers
on the subject: 'Enforcement of a promise does not necessarily mean Specific Performance. It does not necessarily mean Damages for breach. Moreover the
amount allowed as Damages may be determined by the plaintiff's expenditures
or change of position in reliance as well as by the value to him of the promised
performance. Restitution is also an 'enforcing' remedy, although it is often said
to be based upon some kind of a rescission. In determining what justice requires,
the court must remember all of its powers, derived from equity, law merchant,
and other sources, as well as the common law. Its decree should be molded accordingly.' 1A Corbin, Contracts, p. 221, sec. 200. 'The wrong is not primarily
in depriving the plaintiff of the promised reward but in causing the plaintiff to
change position to his detriment. It would follow that the damages should not
exceed the loss caused by the change of position, which would never be more in

---

2. See Boyer, 98 University of Pennsylvania Law Review (1950), 459, 460. 'Enforcement' of the promise embraces an award of damages for breach as well as decreeing specific
performance.

amount, but might be less, than the promised reward.' Seavey, Reliance on Gratuitous Promises or Other Conduct, 64 Harvard Law Review (1951), 913, 926. 'There likewise seems to be no positive legal requirement, and certainly no legal policy, which dictates the allowance of contract damages in every case where the defendant's duty is consensual.' Shattuck, Gratuitous Promises—A New Writ?, 35 Michigan Law Review (1936), 908, 912. [3]

[The Court disallowed profits that plaintiffs might have made and allowed only monetary losses plaintiffs suffered in reliance on defendant's promises. These included sale at a loss of their on going business.]

Note on Franchising

This is a fairly early franchise case. Franchising is a very big business today. Many issues exist in franchising situations. Usually, the franchisor, here Red Owl, tries to retain as much control over the franchisee without allowing the franchisee to become an agent of Red Owl. This is because a principal is very often responsible for an agent's actions, negligence, liabilities in general if these liabilities are created in the course of the agency relationship. The key to discovering whether someone is an agent is to ask how much control one person has over another. The more control the more an agency relationship is likely — a familiar type of agency relationship is employer/employee. At the opposite end of the spectrum is the independent contractor. This is a person who is hired to do something but the person who does the hiring retains no control over how it is done. For example: if I hire a painting contractor to paint my house, tell her what colors I want etc. and let her do it her own way, probably an independent contracting relationship has been created. If, however, I tell her how I want it done, in all details, what kind of ladders to use, when and how to put them up, how to mix the paint etc. the relationship is probably employer/employee — agency.

In *Red Owl* the problem was one of stringing along the would be franchisee without incurring liability. As you know, the franchisor failed.

What promise(s) did the franchisor make? Why was a suit in contract not possible? What does the court mean that the promise to support a promissory estoppel action need not be "so comprehensive in scope as to meet the requirements of an offer?"

In *Gorham v. Benson Optical, 539 N.W.2d 798 (Minn. Ap. 1995)*, Gorham received a phone call from Ed Iwinski who had "apparently" (the court's word) been offered the job of chief operating officer (COO) for Benson Optical. Iwinski told Gorham that he was not yet part of the decision-making process at Benson but that he would put Gorham's name forward. Gorham was interviewed by Sue Ophale who later offered him a job with Benson. Gorham accepted but was almost immediately terminated when Iwinski did not join the Benson team.

---

3. For expression of the opposite view, that courts in promissory estoppel cases should treat them as ordinary breach of contract cases and allow the full amount of damages recoverable in the latter, see note, 13 Vanderbilt Law Review (1960), 705.

Gorham sued in Contract, Promissory Estoppel and Fraud. The trial court granted summary judgment to defendant on all three claims. The appeals court reversed on the promissory estoppel claim.

The appeals court found that although there had been a contract formed, because it was "at will" and not for the 90 day term that Gorham thought it was, summary judgment was proper. While the court did not discuss this issue in detail, in almost every American jurisdiction if an employment contract is not for a specific time period, or is not clearly stated to be during the satisfactory performance of duties, then it is "at will." This means that the employer can discharge the employee at any time for any or no reason at all. Almost all employment contracts are of this type. When the employer says "we are all one big happy family" she means until I decide to dissolve it. Thus, although there was a contract for a specific salary, employer could terminate it at any time, as could employee. The ninety days mentioned in the letter was discussed by the court as follows: "The hiring letter, however, fell short as a matter of law of guaranteeing Gorham employment for 90 days as he claims. The relevant statement merely informed Gorham that he needed to produce in 90 days or face termination." The fraud claim was likewise dismissed because for fraud to exist the employer must have made a misrepresentation about a past or present material fact which the employer knows is false or which the employer makes without knowing whether it is true or not with the intent of inducing the employee's action and on which the employee acts to his damage. The statements made here were found to be related to the future not the present or the past.

As to promissory estoppel, the appeals court reversed the trial court's grant of summary judgment to the defendant.

"Gorham alternatively contends that the district court erred in granting summary judgment for Benson Optical on the promissory estoppel claim. We agree.

The elements of promissory estoppel are: A promise which the promisor should reasonably expect to induce action or forbearance...on the part of the promisee and which does induce such action or forbearance is binding if injustice can be avoided only by enforcement of the promise. Restatement of Contracts § 90 (1932), quoted in Grouse v. Group Health Plan, Inc., 306 N.W.2d 114, 116 (Minn.1981).

Respondents argue that promissory estoppel is not available when a contract exists. This is true (but with one exception). See Banbury v. Omnitrition Int'l, 533 N.W.2d 876, 881 (Minn.App.1995) (holding promissory estoppel applies only where contract does not exist). In Grouse, however, the supreme court in effect found an exception to this rule. The exception applies when the contract is of a type that provides no basis for a contract recovery, i.e., an at-will employment contract. 306 N.W.2d at 116. Then there is no bar to a promissory estoppel claim. Id.

Significant to this case, the Grouse court stated, in dictum: '[U]nder appropriate circumstances we believe section 90 [of the Restatement] would apply even after employment has begun.' 306 N.W.2d at 116. Gorham presents the specific hypothetical situation the Grouse court's dictum addressed—a short time actually on the job. And, independent of the hypothetical and like Grouse himself, Gorham relied on the promise of a new job when he quit his job with LensCrafters and declined any renegotiations with them. Gorham came to Minneapolis to begin work on October 4, believing that he had been hired. Within a day, Benson Optical terminated him. These facts show Gorham's reasonable reliance on Benson Optical's promise of employment, his declining any other job in deference to his new job with Benson Optical, and the injustice to him when, on his first day of "employment," he went through a hostile re-interview process that led to his immediate termination.

Grouse was explained in terms of implied contract. We consider it now more appropriate, however, to root our decision on pure promissory estoppel doctrine. We do this based on developments in the law of promissory estoppel since Grouse and to reduce the risk of an inappropriate use of an expectation measure for damages. See E. Allan Farnsworth, Farnsworth on Contracts § 2.19, at 143-46 (1990) (discussing reliance versus expectation interests as measures of damage in promissory estoppel claims); see also Michael B. Metzger & Michael J. Phillips, The Emergence of Promissory Estoppel as an Independent Theory of Recovery, 35 Rutgers L.Rev. 472, 511-12 (1983) (discussing treatment of promissory estoppel as not just a substitute for elements of contract, but an independent theory of recovery). We point also to developments in the doctrine of good faith since the supreme court issued Grouse. See, e.g., Deborah A. Schmedemann, Working Backwards: The Covenant of Good Faith and Fair Dealing in Employment Law, 16 Wm.Mitchell L.Rev. 1119 (1990) (exploring evolving principles of good faith in Minnesota employment law).

The doctrine of promissory estoppel allows Gorham to recover good faith reliance damages when Benson Optical terminated him on his first day of employment, after Gorham had detrimentally and reasonably relied on the promise of new employment.

Affirmed in part, reversed in part, and remanded."

Question.

1. What might reliance damages include? What would be the difference between reliance and expectancy?

In *Wheeler v. White, 398 S.W.2d 93 (Tex., 1965)* Wheeler sued White in contract and promissory estoppel for White's failure to secure a loan or furnish money for Wheeler to make improvements on real property. The trial court and intermediate court dismissed Wheeler's petition. The Supreme Court of Texas affirmed the dismissal of the contract count but reversed and remanded for trial on the promissory estoppel. The contract count was dismissed because it did not contain essential elements for its enforceability, including the amount of monthly installments, and the amount of interest, how it would be computed or paid. This indefiniteness, the Texas Supreme Court agreed ruined the contract count. The action for promissory estoppel was not barred by this indefiniteness. After the "contract" was signed in which White agreed to obtain a loan for Wheeler or loan Wheeler money, White urged Wheeler to demolish buildings on the land which was to be improved by the loan. The buildings which were demolished had a reasonable value of $58,000 and a rental value of $400 per month. "By way of reassurance, White stressed the fact that in the event the money was unobtainable elsewhere, he would make the loan himself." The court further stated that promissory estoppel "does not create a contract where none existed before, but only prevents a party from insisting on his strict legal rights when it would be unjust to allow him to enforce them.... The function of promissory estoppel is, under our view, defensive in that it estops a promisor from denying the enforceability of the promise.... Under this theory, losses of expected profits will not be allowed even if expected profits are provable with certainty.... We agree with the reasoning...that...where there is actually no contract the promissory estoppel theory may be invoked, thereby supplying a remedy which will enable the injured party to be compensated for his foreseeable, definite and substantial reliance." A concurring justice stated that the contract was not too indefinite to support an action for damages although it might be too indefinite to support an action for specific performance.

Note on Specific Performance

Actions for specific performance will not be allowed where personal services are involved. Also, specific performance is available only where the remedy at law is inadequate. Using these principles, why might the concurring justice in *Wheeler* say that a rule demanding specificity in cases where specific performance is involved ought not to be followed where damages are sought?

Is there a way in which the *Wood* doctrine of implied contract might have been used to create the specificity required? What might the parties in *Wheeler* have impliedly agreed to without writing it down about the amount of payments and the interest? If an implied agreement had been found how would that have affected the definiteness issue? If the contract had been found to be sufficiently definite to be enforced, how would that have affected Wheeler's remedy?

Note on Types of Recovery

What is the effect of the doctrine of promissory estoppel on defenses such as the Statute of Frauds. In the next two cases, the impact is considered in the context of a lease of land and an employment situation. Statutes of Frauds routinely allow persons who have not signed writings reflecting a contract to raise such lack of signing or of a writing where a sale of land or a lease of land for one year or more, or employment or other personal services which by the terms of the contracting creating it must be for one or more years. Although a person may raise the Statute of Frauds as a defense to a contract action in such cases, is the defense available where promissory estoppel is pleaded? The issue is much like the definiteness issue in the *Wheeler* case. Remember, look at this from the point of view of plaintiff seeking a recovery and defendant seeking to avoid liability. Plaintiff may try to sue on express contract—where all the terms have been expressed; on implied contract where one or more terms have not been expressed but can be implied from circumstances; on quantum meruit where there has been a request for a benefit but no promise to pay for it and no terms spelled out; on quasi contract if the law would require payment for a benefit even if it were not requested; or on promissory estoppel if there is a promise but no bargained for exchange (consideration).

The allowable recovery for a plaintiff will often dictate what remedy plaintiff prefers. For contract—express or implied—the recovery is expectancy. What was promised? What is that promise worth in dollars? For quantum meruit, depending on the jurisdiction, restitution or reliance but not expectancy. While reliance is now sometimes given for quantum meruit, restitution was the common law recovery. This meant at earliest common law that the plaintiff could only recover from the defendant the value of the benefit to the defendant. Later recovery was based solely on the value of the benefit in the marketplace, independent of any value that might have been conferred upon defendant. Finally, reliance damages were given according to the amount that plaintiff lost based on market valuation whether or not defendant benefited. Promissory estoppel is routinely a reliance measure of damages: How much did plaintiff lose by relying on the promise? For example, in *Wheeler*, if plaintiff could have recovered in contract the measure of damages would be expectancy—how much did plaintiff expect to make as a result of the improvements made possible by defendant's loan. If plaintiff could prove this, plaintiff would recover it. For example, if plaintiff were planning to put up a housing subdivision and could prove how much profit she would have made on it that would be the recovery. Proving this can sometimes be difficult—it is called speculative and not allowed in many cases—but if other housing subdivisions had been built and made a profit, especially if plaintiff had built them thus showing that plaintiff was likely to have succeeded, then such profit is very possible. Two other doctrines may cut down on an expectancy recovery even where it is allowed. One is mitigation. Could plaintiff have obtained a loan from someone else and thus "mitigaged" the harm caused by defendant breaching the contract? If plaintiff could have "mitigated" then she may not charge this loss to defendant. The other is foreseeability. Under the doctrine of *Hadley v. Baxendale, 156 Eng.Rep 145, (1854)*, if the harm caused by defendant's breach was not foreseeable to defendant, then plaintiff may not recover for this harm from defendant. If, however, plaintiff overcomes these hurdles the damages can be very high indeed.

Where plaintiff cannot prove the existence of a contract—failure of consideration, lack of definiteness—or is prevented from attempting to prove the existence of a contract because the alleged contract is unenforceable if not in writing (Statute of Frauds)—quantum meruit, quasi contract and promissory estoppel exist. Quantum meruit and quasi contract may be the least desirable remedies in jurisdictions where restitution is the measure of recovery. Here, a request could be proved on the part of defendant for plaintiff to demolish existing buildings. But of what benefit was this to defendant—measured either as a benefit to defendant subjectively or measured by the value of the benefit in the market place? Probably zero. A creative counsel might try to say that the cost of demolition if paid by defendant would have cost defendant so much and this is the measure of the benefit to defendant. Defendant requested demolition—the market cost of demolition experts could be the measure of plaintiff's recovery. Even so, how much would this be?

In promissory estoppel the measure of damages is reliance. Use the facts in *Wheeler*. How much might plaintiff recover? How much did plaintiff lose as a result of relying on defendant's promise? How is plaintiff's loss related to plaintiff's recovery from defendant? How does it differ from plaintiff's expectancy?

All efforts at contract recovery, though not quantum meruit or quasi contract, can founder on the reefs of the Statute of Frauds. Does the same result occur when the theory of recovery is promissory estoppel?

In *Moore Burger, Inc. v. Phillips Petroleum Co., 492 S.W.2d 934 (Tex,. 1972)* the Texas Supreme Court held the defendants, two realtors, (Dowd and Craus) may be estopped to deny the enforceability of a contract because of the lack of a writing in the same way that Dowd and Craus could be estopped to deny the existence of liability because of indefiniteness which would prevent the existence of a contract. Dowd and Craus had represented to Moore Burger Inc., the plaintiff, that if Moore would not bid on a tract of land then Dowd and Craus would purchase it and later lease it to Moore. A contract to this effect was drawn up and signed by Moore but not the realtors. When Moore told Dowd and Craus that Moore would bid on the property unless the realtors signed the contract, they promised to sign it. In the court's words: "The entire time these negotiations were going on, Dowd and Craus had a contract to sell the property to Broadway Oil Company which planned to build a service station for Phillips Petroleum Company. Phillips later bought this contract of sale from Broadway Oil Company." Once Dowd and Craus had bought the property they sold it to Phillips and when Moore asked about it, the realtors denied any knowledge of it and refused to perform obligations under it. The court discussed promissory estoppel.

"The foregoing recitation of summary judgment evidence is legally sufficient to raise fact issues that: (1) the promisors should reasonably have expected that their promise to sign the lease (2) would induce 'Moore' Burger to forbear bidding on the City property (3) which was a forbearance of a definite and substantial character (4) induced by the promise, and (5) that injustice to 'Moore' Burger can only be avoided by enforcement of the promise. See Cooper Petroleum Co. v. LaGloria Oil and Gas Co., 436 S.W.2d 889, 896 (Tex.1969).

Respondents argue that the doctrine of promissory estoppel, although approved and applied in Wheeler v. White, should not be extended so as to enforce contracts for the sale of land, or for the lease of land for a term of more than one year, in the absence of proof of the (1) taking of possession, (2) furnishing of consideration, and (3) making of valuable improvements, as required by the rule of Hooks v. Bridgewater, Supra. But the court recognized in Hooks v. Bridgewater that contracts may be enforced if application of the statute 'would, itself, plainly amount to a fraud.' 229 S.W. 1116. If the evidence tendered in this case by 'Moore' Burger be accepted as true, enforcement of the statute of frauds 'would, itself, plainly amount to a fraud' on 'Moore' Burger's rights. We hold, therefore, that as to Dowd and Craus the take-nothing summary judgment was erroneously rendered and must be reversed."

Stearns v. Emery-Waterhouse Co.

(596 A.2d 72)
Maine, 1991.

ROBERTS, Justice.

Emery-Waterhouse Co. appeals from a judgment of the Superior Court awarding damages to Timothy B. Stearns for breach of an oral contract to employ Stearns for a definite term greater than one year. The court held Emery-Waterhouse estopped to assert its defense under the statute of frauds, 33 M.R.S.A.

§ 51(5)(1988), by the extent of Stearns's detrimental reliance on the oral contract. Because Stearns did not produce clear and convincing evidence of fraud on the part of his employer, we hold that enforcement of the oral contract was barred by the statute of frauds. Accordingly, we vacate the judgment.

Emery-Waterhouse is a Portland hardware wholesaler that also franchises "Trustworthy" hardware stores throughout the Northeast and owns several such stores. In December, 1984 the Employer's president, Charles Hildreth, met with Timothy Stearns in Massachusetts to discuss hiring him to run the Employer's retail stores. Stearns was managing a Sears-Roebuck & Company store in Massachusetts, had done retail marketing for Sears for twenty-seven years, and was then fifty years old. He was earning approximately $99,000 per year, owned his home in Massachusetts, and also owned property in Maine. Stearns had some dissatisfactions with Sears but was concerned about retaining his Sears job security and was aware that his age would make it hard to find another marketing job. After the initial meeting Stearns came to Maine, inspected some stores, and met with Hildreth in Portland. The substance of this second meeting was disputed, but the jury found that Hildreth gave Stearns an oral contract of employment to age fifty five at a guaranteed salary of $85,000 per year. This contract was never reduced to writing.

Stearns resigned from Sears, moved to Maine, and became Emery- Waterhouse's director of retail sales. His employer retained Stearns in this position at $85,000 for nearly two years. In December, 1986 Hildreth advised Stearns that he was being removed, but Stearns was given a different job as the national accounts manager the next day. Stearns remained in this new position at an annual salary of $68,000 for six months. Hildreth then succeeded in his efforts to acquire a national marketing firm, eliminated Stearns's position as a result, and terminated his employment before he reached age fifty five. Stearns eventually filed a complaint in the Superior Court for breach of contract. The court denied summary judgment based on the possibility that the employer might be estopped to assert its defense under the statute of frauds by Stearns's detrimental reliance. At trial the court held that such an estoppel applied. The jury established the oral contract and breach by special findings and the court assigned damages in equity pursuant to Restatement (Second) of Contracts § 139. Following the denial of its post trial motions Emery-Waterhouse brought this appeal.

The appeal presents a question of first impression in Maine: whether an employee may avoid the statute of frauds based solely upon his detrimental reliance on an employer's oral promise of continued employment.[1] Other jurisdictions have divided on this question. Some have permitted avoidance based on theories of promissory estoppel, equitable estoppel, or part performance. Others have rejected such an avoidance as contrary to the policy of the statute, or as unsupported by sufficient evidence to verify the oral promise. Stearns contends that our case law permits him to avoid the statute of frauds under the promissory estoppel theory of section 139 of the Restatement (Second) of Contracts.[2] We disagree.

---

1. It is undisputed that the oral contract with Stearns, if any, was for a period longer than one year and therefore was within the statute of frauds.

2. Restatement (Second) of Contracts § 139(1) provides as follows: (1) A promise which the promisor should reasonably expect to induce action or forbearance on the part of the promisee or a third person and which does induce the action or forbearance is enforceable

In Chapman v. Bomann, 381 A.2d 1123 (Me.1978), we adopted promissory estoppel as a substitute for consideration, Restatement (Second) of Contracts § 90, but did not decide whether it would permit a direct avoidance of the statute of frauds. Id. § 139. Chapman involved an oral promise to make a writing satisfying the statute of frauds that was ancillary to a contract for the sale of land. We considered whether this ancillary promise could be enforced under the equitable principle that the statute of frauds may not itself become an instrument of fraud. Focusing on the conduct of the defendant, we concluded that an actual, subjective intention to deceive can estop the operation of the statute. In addition, an oral, ancillary promise may be enforced if the circumstances show objectively that "a fraud, or a substantial injustice tantamount to a fraud" would result from strict application of the statute. Chapman, 381 A.2d at 1123. Thus, although we invoked the rubric of promissory estoppel, our decision in Chapman actually applied an equitable estoppel and extended it only to an ancillary promise to make a writing. See 381 A.2d at 1130 n. 6.

We affirm that equitable estoppel, based upon a promisor's fraudulent conduct, can avoid application of the statute of frauds and that this principle applies to a fraudulent promise of employment. But we decline Stearn's invitation to accept promissory estoppel as permitting avoidance of the statute in employment contracts that require longer than one year to perform. Although section 139 of the Restatement may promote justice in other situations, in the employment context it contravenes the policy of the Statute to prevent fraud. It is too easy for a disgruntled former employee to allege reliance on a promise, but difficult factually to distinguish such reliance from the ordinary preparations that attend any new employment. Thus, such pre- employment actions of reliance do not properly serve the evidentiary function of the writing required by the statute. An employee who establishes an employer's fraudulent conduct by clear and convincing evidence may recover damages for deceit, Boivin v. Jones & Vining, Inc., 578 A.2d 187, 189 (Me.1990), or may avoid the statute of frauds and recover under an oral contract. The policy of the statute commands, however, that the focus remain upon the employer's conduct rather than upon the employee's reliance.

For similar reasons we reject the part performance doctrine as an avenue for avoidance of the statute of frauds in the employment context. We have recognized in other circumstances that a promisor's acceptance of partial performance may estop a defense under the statute on the ground of equitable fraud. Under this doctrine, too, our focus has been upon the conduct of the promisor. Moreover, an employee's preparations to begin a new assignment generally convey no direct benefit to an employer so it is particularly inappropriate to remove from an employer the protections of the statute. An employee can recover for services actually performed in quantum meruit. But to enforce a multi-year employment contract an employee must produce a writing that satisfies the statute of frauds or must prove fraud on the part of the employer.

Stearns has neither alleged nor proved fraud on the part of Emery-Waterhouse. Stearns does not dispute that he was adequately compensated for the time

notwithstanding the Statute of Frauds if injustice can be avoided only by enforcement of the promise. The remedy granted for breach is to be limited as justice requires.

that he actually worked. We conclude that his action for breach of contract is barred by the statute of frauds. Our holding renders it unnecessary to address the employer's other contentions on appeal.

The entry is:

Judgment vacated.

Case remanded with direction to enter judgment for the defendant. Because of the novel question presented, no costs are awarded to either party.

Questions

1. What is the difference between promissory and equitable estoppel and part performance? How might Stearns have fit himself within equitable estoppel or part performance?

2. What would Stearns have had to prove to meet the standard of "actual, subjective intention to deceive" stated by the court to be the standard set by *Chapman*?

3. Would the Maine court have come out the same way as the Texas court in *Moore Burger* based on the standards set up in *Chapman*?

4. Could an intent to deceive have been found more easily in *Moore Burger* than in *Stearns*? If an intent to deceive did exist, would that amount to fraud? What is the difference between fraud and equitable estoppel?

5. How can these cases help solve the Problem on page 3?

F. A Multi-million Dollar Case History — Bethlehem Steel

The following case between Bethlehem Steel and Litton Industries is a 95 million dollar dispute focusing on whether or not the two parties intended to contract. As you read the Pennsylvania Supreme Court decision ask yourself whether you agree with the majority or dissent. Keep in mind, that the Pennsylvania Supreme Court could not answer the question as they were evenly divided 2-2 on the issue on intent to enter into contractual relations between the two companies. Also consider the problem beginning on page 3. What issues does the problem raise? What is its resolution likely to be? What other facts would you like to learn to help you decide how it will come out.

At the center of this dispute are two letters exchanged between the two companies. Relevant portions are taken from the Superior Court decision, (468 A.2d 748) and reprinted below.

"The primary and fundamental question now before the Court is whether or not there has been an option contract. The plaintiff's claim is based upon the following two-page letter:

'ERIE MARINE, INC.
ERIE, PENNSYLVANIA

April 25, 1968
Bethlehem Steel Corporation
Bethlehem, Pennsylvania
Attn: Ralph K. Smith
Gentlemen:

Reference is made to the ship construction contract signed by our companies this date for the construction by us of a 1,000' self-unloading ore vessel for you. Reference is also made to my letter to you of this date extending to you an option to purchase either one or two additional vessels upon the terms therein set forth.

We hereby extend to you an offer to enter into an option agreement to have us construct for you from one to five additional vessels in accordance with "Specifications covering the Construction of a Self-Unloading Bulk Carrier for Bethlehem Steel Corporation" (Number Y 917) dated March 1968, addendum number 1 thereto dated March 28, 1968 and addendum number 2 thereto dated April 17, 1968. This offer to enter into an option agreement shall be firm and irrevocable until December 31, 1968 at 5:00 P.M. E.S.T.

The terms of the option agreement are to be as follows: (a) The specifications for the vessels shall be the specifications referred to above, except for mutually agreeable reduced test schedules of the vessels, if the testing of the vessel to be delivered under the contract executed this date proves successful. (b) Bethlehem to have the right at any time within five years after the effective date of the option agreement to order from one to not more than a total of five vessels, for delivery within 24 months from the date of the order for the first vessel ordered and for delivery within 24 months plus 4 months for each additional vessel ordered within any one calendar year; provided however no vessel shall be scheduled for delivery between November 31 and March 31. (c) The price of the vessel shall be as follows: 1st vessel ordered $22,400,000.00 2nd '''' '''' $21,400,000.00 3rd '''' '''' $20,400,000.00 4th '''' '''' $19,400,000.00 5th '''' '''' $18,400,000.00 (d) The vessel prices are subject to escalation for both labor and material for a base price of $20,400,000.00 for each vessel and based upon Fourth Quarter 1968 mutually agreed upon index such as: Material—Material index for Bureau of Ships steel vessel contracts" furnished to the Naval Ship Systems Command by the Bureau of Labor Statistics of the U.S. Department of Labor. Labor—'Index of changes in straight-time average hourly earnings for selected shipyards' (June 1962 = 100) for steel ship construction, furnished to the Naval Ship Systems Command by the Bureau of Labor Statistics of the U.S. Department of Labor. At the time of exercise of the option for any vessel, the escalation shall be computed to the date of contract execution, and an appropriate contract clause will be included therein providing for quarterly escalation thereafter. We will furnish you the labor and material percentages subject to escalation by May 15, 1968. (e) The terms and conditions of the ship construction contracts to be in accordance with the attached terms and conditions and any other mutually agreed to terms and conditions and shall contain a clause giving to Bethlehem the right to cancel at any time upon the payment of all of our costs incurred to date of cancellation, including similar vendor and subcontractor cancellation charges, plus 15% of such costs. Very truly yours, George K. Geiger'

"In response to this letter, a letter dated December 31, 1968 was sent by Bethlehem to Erie which stated in part 'We hereby accept your offer of an option to have you construct for us from one to five additional vessels...' In all other respects, the letter of December 31, 1968 is merely identical repetition of the language in the letter of April 25, 1968. This letter of December 31, 1968 appears in the record as PX-1." [The letter of April 25, 1968 appeared in the record as PX-4].

Both of these communications will be discussed and referred to at length in the Supreme Court decision.

Bethlehem Steel Corporation, v. Litton Industries, Inc.

507 Pa. 88, 488 A.2d 581
Supreme Court of Pennsylvania, 1985.

FLAHERTY, Justice.

On April 25, 1968 Litton Industries, Inc., its wholly owned subsidiary, Erie Marine, [Litton] Inc. and Bethlehem Steel Corporation met to formally exchange an already agreed upon contract for the construction of a multi-million dollar ore vessel. This boat, the Cort, was unique in size and design. At this same meeting where the contractual formalities for the Cort were exchanged, Litton initiated a proposal that the parties enter into a further agreement which would give Bethlehem a five year option to purchase an additional five vessels identical to the one just contracted for, and the parties jointly prepared the following letter on that subject: [See Superior Court Opinion—Letter of 4/25/68, *infra,* preceding page]

The construction contract referred to in paragraph one consists of approximately 500 pages of specifications for the construction of the Cort, which was built on a fixed price basis. In response to this letter, Bethlehem, on December 31, 1968, wrote: "We hereby accept your offer of an option to have you construct for us from one to five additional vessels...." In all other pertinent respects, the Bethlehem letter repeated the substance of the letter from Geiger, except that Bethlehem's letter was countersigned at its conclusion as follows:

AGREED TO:
ERIE MARINE, INC.

by George K. Geiger, President

Although the parties never reached agreement as to any of the open terms contained in this writing, in 1973, Bethlehem formally notified Litton that it was exercising its option to purchase three more ore ships of the type specified in the December 31, 1968 letter. Litton refused to perform under the terms of the 1968 letter, and Bethlehem brought an action against Litton claiming that it had repudiated its obligations under the 1968 letter, which Bethlehem characterized as an "option agreement," and that its actions constituted an anticipatory breach of this agreement. Bethlehem's damages for the alleged breach were stated at $95 million. Litton filed counterclaims in assumpsit for lost profits which it allegedly would have made on the building of the three vessels, had Bethlehem negotiated in good faith, and in trespass, for consequential and punitive damages for Bethlehem's alleged failure to negotiate in good faith.

A trial was then conducted in the Allegheny County Court of Common Pleas before Judge Maurice Louik. The proceedings lasted some nine months and produced more than 12,000 pages of testimony and 500 exhibits. It can hardly escape notice that the proceedings were somewhat protracted. As counsel for Litton noted during final argument, "May it please the court. Now...we enter into the fourth season in this case—we started in summer, went through the fall and winter and it's now spring, although the snowflakes are still falling...." In spite of the complexity of the case and the length of the litigation, or perhaps because of it, the parties were able to agree that the trial should be bifurcated on the issues of liability and damages. The trial court, without reaching the issue of damages, decided the liability issue against Bethlehem. On appeal, a divided Superior Court affirmed, Judges Hester, Rowley and Wieand dissenting. 321 Pa.Super. 357, 468 A.2d 748. We granted allocatur.

Judge Louik held that Bethlehem's action must fail because there was no enforceable agreement between the parties since the price term was so indefinite as to render the court unable to fill the gap. The Superior Court majority stated that the trial court "held that the plaintiff-appellant had not sustained its burden of proving that the parties intended to be contractually bound." At 359, 468 A.2d at 748. The Superior Court majority also observed that the intent to contract is a question of fact which must be affirmed on review if the lower court's finding that there was no intent to contract was supported by competent evidence. After reviewing the evidence, Superior Court held that the trial court's finding as to the intent of the parties must be affirmed because it was supported by competent evidence and because the lower court had not abused its discretion. Superior Court also noted the lower court's determination that the parties had not included the terms necessary to calculate the escalation in price referred to in the contract. These open terms, according to Superior Court, supported an inference that the parties did not intend to be legally bound.[1]

The dissent, however, observed that under the Uniform Commercial Code, a contract may be made in any manner which indicates agreement, including conduct, and that when a contract exists, it will not fail if there is a "reasonably certain basis" for fashioning a remedy. 13 Pa.C.S.A. § 2204. The dissent then determined that the conduct of the parties indicated an intent to enter a legally binding contract and that under 13 Pa.C.S.A. § 2305, the section of the code concerning contracts containing an "open price term," a "reasonable price at the time of delivery" is the proper remedy and that the court is capable of fashioning such a remedy.

---

1. There seems to be a dispute as to whether the trial court held that the parties did not intend to be contractually bound, or merely that the terms of the purported agreement were so indefinite that the court could not fill the gap. The trial judge himself disclaimed what was to become the view of the Majority of the Superior Court when, at post-trial motions, the following exchange took place. MR. KAUFFMAN [attorney for Litton]: There are two independent grounds. The opinion went off on two separate and independent grounds. One, there is no contract. Two, even if there were a contract, the gaps are so complex and so wide that the Court can't fill them in and therefore there is no enforceable agreement. HON LOUIK [The trial judge]: I didn't say that. I said there was no evidence in the record for which the Court could fill in the gaps. Repr.Rec. at 6958a. Judge Louik's remark notwithstanding, Superior Court's interpretation of the adjudication is plausible. Although the trial court made no factual finding that the parties intended not to contract, a fair inference may be drawn from the court's "Discussion" section of the adjudication that no contractual intent existed. We adopt that inference.

STANDARD OF REVIEW

It is axiomatic, of course, that this Court will not disturb the factual findings of a trial court if there is competent evidence of record to support the findings and if the court has not abused its discretion. Further, when intent to contract is at issue, the lower court's determinations of intent will not be disturbed if supported by competent evidence and if the court did not abuse its discretion.

Although the dissent in Superior Court characterized the determination of contractual intent as one of ultimate fact, or one of inference drawn from facts, and therefore reversible by an appellate court, it is nevertheless true that Pennsylvania law has traditionally treated such determinations as factual: The first issue involves the Chancellor's [finding that the parties entered into a particular oral agreement]. We are mindful that the findings of the Chancellor will not be reversed unless it appears that he has clearly abused his discretion or committed an error of law...and that the findings have the full force of a jury verdict and, if supported by sufficient evidence and if affirmed by the court en banc, will not be disturbed on appeal....As we stated in Masciantonio Will..."The test is not whether we, the appellate court, would have reached the same result had we been acting as the hearing judge who saw and heard the witness, 'but rather whether a judicial mind, on due consideration of the evidence, as a whole, could reasonably have reached the conclusion of the chancellor.' " Yuhas v. Schmidt, 434 Pa. 453-54, 258 A.2d 616, 619-20 (1969). While the dissent's point is well taken that a finding of contractual intent is an inference drawn from facts, it is also an inference drawn in the context of the whole record, including matters of credibility, and such matters are clearly for the trial court to determine. Thus, our standard of review is to ask whether the findings of fact, including the determination of contractual intent, are supported by any competent evidence of record which a reasonable judicial mind could find as supportive of the determination made by the fact finder.

Within the context of this standard of review, the two issues which this Court must address in the present case are whether the parties intended to enter into a legally enforceable option contract for the sale of ore vessels; and whether, if the parties intended that such a contract exist, its terms are sufficiently clear to be enforceable. Among the evidence of record which has a bearing on these issues are: (1) the writings themselves; (2) statutory provisions concerning the formation of contracts with open terms; (2)(a) conduct having a bearing on the determination of contractual intent; (2)(b) open terms which may have a bearing both on intent and ability of the court to fashion a remedy.

(1) THE LETTERS OF APRIL 25, 1968 and DECEMBER 31, 1968

It is possible, of course, that a clear indication of contractual intent might be gleaned from the documents themselves, and to that end, they must be considered. Litton's letter of April 25, 1968 reads: "We hereby extend you an offer to enter into an option agreement....This offer to enter into an option agreement shall be firm and irrevocable until December 31, 1968 at 5:00 P.M. E.S.T." Bethlehem on December 31, 1968 responded: "We hereby accept your offer of an option...."

As the trial court indicated, if Bethlehem had accepted what was offered, it would have accepted "your offer to enter into an option agreement," not "your offer of an option." By purporting to accept an option, Bethlehem, was, as the trial court put it, accepting more than was offered. Thus, it cannot be said from an examination of the documents alone that the parties intended to be contractually bound to the terms of the writings, for one was offering we know not what and the other was accepting something that was not offered.

Moreover, the writings contain a number of open terms: (a) an excalation index (a multiplier which adjusts the price of labor and materials for inflation), (b) "an appropriate contract clause" providing for quarterly escalation after the option is exercised (hereinafter referred to as an "apportionment clause" because it determines the manner in which escalation will be paid or apportioned over each quarter of the contract period); (c) "any other mutually agreed to terms and conditions."

Nevertheless, regardless of the ambiguity of the writings, because the parties' conduct, under the provisions of the Uniform Commercial Code, may indicate that the parties did in fact intend to be contractually bound and, because under the Code the missing terms may be able to be supplied by a court, we must examine the principles of the law under the Code which govern the formation of sales contracts.

(2) FORMATION OF A CONTRACT WITH OPEN TERMS

The section of the Uniform Commercial Code, as enacted in Pennsylvania, concerning formation of contracts provides: § 2204 Formation in General (a) General rule—A contract for sale of goods may be made in any manner sufficient to show agreement, including conduct by both parties which recognizes the existence of such a contract. * * * (c) Effect of open terms—Even though one or more terms are left open a contract for sale does not fail for indefiniteness *if the parties have intended to make a contract and there is a reasonably certain basis* for giving an appropriate remedy. 13 Pa.C.S.A. § 2204. (Emphasis supplied). The Comment to subsection (c) states: "Subsection [(c)] states the principle as to 'open terms' underlying later sections of the Article. If the parties intend to enter into a binding agreement, this sub-section recognizes that agreement as valid in law, despite missing terms, if there is any reasonably certain basis for granting a remedy. The test is not certainly as to what the parties were to do nor as to the exact amount of damages due the plaintiff. Nor is the fact that one or more terms are left to be agreed upon enough of itself to defeat an otherwise adequate agreement. Rather, commercial standards on the point of 'indefiniteness' are intended to be applied, this Act making provision elsewhere for missing terms needed for performance, open price, remedies and the like. The more terms the parties leave open, the less likely it is that they have intended to conclude a binding agreement, but their actions may be frequently conclusive on the matter despite the omissions."

For purposes of this case, the significance of § 2204 and its comment is that, generally, it tells us a contract may be formed "in any manner sufficient to show agreement, including conduct by both parties which recognizes the existence of such a contract," and that even if some terms of the contract are left open, the contract will not fail for indefiniteness if there is a contractual intent and a "reasonably certain" basis to give a remedy. Further, the comment tells us that the general purpose of this section is to give effect to agreements which the parties intended to be effective, even if there are missing terms, but only if there is—again—a "reasonably certain" basis for fashioning a remedy. The comment goes on to observe that the more terms there are which are left open, the less likely it is that the parties intended a contract, but the comment leaves open the possibility that the parties' actions might so blatantly acknowledge the intent to be contractually bound that an inference of contractual intent may be drawn in spite of the number of terms left open.

Applying these principles to the present case, we must determine whether the parties intended to create a contract and whether there is a "reasonably certain basis" for supplying a remedy if they did so intend. In making the determination as to intent, we may consider the conduct of the parties and the number and nature of terms left open.

(2)(a). INFERENCES AS TO CONTRACTUAL INTENT WHICH MAY BE DRAWN FROM THE CONDUCT OF THE PARTIES

The dissenting opinion of Judge Hester in Superior Court notes a number of matters which, in the dissent's view, constitute conduct indicating an intent to be contractually bound. Two of these items are worthy of comment: 9. In its financial plan of July, 1973, Litton acknowledged the outstanding option as follows: "It should be noted that Bethlehem has an option for construction of up to five (5) new vessels. That option will not expire until December 31, 1973. The terms of the option, if exercised by Bethlehem, would result in substantial losses by Litton." 14. In a letter of March, 1970, from Litton to Bethlehem, Litton stated as follows: "Bethlehem already has an option agreement covering the next five vessels of the L.S.C. [Litton Super Carrier] type. We assume that you continually weigh the escalating cost of exercising these options against the projected going rate, your own fleet cost, the cost and benefits of postponing the decision further, and other investment opportunities in Bethlehem." Slip Op. at 40, 41. Item # 9 overtly acknowledges that "Bethlehem has an option," and item # 14 similarly states, "Bethlehem already has an option agreement covering the next five vessels...." Such language clearly indicates that at least some Litton people believed there was an option contract, and if there were nothing more, would constitute conduct of a party indicative of an intent to be contractually bound.

On the other hand, other items listed by the dissent in Superior Court as indicative of contractual intent, are not so indicative.

In all, the dissent below lists a total of sixteen items which allegedly illustrate conduct of the parties indicative of an intent to be contractually bound. Some of these items, in fact, support that inference; others do not. The importance of this observation is only that if there is a case to be made supporting the inference of Litton's intent to be contractually bound derived from Litton's conduct, the case is not so strong as the dissent would have it.

Concerning Bethlehem's conduct, it is self-evident that the letter of August 21, 1973 from A.K. Smith, Bethlehem's Purchasing Agent, indicating that Bethlehem intended to exercise its "options," constituted conduct consistent with an intent to be contractually bound. Further, it cannot be said that Bethlehem's failure to bargain earlier as to the open terms of the option necessarily is conduct which is inconsistent with an intent to be contractually bound. However, even in the August 21, 1973 letter, Bethlehem's Purchasing Agent stated: Several aspects of the referenced agreement are subject to the mutual agreement of the parties and we request an early meeting with you to resolve these matters. Please let us have your early reply. Thus, the very letter in which Bethlehem announces its intent to exercise its purported option specifically acknowledges that the agreement has open terms which must be mutually agreed to as a condition precedent to the effectiveness of the agreement. Additionally, Bethlehem's Purchasing Agent admitted at trial: "We indicated on August 21, we intended to exercise our options and there were things that had to be resolved before we actually could have a commitment."

This same witness also testified, as follows: Q. Why didn't you make the downpayment at the time you sent the letter [purporting to exercise Bethlehem's option]? A. Because, we didn't have an agreement with you. There were clauses that we agreed—there were clauses that we agreed would have to be mutually agreed to. Q. Is it your testimony that the only reason you didn't make a downpayment was because no invoice was submitted? A. No. There wasn't a contract signed at that point in time. Why should we pay the ten percent? Repr.Rec. 2736a, 2739a-40a.

It would be fair to say that such conduct, as explained by this witness, a key Bethlehem employee, was inconsistent with a belief that the parties were contractually bound. Rather, it was consistent with a desire to become contractually bound.

The record literally bulges with letters, conversations and explanations on the part of both parties—all of which might generally be classified as "conduct" and explanations of conduct—which indicate both that the parties did and also that they did not intend to be contractually bound. When there is important conduct and explanatory testimony on the part of the parties that both supports and negates the inference of intent to be contractually bound, as there is in this case, an inference of contractual intent may not be drawn, and plaintiff has not met its burden of proof by a preponderance of evidence.

Thus, there was competent evidence of record indicating that the conduct of the parties was inconsistent with an intent to be contractually bound, and the trial court's adjudication could be supported on this alone, for 13 Pa.C.S.A. §2204 requires that in order for a contract to be formed, there must be both contractual intent and a reasonably certain basis for awarding a remedy. When one of these necessary elements is missing, there is no contractual intent and any purported agreement is not enforceable as a contract.[2]

It will be recalled that under the provisions of §2204, the existence of open terms in a writing will not necessarily defeat the enforceability of a contract so long as there is a contractual intent. However, the number of open terms may have a bearing on a determination of contractual intent, and whether there is a reasonably certain basis for fashioning a remedy will determine whether the contract will fail for indefiniteness.

---

2. The dissent in Superior Court relies in part on another section of the code, 2-305, 13 Pa.C.S.A. §2305: "§2305. **Open price term** (a) **General rule.**—The parties if they so intend can conclude a contract for sale even though the price is not settled. In such a case the price is a reasonable price at the time for delivery if: (1) nothing is said as to price; (2) the price is left to be agreed by the parties and they fail to agree; or (3) the price is to be fixed in terms of some agreed market or other standard as set or recorded by a third person or agency and it is not so set or recorded." As the discussion in (2) and (2)(a) above indicates, a necessary condition of contract formation is contractual intent. That is also required by §2305(a). Since no contractual intent may be inferred, the contract fails both under §2304 [sic] and §2305.

Although we have already seen that there is an adequate basis in the record for determining that the parties did not intend to contract, if we assume arguendo that they did, we must then look at the open terms in the parties' writings, which are: (1) the indexes to be used for the escalation of labor and material; (2) the apportionment of this escalation on a quarterly basis; (3) other terms mutually agreed to terms and conditions.

As to (1), the indexes which provide for escalation of labor and material costs in line with inflation, the evidence of record established, and the trial court found, that there are no standard escalation indexes. The record indicates that during the years relevant to this case, there were thousands of published independent indexes which could be used to formulate escalation clauses, Repr.Rec. 5810a; that even if one considered only a single index, for example the NAVships material index for iron and steel, approximately 125 individual indexes are aggregated to form the composite index for iron and steel; and that in the same NAVships index, 140 separate commodity indexes comprise the general purpose machinery and equipment index. Repr.Rec. 5847a-5851a. The importance of this information is that since there is no "standard" index to use, and since an individual index may be constructed by using one or many individual indexes (weighted, for example, for the commodities used in the project being contracted for, and even for the geographical location of the project), there is no "reasonably certain" way to know which of the thousands of possibilities for constructing an index the parties would have agreed upon.

Item (2) concerns the apportionment schedule. Once an escalation index is agreed upon and that is applied to the base price (here $20,400,000.00), then the parties must agree upon the amount to be escalated during each quarter of the contract. The reason for this is that if an apportionment schedule is constructed which requires the buyer to pay a larger percentage of the apportionment at the end of the contract period, when prices and costs have gone up because of inflation, the buyer will pay significantly more escalation dollars than if he had paid early in the contract period. Thus, it is in the shipbuilder's interest to delay the apportionment schedule until the end of the contract period, but it is in the buyer's interest to pay as much of the apportionment as possible in the early quarters. In one hypothetical calculation of delivered price based on 93% of the escalation amount being paid in the last quarter, the shipbuilder's price, using this variable alone to calculate the delivered price of one ship, was $5,493,000 more than the buyer's calculated price as indicated in one of the buyer's exhibits. Repr.Rec. 6037a. Since the writing in question concerned five ships, by varying the apportionment term in the shipbuilder's favor, the contract price for five ships would increase more than $25,000,000.

Thus, the record not only supports the trial court's finding that there is no standard or "typical" apportionment of escalatable costs, but it demonstrates as well that the apportionment schedule alone, forgetting all of the other variables represented by the open terms, may make a difference of millions of dollars on the delivered price of even a single boat.

Item (3), concerns other mutually agreed to terms which may be added by the parties. The trial court found and the record supports the finding that in September of 1973 Bethlehem submitted to Litton a draft construction contract which contained 12 additional terms beyond those contained in the sample contract which was referred to in Bethlehem's letter of December 31,

1968. These additional terms included various warranties, a provision for liquidated damages, a revision of the payment schedule, retainage of an amount of the contract price after delivery, a buy-American clause, a drydocking-repair provision, and a clause that would prevent Erie from merging or consolidating with any other corporation without Bethlehem's consent. It is self-evident that some if not all of these matters are significant and might well be the subject of disagreement between the parties. Taking only one item as an illustration, a Bethlehem official was questioned as follows about the buy-American clause: Q. And the buy-American provision was inserted in the Defendants' Exhibit 12 [a draft ship construction contract submitted by Bethlehem to Litton at a meeting of September 24, 1973] in Paragraph 16.4. Is that correct? A. Yes, sir. Q. There was no buy-American provision in Plaintiff's Exhibit 2 [sample ship construction contract exchanged between the parties when Litton's April 25, 1968 letter was delivered] was there? A. No, sir. Q. And the buy-American provision was a matter of serious concern to you? Wasn't it? A. Yes, sir. Q. And that was something that you told Litton and Erie? Wasn't it? A. Yes, sir, yes, it was. Q. And you told them that in accordance with the policy of Bethlehem Steel Corporation that you, as a representative of Bethlehem Steel Corporation, wanted a buy-American provision in the contract or any contract for additional vessels? Isn't that correct? A. That we would want such a clause included, a buy-American clause included in the contract, yes, sir. Q. And there were other clauses such as liquidated damages and guarantees and others, and I'm not going to compare D-12 with P-2, . . . But there were other clauses that were included in D-12—that were placed in D-12 that were not in Plaintiff's Exhibit 2? Isn't that right? A. That's right. Q. Now, on or prior to December 31, 1973, did anyone from Bethlehem tell anyone from Litton and Erie that with respect to acquiring additional vessels from Erie, that Bethlehem was agreeable to signing a contract with the terms contained in P-2 sample form of contract without any additional terms? A. I don't recall any such statement that included "without any additional terms..." Repr.Rec. 3070a-3072a.

Without going into a protracted discussion of each of Bethlehem's proposed additional terms, it suffices, for purposes of determining contractual intent, to note that there were twelve such terms, that at least one of them was described by a Bethlehem official as a matter of "serious" concern, and that Bethlehem apparently made no offer to enter into an agreement without such additional terms. Under these conditions, the parties can hardly be said to have agreed on what additional terms, if any, would be included in a contract.

Moreover, and this is the final point, all of these open terms are interrelated. It may have been that if Bethlehem would agree to omit some or all of its additional terms, Litton would agree to an escalation index proposed by Bethlehem, or that Litton would agree to the index if an additional concession were made by Bethlehem that the quarterly apportionment of escalation amounts would be weighted toward the end of the contract period. The point is that far from leaving open terms which could be easily filled by a court, the parties left open what amounted to gaping holes in a multi-million dollar contract that no one but the parties themselves could fill. There is no "reasonably certain" basis upon which any court could fill the gaps, and thus the trial court's findings as to the open terms are supported by competent evidence of record.

In sum, a review of the record indicates that there is more than ample evidence to support the trial court's findings that there was no contractual intent and that the open terms could not be filled by the court. The writings themselves are ambiguous as to what the parties intended. Moreover, the conduct of the parties offers no more certain guidance than the writings as to intent, and the nature of the open terms argues against contractual intent. But even if contractual intent were assumed, the contract would fall for indefiniteness because the open terms may not be filled by the court on the required "reasonably certain" basis, or in fact, on any basis at all short of sheer speculation.

HUTCHINSON, J., joins this Opinion in Support of Affirmance and files an Opinion in Support of Affirmance.

OPINION IN SUPPORT OF AFFIRMANCE

HUTCHINSON, Justice.

In his opinion in support of affirmance, Mr. Justice Flaherty distinguishes an "option" from an "option agreement." For the following reasons I believe that distinction supplies an adequate alternative supporting ground for the lower court's opinion that these parties did not contract. I therefore join him in support of affirmance.

An option agreement, although it may seem to have only the characteristics of an offer, is nevertheless a contract. As a contract, the option agreement requires contract formalities, including consideration. In cases involving the sale of goods, the U.C.C. has modified the common law of offer and acceptance by creating what it calls firm offers in § 2-205, 13 Pa.C.S. § 2205, which bind the offeror, in a limited sense, without consideration. Such an offer, if it states that it will be held open for a definite time, not in excess of a statutorily limited period, does not fail for lack of consideration, i.e. it is not revocable during the period set up to the statutory limit. This Code section limits the time a firm offer can be held irrevocable to three months. Option contracts, however, are not governed by 13 Pa.C.S. § 2205. The firm offer which Code § 2-205 makes irrevocable for a limited time is sometimes loosely called an "option," but it has a different character than the option contract recognized at common law. The Code discloses no legislative intent to eliminate the option contract, with its requirement of consideration. Hence, the necessary distinction between the "option" which is in reality a firm offer and the option contract.

In this case, appellee may have extended a firm offer to Bethlehem. The letter set forth in Exhibit PX-4 stated that its offer would be firm and irrevocable until December 31, 1968, five months beyond the U.C.C. limitation. Because Bethlehem did not accept within the three-month limit the Code sets, Litton's firm offer became revocable after July 25, 1968. Bethlehem's letter of December 31 may be treated as an attempt to accept the original offer. As an acceptance of a firm offer it came too late. If timely, however, as a common law acceptance of an unrevoked offer for an option contract, it required consideration. By conforming to the requirements of § 2205 Bethlehem could at best only tender a new firm offer, this one subject to Litton's, not Bethlehem's, timely acceptance. While Litton's counter-signature on this December 31 letter from Bethlehem comes within the Code's three-month irrevocability period if it is itself considered a firm offer and not an acceptance of Litton's expired firm offer, the underlying option contract must still be supported by consideration.

Thus, although Litton's counter-signature on this letter may arguably evidence an intent to accept a firm offer from Bethlehem and create an option contract, it is nevertheless ineffective to do so. Consideration was lacking because Bethlehem offered no payment or other consideration for the option contract, either in December of 1968 or at any time. In short, there was no exchange and Bethlehem remained free to act entirely in accordance with its own will, judgment and interest. It would bind Litton, while leaving itself free. The acceptance here did not supply consideration in the form of a promise because Bethlehem did not commit itself to purchase any vessels, or undertake any obligation. It was free to let the option lapse. This lack of consideration precludes the offer, firm or otherwise, from ripening into a contract by either party's timely acceptance. This is so, not because Bethlehem's promise was illusory or because there was no mutuality of obligation, but because Bethlehem made no promise at all. The simple problem with Bethlehem's case is that it did not offer to buy any additional ships now or pay for the right to require Litton to make one in the future under the terms of Litton's offer, whatever those terms may be.

Bethlehem's assertion, that the option is part of one overall contract for the construction of ore ships and thus supported by the consideration relating to the ceremonial contract for the construction of the CORT, is not in accordance with the language of PX-4. That document says "we hereby extend to you an offer to enter into an option agreement to have us construct for you from one to five additional vessels in accordance with the specifications covering the construction of a self-unloading boat carrier for Bethlehem Steel Corporation. (No. Y 917) Dated March 1968,...." By that language it becomes plain that there was no intention to make the option a part of an overall contract for the construction of ships but simply the extension of an offer to contract separately for additional ships. This becomes even plainer when we consider Litton's agreement to the extension of an additional so-called shorter term option to Bethlehem for the purchase of two ships.

I agree with Bethlehem that it is unnecessary to have a separate consideration for an option which is part of one overall transaction, and that such an option need not be a part of the writing setting out the terms of the main agreement. It is necessary that both writings be intended as part of one overall agreement supported by a single consideration. No such intention appears from the language of PX-4 or its relationship to the other documents. Indeed, its language speaks to an irrevocable offer to enter into an independent option agreement. As such, that agreement required a separate consideration.

I have also carefully considered Bethlehem's argument that we can find consideration for an option contract in the form of promissory estoppel or detrimental reliance under § 90 of Restatement (Second) of Contracts. In that connection we are referred to expenses which Bethlehem "obviously incurred" in its efforts to obtain additional ships from Litton. These obvious expenses are not specified and for them we are referred only to Bethlehem's offer to perform the obligations specified in the exchange of letters. However, these tenders of performance come approximately five years after December 31, 1968, the latest date on which the contract could have been created, leaving nothing to show significant detriment or restrictions on Bethlehem's will during the intervening five years. Under such circumstances I do not believe § 90 furnishes a basis for finding the detrimental reliance which may be substituted for the consideration otherwise necessary to support this contract.

Such a lack of consideration or a substitute for it aborts any intended contract, despite the provisions of U.C.C. § 2-204(3), 13 Pa.C.S. § 2204(c). That section modified the common law rule that a contract which lacks a material term was too indefinite to be enforced. In such cases the Code saves the contract by implying a good faith obligation to agree more precisely on the nature of the indefinite term. We might speculate that good faith discussions by these parties would have produced mutual agreement on an index commonly acceptable for long term ship building contracts. However, no such further negotiation would supply consideration. It could have been supplied only if Bethlehem was required to pay or promise something. In the absence of Bethlehem's payment or promise, a promise by Litton could not create a contract.

Thus, whether or not the parties intended to be bound by the writings, an issue on which considerable deference is due the fact finder, there is no evidence on the record to show that the purported contract would have been supported by consideration. On this alternate ground I agree with Mr. Justice FLAHERTY that the orders of the courts below must be affirmed.

OPINION IN SUPPORT OF REVERSAL

ZAPPALA, J. joined by LARSEN, J. DISSENTING

The question before the Court is whether or not there was an option contract between the parties.

The focus of the documentary and testimonial evidence at trial was a pair of letters, the first from Litton to Bethlehem dated April 25, 1968, and the second from Bethlehem to Litton dated December 31, 1968, respectively designated Plaintiff's Exhibits (PX-) 4 and 1.

The Court of Common Pleas of Allegheny County in its Findings of Fact concluded that on April 25, 1968, Litton and Bethlehem were in agreement that "the concept of escalation would be included in any ship construction contract they might subsequently agree upon," although they did not agree at that time on the terms of such escalation, nor were they then prepared to negotiate on such a clause, recognizing it as a subject for future negotiation and agreement.

At the outset of the analysis, it is well to note that the scope of our review of a finding on contractual intent, such being a finding of fact, is narrowly circumscribed. Although purporting to apply the "abuse of discretion" standard of review in assessing the lower court's findings on contractual intent, the Opinion in Support of Affirmance acknowledges that "the trial court made no factual finding that the parties intended not to contract." At 585 n. 2 (Emphasis added). Indeed the trial court expressly denied having determined that there was no contract and specifically stated that its determination was simply that "there was no evidence in the record for [sic] which the Court could fill in the gaps." Despite this express statement, Justice Flaherty's Opinion in Support of Affirmance adopts what is described as a "fair inference" drawn from the "Discussion" section of the lower court's opinion "that no contractual intent existed." Id. I cannot agree that this Court is bound to accept such "inferences" from the court's discussion of the facts in the same manner as we are bound to accept the facts themselves.

There is no dispute that the parties did not execute a final document containing all the terms which the parties contemplated would constitute their final ship construction agreement. To say this, however, is not to say that the parties did not have an enforceable contract. Neither is it to say that the parties' contractual intent as to ship construction is properly determined by viewing the evidence solely in relation to the documents which the parties had executed regarding the option agreement.

"An option contract is a promise which meets the requirements for the formation of a contract and limits the promisor's power to revoke an offer." Restatement (Second) of Contracts § 25 (emphasis added). Reduced to its simplest elements, PX-4 contains an offer by Litton to Bethlehem of an option agreement. (This offer was, by its own terms, made irrevocable until December 31, 1968.) The basic terms of the offer which was to be kept open by this option agreement were that Litton would build up to five ships for Bethlehem at any time over the five years following acceptance of the option agreement, according to certain specifications, and at certain prices which would be subject to escalation based upon an index to be mutually agreed upon. In other words, by PX-4 Litton made an offer to Bethlehem to build up to five ships and gave Bethlehem the opportunity to make this offer irrevocable for a period of five years by offering an option agreement. Bethlehem unequivocally accepted the offered option agreement by its letter of December 31, 1968, PX-1. Once again it is emphasized that the sole purpose of this agreement, the option agreement, was to keep open for five years Litton's offer to build up to five ships for Bethlehem.

We have previously accepted as the law of this Commonwealth the principle stated in Restatement (Second) of Contracts § 205 that "[e]very contract imposes upon each party a duty of good faith and fair dealing in its performance and its enforcement." Atlantic Richfield Co. v. Razumic, 480 Pa. 366, 378 n. 7a, 390 A.2d 736, 742 n. 7a (1978) (referring to § 231 of Restatement (Second) of Contracts Tent. Draft No. 5 1970 now § 205). Likewise, the Uniform Commercial Code provides that "[e]very contract...within this title imposes an obligation of good faith in its performance or enforcement," 13 Pa.C.S. § 1203.

Application of this legal analysis changes the relative significance of the facts as found by the trial court. The most significant fact is not that the important escalation clause of the ship construction contract was never agreed upon, or that the parties would not have executed a written ship construction contract without agreement on an escalation index. Rather the most important finding is that Bethlehem was willing to consider a number of indices for the escalation clause, but Litton "did not intend to develop any language regarding a proposed ship construction contract," Findings of Fact 30, 31, 33; Opinion at 9-10. In effect, when Bethlehem sought to "exercise its option" by accepting Litton's outstanding offer to build ships, Litton prevented execution of a ship construction contract by failing to bargain in good faith on the open terms. This constituted a breach of the agreement formed by Bethlehem's 1973 letter acceptance of Litton's offer contained in the letter of April 25, 1968 and renewed by Litton's agreement to its restatement in the letter of December 31, 1968.

Justice Flaherty's Opinion in Support of Affirmance also errs, as did the trial court, in the manner in which it interprets and applies the "open terms" provisions of the Uniform Commercial Code. Section 2204 provides: "§ 2204 **Formation in General** (a) General rule—A contract for sale of goods may be made in any manner sufficient to show agreement, including conduct by both parties which recognizes the existence of such a contract...."

(c) Effect of open terms—Even though one or more are left open a contract for sale does not fail for indefiniteness *if the parties have intended to make a contract and* there is a *reasonable certain basis for giving an appropriate remedy.*" 13 Pa.C.S. § 2204. (Emphasis added). Subsection (c), explains the Comment, "states the principle as to 'open terms' underlying later sections of the Article. If the parties intend to enter into a binding agreement, this sub-section recognizes that agreement as valid in law, despite missing terms, if there is any reasonably certain basis for granting a remedy. *The test is not certainty as to what the parties were to do nor as to the exact amount of damages due the plaintiff.*" (Emphasis added).

Section 2305 provides: **Open price term** (a) General rule.—The parties if they so intend can conclude a contract for sale even though the price is not settled. *In such a case the price is a reasonable price at the time for delivery if*: (1) nothing is said as to price; (2) *the price is left to be agreed by the parties and they fail to agree*; (3) the price is to be fixed in terms of some agreed market or other standard as set or recorded by a third person or agency and it is not so set or recorded. 13 Pa.C.S. § 2305. (Emphasis added).

The trial court concluded that "because of the nature of the gaps...the parties are the exclusive entities capable of *filling the gaps*," and "[b]ecause the gaps are so wide the Court cannot *make a new contract* for the parties." (Emphasis added). Justice Flaherty's Opinion in Support of Affirmance similarly finds that "there is no 'reasonably certain' way to know which of the thousands of possibilities for constructing an index the parties would have agreed upon." Were the remedy being sought specific performance of a contract, these difficulties would indeed make the determination of an "appropriate remedy" well nigh impossible. Because there is an available remedy in monetary damages, however, the proper inquiry is not what the parties would have agreed to, but what is reasonable. The court's role in this situation is not to form a contract as the parties would have done, but to determine a remedy for the wrongful failure of the parties to reach agreement. The result of this confusion is painfully demonstrated in the present case, where it is not even the entire price term which was left open, but only the "extras" to be added on to an already agreed upon price. The court would have no difficulty in determining from the stated base price of $20,400,000 per ship that an "appropriate remedy" for a breach involving three ships would be *at least* $61,200,000. Yet because of the open escalation clause of the price term, the result is that *no* remedy is awarded. I find this result to be absurd and unconscionable.

For the foregoing reasons I would reverse the Order of the Superior Court. Because the trial court bifurcated this case as to liability and damages, I would remand the case for determination of damages on Bethlehem's claim against Litton.

Questions

1. What is the result of this case? Did Justice Flaherty find intent to enter a contract by the parties or did he not reach that question?

2. What issue do the three opinions identify as the basis for their ultimate decision? Which one do you agree with?

3. Suppose Justice Hutchinson found detrimental reliance. What measure of damages would he be likely to award Bethlehem? Compare that to the damage awards given in the cases on promissory estoppel.

4. Using Justice Hutchinson's logic, is it possible to find a contract based solely on detrimental reliance and no consideration?

5. Did Justice Zappala omit a significant portion of Subsection (c) to the Comment to § 2204? See Justice Flaherty's opinion.

6. Justice Zappala believes that there is a reasonably certain way to estimate damages, but not to give specific performance. Why? Reread the Note on Specific Performance *supra* Part E.

7. What does Justice Zappala mean by the following sentence: "The court's role in this situation is not to form a contract as the parties would have done, but to determine a remedy for the wrongful failure of the parties to reach agreement." Do you agree with that interpretation?

8. Justice Zappala speaks of an "apparent remedy" for breach being at least $61,200,000. Review the text of damage recovery from Question 4 following the *Petroleum Refractionating* case, *supra* Part D . What is missing from his conclusion?

Part II

Offer and Acceptance

Introduction

In Part I (Parts C and D) we considered offer and acceptance in terms of consideration. An offeror seeks to have the offeree either do or refrain from doing something, or promise to do or refrain from doing something. The action or promise which is sought and which the offeree gives constitutes consideration for the promise of the offeror just as the promise of the offeror constitutes consideration for the promise of the offeree, if a promise is what the offeror sought.

It is often said that the offeror controls the contract. This is because of the common law "mirror image" rule, whereby to create a contract the offeree must respond to the offer by doing or promising exactly what the offeror requires. If the offeree does not exactly respond in the manner requested then she has not accepted the offer and no contract results. However, under the Uniform Commercial Code (U.C.C.) an offeree who does not give the exact response sought by the offeror may still have accepted the contract. We will examine this approach in Part F.

Often a person responds to an offer not by accepting it, but by making an offer of their own (counter offer). X tells Y "I will buy your concert ticket from you for $20." Y responds "I will sell it for $25," to which X agrees. X the original offeror (he offered to buy the ticket for $20) became the offeree when Y responded by asking for $25. Y, the original offeree became the offeror. X accepted her counter offer to sell the ticket for $25. While X initiated the talks, Y's terms controlled the sale. Thus, roles can be reversed and the offeree can become the offeror. Because the offeror's terms control at common law and also control under the U.C.C. in almost all cases, it is always important to identify which party is the offeror and which is the offeree.

Offers are normally revocable, but can be made in such a way that they are irrevocable. The *Bethlehem* case discussed this in detail. Under U.C.C. section 2-205, certain offers are valid and irrevocable for up to 90 days without any consideration being paid for them. If consideration is paid to keep an offer open or if an offer is under seal, then in essence you have a contract in which the offeror promises to keep an offer for a separate contract open. We examined this in the section on seals in Part I. In theory if a person breaks a contract in which he has promised to keep an offer open, the injured party should be able to sue for breach. In practice, if a person contracts to keep an offer open, he cannot revoke

107

it—the offeree may accept the offer even though the offeror is objecting and stating that there is no longer an offer. Here again, we see the objective and subjective aspects of contract formation coming into play. In the 19th century a subjective "meeting of the minds" was necessary to create a contract. Both parties had to "intend" in their own minds to make a contract. We saw in *Embry* and elsewhere that the modern courts' focus is on the objective manifestation of intent. Here again in the firm offer/option contract setting we see the objective vs. the subjective with the objective winning. If a person makes a "firm offer" or enters an option contract the offer stays open, regardless of the offeror's subjective intent to revoke it.

Another way in which an offer can be deemed to be kept open, despite the attempt of the offeror to revoke it, is if it is relied upon by the offeree. If the offeror makes an offer to enter into a bilateral contract and the offeror has reason to know that the offeree before accepting the offer may take action in reliance on it and the offeree does so act, an option contract can result—that is, the offeror may not be allowed to withdraw the offer and the offeree can accept it. Where the offer is not deemed to be kept open despite the offeree's reasonable reliance on it, the offeree may be able to recover reliance damages for the revocation of it by the offeror. This issue arose in the *Empro* case (*supra* Part I-A) although damages were not allowed.

Where the offeror is making an offer to enter into a unilateral contract and should know that the offeree expects the offer to be kept open and the offeree in reliance on its being kept open undertakes expenditures in preparation for the performance of the contract, the Restatement allows reliance damages for the preparation cost. (Restatement § 87(2).) Where the performance has actually begun, if the offer is for a unilateral contract, Restatement § 45 requires the offeror to keep the offer open but does not require the offeree to finish performance. If the offer is one which can be accepted by either performing or promising and the offeree begins performance, this beginning of performance acts as an acceptance in which the offeree and the offeror are both bound to a contract. (See Restatement § 62) Although these Restatement rules are not nearly as widespread among the jurisdictions as the word "Restatement" implies, most courts do not now follow the strict common law interpretation of a unilateral contract that says the offeror may revoke the offer until the full performance is completed and that the offeree has no action either for preparation costs or for actually beginning performance. Usually, but by no means always, some relief is given. An illustration of the type of unilateral contract where beginning performance creates an option in which the offeror cannot revoke the offer would be where an offeror says to an offeree: "If you paint my house, I will pay you $10,000." Assuming that the offer is not too indefinite, if the offeree begins painting the house the offeror cannot revoke the offer. If, on the other hand, the offeree buys paint and brushes and ladders to do the job but has not yet started work, the offeror may revoke the offer but the offeree may be able to recover reliance damages for the out of pocket cost of the paint, brushes and ladders. The ability to use them on other jobs may mitigate the amount of damages. If the offeror said: "If you paint my house or promise to paint my house, I will pay you $1,000 " and the offeree begins to paint the house, the beginning acts as a promise to finish the job and the offeree is bound to finish the job. In this last case it is not a question of the offer being kept open; rather, once the offeree begins work the offeree accepts the offer and a contract is formed—the offer merges with the acceptance to create a bilateral contract.

These convoluted rules were devised by the draftspersons of the Restatement to avoid the results of the very few cases where they believed the court reached an unfair result. If an offeror could revoke an offer at any time prior to the complete performance being given by the offeree, an offeree might complete 90% of the performance and the offeror simply revoke. While a quantum meruit recovery might be available to the offeree, this would not be an expectancy remedy but at most a reliance measure of damages and more likely a restitution measure which might give the offeree little or nothing in terms of a monetary recovery. An old example is the offeror who says to the offeree, "If you walk across the Brooklyn Bridge I will pay you $100." Just before the offeree reaches the other side, the offeror says "I revoke." The offeree has not done what the offeror requested before the offer was revoked. Therefore, there is no contract and there can be no damages for breach of contract, unless some exception to this common law approach, as mentioned in the previous paragraph, is created. How could the offeree protect him/herself from such a result?

In the *Bethlehem* opinions, the key issue was whether the parties intended to contract. Collateral to this was whether there was an option contract or a firm offer, whether there was consideration for this offer, whether it was accepted, whether the alleged contract had enough definiteness to be enforceable, whether the U.C.C. should apply and if so whether or not it should apply exclusively to help resolve this. All of these issues become intertwined. As you consider what an offer is, an acceptance, a rejection, a counteroffer and also the impact of the U.C.C., keep in mind what you have learned previously about promissory estoppel, consideration, the seal. All the doctrines interrelate. Your job will be to solve problems for clients. Do not learn rules and principles in a vacuum; do not separate ideas. Note their interrelation.

Problem to Part II

Joanne Jones wants to buy software for her computer. She telephones several companies, one of which is Interworld Computer & Machine (ICM). The ICM representative she speaks to is Sylvia Robins, who tells her that they have the best and newest software for her needs. She describes it in great detail for Jones who finally says: "Well, I certainly would like to see and try it." Robins says: "I can send it to you and if you don't like it, return it in 30 days and no one is out anything." Jones said: "The price you advertise is $150, is that right?" Robins said "Yes." Jones said: "OK send it." ICM sends the software which Jones uses in her business. She ignores the pamphlet which came inside the box and also does not read the writing on the box. The writing on the box says that ICM "is not liable for any damages caused by the failure of this software to meet user needs except for the return of the purchase price." The U.C.C. in Jones' jurisdiction allows a buyer to recover damages for failure of goods to perform as warranted by the seller and where no warranty is given the U.C.C. implies a warranty of merchantability that the goods are at least as good as those generally sold in the trade, generally as good as other brands. The U.C.C. in her state and also federal law allow a seller to exclude all warranties and/or to limit damages to a return of the purchase price. Inside the box, in a rather lengthy pamphlet, the clause found on the box plus the following two statements are found: "In any dispute buyer agrees to arbitrate all differences with seller by use of arbitrators from the American Arbitration Association," and "This product shall not be used for any commercial purpose but is restricted to personal, non-profit use."

The product fails to function as well as others in the trade. Jones sues ICM for breach of warranty of merchantability and also for failure to perform as Robins said it would. ICM responds that (1) there is no contract; (2) if there is a contract, Jones is bound by the clauses in the pamphlet; (3) if Jones is not bound by the clauses in the pamphlet, she is bound by the clause on the box. Jones replies that the contract was formed by the phone call between Jones and Robins and that all other clauses are irrelevant.

You are the trial court judge assigned to decide the case. What outcome should result? What other facts would you like to or might you need to know? Why? Who is the offeror? Offeree? Does it matter?

A. The Offer

Introduction

An offer is a communication capable of acceptance so that a contract can be formed. The communication is usually in words although this is not always the case. An example where an offer is communicated without words is where custom or habit shows a routine. If a person has done business with someone frequently and has always simply sent goods to that person who either takes them and sends a check for their amount or returns them, then by a long course of dealing the simple sending may be an offer to sell for whatever reasonable price the recipient wishes to pay and the sending of the check an acceptance. If a price is stated with the goods when they are sent, this would be part of the offer and the offeree would have to send a check for that amount to constitute an acceptance.

Most often, however, offers will be made with words either written or spoken. The difficulty is distinguishing an offer from a mere inquiry, a negotiation, a suggestion, or a request for someone else to make an offer. As we discovered in Part I, the key to determining an offer from some other form of communication is intent. Intent, however, is not measured by a person's subjective mental set — it is objective. Therefore, I may think that I am just encouraging you, to come in and buy my product or to not be afraid and let me perform a surgical operation, making an inquiry or requesting you to make an offer or just discussing the possibility of a contract, but if objectively a person could reasonably interpret my words as an offer and if the person does so and acts on it by accepting the offer, a contract results. Think again about the cases in Part I; *Carlill, Empro, Van Zee.* While lawyers often say and write a lot, they tend as a group to be careful about what they say and even more careful about what they write. What you mean doesn't count for much. What your words could mean, counts for a lot.

What then are the hallmarks of an offer? It is definite in its terms and shows a wish on the part of the person making it to be bound to do something in the future. More than that, it indicates a wish to be bound to a particular person, and to do or not to do something for that person or for someone else. At the end of Shakespeare's play *Richard III*, the king shouts "A horse, a horse, my kingdom for a horse." What if someone had brought him a horse? Are the elements of offer there? In the Bible when King Herod was pleased by the dance of the seven veils, he said the dancer could ask what she wanted up to half his kingdom. (She asked for and got the head of John the Baptist.) Why was that not an offer? Whenever a reward is posted, it is usually addressed to the world at large. Often it speaks of information leading to the arrest and conviction etc. Is this a very narrow form of offer?

The following cases consider some aspects of offer.

Miller-Dunn Co., Inc., v. Green
154 Fla. 72, 16 So.2d 637
Supreme Court of Florida, 1944.

TERRELL, Justice.

The declaration in this case filed by appellee alleges in substance that Miller-Dunn Company, Inc., a corporation, employed Perry Green to manufacture 850 small metal pumps, Miller-Dunn Company, Inc., to furnish all material and pay $12 for each pump and Green to furnish all labor. Some material was delivered to Green; he began work on the pumps but Miller-Dunn Company, Inc., breached its contract by removing the material from Green's premises.

Numerous questions are argued but we rest this decision on that of whether or not there was a contract between appellant and appellee. We have reached the conclusion that question must be answered in the negative.

As to whether or not there was a contract between the parties, the evidence shows nothing more than an inquiry by appellant as to whether Perry Green could make the pumps in question. The declaration relies on an express promise by oral agreement. It is shown that an agent of Miller-Dunn Company asked Green if he could make 850 pumps or words to that effect but this without more did not constitute an offer with an acceptance which is necessary to constitute an enforceable contract. In other words, we find nothing based on a valuable consideration whereby Miller-Dunn Company binds itself to perform or forbear to perform an act that gives Green a right to demand and enforce performance. Moulton v. Kershaw, 59 Wis. 316, 18 N.W. 172, 48 Am.Rep. 516.

In this pronouncement, we do not overlook the fact that three other similar contracts had been made and performed by the parties. Green relying on this and the fact that some materials were delivered to him by appellant contends that by inference, an offer and an acceptance were completed and thereby a contract closed. The answer to this is that the declaration and the evidence relies on an express contract and will not support an implied one. Even if this were not true, a contract to construct 850 pumps will not be implied by delivery of material for less than one fourth of that many.

Questions

1. Would quantum meruit, implied contract, promissory estoppel, or quasi-contract have been of any use to plaintiff? Review Note on Implied Promises and Note on Types of Recovery in Part I.

2. What is the difference between an inquiry and an offer? What fact(s) indicate that an inquiry and not an offer is involved here?

3. Why did the Court not put more weight on the delivery of material to Green and on the earlier contracts? Do you think it should have?

4. If you were Green's lawyer, what facts would you try to discover to establish implied contract? promissory estoppel? quantum meruit? quasi-contract? Which of these recoveries would you prefer? Which facts that you already have lend themselves to the establishment of any of these remedies?

5. In some cases part performance can take a contract out of the Statute of Frauds (see *e.g.* U.C.C. § 2-201 (1) and (2)(a).) Part performance of a substantial character can also act to make or convert an offer for a unilateral contract into an option contract where the performing party has the option to either continue performance or not without breaching the contract but the offering party cannot revoke the offer. See Restatement of Contracts § 45 and also the Introduction to Part II. Why would part performance not be applicable here?

Academy Chicago Publishers, v. Cheever
144 Ill.2d 24, 578 N.E.2d 981, 161 Ill.Dec. 335
Supreme Court of Illinois, 1991.

Justice HEIPLE delivered the opinion of the court:

This is a suit for declaratory judgment. It arose out of an agreement between the widow of the widely published author, John Cheever, and Academy Chicago Publishers. Contact between the parties began in 1987 when the publisher approached Mrs. Cheever about the possibility of publishing a collection of Mr. Cheever's short stories which, though previously published, had never been collected into a single anthology. In August of that year, a publishing agreement was signed which provided, in pertinent part: "Agreement made this 15th day of August 1987, between Academy Chicago Publishers or any affiliated entity or imprint (hereinafter referred to as the Publisher) and Mary W. Cheever and Franklin H. Dennis of the USA (hereinafter referred to as Author). Whereas the parties are desirous of publishing and having published a certain work or works, tentatively titled The Uncollected Stories of John Cheever (hereinafter referred to as the Work):

* * *

2. The Author will deliver to the Publisher on a mutually agreeable date one copy of the manuscript of the Work as finally arranged by the editor and satisfactory to the Publisher in form and content.

* * *

5. Within a reasonable time and a mutually agreeable date after delivery of the final revised manuscript, the Publisher will publish the Work at its own expense, in such style and manner and at such price as it deems best, and will keep the Work in print as long as it deems it expedient; but it will not be responsible for delays caused by circumstances beyond its control."

Academy and its editor, Franklin Dennis, assumed the task of locating and procuring the uncollected stories and delivering them to Mrs. Cheever. Mrs.

Cheever and Mr. Dennis received partial advances for manuscript preparation. By the end of 1987, Academy had located and delivered more than 60 uncollected stories to Mrs. Cheever. Shortly thereafter, Mrs. Cheever informed Academy in writing that she objected to the publication of the book and attempted to return her advance.

Academy filed suit in the circuit court of Cook County in February 1988, seeking a declaratory judgment: (1) granting Academy the exclusive right to publish the tentatively titled, "The Uncollected Stories of John Cheever"; (2) designating Franklin Dennis as the book's editor; and (3) obligating Mrs. Cheever to deliver the manuscript from which the work was to be published. The trial court entered an order declaring, inter alia: (1) that the publishing agreement executed by the parties was valid and enforceable; (2) that Mrs. Cheever was entitled to select the short stories to be included in the manuscript for publication; (3) that Mrs. Cheever would comply with her obligations of good faith and fair dealing if she delivered a manuscript including at least 10 to 15 stories totaling at least 140 pages; (4) Academy controlled the design and format of the work to be published, but control must be exercised in cooperation with Mrs. Cheever.

Academy appealed the trial court's order, challenging particularly the declaration regarding the minimum story and page numbers for Mrs. Cheever's compliance with the publishing agreement, and the declaration that Academy must consult with defendant on all matters of publication of the manuscript.

The appellate court affirmed the decision of the trial court with respect to the validity and enforceability of the publishing agreement and the minimum story and page number requirements for Mrs. Cheever's compliance with same. The appellate court reversed the trial court's declaration regarding control of publication, stating that the trial court erred in considering extrinsic evidence to interpret the agreement regarding control of the publication, given the explicit language of the agreement granting exclusive control to Academy. (200 Ill.App.3d 677, 146 Ill.Dec. 386, 558 N.E.2d 349.) Appeal is taken in this court pursuant to Supreme Court Rule 315(a) (134 Ill.2d R. 315(a)).

The parties raise several issues on appeal; this matter, however, is one of contract and we confine our discussion to the issue of the validity and enforceability of the publishing agreement.

While the trial court and the appellate court agreed that the publishing agreement constitutes a valid and enforceable contract, we cannot concur. The principles of contract state that in order for a valid contract to be formed, an "offer must be so definite as to its material terms or require such definite terms in the acceptance that the promises and performances to be rendered by each party are reasonably certain." (1 Williston, Contracts §§ 38 through 48 (3d ed. 1957)) Although the parties may have had and manifested the intent to make a contract, if the content of their agreement is unduly uncertain and indefinite no contract is formed.

The pertinent language of this agreement lacks the definite and certain essential terms required for the formation of an enforceable contract. A contract "is sufficiently definite and certain to be enforceable if the court is enabled from the terms and provisions thereof, under proper rules of construction and applicable principles of equity, to ascertain what the parties have agreed to do." The provisions of the subject publishing agreement do not provide the court with a means of determining the intent of the parties.

In rendering its judgment, the trial court supplied minimum terms for Mrs. Cheever's compliance, including story and page numbers. It is not uncommon for a court to supply a missing material term, as the reasonable conclusion often is that the parties intended that the term be supplied by implication. However, where the subject matter of the contract has not been decided upon and there is no standard available for reasonable implication, courts ordinarily refuse to supply the missing term. No suitable standard was available for the trial court to apply. It is our opinion that the trial court incorrectly supplied minimum compliance terms to the publishing agreement, as the agreement did not constitute a valid and enforceable contract to begin with. As noted above, the publishing agreement contains major unresolved uncertainties. It is not the role of the court to rewrite the contract and spell out essential elements not included therein.

Reversed.

Questions

1.   What was the basis for the Supreme Court's reversal?

2.   Was there any doubt as to the grounds for reversal? In *Bethlehem* at least one judge felt that the trial court had based its determination of no contract on indefiniteness and not on a lack of intent to contract. Using U.C.C. principles as discussed in that and other cases, how is indefiniteness dealt with? Is this such a radical departure from established law? See *Wood*. Why would the Supreme Court not supply terms in *Academy*? What is the meaning of the sentence: "The provisions of the subject publishing agreement do not provide the court with the means of determining the intent of the parties."

3.   How are intent to contract and definiteness intertwined? How are they distinct issues?

4.   What did the court mean when it wrote that "the subject matter of the contract had not been decided upon and there is no standard available for reasonable implication"?

In *Moulton v. Kershaw, 18 N.W. 172, (Wis., 1884)*, according to Moulton's complaint the following facts existed. Both parties were dealers in salt. The defendant (Kershaw) sent a letter to Moulton as follows: "In consequence of a rupture in the salt trade, we are authorized to offer Michigan fine salt, in full car-load lots of 80 to 100 bbls., delivered at your city, at 85 cents per bbl., to be shipped per C. & N.W.R.R. Co. only. At this price it is a bargain, as the price in general remains unchanged. Shall be pleased to receive your order." Moulton ordered 2,000 barrels and Kershaw refused to ship it. Two thousand barrels was a reasonable quantity for Moulton to order and not in excess of what Kershaw might expect. Moulton sued Kershaw for breach of contract. Kershaw's demurrer to the complaint was upheld by the appeals court. The court said that the language used by Kershaw did not reflect what business people would say in an offer but that it was instead general language in the nature of an advertisement to attract the attention of the public (the word "sell" was missing), that from the face of the communications reasonable quantities could not be determined and therefore a jury would have to make inquiries into the nature and extent of the business of both parties resulting in a contract not expressed in the writings. Moulton said that it should be construed to mean that Kershaw was offering to sell such quantity as Kershaw from its knowledge of Moulton's business might expect Moulton to order. The court refused to do this and said: "Rather than introduce such an element of uncertainty into the contract, we deem it much more reasonable to construe the letter as a simple notice to those dealing in salt that the appellants [Kershaw] were in a condition to supply that article for the prices named, and requesting the person to whom it was addressed to deal with them." The court quoted another case where it was said: "That care should always be taken not to construe as an agreement letters which the parties intended only as preliminary negotiations."

Questions

1. Was the court fair to Moulton? How does this case differ from *Carlill*? from *Empro*? In Part III we will learn that courts are more willing today to go outside the writing to find the contract but that once a writing is found to embody the intent of the parties to form a contract, it cannot be ignored. Look at Kershaw's letter. What facts about it make it seem like an offer? Did counsel for Moulton have a good point about quantities that from Kershaw's knowledge Moulton might order? Compare later cases with this one.

2. Once again, how do we tell a preliminary negotiation from an offer?

Lefkowitz v. Great Minneapolis Surplus Store, 86 N.W.2d 689, (Minn., 1957) also dealt with the issue of whether advertisements can constitute offers which can be accepted forming a binding contract. How is this different from *Moulton*? similar to *Carlill*?

"There are numerous authorities which hold that a particular advertisement in a newspaper or circular letter relating to a sale of articles may be construed by the court as constituting an offer, acceptance of which would complete a contract. [cites omitted]

The test of whether a binding obligation may originate in advertisements addressed to the general public is 'whether the facts show that some performance was promised in positive terms in return for something requested.' 1 Williston, Contracts (Rev. ed.) § 27.

The authorities above cited emphasize that, where the offer is clear, definite, and explicit, and leaves nothing open for negotiation, it constitutes an offer, acceptance of which will complete the contract.

Whether in any individual instance a newspaper advertisement is an offer rather than an invitation to make an offer depends on the legal intention of the parties and the surrounding circumstances."

Izadi, v. Machado (Gus) Ford, Inc.
550 So.2d 1135
Court of Appeal of Florida, 1989.

1. Breach of Contract. We first hold, on two somewhat distinct but closely related grounds, that the complaint states a cause of action for breach of an alleged contract which arose when Izadi accepted an offer contained in the advertisement, which was essentially to allow $3,000 toward the purchase of the

Ranger for any vehicle the reader-offeree would produce, or, to put the same proposed deal in different words, to sell the Ranger for $3,595, plus any vehicle.

(a) It is of course well settled that a completed contract or, as here, an allegedly binding offer must be viewed as a whole, with due emphasis placed upon each of what may be inconsistent or conflicting provisions. NLRB v. Federbush Co., 121 F.2d 954, 957 (2d Cir.1941) ("Words are not pebbles in alien juxtaposition; they have only a communal existence; and not only does the meaning of each interpenetrate the other, but all in their aggregate take their purport from the setting in which they are used...."); Transport Rental Systems, Inc. v. Hertz Corp., 129 So.2d 454, 456 (Fla.3d DCA 1961) ("The real intention, as disclosed by a fair consideration of all parts of a contract, should control the meaning given to mere words or particular provisions when they have reference to the main purpose."); 11 Fla.Jur. 2d Contracts § 121 (1979). In this case, that process might well involve disregarding both the superfine print and apparent qualification as to the value of the trade-in, as contradictory to the far more prominent thrust of the advertisement to the effect that $3,000 will be allowed for any trade-in on any Ford. Transport Rental Systems, Inc. v. Hertz Corp., 129 So.2d at 456 ("If a contract contains clauses which are apparently repugnant to each other, they must be given such an interpretation as will reconcile them."); see supra notes 1-3, and accompanying text. We therefore believe that the complaint appropriately alleges that, objectively considered, the advertisement indeed contained just the unqualified $3,000 offer which was accepted by the plaintiff.

Of course, if an offer were indeed conveyed by an objective reading of the ad, it does not matter that the car dealer may subjectively have not intended for its chosen language to constitute a binding offer. As Williston states: [T]he test of the true interpretation of an offer or acceptance is not what the party making it thought it meant or intended it to mean, but what a reasonable person in the position of the parties would have thought it meant. 1 Williston on Contracts § 94, at 339-340. That rule seems directly to apply to this situation.

(b) As a somewhat different, and perhaps more significant basis for upholding the breach of contract claim, we point to the surely permissible conclusion from the carefully chosen language and arrangement of the advertisement itself that Machado—although it did not intend to adhere to the $3,000 trade-in representation—affirmatively, but wrongly sought to make the public believe that it would be honored; that, in other words, the offer was to be used as the "bait" to be followed by a "switch" to another deal when the acceptance of that offer was refused.[1] Indeed, it is difficult to offer any other explanation for the blanket representation of a $3,000 trade-in for any vehicle—which is then hedged in sub-microscopic print to apply only to two models which were not otherwise referred to in the ad—or the obvious non-coincidence that the only example of the trade-in for the three vehicles which was set out in the ad was the very same $3,000. This situation invokes the applicability of a line of persuasive authority that a binding offer may be implied from the very fact that deliberately misleading advertising intentionally leads the reader to the conclusion that one exists. In short, the

---

1. "'Bait and switch' describes an offer which is made not in order to sell the advertised product at the advertised price, but rather to draw the customer to the store to sell him another similar product which is more profitable to the advertiser." Tashof v. Federal Trade Commission, 436 F.2d 707, 709 n.3 (D.C.Cir.1970)

dealer can hardly deny that it did not mean what it purposely misled its customer into believing. This doctrine is expressed in the Restatement (Second) of Contracts which states:

§ 20. Effect of Misunderstanding

(2) The manifestations of the parties are operative in accordance with the meaning attached to them by one of the parties if (a) that party does not know of any different meaning attached by the first party[.] Restatement (Second) of Contracts § 20(2)(a) (1981); Restatement (Second) of Contracts § 20(2)(a) comment d ("[I]f one party knows the other's meaning and manifests assent intending to insist on a different meaning, he may be guilty of misrepresentation. Whether or not there is such misrepresentation as would give the other party the power of avoidance, there is a contract under Subsection (2)(a), and the mere negligence of the other party is immaterial.").

Cobaugh v. Klick-Lewis Inc., 561 A.2d 1248,(Pa. Super., 1989).

[Cobaugh was playing golf when he saw the following sign, "HOLE-IN-ONE Wins this 1988 Chevrolet Beretta GT Courtesy of KLICK-LEWIS Buick Chevy Pontiac." Cobaugh aced the ninth hole and attempted to claim his prize, but the dealer refused, saying the sign had been put up for a charity golf tournament two days before and had not been removed.]

WIEAND, Judge:

The facts in the instant case are not in dispute. To the extent that they have not been admitted in the pleadings, they have been stipulated by the parties. Therefore, we must decide whether under the applicable law plaintiff was entitled to judgment as a matter of law.

An offer is a manifestation of willingness to enter into a bargain, so made as to justify another person in understanding that his assent to that bargain is invited and will conclude it. Restatement (Second) of Contracts § 24.

Consistent with traditional principles of contract law pertaining to unilateral contracts, it has generally been held that "[t]he promoter of [a prize-winning] contest, by making public the conditions and rules of the contest, makes an offer, and if before the offer is withdrawn another person acts upon it, the promoter is bound to perform his promise." The only acceptance of the offer that is necessary is the performance of the act requested to win the prize.

Appellant argues that it did nothing more than propose a contingent gift and that a proposal to make a gift is without consideration and unenforceable. See: Restatement (Second) of Contracts § 24, Comment b. We cannot accept this argument. Here, the offer specified the performance which was the price or consideration to be given. By its signs, Klick-Lewis offered to award the car as a prize to anyone who made a hole-in-one at the ninth hole. A person reading the signs would reasonably understand that he or she could accept the offer and win the car by performing the feat of shooting a hole-in-one. There was thus an offer which was accepted when appellee shot a hole-in-one.

The contract does not fail for lack of consideration. The requirement of consideration as an essential element of a contract is nothing more than a requirement that there be a bargained for exchange. Consideration confers a benefit upon the promisor or causes a detriment to the promisee. By making an offer to award one of its cars as a prize for shooting a hole-in-one at the ninth hole of the Fairview Golf Course, Klick-Lewis benefited from the publicity typically generated by such promotional advertising. In order to win the car, Cobaugh was required to perform an act which he was under no legal duty to perform. The car was to be given in exchange for the feat of making a hole-in-one. This was adequate consideration to support the contract.

[Affirmed]

[As to dealer's mistake claim, the court said the sign did not mention that the prize was only for an earlier tournament and that a unilateral (as opposed to mutual) mistake where the party seeking to rescind is negligent will not permit relief. We will study mistake later in Part V].

Question

1. What if an offer were made during a television show in which the offeror said, "If you call in with the right answer to the studio before this broadcast ends I will pay you $5,000." Without the knowledge of the offeror the show is taped and rebroadcast at a later time during which rebroadcast someone calls in with the correct answer?

Petterson v. Pattberg
248 N.Y. 86, 161 N.E. 428
Court of Appeals of New York, 1928.

KELLOGG, J.

Facts: John Petterson was the owner of a parcel of real estate. The defendant [Pattberg], was the owner of a bond executed by Petterson, which was secured by a third mortgage upon the parcel. On April 4, 1924, there remained unpaid upon the principal the sum of $5,450. This amount was payable in installments. The bond and mortgage had more than five years to run before the entire sum became due. Defendant wrote Petterson as follows: 'I hereby agree to accept cash for the mortgage which I hold. I will allow you $780 providing said mortgage is paid on or before May 31, 1924.'

In the latter part of May, 1924, Petterson presented himself at the defendant's home, and knocked at the door. The defendant demanded the name of his caller. Petterson replied: 'It is Mr. Petterson. I have come to pay off the mortgage.' The defendant answered that he had sold the mortgage. Petterson stated that he would like to talk with the defendant, so the defendant partly opened the door. Thereupon Petterson exhibited the cash, and said he was ready to pay off the mortgage. The defendant refused to take the money. Prior to this conversation, Petterson had made a contract to sell the land to a third person free and clear of the mortgage to the defendant. Meanwhile, also, the defendant had sold the bond and mortgage to a third party. It therefore became necessary for Petterson to pay to such person the full amount of the bond and mortgage. It is claimed that he thereby sustained a loss of $780, the sum which the defendant agreed to allow upon the bond and mortgage, if payment in full of principal, less that sum, was made on or before May 31, 1924. The plaintiff has had a recovery for the sum thus claimed, with interest.

Clearly the defendant's letter proposed to Petterson the making of a unilateral contract, the gift of a promise in exchange for the performance of an act. The thing conditionally promised by the defendant was the reduction of the mortgage debt. The act requested to be done, in consideration of the offered promise, was payment in full of the reduced principal of the debt prior to the due date thereof. 'If an act is requested, that very act, and no other, must be given.' Williston on Contracts, § 73. It is elementary that any offer to enter into a unilateral contract may be withdrawn before the act requested to be done has been performed. A bidder at a sheriff's sale may revoke his bid at any time before the property is struck down to him. The offer of a reward in consideration of an act to be performed is revocable before the very act requested has been done. So, also, an offer to pay a broker commissions, upon a sale of land for the offeror, is revocable at any time before the land is sold, although prior to revocation the broker performs services in an effort to effectuate a sale.

An interesting question arises when, as here, the offeree approaches the offeror with the intention of proffering performance and, before actual tender is made, the offer is withdrawn. Of such a case Williston says: 'The offeror may see the approach of the offeree and know that an acceptance is contemplated. If the offeror can say 'I revoke' before the offeree accepts, however brief the interval of time between the two acts, there is no escape from the conclusion that the offer is terminated.' Williston on Contracts, § 60b.

In this instance Petterson, standing at the door of the defendant's house, stated to the defendant that he had come to pay off the mortgage. Before a tender of the necessary moneys had been made, the defendant informed Petterson that he had sold the mortgage. That was a definite notice to Petterson that the defendant could not perform his offered promise, and that a tender to the defendant, who was no longer the creditor, would be ineffective to satisfy the debt. 'An offer to sell property may be withdrawn before acceptance without any formal notice to the person to whom the offer is made. It is sufficient if that person has actual knowledge that the person who made the offer has done some act inconsistent with the continuance of the offer, such as selling the property to a third person.' Dickinson v. Dodds, 2 Ch. Div. 463, headnote. Thus it clearly appears that the defendant's offer was withdrawn before its acceptance had been tendered. It is unnecessary to determine, therefore, what the legal situation might have been had tender been made before withdrawal. It is the individual view of the writer that the same result would follow. This would be so, for the act requested to be performed was the completed act of payment, a thing incapable of performance, unless assented to by the person to be paid. Clearly an offering party has the right to name the precise act performance of which would convert his offer into a binding promise. Whatever the act may be until it is performed, the offer must be revocable. However, the supposed case is not before us for decision. We think that in this particular instance the offer of the defendant was withdrawn before it became a binding promise, and therefore that no contract was ever made for the breach of which the plaintiff may claim damages.

The judgment of the Appellate Division and that of the Trial Term should be reversed, and the complaint dismissed, with costs in all courts.

LEHMAN, J. (dissenting).

The defendant's letter to Petterson constituted a promise on his part to accept payment.

The promise made by the defendant lacked consideration at the time it was made. Nevertheless, the promise was not made as a gift or mere gratuity to the plaintiff. It constituted an offer which was to become binding whenever the plaintiff should give, in return for the defendant's promise, exactly the consideration which the defendant requested.

Here the defendant requested no counter promise from the plaintiff. The consideration requested by the defendant for his promise to accept payment was, I agree, some act to be performed by the plaintiff. Until the act requested was performed, the defendant might undoubtedly revoke his offer. Our problem is to determine from the words of the letter, read in the light of surrounding circumstances, what act the defendant requested as consideration for his promise.

The defendant undoubtedly made his offer as an inducement to the plaintiff to 'pay' the mortgage before it was due. Therefore, it is said, that 'the act requested to be performed was the completed act of payment, a thing incapable of performance, unless assented to by the person to be paid.' In unmistakable terms the defendant agreed to accept payment, yet we are told that the defendant intended, and the plaintiff should have understood, that the act requested by the defendant, as consideration for his promise to accept payment, included performance by the defendant himself of the very promise for which the act was to be consideration. So construed, the defendant's promise or offer, though intended to induce action by the plaintiff, is but a snare and delusion.

I cannot believe that a result so extraordinary could have been intended when the defendant wrote the letter. If the defendant intended to induce payment by the plaintiff and yet reserve the right to refuse payment when offered he should have used a phrase better calculated to express his meaning than the words: 'I agree to accept.' A promise to accept payment, by its very terms, must necessarily become binding, if at all, not later than when a present offer to pay is made.

I recognize that in this case only an offer of payment, and not a formal tender of payment, was made before the defendant withdrew his offer to accept payment. Even the plaintiff's part in the act of payment was then not technically complete. Even so, under a fair construction of the words of the letter, I think the plaintiff had done the act which the defendant requested as consideration for his promise. The plaintiff offered to pay, with present intention and ability to make that payment. If the defendant acted in good faith in making his offer to accept payment, he could not well have intended to draw a distinction in the act requested of the plaintiff in return, between an offer which, unless refused, would ripen into completed payment, and a formal tender.

The judgment should be affirmed.

Questions

1. What was the consideration Pattberg sought?

2. The majority opinion seems to believe a sheriff's sale, a reward, and a real estate sale and the case at bar as similar to each other. Are they similar? If not, do these examples really work against the majority's thesis?

3. What is the difference between an offer of payment and a formal tender? Why does Judge Kellogg say that even a formal tender would not be the act requested?

4. What is the relevance of "good faith" in the dissent?

5. If an offer is printed on a cereal box: "Send for free stamps—if not satisfied just keep the stamps, notify us and you owe us nothing and we will send no more. Otherwise, each month we will send and bill you for a selection of stamps...." What does the offeror hope you will do? What if you send for the free stamps and immediately cancel even though you are satisfied with them. Is good faith relevant here?

6. Did plaintiff rely on Pattberg's offer?

7. Did plaintiff reasonably rely on Pattberg's offer?

8. Should plaintiff's reliance, if any, have a bearing on plaintiff's recovery? See *Pavel Enterprises infra*, and the court's discussion of Restatement §§ 87 and 90 therein. Is plaintiff's reliance different from that in *Pavel*? See also the discussion in the introduction to Part II.

9. Should plaintiff receive reliance damages based on any theories developed in *Pavel, infra*, or *Empro, supra*.

Note on Offers

Offers can be made in many ways. At an auction, a person making a slight movement of her hand may be making an offer to buy the item being auctioned. This is true at the sale of hogs as well as paintings. Where words are used, offers can be in writing or oral. An offer has no force until it is communicated to the offeree. Thus, if I shout an offer into the telephone but the line at that moment goes dead, my offer is ineffective—I have not made an offer.

How are offers terminated? We will consider "revocation" in more detail later in this Part along with the doctrine of the offeror as "master of the offer," which means that the offeror controls the terms of the contract. An offer may be terminated in several ways. One method of terminating an offer is if the offeree rejects it. Offers can also be terminated by the mere passage of time, either through the expiration of a "reasonable time", or expiration of a the time limit explicitly stated in the offer. This second scenario is often true of real estate offers in which it will be stated *e.g.* "This offer is only good until 5:00 P.M. December 1, 2000." Chances are there will also be language stating that the offer can only be accepted by communicating the acceptance to the offeror so that the offeror actually receives it at or before 5:00 P.M. December 1, 2000. The offer may even say how the acceptance must be communicated—in writing for example. It may state to what address it must be sent or into whose hands it must be put or whether an acknowledgment in writing of its receipt from the offeror must be obtained. It is important to identify whether the offeror is explicitly stating terms of accepting her offer because any terms stated must be fulfilled by the offeree for legal obligations to result. Without any stipulations, the offeree is deemed to accept the offer when the acceptance is sent, not when it is received. Thus, if no language were included on the manner of acceptance, the offeree could mail a letter at 5:00 P.M. December 1, 2000, by simply dropping it properly stamped into the mail box, and at that moment the offer is accepted and a contract is formed even if the offeror does not receive the acceptance for days or perhaps a week or more.

Offers are also terminated when the offeror does anything inconsistent with the continued making of the offer and this action is learned, discovered by or communicated to the offeree. If I offer to sell you Blackacre and after I make my offer and before you accept it you learn that I have sold Blackacre to someone else, you cannot accept my offer and then sue me for specific performance and for breach of contract. Your learning that I sold it to someone else is as effective a termination as my communicating to you my cancellation of my offer. The offeror's death and in some states the offeror's insanity terminate offers. These latter terminations are a throwback to the 19th century subjective "meeting of the minds" theories of contracts, when it was said that when two minds met on an offer and acceptance a contract resulted. Thus, subjectively a person making an offer had to will that the offer continually be sent until the offeree accepted it. If a person died or became mentally disabled (s)he no longer had a mind capable of forming and transmitting an offer—thus, the offer died with the person and no contract could be formed. The subjective meeting has been largely replaced by an objective understanding, but death and often insanity still act to revoke offers.

Problem [Based on Davis v. Jacoby, 34 P.2d 1026, (Supreme Court of California, 1934)].

Caro Davis ("Caro") was the niece of Blanche Whitehead ("Blanche"). Blanche was very fond of Caro and spent much time visiting with her over a period of 20 years even though Caro lived with her husband in another country. In addition to visits, there was much correspondence showing a loving relationship. Blanche and her husband, Rupert Whitehead ("Rupert") were childless. In 1930 Blanche became seriously ill. Rupert placed her in a private hospital in 1931 after she had suffered several strokes and her mind began to fail. During her stay she emotionally indicated to Rupert (by bursting into tears when Rupert asked if she wanted to see Caro) her desire to see Caro. This was early in 1931. A court later found that at this time Rupert was also in poor health and in need of assistance with his wife and his business, and that he did not trust his friends. On March 18, 1931 Rupert wrote to Caro telling her of his problems and about his wife's crying fit. "Evidently that [Caro's coming to visit]," he wrote, "is what is on her [Blanche's] mind. It is a very difficult matter to decide. If you come it will mean that you will have to leave again and then things may be serious." He added later that he had consulted Blanche's doctor who thought a visit by Caro could do some good. He wrote again further explaining his and Blanche's physical condition. On March 24 Frank Davis ("Frank"), who was Caro's husband, at Caro's request telegraphed Rupert saying Caro could come. On March 30 Rupert wrote again discussing his and Blanche's health. He also mentioned that although his cash was down he still had real estate. He said he needed help with his wife and with his business affairs and suggested Frank might help him. He added that all his property would go to Blanche under his will and he believed that under Blanche's will it would all go to Caro. On April 9, 1931 Rupert wrote Caro and Frank and said he needed someone he could trust to help him. He pointed out that he would have about $150,000 left if his affairs were properly handled.

The following is taken directly from the opinion:

"Three days later, on April 12, 1931, Mr. Whitehead [Rupert] again wrote, addressing his letter to 'Dear Frank and Caro,' and in this letter made the definite offer, which offer it is claimed was accepted and is the basis of this action. In this letter he first pointed out that Blanche, his wife, was in a private hospital and that 'she cannot last much longer...my affairs are not as bad as I supposed at first. Cutting everything down I figure 150,000 can be saved from the wreck.' He then enumerated the values placed upon his various properties and then continued:

'My trouble was caused by my friends taking advantage of my illness and my position to skin me.

'Now if Frank could come out here and be with me, and look after my affairs, we could easily save the balance I mention, provided I dont get into another panic and do some more foolish things.

'The next attack will be my end, I am 65 and my health had been bad for years, so, the Drs. dont give me much longer to live. So if you can come, Caro will inherit everything and you will make our lives happier and see Blanche is provided for to the end.

'My eyesight had gone back on me, I cant read only for a few lines at a time. I am at the house alone with Stanley [the chauffeur] who does everything for me and is a fine fellow. Now, what I want is some one who will take charge of my affairs and see I dont lose any more. Frank can do it, if he will and cut out the booze.

'Will you let me hear from you as soon as possible, I know it will be a sacrifice but times are still bad and likely to be, so by settling down you can help me and Blanche and gain in the end. If I had you here my mind would get better and my courage return, and we could work things out.'"

Frank received this letter at his office on April 14th, read it to Caro over the telephone, received her opinion that they must go to Blanche and wrote Rupert a letter. Although the letter was lost, Frank testified that in it he unequivocally accepted Rupert's proposition. They said they would leave to be with him on April 25th and could not come before then because Frank had to be in court as an executor of his mother's estate on April 22.

On April 15, 1931 Rupert wrote to Frank:

"Your letter by air mail received this a.m. Now, I am wondering if I have put you to unnecessary trouble and expense, if you are making any money don't leave it, as things are bad here.... You know your business and I dont and I am half crazy in the bargain, but I dont want to hurt you or Caro. Then on the other hand if I could get some one to trust and keep me straight I can save a good deal, about what I told you in my former letter."

Frank received this letter on April 17th and that day telegraphed to Rupert: "Cheer up we will soon be there — we will wire you from the train." Until April 22 Caro and Frank were preparing to go. On April 22 Rupert committed suicide. Frank and Caro immediately went to Blanche and "cared for her and administered to her wants as a natural daughter would have done toward and for her mother" in the words of the court which noted that this was not contradicted. Blanche died on May 30, 1931. It was then discovered that Rupert on February 28, 1931 had bequeathed everything to Blanche for life with the remainder to two nephews on her death. Caro and Frank sued in essence to set aside the will and make the beneficiaries trustees for Caro on the basis that Rupert had made a contractual obligation to make a will whereby "Caro would inherit everything." On the basis that a decedent's property goes first to creditors, Caro was claiming to be a creditor on the basis of contract.

In the jurisdiction where suit took place the courts followed the Restatement of Contracts 1st, which, like Restatement 2nd., indicates that where there is doubt as to whether an offeror is requesting an act or a promise a bilateral contract is favored over a unilateral contract because a bilateral contract "immediately and fully protects both parties." Two courts reviewed the facts in this case. One found an offer to enter into a unilateral and the other an offer to enter into a bilateral contract.

Questions

1. Do you see an offer here? Where?

2. Are there any grounds for saying that no offer was ever made?

3. If an offer was made who made it?

4. What effect does Rupert's suicide have on the alleged offer?

5. Assume that Rupert made an offer for a unilateral contract in all those confused letters and that he did not commit suicide. Consider the alternate scenarios below.

   (a) As Caro and Frank get off the train, Rupert meets them with his lawyer and says: "No deal. Blanche is better. We don't need you."

   (b) As Caro and Frank are walking up to the front door of Rupert's house he opens the door and says: "You shouldn't have come. My psychiatrist tells me I've got to stand on my own feet. I'll pay your expenses to go home."

   (c) As Caro, Frank and Rupert enter Blanche's hospital room, Rupert says to Blanche, "Look dear, Caro's here." Blanche says "Caro who?"

   (d) Caro cares for Blanche for a few days and Blanche becomes very upset and tells Rupert that she can't stand having Caro around, that Caro reminds her of a vulture and that she is sure that Caro and Frank are just waiting for her to die and she wants them to go away.

Centerville Builders, Inc. v. Wynne, 683 A.2d 1340, (R.I., 1996). Buyer signed a document captioned "Offer to Purchase." There were several conditions in the document including # 9 "Subject to seller ceasing negotiations with any and all parties on the purchase of subject property." Before seller signed, he (with buyer's consent) deleted this. Condition # 6 remained: "Subject to satisfactory purchase and sale agreement between seller and buyer." The court said that mutuality of obligation was essential for contract formation. "However, when the promises of the parties depend on the occurrence of some future event within the unilateral control of the promisor, the promises are illusory and the agreement is nonbinding." The court found the presence of #6 and the seller's crossing out of #9 evidenced lack of mutuality of obligation.

How does mutuality of obligation relate to consideration?

Note on Revocation

Petterson v. Pattberg is one of those cases which troubles scholars because it seems so unfair. The note case which follows briefly considers revocation. It is common law that an offer is revocable until acceptance. This used to be true even if someone paid you a consideration to keep an offer open. Because contract formation before the 20th century was considered a subjective happening, in theory a person who was paid a consideration to keep an offer open could nevertheless revoke it, but would then be liable in damages for breach of contract to keep an offer open. Instead, courts decided that if a consideration was paid (or a seal affixed) to an offer it could not be revoked and therefore the offeree could "accept" it even as the offeror was screaming "I revoke."

Consider again the classic illustration of the unfairness of the right to revoke an offer to enter into a unilateral contract after the offeree had begun performance, the case of the offer to pay someone to walk across the Brooklyn Bridge and then just as the person is about to reach the other side shout "I revoke." To my mind an even better example would be to offer to pay someone to "jump off the Brooklyn Bridge and into the water" and then after they jump and just before they reach the water shout "I revoke!"

Examples like this are amusing but not very enlightening. As you read the following note case and the cases in Section B on Options, ask yourself if offerees of offers to enter unilateral contracts need protection. Can they not protect themselves some other way?

Dura Chemical Co., Inc. v. Dalton-Cooper, Inc., 107 N.Y.S.2d 280, (N.Y. Sup. Ct., 1951). Dura Chemical Co. ("Dura") sues Dalton-Cooper, Inc. ("Dalton") for breach of contract. Prior to Dura's mailing an acceptance to Dalton, Dalton told Dura that because Dalton's shipper was unable to get goods to Dalton that Dalton could not ship to Dura. Dalton further told Dura that Dura had taken too long to return the letter and establish a letter of credit. The court said: "'Any statement which clearly implies unwillingness to contract according to the terms of the offer is sufficient though the word 'revoked' is not used.' Restatement, Contracts § 41....It is elementary that since this offer was not given for a consideration it could be revoked at any time before the acceptance, *Petterson v. Pattberg*....'"

B. Option Contract

1. Options Supported by Consideration

As we will see in this section on option contracts, an option contract will remain exercisable for the time it is stated to be open so long as the optionee pays adequate consideration to the optioner. In *Hamilton Bancshares Inc v. Leroy*, plaintiff sues defendant for specific performance of an agreement that guaranteed options to buy stock. Defendant argues that the option agreement to buy stock was revocable, and in fact was revoked, because plaintiff failed to provide adequate consideration.

Hamilton Bancshares, Inc., v. Leroy

131 Ill.App.3d 907, 476 N.E.2d 788, 87 Ill.Dec. 86
Appellate Court of Illinois, 4th. District, 1985.

[On June 11, 1981, Plaintiff entered into an 80 day agreement with Defendant whereby Plaintiff had the option to purchase stock. This agreement was purportedly granted "in consideration of the sum of One Dollar and other good and valuable consideration." Following the defendants' signatures on each option there was included the statement "I Lloyd Edwards [plaintiff's president], have this day paid to the optioner the sum of $5,000.00 earnest money, to be applied to the purchase price of the shares subject to this option in the event that the option is exercised and to be refunded to me in the event that this option is not exercised."

On July 17, 1981, defendant sent notice to plaintiff withdrawing the options. On August 19, 1981, plaintiff wrote to defendant to exercise the agreement, and brought this action for specific performance of the options.

Plaintiff admits that the "One Dollar" consideration was not paid, but contends that the transfer of earnest money was adequate consideration. Furthermore defendants possessed control of plaintiff's $10,000 earnest money, meaning plaintiff was denied its benefit or use. Defendants moved for summary judgment alleging no consideration for the options was ever given, and therefore the option "merely constituted an offer which could be withdrawn at any time prior to a tender of compliance." Defendants also contended the earnest money was of no benefit to them since it "was to be applied toward the purchase price if the option was exercised, but refunded if not exercised." The trial court agreed with Defendant, and Plaintiff appeals.]

McCULLOUGH, Justice:

We therefore proceed to the merits of plaintiff's argument. Generally, to justify specific performance a contract must be clear, certain, unambiguous, and free from doubt. A contract, by ancient definition, is an agreement between competent parties, upon a consideration sufficient in law, to do or not to do a particular thing. The validity of consideration for an instrument must be evaluated as it relates to the entire record and not as perceived in a vacuum of either terms or definitions. The burden of proving the validity of the affirmative defense of want of consideration is clearly upon the party asserting it.

The general principles applicable to option contracts were reviewed in Hermes v. Wm. F. Meyer Co. (1978), 65 Ill.App.3d 745, 749, 22 Ill.Dec. 451, 454-55, 382 N.E.2d 841, 844-45: "The general principles applicable to option contracts have been long established. An option contract has two elements, an offer to do something, or to forbear, which does not become a contract until accepted; and an agreement to leave the offer open for a specified time or for a reasonable time. An option contract must be supported by sufficient consideration; and if not, it is merely an offer which may be withdrawn at any time prior to a tender of compliance. If a consideration of 'one dollar' or some other consideration is stated but which has, in fact, not been paid, the document is merely an offer which may be withdrawn at any time prior to a tender of compliance. The document will amount only to a continuing offer which may be withdrawn by the offeror at any time, before acceptance. The consideration to support an option consists of 'some right, interest, profit or benefit accruing to one party, or some forbearance, detriment, loss or responsibility given, suffered or undertaken by the other' or otherwise stated, 'Any act or promise which is of benefit to one party or disadvantage to the other * * *.' In Steinberg v. Chicago Medical School (1976), 41 Ill.App.3d 804, 807, 354 N.E.2d 586, 589, aff'd in part, rev'd in part (1977), 69 Ill.2d 320, 13 Ill.Dec. 699, 371 N.E.2d 634, the court stated:

"Money is a valuable consideration and its transfer or payment or promises to pay it or the benefit from the right to its use, will support a contract."

Consideration adequate to support an option is discussed at 1 Corbin, Contracts sec. 127, at 550-51 (1950): "A very small consideration is sufficient to support the promise of an option-giver, for a different reason. Suppose that A pays 25 cents in return for B's promise to sell and convey Blackacre for the price of $10,000 at any time within 30 days. The sum of 25 cents is not 'inadequate' as an exchange for B's promise, although it would be exceedingly inadequate as an exchange for Blackacre. But it is not being exchanged for Blackacre, or even for a promise to convey Blackacre; it is being exchanged for a promise to exchange Blackacre for $10,000. B has bought a power to compel the exchange of Blackacre for $10,000, a power continuing 30 days; for this power he has paid 25 cents, a small sum. We can not say that it is an 'inadequate' price to pay for such a power until we know the 'market' for it—the opinions of other dealers as to its value in money. There may or may not be such a 'market'. It is true, however, under our existing law, that B's promise to A is enforceable even though it is proved that other dealers in land would gladly have paid $1,000 for the 'option' that A got for 25 cents. Nor is B's promise made unenforceable by the fact that the other dealers would gladly have paid $50,000 for Blackacre." 1A Corbin, Contracts sec. 263, at 501 (1950) states: "If, however, the consideration is nominal in fact as well as in amount—that is, it is merely named and is in fact neither given nor promised, then there is no consideration at all, and the option giver has power of revocation as in the case of other revocable offers." The legal concepts of "detriment" and "benefit" are discussed at 1 Williston, Contracts sec. 102A at 380-82 (3d ed. 1957): "Both benefit and detriment have a technical meaning. Neither the benefit to the promisor nor the detriment to the promisee need be actual. 'It would be a detriment to the promisee, in a legal sense, if he, at the request of the promisor and upon the strength of that promise, had performed any act which occasioned him the slightest trouble or inconvenience, and which he was not obliged to perform.' Benefit correspondingly must mean the receiving as the exchange for his promise of some performance or forbearance which the promisor was not previously entitled to receive. That the promisor desired it for his own advantage and had no previous right to it is enough to show that it was beneficial." This view of "benefit" and "detriment" as constituting valuable consideration has long been accepted in Illinois. It is not essential that it import a certain gain or loss to either party, but is sufficient if the party in whose favor the contract is made parts with a right which he might otherwise exert. (Miller Ice Co. v. Crim (1939), 299 Ill.App. 615, 20 N.E.2d 347.) Common sense dictates that plaintiff's parting with $5,000 earnest money under each option contract for more than 30 days constituted a legal detriment to plaintiff.

Reversed and remanded.

Questions

1. Who is making the offer in the above case?

2. What is the consideration which keeps the offer open? If it was not the "One Dollar" then what was its use? If Plaintiff had paid Defendant the requested dollar would that have affected the court's reasoning?

3. Was the consideration bargained for? Was it the motive for the offeror promising to keep the offer open? Does this appear to matter to the court?

4. In the court's view, was the consideration a benefit to the defendant or a detriment to the plaintiff?

5. Who was to have received the interest on the $10,000 if the money was returned? Could this shed light on consideration?

Turner v. Gunderson, 60 *Wash.App.* 696, 807 *P.2d* 370 (*Wash. Ct. App.*, 1991) concerned an option to purchase real estate. The court in part discussed how the relationship of the parties is changed once the option is exercised by the holder of the option, the one who paid for it. "Once an option is exercised, a new contract is created. As explained in 1A A. Corbin, Contracts § 264, at 507-08, 510, 512 (1963): 'Although an option contract is itself binding—that is, it is a contract before the option holder makes his choice and exercises his power— nevertheless, the exercise of the power changes the legal relations of the parties.... [The notice of intent to exercise the option is] both an acceptance of the offer and the performance of a condition precedent to [the option giver's] duty of immediate conveyance of the land....In the bilateral contract existing after notice...each party now being bound by a promise, the duty of each is still a conditional duty. [The option giver's] duty of immediate conveyance by deed is conditional upon tender of [the price] by [the option holder] within a reasonable time; and [the option holder's] duty...is conditional upon tender of a deed of conveyance of marketable title. These acts are made conditions of the two duties, not by the express words of either party, but by usage and the prevailing judicial notions of what is just. Once an option is exercised, it becomes a new contract of 'purchase and sale.'"

In the case at bar, the option offer was accepted and the option was exercised on March 13, 1986. The handwritten memorandum prepared and signed on that date constituted a binding bilateral contract of purchase and sale. Once the option is exercised and the bilateral contract is formed, there is still a "condition" which must be fulfilled by the buyer before the seller has a duty to convey the land and a condition which must be fulfilled by the seller before the buyer has a duty to tender the price. In Part IV we will consider the order in which conditions must be fulfilled. In real estate contracts they must normally be fulfilled concurrently on the date set for closing—that is the date set for the conveyance of the land and the receipt of the price. Note that the court says these duties are not always expressly spelled out in the contract. Where do they come from?

2. Options Not Supported by Consideration

The *Pavel* case, the first case in this section, is reprinted almost in its entirety because it illustrates the theories under which offers are said to be kept open, *i.e.* options are created, even when a consideration has not been paid. *Pavel* deals with a construction contract, a contract between an outside party with a general contractor ("general") and a series of contracts between the general and subcontractors ("subs"). An example of how this interaction works is, *e.g.*, a general contractor was seeking to contract with the federal government for the construction of a Post Office. The general makes an offer to the government for the cost of construction. Within this offer by the general contractor is included the amounts charged by subcontractors for individual portions of the construction, *i.e.*, plumbing, electricity, plaster, paint etc. The subs make bids to the general, who uses the subcontractors' bids (offers) in determining how much it will charge the government for the overall project. So, the general's bid submitted to the government consists of a conglomeration of offers from the subs. The general's offer is binding and cannot be withdrawn, creating, in essence, an option contract under which the general contractor is bound to leave its offer open, but the government is not bound to accept it.

Problems would exist if the subcontractors who had made bids could then withdraw their bids, since the general could then be bound to the government, but have no remedy for increased costs against the subs who had withdrawn bids. For example, if the general is selected to build a post office, and the subs could later withdraw their bids to the general, the general is still liable to the government to build the post office for the amount stated in its bid, even if actual costs are higher due to subs' cancellation. Another problem, perhaps more damaging to the general, is that if subs could withdraw bids (even if the general could withdraw its bid) the general contractor would then lose its opportunity to build the project and might damage its reputation as a reliable builder. Because the general contractor does not accept the subcontractors' bids until after its own bid has been accepted, the general contractor might be bound to build something and before it could accept the subcontractors' bids, one or more of the subs might withdraw their bids.

In cases like *Baird* and *Drennan*, discussed at length in *Pavel*, courts were concerned about the relationship between general and subcontractors. General contractors would rely on the bids (offers) of subcontractors in submitting their (the generals') overall bids to whomever they were seeking to contract with. The *Baird* case was criticized because it held that the subcontractor could withdraw its bid without liability to the general contractor even though the general contractor had already used the sub's bid in making its (the general's) bid.

Sympathy for the general contractor caused much criticism of the *Baird* case. On the other hand, if the sub is bound to its offer but the general is not bound to take it, the general then can bid shop etc. trying to cut down on the cost, after the general receives the contract from the government, knowing that the subcontractor whose bid the general has used cannot withdraw its bid. Because there is now more sympathy for subcontractors who are perceived as being at the mercy of general contractors, there is less inclination to find ways to hold them to their offers.

In terms of legal theory, there is no way to bind a subcontractor to its offer at common law unless a consideration is paid or a seal is used. In *Pavel* the doctrine of reliance on the offer is used as a variant on this, although without success. Where reliance is found and used to hold offers open, a person can be estopped from withdrawing his/her offer if the offeree relies on its being held open. This is a variant on the doctrine of promissory estoppel in which a person cannot deny the enforceability of a promise even if no consideration supports it if someone reasonably relies on it. As you read this and other cases note the use of Restatement sections 90 (promissory estoppel) and 87 (offertory estoppel) in the context of holding an offeror (subcontractor) to his/her offer. Note in *Drennan* how the court finds that the offeror makes an implied promise to keep the offer open; when the general contractor uses the offer she relies on that promise and the reliance in effect acts as a substitute for consideration making it impossible for the offeror (the subcontractor) to withdraw the offer. The promise is implied from the circumstances. The sub knows that the general will use the offer and must be able to rely on its being kept open because the general's overall bid is made up of a combination of all the subcontractor's bids plus the general's profit. From this knowledge that the subcontractor's bid is worthless if not kept open can be implied the subcontractor's promise to keep it open. The general contractor's actually using the bid is the general's reliance. Presumably up to the use of it by the general the sub could withdraw it without liability. Note that in *Baird*, an earlier case, the court would not find reliance as a possible substitute for consideration.

Pavel opens many possibilities. When the subcontractor makes a bid it makes an offer. Would it be possible to say that the subcontractor is bargaining with the general contractor and saying: "If you use my offer in your bid I promise to keep it open" thus creating a unilateral contract once the general performs the act requested and uses it. Some courts do not find this persuasive because the sub is not really bargaining for the general to use the bid. The sub is bargaining for the general to accept the sub's bid. Other courts say if the general wants to bind the sub it should pay a consideration to keep the bid open or have the sub use a sealed bid. Some say that when the general uses the bid the general is impliedly promising to the sub 'if my general offer is accepted, I will accept your offer.'

There are many theories. *Pavel* opens the door to some of them. Study it carefully including the footnotes.

Pavel Enterprises, Inc. v. A.S. Johnson Company, Inc.

674 A.2d 521

Court of Appeals of Maryland, 1996.

KARWACKI, Judge.

In this case we are invited to adapt the "modern" contractual theory of detrimental reliance[1] , or promissory estoppel, to the relationship between general contractors and their subcontractors. Although the theory of detrimental reliance is available to general contractors, it is not applicable to the facts of this case. For that reason, and because there was no traditional bilateral contract formed, we shall affirm the trial court.

I

The National Institutes of Health [hereinafter, "NIH"], solicited bids for a renovation project on Building 30 of its Bethesda, Maryland campus. The proposed work entailed some demolition work, but the major component of the job

---

1. We prefer to use the phrase detrimental reliance, rather than the traditional nomenclature of "promissory estoppel," because we believe it more clearly expresses the concept intended. Moreover, we hope that this will alleviate the confusion which until now has permitted practitioners to confuse promissory estoppel with its distant cousin, equitable estoppel. See Note, The "Firm Offer" Problem in Construction Bids and the Need for Promissory Estoppel, 10 WM & MARY L.REV. 212, 214 n. 17 (1968) [hereinafter, "The Firm Offer Problem "].

was mechanical, including heating, ventilation and air conditioning ["HVAC"]. Pavel Enterprises Incorporated [hereinafter, "PEI"], a general contractor from Vienna, Virginia and appellant in this action, prepared a bid for the NIH work. In preparing its bid, PEI solicited sub-bids from various mechanical subcontractors. The A.S. Johnson Company [hereinafter, "Johnson"], a mechanical subcontractor located in Clinton, Maryland and the appellee here, responded with a written scope of work proposal on July 27, 1993[2] . On the morning of August 5, 1993, the day NIH opened the general contractors' bids, Johnson verbally submitted a quote of $898,000 for the HVAC component[3] . Neither party disputes that PEI used Johnson's sub-bid in computing its own bid. PEI submitted a bid of $1,585,000 for the entire project.

General contractors' bids were opened on the afternoon of August 5, 1993. PEI's bid was the second lowest bid. The government subsequently disqualified the apparent low bidder however, and in mid-August, NIH notified PEI that its bid would be accepted.

With the knowledge that PEI was the lowest responsive bidder, Thomas F. Pavel, president of PEI, visited the offices of A.S. Johnson on August 26, 1993, and met with James Kick, Johnson's chief estimator, to discuss Johnson's proposed role in the work. Pavel testified at trial to the purpose of the meeting: "I met with Mr. Kick. And the reason for me going to their office was to look at their offices, to see their facility, to basically sit down and talk with them, as I had not done, and my company had not performed business with them on a direct relationship, but we had heard of their reputation. I wanted to go out and see where their facility was, see where they were located, and basically just sit down and talk to them. Because if we were going to use them on a project, I wanted to know who I was dealing with."

Pavel also asked if Johnson would object to PEI subcontracting directly with Powers for electric controls, rather than the arrangement originally envisioned in which Powers would be Johnson's subcontractor. Johnson did not object.

Following that meeting, PEI sent a fax to all of the mechanical subcontractors from whom it had received sub-bids on the NIH job. The text of that fax is reproduced:

Pavel Enterprises, Inc.

TO: PROSPECTIVE MECHANICAL SUBCONTRACTORS FROM: ESTIMATING DEPARTMENT REFERENCE: NIH, BLDG 30 RENOVATION We herewith respectfully request that you review your bid on the above referenced project that was bid on 8/05/93. PEI has been notified that we will be awarded the project as J.J. Kirlin, Inc. [the original low bidder] has been found to be nonresponsive on the solicitation. We anticipate award on or

---

2. The scope of work proposal listed all work that Johnson proposed to perform, but omitted the price term. This is a standard practice in the construction industry. The subcontractor's bid price is then filled in immediately before the general contractor submits the general bid to the letting party.

3. PEI alleged at trial that Johnson's bid, as well as the bids of the other potential mechanical subcontractors contained a fixed cost of $355,000 for a sub-sub-contract to "Landis and Gear Powers" [hereinafter, "Powers"]. Powers was the sole source supplier of the electric controls for the project.

around the first of September and therefor request that you supply the following information. 1. Please break out your cost for the "POWERS" supplied control work as we will be subcontracting directly to "POWERS". 2. Please resubmit your quote deleting the above referenced item. We ask this in an effort to allow all prospective bidders to compete on an even playing field. Should you have any questions, please call us immediately as time is of the essence.

On August 30, 1993, PEI informed NIH that Johnson was to be the mechanical subcontractor on the job. On September 1, 1993, PEI mailed and faxed a letter to Johnson formally accepting Johnson's bid. That letter read:

Pavel Enterprises, Inc.

September 1, 1993 Mr. James H. Kick, Estimating Mngr. A.S. Johnson Company 8042 Old Alexandria Ferry Road Clinton, Maryland 20735 Re: NIH Bldg 30 HVAC Modifications RC: IFB # 263-93-B (CM)—0422 Subject: Letter of Intent to award SUBJECT: Subcontract Dear Mr. Kick; We herewith respectfully inform your office of our intent to award a subcontract for the above referenced project per your quote received on 8/05/93 in the amount of $898,000.00. This subcontract will be forwarded upon receipt of our contract from the NIH, which we expect any day. A preconstruction meeting is currently scheduled at the NIH on 9/08/93 at 10 AM which we have been requested that your firm attend. As discussed with you, a meeting was held between NIH and PEI wherein PEI confirmed our bid to the government, and designated your firm as our HVAC Mechanical subcontractor. This action was taken after several telephonic and face to face discussions with you regarding the above referenced bid submitted by your firm. We look forward to working with your firm on this contract and hope that this will lead to a long and mutually beneficial relationship. Sincerely, /s/ Thomas F. Pavel, President

Upon receipt of PEI's fax of September 1, James Kick called and informed PEI that Johnson's bid contained an error, and as a result the price was too low. According to Kick, Johnson had discovered the mistake earlier, but because Johnson believed that PEI had not been awarded the contract, they did not feel compelled to correct the error. Kick sought to withdraw Johnson's bid, both over the telephone and by a letter dated September 2, 1993:

A.S. Johnson Co.

September 2, 1993 PEI Construction 780 West Maples Avenue, Suite 101 Vienna, Virginia 22180 Attention: Thomas Pavel, ATTENTION: President Reference: NIH Building 30 HVAC Modifications Dear Mr. Pavel, We respectfully inform you of our intention to withdraw our proposal for the above referenced project due to an error in our bid. As discussed in our telephone conversation and face to face meeting, the management of A.S. Johnson Company was reviewing this proposal, upon which we were to confirm our pricing to you. Please contact Mr. Harry Kick, General Manager at [telephone number deleted] for any questions you may have. Very truly yours, /s/ James H. Kick Estimating Manager

PEI responded to both the September 1 phone call, and the September 2 letter, expressing its refusal to permit Johnson to withdraw.

On September 28, 1993, NIH formally awarded the construction contract to PEI. PEI found a substitute subcontractor to do the mechanical work, but at a cost of $930,000.[6] PEI brought suit against Johnson in the Circuit Court for Prince George's County to recover the $32,000 difference between Johnson's bid and the cost of the substitute mechanical subcontractor.

The case was heard by the trial court without the aid of a jury. The trial court made several findings of fact, which we summarize: 1. PEI relied upon Johnson's sub-bid in making its bid for the entire project; 2. The fact that PEI was not the low bidder, but was awarded the project only after the apparent low bidder was disqualified, takes this case out of the ordinary; 3. Prior to NIH awarding PEI the contract on September 28, Johnson, on September 2, withdrew its bid; and 4. PEI's letter to all potential mechanical subcontractors, dated August 26, 1993, indicates that there was no definite agreement between PEI and Johnson, and that PEI was not relying upon Johnson's bid.

The trial court analyzed the case under both a traditional contract theory and under a detrimental reliance theory. PEI was unable to satisfy the trial judge that under either theory that a contractual relationship had been formed.

PEI appealed to the Court of Special Appeals, raising both traditional offer and acceptance theory, and "promissory estoppel." Before our intermediate appellate court considered the case, we issued a writ of certiorari on our own motion.

II

The relationships involved in construction contracts have long posed a unique problem in the law of contracts. A brief overview of the mechanics of the construction bid process, as well as our legal system's attempts to regulate the process, is in order.

A. CONSTRUCTION BIDDING.

Our description of the bid process in Maryland Supreme Corp. v. Blake Co., 279 Md. 531, 369 A.2d 1017 (1977) is still accurate: "In such a building project there are basically three parties involved: the letting party, who calls for bids on its job; the general contractor, who makes a bid on the whole project; and the subcontractors, who bid only on that portion of the whole job which involves the field of its specialty. The usual procedure is that when a project is announced, a subcontractor, on his own initiative or at the general contractor's request, prepares an estimate and submits a bid to one or more of the general contractors interested in the project. The general contractor evaluates the bids made by the subcontractors in each field and uses them to compute its total bid to the letting party. After receiving bids from general contractors, the letting party ordinarily awards the contract to the lowest reputable bidder." Id. at 533-34, 369 A.2d at 1020-21 (citing The Firm Offer Problem)

B. THE CONSTRUCTION BIDDING CASES—AN HISTORICAL OVERVIEW.

The problem the construction bidding process poses is the determination of the precise points on the timeline that the various parties become bound to each

---

6. The record indicates that the substitute mechanical subcontractor used "Powers" as a sub-subcontractor and did not "break out" the "Powers" component to be directly subcontracted by PEI.

other. The early landmark case was **James Baird Co. v. Gimbel Bros., Inc.,** 64 F.2d 344 (2d Cir.1933). The plaintiff, James Baird Co., ["Baird"] was a general contractor from Washington, D.C., bidding to construct a government building in Harrisburg, Pennsylvania. Gimbel Bros., Inc., ["Gimbel"], the famous New York department store, sent its bid to supply linoleum to a number of bidding general contractors on December 24, and Baird received Gimbel's bid on December 28. Gimbel realized its bid was based on an incorrect computation and notified Baird of its withdrawal on December 28. The letting authority awarded Baird the job on December 30. Baird formally accepted the Gimbel bid on January 2. When Gimbel refused to perform, Baird sued for the additional cost of a substitute linoleum supplier. The Second Circuit Court of Appeals held that Gimbel's initial bid was an offer to contract and, under traditional contract law, remained open only until accepted or withdrawn. Because the offer was withdrawn before it was accepted there was no contract. Judge Learned Hand, speaking for the court, also rejected two alternative theories of the case: unilateral contract and promissory estoppel. He held that Gimbel's bid was not an offer of a unilateral contract that Baird could accept by performing, i.e., submitting the bid as part of the general bid; and second, he held that the theory of promissory estoppel was limited to cases involving charitable pledges.

Judge Hand's opinion was widely criticized, see Note, Contracts-Promissory Estoppel, 20 VA.L.REV. 214 (1933) [hereinafter, "Promissory Estoppel"]; Note, Contracts-Revocation of Offer Before Acceptance-Promissory Estoppel, 28 ILL.L.REV. 419 (1934), but also widely influential. The effect of the James Baird line of cases, however, is an "obvious injustice without relief of any description." Promissory Estoppel, at 215. The general contractor is bound to the price submitted to the letting party, but the subcontractors are not bound, and are free to withdraw.[8] As one commentator described it, "If the subcontractor revokes his bid before it is accepted by the general, any loss which results is a deduction from the general's profit and conceivably may transform overnight a profitable contract into a losing deal." Franklin M. Schultz, The Firm Offer Puzzle: A Study of Business Practice in the Construction Industry, 19 U.CHI.L.REV. 237, 239 (1952).

The unfairness of this regime to the general contractor was addressed in **Drennan v. Star Paving,** 333 P.2d 757, 51 Cal.2d 409 (1958). Like James Baird, the Drennan case arose in the context of a bid mistake.[9] Justice Traynor, writing

---

8. Note that under the Baird line of cases, the general contractor, while bound by his offer to the letting party, is not bound to any specific subcontractor, and is free to "bid shop" prior to awarding the subcontract. Michael L. Closen & Donald G. Weiland, The Construction Industry Bidding Cases: Application of Traditional Contract, Promissory Estoppel, and Other Theories to the Relations Between General Contractors and Subcontractors, 13 J. MARSHALL L.REV. 565, 583 (1980). At least one commentator argues that although potentially unfair, this system creates a necessary symmetry between general and subcontractors, in that neither party is bound. Note, Construction Contracts—The Problem of Offer and Acceptance in the General Contractor-Subcontractor Relationship, 37 U.CINN.L.REV. 798 (1980) [hereinafter, "The Problem of Offer and Acceptance "].

9. Commentators have suggested that the very fact that many of these cases have arisen from bid mistake, an unusual subspecies, rather than from more typical cases, has distorted the legal system's understanding of these cases. Comment, Bid Shopping and Peddling in the Subcontract Construction Industry, 18 UCLA L.REV. 389, 409 (1970) [hereinafter, "Bid Shopping "]. See also note, Once Around the Flag Pole: Construction Bidding and Contracts

for the Supreme Court of California, relied upon § 90 of the Restatement (First) of Contracts:

"A promise which the promisor should reasonably expect to induce action or forbearance of a definite and substantial character on the part of the promisee and which does induce such action or forbearance is binding if injustice can be avoided only by enforcement of the promise." Restatement (First) of Contracts § 90 (1932).[10]

Justice Traynor reasoned that the subcontractor's bid contained an implied subsidiary promise not to revoke the bid. As the court stated: "When plaintiff [, a General Contractor,] used defendant's offer in computing his own bid, he bound himself to perform in reliance on defendant's terms. Though defendant did not bargain for the use of its bid neither did defendant make it idly, indifferent to whether it would be used or not. On the contrary it is reasonable to suppose that defendant submitted its bid to obtain the subcontract. It was bound to realize the substantial possibility that its bid would be the lowest, and that it would be included by plaintiff in his bid. It was to its own interest that the contractor be awarded the general contract; the lower the subcontract bid, the lower the general contractor's bid was likely to be and the greater its chance of acceptance and hence the greater defendant's chance of getting the paving subcontract. Defendant had reason not only to expect plaintiff to rely on its bid but to want him to. Clearly defendant had a stake in plaintiff's reliance on its bid. Given this interest and the fact that plaintiff is bound by his own bid, it is only fair that plaintiff should have at least an opportunity to accept defendant's bid after the general contract has been awarded to him." Drennan, 51 Cal.2d at 415, 333 P.2d at 760. The Drennan court however did not use "promissory estoppel" as a substitute for the entire contract, as is the doctrine's usual function. Instead, the Drennan court, applying the principle of § 90, interpreted the subcontractor's bid to be irrevocable. Justice Traynor's analysis used promissory estoppel as consideration for an implied promise to keep the bid open for a reasonable time. Recovery was then predicated on traditional bilateral contract, with the sub-bid as the offer and promissory estoppel serving to replace acceptance.

The Drennan decision has been very influential. Many states have adopted the reasoning used by Justice Traynor.

Despite the popularity of the Drennan reasoning, the case has subsequently come under some criticism. The criticism centers on the lack of symmetry of detrimental reliance in the bid process, in that subcontractors are bound to the general, but the general is not bound to the subcontractors.[12] The result is that

---

at Formation, 39 N.Y.U.L.REV. 816, 818 (1964) [hereinafter, "Flag Pole "] (bid mistake cases generally portray general contractor as victim, but market reality is that subs are usually in weaker negotiating position).

10. This section of the Restatement has been supplanted by the Restatement (Second) of Contracts § 90(1) (1979). That provision will be discussed, infra.

12. See Williams v. Favret, 161 F.2d 822, 823 n. 1 (5th Cir.1947); Merritt-Chapman & Scott Corp. v. Gunderson Bros. Eng'g Corp., 305 F.2d 659 (9th Cir.1962). But see Electrical Constr. & Maintenance Co. v. Maeda Pac. Corp., 764 F.2d 619 (9th Cir.1985) (subcontractor rejected by general contractor could maintain an action in both traditional contract or promissory estoppel). See Bid Shopping, at 405-09 (suggesting using "promissory estoppel" to bind generals to subcontractors, as well as subs to generals, in appropriate circumstances).

the general is free to bid shop,[13] bid chop[14], and to encourage bid peddling,[15] to the detriment of the subcontractors. One commentator described the problems that these practices create:

"Bid shopping and peddling have long been recognized as unethical by construction trade organizations. These 'unethical,' but common practices have several detrimental results. First, as bid shopping becomes common within a particular trade, the subcontractors will pad their initial bids in order to make further reductions during post-award negotiations. This artificial inflation of subcontractors' offers makes the bid process less effective. Second, subcontractors who are forced into post-award negotiations with the general often must reduce their sub-bids in order to avoid losing the award. Thus, they will be faced with a Hobson's choice between doing the job at a loss or doing a less than adequate job. Third, bid shopping and peddling tend to increase the risk of loss of the time and money used in preparing a bid. This occurs because generals and subcontractors who engage in these practices use, without expense, the bid estimates prepared by others. Fourth, it is often impossible for a general to obtain bids far enough in advance to have sufficient time to properly prepare his own bid because of the practice, common among many subcontractors, of holding sub-bids until the last possible moment in order to avoid pre-award bid shopping by the general. Fifth, many subcontractors refuse to submit bids for jobs on which they expect bid shopping. As a result, competition is reduced, and, consequently, construction prices are increased. Sixth, any price reductions gained through the use of post-award bid shopping by the general will be of no benefit to the awarding authority, to whom these price reductions would normally accrue as a result of open competition before the award of the prime contract. Free competition in an open market is therefore perverted because of the use of post-award bid shopping." Bid Shopping, at 394-96 (citations omitted). See also Flag Pole, at 818 (bid mistake cases generally portray general contractor as victim, but market reality is that subs are usually in weaker negotiating position). These problems have caused at least one court to reject promissory estoppel in the contractor-subcontractor relationship. But other courts, while aware of the limitations of promissory estoppel, have adopted it nonetheless. See, e.g., Alaska Bussell Elec. Co. v. Vern Hickel Constr. Co., 688 P.2d 576 (Alaska 1984)[16].

The doctrine of detrimental reliance has evolved in the time since Drennan was decided in 1958. The American Law Institute, responding to Drennan,

---

13. Bid shopping is the use of the lowest subcontractor's bid as a tool in negotiating lower bids from other subcontractors post-award.

14. "The general contractor, having been awarded the prime contract, may pressure the subcontractor whose bid was used for a particular portion of the work in computing the overall bid on the prime contract to reduce the amount of the bid." Closen & Weiland, at 566 n. 6.

15. An unscrupulous subcontractor can save estimating costs, and still get the job by not entering a bid or by entering an uncompetitive bid. After bid opening, this unscrupulous subcontractor, knowing the price of the low sub-bid, can then offer to perform the work for less money, precisely because the honest subcontractor has already paid for the estimate and included that cost in the original bid. This practice is called bid peddling.

16. The critical literature also contains numerous suggestions that might be undertaken by the legislature to address the problems of bid shopping, chopping, and peddling. See Note, Construction Bidding Problem: Is There a Solution Fair to Both the General Contractor and Subcontractor?, 19 ST. LOUIS L.REV. 552, 568-72 (1975) (discussing bid depository and bid listing schemes); Flag Pole, at 825-26.

sought to make detrimental reliance more readily applicable to the construction bidding scenario by adding § 87. This new section was intended to make subcontractors' bids binding: "§ 87. Option Contract...(2) An offer which the offeror should reasonably expect to induce action or forbearance of a substantial character on the part of the offeree before acceptance and which does induce such action or forbearance is binding as an option contract to the extent necessary to avoid injustice." Restatement (Second) of Contracts § 87 (1979)[17].

Despite the drafter's intention that § 87 of the Restatement (Second) of Contracts (1979) should replace Restatement (First) of Contracts § 90 (1932) in the construction bidding cases, few courts have availed themselves of the opportunity. Section 90(1) of the Restatement (Second) of Contracts (1979) modified the first restatement formulation in three ways, by: 1) deleting the requirement that the action of the offeree be "definite and substantial;" 2) adding a cause of action for third party reliance; and 3) limiting remedies to those required by justice.[18]

Courts and commentators have also suggested other solutions intended to bind the parties without the use of detrimental reliance theory. The most prevalent suggestion[19] is the use of the firm offer provision of the Uniform Commercial Code. Maryland Code (1992 Repl.Vol.), § 2-205 of the Commercial Law Article. That statute provides:

"An offer by a merchant to buy or sell goods in a signed writing which by its terms gives assurance that it will be held open is not revocable, for lack of consideration, during the time stated or if no time is stated for a reasonable time, but in no event may such period of irrevocability exceed three months; but any such term of assurance on a form supplied by the offeree must be separately signed by the offeror."

In this manner, subcontractor's bids, made in writing and giving some assurance of an intent that the offer be held open, can be found to be irrevocable.

The Supreme Judicial Court of Massachusetts has suggested three other traditional theories that might prove the existence of a contractual relationship between a general contractor and a sub: conditional bilateral contract analysis; unilateral contract analysis; and unrevoked offer analysis. Loranger Constr. Corp. v. E.F. Hauserman Co., 384 N.E.2d 176, 376 Mass. 757 (1978). If the general contractor could prove that there was an exchange of promises binding the parties to

---

17. This provision was derived from Restatement (Second) of Contracts § 89B(2) (Tent.Drafts Nos. 1-7, 1973). There are cases that refer to the tentative drafts. See Loranger Constr. Corp. v. E.F. Hauserman Co., 384 N.E.2d 176, 179, 376 Mass. 757, 763 (1978). See also Closen & Weiland, at 593-97.

18. Section 90 of the Restatement (First) of Contracts (1932) explains detrimental reliance as follows: "A promise which the promisor should reasonably expect to induce action or forbearance of a definite and substantial character on the part of the promisee and which does induce such action or forbearance is binding if injustice can be avoided only by enforcement of the promise." Section 90(1) of the Restatement (Second) Contracts (1979) defines the doctrine of detrimental reliance as follows: "A promise which the promisor should reasonably expect to induce action or forbearance on the part of the promisee or a third person and which does induce such action or forbearance is binding if injustice can be avoided only by enforcement of the promise. The remedy granted for breach may be limited as justice requires."

19. See Bid Shopping and Peddling at 399-401; Firm Offer Problem at 215; Closen & Weiland, at 604 n. 133.

each other, and that exchange of promises was made before bid opening, that would constitute a valid bilateral promise conditional upon the general being awarded the job. Loranger, 384 N.E.2d at 180, 376 Mass. at 762. This directly contrasts with Judge Hand's analysis in James Baird [an analysis which Hand dissmissed], that a general's use of a sub-bid constitutes acceptance conditional upon the award of the contract to the general. James Baird, 64 F.2d at 345-46.

Alternatively, if the subcontractor intended its sub-bid as an offer to a unilateral contract, use of the sub-bid in the general's bid constitutes part performance, which renders the initial offer irrevocable under the Restatement (Second) of Contracts § 45 (1979). This resurrects a second theory dismissed by Judge Learned Hand in James Baird.

Finally, the Loranger court pointed out that a jury might choose to disbelieve that a subcontractor had withdrawn the winning bid, meaning that acceptance came before withdrawal, and a traditional bilateral contract was formed. Loranger, 384 N.E.2d at 180, 376 Mass. at 762-63.[20]

Another alternative solution to the construction bidding problem is no longer seriously considered—revitalizing the common law seal. Because a sealed option contract remains firm without consideration this alternative was proposed as a solution to the construction bidding problem.[21]

It is here that the state of the law rests.

III

If PEI is able to prove by any of the theories described that a contractual relationship existed, but Johnson failed to perform its end of the bargain, then PEI will recover the $32,000 in damages caused by Johnson's breach of contract. Alternatively, if PEI is unable to prove the existence of a contractual relationship, then Johnson has no obligation to PEI. We will test the facts of the case against the theories described to determine if such a relationship existed.

The trial court held, and we agree, that Johnson's sub-bid was an offer to contract and that it was sufficiently clear and definite. We must then determine if PEI made a timely and valid acceptance of that offer and thus created a traditional bilateral contract, or in the absence of a valid acceptance, if PEI's detrimental reliance served to bind Johnson to its sub-bid. We examine each of these alternatives, beginning with traditional contract theory.[22]

---

20. For an excellent analysis of the Loranger case, see Closen & Weiland at 597-603.

21. Of course, general contractors could require their subcontractors to provide their bids under seal. The fact that they do not is testament to the lack of appeal this proposal holds.

22. Because they were not raised, either below or in this Court, we need not address the several methods in which a court might interpret a subcontractor's bid as a firm, and thus irrevocable, offer. Nevertheless, for the benefit of bench and bar, we review those theories as applied to this case. First, PEI could have purchased an option, thus supplying consideration for making the offer irrevocable. This did not happen. Second, Johnson could have submitted its bid as a sealed offer. Md.Code (1995 Repl.Vol.), § 5-102 of the Courts & Judicial Proceedings Article. An offer under seal supplants the need for consideration to make an offer firm. This did not occur in the instant case. The third method of Johnson's offer becoming irrevocable is by operation of Md.Code (1992 Repl.Vol.), § 2-205 of the Commercial Law Article. We note that Johnson's sub-bid was made in the form of a signed writing, but without further evidence we are unable to determine if the offer "by its terms gives as-

A. TRADITIONAL BILATERAL CONTRACT

The trial judge found that there was not a traditional contract binding Johnson to PEI. A review of the record and the trial judge's findings make it clear that this was a close question. On appeal however, our job is to assure that the trial judge's findings were not clearly erroneous. Maryland Rule 8-131(c). This is an easier task.

The trial judge rejected PEI's claim of bilateral contract for two separate reasons: 1) that there was no meeting of the minds; and 2) that the offer was withdrawn prior to acceptance. Both need not be proper bases for decision; if either of these two theories is not clearly erroneous, we must affirm.

There is substantial evidence in the record to support the judge's conclusion that there was no meeting of the minds. PEI's letter of August 26, to all potential mechanical subcontractors, reproduced supra, indicates, as the trial judge found, that PEI and Johnson "did not have a definite, certain meeting of the minds on a certain price for a certain quantity of goods...." Because this reason is itself sufficient to sustain the trial judge's finding that no contract was formed, we affirm.

Alternatively, we hold, that the evidence permitted the trial judge to find that Johnson revoked its offer prior to PEI's final acceptance. We review the relevant chronology. Johnson made its offer, in the form of a sub-bid, on August 5. On September 1, PEI accepted. Johnson withdrew its offer by letter dated September 2. On September 28, NIH awarded the contract to PEI. Thus, PEI's apparent acceptance came one day prior to Johnson's withdrawal.

The trial court found, however, "that before there was ever a final agreement reached with the contract awarding authorities, that Johnson made it clear to [PEI] that they were not going to continue to rely on their earlier submitted bid." Implicit in this finding is the judge's understanding of the contract. Johnson's sub-bid constituted an offer of a contingent contract. PEI accepted that offer subject to the condition precedent of PEI's receipt of the award of the contract from NIH. Prior to the occurrence of the condition precedent, Johnson was free to withdraw. See 2 Williston on Contracts § 6:14 (4th ed.). On September 2, Johnson exercised that right to revoke.[23] The trial judge's finding that withdrawal preceeded valid final acceptance is therefore logical and supported by substantial evidence in the record. It was not clearly erroneous, so we shall affirm.

B. DETRIMENTAL RELIANCE

PEI's alternative theory of the case is that PEI's detrimental reliance binds Johnson to its bid. We are asked, as a threshold question, if detrimental reliance

surance that it will be held open" and if the sub-bid is for "goods" as that term is defined by Md.Code (1994 Repl.Vol.), § 2-105(1) of the Commercial Law Article and by decisions of this Court, including Anthony Pools v. Sheehan, 295 Md. 285, 455 A.2d 434 (1983) and Burton v. Artery Co., 279 Md. 94, 367 A.2d 935 (1977).

23. We have also considered the possibility that Johnson's offer was not to enter into a contingent contract. This is unlikely because there is no incentive for a general contractor to accept a non-contingent contract prior to contract award but it would bind the general to purchase the subcontractor's services even if the general did not receive the award. Moreover, PEI's September 1 letter clearly "accepted" Johnson's offer subject to the award from NIH. If Johnson's bid was for a non-contingent contract, PEI's response substantially varied the offer and was therefore a counter-offer, not an acceptance. Post v. Gillespie, 219 Md. 378, 385-86, 149 A.2d 391, 395-96 (1959); 2 Williston on Contracts § 6:13 (4th ed.).

applies to the setting of construction bidding. Nothing in our previous cases suggests that the doctrine was intended to be limited to a specific factual setting. The benefits of binding subcontractors outweigh the possible detriments of the doctrine.[24]

This Court has decided cases based on detrimental reliance as early as 1854, and the general contours of the doctrine are well understood by Maryland courts. The historical development of promissory estoppel, or detrimental reliance, in Maryland has mirrored the development nationwide. It was originally a small exception to the general consideration requirement, and found in "cases dealing with such narrow problems as gratuitous agencies and bailments, waivers, and promises of marriage settlement." Jay M. Feinman, Promissory Estoppel and Judicial Method, 97 HARV.L.REV. 678, 680 (1984). The early Maryland cases applying "promissory estoppel" or detrimental reliance primarily involve charitable pledges.

The leading case is Maryland Nat'l Bank v. United Jewish Appeal Fed'n of Greater Washington, 286 Md. 274, 407 A.2d 1130 (1979), where this Court's opinion was authored by the late Judge Charles E. Orth, Jr. In that case, a decedent, Milton Polinger, had pledged $200,000 to the United Jewish Appeal ["UJA"]. The UJA sued Polinger's estate in an attempt to collect the money promised them. Judge Orth reviewed four prior decisions of this Court and determined that Restatement (First) of Contracts § 90 (1932) applied. Id. at 281, 407 A.2d at 1134. Because the Court found that the UJA had not acted in a "definite or substantial" manner in reliance on the contribution, no contract was found to have been created. Id. at 289-90, 407 A.2d at 1138- 39.

Detrimental reliance doctrine has had a slow evolution from its origins in disputes over charitable pledges, and there remains some uncertainty about its exact dimensions.[27] Two cases from the Court of Special Appeals demonstrate that confusion.

The first, Snyder v. Snyder, 79 Md.App. 448, 558 A.2d 412 (1989), arose in the context of a suit to enforce an antenuptial agreement. To avoid the statute of frauds, refuge was sought in the doctrine of "promissory estoppel."[28] The court

---

24. General contractors, however, should not assume that we will also adopt the holdings of our sister courts who have refused to find general contractors bound to their subcontracters. See, e.g., N. Litterio & Co. v. Glassman Constr. Co., 319 F.2d 736 (D.C.Cir.1963).

27. Other cases merely acknowledged the existence of a doctrine of "promissory estoppel," but did not comment on the standards for the application of this doctrine. See, e.g., Chesapeake Supply & Equip. Co. v. Manitowoc Eng'g Corp., 232 Md. 555, 566, 194 A.2d 624, 630 (1963).

28. Section 139 of the Restatement (Second) of Contracts (1979) provides that detrimental reliance can remove a case from the statute of frauds: "Enforcement by Virtue of Action in Reliance (1) A promise which the promisor should reasonably expect to induce action or forbearance on the part of the promisee or a third person and which does induce the action or forbearance is enforceable notwithstanding the Statute of Frauds if injustice can be avoided only by enforcement of the promise. The remedy granted for breach is to be limited as justice requires. (2) In determining whether injustice can be avoided only by enforcement of the promise, the following circumstances are significant: (a) the availability and adequacy of other remedies, particularly cancellation and restitution; (b) the definite and substantial character of the action or forbearance in relation to the remedy sought; (c) the extent to which the action or forbearance corroborates evidence of the making and terms of the promise, or the making and terms are otherwise established by clear and convincing evi-

held that "promissory estoppel" requires a finding of fraudulent conduct on the part of the promisor.

The second, Kiley v. First Nat'l Bank, 102 Md.App. 317, 649 A.2d 1145 (1994), the court stated that "[i]t is unclear whether Maryland continues to adhere to the more stringent formulation of promissory estoppel, as set forth in the original Restatement of Contracts, or now follows the more flexible view found in the Restatement (Second) Contracts." Id. at 336, 649 A.2d at 1154.

To resolve these confusions we now clarify that Maryland courts are to apply the test of the Restatement (Second) of Contracts § 90(1) (1979), which we have recast as a four-part test: 1. a clear and definite promise; 2. where the promisor has a reasonable expectation that the offer will induce action or forbearance on the part of the promisee; 3. which does induce actual and reasonable action or forbearance by the promisee; and 4. causes a detriment which can only be avoided by the enforcement of the promise.[29]

In a construction bidding case, where the general contractor seeks to bind the subcontractor to the sub-bid offered, the general must first prove that the subcontractor's sub-bid constituted an offer to perform a job at a given price. We do not express a judgment about how precise a bid must be to constitute an offer, or to what degree a general contractor may request to change the offered scope before an acceptance becomes a counter-offer. That fact-specific judgment is best reached on a case-by-case basis. In the instant case, the trial judge found that the sub-bid was sufficiently clear and definite to constitute an offer, and his finding was not clearly erroneous.

Second, the general must prove that the subcontractor reasonably expected that the general contractor would rely upon the offer. The subcontractor's expectation that the general contractor will rely upon the sub-bid may dissipate through time.[30]

In this case, the trial court correctly inquired into Johnson's belief that the bid remained open, and that consequently PEI was not relying on the Johnson bid. The judge found that due to the time lapse between bid opening and award, "it would be unreasonable for offers to continue." This is supported by substan-

---

dence; (d) the reasonableness of the action or forbearance; (e) the extent to which the action or forbearance was foreseeable by the promisor."

29. This comports with the formulation given by the United States District Court for the District of Maryland in Union Trust Co. of Md. v. Charter Medical Corp., 663 F.Supp. 175, 178 n. 4 (D.Md.1986) aff'd w/o opinion, 823 F.2d 548 (4th Cir.1987). We have adopted language of the Restatement (Second) of Contracts (1979) because we believe each of the three changes made to the previous formulation were for the better. As discussed earlier, the first change was to delete the requirement that the action of the offeree be "definite and substantial." Although the Court of Special Appeals in Kiley v. First Nat'l Bank, 102 Md.App. 317, 336, 649 A.2d 1145, 1154 (1994) apparently presumed this to be a major change from the "stringent" first restatement to the "more flexible" second restatement, we perceive the language to have always been redundant. If the reliance is not "substantial and definite" justice will not compel enforcement. The decisions in Snyder v. Snyder, 79 Md.App. 448, 558 A.2d 412 (1989) and Friedman & Fuller v. Funkhouser, 107 Md.App. 91, 666 A.2d 1298 (1995) to the extent that they required a showing of fraud on the part of the offeree are therefore disapproved.

30. We expect that evidence of "course of dealing" and "usage of the trade," see Restatement (Second) of Contracts ss 219-223 (1979), will provide strong indicies of the reasonableness of a subcontractor's expectations.

tial evidence. James Kick testified that although he knew of his bid mistake, he did not bother to notify PEI because J.J. Kirlin, Inc., and not PEI, was the apparent low bidder. The trial court's finding that Johnson's reasonable expectation had dissipated in the span of a month is not clearly erroneous.

As to the third element, a general contractor must prove that he actually and reasonably relied on the subcontractor's sub-bid. We decline to provide a checklist of potential methods of proving this reliance, but we will make several observations. First, a showing by the subcontractor, that the general contractor engaged in "bid shopping," or actively encouraged "bid chopping," or "bid peddling" is strong evidence that the general did not rely on the sub-bid. Second, prompt notice by the general contractor to the subcontractor that the general intends to use the sub on the job, is weighty evidence that the general did rely on the bid.[31] Third, if a sub-bid is so low that a reasonably prudent general contractor would not rely upon it, the trier of fact may infer that the general contractor did not in fact rely upon the erroneous bid.

In this case, the trial judge did not make a specific finding that PEI failed to prove its reasonable reliance upon Johnson's sub-bid. We must assume, however, that it was his conclusion based on his statement that "the parties did not have a definite, certain meeting of the minds on a certain price for a certain quantity of goods and wanted to renegotiate...." The August 26, 1993, fax from PEI to all prospective mechanical subcontractors, is evidence supporting this conclusion. Although the finding that PEI did not rely on Johnson's bid was indisputably a close call, it was not clearly erroneous.

Finally, as to the fourth prima facie element, the trial court, and not a jury, must determine that binding the subcontractor is necessary to prevent injustice. This element is to be enforced as required by common law equity courts— the general contractor must have "clean hands." This requirement includes, as did the previous element, that the general did not engage in bid shopping, chopping or peddling, but also requires the further determination that justice compels the result. The fourth factor was not specifically mentioned by the trial judge, but we may infer that he did not find this case to merit an equitable remedy.

Because there was sufficient evidence in the record to support the trial judge's conclusion that PEI had not proven its case for detrimental reliance, we must, and hereby do, affirm the trial court's ruling.

IV

In conclusion, we emphasize that there are different ways to prove that a contractual relationship exists between a general contractor and its subcontractors. Traditional bilateral contract theory is one. Detrimental reliance can be another. However, under the evidence in this case, the trial judge was not clearly erroneous in deciding that recovery by the general contractor was not justified under either theory.

---

31. Prompt notice and acceptance also significantly dispels the possibility of bid shopping, bid chopping, and bid peddling.

JUDGMENT AFFIRMED, WITH COSTS.

Questions

1. What should P.E.I. have done to hold Johnson to its bid?

2. What should P.E.I. have avoided doing if they wanted to hold Johnson to its bid?

3. Why did the appellate court keep referring to "close calls?" What is the counseling point here for you as a lawyer in so far as you are evaluating your chances of winning on appeal if you lose in the trial court?

4. What does the appellate court mean when it refers to the trial judge's findings (what is a "finding?") as "not clearly erroneous, so we shall affirm"?

In *Chrysler Motors Corporation v. Tom Livizos Real Estate Inc , 210 A.2d 299 (Del. Ch., 1965)*. Defendant signed an option which was under seal and which also recited a consideration of $1.00, granting to plaintiff, Chrysler, the right to purchase certain real estate. In a later dispute, defendant challenged the right of plaintiff to exercise the option after defendant's attempted withdrawal of it because a consideration of $1.00 had not in fact been paid. Defendant's view that while the seal alone would have made the option irrevocable, because a consideration of $1.00 had been stated but not paid, this made the alleged option no more than an offer which could be withdrawn at any time. The court disagreed and upheld the right of plaintiff to exercise the option.

What would you counsel your client to do if the client was seeking an option from someone and the option form recited a consideration of $1.00? Is $1.00 really a valuable consideration? Why isn't it just nominal and of no effect? Would the decision be different if the option was not under seal in addition to the one dollar not being paid.

Johnson v. Norton Housing Authority, 375 Mass 192, 375 N.E. 2d 1209 (Mass., 1978). In this case for damages when real property was taken by eminent domain by a state agency, the court ruled that damages were limited by the amount stated in the option agreement ($20,000) and not a jury award of $53,000 which was based on the land's value. The court found that the lower award was proper because the option agreement had stated that this would be the consideration, and that it was the fair market value, if the option was exercised or if the state proceeded by eminent domain during the option period. The estate of the seller tried to state that the option was not valid because while it stated in part "in consideration of the sum of One Dollar ($1) and other valuable consideration in hand to the undersigned [the grantor of the option] paid" the dollar was never paid. The Massachusetts Supreme Judicial Court met this in two ways. First, the option was under seal and this was sufficient to make it enforceable. It recited 'WITNESS OUR HANDS AND SEALS" which the court said is a recital of sealing within the Massachusetts statute. "A recital that it [the option agreement] was signed under seal...has the effect of a sealed instrument." Second, "[t]he mere nonpayment of the dollar does not show conclusively that there was no consideration. It would be sufficient if it could be shown that the dollar was bargained for and that the parties intended that it would be paid in the future."

Once again, to avoid litigation, what should the optionee do if a dollar is recited as consideration?

Berryman v. Kmoch, 221 Kan. 304, 559 P.2d 790 (Kan., 1977). In this case the optioner's attempted revocation of the offer contained in the option during the option period (120 days) was a success. The court found that the nonpayment of the $10 stated as consideration, and the failure of the optionee to establish that money spent by him to interest others in joining him in the purchase of the land could be considered "other valuable consideration" which was also recited in the contract made the option fail for lack of consideration. The optionee also failed in an attempt to establish promissory estoppel as an alternate ground for making the option enforceable, as the court rejected his argument that expenses incurred showed reliance upon the promise.

"In order for the doctrine of promissory estoppel to be invoked as a substitute for consideration the evidence must show (1) the promise was made under such circumstances that the promisor reasonably expected the promisee to act in reliance on the promise, (2) the promisee acted as could reasonably be expected in relying on the promise, and (3) a refusal by the court to enforce the promise must be virtually to sanction the perpetration of fraud or must result in other injustice.

The requirements are not met here. This was an option contract promising to sell the land to appellant. It was not a contract listing the real estate with Kmoch for sale to others. Kmoch was familiar with real estate contracts and personally drew up the present option. He knew no consideration was paid for the same and that it had the effect of a continuing offer subject to withdrawal at any time before acceptance. The acts which appellant urges as consideration conferred no special benefit on the promisor or on his land. The evidence which appellant desires to introduce in support of promissory estoppel does not relate to acts which could reasonably be expected as a result of extending the option promise. It relates to time, effort, and expense incurred in an attempt to interest other investors in this particular land. The appellant chose the form of the contract. It was not a contract listing the land for sale with one entrusted with duties and obligations to produce a buyer. The appellant was not obligated to do anything and no basis for promissory estoppel could be shown by the evidence proposed.

An option contract can be made binding and irrevocable by subsequent action in reliance upon it even though such action is neither requested nor given in exchange for the option promise. An option promise is no different from other promises in this respect but cases are rare in which an option holder will be reasonably induced to change his position in reliance upon an option promise that is neither under seal nor made binding by a consideration, or in which the option promisor has reason to expect such change of position. (1A Corbin on Contracts, § 263, pp. 502-504.)

When an option is conditioned upon a performance of certain acts, the performance of the acts may constitute a consideration to uphold a contract for option; but there is no such condition imposed if the acts were not intended to benefit nor were they incurred on behalf of the optionor.

Now we turn to the question of revocation or withdrawal of the option-promise before acceptance.

Where an offer is for the sale of an interest in land or in other things, if the offeror, after making the offer, sells or contracts to sell the interest to another person, and the offeree acquires reliable information of that fact, before he has exercised his power of creating a contract by acceptance of the offer, the offer is revoked.

In Restatement of the Law, Second, Contracts, § 42, p. 96, it is said: 'An offeree's power of acceptance is terminated when the offeror takes definite action inconsistent with an intention to enter into the proposed contract and the offeree acquires reliable information to that effect.'

The appellant in his deposition admitted that he was advised in July, 1973, by telephone that Berryman no longer wanted to be obligated by the option. Appellant further admitted that he was advised in August, 1973, by a representative of the Federal Land Bank, which held a substantial mortgage on the land, that Berryman had disposed of this land. The appellant's power of acceptance was terminated thereby and any attempted exercise of the option in October came too late when you consider the appellant's own admissions.

Summary judgment was therefore proper and the judgment is affirmed."

Questions

1. If the court had found the option given by Berryman to be enforceable either because supported by consideration or made irrevocable because of promissory estoppel, and Berryman sold the land with Kmoch's knowledge prior to Kmoch exercising it, would the result be the same as in the case?

2. Is fraud normally an element of promissory estoppel?

3. Options Created by Statute

Norca Corporation, v. Tokheim Corporation
N.Y.S.2d 139
Supreme Court, Appellate Division, 2nd. Department, 1996.

MEMORANDUM BY THE COURT.

In an action, inter alia, to recover damages for breach of contract, the plaintiff appeals from an order and judgment (one paper) of the Supreme Court, Nassau County (Alpert, J.), entered April 11, 1995, which, inter alia, granted the respective motions of the defendants for summary judgment dismissing the complaint.

ORDERED that the order and judgment is affirmed, with costs.

If a firm offer is made for a specified period which is in excess of three months, the offer is subject to revocation at the expiration of the three month period (see, Uniform Commercial Code § 2-205, Official Comment 3; Uniform Commercial Code, § 2-205:11, at 242). An offer may be terminated by indirect revocation (see, Calamari & Perillo, Contracts, § 2-20, at 97 [3d ed.]). An offeror need not say "revoke" to effectuate a revocation (1 Farnsworth, Contracts § 3.17, at 249 [1990]). Where an offeror takes "definite action inconsistent with an intention to enter into the proposed contract", such action is considered a valid revocation (Restatement [Second] of Contracts § 43; see also, 1 Farnsworth, Contracts § 3.17, at 250 [1990]).

In the instant case, the defendant Saint Switch, Inc. (hereinafter Saint Switch), agreed to purchase the assets of the manufacturing pump division of the defendant Tokheim Corporation. On April 14, 1993, Saint Switch offered, on Tokheim Corporation letterhead, to sell fuel pumps to the appellant. The offer was firm until July 31, 1994. On August 18, 1993, more than three months after the original offer was made, Saint Switch forwarded to the appellant a new offer stating different price terms for the fuel pumps. On November 4, 1993, the appellant attempted to accept the original offer made on April 14, 1993.

We find that the offer made by Saint Switch on August 18, 1993, revoked its earlier offer made on April 14, 1993. The offer made on August 18, 1993, was inconsistent with the original offer in that it had a different price term (see, Restatement [Second] of Contracts § 43; see also, 1 Farnsworth, Contracts § 3.17, at 249-250 [1990]). In addition, it was made prior to any effective acceptance on the part of the appellant. Accordingly, the Supreme Court properly granted the respective motions of the defendants for summary judgment.

The appellant's remaining contentions are without merit.

Cardin v. Outdoor East, 481 S.E. 2d 872 (Ga.Ct. App., 1997) On a form lease lessor (appellant) granted to lessee (appellee) an 18 year lease at $2,500 per year. In the lease "appellant as lessor made various promises in writing to appellee, but the appellee made no mutual promise in return of any kind on the written form." After two years, appellee gave notice that it would not be renewing the lease and appellant sued for breach of contract. Appellant lost in both the trial and appellate courts. "The agreement is a unilateral contract in which appellant makes various promises in consideration of performance by appellee.... Appellant had a landlord-tenant relationship with appellee on a year-to-year renewable option. Appellee gave timely notice that it was canceling the agreement, which notice terminated appellee's liabilities to appellant, not only under the unilateral contract but also as imposed by statute as a tenant."

Does this mean that if appellee had wanted to stay for the whole 18 year term it could and appellant could not dislodge it but that appellee could get out at any time during the lease? Does this violate mutuality of obligation? Who is the offeror here? Who is the offeree?

C. Acceptance

Houston Dairy, Inc., v. John Hancock
Mutual Life Insurance Company

643 F.2d 1185
United States Court of Appeals, 5th Cir., 1981.

AINSWORTH, Circuit Judge:

This is an appeal from a Mississippi diversity action in which appellant Houston Dairy, Inc. attempted to recover $16,000 sent to appellee John Hancock Mutual Life Insurance Company as a "Good Faith Deposit" on a loan application which Houston Dairy claims never became binding. At the conclusion

of the nonjury trial, the district court ruled that there was a binding contract between the parties and that the $16,000 deposit represented valid, liquidated dam-
ages forfeited by Houston Dairy when it breached the contract. We reverse.

I. Facts

John Hancock mailed a commitment letter to Houston Dairy on December 30,
1977 in which it agreed to lend Houston Dairy $800,000 at 9¼% provided that
within seven days Houston Dairy would return the commitment letter with a written acceptance and enclose either a letter of credit or a cashier's check in the amount
of $16,000. The commitment letter stated the $16,000 was a "Good Faith Deposit"
and was the appropriate measure of liquidated damages to be awarded John Hancock should Houston Dairy default. Dr. Dyer, president and principal shareholder
of Houston Dairy, did not execute the letter until eighteen days later, on January 17,
1978. Along with the letter, Houston Dairy mailed a $16,000 cashier's check.

Upon receiving the returned commitment letter on January 23, an agent for
John Hancock mailed the cashier's check to the John Hancock Depository and Service Center in Champaign, Illinois, for deposit and sent the loan-closing attorney,
Harvey Henderson, the necessary information to close the loan. Meanwhile, Dr.
Dyer delivered a copy of the commitment letter to Houston Dairy's attorney and
asked him to call Henderson to ascertain his fee for closing the loan. On January 28,
the two attorneys talked and agreed to the method they would use to close the loan
and the manner in which the fee would be charged. However, on January 30, Houston Dairy was able to obtain a 9% loan from a state bank. Houston Dairy then requested a refund of its $16,000 deposit, which was refused by John Hancock.

In the district court, Houston Dairy contended that the return of the commitment letter constituted a counter offer since the seven-day time period for acceptance had expired, that John Hancock never communicated its acceptance of the
counter offer, thus allowing Houston Dairy to revoke the counter offer, which it
did on January 31. Therefore, the argument proceeds, no contract was ever
formed and Houston Dairy was entitled to a refund of $16,000.

The district court disagreed, finding that John Hancock had both waived the
seven-day limitation and validly accepted a counter offer. Accordingly, the court
held that the parties had entered into a binding contract and awarded John Hancock the $16,000 deposit as valid, liquidated damages for breach of the loan
agreement.

II. Was there a contract?

It is fundamental that a contract is formed only upon acceptance of an offer.
Just as basic is the principle that an offeror is free to limit acceptance to a fixed
time period. Restatement of Contracts § 40 (1932). Once the time period has expired, a belated attempt to accept would be ineffective. However, such an untimely attempt to accept normally constitutes a counter offer which would shift
the power of acceptance to the original offeror. 1 Corbin § 74; Restatement § 73.
Additionally, acceptance of a counter offer is established only by conforming to
the rules governing acceptance, not a separate theory of "waiver and ratification." Kurio v. United States, 429 F.Supp. 42, 64 (S.D.Tex.1970).[4]

---

4. In Kurio, the court considered an issue in contract law similar to the instant case. An
offer had been terminated by lapse of time and a belated attempt to accept the offer was

It is therefore clear in the instant case that upon expiration of the seven-day time period, John Hancock's offer terminated. Thus the action taken by Houston Dairy in signing and returning the commitment letter subsequent to the termination of the offer constituted a counter offer which John Hancock could accept within a reasonable time.

In Mississippi, the courts have long recognized that for acceptance to have effect, it must be communicated to the proposer of the offer. John Hancock contends it did accept Houston Dairy's counter offer and that the acceptance was communicated to Houston Dairy.

According to John Hancock, depositing Houston Dairy's check was itself sufficient to operate as communication of its acceptance of the counter offer. John Hancock argues that its silence plus retention of Houston Dairy's money constituted acceptance and notification. Indeed, Mississippi has specifically recognized the validity of acceptance by silence within the guidelines laid down in Restatement § 72.[5] However, the present facts do not fit within these guidelines. Houston Dairy neither had previous dealings nor had otherwise been led to understand that John Hancock's silence and temporary retention of its deposit would operate as acceptance. In addition, Houston Dairy had no knowledge that its check had been deposited in John Hancock's depository. Since Houston Dairy sent a cashier's check, it could not have known the check had even been deposited unless notified by John Hancock or its bank. No such notice arrived from John Hancock and none is required from the bank.

The Mississippi Supreme Court held in L. A. Becker v. Clardy, 96 Miss. 301, 51 So. 211 (1910) that the mere depositing of a check was insufficient to constitute acceptance of an offer. There, an offeror sent a $100 downpayment along with its order for merchandise to the offeree. As was its policy, the offeree immediately deposited the check in its account, which was later paid in due course by the bank upon which the check was drawn. However, the offeree subsequently mailed a letter to the offeror rejecting the offer and enclosed a check for $100.

---

construed as a counter offer. As in the present case, an argument was made that the original offeror could waive the untimeliness of the acceptance. After outlining the basic requirements for formation of a contract and acceptance of a counter offer, the court dismissed the "waiver" argument stating that the original offer cannot be revived once it is terminated. The original offeror may only renew the original offer or accept the counter offer implicit in the defective acceptance. Consequently, once an offer's time period has terminated, a contract may be formed only by formal acceptance of the counter offer and not by a theory of waiver of the expired time limitation. 429 F.Supp. at 63-65.

5. Restatement § 72 states as follows: § 72. Acceptance by Silence or Exercise of Dominion. (1) Where an offeree fails to reply to an offer, his silence and inaction operate as an acceptance in the following cases and in no others: (a) Where the offeree with reasonable opportunity to reject offered services takes the benefit of them under circumstances which would indicate to a reasonable man that they were offered with the expectation of compensation. (b) Where the offeror has stated or given the offeree reason to understand that assent may be manifested by silence or inaction, and the offeree in remaining silent and inactive intends to accept the offer. (c) Where because of previous dealings or otherwise, the offeree has given the offeror reason to understand that the silence or inaction is intended by the offeree as a manifestation of assent, and the offeror does so understand. (2) Where the offeree exercises dominion over things which are offered to him, such exercise of dominion in the absence of other circumstances showing a contrary intention is an acceptance. If circumstances indicate that the exercise of dominion is tortious the offeror may at his option treat it as an acceptance, though the offeree manifests an intention not to accept.

The court held that upon receipt of the order and downpayment, the offeree was "entitled to a reasonable time in which to examine and determine whether it would accept or reject (the order)....Depositing the check for collection, therefore, did not constitute acceptance of the order." Id., 51 So. at 213.[6]

John Hancock also contends that Houston Dairy was notified of its acceptance in the conversation between the attorneys for both parties on January 28. However, a review of the testimony concerning that conversation shows no communication of acceptance. Indeed, John Hancock's closing attorney testified that at the time of his conversation with Houston Dairy's attorney, he had not received the executed commitment letter and had no knowledge a counter offer had even been made. His conversation only concerned the method to be used to close the loan and the distribution of the fee to be charged, not acceptance of the counter offer. Houston Dairy cannot be deemed to have knowledge of John Hancock's acceptance simply by requesting and receiving information on the procedures for closing a loan should an agreement be reached.

III. Conclusion

In summary, Houston Dairy could not accept John Hancock's offer once the time period had lapsed. Thus, when Houston Dairy executed and returned the commitment letter several days late, it was proposing a counter offer which John Hancock could either accept or reject. Since the actions and policies of John Hancock were unknown to Houston Dairy, mere silence was not operative as an acceptance of the counter offer, no communication of acceptance having been received. Houston Dairy therefore was entitled to revoke its counter offer, which it did on January 31. Accordingly, we reverse the judgment of the district court and render in favor of Houston Dairy for the amount of its deposit, $16,000.

REVERSED.

Questions

1. What is a "commitment letter?" Is it different from a contract?
2. What is a "counter-offer?"
3. What is the significance of a cashier's check as opposed to an ordinary check?
4. What is the significance of footnote 4?

Note on Liquidated Damages

Liquidated damages are a sum of money agreed by the parties in the original contract to represent their best estimate, in advance of any breach of contract, of

---

6. John Hancock attempts to distinguish L. A. Becker by stating that the offeree in L. A. Becker did not have a policy of immediately returning checks on offers it did not wish to accept, as was John Hancock's policy here. With this argument, John Hancock suggests that since the $16,000 deposit was not returned immediately in accord with its policy, then Houston Dairy had notice the counter offer had been accepted. This argument is valid only if Houston Dairy first had knowledge of John Hancock's policy. Upon a review of the record, we have found no previous dealings or statements that would indicate knowledge by Houston Dairy of John Hancock's policy concerning offers it would not accept.

the harm that will be caused to the non-breaching party by a breach. At common law a liquidated damages clause would not be upheld unless at the time the contract was entered into the parties would have a great deal of difficulty estimating how much a breach would "cost," and the amount set out in the contract as liquidated damages was in fact a reasonable estimate of the harm which at the time of contracting one might expect to occur. The fact that a breach caused much less or much more harm was irrelevant if the clause was upheld. More recent statutory enactments (see *e.g.* Uniform Commercial Code § 2-718) uphold clauses where the amount stated in them is *either* a reasonable estimate made at the time of contracting of the harm which actually occurred *or* whether the estimate is reasonable or not the harm actually occurring is close to the amount stated in the contract. The value of such clauses is that if upheld the parties know in advance the amount for which one will be liable and the other receive and the costliness of proving damages at a trial is avoided.

Note on Waiver and Equitable Estoppel

Waiver and equitable estoppel are very important topics. We will return to them in Part IV. For the most part equitable estoppel refers to actions or statements of fact which someone relies upon as true or accurate, but in fact are not. The person making the statement may be estopped to deny its accuracy or truth. For example, someone says to me: "Is that your signature on this check?" I say "Yes." My questioner takes the check in payment of goods. The check later turns out to be a forgery of my name and the merchant sues me. I may be "estopped" (which simply means stopped) from denying that the signature is mine because I misled someone. Waiver on the other hand is not an action or misstatement of fact which causes another harm. Rather, waiver is the known and intentional relinquishment of a known right. For example, if in a contract with me there is a clause obligating you to give me a payment by the 5th day of each month and you come to me and say: "Is it OK if I make the payment on the 10th from now on" and I say "OK" we probably have a waiver. What if I later change my mind? At common law I could not retract it. Under the U.C.C. § 2-209(5) I can unless you have changed position in reliance on it. If a position were changed as a result of estoppel—for months you paid me on the 10th and I never objected—I could give you notice and demand that you pay on the 5th under both common law and the U.C.C. unless you had changed position in reliance. In either case, I could not sue you for failure to pay on the 5th nor could I cancel the contract for breach so long as the estoppel or waiver was in effect.

How does equitable estoppel differ from promissory estoppel?

Note on Acceptance

Normally a mailed acceptance is effective when sent. You deposit a written acceptance in a mailbox and it is effective when it goes into the mailbox, not when the addressee receives it. With option contracts, courts often say the acceptance is only effective when received. (See Restatement § 62). This distinction can be important when the optionee waits until almost the end of the option period to act. Also, proving it was sent may not constitute proof it was ever received. Certified mail, return receipt, is a good counseling point.

Anand v. Marple, 522 N.E.2d 281, (Ill. App. Ct., 1988). "The basic issue presented by this appeal is whether the disputed document is a valid, enforceable contract or merely preliminary negotiation, and this depends on the intent of the parties. The determination of the intent of the parties may be a question of law or fact, depending on the language set forth in the document. If the language in the document is unambiguous, construction of the alleged contract is a question of law. Interway, Inc. v. Alagna (1980), 85 Ill.App.3d 1094, 41 Ill.Dec. 117, 407 N.E.2d 615.

We note that the defendant signed the document on January 22 when she presented her counteroffer, but she did not sign it again after the plaintiff countered on January 23. It is elementary that for a contract to exist there must be an offer and acceptance, and the acceptance must comply strictly with the terms of the offer. A conditional acceptance or one which introduces new terms that vary from those offered constitutes a rejection of the original offer and becomes a counterproposal which must be accepted by the original offeror before a valid contract is formed. In this case, there was an original offer and two counteroffers, but there is no indication of mutual assent to any or all of the terms contained in the document."

Problem

Plaintiff (CTV) sought a loan of $1 million from defendant, bank, to develop a cable television system. Bank sent CTV a "commitment letter" in which it stated it would approve the loan if CTV (1) met certain conditions—including a deposit of $125,000 in escrow to cover labor costs, and the receipt by CTV of absolute non-cancelable pole line rights; and (2) accepted the commitment in writing before August 30, 1997. CTV did not meet any of the conditions nor did it send its acceptance in writing by August 30th. It went ahead and began constructing its cable system and sued bank for the loan. Bank defended saying that there was no contract because its commitment letter was really an offer which CTV could only accept by following and complying with the terms of the offer. CTV says that on August 13th., at a meeting, both representatives of CTV and bank orally agreed to a contract. CTV also states that at a public meeting a bank representative stated that bank "is committed to lending CTV sufficient funds to start the operation" and that the bank would make the loan "as soon as the paperwork is done." Bank moves for summary judgment. It quotes caselaw that "where parties do not intend to be bound until a written contract is executed no valid and enforceable contract arises on an oral understanding." Bank also relies on Restatement of Contracts 2nd § 58 which states that if an offer prescribes the manner of acceptance, the offeree must comply with its terms in order to create a contract.

If you represented CTV what would be your argument? What other facts would you look for to help support your position? If you represented bank what would be your argument? What facts would you look for to help support your position.

For additional information on this problem see *Fender & Latham, Inc. v. First Union Nat'l Bank, 446 S.E.2d 448 (Ct. Ap. S.C., 1994); Allied Steel Conveyors v. Ford Motor Co., 277 F.2d 907 (6th Cir. 1960).*

Buchbinder Tunick & Co. v. Manhattan Nat'l Life Ins. Co., 631 N.Y.S.2d 148 (A.D. 1st Dept.,, 1995). "While a revocable offer to a bilateral contract may be revoked at any time prior to acceptance, that revocation, or rejection, is effective at the moment of receipt . On the other hand, acceptance is effective upon dispatch. '[T]he contract springs into existence at the time of such mailing or sending [by the offeree], because of implied authority in the carrier of the message to receive the reply' (Wester v. Casein Co. of Am., 206 N.Y. 506, 513, 100 N.E. 488).

While the offeror may dictate that acceptance is effective only upon receipt by the offeror, that intention must be expressly stated. In this case, there was no such express requirement. In fact, the back-page disclaimer to the first late notice (the only notice that refers to a mode of communicating payment) states that '[p]ayments mailed later than 31 days after the due date will not be applied to payment of premium', thereby indicating that the payment, or in this case acceptance, could arrive after the expiration of the grace period and still have to be accepted."

Pacific Photocopy, Inc. v. Canon U.S.A., Inc., 646 P.2d 647 (Ct. Ap. Ore. 1982). Defendant, Canon, held long negotiations with plaintiff, Pacific Photocopy, over Pacific becoming one of Canon's dealers. Finally a representative of Pacific signed a credit application, a purchase order and a dealership agreement. The agreement included the following provisions: "(5) Dealer shall not be legally obligated to purchase the minimum quantities set forth in schedule A or as they may be changed from year to year;" "(6) Notwithstanding any provisions of this Agreement, Manufacturer shall not be required to fill any order placed by Dealer, and each of Dealer's orders is subject to acceptance by Manufacturer at its home office in the state of New York;" "(23) This agreement shall become effective only upon affixing the Dealer's signature, properly witnessed, followed by approval of this agreement at the Executive Office of Manufacturer by its duly authorized representative." There were signature lines for both Canon and Pacific. Canon never signed. Pacific, in the time between its signing and learning of Canon not signing, had its credit approved by Canon, was told by a District Manager that Pacific was approved as a Canon dealer, enrolled its manager in Canon's training school, received a dealer number and was put on Canon's mailing list as a dealer. About two weeks after this Pacific was informed that Canon's general manager in New York would not sign the agreement. Pacific sued for breach of contract. The trial court after hearing Pacific's evidence dismissed Pacific's case. Pacific appeals solely on the issue of whether a valid enforceable contract exists despite the lack of a writing signed by defendant.

Questions

1. Do you think the appeals court should reverse?

2. Is there a jury question here somewhere?

3. Does clause 23 require approval in writing? Could Canon's actions indicate approval? Does clause 23 allow for approval by action?

4. What effect do clauses 5 and 6 have on contract issues?

5. Do you agree with the following statement by the appellate court:

"It a fundamental rule of contract law that the provisions of an offer as to the place and manner of acceptance must be complied with. When the evidence establishes that both parties contemplated a formal written contract together with written approval by the home office of the principal, approval in those terms cannot be dispensed with, at least under the facts at bar.

We do not reach the statute of frauds issue, and we need not resolve this point.

Affirmed."

The Oregon version of Uniform Commercial Code section 2-201(1) [Statute of Frauds] provides:

"(1) Except as otherwise provided in this section a contract for the sale of goods for the price of $500 or more is not enforceable by way of action or defense unless there is some writing sufficient to indicate that a contract for sale has been made between the parties and signed by the party against whom enforcement is sought or by his authorized agent or broker. A writing is not insufficient because it omits or incorrectly states a term agreed upon but the contract is not enforceable under this subsection beyond the quantity of goods shown in such writing."

Can you think of a way to avoid the application of the Statute of Frauds? What would you like to learn about the nature of the alleged contract?

Collins, v. Thompson

679 F.2d 168
United States Court of Appeals, 9th. Cir., 1982.

[Prisoners at a state of Washington correctional facility brought a class action against the state for a reduction in the prison population because of alleged overcrowding. A consent decree was reached which provided for a reduction in the population to 656 over a period of about two and one half years with the first reduction to be to 865 by March 1, 1981, according to the consent decree. The proposed consent decree was "submitted by the state" on January 19, 1981. On February 6th the state discovered an error in that the first reduction according to a master plan attached to the decree "and incorporated by reference" referred to the initial reduction to 865 to take place by April 1, 1981 and not March 1. On February 13th the state submitted a revised consent decree listing April 1 as the correct date. On February 26th the prisoners moved for "approval of the consent decree with the March 1, 1981 date intact, or in the alternative for issuance of an amended notice to class reflecting the modification to the April 1, date." The state moved to incorporate the April 1 date. The magistrate who heard this on March 4th denied both side's motions, finding that no meeting of the minds had occurred. On May 15th the prisoners filed a notice of acceptance of the April 1 date. The magistrate found that this was an acceptance of the state's offer of February 13th, that the prisoners' attempt to obtain a March 1 date did not constitute a rejection of that offer, and that the state had not revoked its offer prior to acceptance. The state appealed this insofar as the order required a reduction of the prison population below 850.]

SKOPIL, Circuit Judge:

The state appeals from the district court's order approving a consent decree regarding the reduction of inmate population at Washington State Reformatory. We affirm.

Questions regarding formation of consent decrees are to be resolved by general contract principles. A consent decree is essentially an agreement of the parties to resolve their dispute, and the facets of agreement are analyzed by applying contract principles.

A.   The state argues that the proposed consent decree dated February 13th was not an offer. However, the state never raised this argument below. In fact, in the only memorandum in opposition to the motion for the order granting preliminary approval of the consent decree, the state called the February 13, 1981 consent decree an "offer".

Issues not presented to the trial court should not be considered on appeal, Inman-Poulsen Lumber Co. v. Internal Revenue Service, 219 F.2d 159 (9th Cir. 1955), unless injustice might otherwise result, Roberts v. Hollandsworth, 582 F.2d 496 (9th Cir. 1978), or where the issue involves only questions of law. Telco Leasing, Inc. v. Transwestern Title Co., 630 F.2d 691, 693 (9th Cir. 1980). Whether the proposed decree is an offer is a question of fact. None of the exceptions to the rule apply, and this point cannot be raised on appeal.

B.   The state argues that the prisoners' actions in strenuously pursuing the enforcement of the proposed consent decree with the March 1, 1981 date constituted a rejection of the February 13, 1981 offer.

Generally, a rejection or counteroffer ordinarily terminates the power to accept the previously-made offer. 1 Jaeger, Williston on Contracts § 51 (3d ed. 1957); 1 Corbin, Contracts § 90 (1963 & Supp.1980). However, "The offeree (has) the power to prevent his counteroffer (or even a rejection) from terminating his power of acceptance. Suppose he should say: 'I am still considering your offer; but meantime I am now willing to buy the property you offer if you will reduce your price by $500.' There is no reason why this should lead the offeror into a change of position, or why it should operate to terminate the power of accepting the original offer still under consideration." 1 Corbin, Contracts § 92. The Restatement also agrees with the above contract principle: "A manifestation of intention not to accept an offer is a rejection unless the offeree manifests an intention to take it under further advisement." Restatement (Second) of Contracts § 38 (1981).

On February 26, 1981 the prisoners moved for either (1) approval of the consent decree with the March 1, 1981 date, or, in the alternative (2) a notice to the class to reflect the change in the decree to April 1, 1981.

The district court found that "The plaintiffs' alternative motion on February 26, 1981 for a new notice to the class clearly indicated that the plaintiffs were not rejecting the entire settlement and that they fully intended settlement even if the date were the April 1st date." There is sufficient evidence such that this finding cannot be held clearly erroneous. As stated above, the objective test is used to determine questions of contract formation. The February 26th motion would not clearly indicate to a reasonable person that the prisoners were rejecting the proposed settlement offer with the April 1st date. In point of fact, the prisoners in this motion specifically indicated they were still considering the April 1st date.

The cases cited by the state for the proposition that attempts to accept a previously-rejected offer after trial or arbitration had commenced are not on point. In both cited cases, the trial court found that the plaintiffs had explicitly rejected the offer. In neither case did the offeree "manifest an intention to take (the offer) under further advisement." Restatement (Second) of Contracts § 38. In the present case, the prisoners indicated by their alternative motion that they did not consider the offer terminated.

C.   A revocation can be made by any statement which clearly implies unwillingness to contract according to the terms of the offer.

Prior to the filing of their Notice of Acceptance on May 15, 1981 the prisoners attempted to take an interlocutory appeal of the district court's refusal to approve the decree with the March 1 date. That appeal became a factor in the parties' negotiations. The state argues that its counsel's statement to the prisoners' attorney that "defendants would not discuss entry of any consent decree until plaintiffs dropped their appeal of the proposed consent decree" was a clear revocation.

The district court found that "such comments... do not indicate a clear intent to revoke, especially since defendants' counsel continually reiterated that it was their intent to enter into the agreement with the terms contained in the February 13, 1981 offer. There is no indication in the record that any action was taken by defendants prior to plaintiffs' May 15, 1981 acceptance and acquiescence which would indicate that the February 13 offer was not still open."

The statement by state counsel is clearly subject to the interpretation given by the district court, which is that the offer remained open, but that the state was unwilling to discuss the specifics of the procedure of entering into a consent decree while there was litigation pending concerning the interpretation of the previous consent decree. We cannot say that the district court's finding is clearly erroneous.

[AFFIRMED.]

Panhandle Eastern Pipeline Co. v. Smith, 637 P.2d 1020 (Wyo., 1981.) Smith, an employee of Panhandle, sued Panhandle for damages for breach of contract and won. Panhandle appealed. The suit arose out of a dispute with Panhandle. Smith was about to be discharged when Panhandle sent him a letter saying that they would not discharge him if he would agree to certain conditions set forth in the letter. Smith signed the letter, "added some handwritten notations" and again signed his name. Panhandle claimed that because Smith used a different "mode of acceptance" than that called for and because he added something to his acceptance, it was not an acceptance and there was no contract. The court stated that an exclusive "mode of acceptance" can be dictated by the offeror because the offeror controls the offer and can set any terms it wishes. It can be an unreasonable or difficult mode so long as the offeror makes it clear. Here, the offer did not make clear that Smith could add no words. Panhandle testified that in an oral conversation with Smith it made clear he should add nothing. Smith did not understand the conversation this way and the court accepts Smith's understanding. Therefore, the offeror did not make it clear that nothing could be added to the signature. The appellate court then stated:

"The requirement that no terms or conditions be added to change the contract is a different matter. The law of contract formation dictates that one who modifies an offer has usually rejected the offer and made a counteroffer, and that no contract exists unless the original offeror accepts the counteroffer. Panhandle contends that Mr. Smith made a counteroffer by adding a request on the letter to see his personnel file and to contest any mistakes he found there. An offer must be accepted unconditionally; but there is, as always, an exception to the rule. An acceptance is still effective if the addition only asks for something that would be implied from the offer and is therefore immaterial. A Panhandle supervisor, Mr. Smith, and a company machinist, who was also a union representative, all testified that all Panhandle employees had the right to see their personnel files. Panhandle's offer to withdraw its discharge and eventually reinstate Mr. Smith carried with it the implication that he would be able to see his personnel record when he was once again an active employee.

Besides reserving the right to see his personnel file, Mr. Smith wrote that his personnel file contained mistakes, and that he was having financial problems, apparently as a result of the company's actions. Williston has described the kind of acceptance Mr. Smith made as one showing 'an abundance of caution,' and Corbin has called it a 'grumbling acceptance,' which in this case it certainly appeared to be. The acceptance was unenthusiastic to be sure, but it was an acceptance nevertheless. Mr. Smith signed his name under the words "Understood, Agreed To and Accepted." He wrote that he agreed to the terms and conditions. He began performance by seeking medical help and by sending in a check to keep his insurance current. Mr. Smith wanted to be sure that he would be able to see his personnel file when he returned to work. His effort to insure that right should not block him from benefits that Panhandle had already offered to him. His 'grumbling acceptance' should stand."

Note on Employment Contracts

Employment contracts are almost always "at will." This means that the employer may fire the employee without cause at any time and the employee is free to leave at any time. This is true even if the employer promises "permanent" employment. Unless the employee gives the employer some special consideration in addition to taking a job, such statements are not considered enforceable at common law. To avoid the at will presumption, employment must be stated to be for a term of years or tenured or some definite statement as to time. Occasionally, an at will employee will argue that the terms of an employment booklet should be considered part of the employer/employee contract. These booklets most often speak in general terms about company policies, the desire for harmony etc. Occasionally, they include specifics such as no employee will be fired without a hearing, or the company's plan to set up a medical insurance or pension plan. Often the statements are so general that it is hard to find any promise but occasionally there are grounds to say that something was promised. Then, the dispute arises. Can the employee use the promise in the booklet as the basis for a lawsuit against the company. Various theories have been tried in various jurisdictions with varying degrees of success. If the employee is given the booklet before hiring, it is easy to say the booklet induced the employee to take the job and became part of the offer. But what if the employee is hired first on an at will basis and then handed the booklet which says that there are no dismissals except for cause and after a hearing? Some courts go on contract modification principles but the problem of consideration quickly looms. Faced with this, some courts use U.C.C. § 2-209(1) by analogy. That provision says a contract needs no consideration to be modified. By the way do you see why at common law consideration was needed for a modification? Other courts turned to promissory estoppel — the person relied on the promise to her detriment. Proving the detriment might be hard. The following two note cases turned to unilateral contract principles.

Pine River State Bank v. Mettille, 333 N.W.2d 622 *(Minn., 1983.)*

"Generally speaking, a promise of employment on particular terms of unspecified duration, if in form an offer, and if accepted by the employee, may create a binding unilateral contract. The offer must be definite in form and must be communicated to the offeree. Whether a proposal is meant to be an offer for a unilateral contract is determined by the outward manifestations of the parties, not by their subjective intentions. An employer's general statements of policy are no more than that and do not meet the contractual requirements for an offer. Thus, in Degen v. Investors Diversified Services, Inc., 260 Minn. 424, 110 N.W.2d 863 (1961), where the employee was told he had a great future with the company and to consider his job as a "career situation," we said these statements did not constitute an offer for a lifetime employment contract.

If the handbook language constitutes an offer, and the offer has been communicated by dissemination of the handbook to the employee, the next question is whether there has been an acceptance of the offer and consideration furnished for its enforceability. In the case of unilateral contracts for employment, where an at-will employee retains employment with knowledge of new or changed conditions, the new or changed conditions may become a contractual obligation. In this manner, an original employment contract may be modified or replaced by a subsequent unilateral contract. The employee's retention of employment constitutes acceptance of the offer of a unilateral contract; by continuing to stay on the job, although free to leave, the employee supplies the necessary consideration for the offer. We have so held in Stream v. Continental Machines, Inc., 261 Minn. 289, 293, 111 N.W.2d 785, 788 (1961), and Hartung v. Billmeier, 243 Minn. 148, 66 N.W.2d 784 (1954) (employer's promise of a bonus made after the employee started working held enforceable).

An employer's offer of a unilateral contract may very well appear in a personnel handbook as the employer's response to the practical problem of transactional costs. Given these costs, an employer, such as the bank here, may prefer not to write a separate contract with each individual employee. See Note, Protecting At Will Employees against Wrongful Discharge: The Duty to Terminate Only in Good Faith, 93 Harv.L.Rev. 1816, 1830 (1980). By preparing and distributing its handbook, the employer chooses, in essence, either to implement or modify its existing contracts with all employees covered by the handbook. Further, we do not think that applying the unilateral contract doctrine to personnel handbooks unduly circumscribes the employer's discretion. Unilateral contract modification of the employment contract may be a repetitive process. Language in the handbook itself may reserve discretion to the employer in certain matters or reserve the right to amend or modify the handbook provisions.

We conclude, therefore, that personnel handbook provisions, if they meet the requirements for formation of a unilateral contract, may become enforceable as part of the original employment contract."

Brodie v. General Chem. Corp., 934 P.2d 1263 (Wyo., 1997.) This case resolved the question of whether, once a handbook became part of the employment contract on unilateral contract or other principles, the employer could unilaterally modify the employment handbook so as to remove job security from the contract. The court said no. "A valid modification requires an offer, acceptance and consideration. Consideration to modify an employment contract to restore at-will status would consist of either some benefit to the employee, detriment to the employer or a bargained for exchange. The question of what type of consideration is sufficient cannot be answered with specificity because we have long held that absent fraud or unconscionability we will not look into the adequacy of consideration. As long as the consideration given meets the definition of legal consideration, it will be considered sufficient consideration."

Is the court's definition of consideration in accord with common law principles ("some benefit to the employee, detriment to the employer or a bargained for exchange")? Does that "or" create a problem? Note that in this case it is not a modification from at-will to something else that is at issue, but an employee with "job security" being transformed to at-will against his/her wishes.

Simmons v. United States of America, 308 F.2d 160 (4th Cir., 1962). This case concerned a fisherman who caught a specially tagged fish worth $25,000. The fish had been placed in Chesapeake Bay by the American Brewery, Inc. and state of Maryland Fish and Game officials to be part of the Third Annual American Beer Fishing Derby. Simmons claimed that he knew of the contest but did not go fishing for the express purpose of catching that fish. Indeed, for sometime after catching it he did not realize he had. In the course of discussing several issues, including Simmons liability for tax unless the prize money could be considered a gift, the court considered the requirements of acceptance of an offer to enter into a unilateral contract.

"[U]nder accepted principles of contract law on which we may rely in the absence of pertinent Maryland cases, the company was legally obligated to award the prize once Simmons had caught the fish and complied with the remaining conditions precedent. The offer of a prize or reward for doing a specified act, like catching a criminal, is an offer for a unilateral contract. For the offer to be accepted and the contract to become binding, the desired act must be performed with knowledge of the offer. The evidence is clear that Simmons knew about the Fishing Derby the morning he caught Diamond Jim III. It is not fatal to his claim for refund that he did not go fishing for the express purpose of catching one of the prize fish. So long as the outstanding offer was known to him, a person may accept an offer for a unilateral contract by rendering performance, even if he does so primarily for reasons unrelated to the offer. Consequently, since Simmons could require the company to pay him the prize, the case is governed by Robertson v. United States, 343 U.S. 711, 713-714, 72 S.Ct. 994, 96 L.Ed. 1237 (1952). There, the Supreme Court held that, since the sponsor of a contest for the best symphonies submitted was legally obligated to award prizes in accordance with his offer, the payment made was not a gift to the recipient."

Note on Silence as Acceptance

In footnote 2 of *Houston Dairy, supra,* the court discussed silence as acceptance. In *Acstar, Berjian* and *Anderson* the issue arises again. In the very last section of Part II we will find the same basic issue in slightly altered context. In a way, in these cases, silence in the circumstances is a form of conduct just as inaction may be a form of action. Do you agree with the approach of these cases? Is contract formation becoming too vague, nebulous, uncertain when a person by doing nothing does something—accepts an offer and thereby undertakes contractual liability.

Acstar Insurance Company v. American Mechanical Contractors, Inc.

621 So.2d 1227
Supreme Court of Alabama, 1993.

PER CURIAM.

The defendant/third-party plaintiff Acstar Insurance Company ("Acstar"), appeals from a summary judgment for the defendant American Mechanical Contractors, Inc. ("AMCI"), the defendant-intervenor Highland Bank ("Highland"), and the third-party defendants Roy F. Bragg and Carolyn B. Bragg and Wade M. Cline and Anita Cline.

Facts

The facts are essentially undisputed. Harbert International, Inc. ("Harbert"), a Delaware corporation specializing in public and private construction, was awarded contracts by the United States Government in early 1989 for the construction of a "multi-storage training facility" in Virginia Beach, Virginia (the "Virginia Project") and a mail processing center in Lake Mary, Florida (the "Florida Project"). AMCI, a mechanical contracting company, submitted bids to Harbert for the mechanical and plumbing work on the projects. AMCI was awarded subcontracts on the Virginia Project, on its low bid of $854,000, and on the Florida Project, on its low bid of $3,087,000.

Both subcontracts specifically required AMCI to furnish Harbert performance and payment bonds before any commencement of subcontractor's work at the job site. AMCI contacted its insurance brokers, McGriff, Seibels & Williams, Inc. ("McGriff-Seibels"), to obtain the necessary bonds. McGriff-Seibels then contacted Acstar, an Illinois corporation with its principal place of business in Connecticut. Acstar was actively involved in writing payment and performance bonds and was licensed to do business in Alabama.

On April 25, 1989, Acstar, in a letter to McGriff-Seibels, agreed to execute bonds on the projects in return for premiums in the amount of 2.4% of the contract price and "an irrevocable letter of credit in the amount of $250,000 plus executed indemnification agreement."

AMCI and Roy F. Bragg and Carolyn B. Bragg and Wade M. Cline and Anita Cline ("indemnitors"), executed an indemnity agreement. The indemnitors were the stockholders of AMCI and their spouses. The agreement contained the following provisions: "2) The Indemnitors will (a) perform all the conditions of each said bond or obligation, and any and all alterations, modifications, renewals, continuations and extensions thereof."…. "6) The Surety shall have the exclusive right to determine for itself and the Indemnitors whether any claim or suit brought against the Surety or the principal upon any such bond shall be settled or defended and the Surety's decision shall be final and binding upon the indemnitors. "7)...[I]t is expressly understood that all monies due and to become due under any contract or contracts covered by the bonds shall be held in trust, whether such monies are in the possession of the Indemnitors or otherwise, for the benefit of and for payment of all such obligations in connection with any such contract or contracts for which the Surety would be liable under any of said bonds."

Citizens and Southern National Bank ("C & S Bank") issued a $250,000 irrevocable letter of credit to Acstar on behalf of AMCI. C & S Bank subsequently assigned its rights under this letter of credit to Highland Bank. The letter of credit was to become effective upon issuance of the payment and performance bonds. Acstar's ability to draw down on the letter of credit was conditioned "in the event you deem it necessary by reason of your having executed bond(s) on behalf of American Mechanical Contractors, Inc."

Acstar issued payment and performance bonds for the two projects on May 18, 1989. On June 1, 1989, Acstar forwarded the invoice for premiums in the sum of $85,126.50 to McGriff-Seibels.

The bonds, properly executed by Acstar and AMCI, were subsequently delivered to Harbert by AMCI. On June 5, 1989, Harbert wrote to AMCI, acknowledging receipt of the bonds and pointing out that "[t]he bonding company, Acstar, is not on our list of acceptable companies." The letter further stated: "At this point, the bonds, as submitted, are not acceptable because we have no information to judge the capability of Acstar to support the liability the two bonds represent. I suggest we meet on Thursday, June 8, 1989, to discuss the matter further."

AMCI forwarded a copy of this letter, via facsimile, to Acstar on June 7, 1989, with the notation "any help you can give us is needed. We need this information for our meeting on Thursday." Responding the same day, Acstar wrote to AMCI, providing three paragraphs of financial information, including its listing in "Best's Property-Casualty Insurance Reports" (1988 edition), its proposed treasury listing on or before June 30, 1989, and a statement that its "statutory surplus is one of the highest of the approximately 600 surety companies admitted for writing surety bonds." In conclusion, the letter stated: "In view of the Harbert, June 5, 1989, letter and because you have not paid for the bonds as promised, we expect that you immediately return the original copies of the bonds for cancellation as they are null and void due to Harbert's rejection and due to your nonpayment of the premiums as agreed. "We expect return of the bond documents immediately."

AMCI did not seek return of the bonds. Harbert replied on June 13, 1989: "[A]fter receipt of additional information on Acstar Insurance Company, we have decided to accept the bonds as submitted by your firm for the above-referenced projects." The bonds, accordingly, were not returned.

On June 22, 1989, Acstar wrote to Harbert, stating, "Harbert's rejection of the bonds in its letter of June 15, 1989 to American Mechanical rendered the bonds null and void." A handwritten notation on this letter indicates that it was received on June 26, 1989.

AMCI then wrote to Acstar on June 26, 1989, confirming that "[p]ayment for the two bonds on the above-referenced jobs will be sent to your office tonight via Federal Express" and stating, "We have been given an acceptance by Harbert

International. If you are not willing to accept our check, please give me a call." A July 8, 1989, notation on this letter reads "please file in underwriting file."

On June 27, 1989, Harbert wrote to AMCI and Acstar, stating: "The bonds were never rejected by Harbert. Acceptability of the bonds was questioned, subject to receipt of additional information from Acstar. Once this information was received the bonds were fully accepted.... Acstar cannot unilaterally cancel the bonds. We have executed bonds in hand and consider them in full force and effect." Acstar did not refuse the premium payment and did not thereafter declare the bonds null and void or seek their return. Acstar did not return the premium check or call AMCI. Acstar's president, Henry Nozko, Jr., acknowledged that Acstar made no request for the return of the bonds after June 27, 1989. The bonds remained in the possession of Harbert.

Beginning in the last quarter of 1989 and continuing into the spring of 1990, AMCI went into default on both projects in terms of payment and performance, and Harbert was required to expend substantial additional sums to complete AMCI's work and to pay debts due and owing to AMCI's materialmen and suppliers. During the spring of 1990, Harbert declared AMCI in default on both the Virginia Project and the Florida Project. AMCI admitted in its answer to Harbert's complaint that it had failed to make timely payments to suppliers of labor and material and had failed to prosecute and complete its work in a timely manner. When claims by AMCI's creditors were ultimately made on the subject bonds, Acstar denied its surety obligations, reaffirmed its cancellation of the bonds, and restated its position that the bonds were both null and void.

By two letters dated April 24 and April 26, 1990, Acstar subsequently drew on the full amount of the letter of credit. The documentation presented to C & S Bank as support for the draw upon the letter of credit stated that the bonds issued by Acstar on behalf of AMCI were "still outstanding."

On June 15, 1990, Acstar notified Harbert that the payment and performance bonds were null and void. Acstar wrote to Harbert and explained that Harbert had rejected the bonds on June 7, 1989, and that Acstar had subsequently withdrawn its offer, making the bonds null and void. Thereafter, Acstar informed claimants that the performance and payment bonds were null and void. While Acstar stated that the bonds were null and void, it understood that there was exposure under the bonds because Harbert was contending that the bonds were still in force.

Acstar's denial of all claims made on the subject bonds, and its insistence that the bonds had been canceled and rendered null and void pursuant to Harbert's letter of June 5, 1989, prompted Harbert to institute this action on June 27, 1990. Harbert alleged that it had suffered losses, damage, and costs in excess of $1,000,000 on the bonds. Harbert also claimed punitive damages, alleging that Acstar's refusal to pay under the bonds had been in bad faith. Each of the defendants, Acstar and AMCI, then filed cross-claims against each other. Defendant Acstar also filed a third-party claim against the indemnitors, seeking indemnity under their indemnity agreement. Highland Bank, having been assigned the rights of C & S Bank under the $250,000 letter of credit, petitioned the court to intervene as a party defendant and to assert a cross-claim against Acstar.

In September 1991, Acstar and Harbert entered into a settlement agreement whereby Acstar, in an effort to mitigate potential exposure, paid Harbert

$680,000. Under the settlement agreement, Acstar received an assignment of Harbert's claim against AMCI for the amount of $680,000. Acstar remained exposed to claims by labor and material suppliers under the payment bonds.

I. The Validity of the Bonds

In spite of Acstar's position, during the course of this litigation, that the bonds were never in effect, Acstar now contends that the bonds were never rendered null and void, because, it says, Acstar and AMCI, after Acstar's alleged cancellation of the bonds, treated the bonds in all respects as if they were legal, binding, and in full force in effect. However, AMCI asserts, and the trial court agreed, that testimony taken from officials of Acstar indicated that the bonds had been canceled before acceptance, were never in force and effect, and were at all times null and void.

This cause came before the trial court on cross motions for summary judgment. The defendant AMCI and the indemnitors, as third-party defendants, filed their motion for partial summary judgment against Acstar, and in support of that motion regarding the validity of the bonds, submitted testimony of two of Acstar's officers, Henry W. Nozko, Jr., its president, and Robert Frazer, its vice president.

Nozko stated in his deposition: "Q. . . . My question is, what is your understanding of the position that Acstar Insurance Company has taken and takes today concerning the bonds that appear to have been issued? "A. Our position is that the bonds are null and void. "Q. And for what period of time has that been your position? "A. Since their issuance. "Q. Is it your testimony that Acstar, that any bonds issued by Acstar were never in force or effect? "A. Correct." Nozko deposition, p. 24.

The "intention of the parties at the time of making [a] contract controls, not subsequent perceptions." This Court stated in Lilley v. Gonzales, 417 So.2d 161, 163 (Ala.1982), that "the law of contracts is premised upon objective rather than subjective manifestations of intent." Additionally, the Eleventh Circuit Court of Appeals has stated that "it is well recognized in all areas of the law, that a subjective intent on the part of the actor will not alter the relationship or duties created by an otherwise objectively indicated intent."

According to those legal principles, even though Acstar's president, Nozko, testified in his deposition that the bonds issued by Acstar on May 18, 1989, were null and void, his testimony as to validity was merely a contention and should not be conclusive on the issue of whether the bonds were valid. To determine whether the bonds were valid, the trial court should have analyzed the evidence before it, which showed Acstar's objective manifestations of intent to validate the bonds when it accepted AMCI's premium payment. A detailed analysis of the communications between AMCI, Acstar, and Harbert regarding the bonds establishes that, as of June 27, 1989, when Acstar accepted AMCI's premium payment, Acstar intended that the bonds issued on May 18, 1989, be valid.

On April 25, 1989, Acstar wrote to AMCI, confirming an agreement between them that Acstar would issue two payment and performance bonds to Harbert on AMCI's behalf. That letter stated: "It is our understanding that you will forward the contracts amounting to $3,100,000 and $850,000 and an irrevocable letter of credit in the amount of $250,000, plus executed indemnification agreement. Upon receipt, we will execute payment and performance bonds at the agreed rate of 2.4%." On April 26, 1989, the indemnitors executed an indemnity agreement with Acstar on AMCI's behalf, and on May 17, 1989, C & S Bank, on behalf of AMCI, established an irrevocable letter of credit in Acstar's favor. On May 18, 1989, Acstar issued the bonds to Harbert.

On June 5, 1989, Harbert wrote AMCI a letter acknowledging receipt of the bonds, and stating: "The bonding company Acstar is not on our list of acceptable companies. At this point, the bonds, as submitted, are not acceptable because we have no information to judge the capability of Acstar to support the liability the two bonds represent." AMCI forwarded a copy of this letter to Acstar on June 7, 1989, with a notation that "any help you can give us is needed." Acstar responded the same day with a letter to AMCI providing three paragraphs of financial information. Acstar's letter stated: "In view of the Harbert, June 5, 1989, letter and because you have not paid for the bonds as promised, we expect that you immediately return the original copies of the bonds for cancellation as they are null and void due to Harbert's rejection and due to your nonpayment of the premiums as agreed."

Harbert, apparently unaware that Acstar had declared the bonds null and void, wrote to AMCI on June 13, 1989, stating, "[A]fter receipt of the additional information on Acstar...we have decided to accept the bonds...." Then, Acstar, apparently unaware that Harbert had accepted the bonds, wrote to Harbert on June 22, 1989, stating, "Harbert's rejection of the bonds in its letter of June 5, 1989,...rendered the bonds null and void." On June 26, 1989, AMCI wrote to Acstar as follows: "Payment for the two bonds...will be sent to your office tonight....We have been given an acceptance by Harbert....If you are not willing to accept our check, please give me a call."

On June 27, 1989, Harbert wrote to Acstar and AMCI, stating: "We have executed the bonds in hand and consider them in full force and effect." As promised, AMCI forwarded the premium payment to Acstar. Acstar accepted AMCI's premium payment, and from June 27, 1989, until this action was filed on June 27, 1990, Acstar never again asserted that the bonds issued on May 18, 1989, were null and void. During that time, all of the parties relied on the bonds as valid and enforceable. Acstar even stated in a letter dated October 9, 1989, to McGriff, Seibels & Williams, Inc., AMCI's insurance brokers, that AMCI was bonded by Acstar.

The foregoing correspondence establishes that AMCI and Acstar had a valid agreement, confirmed in the letter Acstar wrote to AMCI on April 25, 1989, that Acstar would undertake the role of surety in a relationship between AMCI, Acstar, and Harbert. As of May 18, 1989, AMCI had partially performed its part of the agreement by securing a letter of credit and having the indemnitors execute an indemnity agreement on its behalf. Likewise, Acstar, in performing its part of the agreement, had issued the bonds. Impliedly, Acstar was obligated to give Harbert a good faith opportunity to accept Acstar as a bonding company. The fact that Acstar, in its letters to AMCI on June 5, 1989, and June 22, 1989, may have declared the bonds issued on May 18, 1989, null and void did not relieve Acstar of its obligation under the original agreement between Acstar and AMCI to undertake the role of surety. Acstar's behavior upon learning that Harbert had approved it as a bonding company evidences the fact that Acstar understood that, upon Harbert's approval, Acstar was obligated to issue the bonds on AMCI's behalf.

In AMCI's letter to Acstar dated June 26, 1989, AMCI notified Acstar that Harbert had accepted Acstar as a bonding company and stated that payment for the bonds would be forthcoming unless Acstar objected. We conclude that AMCI's letter is prima facie evidence that on June 26, 1989, AMCI extended to Acstar an offer to validate the bonds issued on May 18, 1989, and, further, that Acstar, by its silent acceptance of AMCI's premium payment, accepted AMCI's offer to validate the outstanding bonds. Even though Nozko denied the validity of the bonds in his deposition testimony taken after Harbert commenced this action, Nozko's subjective contentions do not alter Acstar's objective manifestations of intent to create a suretyship by validating the outstanding bonds. AMCI presented no substantial evidence to rebut Acstar's showing that the bonds were valid.

Based on the foregoing, we hold that the performance and payment bonds issued by Acstar on May 18, 1989, were valid, and, for that reason, the summary judgment for AMCI is due to be reversed.

Conclusion

Based on the foregoing, we hold that the trial court improperly entered the summary judgment in favor of AMCI, the indemnitors, and Highland Bank. We hold that the trial court erred in holding that the bonds were null and void. Likewise, because we hold that the bonds were valid and enforceable, the underlying indemnity agreement did not fail for want of consideration. In addition, we also hold that Acstar was legally entitled to draw the funds under the letter of credit.

Therefore, the judgment of the trial court is hereby reversed and the cause remanded.

REVERSED AND REMANDED.

MADDOX, Justice (dissenting).

The conclusion reached by the majority appears on its face to be correct, but in reaching that conclusion the majority must apply equitable principles that were neither presented, nor argued, to the trial court. The trial court's ruling was based upon uncontradicted evidence that the bonds were null and void. To permit Acstar Insurance Company to argue before the trial court that the bonds were null and void and then to argue on appeal that they were valid seems legally inappropriate. Consequently, I must respectfully disagree with the holding of the majority.

The uncontroverted evidence shows that in the action underlying this appeal Acstar took the position that the bonds made the basis of this action had been canceled, were of no force and effect, and were at all times null and void. In fact, Acstar, on numerous occasions, requested the trial court to make a finding of fact that the bonds were null and void. As Acstar requested, the trial court found that the bonds were indeed null and void. Consequently, based on this holding, no principal-surety relationship could have existed between AMCI and Acstar.

In view of my opinion that the bonds were null and void, I likewise am of the opinion that the trial court correctly decided that the indemnity agreement executed by the indemnitors must fail for lack of consideration. Acstar's claim of indemnity against AMCI as principal and against the Braggs and the Clines as indemnitors was derived solely from the bonds, which, by Acstar's admission, were canceled and rendered null and void. The law is clear that Acstar cannot recover against the principal or an indemnitor on an indemnity agreement that is predicated upon an underlying contract that is null and void; if the underlying contract was null and void, then there was no consideration for the contract with Acstar. As a result, there can be no indemnity from either the principal or the indemnitors.

Because I believe the trial court correctly ruled that the bonds were null and void, I must also disagree with the majority's holding regarding the letter of credit proceeds recovered by Highland Bank. In short, I am of the opinion that the trial court properly entered the summary judgment in favor of AMCI and the indemnitors, holding that (1) the bonds were null and void; (2) the indemnity agreement failed for want of consideration; and (3) Acstar was not legally entitled to the funds under the letter of credit. However, I also believe that the trial court improperly ignored Acstar's settlement and assignment of rights from Harbert. Acstar had an assignment of Harbert's rights to the extent of its $680,000 settlement payment. Any monies due to be refunded to AMCI should have been set-off against this settlement payment. This includes the unearned premium payment on the bonds, plus legal interest of $98,323.07 that the trial court ordered Acstar to refund.

In addition, although the trial court, at first glance, appears to have reached the correct legal conclusion in regard to the letter of credit proceeds, I think that the court erred when it failed to consider Acstar's rights under the settlement agreement. This amount, $276,250, was also due to be set-off against Acstar's $680,000 settlement payment. The trial court failed to consider Acstar's rights under the assignment and improperly allowed AMCI, which was directly obligated for this indebtedness, to recover this money on behalf of Highland Bank.

Questions

1. Why the quick reverse by Acstar saying the bonds are good after saying they were void?

2. What role do Clines and Braggs have in the case?

3. Do you agree with the court that on June 26 AMCI made an offer to Acstar? What language used by AMCI supports that?

4. How is Acstar's keeping the check an acceptance when in *Houston Dairy* it was not?

Berjian v. Ohio Bell Telephone. Co., 375 N.E.2d 410 (Ohio, 1978.) A doctor placed an advertisement in the yellow pages of the phone book. His name was misspelled and he sued. The defendant telephone company used a limitation of liability clause as a defense. The plaintiff said that he was not bound by that clause because he never accepted the offer in which it was embodied. The court said:

"The third preliminary issue confronting this court is whether the provisions of the directory advertising agreement are enforceable since Dr. Berjian did not formally express his acceptance by signing the agreement. However, simply because the customer did not signify his acceptance by executing the agreement does not necessarily result in its unenforceability.

Although in the usual situation an offeror cannot cause the silence of the offeree to constitute an acceptance, where the relation between the parties justifies the offeror's expectation of a reply, such silence may constitute an acceptance on the part of the offeree. See Restatement of Contracts 2d § 142.

In the cause at bar, the evidence reflects that Ohio Bell, pursuant to the office manager's placement of an order for advertising in the yellow pages, sent a copy of the directory-advertising agreement to the doctor's office. Accompanying the order was a card calling to the customer's attention the terms and conditions of the agreement, and requesting notification of any changes or corrections to be made. Without further instructions from the customer, Ohio Bell proceeded to act on the order placed by the office manager.

At trial, the doctor's office manager admitted that she read both the card and the terms and conditions contained on the reverse side of the directory-advertising agreement, and that her subsequent contact with the telephone company was only for the purpose of requesting that the abbreviation "Inc." be added to the doctor's name in the yellow-pages listing.

It is clear that Ohio Bell was justified in believing that the offeree had accepted the terms and conditions of the written agreement. Not only did the doctor not notify Ohio Bell of any proposed changes, through his silence he demonstrated a willingness to accept the service at the stated rates, as evidenced by his payment of the monthly charge. As set forth in Corbin on Contracts, supra, at page 321:

'Frequently, services are rendered under circumstances such that the party benefited thereby knows the terms on which they are being offered. If he receives the benefit of the services in silence, when he had a reasonable opportunity to express his rejection of the offer, he is assenting to the terms proposed and thus accepts the offer.'

[T]he terms and conditions contained in the directory-advertising agreement constituted the contractual agreement between the parties."

Question.

1. What did the court rely on as authority for its conclusion?

Anderson Chevrolet/Olds Inc. v. Higgins, 292 S.E.2d 159 (N.C. Ct. App., 1982). Defendant leased a vehicle and failed to service it as required in the lease contract. As a result the engine was severely damaged and had to be replaced. When the vehicle first stopped running, defendant had it towed to the lessor (plaintiff's) garage. Defendant authorized plaintiff to disassemble the vehicle and determine what was wrong. Defendant's employees, at defendant's direction, examined the parts of the disassembled vehicle. Defendant did not expressly authorize plaintiff to fix the vehicle but instead did nothing. After waiting 22 days, and having heard nothing, plaintiff fixed it and presented defendant with a bill. Defendant tried to obtain possession of the vehicle without paying the bill. The court found that an implied contract existed from defendant's having the vehicle towed to plaintiff's garage, having had employees examine it, making no effort to remove it from the garage, and seeking to obtain possession of it after it was repaired.

D. Rejection

In several preceding cases we saw that occasionally silence can mean acceptance. This is, however, a rare occurrence. Most often acceptance requires some positive act, some manifestation by the offeree that the offeree wants to have a contractual relationship with the offeror. This is more true where an objective interpretation of contract controls over a subjective. How can nothing be an objective manifestation of something, an acceptance?

Rejection, on the other hand, at common law occurred very easily and often without the parties realizing it. A person responding with any different terms was deemed not to have accepted what was offered; if you didn't accept, you rejected. "Will you take a check?" or "Can I make installment payments" could be construed as "No." Sometimes, courts would say that a person responding in this way was making an inquiry or a suggestion and intended to leave the offer open, not reject it, until she could learn whether or not the offeror would respond favorably to the inquiry. If the offeror said no, the original offer was still open. Very often, however, any inquiry, suggestion, change from the original terms offered resulted in courts saying that the offer was rejected. Once rejected, it was gone — the offeree could not turn around and accept it.

In Part F we will consider the impact of the U.C.C. on these common law Rules. Basically the U.C.C. turns outright rejection into an acceptance with suggestions for additional or different terms. This stands the common law on its head. At common law the most that could happen when the offeree responded with a new term was to find that the new term did not act to reject the offer. Under the U.C.C. if the response looks like an acceptance except for the new term (see introduction to Parts E and F) the Code treats it as an acceptance and the new term as a suggestion for an addition or change to the contract.

In the next case we see the common law rule at work.

In re Pago Pago Aircrash of January 30, 1974
Dibley, Van Boxtel, v. Pan American World Airways, Inc.

637 F.2d 704
United States Court of Appeals, 9th Cir., 1981.

PER CURIAM:

Pan American World Airways, Inc. (Pan Am) appeals the judgments in favor of the survivors of passenger Dibley and the Estate of passenger Van Boxtel, respectively, for a settled amount of general damages, attorney's fees, costs incurred in post-settlement discovery and pre-judgment interest as entered by the District Court on February 16, 1979. We note jurisdiction under 28 U.S.C. § 1291 and vacate the judgments and remand the causes for trial on the issue of damages.

I. BACKGROUND

On January 30, 1974, a Pan Am Boeing 707 crashed near Pago Pago. Passengers Dibley and Van Boxtel died in the accident. Numerous suits arising from this accident were filed against Pan Am. The Judicial Panel on Multidistrict Litigation consolidated these suits for pretrial proceedings in the Central District of California, and later the parties stipulated that the actions be transferred there for all purposes. Boeing was a co-defendant, and Pan Am named the United States as a third party defendant. Because both cases involved here raise identical issues, we reference Dibley only.

In the bifurcated trial during the summer of 1978, the jury returned a verdict against Pan Am on the issue of liability. Settlement negotiations followed between Alpert, associate director of claims for Pan Am's insurance company, and Cathcart, attorney for the Dibleys. The negotiations culminated on August 15, 1978, in settlement offers contingent on acceptance by Dibley of numerous conditions.[1] September 1, 1978 was the deadline for acceptance of these offers.

On August 31, 1978, Cathcart sent a letter (Dibley's reply) to Tucker, attorney for Pan Am, which allegedly accepted the settlement offers.[2] On September 6, 1978, Alpert telephoned Cathcart's office and withdrew the offers, stating that the offers had not been accepted under the conditions proposed. A letter followed reiterating the withdrawal of the offers.

In a summary proceeding on December 18, 1978, the District Court granted Dibley's motion to enforce the settlement agreement.

II. ISSUE

We find the dispositive issue to be the validity of Dibley's reply as an acceptance of Pan Am's offer.

III. DISCUSSION

We find that the validity of the reply as an acceptance must be determined by California law. The parties stipulated to transfer these actions to the Central District of California for all purposes. Pan Am has argued that California law ought to apply. Appellees have not contested this issue. California law definitively states: An acceptance must be absolute and unqualified, or must include in itself an acceptance of that character which the proposer can separate from the rest, which will conclude the person accepting. A qualified acceptance is a new pro-

---

1. The only condition relevant to our decision is condition 1): "Conditions precedent to the settlement of any passenger claims arising out of the captioned accident. "1) A complete release of all defendants including, but not limited to, Pan American, the Estates of the deceased crew members, The Boeing Company, the United States of America and their agents, servants and employees."

2. The full text of Dibley's reply is as follows: "I have been instructed by my referring counsel to accept the following offers of settlement:

"HILL	$130,000.00
DIBLEY	150,000.00
IAFETA	75,000.00
TANIELA	200,000.00
VAN BOXTEL	250,000.00

"All of the other offers of settlement are not acceptable. It is my understanding Mr. Alpert wishes releases executed in favor of the United States, Boeing and Pan American. It is my further understanding that neither the United States nor Boeing has authorized Mr. Alpert to negotiate on their behalf. Assuming that Judge Byrne follows the verdict of the advisory jury, there will be an outstanding cost bill of the United States and Boeing for which the settling parties would remain liable, thus, unless Mr. Alpert can get Boeing and the United States to forego their cost bills, at least as to the settling parties, we have serious problems with these added conditions. My clients are willing that a release of all three parties be given as long as there is no further potential liability on their part for costs. Accordingly, if you will forward to me appropriate releases, I will see that they are executed and, where necessary, seek Court approval of these settlements."

posal." Cal.Civ.Code § 1585 (West). If the acceptance contains conditions not embraced in the offer or adds new terms, there is no meeting of the minds and no acceptance.

Here, Pan Am made its settlement offer contingent on eight written conditions as stated, only one of which is relevant here: "A complete release of all defendants including, but not limited to, Pan American, the Estates of the deceased crew members, The Boeing Company, the United States of America and their agents, servants and employees." Dibley's reply to Pan Am's offer and conditions stated: "(U)nless Mr. Alpert can get Boeing and the United States to forego their cost bills, at least as to the settling parties, we have serious problems with these added conditions. My clients are willing that a release of all three parties be given as long as there is no further potential liability on their part for costs."

Dibley contends that the quoted language was merely an inquiry about the relationship between Dibley, Boeing, and the United States. Since Alpert had no authority to negotiate on behalf of Boeing or the United States, Dibley argues, the "complete release of all defendants" condition was meaningless. Pan Am, on the other hand, argues that it could condition its offer on any terms it chose. Since Dibley's reply did not accept the release condition, Pan Am contends, the letter was not a valid acceptance.

We do not find Dibley's inquiry theory persuasive. Pan Am's offer was contingent on Dibley's release of all the defendants. Pan Am did not need authority from Boeing and the United States to make this condition because Pan Am was not bargaining away anything on their behalf. In response, Dibley proposed a quid pro quo: He would release all defendants if Boeing and the United States agreed to forego the costs outstanding against him. This added a new term, rendering Dibley's response a qualified acceptance and a new proposal. Cal.Civ.Code § 1585 (West). Therefore, as a matter of law, the Dibley reply was not a valid acceptance.[3]

Because we find no valid contract of settlement, we need not reach the other issues raised by this appeal.

The judgments of the District Court are vacated and the cause is remanded to the District Court for trial on the damage issues.

VACATED.

Questions

1. If Dibley did not give an acceptance, did he make a counteroffer?

2. Is every rejection, other than just a "NO" a counteroffer?

3. What is a counteroffer?

---

3. Dibley attempts to salvage the settlement by claiming that Alpert's written response of September 7 "validated" Dibley's reply as an acceptance. Alpert's September 7th letter, however, reiterated the same conditions precedent to the consummation of any settlement. Thus, because Alpert continued to assert the necessity of all eight conditions in any agreement, we reject Dibley's validation theory.

E. Counteroffer

Acceptance, rejection and counteroffer are all linked together. X makes an offer to sell goods to Y. If Y says "No" or "I reject" or "No thanks" or anything else that indicates no intention to have a contract, there is a rejection. If Y says nothing, there is very probably no contract, because while silence can lead to contractual liability, as noted in the introduction to Part D, this is rare.

Often, however, Y will not just say "No." Y will say something like: "$100 seems like a lot—will you take $80?" Clearly here Y has not accepted, but has Y only rejected or has Y made a counteroffer? If X says "Yes" to Y's response, is there a contract? All of this turns on intent. Was Y making an inquiry, or was Y making an offer of her own?

Remembering that the offeror controls the terms of the offer what if X and Y go back and forth with offers and counteroffers and finally X ships the goods to Y. If the last communication to be made was made by X and courts determine that it was an offer or counteroffer and that Y accepted the goods after receiving this communication, then probably Y, at common law, accepted X's terms when Y accepted the goods.

The U.C.C. tends to turn counteroffers into acceptances. (See introduction to Part D.) Under section 2-207 if the offeree responds with a communication that indicates a desire to contract (e.g.: "we are pleased to fill your order and will do so on the following terms" and then fills in blanks with the same quantity, price, shipping date etc. that are in the buyer's offer) but puts in different or additional terms ("it is understood that these goods are sold without warranties and seller will not be responsible for their failure to function properly") at common law we have a counteroffer. Under the U.C.C. we have an acceptance. Furthermore, the offeree's new terms are usually only suggestions which do not become part of the contract. More on this in Part F.

For now—at common law, and common law still governs most contracts, a response which deviates from the offer is not only a rejection but if it contains new terms may very well be a counteroffer which the other party can accept. Counseling point: say no to the offer and introduce your next words with "I'd be willing to talk over and consider some other terms, however; for example, without making this an offer what do you think of…" If responding in writing: "I cannot agree to the terms of your offer but would like to consider other possibilities with you. For purposes of negotiation only and not as an offer what do you think of…."

Often preprinted forms are used. Offerors and Offerees just fill in blanks and have printed terms that favor the user of the form. At common law, these would never create a contract. Under the U.C.C. they may. If the Code were in effect and applied to the *Craddock* case might it have led to a different result?

G. H. Craddock, v. Greenhut
Construction Company, Inc.

423 F.2d 111
United States Court of Appeals, 5th. Cir., 1970.

GEWIN, Circuit Judge:

Appellant, G. H. Craddock, d/b/a Southern Heat Pump Company, brought an action in the United States District Court for the Northern District of Florida against appellee, Greenhut Construction Company, Inc., for breach of contract to employ Craddock as a subcontractor on a construction project. This appeal is taken from an order of the district court granting Greenhut's motion for summary judgment. We reverse.

The controversy arises from Craddock's thwarted efforts to obtain the subcontract for the heating and air-conditioning of 300 housing units to be constructed at Eglin Air Force Base, Pensacola, Florida. Craddock is a mechanical contractor. For the five years immediately prior to the critical events, he was primarily engaged in construction work in the Panama Canal Zone. While between jobs in Panama, Craddock came to the States in search of work. He met Dudley Greenhut, appellee's president, in Charleston, South Carolina, where both had come to bid on another government project. There they discussed Greenhut's plan to submit a bid for the general contract for the forthcoming Eglin project, and it was agreed that Craddock would furnish Greenhut with a bid for the heating and air-conditioning portion of the work.

On 21 June 1967, Craddock sent Greenhut a bid of $322,500.00 not including the cost of a payment and performance bond. A second bid letter dated 17 July 1967 quoted the lump sum of $328,000.00 including the cost of acquiring the bond. Greenhut used Craddock's June 21 bid plus the normal cost of a bond in preparing its bid on the general contract. On 20 July 1967, Craddock sought and obtained a letter from Greenhut which provided in part:

"We wish to advise, at this time, that in the event that we are awarded the above subject contract, that we will award you a contract covering Section 28, HEATING AND AIR CONDITIONING, as outlined in your letter of June 21, 1967, providing that we are furnished with a Performance Bond two (2) weeks thereafter. This bond must be furnished with good and sufficient surety or securities acceptable to the General Contractor and the Government."

On 8 August 1967, Greenhut was awarded the general contract for the Eglin project. It informed Craddock, by means of a letter from its president dated 12 August 1967, that unless it received the performance bond by 17 August 1967 it would 'of necessity consider the matter closed.' Craddock received this letter on 15 August 1967, and replied by a letter bearing that date. Craddock referred to the Greenhut letter of 20 July 1967, and reaffirmed his intention to comply with its terms. In reference to the letter of 12 August, he stated that he would do his best to expedite the bonding procedure. On 15 August 1967, Greenhut sent Craddock a telegram noting that it had been requested by the government to furnish the name of the mechanical subcontractor and stating:

"Due to your inability to furnish a performance and payment bond, which we have requested from you several times, we deem it necessary to consider another source for the project."

The bonding company that Craddock had previously used was not licensed to issue bonds in the United States. Consequently, Craddock had been negotiating with Fidelity & Deposit Company of Maryland for the payment and performance bond. On 16 August 1967, an agent of this company called Dudley Greenhut and informed him that Fidelity & Deposit was prepared to issue a bond for Craddock. Greenhut stated that it would be unnecessary to furnish the bond, since Greenhut was obtaining another subcontractor for the project.

Craddock, through his counsel, sought a clarification of the situation by a letter of 22 August 1967. Greenhut received the letter but made no response. Subsequently, Craddock filed suit alleging breach of contract. Greenhut denied the existence of a contract and counterclaimed for the additional cost of the subcontractor who replaced Craddock.[2] Both parties filed motions for summary judgment.

The court determined that Greenhut's letter of 20 July 1967 was a rejection of the offers embodied in Craddock's bid letters, and a counteroffer to Craddock. This counteroffer was found to call for acceptance by the act of furnishing an acceptable performance bond. The manifestations by Craddock of his intention to furnish the bond were held insufficient to form a contract since the terms of the offer required the act itself. By the court's reasoning, Greenhut was free to withdraw its offer, and did withdraw it prior to effective acceptance.

Craddock contends that the court erred in classifying the parties' dealings as an abortive unilateral contract. Quite to the contrary, he argues that the circumstances clearly reveal a bilateral agreement to which the obtaining of a performance bond was a condition subsequent.

In determining that Greenhut's offer contemplated a unilateral contract, the district court cited Ballou v. Campbell, as announcing rules which were dispositive. In Ballou, the plaintiff alleged that a shareholder of a failing corporation had promised to give all his capital stock to the plaintiff if he would take over management of the corporation and make it financially successful. Plaintiff allegedly accomplished the corporate rejuvenation and sued the estate of the since-deceased shareholder for specific performance. Faced with a classic unilateral contract, the court was primarily concerned with questions of consideration and mutuality. While Ballou is relevant for its citation of the definition of 'unilateral' and 'bilateral' contracts found in the Restatement of Contracts, it is of little help in resolving the precise issue of the present case.

The parties are in agreement that the district court properly determined Greenhut's 20 July 1967 letter to be a rejection of the offer in Craddock's bid letters. The wisdom of this concession is borne out by the Florida cases requiring strict conformity to an offer to accomplish an effective acceptance. There is also agreement that the Greenhut letter constituted a counteroffer to Craddock. The controversy centers on the interpretation of this counteroffer. The precise issue is

---

2. Greenhut did not prosecute this counterclaim in the district court or on appeal, and the judgment of the district court did not treat it. We observe that the claim is apparently inconsistent with Greenhut's contention that no contract was formed.

whether the phrase, 'providing that we are furnished with a Performance Bond two (2) weeks thereafter,' constituted the exclusive means for accepting the offer, or expressed a condition subsequent modifying Greenhut's obligation to award the subcontract.

We deem neither interpretation of the phrase to be patently required by the language of the letter. Its wording lies somewhere between the clearest expression of either intention. In this situation, we consider the application of two canons of construction appropriate. § 31 of the Restatement of Contracts provides:

"In case of doubt it is presumed that an offer invites the formation of a bilateral contract by an acceptance amounting in effect to a promise by the offeree to perform what the offer requests, rather than the formation of one or more unilateral contracts by actual performance on the part of the offeree."

The expression of a similar position by one commentator explains the policy behind the presumption:

"Whenever possible...a court would and should interpret an offer as contemplating a bilateral rather than a unilateral contract, since in a bilateral contract both parties are protected from a period prior to the beginning of performance on either side."

A second guidepost for resolution of such a doubtful situation requires that unclear language be resolved against the draftsman or the party for whose benefit the term is inserted. The letter of 20 July 1967 was composed and given by Greenhut, and the bonding provisions were inserted exclusively for its benefit. It had the power and the ability to clearly require that its offer must be accepted by the act of furnishing the bond. These considerations lead us to conclude that the critical phrase was a condition subsequent which would limit Greenhut's obligations under the contract, and that the district court erred in interpreting it as defining the exclusive means of accepting the counteroffer.

Under our construction of the counteroffer, acceptance would entitle Craddock to the subcontract in the event Greenhut received the general contract. In return Craddock would be bound to the price quoted in its bid. Greenhut is still assured of receiving a bond, since the unexcused failure of Craddock to satisfy the condition would terminate Greenhut's contractual obligations. Greenhut has not contended that Craddock failed to manifest assent to its counteroffer, but adhering to its unilateral theory, has contended that these manifestations were legally insufficient. Craddock's acceptance is documented in his letter of 15 August 1967.[9]

Having decided that a bilateral contract was contemplated and formed, it remains to be determined whether Craddock's failure to satisfy the condition of furnishing a performance bond relieves Greenhut of its obligation to award the subcontract to Craddock. § 306 of the Restatement of Contracts states in part:

---

9. This letter states in part: Reference is made to your letter of 20 July 1967, wherein you state that if you are awarded the above subject contract that you will in turn award Southern Heat Pump Company a contract covering Section 28C, Heating and Air Conditioning, as outlined in my letter of 21 June 1967, provided you are furnished with a performance and payment bond two (2) weeks thereafter. It is my intention to fully comply with this request.

"Where failure of a party to a contract to perform a condition or a promise is induced by a manifestation to him by the other party that he cannot or will not substantially perform his own promise…the duty of such other party becomes independent of performance of the condition or promise."

Greenhut's letter of 12 August 1967 demanded receipt of the bond by 17 August 1967. Its telegram sent on 15 August 1967 stated that it was considering 'another source for the project.' On 16 August 1967, with the possibility of furnishing the bond by Greenhut's accelerated deadline remaining, Dudley Greenhut told the agent of Fidelity & Deposit that it was unnecessary to furnish the bond for Craddock because Greenhut was obtaining another subcontractor for the project. Greenhut made no response to the 22 August 1967 letter from Craddock's counsel seeking a clarification of its position. Dudley Greenhut testified that his conduct was an effort to 'put the club' to Craddock and speed up the bonding process, and that he would have been willing to take him back as mechanical subcontractor at any time before actual work began in September of 1967.[12] Regardless of subjective attitude, we feel Craddock could reasonably assume from Greenhut's arbitrary conduct, that he had lost the subcontract and that the furnishing of the performance bond was a useless gesture.

On the present state of the record, there is a reasonable basis to order that judgment be rendered for Craddock. However, in view of the original summary disposition of the case, and the posture in which it is presented to this court, we remand it for the district court to determine whether there are additional facts which the parties can develop that would lead to a different conclusion. The judgment of the district court is reversed and the cause is remanded for proceedings consistent with this opinion.

Reversed and remanded.

Note on Conditions

The court in *Craddock* refers to conditions subsequent. Although today the distinction between conditions precedent and subsequent is somewhat out of favor, courts and counsel still use the terms. Principally, both refer to the time when someone must act under a contract. In *Craddock* plaintiff and defendant were bound to contractual duties but if plaintiff failed to perform a condition whose performance would arise only after the contract was entered into, the defendant would be free to find another contractee without liability to plaintiff. In short if Craddock didn't provide a performance bond within two weeks, Greenhut could find someone else to do the work without breaking the contract and having liability to Craddock. Note also, that where a condition is involved, as in the case, Craddock is not liable to Greenhut if he cannot get the bond. Craddock has promised to do the heating and air conditioning; Greenhut has promised to

---

12. The deposition of Dudley Greenhut contains the following: A. I can't speak for Mr. Craddock. I think you have had people that found you were probably a little slow in getting something up and used a club if proper to get it, to put you in a corner to try and force you to do something faster, is that not true, sir? Q. But still in all the answer you just gave me, if Mr. Craddock had walked in with the bond on August 30th or September 1st, August 30th, you would have substituted his name for someone else's name and gone on with the job because of his low price, is that correct? A. Very definitely, sir.

pay him for this (see footnote nine and text of opinion at that note.) A bilateral contract was formed subject to a condition subsequent. The condition is that Greenhut is obliged to give the air conditioning and heating work to Craddock only if Craddock provides a bond. If Craddock doesn't get the bond, does this mean that no one has any obligation to do anything? Does this, in turn, mean that Craddock really hasn't promised anything to Greenhut because to get out of the contract all Craddock has to do is not get a bond and therefore because he has made no binding promise to Greenhut there is no consideration for Greenhut's promise? If that were the case, there would be no contract and Greenhut would owe Craddock nothing. How do you conclude the court construed the condition so as to make Craddock's promise a valuable consideration for Greenhut's promise? Review *Wood v. Lucy, Lady Duff Gordon, supra.*

F. Uniform Commercial Code Section 2-207 and the Imperfect Acceptance that Nevertheless Creates a Contract

In the cases thus far in this part we have considered more or less classic contract formation. An offeror seeks either a return promise or a performance. A contract is formed when the offeree gives either the promise or the performance, whatever the offeror requested in the offer. At common law, the acceptance had to exactly conform to the offer—to use the classic phrase be the "mirror image" of the offer. In *Collins, supra* and in *Panhandle, supra*, a serious question arose as to whether or not a response by the offeree was an acceptance because it added new matter. Is a person's response which does more than say "I accept" still an acceptance if it makes an inquiry or if it is a "grumbling" or "cautious" acceptance (see *Panhandle*).

In the cases in this section we look at offers that have responses that would at common law have been called rejections or counteroffers. Here, however, these responses are considered acceptances, even though they contain new or different clauses not in the original offers. This is because U.C.C. § 2-207 has changed the law in contracts involving sales of goods and in other contracts to which courts apply 2-207 by analogy.

As you read these cases consider the impact of § 2-207. It is in three subdivisions but really has four parts. The first part is subdivision (1) up to the "unless clause." This part says that an expression of acceptance is an acceptance even though it contains new terms. At common law new terms turned a response into a rejection, though possibly a counteroffer. The Code says it is an acceptance. *E.g.:* "We were pleased to receive your order and will be happy to ship the goods in accordance with your instructions." [Here the form has blanks for quantity, price, shipping date etc. all of which mirror the offer or order.] Then comes the printed part. "There are no warranties of any kind with these goods and we are not responsible for any damages for equipment or other failures which they may cause." Is this an acceptance? Yes. What happens to the no warranties clause if it conflicts with the order. The second part of § 2-207 found in sub (2) in essence says it drops out. You will see why in the cases. Thus, the offeror gets the goods on her terms. Can the offeree make it clear she wants the no warranties term to control and there is no deal if it does not? Yes—that is the third part of 2-207 found in the "unless" clause of sub (1). The offeree says I accept your offer but only if you expressly accept my different terms found in the acceptance. This acts not as an offer but a counteroffer. What if the offeror does not accept the offeree's terms? Then, there is no contract. What if after sending the form, the offeree ships the goods? If the offeror accepts them, conduct probably creates a contract. What are the terms then? The fourth part of § 2-207 comes into play. Sub (3) says if the writings don't create a contract but conduct does, the terms are those on which the writings agree plus terms added by the Code. The writings don't agree on warranties but the Code implies some (merchantability; fitness, in some cases) warranties. Result: buyer (original offeror) gets some of what it wants.

Counseling point: be the offeror. Read the paperwork.

Columbia Hyundai, Inc., v. Carll Hyundai, Inc.

484 S.E.2d 468
Supreme Court of South Carolina, 1997.

WALLER, Justice:

This is a contract case. The sole issue on appeal is whether the trial judge properly submitted the issue of the existence of a contract to the jury. We find that he did and, accordingly, affirm.

FACTS

In early 1993, appellant, Columbia Hyundai, Inc. (Gibbes)[1] , negotiated with respondent, Carll Hyundai (Carll) to purchase Carll's Hyundai automobile dealership. After several months of negotiations between the parties and their attorneys, and numerous revisions to drafts of a proposed contract, Carll submitted an "Agreement for Purchase and Sale of Assets" to Gibbes on July 20, 1993. The contract contained a provision to the effect that "This Agreement may not be amended, changed or modified except by instrument in writing signed by the parties to be charged." Paragraph 1(a) of the agreement, concerning the assets to be transferred, reads "All of Seller's right title and interest in and to all saleable new Hyundai vehicles in existence at the close of business on the last business day before final closing date...." Gibbes signed the agreement but added the words "current year" such that the agreement now reads "all saleable current year new Hyundai vehicles." Upon receipt of the agreement from Gibbes one week later, Carll advised the "counter-offer" was rejected.[2]

---

1. George Gibbes was president and sole shareholder of Columbia Hyundai. They are referred to collectively herein as Gibbes.

2. The dispute of the parties centers on whether this insertion merely relieved Gibbes of the obligation to purchase any 1992 new vehicles or, as Carll testified, whether insertion of the term "current year" could be interpreted to render Gibbes liable for only 1993 or 1994 new vehicles, but not both. The alteration was critical to Carll as it planned to finance $600,000.00 in new vehicles for Gibbes until such time as Gibbes was approved as a Hyundai dealer. If Gibbes was not obligated to purchase the 1994 vehicles, Carll could be

Gibbes instituted this suit for breach of contract and specific performance. The trial judge submitted the issue to the jury which found there was no contract. Gibbes appeals.

ISSUE

Did the court err in failing to direct a verdict for Gibbes on the ground that, under section 36-2-207 of the South Carolina Uniform Commercial Code, a contract was formed as a matter of law?[3]

DISCUSSION

Gibbes contends a contract was formed as a matter of law under S.C.Code Ann. § 36-2-207 (1976) (hereinafter § 2-207), such that it was entitled to a directed verdict. Under the facts of this case, we find the trial judge properly submitted the issue of the existence of a contract to the jury.

At common law, a purported acceptance containing terms which did not "mirror" those of the offer operated as a rejection thereof and amounted to a counteroffer. S.C.Code Ann. § 36-2-207 [this is the South Carolina version of Uniform Commercial Code § 2-207] was designed to abrogate the rather severe consequences of the "mirror image" rule[4] . It provides, in pertinent part:

"(1) A definite and seasonable expression of acceptance or a written confirmation which is sent within a reasonable time operates as an acceptance even though it states terms additional to or different from those offered or agreed upon, unless acceptance is expressly made conditional on assent to the additional or different terms. (2) The additional terms are to be construed as proposals for addition to the contract. Between merchants such terms become part of the contract unless: (a) the offer expressly limits acceptance to the terms of the offer; (b) they materially alter it; or (c) notification of objection to them has already been given or is given within a reasonable time after notice of them is received."

Adoption of § 2-207 resulted from what is commonly known as "the battle of the forms" in which parties exchange preprinted, standardized forms to finalize their bargain, which forms tend to use "boilerplate language" and omit material terms. Weisz Graphics Division v. Peck Industries, Inc., 304 S.C. 101, 403 S.E.2d 146 (1991). See also Official Comment 1 to § 36-2-207 (typical situation covered by § 2-207 involves memoranda or acknowledgment confirming oral agreement or letter intended as confirmation of agreement which adds further minor suggestions or proposals); Brown, Restoring Peace in the Battle of the

---

forced to sell them for a reduced price, as it would no longer be an "authorized Hyundai dealer."

3. Carll contends section 2-207 is inapplicable as the sale of a business does not involve "goods." This contention was not specifically raised to the trial judge and is therefore not preserved. In any event, although there is a split of authority, the majority view is that the sale of a business is treated as the sale of "goods" under the UCC. See Annotation, 4 A.L.R.4th 912; White and Summers, Uniform Commercial Code §§ 1-2 at p. 5 (4th Ed.1995).

4. Notwithstanding the beneficent intentions surrounding adoption of section 2-207, it has been the subject of much criticism and has been recognized by numerous commentators as "chaotic."

Forms…69 N.C.L.Rev 893; White and Summers, Uniform Commercial Code §§ 1-3 at p. 6 (4th Ed. 1995); Owens-Corning Fiberglas v. Sonic Dev. Corp., 546 F.Supp. 533, 538 (D.C.Kan.1982) (when each party uses their own form, it is to be expected that acceptance will not correspond to terms of offer in all respects); C. Itoh & Co. Inc. v. Jordan Intern. Co., 552 F.2d 1228 (7th Cir.1977) (in battle of forms, each party typically has printed form drafted by his attorney, containing as many terms favorable to him/her as may be envisioned).

However, there are some situations which simply do not warrant application of § 2-207. It has been noted that in the case of non-form agreements, there is no pattern of exchange of printed forms. Under such circumstances, when the parties fully negotiate each provision of a contract, a contract may be "beyond the reach of 2-207 and adrift on the murky sea of common law." White and Summers, §§ 1-3 at p. 29. See also Brown, supra at p. 943 (concluding section 2-207 is inapplicable if no form is used or if the disputed term was the subject of precontract negotiation). We find the present case presents such a situation. The parties met and negotiated the provisions of their contract, through their attorneys, for several months. They exchanged at least four draft proposals, making numerous changes. The contract specifically contained a negotiated provision to the effect that it could not be amended or changed except by instrument in writing signed by the parties.

Under the limited factual circumstances presented here, we find this is simply not a "battle of the forms" case; on the contrary, this was merely one more in a series of contract negotiations. Accordingly, we find section 2-207 inapplicable to the present facts. Therefore, we find the matter of the existence of a contract was properly submitted to the jury[5] . Player v. Chandler, 299 S.C. 101, 382 S.E.2d 891 (1989) (South Carolina common law requires that, in order to have a valid and enforceable contract, there must be a meeting of the minds between the parties with regard to all essential and material terms of the agreement).

[AFFIRMED.]

Questions

1. Why, "adrift on the murky sea of common law," was there no contract when Gibbes added the words "current year?" What, at common law, was the effect of adding them?

2. Gibbes contended that under § 2-207 a contract was formed as a matter of law. Review the provisions of that section which appear just following footnote #4 in the text of the opinion. Could Gibbes be right? How does S.C. 36-2-207(1) affect this?

3. If a contract were formed, would the terms include "current year?" In this connection what is the meaning of S.C. 36-2-207(2)(b)? Does it have an impact on the term "current year"?

4. What is the effect of the language in the "Agreement of Purchase and Sale…" found in the first paragraph of the text, "This Agreement may not be amended, changed or modified except by instrument in writing signed by the parties to be charged"? What is the effect of S.C. 36-2-207(2)(a) and also (2)(c) on this?

---

5. The trial court charged the jury concerning the common law of contract formation and meeting of the minds.

5. Review again your answers to questions 2 through 4. If the U.C.C. applied would there be a contract? Would the phrase "current year" be part of it?

6. What is the argument given in the opinion for not applying the U.C.C. to this case? To what does this "battle of the forms" argument refer? The court seems to imply that § 2-207 does not look to a "meeting of the minds" while common law does. Would it be more accurate to say that where forms are used, both sides want a contract on the best possible terms, that there is a meeting of the minds on the intent to contract, but no meeting on the details of the contract and that § 2-207 sets up a legal framework by which the forms fill in the details? Review the *Bethlehem* case, *supra* Part I-F, note 1 and accompanying text.

7. Where in S.C. § 2-207 is there any reference to forms? In paragraph 3 under "Discussion" there is a reference to Comment 1. Does that situation fit the facts of this case?

Note on Determination of Contract Existence

Who determined here whether a contract existed, court or jury? In some jurisdictions a jury would not have been needed. The facts seem to be undisputed and because in many (perhaps most) jurisdictions the existence of a contract and the meaning of its terms are questions of law, in those jurisdictions no jury would need to be impaneled to determine if a contract existed. This is the reason that in the United States it is important to be familiar with the differences among jurisdictions if you are practicing in more than one of them and the reason that each state has its own bar examination. Differences do exist although the common law is the basis for American jurisprudence in all states but one.

Steiner, v. Mobil Oil Corporation
20 Cal.3d 90, 569 P.2d 751, 141 Cal.Rptr. 157
Supreme Court of California, 1977.

[The basic facts were simple. Steiner wanted to buy the real property which he had been leasing for his service station and which was for sale. Steiner had been a Mobil products purchaser. Mobil agreed to help Steiner purchase the property and as part of the deal two Mobil representatives put together a package of "documents" which reflected various aspects of it and which Steiner signed. One feature very important to Steiner was a 10 year discount of 1.4 cents per gallon from the basic "tank wagon" (wholesale) price to dealers. This was not in the documents and one document which came to Steiner's attention but which "did not require Steiner's signature" and which he in fact did not sign indicated that the discount could be changed or discontinued at any time. Steiner immediately phoned one of the two representatives with whom he had been dealing and in effect said that if the discount was not guaranteed for 10 years he would not go ahead with the deal. This representative, although he did not have the authority to make such a deal, sent Steiner a letter which said that if Mobil did not accept Steiner's terms for a 10 year discount "the above mentioned contract [between Steiner and Mobil] will be void." The representatives failed to send a copy of this letter to the Manager who had authority to contract with Steiner but the trial court found that the representatives had authority to write it on Mobil's behalf and that therefore, because they were properly acting as Mobil's agents in receiving Steiner's demands and in writing the letter, Mobil knew that Steiner would not enter into the deal if the guaranteed discount were not part of it. Therefore, they also knew that the 1.4 cent per gallon discount was part of Steiner's offer. The Manager received a package of documents from the two representatives which included a revocable 1.4 cent discount. The Manager approved the deal on this basis and a package of documents "numerous and complex in nature", which had no index, and which included the revocable 1.4 cent provision which was not called to Steiner's attention and which Steiner never read, was delivered to Steiner. Based on his supposed deal with Mobil, Steiner purchased the realty for his service station. Less than a year and a half later Mobil informed Steiner that the discount was being reduced to .5 cent per gallon.

Steiner brought this suit in the Los Angeles County Superior Court, seeking declaratory and monetary relief. The trial court, sitting without a jury, found that Mobil "had reason to know" that Steiner would not enter into an agreement unless Mobil agreed that he "was to have a non-cancelable ... competitive allowance ... to run as long as the distributor agreement was in force." Moreover, the trial court found, in returning the package of documents to Steiner, "Mobil intended to make a contract, not to make a counter offer." The trial court concluded that "in the exercise of good faith and reasonable care and diligence Mobil was required to specifically bring to the attention of plaintiff the statements concerning the cancelable condition of the competitive allowance."]

TOBRINER, Justice.

In this case, over one year after apparently accepting plaintiff's offer, the Mobil Oil Corporation sought to impose upon plaintiff the very contractual terms which plaintiff expressly rejected in his offer. As justification for its conduct, Mobil asserted that the crucial provision of plaintiff's offer was lost in the labyrinth of the Mobil bureaucracy, and thus that Mobil decisionmakers had no opportunity to pass on plaintiff's offer as such. As we shall see, however, the trial court correctly concluded that section 2207 of the California Uniform Commercial Code bars Mobil from in this way converting its own error into plaintiff's misfortune.

Section 2207, subdivision (1), provides that parties may form an agreement, even if the terms of offer and acceptance do not entirely converge, if the offeree gives a definite expression of acceptance, and if the terms of acceptance do not explicitly condition agreement upon the offeror's consent to the offeree's new proposed terms. In this case, as the trial court found, defendant Mobil did not condition its acceptance of plaintiff's offer upon plaintiff's agreement to Mobil's alteration of plaintiff's offer and thus a contract was formed. Section 2207, subdivision (2), provides in turn that, if the terms of the offer and acceptance differ, the terms of the offer become part of a contract between merchants if the offer expressly limits acceptance to its own terms, or if the varying terms of the acceptance materially alter the terms of the offer. As the trial court found, under either of these clauses, the terms of Steiner's offer must prevail, because Steiner's offer was expressly conditional upon Mobil's agreement to provide a guaranteed discount, and Mobil's substitution of a discount terminable at its discretion materially affected Steiner's interests.

Accordingly, the trial court did not err in granting judgment for plaintiff, and we shall thus affirm its judgment.

The trial court ruled that, under California Uniform Commercial Code section 2207, Mobil had entered into a contract with Steiner which guaranteed Steiner a 1.4 cents per gallon discount for 10 years. "Mobil made a definite and seasonable expression of acceptance of plaintiff's offer, although its reply contained a material term different from that offer." Moreover, "(i)n accepting plaintiff's offer Mobil did not either orally or in writing expressly condition its acceptance upon plaintiff's assent to the different terms as to the competitive allowance in Mobil's acceptance." The trial court granted Steiner a declaratory judgment to that effect, and awarded Steiner damages of $4,953.63. Mobil appeals the trial court's judgment.

2. Under California Uniform Commercial Code section 2207, Steiner's contract with Mobil grants Steiner a 1.4 cents per gallon discount for the duration of the contract.

Neither Mobil nor Steiner disputes the trial court's conclusion that the sales provisions of the California Uniform Commercial Code apply in this case[4] . Moreover, Mobil and Steiner do not challenge the trial court's conclusion that the outcome of this case turns on the applicability of section 2207.[5] As we shall see, the relevant provisions of that statute confirm the trial court's conclusion that Mobil breached its agreement with Steiner when it unilaterally reduced Steiner's competitive discount. Initially, we shall identify the considerations which underlie section 2207 and thus structure our interpretation of the statute. Thereafter, we shall proceed to the application of section 2207 itself.

Under traditional common law, no contract was reached if the terms of the offer and the acceptance varied.

Section 2207 rejects the "mirror image" rule.

In place of the "mirror image" rule, section 2207 inquires as to whether the parties intended to complete an agreement: "Under this Article a proposed deal which in commercial understanding has in fact been closed is recognized as a contract." (§ 2207, U.C.C. com. 2.)

---

4. Section 2102 states that "this division applies to transactions in goods; it does not apply to any transaction which although in the form of an unconditional contract to sell or present sale is intended to operate only as a security transaction...." Section 2105 defines "goods" as "all things (including specially manufactured goods) which are moveable at the time of identification to the contract for sale...." The gasoline which Steiner agreed to purchase from Mobil plainly falls within that definition.

5. Section 2207 provides in full: "(1) A definite and seasonable expression of acceptance or a written confirmation which is sent within a reasonable time operates as an acceptance even though it states terms additional to or different from those offered or agreed upon, unless acceptance is expressly made conditional on assent to the additional or different terms. "(2) The additional terms are to be construed as proposals for addition to the contract. Between merchants such terms become part of the contract unless: (a) The offer expressly limits acceptance to the terms of the offer; (b) They materially alter it; or (c) Notification of objection to them has already been given or is given within a reasonable time after notice of them is received. (3) Conduct by both parties which recognizes the existence of a contract is sufficient to establish a contract for sale although the writings of the parties do not otherwise establish a contract. In such case the terms of the particular contract consist of those terms on which the writings of the parties agree, together with any supplementary terms incorporated under any other provisions of this code."

Section 2207 is thus of a piece with other recent developments in contract law. Instead of fastening upon abstract doctrinal concepts like offer and acceptance, section 2207 looks to the actual dealings of the parties and gives legal effect to that conduct.

Section 2207, subdivision (1), provides: "A definite and seasonable expression of acceptance or a written confirmation which is sent within a reasonable time operates as an acceptance even though it states terms additional or different from those offered or agreed upon, unless acceptance is expressly made conditional on assent to the additional or different terms." (§ 2207, subd. (1).)

In this case, as the trial court found, Mobil provided "(a) definite and seasonable expression of acceptance." Steiner offered to enter into a 10-year dealer contract with Mobil only if Mobil agreed to give Steiner a 1.4 cents per gallon competitive discount on the price of Mobil gasoline for the duration of the contract. When Steiner telephoned Chenen, Mobil's employee,[one of the two representatives with whom Steiner had dealt] to inquire as to the fate of Steiner's offer, Chenen told Steiner that Mobil had a check for him, that he should open an escrow account, and that he should go ahead with the purchase of the service station property in context a clear statement that Mobil had approved the deal.

Moreover another Mobil employee returned to Steiner various executed documents in an envelope unaccompanied by any cover. The documents provided written confirmation of the deal. The fact that Mobil returned the documents without in any way calling Steiner's attention to them is further evidence that Mobil regarded the process of negotiation as over and the deal as complete.

As the trial court also found, Mobil did not in any way make its acceptance "expressly...conditional" on Steiner's "assent to the additional or different terms." Chenen, in telling Steiner to go ahead with the purchase, did not suggest that Mobil had conditioned its acceptance. In returning the executed documents, Mobil enclosed no cover letter; again, it did not use the occasion in any way to condition expressly its acceptance.

Thus, neither of the restrictions which limit section 2207, subdivision (1)'s application are relevant in this case. Despite the fact that the terms of Mobil's acceptance departed partially from the terms of Steiner's offer, Mobil and Steiner did form a contract. To determine the terms of this contract, we turn to section 2207, subdivision (2).

Section 2207, subdivision (2), provides: "...additional terms are to be construed as proposals for addition to the contract. Between merchants such terms become part of the contract unless: (a) The offer expressly limits acceptance to the terms of the offer; (b) They materially alter it; or (c) Notification of objection to them has already been given or is given within a reasonable time after notice of them is received."

Under section 2207, subdivision (2), Mobil's revocable discount provision does not become part of the agreement between Steiner and Mobil. In order to become part of the agreement, Mobil's provision must not fall within any of the categories defined by section 2207, subdivision (2), subsections (a), (b), and (c). Mobil's term, however clearly comes within subsections (a) and (b).

Subsection (a) provides that no additional term can become part of the agreement if Steiner's offer "expressly limit(ed) acceptance to the terms of the offer." (§ 2-207, subd. (2)(a).) Mobil concedes that Steiner's offer provided that the competitive allowance of 1.4 cents per gallon would run for the full length of the 10-year dealer contract. Chenen's December 2 letter to Steiner explicitly acknowledges Mobil's awareness that "(i)f Mobil management does not accept in full the above conditions outlined in your competitive offer, the above mentioned contract is void."

Moreover, Mobil's acceptance falls within subsection (b) since without question the acceptance "materially alter(ed)" the terms of Steiner's offer. (See § 2-207, subd. (2)(b).) The Uniform Commercial Code comment notes that a variation is material if it would "result in surprise or hardship if incorporated without express awareness by the other party...." (§ 2-207, UCC com. 4.) Here, Steiner clearly indicated to Mobil in the course of the negotiations that, without the 1.4 cents per gallon discount, he could not economically operate the service station. Mobil's alteration, therefore, amended the terms of the offer to Steiner's significant detriment; accordingly, the alteration was necessarily "material."

To reiterate, subsections (a), (b), and (c) of section 2207, subdivision (2), operate in the alternative. If any one of the three subsections applies, the variant terms of an acceptance do not become part of an agreement. Here, as we have seen, the provisions of both subsections (a) and (b) are met. Mobil's declaration that the 1.4 cents per gallon discount was terminable at Mobil's discretion did not become part of the contract. Instead, Steiner and Mobil formed a contract incorporating the terms of Steiner's offer: Under this contract, Steiner was guaranteed a 1.4 cents per gallon discount throughout the 10-year period of the dealer contract.[6]

[Mobil then tried to state that § 2-204 (reproduced in footnote 7) requires that the parties agree to all "essential" terms or no contract can result; therefore § 2-207(1) means that Mobil's response to Steiner's offer was not an acceptance but a counter-offer.]

As we shall explain, Mobil's arguments do not survive scrutiny. The official comments accompanying section 2204, other provisions of the code, and the case law interpreting section 2204, all support the conclusion that section 2204 does not require mutual assent to all essential terms.

a. California Uniform Commercial Code section 2204 does not incorporate the traditional requirement of mutual assent to all essential terms.

Section 2204 incorporates three subdivisions.[7] The third of these subdivisions directly refutes Mobil's claims. "Even though one or more terms are left

---

6. The parties do not challenge the finding of the trial court that both Steiner and Mobil are "merchants within the meaning of section 2104, subdivision (1), and thus within the meaning of section 2207, subdivision (2), as well.

7. Section 2204 provides in full: "(1) A contract for sale of goods may be made in any manner sufficient to show agreement, including conduct by both parties which recognizes the existence of such a contract. (2) An agreement sufficient to constitute a contract for sale may be found even though the moment of its making is undetermined. (3) Even though one or more terms are left open a contract for sale does not fail for indefiniteness if the parties have intended to make a contract and there is a reasonably certain basis for giving an appropriate remedy."

open a contract for sale does not fail for indefiniteness if the parties have intended to make a contract and there is a reasonably certain basis for giving an appropriate remedy." (s 2204, subd. (3).)

4. Conclusion.

In this case, as we have seen, the trial court correctly concluded that under section 2207 the guaranteed discount included in the terms of Steiner's offer, and not Mobil's standard revocable discount provision, became part of the agreement between Mobil and Steiner. Mobil cannot assert as a defense the failure of its own bureaucracy to respond to, or even fully recognize, Steiner's efforts to modify the standard Mobil dealer contract.

The judgment is affirmed.

Questions

1. If the U.C.C. had not been in effect, what would have been the result? Would it be possible to say that Mobil would have made a counter-offer of a 1.4 cent *revocable* discount which Steiner then accepted by going ahead and buying the station, and continuing to deal with Mobil? Would it be possible to say that Mobil made a counter offer which never ripened into a contract and that Steiner's orders for gasoline were just a series of offers which Mobil accepted when they shipped the gasoline?

2. What if Steiner had read the documents which Mobil sent to him after he had made his offer of a 1.4 cent non-revocable discount? Would that have changed the result?

In reading the 2-207 note cases below, use the version of 2-207 found in footnote 5 of *Steiner*.

Boese-Hilburn Co. v. Dean Machinery, 616 S.W. 2D 520 (Mo.Ct. App., 1981). In a purchase order a seller of machinery wrote: "the equipment we have proposed above may or may not meet the specifications as written and is subject to engineers approval." This 'order' was found to be an offer. The buyer wrote back "Accepted subject to above." The above included "[Seller] warrants that he will provide equipment to meet specifications."

Make your best argument based on § 2-207 first for seller and then for buyer.

Air Products v. Fairbanks Morse, 58 Wis.2d 193, 206 N.W.2d 414 (Wis., 1973). This case turned on the "unless" clause in § 2-207(1). The buyer in its order for several expensive electric motors did not expressly request warranties but the court found that the U.C.C. implied in all contracts where the merchant is a seller a warranty of merchantability, found in § 2-314, which basically says that what a merchant sells must be fit for the ordinary uses for which such goods are used and must pass in the trade as being of at least fair, average quality. As more colorfully phrased by an English jurist a century or two ago: "The buyer must not be supposed to purchase goods in order to put them on a dung heap." As a result the buyer's order contained by implication a warranty of merchantability. The seller in its acceptance (which it termed an "Acknowledgment") had the following clause: "The Company nowise assumes any responsibility or liability with respect to use, purpose, or suitability, and shall not be liable for damages of any character for defect, delay or otherwise...." The court found for the buyer when the seller's goods were deemed not to be merchantable. The court found that the "unless" clause in 2-207(1) was not fulfilled, that the response of the seller was therefore an acceptance and that under 2-207(2)(b) the seller's clause was not part of the contract with the result that the seller was liable to the buyer for damages for the malfunctioning electric motors. The seller vigorously and unsuccessfully tried to state that "implied" as opposed to express warranties did not become part of buyer's offer. What would have been the result if seller had succeeded on this point?

Hohenberg Bros. v. Killebrew, 505 F.2d 643 (5th. Cir., 1974). Mississippi cotton farmer sends a one page document (which court finds to be an offer) to Memphis cotton buyer offering to sell farmer's 400 acres of cotton. Buyer sends back three page document which is intended to close deal which is found to be substantially similar to the one page document but has some terms not found in the one page document. Farmer claims no contract. Is he right?

Problem

Buyer sends order to seller for goods, stating "this order is good only for 15 days and cannot be accepted thereafter." Following several phone conversations, in which buyer and seller only discussed how the goods should be paid for and in which buyer said to seller "OK send the goods," and more than 15 days after the order was both sent and received, seller sent an "acknowledgment" to buyer which had the same terms as the order and the same terms as were discussed on the telephone except that it said, "there are no warranties with these goods, either express or implied, and seller is responsible for no damages of any kind." The order was silent on the subject of warranties. After sending the "acknowledgment" seller sent the goods requested in the "order." The buyer never sent any other writing to the seller. These goods were received by buyer after the acknowledgment had been received. Assume that under the U.C.C. a disclaimer of warranties clause will be upheld if part of the contract. The goods are defective. Buyer sues seller. Seller's lawyer claims that the acknowledgment is really an offer which buyer accepted by taking the goods after receiving it—therefore the "no warranties" controls and seller is not liable. Buyer says in the alternative [assume that in buyer's jurisdiction you may plead in the alternative as for example an alleged criminal pleads (a) I didn't do it; (b) if I did it I was justified in doing it, (c) I did it but was mentally not responsible at the time] (1) no contract was formed because the acknowledgment did not mirror the offer embodied in the order; (2) there was a contract but the acknowledgment has different material terms than the order (offer) and these terms drop out so that warranties are implied; (3) the telephone conversation formed the contract and although nothing was said in it about warranties, a warranty of merchantability is implied, and the seller's acknowledgment acted as an acceptance containing a material alteration which drops out; (4) the telephone conversation which contained the words by the buyer "OK send the goods" constituted an oral offer which by implication included the terms of the written offer, and seller's acceptance contained a term different from this offer which would act to materially change the offer so there is a contract without the materially changing term which under 2-207(2)(b) drops out. Seller responds: "I sent the goods along with an acknowledgment which constituted the offer. When buyer took the goods buyer accepted my terms. Buyer responds: Under 2-207(3) if the writings don't create a contract then the contract consists of the terms the writings agree on and the U.C.C. fills in the other terms and one of the terms filled in is the implied warranty of merchantability. Therefore seller is liable to buyer.

Consider the case [problem] from the vantage point of either buyer or seller or both. Presume you are the lawyer for either one. Try to work out the strongest case for your client and predict the strongest case your adversary will present. Use the arguments above and any others you consider relevant. Do *not* give in to the lawyer's temptation to just settle the whole thing and forget it. Remember, if you are going to settle, settle from strength—which translates into preparation. If you had a contract like the one a parking garage once had with a lessor of a building according to which the lessor would pay for all outside damage and the lessee all inside damage to the building, and vandals broke windows, you might do as they did—each side pay 50% and forget it. Assume here that clients want answers. Who has the better argument? Why?

Cases that might help include *CBS v. Auburn Plastics, 67 A.D.2d 811, 413 N.Y.S.2d 50 (4th Dep't. 1979); Dorton v. Collins and Aikman Corp., 453 F.2d 1161(6th Cir. 1972); Roto-Lith Ltd. v. Bartlett, 297 F.2d 497 (1st Cir. 1962).* [Note: Roto-Lith has been much criticized over the years, perhaps unfairly. At the time it was decided subdivision (3) to U.C.C. 2-207 was not in effect.] You are not expected to read these cases unless you want further enlightenment. Whether you read them or not, work out the problem.

Construction Aggregates Inc. v. Hewitt-Robins, Inc., 404 F.2d 505 (5th Cir. 1968). This case concerned two companies which exchanged writings. Buyer (CAC) sent a writing to seller (HR) which responded with a writing that contained a very limited warranty clause. Buyer argued that seller's clause came within the "unless" clause of 2-207 and was therefore a counter offer and could not create a contract and that therefore 2-207(3) which would include implied warranties applied. The court disagreed.

"Section 2-207(3) recognizes that the subsequent conduct of the parties can establish a contract for sale. Since CAC's July 3 purchase order and H-R's July 20 counter-offer did not in themselves create a contract, Section 2-207(3) would operate to create one because the subsequent performance by both parties constituted 'conduct by both parties which recognized the existence of a contract.' Such a contract by operation of law would consist only of 'those terms on which the writings of the parties agree, together with any supplementary terms incorporated under other provisions of this Act.' There having been no agreement on the warranty terms, the implied warranties provided in Sections 2-314 and 2-315 (Ill.Rev.Stats.1967, ch. 26, §§ 2-314 and 2-315) would then ordinarily become applicable. Here, however, there is no occasion to create a contract by operation of law in default of further actions by the negotiating parties, for CAC can be said to have accepted the terms of H-R's counter-offer. [After receiving H-R's counteroffer] CAC sought a change only in the payment terms of the counter-offer, raising no objection to H-R's other modifications of the original purchase order. H-R granted CAC's requested change in a "letter of July 31 and could reasonably have assumed that CAC's single objection was a an acquiescence in the remaining terms of the counter-offer. CAC did not object to this implication in

H-R's July 31st letter reference to the terms of its counter-offer and therefore CAC could appropriately be held to the terms of the July 20th letter. In this setting, the jury could determine that CAC had accepted H-R's July 20 terms."

The Illinois version of § 2-207 which was quoted and used in *Construction Aggregates* is reproduced here.

"Section 2-207 provides (Ill.Rev.Stats.1967, ch. 26, § 2-207): 'Additional Terms in Acceptance or Confirmation. (1) A definite and seasonable expression of acceptance or a written confirmation which is sent within a reasonable time operates as an acceptance even though it states terms additional to or different from those offered or agreed upon, unless acceptance is expressly made conditional on assent to the additional or different terms. (2) The additional terms are to be construed as proposals for addition to the contract. Between merchants such terms become part of the contract unless: (a) the offer expressly limits acceptance to the terms of the offer; (b) they materially alter it; or (c) notification of objection to them has already been given or is given within a reasonable time after notice of them is received. (3) Conduct by both parties which recognizes the existence of a contract is sufficient to establish a contract for sale although the writings of the parties do not otherwise establish a contract. In such case the terms of the particular contract consist of those terms on which the writings of the parties agree, together with any supplementary terms incorporated under any other provisions of this Act.' "

G. The Outer Limits — Other Cases Where Acceptance Does Not Follow Common Law Rules but Is Effective

Hill, v. Gateway 2000, Inc.
105 F.3d 1147
United States Court of Appeals, 7th. Cir., Jan. 6, 1997.

EASTERBROOK, Circuit Judge.

A customer picks up the phone, orders a computer, and gives a credit card number. Presently a box arrives, containing the computer and a list of terms, said to govern unless the customer returns the computer within 30 days. Are these terms effective as the parties' contract, or is the contract term-free because the order-taker did not read any terms over the phone and elicit the customer's assent?

One of the terms in the box containing a Gateway 2000 system was an arbitration clause. Rich and Enza Hill, the customers, kept the computer more than 30 days before complaining about its components and performance. They filed suit in federal court arguing, among other things, that the product's shortcomings make Gateway a racketeer (mail and wire fraud are said to be the predicate offenses), leading to treble damages under RICO for the Hills and a class of all other purchasers. Gateway asked the district court to enforce the arbitration clause; the judge refused, writing that "[t]he present record is insufficient to support a finding of a valid arbitration agreement between the parties or that the plaintiffs were given adequate notice of the arbitration clause." Gateway took an immediate appeal, as is its right. 9 U.S.C. § 16(a)(1)(A).

The Hills say that the arbitration clause did not stand out: they concede noticing the statement of terms but deny reading it closely enough to discover the agreement to arbitrate, and they ask us to conclude that they therefore may go to court. Yet an agreement to arbitrate must be enforced "save upon such grounds as exist at law or in equity for the revocation of any contract." 9 U.S.C. § 2. Doctor's Associates, Inc. v. Casarotto, — U.S. —, 116 S.Ct. 1652, 134 L.Ed.2d 902 (1996), holds that this provision of the Federal Arbitration Act is inconsistent with any requirement that an arbitration clause be prominent. A contract need not be read to be effective; people who accept take the risk that the unread terms may in retrospect prove unwelcome. Terms inside Gateway's box stand or fall together. If they constitute the parties' contract because the Hills had an opportunity to return the computer after reading them, then all must be enforced.

ProCD, Inc. v. Zeidenberg, 86 F.3d 1447 (7th Cir. 1996), holds that terms inside a box of software bind consumers who use the software after an opportunity to read the terms and to reject them by returning the product. Likewise, Carnival Cruise Lines, Inc. v. Shute, 499 U.S. 585, 111 S.Ct. 1522, 113 L.Ed.2d 622 (1991), enforces a forum-selection clause that was included among three pages of terms attached to a cruise ship ticket. ProCD and Carnival Cruise Lines exemplify the many commercial transactions in which people pay for products with terms to follow; ProCD discusses others. 86 F.3d at 1451-52. The district court concluded in ProCD that the contract is formed when the consumer pays for the software; as a result, the court held, only terms known to the consumer at that moment are part of the contract, and provisos inside the box do not count. Although this is one way a contract could be formed, it is not the only way: "A vendor, as master of the offer, may invite acceptance by conduct, and may propose limitations on the kind of conduct that constitutes acceptance. A buyer may accept by performing the acts the vendor proposes to treat as acceptance." Id. at 1452. Gateway shipped computers with the same sort of accept-or-return offer ProCD made to users of its software. ProCD relied on the Uniform Commercial Code rather than any peculiarities of Wisconsin law; both Illinois and South Dakota, the two states whose law might govern relations between Gateway and the Hills, have adopted the UCC; neither side has pointed us to any atypical doctrines in those states that might be pertinent; ProCD therefore applies to this dispute.

Plaintiffs ask us to limit ProCD to software, but where's the sense in that? ProCD is about the law of contract, not the law of software. Payment preceding the revelation of full terms is common for air transportation, insurance, and many other endeavors. Practical considerations support allowing vendors to enclose the full legal terms with their products. Cashiers cannot be expected to read legal documents to customers before ringing up sales. If the staff at the other end of the phone for direct-sales operations such as Gateway's had to read the four-page statement of terms before taking the buyer's credit card number, the droning voice would anesthetize rather than enlighten many potential buyers. Others would hang up in a rage over the waste of their time. And oral recitation would not avoid customers' assertions (whether true or feigned) that the clerk did not read term X to them, or that they did not remember or understand it. Writing provides benefits for both sides of commercial transactions. Customers as a group are better off when vendors skip costly and ineffectual steps such as telephonic recitation, and use instead a simple approve-or-return device. Competent adults are bound by such documents, read or unread. For what little it is worth, we add that the box from Gateway was crammed with software. The computer came with an operating system, without which it was useful only as a boat anchor. See Digital Equipment Corp. v. Uniq Digital Technologies, Inc., 73 F.3d 756, 761 (7th Cir.1996). Gateway also included many application programs. So the Hills' effort to limit ProCD to software would not avail them factually, even if it were sound legally—which it is not.

For their second sally, the Hills contend that ProCD should be limited to executory contracts (to licenses in particular), and therefore does not apply because both parties' performance of this contract was complete when the box arrived at their home. This is legally and factually wrong: legally because the question at hand concerns the formation of the contract rather than its performance, and factually because both contracts were incompletely performed. ProCD did not depend on the fact that the seller characterized the transaction as a license rather than as a contract; we treated it as a contract for the sale of goods and reserved the question whether for other purposes a "license" characterization might be preferable. 86 F.3d at 1450. All debates about characterization to one side, the transaction in ProCD was no more executory than the one here: Zeidenberg paid for the software and walked out of the store with a box under his arm, so if arrival of the box with the product ends the time for revelation of contractual terms, then the time ended in ProCD before Zeidenberg opened the box. But of course ProCD had not completed performance with delivery of the box, and neither had Gateway. One element of the transaction was the warranty, which obliges sellers to fix defects in their products. The Hills have invoked Gateway's warranty and are not satisfied with its response, so they are not well positioned to say that Gateway's obligations were fulfilled when the motor carrier unloaded the box. What is more, both ProCD and Gateway promised to help customers to use their products. Long-term service and information obligations are common in the computer business, on both hardware and software sides. Gateway offers "lifetime service" and has a round-the-clock telephone hotline to fulfill this promise. Some vendors spend more money helping customers use their products than on developing and manufacturing them. The document in Gateway's box includes promises of future performance that some consumers value highly; these promises bind Gateway just as the arbitration clause binds the Hills.

Next the Hills insist that ProCD is irrelevant because Zeidenberg was a "merchant" and they are not. Section 2-207(2) of the UCC, the infamous battle-of-the-forms section, states that "additional terms [following acceptance of an offer] are to be construed as proposals for addition to a contract. Between merchants such terms become part of the contract unless...". Plaintiffs tell us that ProCD came out as it did only because Zeidenberg was a "merchant" and the terms inside ProCD's box were not excluded by the "unless" clause. This argument pays scant attention to the opinion in ProCD, which concluded that, when there is only one form, "sec. 2-207 is irrelevant." 86 F.3d at 1452. The question in ProCD was not whether terms were added to a contract after its formation, but how and when the contract was formed—in particular, whether a vendor may propose that a contract of sale be formed, not in the store (or over the phone) with the payment of money or a general "send me the product," but after the customer has had a chance to inspect both the item and the terms. ProCD answers "yes," for merchants and consumers alike. Yet again, for what little it is worth we observe that the Hills misunderstand the setting of ProCD. A "merchant" under the UCC "means a person who deals in goods of the kind or otherwise by his occupation holds himself out as having knowledge or skill peculiar to the practices or goods involved in the transaction", § 2-104(1). Zeidenberg bought the product at a retail store, an uncommon place for merchants to acquire inventory. His corporation put ProCD's database on the Internet for anyone to browse, which led to the litigation but did not make Zeidenberg a software merchant.

At oral argument the Hills propounded still another distinction: the box containing ProCD's software displayed a notice that additional terms were within, while the box containing Gateway's computer did not. The difference is functional, not legal. Consumers browsing the aisles of a store can look at the box, and if they are unwilling to deal with the prospect of additional terms can leave the box alone, avoiding the transactions costs of returning the package after reviewing its contents. Gateway's box, by contrast, is just a shipping carton; it is not on display anywhere. Its function is to protect the product during transit, and the information on its sides is for the use of handlers rather than would-be purchasers.

Perhaps the Hills would have had a better argument if they were first alerted to the bundling of hardware and legal-ware after opening the box and wanted to return the computer in order to avoid disagreeable terms, but were dissuaded by the expense of shipping. What the remedy would be in such a case—could it exceed the shipping charges?—is an interesting question, but one that need not detain us because the Hills knew before they ordered the computer that the carton would include some important terms, and they did not seek to discover these in advance. Gateway's ads state that their products come with limited warranties and lifetime support. How limited was the warranty—30 days, with service contingent on shipping the computer back, or five years, with free onsite service? What sort of support was offered? Shoppers have three principal ways to discover these things. First, they can ask the vendor to send a copy before deciding whether to buy. The Magnuson-Moss Warranty Act requires firms to distribute their warranty terms on request, 15 U.S.C. § 2302(b)(1)(A); the Hills do not contend that Gateway would have refused to enclose the remaining terms too. Concealment would be bad for business, scaring some customers away and leading to excess returns from others. Second, shoppers can consult public sources (computer magazines, the Web sites of vendors) that may contain this information. Third, they may inspect the documents after the product's delivery. Like Zeidenberg, the Hills took the third option. By keeping the computer beyond 30 days, the Hills accepted Gateway's offer, including the arbitration clause.

The Hills' remaining arguments, including a contention that the arbitration clause is unenforceable as part of a scheme to defraud, do not require more than a citation to Prima Paint Corp. v. Flood & Conklin Mfg. Co., 388 U.S. 395, 87 S.Ct. 1801, 18 L.Ed.2d 1270 (1967). Whatever may be said pro and con about the cost and efficacy of arbitration (which the Hills disparage) is for Congress and the contracting parties to consider. Claims based on RICO are no less arbitrable than those founded on the contract or the law of torts. Shearson/American Express, Inc. v. McMahon, 482 U.S. 220, 238-42, 107 S.Ct. 2332, 2343-46, 96 L.Ed.2d 185

(1987). The decision of the district court is vacated, and this case is remanded with instructions to compel the Hills to submit their dispute to arbitration.

Questions

1. What if the return clause was three not thirty days and return was at buyer's expense?

2. Does the opinion say that travel, insurance, goods contracts may all have "secret" terms and that you must cancel according to the seller's requirements to avoid them?

3. When is the contract formed? Read also the ProCD case which follows.

ProCD, Inc. v. Zeidenberg, 86 F.3d 1447 (7th Cir. 1996) Plaintiff (ProCD) compiled data from telephone directories into a database on compact disc. Wishing to sell the data for more money to commercial than consumer users, and having no other effective way to do this, plaintiff resorted to contract. If someone buys at the consumer price a statement enclosed with the product but not accessible at the time of purchase states that it may be used only for non-commercial purposes. However, on the outside of the box is a statement that the "softwear[cd] comes with restrictions stated in an enclosed license." Zeidenberg bought at the consumer price from a retail outlet and used it commercially. The trial court held that Zeidenberg could not be held to terms (no commercial use) which were "secret at the time of purchase." The appellate court agreed that a contract only includes the terms on which the parties have agreed but nevertheless reversed the trial court. The appellate court said in part:

"What then does the current version of the UCC have to say? We think that the place to start is § 2-204(1): "A contract for sale of goods may be made in any manner sufficient to show agreement, including conduct by both parties which recognizes the existence of such a contract." A vendor, as master of the offer, may invite acceptance by conduct, and may propose limitations on the kind of conduct that constitutes acceptance. A buyer may accept by performing the acts the vendor proposes to treat as acceptance. And that is what happened. ProCD proposed a contract that a buyer would accept by using the software after having an opportunity to read the license at leisure. This Zeidenberg did. He had no choice, because the software splashed the license on the screen and would not let him proceed without indicating acceptance. So although the district judge was right to say that a contract can be, and often is, formed simply by paying the price and walking out of the store, the UCC permits contracts to be formed in other ways. ProCD proposed such a different way, and without protest Zeidenberg agreed. Ours is not a case in which a consumer opens a package to find an insert saying 'you owe us an extra $10,000' and the seller files suit to collect. Any buyer finding such a demand can prevent formation of the contract by returning the package, as can any consumer who concludes that the terms of the license make the software worth less than the purchase price. Nothing in the UCC requires a seller to maximize the buyer's net gains.

Section 2-606, which defines 'acceptance of goods', reinforces this understanding. A buyer accepts goods under § 2-606(1)(b) when, after an opportunity to inspect, he fails to make an effective rejection under § 2-602(1). ProCD extended an opportunity to reject if a buyer should find the license terms unsatisfactory; Zeidenberg inspected the package, tried out the software, learned of the license, and did not reject the goods. We refer to § 2-606 only to show that the opportunity to return goods can be important; acceptance of an offer differs from acceptance of goods after delivery, but the UCC consistently permits the parties to structure their relations so that the buyer has a chance to make a final decision after a detailed review."

Manhattan Construction Co. V. Rotek

905 F. Supp. 971
United States District Court, N.D. Oklahoma, 1995.

HOLMES, District Judge.

This matter comes before the Court on a Motion to Stay Proceedings Pending Arbitration by Defendant Rotek, Inc. ("Rotek"). Pursuant to Section Three of the Federal Arbitration Act ("FAA"), Rotek asserts that Plaintiff's claims are arbitrable and that the Court should stay this lawsuit until the conclusion of such arbitration.[1] Plaintiff objects to arbitration.

I.

The facts necessary for the Court to resolve Rotek's Motion are not in dispute. See Rotek's Reply in Support of Its Motion to Stay Proceedings Pending Arbitration at 2.

Prior to August 19, 1993, Plaintiff Manhattan Construction Company ("Manhattan") contacted Rotek to determine whether Rotek could inspect, test, and, if necessary, repair a ring gear that is used in a tower crane. On August 19, 1993, prior to inspecting the ring gear, Rotek sent a one page quote to Manhattan via facsimile. The quote contained the following information: "Gentlemen: We are pleased to quote as follows: Model No.: 061.50.1637.000.49.1504 Description: Inspect, re-engineer and refurbish customer bearing to like new condition, inspect and test the completed unit as required. The repair involves some combination of the following: —New inner ring to match existing outer ring. — Sand blast. —Non-destructive tests, measurements and visual examination to determine sequence of operations. —Furnace draw-back the case hardness. — Reround and flatten. —Machine to virgin material. —Reinduction harden. —Reround and flatten. —Remachine and/or grind. —Non-destructive tests. — Hand detail and fit the assembly. —Inspect and test. —Prepare for shipment. *See below Inner ring is cracked/scrap. Note: Regardless of the great care taken to determine the degree of wear/distress and the possibility of repair, there is always the possibility of uncovering a deeper than expected damage which negates the possibility [sic] of a successful repair. Quantity: 1 Net Price Each: $5000.00 Terms: Net 30 days after date of invoice, subject to credit approval. F.O.B.: Aurora, OH Delivery: 9 Weeks ARO THIS QUOTATION IS MADE SUBJECT TO

---

1. The statute provides that: [i]f any suit of proceeding be brought in any of the courts of the United States upon any issue referable to arbitration under an agreement in writing for such arbitration, the court in which suit is pending, upon being satisfied that the issue involved in such suit or proceeding is referable to arbitration under such an agreement, shall on application of one of the parties stay the trial of the action until such arbitration has been had in accordance with the terms of the agreement, providing the applicant for the stay is not in default in proceeding with such arbitration.

THE TERMS AND CONDITIONS SET FORTH ON THE REVERSE SIDE HEREOF— All recommendations or opinions with reference to choice of products and installation of such products are offered without charge and without obligation. Of necessity we cannot be responsible for performance of our products beyond our warranty of satisfactory material and workmanship." The quote was signed by Todd Troyer, Service Technician. Despite the reference on the quote to the "terms and conditions set forth on the reverse side hereof," Manhattan did not receive the reverse side of the quote. Further, the facsimile transmission was not followed by a hard copy of the quote.

On August 23, 1993, Jim Adams, Equipment Manager for Manhattan, contacted Rotek and authorized Rotek to make the required repairs. At that time, Manhattan sent the ring gear to Rotek. Prior to September 30, 1993, Rotek performed the agreed-upon work and returned the ring gear to Manhattan. On September 30, 1993, Rotek mailed an invoice to Manhattan covering the work performed. The reverse side of the invoice contained language styled as "TERMS AND CONDITIONS FOR SALE". Paragraph (10) provides: "ARBITRATION. Any controversy or claim arising out of or relating to this agreement, or the breach thereof, shall be settled by arbitration in accordance with the Rules of the American Arbitration Association, and judgment upon the award rendered by the arbitrator may be entered in any court having jurisdiction thereof. The arbitration shall be conducted in Cleveland, Ohio, or at such other place as the parties may agree, by one arbitrator independent of the parties appointed by them by mutual agreement or by the President of the American Arbitration Association." Manhattan then paid the invoice in full without questioning any of the terms and conditions on the back of the invoice.

II.

The Federal Arbitration Act embodies a "strong pro-arbitration policy". Marlin Oil Corp. v. Colorado Interstate Gas Co., 700 F.Supp. 1076, 1078 (W.D.Okla. 1988). The party seeking the stay pending arbitration under Section Three has the burden of proving that: (1) the issue is one which is referable to arbitration under an agreement in writing for such arbitration; and (2) the party applying for the stay is not in default in proceeding with such arbitration. Further, "the question of whether the parties agreed to arbitrate is to be decided by the court." AT & T Technologies, Inc. v. Communications Workers of America, 475 U.S. 643, 649, 106 S.Ct. 1415, 1418, 89 L.Ed.2d 648 (1986).

To effectuate the purposes of the Federal Arbitration Act, courts generally "resolve all doubts regarding the arbitrability of issues in favor of arbitration." Marlin Oil Corp., 700 F.Supp. at 1078-79. However, a party cannot be compelled to arbitrate a dispute unless he or she has agreed to do so. AT & T Technologies, Inc., 475 U.S. at 648-49, 106 S.Ct. at 1418-19; McKinley, 722 F.Supp. at 702.[2] "The central focus of arbitrability analysis is, of course, the parties' intent." Marlin Oil Corp., 700 F.Supp. at 1079 n. 4.

---

2. E.g., Kaplan v. First Options of Chicago, Inc., 19 F.3d 1503, 1512-16 (3d Cir.1994) (individuals who were principals of options market maker and who signed Letter Agreement which was part of workout were not bound by arbitration provision in another workout document which individuals had not signed), aff'd, — U.S. —, 115 S.Ct. 1920, 131 L.Ed.2d 985 (1995).

It is clear that Manhattan and Rotek reached an agreement regarding the repair of the ring gear. Based upon the arbitration provision on the reverse side of the invoice, which provision was sent to Manhattan after Rotek performed under the parties' agreement, Rotek asserts that Plaintiff's claims must now be arbitrated. Plaintiff, however, argues that it did not agree to arbitration. The dispositive issue is thus whether the parties' agreement regarding the repair of the ring gear included the arbitration provision upon which Rotek now relies.

To determine the arbitrability of this dispute, the Court must analyze the parties' agreement under applicable contract formation principles. Manhattan analyzes the contract between the parties as follows: (1) the facsimile quote dated August 19, 1993 constituted an offer and (2) Manhattan's authorization for Rotek to perform the repair and the shipping of the ring gear to Rotek constituted an acceptance.

To the contrary, Rotek asserts that the terms of the facsimile quote were not sufficiently certain to constitute an offer. Rotek offers two competing views of the contract formation: either (1) Manhattan's authorization for Rotek to repair the ring gear was the offer; (2) the invoice dated September 30, 1993, which imposed new terms and materially altered the contract, was a counter-offer; and (3) Manhattan accepted the counter-offer when it paid the invoice without objecting to its terms; or (1) the Rotek invoice was the offer and (2) Manhattan's payment of the invoice evidenced its acceptance. Under either of Rotek's analyses, the parties' agreement may include the arbitration provision because the provision, set forth in either the offer or the counter-offer which was then accepted, was a term of the contract.

If, on the other hand, the Court adopts the reasoning of Manhattan, then the agreement does not include an arbitration provision because it is undisputed that the facsimile quote, the alleged offer, did not contain an arbitration provision. Therefore, to resolve this dispute, the Court must determine at which point the contract to repair the ring gear was formed under the circumstances presented here.

Generally, a price quotation is not an offer but is rather "an invitation to enter into negotiations or a preliminary solicitation of an offer." Master Palletizer Sys., Inc. v. T.S. Ragsdale Co., 725 F.Supp. 1525, 1531 (D.Colo. 1989), aff'd without op., 937 F.2d 616 (10th Cir. 1991); e.g., Berquist Co. v. Sunroc Corp., 777 F.Supp. 1236, 1248 (E.D.Pa.1991)..However, if sufficiently detailed, price quotations "can amount to an offer creating the power of acceptance". Id.

Therefore, in the first instance, the Court must determine whether the facsimile quote dated August 19, 1993 was sufficiently detailed to constitute an offer. See, e.g., Gulf States Utils. Co., 819 F.Supp. at 549 (To amount to an offer, it must reasonably appear from the quote "that assent to the quote is all that is needed to ripen the offer into a contract.").[3]

In deciding this same issue, the *Master Palletizer* court examined the language of the quote, its cover letter, the subsequent purchase order, and the acceptance letter: "The cover letter accompanying the proposal mentioned that Smith Ragsdale should contact Master 'to discuss the operation' and that different options are available. Thus, when Ragsdale submitted its purchase order on August

---

3. "A price quotation that is subject to the seller's confirmation is not an offer because the buyer's assent will not consummate the contract." Gulf States Utils. Co., 819 F.Supp. at 549; Quaker State Mushroom Co., 635 F.Supp. at 1284.

31, 1985, it offered to purchase the system from Master. Master accepted Ragsdale's offer in its September 10, 1985 letter which stated, '[t]he following letter is being submitted as Master Conveyor's *acceptance* of referenced purchase orders.'" (emphasis in original). 725 F.Supp. at 1531.

The *Bergquist* court also discussed whether a quote was an offer under the circumstances presented by that case: "...many factors...would support a finding that the price quotation is an offer. The price quotation was developed after some negotiation between the parties and after Sunroc had submitted its own specifications. This is not a situation where a price quote was unsolicited; rather, it was a specific response to McShane's request. The price quotation is detailed and includes a description of the product, a listing of various quantities at various prices, a die charge, delivery terms, and payment terms. The price quotation states: 'This quotation is *offered for your acceptance* within 30 days....' (emphasis in original). Thus, it appears Bergquist may have intended this price quotation to be an offer inviting acceptance...Finally, the price paid by Sunroc for the first purchase Q Pad II was that listed in the price quotation rather than the lesser price appearing in Sunroc's purchase order. This certainly shows the parties had the price quotation in mind during the transaction.

Yet there is also strong evidence the price quotation was not an offer. It is labeled 'price quotation' in six places. The list of quantities and prices available for the Q Pad II resembles a menu rather than a specific offer to sell a particular quantity at a particular price...Most important is the ambiguous small print at the bottom of the quotation. It states: 'This quotation is offered for your acceptance within 30 days and *is subject to material availability and price in effect at time of shipment....*' (emphasis in original). This clause suggests Bergquist did not intend to be bound by the terms of the price quotation, but reserved the right to change the price up to the time of shipment." 777 F.Supp. at 1249 (court left question to the jury to decide based upon the document itself and the surrounding circumstances at the time of its issuance).

Here, there is strong evidence that Rotek intended the quote to be an offer.[4] The price quote was not unsolicited; rather, it was a specific response to Manhattan's request. The Court finds the quote to be quite detailed, as it included a model number, an elaborate description of services to be performed, the quantity and price, and delivery and payment terms. Finally, the price paid by Manhattan was the price listed in the quote—$5,000.00.

Further, there is no indication that an immediate acceptance of the quote by Manhattan would not form an agreement. In other words, Rotek did not offer the quote "subject to further approval". And there is nothing in the quote to suggest that Rotek did not intend to be bound by its terms.[5] In fact, Rotek performed in accordance with the quote promptly following Manhattan's acceptance of its terms.

---

4. The parties have not submitted any evidence regarding past bargaining history or course of dealing.

5. The Court is cognizant that "the submission of a purchase order by a buyer in response to a price quotation usually constitutes the offer." Master Palletizer Sys., Inc., 725 F.Supp. at 1531. However, here, Manhattan telephoned Rotek to authorize Rotek to perform the work. This phone call was followed with a one page telecopy cover letter stating: Please go ahead and make the required repairs to our ring gear bearing assembly. Ship to address is above, billing is as follows: Manhattan Construction 111 West 5th St., Suite 1000 Tulsa,

Based upon the foregoing analysis, the Court finds that Rotek has not met its burden of proving that the arbitration clause was encompassed within the parties' agreement. It is probable that the parties intended the facsimile quote to be an offer, which offer was accepted by Manhattan's telephone call to Rotek and one page telecopy cover letter.

The Court notes that, even if the facsimile quote were not an offer as a matter of law, Rotek's Motion still must fail. The Court believes that, even if the parties intended the quote only to be an invitation for an offer, the following occurred: (1) the facsimile quote was an invitation for an offer; (2) the one page telecopy transmission from Manhattan to Rotek, which encompassed the terms of the quote, was the offer; (3) and Rotek accepted Manhattan's offer with performance under the contract—the repair of the ring gear, see, e.g., Consarc Corp. v. Marine Midland Bank, N.A., 996 F.2d 568, 573 (2d Cir.1993) (it is elemental that "a unilateral offer may be accepted by the other party's conduct and thereby give rise to contractual obligations."). Under this analysis as well, the arbitration provision is not a term of the parties' final agreement because it was not injected into the parties' dealings until after the offer and the acceptance of the offer by Rotek's repair of the ring gear.

The Court concludes that, based upon the facts of this case, each of the alternative analyses set forth by the Court above more accurately depicts the intent of the parties than the analyses offered by Defendant. Therefore, the contract was formed no later than the performance by Rotek of the repair of the ring gear. Accordingly, the agreement to repair the ring gear does not contain an arbitration provision. Consequently, this Court may not force Manhattan to resolve its dispute in arbitration when it never agreed to that forum. The Court therefore denies Rotek's Motion to Stay Proceedings Pending Arbitration (Docket # 8).

IT IS SO ORDERED.

Questions

1. Can *Hill* and *ProCD* be reconciled with common law principles or even with U.C.C. § 2-207?

2. If *Manhattan* had been heard in the *Hill* court, do you think the result might have been different?

3. Is there a difference between *Manhattan* and the other two cases?

4. Could it be argued that when Manhattan received Rotek's fax, it had a duty to ask Rotek "What's on the other side?" Would the *Hill* court be likely to require this? Could it be argued for Manhattan that if Rotek doesn't send it Rotek can't expect Manhattan to think it's important?

OK. 74103-4235 Attn: Jim Adams There was a handwritten notation on the telecopy which stated, "P.O. # Verbal: Jim". Manhattan did not submit a detailed purchase order to Rotek. It does not appear that the parties intended that telecopy to be the offer. Manhattan instructed Rotek to "go ahead and make the required repairs". This instruction necessarily refers back to the parties' previous communication—the quote. The one page telecopy does not contain detailed information about the repair—unlike the quote. There is no price information. If the telecopy were the offer, it would fail because its terms are not sufficiently certain.

5. When do you think the contract was formed between Manhattan and Rotek? At what point do you think they considered themselves bound, or would it be better to say at what point objectively would a reasonable person consider them to be bound?

6. Are the contracts in parts F and G sufficiently definite to be enforced? If the courts have to fill in terms how radical is that? Review again the Carbolic smokeball case.

7. What about Mr. Hunter's problems? He and the studio have been waiting. Was there an intent to contract there or not? Can Hunter get a summary judgment or will the studio be able to take its case to a jury? A case very like Hunter's developed in the late spring of 1997. Could a person be held to a contract for services which might take a long time, require foreign travel, involve working with people as directors etc. with whom one might not work well all on a few words at a party? Do the circumstances tell us anything? What advice would you give Hunter? the studio?

8. What about Miss Jones' problems? Is there a contract? What are its terms?

Part III

Interpreting the Contract

Introduction

In Part III we move on from the basic questions of which intents will be enforced (Part I—subjective vs. objective; seal, consideration, promissory estoppel) and how does an offer and an acceptance form a contract (Part II) into questions of interpretation of the contract. Part III is divided into four parts, each dealing with different aspects and questions of what the contract means. Subpart A introduces the subject of interpreting the contract. Subpart B concerns Parol Evidence, probably the most important, and one of the most difficult, areas of contract interpretation. Parol evidence becomes relevant when parties to a writing agree that to some extent the writing was meant to reflect the terms the parties agreed upon. The issue becomes when and to what degree may one party over the other's objection introduce into evidence other writings or oral evidence of the terms of the contract. Put another way: once you have a writing that you agree binds you in some way, are you stuck with whatever is in it, whatever objectively its terms seem to mean, or can you add to, or construe its meaning by things outside the writing. Subpart C discusses modifications of the original agreement. When and how do modifications take place? Does a modification replace the original contract? Does it change it in part? Do you need a separate consideration for a modification? Finally, subpart D considers situations where one of the parties wishes to claim that the writing does not reflect the agreement of the parties—in short, they agreed on one thing but then both signed a writing that didn't reflect that agreement. What controls? The oral agreement or the writing? The usual answer is the writing. Are there ways around this?

These four subparts link together. In the first we consider the basic difference between construction and interpretation of a contract. Broadly speaking construction refers to the court's determining the meaning of the contract by applying rules of law. Interpretation, which is our primary concern and the primary concern in the field, is a matter of determining what the parties intended. In *Semmes, infra*, the question is how to interpret a clause. The Court noted that the insurance company had made its own "hard provision," but it nevertheless went on to indicate that construing it was not merely a matter of determining the intent of the parties but what the law itself would do with it. While it is true that "contract" always refers to the agreement which the law will enforce, and agreement usually refers to the meeting of the minds of the parties on one or more

199

promises, the two usually represent the same; *i.e.* the law will usually enforce what the parties agree. In *Feld, infra*, the parties agreed to what the court called an output contract. The law determined the effect of the agreement by construction; it construed what they agreed to as having a particular effect.

In the second part—parol evidence—we discover how courts determine what can be brought to bear to interpret a written statement of the contract's terms—most often called a written contract. Look up parol in a law dictionary. In short, if a writing exists did the parties intend it to embody none or some or all of the contract's terms. If the court determines that none were embodied the writing can be disregarded. If the court determines that only some of the contract's terms were embodied in the writing, then the question becomes can other terms alleged to have been agreed upon orally or in writing be brought in to add to the agreed terms or to explain them. If all of the terms were embodied, then bringing in other terms is even harder. Distinguish parol evidence which refers to writings or oral statements previous to or contemporaneous with the writing alleged to embody the contract with writings or oral statements coming after such writing. Writings or oral statements *after* the original writing are attempted modifications and are *not* covered by, and therefore *not* excluded by the parol evidence rule. What is the role of ambiguity in determining the admissibility or non-admissibility of parol evidence? Is the law changing there? Do different courts have different rules? What is the U.C.C.'s rule? The section is 2-202. Look it up in the library and read the comments. Use the uniform version or any state's statutory enactment of it. All states except Louisiana have enacted it and most have kept the uniform numbering. Ask the librarians if you need help.

In the third part we consider attempts to modify existing contracts and how the courts interpret these attempts. In the first case in this subpart, *Austin*, the majority of the court found that duress existed. We will discuss this more in Part V. But, the minority found there was no duress. As you read this case see how the defendant would claim it was only trying to modify the contract. Was the majority's determination that the attempt was duress a construction (a legal determination of the effect and significance of events and statements) or was it an interpretation of the intent of the parties? Can construction and interpretation be easily distinguished? Does it matter? What if you are in a jurisdiction where interpretation of words and statements and their effect as to the existence or non existence of the intention of the parties to have a contract is a question of fact and not law? Do some cases leave this interpretation to the jury?

In part four we look at standardized contracts—preprinted writings presented to people on a take it or leave it basis. Most courts still say that the writings are presumed to reflect the intent of the signer, even if the person signing the writing has not read it. The exceptions will be if fraud or trickery (explored in Part V) was employed. Note how courts differ on arbitration clauses.

All four parts go to writings that may or may not by themselves be held to embody the parties' agreement. Part III examines if the agreement can be interpreted or modified. In Part IV we will look at conditions that trigger or cancel liability. In Part V we examine ways to escape liability. Just as the subparts of Part III link together, so do all of the other Parts.

Part III materials are very important. You already know how to create a contract—a binding obligation. Now we consider how you or the courts will interpret what was agreed to by the parties.

Problem to Part III

Sam Smith (Smith) went to an insurance agent, Carolyn Ash (Ash) in order to inquire about Great Equity Life and Casualty Insurance Co. (Great) about which Smith had read, seen and heard ads (newspaper, TV and radio.) The ads for the most part said something like: "Why pay more for the coverage you don't need? See your Great Equity insurance agent for a tailor-made plan that will cost you less—much less. We estimate the average savings for persons transferring their coverage to Great Equity to be at least 20%. Your insurance is in effect from the moment you and your agent sign with us. Try us. You won't be unhappy you did." Smith owned and operated a cleaning and laundry business. Because of the relatively high risk of fire as a result of highly volatile cleaning fluids being kept on the premises, Smith has always paid at the high end of the premium scale for business insurance. On the other hand, because he has always kept excellent fire detection and suppression devices installed and operational at his cleaning plants, his premiums have been lower than they might otherwise have been. Nevertheless, because of increased competition from other cleaning businesses, including one that was pressing Smith to sell out to it, Smith was looking for ways to save money while retaining coverage. With this in mind he went to see Ash.

Smith told Ash that he had seen Great's advertisements and asked if it was true he could keep the same coverage at less cost. Ash assured Smith that this was so. Smith and Ash then sat down and discussed Smith's needs. Among other things, Smith told Ash that he wanted coverage for accident, vandalism and arson, that his plants had large quantities of volatile fluids in stock and that the coverage should be for buildings, equipment and clothing on hand waiting to be cleaned or to be picked up by customers. Furthermore, he wanted sufficient coverage to rebuild his business should one or more plants be wholly or substantially destroyed. He wanted "replacement cost" as opposed to "market value." Smith explained to Ash that because of the relatively large number of cleaning establishments and the competition in the cleaning business there was not much of a market for cleaning plant and equipment. As a result, the "market value" of his plants (what he could sell them for if he put them on the market) was much less than it would cost him to rebuild them if anything happened to them. Therefore, Smith said he wanted "replacement cost" coverage which is what he had now.

Ash took out of copy of Great's form policy and filled in the blanks for the amounts of coverage that Smith said he wanted. The total premium was 22% below what Smith was currently paying. Smith asked Ash if he was covered for all the things he had asked about and Ash told him he was except for arson. Ash wrote "arson" in at the bottom of the policy on one of four blank lines under the heading "Additional coverages requested." A printed statement under the fourth blank line read THESE ADDITIONAL REQUESTED COVERAGES WILL BE IN FORCE ONLY AFTER THE POLICY IS RECEIVED BY ITS HOME OFFICE AND A GENERAL MANAGER OF THE COMPANY OR HIGHER OFFICIAL REVIEWS THE REQUEST AND APPROVES IT AT WHICH TIME A

SURCHARGE MAY BE APPLIED TO THE POLICY. THE COVERAGE WILL BE IN FORCE ONLY WHEN THE SURCHARGE IS ACTUALLY PAID BY THE INSURED AND RECEIVED BY THE INSURER. ALL OTHER COVERAGES AS STATED IN THE POLICY WILL BE IN FORCE IMMEDIATELY UPON SIGNING BY THE INSURED AND A QUALIFIED GREAT EQUITY LIFE AND CASUALTY COMPANY AGENT AND THE PAYMENT OF THE PREMIUM. NO ADDITIONAL COVERAGES AND NO CHANGES FROM THE COVERAGES STATED IN THE PRINTED POLICY WILL HAVE ANY EFFECT UNTIL FORMALLY APPROVED BY A GREAT EQUITY GENERAL MANAGER OR HIGHER OFFICIAL. The writing was in bold type as reproduced here and was larger than the regular type elsewhere in the policy in about the same proportion as the reproduced bold type is to the other type on this page. Smith asked Ash if his coverages would go into effect at once. Ash said that they were effective as soon as Smith signed and gave Ash a check for the premium. Smith and Ash then signed the policy form, Smith paid Ash the premium and canceled his other insurance. Ash told Smith that his coverage was now in effect and that in two to four weeks he would receive a copy of the policy. Two weeks later one of Smith's plants, in which Smith happened to be working at the time, was firebombed — *i.e.* someone threw a highly combustible object [bomb] into the building. The bomb landed in a storage area for cleaning fluid which exploded scattering flaming fluid and embers through much of the building. Smith became unconscious as a result of shock and smoke inhalation and was saved by firemen who responded quickly to the scene. The building, despite the functioning of the fire suppression and alarm systems, was a total loss.

Smith was unconscious in the hospital for three days. Immediately after he became conscious he was questioned relentlessly for four days by police, fire department investigators and federal agents investigating racketeering. At one point Smith was certain that the investigators suspected him of starting the fire and telephoned the law firm in which you are an associate asking the firm to send someone to represent him. A lawyer from the firm talked with the authorities, pointed out that Smith had a spotless character and asked them to back off. They did. That was on the eighth day after the fire. Smith said to the lawyer "I suppose I should tell my insurance company." The lawyer agreed that that would be a good idea. Smith phoned Great from his hospital bed. The person he spoke to at Great told him to send in a written statement as soon as possible. That afternoon Smith wrote out a statement of what happened and had one of the orderlies at the hospital mail it for him to Great.

A week later Smith received a large envelope from Great. In it Smith found a photocopy of the policy that he and Ash had signed. He also found a form letter with a facsimile signature from George Swift (Swift), General Manager of Great Equity, in which he was told that his request for arson coverage was not approved but that all other coverages as stated in the policy form signed by Smith were in full effect as of the date signed by Smith and Ash. Swift expressed his appreciation for Smith bringing his business to them and stated that if he could personally ever be of service to please not hesitate to contact him. A second letter, also signed by Swift (but not by facsimile), stated that because investigators from Great had determined that the cause of the fire was arson, Great had no liability to him.

Smith phoned your firm which agreed to represent him in any action against Great. Smith sent over the policy and the letter from Great. The senior partner who received this turned it over to the junior partner working with her who in turn passed it on to you along with the facts mentioned above. On reading the form (once signed, the policy) you find that it has the following printed clauses in addition to those mentioned above.: "Coverages are all measured by fair market value of the property on the day of the loss or at the time of payment for loss whichever is lower." "Fair market value will be determined by Great Equity appraisers and their judgment shall be accepted as final." "This policy expresses the complete views and agreements of the parties thereto and may not be added to or altered in any way except by a signed writing signed by both parties including a signature by a person of General Managerial rank or higher for Great Equity." "All claims must be made initially within 24 hours of loss and it is the duty of the insured to see that such is done. The initial claim may be made telephonically or by facsimile transmission (Fax) but it is essential that the company receive such notice. Within seven days a full report in writing must be submitted to Great Equity. Failure of the insured to submit either report within the time stated: the lapse of time shall be taken as conclusive evidence that the claim is not valid and shall not be enforced. These notices enable Great Equity to sift valid from invalid claims and are therefore one of the most important factors in Great Equity's being able to offer its premiums at a lower than otherwise possible rate." "All acts of wanton, intentional destruction attributed to fire shall be construed by the parties as being in the nature of arson whether or not an 'arsonist' is ever arrested, charged or convicted. Vandalism shall be confined to random acts of minor harm or inconvenience such as breaking a window, spray-painting a wall, tipping over rubbish cans. Any act or sequence of acts by the same person or persons at or about the same time of destruction which results in damage of $1,000 or more shall be considered "substantial wanton harm" unless it is an act causing any amount of damage by fire in which case it shall be considered, as stated above, arson, and shall not be considered vandalism." "This policy covers loss from vandalism but not from arson, substantial wanton harm, riot, insurrection, invasion, war, atomic attack and like causes." "This policy covers accidental loss. Accidental loss shall be defined and construed by the signatory parties as meaning any loss not caused by the intentional or negligent act of any person and shall include acts occurring in the ordinary course of nature such as windstorm, lightning, and flood."

After you have read the cases in this part, do you think Smith has a case against Great Equity for his loss? If he can recover can he get replacement cost?

A. Interpretation of, as Distinguished from Construction of, the Contract

This section introduces ways in which courts seek out the intent of the contracting parties by interpreting the meaning of the words they use, in essence discovering the meaning they attach to their written words. The court does this in two principal ways. One way is by examining the language of the writing which in whole or part embodies the contract. A second method includes examining the circumstances in which the parties came to their agreement—their negotiations, other writings or oral communications, general usages given to particular words in any trade in which the parties are engaged, dictionary definitions of words. The court does this to arrive at the meaning of the writing which the parties have used to memorialize or establish their agreement.

This effort at interpretation—the effort to discover the meaning of the words of the contract—is distinguished from a court's construing a contract. The construction of a contract means the legal effect the court will give to it and for all practical purposes means how the court will fill in gaps that the parties left. Corbin states (§ 534) that "[w]hen a court is filling gaps in the terms of an agreement, with respect to matters that the parties did not have in contemplation and as to which they had no intention to be expressed, the judicial process should not be called interpretation." Thus, construction refers to how the court will deal with situations that the parties did not think of. To a certain degree construction and interpretation will always overlap. A court seeks the parties' intent by discovering the meaning of their words. Where the intent cannot be found on some point but the court is unwilling to conclude that a contract does not exist the court construes the writing so as to fill in the missing term. In construing, however, the court is also filling in the term as it believes that the parties would if they had included it—it is only that the meaning, the intent cannot be found from the words used or the circumstances in which they were used. Thus, construction depends on interpretation—you go as far as you can interpreting and then construe. In the same way interpretation depends on construction. Courts will not enforce agreements that they believe are unfair, against public policy etc. If a court construes an agreement as being against public policy, it will not enforce it and no amount of interpretation of language to discover the parties' intent will matter. For example, if a court concludes that a contract is a gambling contract, it will not matter what the parties intended if gambling is illegal in that state. We will explore this question of unenforceable contracts (escaping liability) in depth in Part V but for now remember that the meaning which the parties attached to their words and hence their intent may be perfectly clear but the court will not enforce it. There is an interplay between what is agreed and what is enforceable.

One of the clearest examples of "construction" is in the Uniform Commercial Code Article 2—Sales. Here, there are numerous sections which tell the court that if the parties have not agreed on a particular term, then a Code section fills it in. For example, section 2-305 [which we met in earlier—see *e.g. Goldstick* and *Bethlehem supra* Part I] states that a contract is not too indefinite if the price is not determined; in such a case the price the court will use is a "reasonable price." Section 2-306 [which we will meet in *Feld v. Levy, infra* Part III-A] states that if quantity is measured by "output" then it is the actual output that occurs in good faith. If there is no agreement as to how the goods shall be tendered or when payment is due, section 2-307 states that they must be tendered in a single delivery and payment is due on tender. Section 2-308 states that if the place for delivery is not stated then it is seller's place of business or if seller has none then seller's residence. These and other U.C.C. Article 2 sections are called "filler" sections. When a court finds a gap it construes the contract so as to make it enforceable and does so by filling the gap with one of the provisions above. If, however, a party can establish that, for example, a long course of dealing (section 1-205) exists between the parties or, in the absence of that, a trade usage (same section) exists which fills the gap, then the court will use the course of dealing or trade usage. In such a case it is really a matter of interpretation and not construction. Parties are presumed to contract with courses of dealing and trade usages in mind. They do no state them because they assume that they control. Thus, a court is not filling a gap with a statutory gap filler (construction) when it uses a course of dealing or trade usage. Rather, the court is discovering the intent of the parties—it is interpreting the writing in the light of the relevant dealings or usage which both parties presumably intend to be part of the contract because it is well established. Indeed, it is because it is so well established that it is not stated. Of course, in time it will be possible to state that the parties are equally well aware of the "filler" provisions of the U.C.C. and that the courts are therefore not construing the contract to fill in, without regard to their particular intent, provisions which they left out. Rather, because the parties are aware of the 'filler' provisions they contract knowing that what they leave out will be filled in by the courts in accordance with statute—in a sense, they intend to have the statute fill in the gaps. Thus, the court is not construing, it is interpreting because it is finding the parties' intent in the statutory gap filler provisions.

Construction is not our principal concern here although it will exist throughout this part as a counterpoint to interpretation. Nonetheless, you must be familiar with it. At early common law, courts would often refuse to enforce contracts that were not definite in every detail. Today, courts will often construe the contracts by filling in reasonable terms when either none are stated or no trade usage or course of dealing can fill them in. You must be aware of this. One of our first cases, *Carlill*, was a lesson in this. How long did the person have to use the smoke ball? The writing gave no clear statement. A combination of interpretation and construction (interpreting statements which included the words "after having used" and "using") and finally construing the contract to have a "reasonable" time requirement which, however the words were interpreted, the plaintiff met (she contracted the illness after having used and while using the smokeball.) Could it be said that the words of the offer implied a reasonable time and hence the courts were merely interpreting the words of the offer? Construction cannot be overlooked. In Part V we will see how persons, both individual and corporate, can escape liability by reason of the construction the courts put on contractual agreements.

In Part III we look to interpretation. The courts interpret the contract—that is they look for the meaning which the parties attach to their words in order to discover the intent of the parties. The first two cases *Semmes* and *Feld* show how the Court tries to discover the parties' intent (in *Semmes*) and put a reasonable construction (and/or interpretation) on a term. In *Semmes* is the Court determining the parties' liability according to its *own* sense of right and wrong in a situation where the parties have not predicted or made provision for an unexpected situation, the Civil War; or is the Court simply interpreting a provision of the contract to determine the parties' intent when they entered the contract; or is the Court combining construction and interpretation to reach a result? Read the italicized passages, editor's emphasis, with particular care. Can a provision that they would have agreed upon, if they had thought of this situation, be deduced from the writing? Did the Court, therefore, construe the writing in what it considered to be a fair manner or did it refuse to construe the contract at all and simply interpret it so that a provision was held not to apply? In other words, did it by striking down a provision and not replacing it with another resort to interpretation or construction?

In *Feld* do we have a combination of interpretation and construction or is the court simply interpreting the language used by the parties? Output was clearly the contract term. The parties did not, however, spell out what was the obligation of a party that in the ordinary course of its business no longer had an "output" of the product that was called for by the contract. In other words, if A agreed to sell B scrap metal in an amount based on its production of a given item and A decided it no longer wanted to make that item, would A have a duty to B to create scrap just so that there would be "output?" The words of A's and B's contract did not say nor could one glean any intent to cover this situation. Did the court, therefore, begin by interpreting the writing of the parties to determine their intention through the meaning of their words — "output" — and end by construing the contract in accordance with the provisions of the Uniform Commercial Code which so far as we know the parties did not actually have in mind when they entered the contract? Did the court fill the gap regarding a situation that the parties had not foreseen and for which they had not provided, *i.e.* A no longer wanting to sell a product which is creating the scrap called for by its contract with B?

Subsection A, therefore, introduces the problem of interpretation. Do not wrack your brains too hard trying to distinguish between construction and interpretation. Keep the distinction in mind though. Note how the courts try to find the intent of the parties but also how some judges are willing to enforce a contract even when that intent is hard to find.

In subsection B (Parol Evidence) we reach the heart of the problem. How much are we bound by a writing once we sign it? Can other terms be brought in? In C we ask can we and how can we modify a writing? Are there problems in trying to modify it? In D we reach the standardized contract — the printed form — take it or leave it. Is the person who did not draft it and may not have read it bound to its terms?

But first Construction vs. Interpretation.

In reading *Semmes* do not be distracted by terms such as "condition." We will reach these later. Rather view the opinion as a judicial construction of a clause. Pay attention to the italics which were added for emphasis. Why is the court "construing" and not "interpreting" the insurance company's 12 month clause ? What is the difference as that has been described above?

Semmes v. Hartford Insurance Company
80 U.S. 158
December Term, 1871

IN error to the Circuit Court for the District of Connecticut.

Semmes sued the City Fire Insurance Company, of Hartford, in the court below, on the 31st of October, 1866, upon a policy of insurance, for a loss which occurred on the 5th day of January, 1860. The policy as declared on showed as a condition of the contract, that payment of losses should be made in sixty days after the loss should have been ascertained and proved.

The company pleaded that by the policy itself it was expressly provided that no suit for the recovery of any claim upon the same should be sustainable in any court unless such suit should be commenced within the term of twelve months next after any loss or damage should occur; and in that in case a new such suit should be commenced after the expiration of twelve months next after such loss or damage should have occurred, the lapse of time should be taken and deemed as conclusive evidence against the validity of the claim thereby so attempted to be enforced. And that the plaintiff did not commence this action against the defendants within the said period of twelve months next after the loss occurred.

To this plea there were replications setting up, among other things, that the late civil war prevented the bringing of the suit within the twelve months provided in the condition, the plaintiff being a resident and citizen of the State of Mississippi and the defendant of Connecticut during all that time.

The plea was held by the court below to present a good bar to the action, notwithstanding the effect of the war on the rights of the parties.

That court, in arriving at this conclusion, held, first, that the condition in the contract, limiting the time within which suit could be brought, was, like the statute of limitation, susceptible of such enlargement, in point of time, as was necessary to accommodate itself to the precise number of days during which the plaintiff was prevented from bringing suit by the existence of the war. And ascertaining this by a reference to certain public acts of the political departments of the government, to which it referred, found that there was, between the time at which it fixed the commencement of the war and the date of the plaintiff's loss, a certain number of days, which, added to the time between the close of the war and the commencement of the action, amounted to more than the twelve months allowed by the condition of the contract.

Judgment being given accordingly in favor of the company the plaintiff brought the case here.

The point chiefly discussed here was when the war began and when it ceased; Mr. W. Hamersley, for the plaintiff in error, contending that the court below had not fixed right dates, but had fixed the commencement of the war too late and its close too early, and he himself fixing them in such a manner as that even conceding the principle asserted by the court to be a true one, and applicable to a contract as well as to a statute of limitation, the suit was still brought within the twelve months.

The counsel, however, denied that the principle did apply to a contract, but contended that the whole condition had been rendered impossible and so abrogated by the war, and that the plaintiff could sue at any time within the general statutory term, as he now confessedly did.

Mr. R. D. Hubbard, contra.

Mr. Justice MILLER delivered the opinion of the court.

It is not necessary, in the view which we take of the matter, to inquire whether the Circuit Court was correct in the principle by which it fixed the date, either of the commencement or cessation of the disability to sue growing out of the events of the war. For we are of opinion that the period of twelve months which the contract allowed the plaintiff for bringing his suit does not open and expand itself so as to receive within it three or four years of legal disability created by the war and then close together at each end of that period so as to complete itself, as though the war had never occurred.

It is true that, in regard to the limitation imposed by statute, this court has held that the time may be so computed, but there the law imposes the limitation and the law imposes the disability. It is nothing, therefore, but a necessary legal logic that the one period should be taken from the other. If the law did not, by a necessary implication, take this time out of that prescribed by the statute, one of two things would happen: either the plaintiff would lose his right of suit by a *judicial construction* of law which deprived him of the right to sue yet permitted the statute to run until it became a complete bar, or else, holding the statute under the circumstances to be no bar, the defendant would be left, after the war was over, without the protection of any limitation whatever. *It was therefore necessary to adopt the time provided by the statute as limiting the right to sue, and deduct from that time the period of disability.*

Such is not the case as regards this contract. The *defendant has made its own special and hard provision on that subject.* It is not said, as in a statute, that a plaintiff shall have twelve months from the time his cause of action accrued to commence suit, but twelve months from the time of loss; yet by another condition the loss is not payable until sixty days after it shall have been ascertained and proved. The condition is that no suit or action shall be sustainable unless commenced within the time of twelve months next after the loss shall occur, and in case such action shall be commenced after the expiration of twelve months next after such loss, the lapse of time shall be taken and deemed as conclusive evidence against the validity of the claim. Now, this contract relates to the twelve months next succeeding the occurrence of the loss, and *the court has no right*, as in the case of a statute, *to construe it* into a number of days equal to twelve months, to be made up of the days in a period of five years in which the plaintiff could lawfully have commenced his suit. So also *if the plaintiff shows any reason which in law rebuts the presumption*, which, on the failure to sue within twelve months, is, by the contract, made conclusive against the validity of the claim, *that presumption is not revived again by the contract.* It would seem that *when once rebutted fully nothing but a presumption of law or presumption of fact could again revive it. There is nothing in the contract which does it, and we know of no such presumptions of law.* Nor does the same evil consequence follow from removing absolutely the bar of the contract that would from removing absolutely the bar of the statute, for when the bar of the contract is removed there still remains the bar of the statute, and though the plaintiff may show by his disability to sue a sufficient answer to the twelve months provided by the contract, he must still bring his suit within the reasonable time fixed by the legislative authority, that is, by the statute of limitations. [Emphasis added.]

We have no doubt that the disability to sue imposed on the plaintiff by the war relieves him from the consequences of failing to bring suit within twelve months after the loss, because it rendered a compliance with that condition impossible and removes the presumption which that contract says shall be conclusive against the validity of the plaintiff's claim. That part of the contract, therefore, presents no bar to the plaintiff's right to recover.

As the Circuit Court founded its judgment on the proposition that it did, that judgment must be

REVERSED AND THE CASE REMANDED FOR A NEW TRIAL.

Questions

1.   What is there to be decided at the new trial?

2. In paragraph two of the opinion the Court is discussing judicial construction in relation to the Statute of Limitations. How does the Court deal with the Statute?

3. In paragraph three the Court is dealing with interpreting or construing the contract? The Court deals with the contract differently than with the Statute. Is there a grounds for saying that the Court construed the Statute but interpreted the Contract? Would it be more accurate to say that as to the contract the Court both interpreted the language and then construed its meaning? Did the Court impose a meaning on the contract language or simply follow the intent of the parties?

4. How would you write a clause for the insurance company that would (or at least might) bar someone from suing if they failed to bring suit for any reason within one year?

5. Assume that you have a clause whose intent cannot be mistaken — no matter what the reason plaintiff agrees that no suit will be brought against defendant unless initiated within one year of the loss. Can you think of a reason and/or a way a court might devise to not enforce it?

Feld v. Henry S. Levy & Sons, Inc.
37 N.Y.2d 466, 335 N.E.2d 320, 373 N.Y.S.2d 102
Court of Appeals of New York, 1975.

[Plaintiff (Feld), operates the Crushed Toast Company business, and entered into an arrangement with defendant (Henry S. Levy & Sons Inc.), a bread baker, whereby defendant agreed to sell to plaintiff "all bread crumbs produced by the Seller in its factory at 115 Thames Street, Brooklyn, New York" for a one year period. The agreement was to automatically renew itself for successive periods of one year, unless either party canceled by giving at least six months notice to the other by certified mail. Subsequent to the agreement defendant sold over 250 tons of bread crumbs to plaintiff, but defendant, without giving notice, stopped all bread crumb production eleven months into the agreement, stating the operation was "very uneconomical". Not only did defendant not try to obtain more economical equipment, but instead dismantled the toasting oven necessary for bread crumb production so that the space could be used for other business. Defendant also indicated to plaintiff that it would resume crumb production if the price were raised to 7 cents from 6 cents. Defendant then proceeded to sell the raw materials used in making crumbs to animal food manufacturers.]

COOKE, Judge.

Interestingly, the term 'bread crumbs' does not refer to crumbs that may flake off bread; rather, they are a manufactured item, starting with stale or imperfectly appearing loaves and followed by removal of labels, processing through two grinders, the second of which effects a finer granulation, insertion into a drum in an oven for toasting and, finally, bagging of the finished product.

Defendant contends that the contract did not require defendant to manufacture bread crumbs, but merely to sell those it did, and, since none were produced after the demise of the oven, there was no duty to then deliver and, consequently from then on, no liability on its part. Agreements to sell all the goods or services a party may produce or perform to another party are commonly referred to as 'output' contracts and they usually serve a useful commercial purpose in minimizing the burdens of product marketing. The Uniform Commercial Code rejects the ideas that an output contract is lacking in mutuality or that it is unenforceable because of indefiniteness in that a quantity for the term is not specified. Official Comment 2 to section 2—306 states in part: 'Under this Article, a contract for output...is not too indefinite since it is held to mean the actual good faith output...of the particular party. Nor does such a contract lack mutuality of obligation since, under this section, the party who will determine quantity is required to operate his plant or conduct his business in good faith and according to commercial standards of fair dealing in the trade so that his output...will proximate a reasonably foreseeable figure.'

The real issue in this case is whether the agreement carries with it an implication that defendant was obligated to continue to manufacture bread crumbs for the full term. *Section 2—306* of the Uniform Commercial Code, entitled 'Output, Requirements and Exclusive Dealings' provides:

'(1) A term which measures the quantity by the output of the seller or the requirements of the buyer means such actual output or requirements as may occur in *good faith*, except that no quantity unreasonably disproportionate to any stated estimate or in the absence of a stated estimate to any normal or otherwise comparable prior output or requirements may be tendered or demanded.

'(2) A lawful agreement by either the seller or the buyer For exclusive dealing in the kind of goods concerned Imposes unless otherwise agreed an obligation By the seller to use best efforts to supply the goods and by the buyer to use best efforts to promote their sale.'

The Official Comment thereunder reads in part:

'Subsection (2), on exclusive dealing, makes explicit the commercial rule embodied in this Act under which the parties to such contracts *are held to have impliedly*, even when not expressly, bound themselves to use reasonable diligence as

well as good faith in their performance of the contract....An exclusive dealing agreement brings into play all of the good faith aspects of the output and requirement problems of subsection (1). It also raises questions of insecurity and right to adequate assurance under this Article.'

Section 2—306 is consistent with prior New York case law. Every contract of this type *imposes an obligation of good faith* in its performance (Uniform Commercial Code, $1—203$). Under the Uniform Commercial Code, the commercial background and intent *must be read into the language of any agreement* and good faith is demanded in the performance of that agreement (Uniform Commercial Code, $2—306$), and, under the decisions relating to output contracts, it is clearly the general rule that good faith cessation of production terminates any further obligations thereunder and excuses further performance by the party discontinuing production. [Emphasis added.]

This is not a situation where defendant ceased its main operation of bread baking. Rather, defendant contends in a conclusory fashion that it was 'uneconomical' or 'economically not feasible' for it to continue to make bread crumbs. Although plaintiff observed in his motion papers that defendant claimed it was not economically feasible to make the crumbs, plaintiff did not admit that as a fact. In any event, 'economic feasibility', an expression subject to many interpretations, would not be a precise or reliable test.

There are present here intertwined questions of fact, whether defendant performed in good faith and whether it stopped its manufacture of bread crumbs in good faith, neither of which can be resolved properly on this record. The seller's duty to remain in crumb production is a matter calling for a close scrutiny of its motives, confined here by the papers to financial reasons. It is undisputed that defendant leveled its crumb making machinery only after plaintiff refused to agree to a price higher than that specified in the agreement and that it then sold the raw materials to manufacturers of animal food. There are before us no componental figures indicating the actual cost of the finished bread crumbs to defendant, statements as to the profits derived or the losses sustained, or data specifying the net or gross return realized from the animal food transactions.

The parties by their contract gave the right of cancellation to either by providing for a six months' notice to the other. The apparent purpose of such a stipulation was to provide an opportunity to either the seller or buyer to conclude their dealings in the event that the transactions were not as profitable or advantageous as desired or expected, or for any other reason. Correspondingly, such a notice would also furnish the receiver of it a chance to secure another outlet or source of supply, as the case might be. Short of such a cancellation, defendant was expected to continue to perform in good faith and could cease production of the bread crumbs, a single facet of its operation, only in good faith. Obviously, a bankruptcy or genuine imperiling of the very existence if its entire business caused by the production of the crumbs would warrant cessation of production of that item; the yield of less profit from its sale than expected would not. Since bread crumbs were but a part of defendant's enterprise and since there was a contractual right of cancellation, good faith required continued production until cancellation, even if there be no profit. In circumstances such as these and without more, defendant would be justified, in good faith, in ceasing production of the single item prior to cancellation only if its losses from continuance would be more than trivial, which, overall, is a question of fact.

[Affirmed.]

Question

1. What parts of the above case represent the court's construction of the contract language and which parts represent interpretation of it?

Joseph Martin, Jr. Delicatessen v. Schumacher, 417 N.E.2d 541 (N.Y., 1981) concerned a renewal clause in a five year lease of realty. The lease was for five years at rentals that ranged from $500 for the first year to $650 for the fifth year. The renewal clause read: "Tenant may renew this lease for an additional period of five years at annual rentals to be agreed upon." Tenant gave landlord notice of intent to renew, as required by the lease, and landlord made it clear that renewal could be had only at a rental "starting at $900 per month." Tenant's appraiser found a "fair market rental to be $541 per month." Tenant sued for specific performance of the lease "to compel the landlord to extend the lease for the additional term at the appraiser's figure or such other sum as the court would decide was reasonable."

Trial court dismissed the tenant's complaint on the grounds that the agreement to agree on future rent was unenforceable because of uncertainty. The intermediate court [the Appellate Division in New York] reversed and declared that "a renewal clause in a lease providing for future agreement on the rent to be paid during the renewal term is renewable if it is established that the parties' intent was not to terminate in the event of a failure to agree." If the tenant met the burden of proving the intent was not to terminate, the trial court was directed to set a "reasonable rent." One appellate division judge would have skipped the first step and simply ordered the trial court to set a reasonable rent. The Court of Appeals reversed by a 4-1 vote, one of the majority writing a concurring opinion. Three members of the majority held that "unless otherwise mandated by law (e.g. residential emergency rent control statutes), a contract is a private 'ordering' in which a party binds himself to do, or not to do, a particular thing.... This liberty is no right at all if it is not accompanied by freedom not to contract. The corollary is that before one may secure redress in our courts because another has failed to honor a promise, *it must appear that the promisee has assented to the obligation in question.* It also follows that, before the power of law can be invoked to enforce a promise, it must be sufficiently certain and specific so that what was promised can be ascertained." The court pointed out that "if a methodology for determining the rent was to be found within the four corners of the lease" that "would have sufficed." Because there was no "formula" and no other language indicating that the parties intended to be bound to a fair rental, there was no way to enforce the clause. The majority also indicated that while a course of dealing (a previous series of annual renewals) might suffice under the Uniform Commercial Code "to give meaning to an otherwise uncertain term," the U.C.C. applied only to sales of goods and not to realty.

One of the four judges voting to reverse the Appellate Division, wrote separately to concur in the result but stated that if a course of dealing could have been proved in this case he would have voted to allow it to "make a clause providing for renewal at a rental 'to be agreed upon' enforceable."

The dissenter said: "While I recognize that the traditional rule is that a provision for renewal of a lease must be 'certain' in order to render it binding and enforceable, in my view the better rule would be that if the tenant can establish its entitlement to renewal under the lease, the mere presence of a provision calling for renewal at 'rentals to be agreed upon' should not prevent *judicial intervention to fix rent* at a reasonable rate in order to avoid a forfeiture." [Emphasis added.]

Were all of the judges interpreting the language? Was the dissenter construing the contract to give the lessee a remedy even though the language did not show intent? Were all three opinions really just interpreting the language? That is, were the three opinions simply implying different meanings to the words "to be agreed upon" and hence interpreting the language differently but not construing the contract without regard to the expressed intent of the parties?

B. Parol Evidence

Introduction

Parol evidence is at once easy and hard. The concept is easy. The Parol Evidence Rule seeks to bar admission of any writings or oral terms which the parties allegedly agreed to if these terms came *before* a signed writing embodying the terms of a contract, and if they contradict any of the written terms of the contract. The theory is that if persons intend a writing to reflect their agreement then everything leading up to it is negotiation and is not intended to be part of the contract. If it were intended to be part of the contract it would be in the writing. Fraud, duress and mistake can avoid the effect of a writing—but then, they can overcome the apparent agreement of the parties, *i.e.* any of the three can void a contract. (See Part V.)

Problem on Parol Evidence

Problem #1. A and B both sign a writing which says that "A agrees to sell his 1995 Saab to B for $15,000 and B agrees to buy it for that price, A to deliver the Saab to B when B brings cash or a certified check to A, the delivery of the car and check to take place on_____[date specified.]" If B later wants to say that the price was $13,000 and not $15,000 the court will have three inquiries. Did the parties intend the above writing to embody the terms of their contract? Does B's allegation of $13,000 contradict a term of the writing? Did the alleged agreement for $13,000 preceed the signing of the writing? Assume that the answers to all three questions are yes. What result? What if the answer to the first question is no? Today, where goods are involved § 2-202 of the U.C.C. states that any oral statement that is contemporaneous or prior to the writing intended to embody the terms of the agreement or any writing that is prior to the embodying writing will be excluded.

Note on Williston vs. Corbin—Two Approaches to Interpreting the Contract

Even though oral statements and other writings preceding and sometimes contemporaneous with a writing intended to embody the terms of a contract cannot be introduced into evidence if they would contradict the embodying writing, they can often be introduced to "explain" the writing. In this way negotiations that preceded or were contemporaneous with the embodying writing can be introduced not to contradict it but to explain it. Sometimes, oral statements and/or other prior or contemporaneous writings can be introduced to "add" to the embodying writing. Whether or not additional terms can be tacked onto a writing is determined by whether or not the embodying writing was determined to be the complete and/or exclusive statement of the rights of the additional parties. In other words, how much did the parties intend to include in the embodying writing—the whole contract, only part of it, none of it (meaning it is not the embodying writing at all)? How is this determined? There are two major standards: one is endorsed by professor and treatise writer Williston, the other by professor and treatise writer Corbin.

According to Williston, you look within the four corners of the writing to determine the intent of the parties as to whether they intend the writing to embody their agreement or whether it is merely a notation of ideas or a record of negotiations or an exchange of views which are not meant to be binding as an embodiment of an agreement, a contract. Furthermore, if you determine that the writing is intended to embody the agreement in some way, to some extent, you then look within the writing to determine what the parties intended. This in turn involves determining both what they meant and how much of the contract they intended to include in the writing. For example, if the writing is formal in appearance and tone and expresses language of agreement just by looking at it the judge may determine that it is intended to embody to some extent an agreement by the parties. The judge then reads it and if the language is clear the judge uses his/her own knowledge of it plus a dictionary to determine what the parties intended. [Keep in mind the objective vs. subjective standard for determining intent.] Finally the judge decides if the writing was meant to include only a part of an agreement or the whole thing. Once again the judge looks within the writing to find in the language some indication of whether or not the parties intended this writing to exclude other non-contradictory language. In other words, can additional terms be added so long as they don't contradict the writing? The answer is no if the judge in reading the writing concludes it is intended to include everything that was agreed on, the whole contract. Just as the judge (and all of these questions are usually questions of law) looks to formality to determine an intent to have the writing embody some part or all of an agreement, and just as she would use a dictionary to determine the doubtful meaning of words (otherwise using her own understanding of words in common usage), so the judge has certain rules to help her determine if the writing is intended to be an exclusive statement. The easiest way is if the writing says it is: "This writing is the complete and exclusive statement of the rights and liabilities of the parties and embodies their whole agreement." If the writing doesn't say this, how complete is it? Does it cover many aspects of the agreement so that the one alleged to belong with it would normally be expected to be there? If so, why isn't it there? Because it isn't part of the agreement? Also, is the additional term one that is "collateral" to, which is to say related to, parallel to, close to the terms of the writing or is it on a wholly different subject? In this regard, if the term is too close to other terms and if the other terms are quite detailed, the question is "why wasn't it put into the writing?" On the other hand, if it isn't related to the agreement at all, is it likely that it was part of the agreement?

Corbin, unlike Williston, believed that to determine whether or not the writing was intended to be a partial or complete embodiment of the agreement often required the court to go outside the writing to the circumstances, including the discussions, preceding and contemporaneous with the writing. Corbin's views are reflected in U.C.C. 2-202 and in many Restatement of Contracts 2nd sections. For example: did the parties intend the writing to embody at least some of the terms of the agreement? What if one person said: "It looks like a contract [i.e. a writing reflecting a contract] but it's really just a stage in the negotiations. We hadn't really decided to go through with it." Williston would probably not admit this; Corbin probably would on the issue of "was the writing intended to embody all or some of the contract?" Likewise on the issue of what the words mean. Both would allow explanations of ambiguous terms but Corbin would be more relaxed about what an ambiguous term is. For example, how much is a ton; does the word "north" mean true or magnetic. Both Williston and Corbin would probably allow evidence to explain these words where two possible meanings exist. What about a term that has a common meaning but one of the parties said they intended it to have a special meaning? For example, for brevity's sake one of the parties claims, when they used the term "United Kingdom" which everyone agrees includes England, Scotland (though maybe not for long) and Wales, they (the parties) intended to include in it the Republic of Ireland (i.e.

southern as opposed to northern Ireland.) As anyone who has lived in places like Boston, MA for long knows this is not the kind of statement you would make in South Boston on St. Patrick's Day or any other day for that matter. But one of the parties insists that is the meaning they attached to the term. Williston would exclude it as contradicting the known meaning of the term, United Kingdom. Corbin would probably allow evidence to discover what meaning they attached to it. Because the meaning they attached would be a fact question, a jury would probably decide it. The court would then construe/interpret the meaning of the contract based on the factual finding of the jury as to what the word in the writing meant. What about whether or not the writing was intended as the complete and exclusive statement of the parties agreement? Corbin would be far more inclined to let in evidence other than the writing as to the intent of the parties.

When analyzing the following problems assume the problem occurs first in a jurisdiction recognizing Williston's approach, and secondly in a jurisdiction recognizing Corbin's approach. What are the differences?

Additional Problems on Parol Evidence

Problem #2. Back to the Saab. B arrives on the stated day with a cashier's check for $15,000. A cashier's check differs from a certified check in that a cashier's check is a check in which the bank is both the drawer and drawee of the check. A certified check is one in which the person with an account at the bank draws a check on the bank; the depositor is the drawer and the bank is the drawee; the bank then stamps the check "certified" which means that the drawer cannot stop payment on it and furthermore that the bank may be sued by a holder of the check. The only difference between a cashier's check and a certified check is that the depositor issues the certified check and the bank in essence guarantees payment and can be sued on it; the bank issues the cashier's check and can be sued on it. [See U.C.C. §§ 3-408, 3-409, 3-411 and 3-412 (1990 revision) NOTE: these sections are not assigned but are here for your information.] If anything, a cashier's check is a more certain and safe method of payment than a certified check. Nevertheless, A refuses to deliver the Saab to B, claiming that B has breached the contract. [If one party breaches the contract the other party need not perform. We will discuss this more thoroughly in Part IV.] B sues A for damages and wishes to introduce evidence that when the parties wrote "certified" they meant some kind of check either issued or guaranteed by a bank. A moves for summary judgment based on the fact that B's proposed evidence directly contradicts a term of the writing. Decide the case.

Problem (#3). Assume the same facts, but now B sues A for breach because A did not clean the interior, clean and wax the exterior of the car, have the engine tuned, nor remove two dents from a fender. A claims that these terms contradict the writing and in any event would be in the writing if the parties had agreed to them. Decide the case.

Problem (#4). What if B sues A for breach because A did not deliver a U-haul trailer and a set of repair tools which B says are part of the deal. A moves for summary judgment. Decide the case.

Problem (#5). Now, B sues A for breach because A did not deliver a 16" color TV when B brought the $15,000 for the car. B claims that the TV was part of the deal, in fact was an inducement to get B to buy the car. B says that when he and A were about to sign the paper, B said to A "What about the TV" and A said "This paper is only about the car—you'll get the TV." A moves for summary judgment . Decide the case.

Problem #6. Discuss how Corbin and Williston would decide the contract if the writing included the clause: "This writing embodies the complete and exclusive terms of the agreement of the parties."

As a concluding note to this section, the word "integration" appears often in connection with parol evidence. It means the same as embodiment. A partial integration means that part of the contract is embodied in or integrated into the writing. A total integration means that the whole contract is embodied in or integrated into the writing.

Also, do not confuse the parol evidence rule with modification. If, *after* the writing which integrates the contract has been signed, the parties agree to some change in the agreement, the parol evidence rule does not apply. A change made after the agreement is in effect is a modification. The parol evidence rule only applies to oral or written terms which preceded or are contemporaneous with the written integration.

Central Massachusetts Television, Inc., v. Amplicon, Inc.

930 F.Supp. 16
United States District Court, Massachusetts, 1996.

[CMTV filed a multi-count complaint against Amplicon including in part a claim for money damages based on breach of contract (count I). The other two counts were for fraud and deceptive trade practices. Amplicon denied this and counter-claimed that CMTV breached its lease contract with Amplicon by failing to make quarterly rent payments. In 1988 CMTV (which operated Channel 27) decided to upgrade its transmission equipment in two phases. With this purpose CMTV entered into a lease with Amplicon ("the Phase I Lease Agreement") for Amplicon to lease to CMTV transmitter equipment. On October 7, 1988 Amplicon sent the Phase I lease agreement to CMTV. CMTV returned the Phase I lease agreement, which it had signed, to Amplicon on November 2, 1988. In the words of the court: "Amplicon accepted this agreement on January 20, 1989," thus indicating that Amplicon, although it drafted the agreement, sent it unsigned to CMTV making CMTV the offeror. The initial term of the lease was 24 months, from July 1, 1989 to June 30, 1991. It contained a clause which provided that the lease would automatically renew for an additional one year term unless CMTV terminated it 180 days or more before the end of the initial term by certified mail delivered to Amplicon. Paragraph 11 of the lease stated: "Title to any hardware shall at all times remain in the Lessor.... The Leased Property is and shall remain personal property of the Lessor. Upon the expiration or termination of this lease...the Lessee...shall return...Leased Property...to Lessor." Early in 1990 CMTV approached Amplicon with a proposal to lease more TV equipment from it. In April Amplicon forwarded to CMTV a proposed lease agreement ("Phase II") for the additional equipment. As with Phase I, Amplicon would purchase the equipment and lease it to CMTV. The Phase II agreement, which was not signed by Amplicon, stated at the bottom: "Until this document...has been signed by a duly authorized officer of Amplicon, Inc. it shall constitute only an offer by Lessee to enter into this Lease Agreement on the terms stated herein by the Lessor." CMTV, in May of 1990, signed the agreement and returned it with a deposit check. Amplicon never signed the agreement and returned the check in a letter dated January 11, 1991. The letter stated that Amplicon's Finance Committee had not approved the financing for Phase II.

This case resulted from a dispute over CMTV's right to buy the Phase I equipment at the end of the lease period. CMTV contended that, although no such provision appeared in the lease, there was an enforceable agreement between CMTV and Amplicon under which CMTV had the right to purchase the Phase I equipment at the end of the lease term by tendering 10% of its original cost. In three letters a proposed buyout by CMTV was addressed. On October 25, 1988, about three weeks after Amplicon sent the Phase I lease to CMTV, an officer of Amplicon sent a letter to CMTV which stated that the fair market value of the equipment at the end of the Phase I lease period would be about "10% of its original value." In the words of the court: "The letter then presented Amplicon with three options at the end of the lease: 1) cancel the lease and return the equipment, 2) refinance the equipment based on the fair market value at the end of the lease, or 3) buy the equipment based on the fair market value at the end of the lease. Kawar [the Amplicon executive who wrote the letter] closed the October 25 letter by stating that '[he] believe[d] this letter will keep everyone satisfied.'" On October 31, Kawar wrote again to CMTV stating in part: "By selling you the equipment for the ten percent (10%) at the end of the term, we can realize a fair and reasonable return on our investment. The most important reason for retaining the *operating lease structure* is that Amplicon can reclaim the equipment...in the event of bankruptcy or default....If we structure a capital lease *with a stated buyout* then it may be easily argued that the lease is a lease only for security. In case of default, rather than being the owner of the equipment, Amplicon would be treated as a secured lender only, and not as the owner of the equipment." What Amplicon is saying here in these two Catch-22, through the looking glass, Alice in Wonderland letters, is that if it puts a 10% buyout clause in the lease agreement and CMTV goes broke, in a bankruptcy proceeding Amplicon might not be able to get the equipment back because the clause would make it look like Amplicon was selling the equipment to CMTV and only using the lease as a form. To avoid this, Kawar is saying in effect "between us there's a 10% buyout clause but we can't put it in the lease." Note the date on the letters and the date CMTV sent the lease back to Amplicon and the date Amplicon accepted it. What is the significance for CMTV's claim that it had a buyout right? The opinion below will discuss it. Note: the difference between a lease and a sale is that in a lease transaction the lessor keeps title and can reclaim, "get back," the "leased" equipment if the lessee breaches the agreement ("defaults" and/or goes into "bankruptcy.") On the other hand if it is a sale, the seller often cannot get back the "sold" equipment from the buyer; in a sale transaction, title goes to the buyer and if buyer defaults or goes bankrupt, often all seller can do is make a claim against the buyer for the damages but not get the goods (equipment) back.

In another letter on January 4, 1991 from an officer of CMTV's parent company to Amplicon the officer stated in part: "As you agreed, you will provide me with a proposed buyout amount with respect to the [Phase I lease], between [CMTV] and [Amplicon]. I understand that the proposed buyout date will be June 30, 1991, which is the end of the base term of the lease. Although the date is somewhere [d]own the road, I believe that it is a good idea to go ahead and get started with all of the paperwork, since I will have to present your proposal to our Board for [its] confirmation." The court made no finding that Amplicon ever acknowledged or commented on this "understanding" in its January 11, 1991 letter or at any other time. The statement by CMTV in this letter of January 4, 1991 did have significance as will be seen in the opinion.

CMTV initially asserted additional claims based on Amplicon's violation of an alleged contract to enter into a proposed second lease, or in the alternative, for breach of the second lease itself. CMTV later stated in its opposition to Amplicon's motion for summary judgment that it was no longer seeking damages for these alleged breaches.

The following were among other findings of fact made by the court.

"9. The Lease Agreement also included the following integration clause, which plays a crucial role in this case: This is the complete Agreement by and between the parties hereto. This Agreement can only be modified by written addendum duly signed by persons authorized to sign agreements on behalf of the customer (Lessee) and by a duly authorized officer of Amplicon, Inc. (Lessor). No oral or written agreement, guaranty, promise, condition, representation or warranty shall be binding unless made a part of this Agreement by duly executed addendum. Any variance from the terms and conditions of this Agreement, unless duly executed, will be of no force and effect. All agreements, representations, and warranties contained in this Lease, or in any document or certificate delivered pursuant hereto or in connection herewith, shall survive the expiration or other termination of this Lease.... This Lease shall be construed in accordance with, and shall be governed by, the laws of the State of California."

"19. CMTV did not notify Amplicon before January 1, 1991 of its intention to terminate the Phase I Lease Agreement, as required by Paragraph 2 of the Agreement. Amplicon took the position that the lease had been automatically extended for an additional one-year term as provided in Paragraph 2 of the Lease."

"20. In July, 1991, CMTV obtained a preliminary injunction from the Superior Court Division of the Massachusetts Trial Court, preventing Amplicon from repossessing the equipment from CMTV's Boylston facility. The injunction was for a period of four months and required CMTV to pay Amplicon $4,000 per month as rent.

"21. After the preliminary injunction expired, Amplicon repossessed the equipment and eventually sold it for $45,000."]

GORTON, District Judge.

III. The Parol Evidence Rule

The gravamen of CMTV's breach of contract claim (Count I) is that there was an enforceable agreement between the parties that entitled CMTV to purchase the Phase I equipment at the end of the lease term. The determination of that issue is dependent upon this Court's application of California's parol evidence rule.

A. The Rule

California's parol evidence rule provides that: (a) Terms set forth in a writing intended by the parties as a final expression of their agreement with respect to such terms as are included therein may not be contradicted by evidence of any prior agreement or of a contemporaneous oral agreement. (b) The terms set forth in a writing described in subdivision (a) may be explained or supplemented by evidence of consistent additional terms unless the writing is intended also as a complete and exclusive statement of the terms of the agreement.... (d) The court shall determine whether the writing is intended as a final expression of their agreement with respect to such terms as are included therein and whether the writing is intended also as a complete and exclusive statement of the terms of the agreement. Also, the execution of a contract in writing, whether the law requires it to be written or not, supersedes all the negotiations or stipulations concerning its matter which preceded or accompanied the execution of the instrument.

In short, the rule provides that where the parties to a contract have set forth the terms of their agreement in a writing which they intend as the final and complete expression of their understanding, it is deemed integrated and may not be contradicted by evidence of any prior agreement or of a contemporaneous oral agreement.

Despite its name, the parol evidence rule is not merely a rule of evidence concerning the method of proving an agreement. Rather, the rule is one of substantive law making an integrated written agreement between parties their exclusive and binding contract "no matter how persuasive the evidence of additional oral understandings. Such evidence is legally irrelevant and cannot support a judgment." Marani v. Jackson, 183 Cal.App.3d 695, 701, 228 Cal.Rptr. 518 (1986) (citation omitted). The determination of whether the parol evidence rule applies is a question of law to be made by the court.

One of the policies advanced by the rule is the reluctance of courts to permit "clear and unambiguous integrated agreements,... to be rendered meaningless by the oral revisionist claims of a party who, at the end of the game, does not care for the result." Banco, 234 Cal.App.3d at 1011, 285 Cal.Rptr. 870.

B. Application of the Rule

To apply the California parol evidence rule, we need to answer two questions: 1) Was the writing intended to be an integration, i.e., a complete and final expression of the parties' agreement, precluding any evidence of collateral agreements? and 2) Is the agreement susceptible of the meaning contended by the party offering the evidence?

1. Is the Writing intended to be an Integration?

At the first step of the analysis, the crucial issue is whether the contracting parties intended the written instrument to serve as the exclusive embodiment of their agreement. To resolve that threshold issue, the court properly may consider all the surrounding circumstances, including the prior negotiations of the parties. However, in determining the issue of integration, the collateral agreement will be examined only insofar as it does not directly contradict an express term of the written agreement: "it cannot reasonably be presumed that the parties intended to integrate two directly contradictory terms in the same agreement." Gerdlund, 190 Cal.App.3d at 271, 235 Cal.Rptr. 279.

In Banco, the California Court of Appeals enunciated four questions to be answered in making the determination of whether a writing is integrated: 1) Does the written agreement appear on its face to be a complete agreement? 2) Does the collateral agreement directly contradict the written agreement? 3) If the collateral agreement had been actually agreed to, would it certainly have been included in the written instrument? and 4) Would evidence of the collateral agreement be likely to mislead the trier of fact? 234 Cal.App.3d at 1002-03, 285 Cal.Rptr. 870.

In the case at bar, this Court concludes that each of the foregoing questions must be answered affirmatively and thus the Phase I Agreement is an integrated contract. First, the presence of an "integration" clause is" very persuasive, if not controlling," on that issue. Banco, 234 Cal.App.3d at 1003, 285 Cal.Rptr. 870. The Phase I lease contains an integration clause that provides that it is "the complete Agreement by and between the parties".

Moreover, the collateral agreement directly contradicts the written instrument. Amplicon persuasively argues that the suggestion that CMTV had the right to tender 10% of the original cost of the Equipment to Amplicon and keep the Equipment is flatly inconsistent with paragraph 11 of the Lease, which provided that title to the equipment "shall at all times remain in the Lessor....".

Finally, if the collateral agreement had actually been agreed to, it certainly would have been included in the written instrument. That determination is made by examining the entire transaction and confirmed by the fact that the parties were sophisticated and experienced businessmen. As the Court concluded in the Banco case: "[i]f a prior binding commitment had been made, as opposed to incomplete negotiations, it would seem obvious, if not compelling, that the terms of such [an] arrangement would have been included in the very written agreement which purported to fully describe the entire relationship of the parties." Id. at 1007, 228 Cal.Rptr. 518. Accordingly, this Court concludes that the Phase I Agreement is an integrated writing.

2. Is the Written Agreement Reasonably Susceptible to the Meaning Supplied by the Proffered Agreement?

After considering the issue of integration, the Court must next consider whether the evidence of the alleged collateral agreement is nonetheless admissible to explain the meaning of the written contractual language. When the collateral agreement directly contradicts the written instrument, however, "it is not possible to say that the written instrument is reasonably susceptible to the proposed new meaning of the parties' [contractual] relationship which would be supplied by the parol evidence...." Banco, 234 Cal.App.3d at 1008, 285 Cal.Rptr. 870. Indeed, "[t]estimony of intention which is contrary to a contract's express terms...does not give meaning to the contract; rather it seeks to substitute a different meaning." Gerdlund, 190 Cal.App.3d at 273, 235 Cal.Rptr. 279. Inasmuch as the alleged agreement providing CMTV with a 10% buy-out option directly contradicts the written Phase I Agreement, the evidence proffered by CMTV is inadmissible to explain the meaning of the written lease.

C. The Fraud Exception to the Parol Evidence Rule

CMTV next attempts to invoke the "fraud exception" to the parol evidence rule. Although a recognized exception to the parol evidence rule permits a party to introduce evidence of fraud in order to nullify a written contract, that exception is not applicable where that party proffers the parol evidence to demonstrate a fraudulent promise directly at variance with the written agreement. The foregoing rule was articulated by the California Court of Appeals in Bank of America v. Lamb Finance Co., 179 Cal.App.2d 498, 3 Cal.Rptr. 877 (1960), as follows: "[I]f, to induce one to enter an agreement, a party makes an independent promise without intention of performing it, this separate false promise constitutes fraud which may be proven to nullify the main agreement; but if the false promise relates to the matter covered by the main agreement and contradicts or varies the terms thereof, any evidence of the false promise directly violates the parol evidence rule and is inadmissible." Id. at 502, 3 Cal.Rptr. 877. Because, the alleged promise to sell the transmission equipment directly contradicts the terms of the written agreement, CMTV's effort to invoke the fraud exception to the parol evidence rule is unavailing.

In sum, although the October, 1988 letters from Amplicon to CMTV make reference to a possible buyout option, those letters were antecedent to the lease (with its integration provision) which was finally accepted. Because a collateral buyout provision would directly contradict provisions of the Phase I Lease, and because that lease was intended by the parties as a final expression of their agreement, evidence of such a prior agreement is inadmissible. Cal.Civ.Code § 1856(a). Furthermore, the execution of a contract in writing supersedes all negotiations or stipulations concerning its subject matter which "preceded or accompanied" the execution of the contract. Id. at § 1625.

Our conclusion is bolstered by the fact that the January 4, 1991 letter from CMTV to Amplicon stated that "As you agreed, you will provide me with a proposed buyout amount with respect to the lease...," indicating that CMTV understood that such a buyout was not already part of the Phase I Lease. Indeed, that lease provides that: "No oral or written agreement, guaranty, promise, condition, representation or warranty shall be binding unless made a part of this Agreement by duly executed addendum. Any variance from the terms and conditions of this Agreement, unless duly executed, will be of no force and effect."

[Amplicon's motion for summary judgment as to Count I of CMTV's Complaint will be allowed.]

Questions

1. Could the court's language in B 1 concerning title to equipment "at all times" remaining with the Lessor be "explained" as saying that the title is to remain in the Lessor until the end of the lease but had no relevance to what would happen when the lease ended? Could the letters of October 25 and 31 be read together with the lease to mean that the lease only covers the lease term? For its term the equipment belongs to the lessor. But at the end, the lessee has three options. The reference to bankruptcy and default probably nullifies this in terms of third parties. In other words, the lessor does not want third parties to conclude that the lessor has really sold the equipment to the lessee on June 30, 1989 and to avoid that result nothing can be put in the lease to indicate that it is not a lease — a transaction in which the lessee is not the owner. Even if the lease, to a reasonable third person, looks like a writing which excludes any right of the lessee to buy the equipment, could

the lessee say that between themselves while it is a real lease nevertheless the lessee is intended to have a right of buyout. Isn't that seen from the letters of October 25 and 31? In fact, isn't that the most likely construction to put on the letters. Consider this case in the light of *New York Trust* and *Hicks*. No third party is damaged by the "side" agreement. Therefore, why shouldn't it be part of the contract? Is the integration clause mentioned by the court in the preceding paragraph, significant if the intent was to make third parties think there was no buyout and hence no possibility of a sale transaction. The reason it is not all in the lease is clear. Lessor wants to make sure no one can later prevent it from reclaiming the equipment on lessee's default or bankruptcy on the grounds that the lessor is not the owner. Therefore, the lease is not the "integration" of the whole agreement. The court says, in B 1, that all "circumstances" must be considered, and continues that "it cannot reasonably be *presumed* that the parties intended to integrate [put] two directly contradictory terms in the same agreement." [Emphasis added.] Could not the presumption be overcome by the 'joke' approach of *New York Trust* and *Hicks*? Consider this argument as if you were representing CMTV and trying to get by the summary judgment motion made by Amplicon. Is there an issue of fact here to go to the jury? Is it easier to assert and establish than fraud? Why?

2. Refer back to subsections (a) and (d) of California's parol evidence rule in A and the last two paragraphs in B. Does it matter whether the statement concerning the 10% buyout was part of a negotiation or a prior, or even a contemporary, agreement for purposes of its being excluded under the parol evidence rule?

3. Again, referring back to subsection (a) in A, and the court's conclusion in B 1 that the Phase I Agreement is an "integrated writing," how do we know the writing—in this case the lease—is "a writing intended by the parties as a final expression of their agreement?" What if there were no integration clause?

4. Why do you suppose the law of California was used to decide a case brought in the United States District Court in Massachusetts concerning a Massachusetts TV station?

5. Work out a way to get around the parol evidence rule on behalf of CMTV. Even if the "joke" approach didn't move the court, could it be argued that the lease covered only its own time frame and not what would happen when it ended?

6. Note that during January 1991 CMTV was apparently still waiting to hear from Amplicon about Phase II and, while waiting, the 180 days (January 1, 1991) notice period passed leading to an automatic renewal under the lease. How could CMTV get around this or could it? What do you suppose was going on in late 1990 that led CMTV to miss its deadline? What did it presume it could do? Do you see why clients need continuous care in their affairs?

Note on Fraud, Illegality, Duress, Mistake and Accident

The principal case discusses fraud, but not only fraud may be introduced to establish that the writing does not reflect or embody the intent of the parties. In addition to fraud, illegality, duress, mistake, and accident may be introduced to show that the writing does not reflect the intention of the parties to contract because no meeting of the minds has taken place. No objective offer and acceptance has taken place between the two parties. Rather, one party has done something to induce a second to a contract that the second party does not intend to enter into. Go back for a moment to *Embry v. McKittrick*, in Part I. No matter what McKittrick thought when he said to Embry 'You'll be all right. Get your men out" the court saw that as an intent to be bound, whether Embry made the offer and McKittrick accepted it or Embry only made an inquiry and McKittrick said in essence, "If you get your men out you'll be all right, by which I mean you'll have a contract for another year; i,e. I promise you a contract for another year if you'll get back to work."

What if Embry had, instead of talking with McKittrick, taken a weapon with him and threatened McKittrick with bodily harm if McKittrick did not sign a paper which said that Embry had a job for another year and furthermore said: "The parties agree that this contract has not been signed under duress or as a result of any fraud or illegality." If McKittrick wanted to testify that he was threatened and terrified into signing the paper even though he knew its contents, it is doubtful if any court would bar that testimony. What if instead of a threat Embry used trickery? He gave McKittrick the paper saying that it was only a receipt for inventory and McKittrick signed without reading it. Here McKittrick is less likely to win, although in a Pennsylvania case a surviving spouse was able to introduce evidence of negligent misrepresentation against an insurance agent who assured the two spouses at the time they signed it that the policy had coverage sufficient to pay off their $15,000 mortgage. When one spouse died the survivor found the policy only paid $10,000. Three courts upheld the survivor's right to testify to facts in direct contradiction to the writing. The court allowed $10,000 on the policy and $5,000 for the tort of negligent misrepresentation by the agent. Note the interplay between tort and contract here. But for the contract there would be no tort. Nevertheless, although the contract gives rise to the tort, the action is in tort. The court held that the evidence of the misrepresentation was not being introduced to 'add to or vary the legal effect of the writing' but rather "since the prior statements and agreements are highly relevant, indeed material, to the issue of whether Mr. McGibbeny committed the tort of negligent misrepresentation, and since that testimony is not being offered to alter, vary or contradict the terms of the writing, the 'Parol Evidence Rule' does not bar its admission into evidence.'" See *Rempel v. Nationwide Life Ins. Co.*, 323 A.2d 193, 196 , *aff'd* 370 A.2d 366(Pa. Super Ct., 1974). The superior court, in short, found that the evidence of prior oral agreements went to the issue of whether the writing was an integration of the parties' intent. The evidence was not introduced to in some way affect the interpretation of the writing but to say that the writing did not at all embody what the parties agreed; the writing did not integrate the agreement; the writing did not say what the parties had agreed.

Some courts would bar such an action because to allow suit would conflict with the writing. Indeed *Rempel* made reference to an earlier Pennsylvania case (which the Superior Court made no effort to reconcile, by implication disapproved, and did not follow) that said "Merely bringing an action in trespass for deceit instead of an assumpsit for breach of contract will not suffice to circumvent the parol evidence rule" (cited at 323 A.2d 195). This is of course what happened here. A tort action is combined with a contract action. To prove the tort action, the plaintiff must establish that defendant made representations. However, normally the contract would follow and supercede the representations, as would the writing embodying the contract.

The key in *Rempel* is that the plaintiff made no effort to reconcile the representations with the writing. Plaintiff admitted that the writing conflicted with the previous oral statements. Plaintiff did not admit that the writing superseded them. Plaintiff said in essence 'Yes I signed this writing. No I didn't read it. I trusted the insurance man that what we said was in it. No that writing does not embody our agreement." *Rempel* is a Corbin case. Once duress, fraud, mistake, accident or illegality is alleged, anything can be brought in to say 'this writing does not embody what we agreed to.' The earlier Pennsylvania case is a Williston case. Basically the rule which he endorsed is 'you signed it; short of showing that you did not intend to have it embody your agreement when you signed it, *i.e.* you had a gun at your head, or you can establish fraud that induced you to sign it and the fraud does not contradict the writing, you are liable in accord with its terms.' The Corbin rule goes to whether you would have signed it if you read it and understood it—you can produce evidence to show you would not if you had, so long as you can produce a reason for signing without reading and/or understanding. The Williston rule goes not to whether you would have signed if you understood, but rather did you sign; did anyone prevent you from exercising your will not to sign (gun to head), were you tricked into signing by a promise not in conflict with the writing on which you relied ('if you sign this insurance contract, I'll make you a winner in our new car contest' as opposed to 'this insurance contract pays $15,000' when the writing says clearly $10,000). Williston respected the writing more. Corbin less.

In *CMTV* an oral promise which the court found to be at variance with the writing was not allowed. *CMTV* involved two businesses, not two spouses signing a life insurance contract in their home with a salesperson whom they trusted enough to admit to their home. Did this influence the courts? When we work with the cases in Part V we will deal with circumstances that make a contract void or voidable—these are usually factors that take away a person's freedom of the will, the freedom to say no "I won't sign until I have this read over by someone who understands it." Here we assume that no such problems exist; people could say "no" but don't. So, they try to say this writing doesn't embody what we agreed. The older Williston rule in two words says "too bad." If two more words are needed "you're stuck." The newer Corbin rule says, the writing is not magic. You can always bring in evidence to show that it doesn't integrate, embody the agreement, no matter what the writing says.

The next case revolves around the interpretation of an ambiguous sentence from a settlement agreement between Bobby Sid Taylor (Plaintiff) and the State Farm Insurance Company regarding an automobile accident.

"WHEREAS, STATE FARM has agreed that uninsured motorist coverage is available to BOBBY SID TAYLOR and appropriate under the facts surrounding the collision on April 9, 1977, and STATE FARM having been fully apprised in the premises, THEREFORE, in consideration of the mutual [cov]enants contained herein, STATE FARM agrees to pay the sum of $15,000 to BOBBY SID TAYLOR in full satisfaction of all contractual rights, claims, and causes of action he has or may have against STATE FARM under the policy of insurance referred to herein, in connection with the collision on April 9, 1977, and all subsequent matters, and BOBBY SID TAYLOR hereby accepts that sum pursuant to the recitals contained herein."

Both parties interpret the agreement differently......

Taylor, v. State Farm Mutual Automobile Insurance Company
175 Ariz. 148, 854 P.2d 1134
Supreme Court of Arizona, 1993.

FELDMAN, Chief Justice.

FACTS AND PROCEDURAL HISTORY

This insurance bad faith action arises out of an accident that occurred approximately sixteen years ago. Many of the facts are undisputed. The accident involved three vehicles—one occupied by Anne Ring and passenger James Rivers, the second by Douglas Wistrom, and the third by Bobby Sid Taylor. Ring, Rivers, and Taylor all were injured. The facts surrounding the accident are set forth in Ring v. Taylor, 141 Ariz. 56, 59, 685 P.2d 121, 124 (Ct.App.1984). Ring, her husband, and Rivers filed actions against Taylor and Wistrom. These actions were consolidated before trial. Taylor's insurer, State Farm, retained attorney Leroy W. Hofmann to defend Taylor. Taylor also personally retained attorney Norman Bruce Randall, who filed a counterclaim against Ring for Taylor's damages. Taylor, therefore, was represented by both Randall and Hofmann in the matter. Because the Rings and Rivers agreed with Wistrom to a stipulated judgment and covenant not to execute, Taylor was the only party vulnerable to the Ring/Rivers claims. At trial, the Rings and Rivers obtained combined verdicts against Taylor for approximately $2.5 million in excess of his insurance policy limits. The court of appeals affirmed these judgments. Taylor, 141 Ariz. at 59, 71, 685 P.2d at 124, 136.

The Rings eventually settled with State Farm. Taylor, however, sued State Farm for bad faith seeking damages for the excess Rivers judgment, claiming, among other things, that State Farm improperly failed to settle the Rivers matter within policy limits. State Farm moved for summary judgment, asserting that Taylor relinquished his bad faith claim when, in 1981, he signed a release drafted by attorney Randall in exchange for State Farm's payment of $15,000 in uninsured motorist benefits. Taylor also moved for partial summary judgment, seeking a ruling that, as a matter of law, the release did not preclude his bad faith claim. The judge denied both motions, finding that the release was ambiguous and that therefore parol evidence was admissible at trial to aid in interpreting the release. A second judge, who presided at trial, also denied State Farm's motion for directed verdict based on the release. Having been instructed on the interpretation of the release, the jury returned a verdict in favor of Taylor for compensatory damages of $2.1 million. The court also awarded Taylor $300,000 in attorney fees.

The court of appeals reversed, holding that the release agreement was not ambiguous and therefore the judge erred by admitting parol evidence to vary its terms. Based on the agreement's "four corners," the court held that "it clearly release[d] all policy contract rights, claims, and causes of action that Taylor has or may have against State Farm." According to the court, because the release should have been strictly enforced, there was no basis for Taylor's bad faith claim. We believe the court's decision both incorrectly applies settled legal principles and raises unsettled issues of contract interpretation.

DISCUSSION

Much of the dispute in this case centers on the events that surround the drafting of the release and the inferences that can be drawn from those events. As noted, the trial court found that the release was ambiguous and admitted extrinsic evidence to aid in its interpretation. The court of appeals found no ambiguity. In resolving this issue, we must address the scope and application of the parol evidence rule in Arizona and decide whether, under these facts, the trial court properly admitted extrinsic evidence to interpret the release.

A. Legal principles

The application of the parol evidence rule has been the subject of much controversy and scholarly debate. "When two parties have made a contract and have expressed it in a writing to which they have both assented as the complete and accurate integration of that contract, evidence, whether parol or otherwise, of antecedent understandings and negotiations will not be admitted for the purpose of varying or contradicting the writing." 3 Arthur L. Corbin, CORBIN ON CONTRACTS § 573, at 357 (1960) ("CORBIN"). Antecedent understandings and negotiations may be admissible, however, for purposes other than varying or contradicting a final agreement. 3 CORBIN § 576, at 384. Interpretation is one such purpose. 3 CORBIN § 579, at 412-13; Restatement (Second) of Contracts § 214(c) & cmt. b (1979) ("Restatement").

Interpretation is the process by which we determine the meaning of words in a contract. See Restatement § 200. Generally, and in Arizona, a court will attempt to enforce a contract according to the parties' intent. "The primary and ultimate purpose of interpretation" is to discover that intent and to make it effective. 3 CORBIN § 572B, at 421 (1992 Supp.). The court must decide what evidence, other than the writing, is admissible in the interpretation process, bearing in mind that the parol evidence rule prohibits extrinsic evidence to vary or contradict, but not to interpret, the agreement. These substantive principles are clear, but their application has been troublesome.

1. Restrictive view

Under the restrictive "plain meaning" view of the parol evidence rule, evidence of prior negotiations may be used for interpretation only upon a finding that some language in the contract is unclear, ambiguous, or vague. E. Allan Farnsworth, FARNSWORTH ON CONTRACTS § 7.12, at 270 (1990) ("FARNSWORTH"). Under this approach, "if a writing, or the term in question, appears to be plain and unambiguous on its face, its meaning must be determined from the four corners of the instrument without resort to extrinsic evidence of any nature." Calamari & Perillo, § 3-10, at 166-67. Thus, if the judge finds from the face of a document that it conveys only one meaning, parol evidence is neither considered nor admitted for any purpose. The danger here, of course, is that what appears plain and clear to one judge may not be so plain to another (as in this case), and the judge's decision, uninformed by context, may not reflect the intent of the parties.

2. Corbin view

Under the view embraced by Professor Corbin and the Second Restatement, there is no need to make a preliminary finding of ambiguity before the judge considers extrinsic evidence. 3 CORBIN § 542, at 100-05 (1992 Supp.); Restatement § 212 cmt. b. Instead, the court considers all of the proffered evidence to determine its relevance to the parties' intent and then applies the parol evidence rule to exclude from the fact finder's consideration only the evidence that contradicts or varies the meaning of the agreement. According to Corbin, the court cannot apply the parol evidence rule without first understanding the meaning the parties intended to give the agreement. To understand the agreement, the judge cannot be restricted to the four corners of the document. Again, even under the Corbin view, the court can admit evidence for interpretation but must stop short of contradiction.

3. Arizona view

Writing for a unanimous court in Smith v. Melson, Inc., 135 Ariz. 119, 121-22, 659 P.2d 1264, 1266-67 (1983), Chief Justice Holohan expressly committed Arizona to the Corbin view of contract interpretation. We have not, however, fully explored Melson's application. We have held that a court may consider surrounding circumstances, including negotiation, prior understandings, and subsequent conduct, but have not elaborated much further.

According to Corbin, the proper analysis has two steps. First, the court considers the evidence that is alleged to determine the extent of integration, illuminate the meaning of the contract language, or demonstrate the parties' intent. The court's function at this stage is to eliminate the evidence that has no probative value in determining the parties' intent. The second step involves "finalizing" the court's understanding of the contract. Here, the parol evidence rule applies and precludes admission of the extrinsic evidence that would vary or contradict the meaning of the written words.

Even during the first step, the judge may properly decide not to consider certain offered evidence because it does not aid in interpretation but, instead, varies or contradicts the written words. This might occur when the court decides that the asserted meaning of the contract language is so unreasonable or extraordinary that it is improbable that the parties actually subscribed to the interpretation asserted by the proponent of the extrinsic evidence. "The more bizarre and unusual an asserted interpretation is, the more convincing must be the testimony that supports it." 3 CORBIN § 579, at 420. At what point a judge stops "listening to testimony that white is black and that a dollar is fifty cents is a matter for sound judicial discretion and common sense." Id.

When interpreting a contract, nevertheless, it is fundamental that a court attempt to "ascertain and give effect to the intention of the parties at the time the contract was made if at all possible." Polk, 111 Ariz. at 495, 533 P.2d at 662. If, for example, parties use language that is mutually intended to have a special meaning, and that meaning is proved by credible evidence, a court is obligated to enforce the agreement according to the parties' intent, even if the language ordinarily might mean something different. See Restatement § 212 cmt. b, illus. 3 & 4. The judge, therefore, must avoid the often irresistible temptation to automatically interpret contract language as he or she would understand the words. This natural tendency is sometimes disguised in the judge's ruling that contract language is "unambiguous." Words, however, are seldom so clear that they "apply themselves to the subject matter." Restatement § 214 cmt. b. On occasion, exposition of the evidence regarding the intention of the parties will illuminate plausible interpretations other than the one that is facially obvious to the judge. Thus, ambiguity determined by the judge's view of "clear meaning" is a troublesome concept that often obstructs the court's proper and primary function in this area—to enforce the meaning intended by the contracting parties.

Recognizing these problems, we are hesitant to endorse, without explanation, the often repeated and usually over-simplified construct that ambiguity must exist before parol evidence is admissible. We have previously criticized the ambiguity prerequisite in the context of non- negotiated agreements. Moreover, a contract may be susceptible to multiple interpretations and therefore truly ambiguous yet, given the context in which it was negotiated, not susceptible to a clearly contradicting and wholly unpersuasive interpretation asserted by the proponent of extrinsic evidence. In such a case, it seems clear that a court should exclude that evidence as violating the parol evidence rule despite the presence of some contract ambiguity. Finally, and most important, the ambiguity determination distracts the court from its primary objective—to enforce the contract as intended by the parties. Consequently, although relevant, contract ambiguity is not the only linchpin of a court's decision to admit parol evidence.

The better rule is that the judge first considers the offered evidence and, if he or she finds that the contract language is "reasonably susceptible" to the interpretation asserted by its proponent, the evidence is admissible to determine the meaning intended by the parties. See Restatement § 215 cmt. b; see also Pacific Gas & Elec. Co. v. G.W. Thomas Dray. & Rigging Co., 69 Cal.2d 33, 69 Cal.Rptr. 561, 564, 566, 567-68, 442 P.2d 641, 644, 645-46 (1968). The meaning that appears plain and unambiguous on the first reading of a document may not appear nearly so plain once the judge considers the evidence. In such a case, the parol evidence rule is not violated because the evidence is not being offered to contradict or vary the meaning of the agreement. To the contrary, it is being offered to explain what the parties truly may have intended. We believe that this rule embodies the concepts endorsed by Corbin and adopted by this court ten years ago in Melson. Other courts more recently have expressed approval of the position taken by Corbin and the Restatement (Second) of Contracts.

A judge may not always be in a position to rule on a parol evidence objection at first blush, having not yet heard enough relevant evidence on the issue. If this occurs, the judge might, for example, admit the extrinsic evidence conditionally, reserve ruling on the issue until enough relevant evidence is presented, or, if the case is being tried to a jury, consider the evidence outside the jury's presence. See, e.g., Ariz.R.Evid. 103(c), 104(b), 104(c), 105. Because the judge is in the best position to decide how to proceed, we leave this decision to his or her sound discretion. As noted also, the judge need not waste much time if the asserted interpretation is unreasonable or the offered evidence is not persuasive. A proffered interpretation that is highly improbable would necessarily require very convincing evidence. In such a case, the judge might quickly decide that the contract language is not reasonably susceptible to the asserted meaning, stop listening to evidence supporting it, and rule that its admission would violate the parol evidence rule. See 3 CORBIN § 542, at 112; § 579, at 420.

We now apply these principles to the facts of this case.

B. Was the release so clear that the trial judge erred in admitting extrinsic evidence to interpret it?

Taylor released "all contractual rights, claims, and causes of action he ha[d] or may have against STATE FARM under the policy of insurance...in connection with the collision...and all subsequent matters." Taylor argued that the bad faith claim sounds in tort and was therefore neither covered nor intended to be covered by the language releasing "all contractual" claims. The trial court found that [p]arts of the document suggest that the parties contemplated the question of the insurer's settlement of claims within policy limits. Yet on page 2 of the document, the release satisfies "all contractual rights, claims, and causes of action." As a matter of statutory or contract construction, the word "contractual" modifies the words "rights," "claims," and the words "causes of action." Although the breach of the duty of good faith and fair dealing arises out of contract, the action itself is a tort claim. Thus, there is ambiguity here. Where there is an ambiguity, parol evidence will be admitted on this issue. The court of appeals held that Taylor's bad faith action was purely contractual and therefore, unlike the trial judge, found no ambiguity in the release language.[7] We must decide whether the release language is reasonably susceptible to Taylor's proffered interpretation in light of the evidence relevant to the parties' intent. If it is, admission of extrinsic evidence supporting his interpretation did not violate the parol evidence rule.

1. Was the release language reasonably susceptible to differing interpretations, including that the bad faith claim was not released despite the contractual quality of such a claim?

First, we address the court of appeals' holding that Taylor's bad faith claim was only contractual and that the trial court erred by finding that the release language, which indisputably covered contractual matters, was unclear, requiring extrinsic evidence for interpretation.

The court of appeals held that to assert a bad faith claim, Taylor first had to establish a "breach of contract"; that is, he must have been able to show that State Farm "denied, failed to pay, or failed to process a valid claim." The court held that at the time Taylor made the release agreement, his bad faith claim was contractual in nature. The release therefore unambiguously included bad faith, and parol evidence supporting the contrary was inadmissible.

We disagree. The proper inquiry is not whether the claim was contractual in nature or whether the judge believed it was contractual but, instead, what the parties intended to release when they used language conspicuously less inclusive than the release of "all claims." Of course, the true doctrinal nature of the claim, if it could be determined, would be relevant evidence in the search for the parties'

---

7. These conflicting rulings illustrate the problems inherent in finding ambiguity. Two trial judges found the agreement ambiguous, that is, "doubtful or uncertain...[or] capable of being understood in two or more possible senses or ways." WEBSTER'S NINTH NEW COLLEGIATE DICTIONARY 77 (1989). Three court of appeals judges, reading the same agreement, found the meaning clear beyond all question. At one time, this court held that if one court found a contract ambiguous and another found it clear, it must be ambiguous. See Federal Ins. Co. v. P.A.T. Homes, Inc., 113 Ariz. 136, 138-39, 547 P.2d 1050, 1052-53 (1976). For obvious reasons, we should discard such doctrine and have done so. See Wilson, 162 Ariz. at 256-58, 782 P.2d at 732-34.

contracting intent. If bad faith was ordinarily and universally thought of as a "contract" claim, it would be very difficult for Taylor to argue that the specific language in the agreement, releasing all "contractual" matters, was reasonably susceptible to his interpretation. In such a case, Taylor would be in the unenviable position of arguing that "X" in fact does not mean "X." This, however, is not the case.

C. Was the parol evidence for the jury?

Whether contract language is reasonably susceptible to more than one interpretation so that extrinsic evidence is admissible is a question of law for the court. We have concluded in the preceding section that the language of the agreement, illuminated by the surrounding circumstances, indicates that either of the interpretations offered was reasonable. Because interpretation was needed and because the extrinsic evidence established controversy over what occurred and what inferences to draw from the events, the matter was properly submitted to the jury. The trial judge, therefore, instructed the jury as follows:... "[State Farm] has alleged the affirmative defense of release. In this regard, [State Farm] contends that the agreement...was intended by the parties thereto to, among other things, release [State Farm] from all bad faith claims.... Whether the parties intended the bad faith claims to be released is for you to determine. If you find that the parties to said agreement intended thereby that [State Farm] be released from bad faith claims, then your verdict must be for [State Farm].....A release is to be construed according to the intent of the parties to it. This intention is to be determined by what was within the contemplation of the parties when the release was executed, which, in turn, is to be resolved in the light of all of the surrounding facts and circumstances under which the parties acted." Reporter's Transcript, Mar. 12, 1987, at 184-85. The instruction states the issue quite clearly. So instructed, the jury resolved the release issue in Taylor's favor. We leave that resolution undisturbed.

CONCLUSION

The trial court properly considered and then admitted extrinsic evidence to interpret the release and determine whether it included Taylor's bad faith claim. That question, in this case, was appropriately left to the trier of fact. There remain other issues not resolved by the court of appeals. We are aware of the frustration that additional delay imposes on all involved, especially in a case as old as this. Nevertheless, because the other issues were initially and fully presented to the court of appeals, prudence dictates that the court of appeals complete its review of this case as expeditiously as possible. The decision of the court of appeals pertaining to the release is vacated and the matter is remanded to the court of appeals for resolution of the remaining issues.

Note on Taylor

This case provides a breakthrough in Arizona for a rule which takes from the judge the ability to throw out alternative scenarios as to the intent of the parties when they use particular words. The court still has a role. It determines the effect of words once the jury determines what the parties meant by them. Allowing parties to suggest to juries that black is white, a dollar is fifty cents or X is not X, arguably creates confusion. Note, however, that the court uses the above illustrations as a limit on what courts must listen to or allow juries to listen to. In other words, ambiguity as a standard is out in Arizona. But, if someone asserts a meaning other than the plain meaning of a word or words, the judge still has the right to put the word(s) through a common sense filter to determine if in the asserted circumstances there is really any chance that the word(s) could have the asserted meaning. In other words, not everything has to go to the jury. Also, the jury decides what was intended by the words used. The legal effect of the words is still up to the court. In a jurisdiction such as decided *Van Zee* where the words used are not in doubt a judge could decide (a) what the parties meant by them and (b) the legal effect of their meaning, leaving a jury question only when there was some doubt as to what was said or written

The Corbin route in theory takes us closer to the true intent of the parties. Does it also tempt parties to come up with meanings no one intended at the time of contracting just to get a jury question on "what did they mean when they used the words 'all contractual rights, claims and causes of action?'" If anyone asked Bobby Sid at the time what it meant, how likely is it he would have distinguished tort from contract? How likely the distinction of a tort first arising in contract? How likely would any of us know the distinction before we entered law school?

Does this raise an ethics question for the lawyer? How far can you go in questioning the client before you begin suggesting things? If you do suggest something that the client latches onto as a way to win are you participating in a fraud on the court? On the other hand, are you properly representing a client if you do not take him/her back to the moment when the contract was created and explain to him/her the importance of remembering accurately what happened, what was said, what was meant etc. as having a crucial bearing on the case? If the client asks: "What does it matter what I thought?" can you say either directly, or in effect, "if you meant only those claims you might have as a result of them breaking a contract but not those where you thought they cheated you you win; on the other hand, if you meant all claims, including those where you thought they cheated you, you lose?" Are you suggesting an answer here? Is that an ethical breach? How different is this from the lawyer back in 1876 in Dakota territory who defended a man who shot a famous gunfighter named 'Wild Bill' Hickock in the back and killed him. The shooter was seized and held for trial. The defendant's lawyer said: "Tell them you shot him because he killed your brother." The defendant said: "I don't have a brother." The lawyer: "They don't know that." Defendant was not acquitted but was only fined $100 and released. Later he was tried and convicted on the same charge by another court and hanged. Double jeopardy did not apply because Dakota territory did not have a recognized judicial system at the time of the trial.

Many a plea is likely to result from this relaxation of the 'four corners' rule.

How, for example, might the application of this rule have helped CMTV in its suit against Amplicon? Note that California law applied in the *CMTV* case. The principal case (*Taylor*) refers to *Pacific Gas and Electric*, a California case. Do you think counsel may have overlooked it when arguing *CMTV, supra*? Or, perhaps, the *CMTV* court ignored it or decided it didn't apply.

In *Pacific Gas and Electric Co. v. Thomas Drayage & Rigging Co., Inc, 442 P.2d 641, (Cal., 1968)*, cited with approval in the principal case, the Supreme Court of California threw out the plain meaning rule, *i.e.* the rule that said extrinsic evidence of meaning is allowed only when there is ambiguity. "[R]ational interpre-

tation requires at least a preliminary consideration of all credible evidence offered to prove the intention of the parties. Such evidence includes testimony as to
the 'circumstances surrounding the making of the agreement... including the object, nature and subject matter of the writing...' so that the court can 'place itself
in the same situation in which the parties found themselves at the time of contracting.'" It was this case which in footnote six noted that in a motion picture
distribution contract the term United Kingdom included Ireland.

In *McAbee Construction, Inc. v. U.S.* 97 F.3d 1431 (Fed. Cir. 1996) the plaintiff
had granted an easement on his land to the United States Army Corps of Engineers
for use as a disposal cite for dredged material. Plaintiff argued, successfully in the
lower court, that the Corps had agreed to place fill on his land to a height of no
more than 165 feet and had breached the contract by returning the property at an
elevation of 183 feet. The writing did not contain a height limitation. The lower
court held that "[t]he missing height restriction term create[d] an ambiguity" and
used extrinsic evidence to find that the Corps had agreed to return the land at an
elevation of no more than 165 feet. Plaintiff recovered $328,000. The contract in-
cluded an integration clause which stated: "all terms and conditions with respect
to this [contract] are expressly contained herein and [plaintiff] agrees that no representative or agent of the United States ha[s] made any representation or promise
with respect to this [contract] not expressly contained herein." The contract clause
in dispute allowed the defendant "to deposit fill, spoil and waste material [on
plaintiff's land]... and to perform any other work necessary and incident to the
construction of the [project]." On appeal, *reversed*. Focusing on the "necessary
and incident" language and taking special note that in the writing plaintiff had
specifically stated that no representations or promises not contained in the writing
had been made, the appeals court criticized the California approach.

"We turn, therefore, to... whether the terms of the contract read as a whole
are ambiguous, whether they are susceptible to more than one reasonable interpretation. We begin with the plain language. ('A contract is read in accordance
with its express terms and the plain meaning thereof.') We must interpret the
contract in a manner that gives meaning to all of its provisions and makes sense.
Thus, if the 'provisions are clear and unambiguous, they must be given their
plain and ordinary meaning' and the court may not resort to extrinsic evidence
to interpret them. ('Extrinsic evidence... should not be used to introduce an ambiguity where none exists.') ('Extrinsic evidence will not be received to change
the terms of a contract that is clear on its face.') To permit other wise would cast
'a long shadow of uncertainty over all transactions' and contracts. Trident Ctr. v.
Connecticut Gen. Life Ins. Co., 847 F.2d 564, 569 (9th Cir. 1988) (criticizing the
California approach, which does not follow the traditional principle that extrinsic evidence is inadmissible to interpret, vary, or add to the terms of an unambiguous integrated instrument.)"

Note: Approaching Parol Evidence in Steps or Integration vs. Interpretation.

The difficulty in determining the standard for admitting and rejecting evidence in addition to the writing to either supplement or explain the writing, and
the equal difficulty in applying the standard, is exacerbated by the need to approach parol evidence in two steps. First: is the writing under consideration an
integration of the alleged agreement of the parties. For example, is it merely an
early negotiated statement of position which neither party intended to be bind-

ing? Is it a statement of intent which is meant as a platform for further discussions, and hence only a negotiation? Does the writing embody the agreement? Does the writing reflect the terms as negotiated by the parties but subject to a condition that it binds no one until some further event occurs?

Discerning whether the writing was intended to embody the terms of a contract is the theoretical first step. If the parties did not intend to have this writing embody the terms of their contract or if there never was a contract, the court will not reach the second step of asking whether oral or written evidence other than the embodying writing contradicts the writing. How does the court determine whether the writing reflects the contract (which implicitly means that the court is assuming at least for purposes of determining the significance of the writing that there is a contract.)? There are two principal means: (1) the court looks at the writing itself. Is either party claiming that he/she did not sign it and a signature is forgery? Is either party claiming that the writing was altered after signing? If these questions are answered no, then does either party deny that to some degree (at least partially) the writing embodies the intent of the parties. If a party does deny this, the court will then examine the writing and want to know "why did you sign it?" This brings up the second means used by the court (2) circumstances. Did someone commit duress, fraud etc. against the other party [see Note on Fraud, *supra*]. Was the writing a preliminary draft? If so why did they sign it? Did both parties read it? If not, why not? Does a party claim that the writing is subject to a condition which must first occur before it becomes effective?

For example, both parties sign a writing which on its face reflects intent to be bound, consideration etc. Both parties agree that there is no binding contract, and hence the writing embodies no binding contract, unless some further event occurs, for example the President is impeached. If the event occurs, the parties agree, there is a binding contract and the writing that they have already signed and that contains all the elements of a contract now embodies that contract. Could either of the parties introduce evidence to establish that the writing, which apparently not only reflects and memorializes but also apparently embodies the agreement of the parties (in other words, it is not just a memo, a note, a reminder of terms but intended to be the piece of paper to whom both parties and the court will look to determine rights), has no value because there is no contract? The answer would seem to be a resounding "yes." This is like the "joke" cases in Part I, *New York Trust* and *Hicks*. If neither party subjectively intended a contract to result, there is no contract, unless the rights of some third party are jeopardized.

However, if the writing said "this writing embodies the full agreement of the parties' and is the exclusive statement thereof and becomes fully effective on signing subject to no conditions," the evidence directly in conflict with the writing would probably be excluded. Although a party could always seek to prove fraud, duress, etc. to say that the writing did not embody the agreement, most courts would not allow the impeachment condition because it directly conflicts with a provision in it.

Thus, if there is a contract but the writing does not reflect the parties intent then, like the "joke" cases, the writing has no effect. If the writing looks valid, complete etc. the court must take evidence concerning the circumstances surrounding its signing. The writing, though it appears complete and has all the terms necessary to reflect a contract, is not some magic force which creates an obligation where none existed.

For example, A and B discuss terms and write them down on a piece of paper. The paper looks to reflect the terms to which both agreed. Both A and B sign copies (two) when B discovers that a term agreed upon has been left out. A agrees that the writing does not reflect the agreement and that a new writing is needed but that the secretaries cannot type it up until morning. B tears up her copy. A keeps hers. No new draft is ever signed. A later claims that the writing reflects the agreement of the parties. Can B introduce evidence to establish that the writing inadvertently left out a term to which both A and B agreed and that both had agreed to sign a new and more accurate writing? In short, can B state that the writing does not integrate the contract of the parties? Yes. (We will discuss this further under mutual mistake in Part V.)

In taking this first step, *i.e.* deciding whether or not the writing integrates (embodies, takes into itself, "becomes") the agreement of the parties, the court may hear any evidence which the court concludes is relevant to determining the parties' intent: (1) Did they intend to contract (Part I); (2) Did they intend this writing to embody that intent or did they intend some other writing to embody it, or did they intend no writing to embody it?

As a further point in step one, did the parties intend the writing to be a partial or a total embodiment of their agreement? For example, in the next case we have an employment agreement. The employee in essence claimed that the employment contract did not embody the "whole" or "complete" terms of the agreement. The employee is saying, 'this agreement is O.K. as far as it goes but there's more.' The employer is saying, 'this agreement not only covers everything stated in it but also everything that is related to the employment whether stated or not.' For example, the writing states that employer will pay employee $1,000 per month for 36 months. If the court passed the threshold that this agreement at least was intended by the parties to embody their agreement as to the explicit terms stated in it, then the employer could not bring in evidence to say the real agreed upon salary was $500 per month and the employee could not bring in testimony that the real salary was $1,500 per month. Such terms would contradict the writing which was found to embody the agreement as to the terms stated in it. Both could try to "explain" $1,000 by saying that when they wrote $1,000 they meant $500 or $1,500 but a court is unlikely to treat that even as a fact question and simply rule that $1,000 means $1,000.

What if the court found the writing to be a partial integration and the writing said nothing about vacation days. Could the employee say that 14 days or 30 days paid vacation per year were part of the contract. Such a term would not contradict the express terms of the contract. Would it contradict an implied term? [See *Hunt Foods v. Doliner, infra* and compare it with *Mitchell v. Lath, infra*]. The court could say that $1,000 per month implies a person will work each month and hence an allegedly "supplemental" term covering vacation days really contradicts, conflicts with, the pay term. A court could also say the salary term is separate from a vacation term and therefore it does not contradict an express term and employee may seek to prove such a term with oral or written evidence other than the written contract.

The court then must move to the second part of step one and ask whether the writing is a complete and exclusive integration, a total integration, of the parties agreement. Using the vacation term as an example, if the court found a total integration it would exclude supplemental terms on the theory that everything related to the contract was intended by the parties to be included in this writing and therefore the writing embodies, speaks definitively of, not only the terms included but any terms that *could* have been included and are not. In the case of the vacation days the court would probably find that such a term would have been included in a full integration and therefore would not allow proof. Thus, the question further becomes what *would* have been included in a total integration, a total statement of the parties' rights as they relate to the subject matter of the contract. All is not lost if one could persuade a court a total integration does not include vacation days because the *subject matter* of the contract is not the employment of the employee but only the employee's wages and the fact that the employee is to be employed for three years. To avoid problems it is often well to state just what the subject matter of the contract is which is being reduced to writing and to state that the writing is the complete and exclusive statement of all rights relating to that subject matter.

Having determined as step one whether or not the writing integrates any or all of the agreement of the parties, and having determined whether that integration is partial or total, the court moves on to step two: the determination of what can be admitted and for what purpose. As noted above if the integration is partial, supplemental terms can usually be *added*. If the integration is total, they cannot.[See *CMTV, supra*]. Some cases will allow an explanation of the meaning of terms without the requirement of any apparent ambiguity in the terms whether the agreement is a total, complete integration or only a partial one. The theory is that people use words differently; there is no magic or universal meaning. Therefore parol evidence is always necessary to know what the parties meant, intended when they used a word. [See *Taylor, supra*; see also footnote 6 in *Pacific Gas and Electric, supra*]. Other cases, such as *McAbee Construction, supra* take a much more traditional view refusing to ignore what the court considers to be a writing's plain meaning. In *Hall, infra* the court would allow parol to "clarify" ambiguous terms but not to vary or contradict terms. There is still some discretion with courts, and there are still differences as to whether interpretation is a fact or law question. Where courts still require ambiguity before allowing explanations of terms there is always the question of what is ambiguous.

In *CMTV* we explored the problems of adding a term when the court found a complete integration and further found that the term sought to be proved would contradict the writing. In *Taylor* one of the parties sought to explain a term. In *Hall* the court takes us through the steps.

As you read *Hall* ask yourself whether Mrs. Hall would have been better off declaring that the whole "employment contract" was a joke rather than trying to say that the writing did not embody all the terms of their agreement but only some. Was it a tactical mistake to admit that the writing embodied part of the agreement [see paragraph three of the decision] because that opened the door (a) to saying that the agreement was a total integration [did the court do this?] and (b) that her testimony would conflict with a definite and specific term of the contract—faithful performance of duties. Remember, appeals court decisions—whether intermediate or final appeals courts—do not tell the whole story. Even the trial record with pleadings and a full transcript of testimony may not—the trial judge may have ruled out testimony he/she considered irrelevant. Mrs. Hall may have tried to prove "joke" and the trial court would not let her pursue it; she may then not have perfected an appeal; or she may have pursued it and either the trial or appeals courts or both ignored the issue when they determined she was in breach. Appellate opinions give only what the court considers significant and relevant.

Consider the result if she could have established: "This whole alleged contract is a fake. My ex-husband wanted it this way for tax purposes. He wanted to deduct the alimony from corporate earnings to lessen corporate tax. I went along. He told me that if I helped him out he'd work with me to make the divorce smooth. So I said OK. He told me to keep the corporate records straight I'd have to sign a standard employment contract. I don't know if it was legal or not and I guess I should have told my lawyer but I didn't. He told me it didn't mean anything and I just signed." If she could establish that he was lying to her and intended all along to fire her, we'd have fraud and as *Hall* says, or implies, fraud creates an exception to the exclusionary impact of the parol evidence rule. Fraud is hard to prove because it requires a dishonest intent at the time the writing, allegedly integrating the contract, was signed. But, proving a joke might be easier. Once again, it is up to counsel to decide on the most honest and effective approach. She apparently tried to say in effect: "Yes I had a job. Yes he employed me. Yes I agreed to work at it. No it didn't mention alimony. So yes the writing tells part of the story." The court then said, in effect, 'you can't contradict the part it tells—and maybe not add to what it says.' Consider the result of the following, which it seems was equally true: "We created a scam to help him out in his business. I don't really understand it but we never intended for me to work at this job and the writing doesn't reflect what we agreed and certainly was never intended to embody anything. It was something to file away in corporate records in case anybody came looking in them."

Your job is to spot these alternatives. The court won't do it, your opponent surely won't do it (not for you—it would be a gross breach of ethics of her duty to her client) and the client can't. In fact the clients in a very few years will be paying you thousands of dollars to find answers.

Hall v. Process Instruments and Control, Inc.

890 P.2d 1024

Supreme Court of Utah, 1995.

[Author's fact summary from the Court of Appeals decision 866 P.2d 604: Mrs Hall had a three year employment contract with her ex-husband entered into about the time of their divorce. She claimed that the employment contract was in lieu of alimony and hence she did not have to show up for work. He fired her. The trial and appeals courts found that the writing embodied the employment contract, *i.e.* was integrated, and was unambiguous. Thus, evidence was not allowed to either "clarify" the terms (not needed in the courts' view because no ambiguity) or to "vary or contradict" them. The Appeals Court [intermediate court] stated: "Further, even if the trial court had found credible Mrs. Hall's assertion that the parties had an oral agreement to the effect that Mrs. Hall did not have to actually work for Process, this parol evidence is still inadmissible. Only 'parol evidence not inconsistent with the writing is admissible to show what the entire contract really was, by supplementing, as distinguished from contradicting the writing.' [citation omitted] The employment agreement stated that Mrs. Hall 'agrees to faithfully perform the duties assigned to her to the best of her ability and to devote such time and skills as shall be necessary therefor' and that '[t]his agreement shall be in effect through and until the month of February 1984.' Parol evidence indicating that Mrs. Hall was not expected to perform any duties at all for Process clearly contradicts the terms of the written agreement Therefore, the trial court correctly held that this parol evidence was inadmissible."]

DURHAM, Justice:

Plaintiff Margaret B. Hall seek[s] review of a court of appeals decision that affirmed the trial court's ruling of no cause of action on her breach of contract claim. The court of appeals concluded that the trial court correctly applied the parol evidence rule to exclude testimony regarding the parties' employment agreement. We affirm.

In February 1981, plaintiff entered into a written employment agreement with defendant Process Instruments and Control, Inc. ("Process"). Under the terms of the employment agreement, Process promised to pay Mrs. Hall $1,000 per month beginning March 1, 1981, and continuing through February 1984. Although Mrs. Hall never went to work for Process, Process paid her for fourteen months. In May 1982, Process informed Mrs. Hall that she had been terminated for failure to show up for work.

Mrs. Hall filed a complaint in May 1982 alleging wrongful discharge, claiming that she had "fully performed the obligations and rendered the services contemplated by [the agreement]" and that she "continue[d] to be able and willing to perform such obligations." She failed to pursue the case until August 1990, at which time she amended her complaint to allege that John A. Hall, her ex-husband and the sole shareholder of Process, had represented to her at the time of the agreement that she would never have to work for Process and that the salary specified in the employment agreement would be paid in return for her promise to forego alimony.[1] The court permitted the amendment.

At trial, the court allowed Mrs. Hall to introduce parol evidence, subject to exclusion, for the limited purpose of establishing whether the agreement was integrated. The court then excluded the evidence, finding that the agreement was "unambiguous" and appeared to be "complete." The court ruled that Mrs. Hall had no cause of action because she had failed to perform her obligations under the employment agreement and had "fail[ed] to establish that the meaning or intent of the employment agreement was anything other than its clearly written terms." Mrs. Hall appealed the trial court's decision to the court of appeals, claiming that parol evidence was necessary to "elucidate the real meaning of the employment agreement since the parties never intended the written contract to be the full and complete expression of their agreement." The court of appeals affirmed the trial court's decision.

---

1. In February 1981, the same month the employment agreement was signed, Mr. Hall filed for divorce. A decree of divorce was entered in June 1981 which provided that no alimony would be awarded to Mrs. Hall. The divorce decree makes no reference to the employment agreement. [Author's note: what is the significance of this footnote? What if the divorce decree had made reference to the employment agreement — how would that have affected the analysis?]

Mrs. Hall now appeals the court of appeals' decision, claiming that the court of appeals erroneously applied the parol evidence rule. She claims that the trial court failed to make the required threshold finding of integration of the contract before excluding her testimony regarding the intent of the parties and therefore that the court of appeals erred in affirming the trial court. Mrs. Hall also claims that the trial court should have allowed the testimony of Brent Turley in making its threshold determination of integration [2]and that the court of appeals erroneously affirmed the exclusion by relying solely on the finding that the agreement was clear and unambiguous.

This court has noted that as a principle of contract interpretation, the parol evidence rule has a very narrow application. Simply stated, the rule operates, in the absence of fraud or other invalidating causes, to exclude evidence of contemporaneous conversations, representations, or statements offered for the purpose of varying or adding to the terms of an integrated contract. Under this general rule, "an apparently complete and certain agreement which the parties have reduced to writing will be conclusively presumed to contain the whole agreement." Eie, 638 P.2d at 1194. Thus, before considering the applicability of the parol evidence rule in a contract dispute, the court must first determine that the parties intended the writing to be an integration. To resolve this question of fact, any relevant evidence is admissible.

Once a court determines that an agreement is integrated, parol evidence, although not admissible to vary or contradict the clear and unambiguous terms of the contract, is admissible to clarify ambiguous terms. The application of the parol evidence rule therefore involves two steps. First, the court must determine whether the agreement is integrated. If the court finds the agreement is integrated, then parol evidence may be admitted only if the court makes a subsequent determination that the language of the agreement is ambiguous.

In this case, the trial court made a conclusion of law that the employment agreement was "clear and unambiguous on its face and not subject to change by parole [sic] evidence." Plaintiff argues that this conclusion related only to the question of ambiguity in the contract and that the trial court failed to make the necessary threshold determination of integration.

We disagree with plaintiff's characterization of the trial court's findings. Although the trial court failed to use the term "integration," it nonetheless made the necessary threshold findings for a correct application of the parol evidence rule. An integrated agreement is defined as "a writing or writings constituting a final expression of one or more terms of an agreement." Restatement (Second) of

---

2. Turley allegedly would have testified that in 1976, Mr. Hall offered him a salaried position with Process, where he would not actually have to work, in lieu of a down payment Mr. Hall owed Mr. Turley. Mrs. Hall claims that Turley's testimony would "clearly have had a tendency to make it more probable that the consideration promised and given by Mrs. Hall in exchange for Defendant's promises under the Employment Agreement was not her promise to go to work for Defendant . . . , but, rather, was her promise to forego her claim to alimony in the Divorce Action." [Author's note: How would this tend to show that her alleged agreement with him was not what the writing made it seem? If Mr. Hall was trying to repay Mr. Turley in a way that would reduce his corporate taxable income — wages are deductible from corporate income; the repayment of a debt, on the other hand, is not — the corporation would first earn money, pay tax on it and have the residue to pay the debt; would not this device seem more plausible in Mrs. Hall's case?]

Contracts § 209 (1981). This court has held that whenever a litigant insists that a writing is an integration and requests application of the parol evidence rule, the court must determine whether the parties adopted a particular writing or writings "as the final and complete expression of their bargain." Eie, 638 P.2d at 1194.

In its findings of fact, the trial court found that the terms of the employment agreement "appear to be complete." Moreover, in its pretrial order, the trial court included as a factual question for trial whether the parties intended the employment agreement "to represent [their] full and complete agreement." Evidently, the use of the term "complete" in place of the term "integrated" has caused some confusion. Notwithstanding this confusion, because the trial court found that the contract was complete, we can infer that the court intended to make the prerequisite finding of integration. Indeed, the trial court listed the following as a finding of fact: "Plaintiff was allowed to introduce parole [sic] evidence, subject to exclusion, in order to attempt to establish that the agreement was not either an integration or a partially integrated contract." (Emphasis added.) This finding clearly indicates that the trial court, prior to excluding the parol evidence, made a determination that the agreement was integrated. Moreover, because this court has described an integrated agreement as a writing which the parties intend as the "final and complete expression of their bargain," we may assume that the trial court intended "complete" and "full and complete" to mean integrated. See id.; see also Union Bank, 707 P.2d at 665 (describing rebuttable presumption of integration: " 'Where the parties reduce an agreement to a writing which in view of its completeness and specificity reasonably appears to be a complete agreement, it is taken to be an integrated agreement unless it is established by other evidence that the writing did not constitute a final expression.' " (quoting Restatement (Second) of Contracts, § 209(3) (1981)). Thus, notwithstanding the trial court's lack of semantic specificity in this case, we are satisfied that its use of the term "complete" was equivalent to a finding of integration. That finding, although contrary to plaintiff's testimony, was amply supported by other testimony and evidence at trial.

Accordingly, the court of appeals did not err in affirming the trial court's application of the parol evidence rule. In its opinion, the court of appeals correctly recognized that when a court is asked to apply the parol evidence rule, it must first determine whether the agreement is integrated. "If a contract is determined to be integrated, the parol evidence rule 'excludes evidence of terms in addition to those found in the agreement.' " Hall, 866 P.2d at 606 (quoting Eie, 638 P.2d at 1194 and citing Restatement (Second) of Contracts § 209(2) (1981)). The court of appeals then addressed the issue of ambiguity, indicating that if a contract is found to be integrated and the terms are unambiguous, then parol evidence is generally not admissible to explain the parties' intent.

After explaining the parol evidence rule, the court of appeals addressed the trial court's findings. The court of appeals noted that after reviewing evidence of the agreement's integration, the trial court found that the terms of the agreement appeared to be "complete and certain." Accordingly, the court of appeals found that the trial court correctly applied the parol evidence rule to exclude Mrs. Hall's testimony. As discussed above, we agree with the court of appeals' conclusion.

Mrs. Hall also contends that the trial court misapplied the parol evidence rule because "both parties...testified that the Employment Agreement was not the full and complete agreement." We read this as a challenge to the trial court's findings of fact. However, Mrs. Hall has failed to meet her burden on appeal to " 'marshal the evidence in support of the findings and then demonstrate that despite this evidence, the trial court's findings are so lacking in support as to be against the clear weight of the evidence, thus making them clearly erroneous.' " State v. A House & 1.37 Acres, 886 P.2d 534, 538 n. 4 (1994) (quoting In re Estate of Bartell, 776 P.2d 885, 886 (Utah 1989)). Absent such a showing, we "assume that the record supports the findings of the trial court and proceed to a review of the accuracy of the lower court's conclusions of law and the application of that law in the case." Id. (citations omitted).

Mrs. Hall also challenges the court of appeals' conclusion that the trial court did not abuse its discretion in excluding Mr. Turley's testimony. We disagree. The trial court did not exceed the bounds of its discretion. We note, however, that the court of appeals' decision causes some confusion by referring to the trial court's finding that the agreement was clear and unambiguous as legitimate grounds for excluding Turley's testimony. Hall, 866 P.2d at 606 n. 2. Indeed, this fails to address Mrs. Hall's contention. Mrs. Hall contends that Turley's testimony[3] was relevant to the issue of integration. All relevant evidence is admissible to prove integration. Eie, 638 P.2d at 1194. Thus, the trial court's finding of clear and unambiguous contract terms should have had no bearing on its decision to exclude testimony regarding the threshold issue of integration, as the court of appeals' opinion seems to imply. Because the court of appeals failed to adequately address Mrs. Hall's argument, we address it here.

We find that the trial court legitimately excluded Turley's testimony as irrelevant to determining whether the agreement was integrated. Trial courts are granted broad discretion in determining the relevance of proffered evidence, and we will find error only if the trial court abused its discretion. The Turley episode was sufficiently attenuated in time and substance from the facts of this dispute to provide little probative value on the issue of integration. Accordingly, we cannot say that the trial court's decision to exclude Turley's testimony was beyond the bounds of reasonability. We therefore affirm the court of appeals' decision to affirm the trial court's ruling on this issue.

Questions

1. Should Turley's testimony been admitted? Could the court have reached a different result if Turley was permitted to testify?

2. Re-read Restatement § 209 quoted by the *Union Bank* case in the opinion to the effect that if an agreement is reduced to a writing that appears to be complete it is presumed to be integrated unless other evidence is presented.

---

3. Turley's testimony allegedly would have shown that Mr. Hall had, on at least one other occasion, attempted to use an employment agreement as consideration for the payment of his personal financial obligations.

Translated into English, does this mean that if you sign something the court will presume you mean it and the burden is on you to prove it is a joke? Or does it mean that if an agreement is found to exist then if it is put into a writing the writing is presumed to embody the whole agreement and not just a part? Notice that this court calls it "a rebuttable presumption of integration." Courts do not always draw fine lines.

3. Did this court find a partial or total integration? Does it matter? Does the whole case really turn on whether Mrs. Hall's parol evidence conflicts with the writing? Does the effectiveness of a writing turn on a presumption that if you sign something you mean it and we presume the writing embodies the agreement? Does this lead to a further presumption, that if you sign something that looks like an agreement, it is an agreement and not a "joke" unless you can prove otherwise? To what counseling point(s) does this lead?

Note on Reversal on Appeal

Remember that no one is entitled to a perfect trial; only to a fair one. This basically means that not every error committed by a trial court will be grounds for reversal. Note further that the trial court has "discretion" in determining relevance of evidence. Combine this with the "clearly erroneous" standard (appellate courts will not overturn fact findings of the fact finder — jury or trial judge — unless clearly erroneous) and the interpretation of an alleged writing to find intent and meaning as a matter of fact and not law and it will be a rare appellant who will win on appeal.

Winning in the trial court is always a good idea. Appellate courts do not like to overturn trial court judgments and rarely do so unless for a clear, indeed obvious, reason.

In *Berg v. Hudesman, 801 P.2d 222 (Wash., 1990)* the court did not have to face the issue of whether or not the disputed term of the contract was contained in the lease. Both parties agreed it was. Nor did they dispute that the lease integrated the parties' intent. The dispute concerned the meaning of the language used in the writing to express intent. The court interpreted the language in this 99 year ground lease not by merely referring to the four corners of the lease or to the plain meaning of the language, but to the circumstances surrounding its signing and also to events occurring *subsequent to* its signing. "Determination of the intent of the contracting parties is to be accomplished by viewing the contract as a whole, the subject matter and objective of the contract, all the circumstances surrounding the making of the contract, the subsequent acts and conduct of the parties to the contract, and the reasonableness of respective interpretations advocated by the parties. This analytic framework for interpreting written contract language has been called the 'context rule.' We now hold that extrinsic evidence is admissible as to the entire circumstances under which the contract was made, as an aid in ascertaining the parties' intent." Whatever it is called it amounts to the court taking evidence of any kind that goes to determine what the parties meant. This means that (1) as to whether the writing integrates the contract of the parties (which would seem to include whether they made a contract at all) the court can look to the circumstances surrounding its signing; (2) as to what the writing means, once it is determined that there is a contract and this writing integrates it, the court can also look to circumstances. Although it appears that the writing has no force at all, in point of fact once the court determines that it embodies the agreement, and if the court determines that it embodies the total agreement, then what can be proved by 'circumstances' is limited. Also, although evidence comes in to explain it, the court (and/or the jury) still determines credibility and meaning. The real question still comes down: Why did you sign it if it doesn't mean anything? If the explanation is off the wall, court and/or jury are unlikely to believe it.

In *Frigaliment Importing Co., v. B.N.S. International Sales Corp, 190 F.Supp 116 (S.D.N.Y., 1960)* the dispute concerned the meaning of the word "chicken." The trial judge, Judge Friendly, stated: "The issue is, what is chicken? Plaintiff says 'chicken' means a young chicken, suitable for broiling and frying. Defendant says 'chicken' means any bird of that genus that meets contract specifications on weight and quality, including what it calls 'stewing chicken' and plaintiff pejoratively terms 'fowl'. Dictionaries give both meanings, as well as some others not relevant here. To support its, plaintiff sends a number of volleys over the net; defendant essays to return them and adds a few serves of its own. Assuming that both parties were acting in good faith, the case nicely illustrates Holmes' remark 'that the making of a contract depends not on the agreement of two minds in one intention, but on the agreement of two sets of external signs— not on the parties' having meant the same thing but on their having said the same thing.' The Path of the Law, in Collected Legal Papers, p. 178. I have concluded that plaintiff has not sustained its burden of persuasion that the contract used 'chicken' in the narrower sense.

"The action is for breach of the warranty that goods sold shall correspond to the description. Since the word 'chicken' standing alone is ambiguous, I turn first to see whether the contract itself offers any aid to its interpretation. Plaintiff says the 1 1/2-2 lbs. birds necessarily had to be young chicken since the older birds do not come in that size, hence the 2 1/2-3 lbs. birds must likewise be young. This is unpersuasive— a contract for 'apples' of two different sizes could be filled with different kinds of apples even though only one species came in both sizes. Defendant notes that the contract called not simply for chicken but for 'US Fresh Frozen Chicken, Grade A, Government Inspected.' It says the contract thereby incorporated by reference the Department of Agriculture's regulations, which favor its interpretation; I shall return to this after reviewing plaintiff's other contentions."

The court then reviewed cablegrams exchanged between the parties during negotiations but found these to be inconclusive. He next reviewed whether trade usage established a definite meaning. Witnesses for both sides testified. One of plaintiff's witnesses testified "on chicken I would definitely understand a broiler." The court however noted that "in his own transactions the witness protected himself by using 'broiler' when that was what he wanted and 'fowl' when he wished older birds. Indeed, there are some indications, dating back to a remark of Lord Mansfield, Edie v. East India Co., 2 Burr. 1216, 1222 (1761), that no credit should be given 'witnesses to usage, who could not adduce instances in verification.' 7 Wigmore, Evidence (3d ed. 1940), § 1954.... While Wigmore thinks this goes too far, a witness' consistent failure to rely on the alleged usage deprives his opinion testimony of much of its effect." A witness for defendant testified that "'chicken' is everything but a goose, a duck and a turkey." The court was unable to find a definite trade usage that was so well established in the trade that its meaning could be used for definition. The court also considered U.S. Dept. of Agriculture regulations as to their definition of chicken because the contract referred to these. Although plaintiff argued that this definition, which supported defendant's interpretation of the word, was not incorporated into the contract, the court noted that "there is force in defendant's argument that the contract made the regulations a dictionary, particularly since the reference to Government grading was already in plaintiff's initial cable to defendant." Defendant also noted that the contract price for the 'chicken' was below the market price for 'broilers,' that it was less than it would have cost defendant to buy them. As the court noted: "Plaintiff must have expected defendant to make some profit. — certainly it could not have expected defendant deliberately to incur a loss."

"When all the evidence is reviewed, it is clear that defendant believed it could comply with the contracts by delivering stewing chicken in the 2 1/2-3 lbs. size. Defendant's subjective intent would not be significant if this did not coincide with an objective meaning of 'chicken.' Here it did coincide with one of the dictionary meanings, with the definition in the Department of Agriculture Regulations to which the contract made at least oblique reference, with at least some usage in the trade, with the realities of the market, and with what plaintiff's spokesman had said. Plaintiff asserts it to be equally plain that plaintiff's own subjective intent was to obtain broilers and fryers; the only evidence against this is the material as to market prices and this may not have been sufficiently brought home. In any event it is unnecessary to determine that issue. For plaintiff has the burden of showing that 'chicken' was used in the narrower rather than in the broader sense, and this it has not sustained.

This opinion constitutes the Court's findings of fact and conclusions of law. Judgment shall be entered dismissing the complaint with costs."

Note on Trade Usage and Good Faith

While a contract which is totally integrated, one which embodies the complete and exclusive statement of the terms of the agreement, cannot be supplemented by additional terms, its intent can almost always be explained or supplemented, but not contradicted, by trade usage or course of dealing. (See U.C.C. 1-205 and 2-202 for contracts involving sales of goods.) Problems still exist in some cases in determining which trade is involved, whether both parties are members of the trade and whether the alleged usage is so established that its use would be assumed by both of the contracting parties. To a great extent trade usage and course of dealing (previous dealings of the parties) are looked to more than dictionary definitions of terms in interpreting contracts. (*See e.g. Nanakuli v. Shell Oil Co.* 664 F.2d 772 (9th Cir., 1980) and *Decker Steel Co. v. Exchange Nat. Bank*, 330 F.2d 82, 85 (7th Cir. 1964).) In *Decker*, the 7th circuit implied in dicta that a contract which called for 36 inch steel could, because of a usage in the steel trade, include steel that measured 37 inches. In testimony it was pointed out that 36 could not mean exactly 36—there is always some variance even if only a very small fraction of an inch. Nothing is exact. For example 8 x 11 paper could vary by 1/100 of an inch or 1/1000. The question then becomes how much of a variance is intended? For this reason contracts often spell out variances. If a contract calls for 1000 bushels of tomatoes it may state that there can be a variance above 1000 but not less than 1000 and to make it plain state no variance under but up to 10 bushels over 1000 will fulfill contract terms. It may also state that this term negates and replaces any trade usage or course of dealing to the contrary and, if such a usage or course of dealing is known to the party, spell out which one or ones are being avoided.

In *Nanakuli* a long term supply contract was involved in which the price to be paid by the buyer was the "posted price" of the seller at the time of delivery. This apparently was the price the seller was generally charging at a particular time and allowed for increases over a long term. Buyer contended successfully that seller was bound by a trade usage that protected buyer under a trade usage of "price protection" for the amount of seller's product for whose use buyer was already committed in contracts with third parties. In short, seller was bound to charge the old, lower, price for quantities of seller's product which buyer was already committed to use in contracts with others. Buyer also pointed out successfully that seller had followed this usage on two prior occasions during the performance of the contract (course of performance) and that this course of performance indicated seller's understanding that "price protection" was a part of the contract. The opinion also indicated that the course of performance could have acted to modify the contract to include the term.

An alternative theory was also accepted by the court. Buyer said that even if price protection was not a term of the contract by reason of trade usage, good faith was. The court pointed out that the U.C.C. which governed the contract provides that "[a] price to be fixed by the seller or by the buyer means a price for him to fix in good faith" (Haw. Rev. Stat. § 490:2-305(2)) and that good faith includes "the observance of reasonable commercial standards of fair dealing in the trade" Id. 490: 2-103(1)(b). The official Code comment to the section states "In the normal case a 'posted price'...satisfies the good faith requirement." The court pointed out that circumstances could make a case not normal and further in this case the manner of putting the price into effect and not the posted price itself were in contention. By not giving buyer reasonable advance notice of a price increase, "a long time usage in the...trade" "the jury could have concluded that [seller's] manner of carrying out the price increase...did not conform to reasonably commercial standards." The court also pointed out that the U.C.C. states "Every contract or duty within this chapter imposes an obligation of good faith in its performance or enforcement." Id. 490:1-203. The comment to this section specifically applies the principle to commercial transactions and that by its definition good faith requires the observance of commercially reasonable standards of fair dealing in the trade.

In a concurring opinion one judge stated:

"The case involves specific pricing practices, not an allegation of unfair dealing generally. Our opinion should not be interpreted to permit juries to import price protection or a similarly specific contract term from a concept of good faith that is not based on well-established custom and usage or other objective standards of which the parties had clear notice. Here, evidence of custom and usage regarding price protection in the asphaltic paving trade was not contradicted in major respects, and the jury could find that the parties knew or should have known of the practice at the time of making the contract. In my view, these are necessary predicates for either theory of the case, namely, interpretation of the contract based on the course of its performance or a finding that good faith required the seller to hold the price. With these observations, I concur."

Was the court adding a term, "price protection" to the contract and then defining it or merely interpreting the meaning of "posted price"?

In *Corenswet Inc. v. Amana Refrigeration, Inc.* 594 F.2d 129 (5th Cir. 1979) the good faith issue arose in the context of a distributorship agreement. The manufacturer terminated the relationship based on a contract clause which stated that the distributorship agreement was terminable by either party at any time "with or without cause." The distributor said that under the U.C.C. which controlled the transaction good faith forbade the termination which the lower court found was "arbitrary and without cause." The upper court let this finding stand but reversed the lower court's judgment for the distributor. "We do not agree that the section 1-203 good faith obligation...can properly be used to override or strike express contract terms."

In *Nanakuli*, *Decker Steel* and *Corenswet* were the courts construing the contract or interpreting contract language? Were any of the courts doing both? Which designation would seem most appropriate in each case? [Review the text in Part A.]

Borg-Warner Corporation, v. Anchor Coupling Co.

16 Ill.2d 234, 156 N.E.2d 513
Supreme Court of Illinois, 1958.

KLINGBIEL, Justice.

This action was brought by Borg-Warner Corporation for specific performance or, in the alternative, money damages, on an alleged contract between plaintiff and Anchor Coupling Co. and its chief officers, Charles L. Conroy and Walter Fritsch. The amended complaint was dismissed on the ground that plaintiff had failed to allege a completed contract capable of specific performance or a cause of action for damages.

This appeal was transferred to this court from the Appellate Court, Second District, for the reason that a freehold is involved, certain real property being among the assets of defendant which were the subject of the alleged contract.

Since the propriety of the lower court's dismissal of the case depends solely on the sufficiency of plaintiff's amended complaint, it is necessary to set forth the facts as alleged in said complaint in some detail.

Plaintiff and defendant, Anchor Coupling Co., hereinafter called Anchor, are corporations organized under the laws of Illinois and engaged in the business of manufacturing. Anchor has issued and outstanding 4,400 shares of stock, owned as follows: Walter Fritsch 1,649 shares, John Fritsch (son of Walter Fritsch) 396 shares, Charles L. Conroy 2,045 shares, Wier (uncle of Charles L. Conroy) 145 shares, and Leubkeman 165 shares. Defendant Fritsch dealt with and represented the stock owned by his son, John Fritsch, as though it were his own, and defendant Fritsch, John Fritsch and defendant Conroy owned at all relevant times 92.96 per cent of Anchor's stock. For ten years defendants Conroy and Fritsch have constituted two of the three directors of Anchor and have dominated and exercised complete control over all the affairs and acts of Anchor with the acquiescence and consent of the other shareholders and the board. The third director, Albrecht, an employee of Anchor, has never owned any shares in the company.

Prior to February 20, 1956, plaintiff engaged in conferences and negotiations with defendants Conroy and Fritsch, as controlling shareholders of Anchor and its chief executive officers and directors, respecting the purchase by plaintiff of all of the property and assets of Anchor. As a result of these negotiations an oral agreement was reached that defendants would sell to plaintiff all of said property and assets for the sum of $4,023,500, if the results of a survey and investigation of Anchor's assets were satisfactory to plaintiff.

On February 20, 1956, plaintiff wrote a letter to Anchor setting forth a detailed agreement giving plaintiff a 60-day option to purchase all of Anchor's business and assets. This was not signed by Anchor, but instead, on February 29, 1956, a letter was sent to plaintiff on Anchor's letterhead and signed by defendants Conroy and Fritsch. Since the decision in this case turns chiefly upon the interpretation to be placed on this letter, we quote its significant parts in full: 'Gentlemen: This letter will outline and confirm our conversation at luncheon today with your Messrs. Porter, Murphy, Steg and Peifer. We are unwilling to enter into a formal option with your company as proposed in your letter of February 20, 1956. This is not for the purpose of horse-trading, but rather to avoid the damage which a turn-down by you would cause both internally and in our market. We would be willing to sell the assets of our company to you for $4,025,000 in accordance with the terms of paragraphs 3, 5, 6, 7, 8, 9, 11, 13, 14 and 17 of your letter of February 20, 1956, if such an offer were made today without the reservations elsewhere contained in that letter, and subject to the exceptions noted below. You may consider this as a letter of intent authorizing you to make the survey you deem necessary to make your offer a firm and binding one; and we assure you of our full cooperation in making it. We suggest that it be completed as quickly as possible. You are assured that should you make a firm offer within fifty days from this date, we are willing to enter into a contract with you on the basis of the terms of the above numbered paragraphs of your letter of February 20, 1956, with the following exceptions: (a) That suitable assurances are given for the retention of the lower level executive personnel; (b) That mutually satisfactory arrangements are made for the continued employment of Charles L. Conroy; (c) That J. D. Leubkeman shall not be a party to any restrictive covenant as outlined in paragraph 8 of your letter of February 20, 1956; and (d) That any purchase price adjustment mentioned in paragraph (7) of your letter of February 20, 1956, shall be made only by mutual agreement between us.'

Plaintiff thereafter inquired of defendants whether their letter of February 29 was correctly understood by plaintiff as a firm offer which would not be revoked during the period stated in said letter (which period was later extended to April 26, 1956) and which plaintiff could accept within said period so as to create a binding contract of sale, and whether plaintiff could make its survey of Anchor's business operations in reliance thereon. In response thereto, defendants Conroy and Fritsch, by their agent, assured plaintiff that plaintiff had 'in effect an option'; that said letter was 'in legal effect...an offer by us (defendants) to enter into a contract with those four very minor things (referring to paragraphs (a) through (d) of defendants' letter of February 29) still to be agreed on'; that the further agreements referred to were not intended to prevent said offer from being a complete offer capable of acceptance but were minor details which, upon the acceptance of said offer, the parties would be obligated to work out in good faith in a reasonable manner, and that if plaintiff within fifty days made an offer in conformity with said letter, defendants would be obligated, subject only to the conditions that the acceptance be delivered within the time limited and that the investigation be conducted in secrecy, to accept such offer.

On March 14, 1956, plaintiff wrote a letter to Conroy, Fritsch and Anchor saying, 'You indicate that our offer on the basis outlined will be accepted if made within fifty days from this date' and asking that the fifty days time be extended to April 26 and that the purchase price be adjusted to $4,024,000. This letter was initialed by Conroy and Fritsch and returned to plaintiff.

Finally, on April 26, 1956, plaintiff wrote to defendants saying that plaintiff had decided to proceed in the acquisition of Anchor's assets. This letter read in part: 'Please consider this our formal offer, therefore, to enter into an agreement in accordance with our letters to you of March 14th, and February 20th and your letter to us of February 29th. Our letter to you of March 14th, the terms of which were accepted by you indicates that this offer will be accepted by you if mailed on April 26th.'

Plaintiff alleges that at this point a completed contract came into existence. Plaintiff also alleges that in various subsequent conversations defendants represented and agreed that there was a complete contract between plaintiff and defendants until on August 1, 1956, defendant Conroy raised objections to the performance of said contract, and on September 27, 1956, refused to perform said contract.

Defendant Fritsch filed an answer admitting the allegations of plaintiff's complaint and stating that 'he did believe that he did enter into a contract and agreement, that the same was fair, open and truly performed on its part by the plaintiff, and this defendant does again reiterate his willingness to perform the same for and on behalf of the shares of stock owned by him and by his son, John Fritsch.' Defendants Conroy and Anchor filed motions to dismiss plaintiff's amended complaint.

On these facts, the trial court dismissed the amended complaint on the ground that it appeared on the face of the pleadings that the parties had failed to agree on material terms of the proposed contract, viz.: (a) The failure to agree on the retention of lower level executive personnel, and (b) failure to make mutually satisfactory arrangements for the continued employment of Conroy. Further, the court held that there was no ambiguity in the written correspondence between the parties and therefore the Statute of Frauds and the parol evidence rule barred consideration of any parol evidence pleaded by plaintiff.

[The court then analyzed the correspondence and found that "[a]lthough defendant in its letter of February 29th spoke in terms of plaintiff making an offer, it must be viewed as an offer itself, asking that plaintiff's acceptance be worded as an offer."]

Was this acceptance sufficient to create a contract at this point or, as defendants contend, did exceptions (a) and (b) prevent the formation of a contract? The answer depends on what the parties intended. Were defendants asking that contracts of employment between plaintiff and the lower level executive personnel and between plaintiff and Conroy actually had to be agreed to as...conditions precedent to the existence of the contract? Or, were defendants merely asking that plaintiff, by a general acceptance, give assurance as to the retention of lower executive personnel and agree that mutually satisfactory arrangements would be made for the employment of Conroy?

In this regard, we find the offer in the February 29 letter to be ambiguous. Thus this case falls within the well-recognized exception to the parol evidence rule that if the terms and provisions of a contract are ambiguous, or if the writings are capable of more than one construction, parol evidence is admissible to explain and ascertain what the parties intended. Street v. Chicago Wharfing & Storage Co., 157 Ill. 605, 41 N.E. 1108; 32 C.J.S. Evidence § 959. This applies to contracts within the Statute of Frauds as well as to any other contract. Plaintiff is not seeking to add terms to the writings by parol, but is merely trying to explain what the parties intended by the written words. The trial court was in error in holding that the parol evidence pleaded by plaintiff could not be considered.

The question then is whether the written correspondence, together with the facts pleaded explaining the terms of the written communications, taken in its most favorable aspect, disclose a contract. We believe the following factors, if proved, are sufficient to support a finding that a completed contract came into existence at the time plaintiff submitted its formal offer on April 26. In so holding, it is impossible to place great reliance on other cases except insofar as they state general principles of law. Contract cases, particularly, must each turn on their own particular facts. As said by Professor Corbin, 'A transaction is complete when the parties mean it to be complete. It is a mere matter of interpretation of their expressions to each other, a question of fact.' 1 Corbin on Contracts, 1st ed. 1950, p. 69.

[The court then noted as "significant" that plaintiff and Fritsch intended that a general acceptance by plaintiff would create a contract. Plaintiff's spending of large sums of money in conducting a survey of defendant's business also shows this belief. Defendant's letter of February 29th was "sprinkled with 'assurances'" and led to plaintiff's belief being reasonable. The court found another "important factor" in the allegation that plaintiff specifically inquired whether the letter of February 29 was intended as a firm offer and defendant's assurance that it was. Also significant were plaintiff's allegations that defendants by "actions and conversations represented that there was a completed contract...subsequent to [plaintiff's] acceptance of April 26." The court held that the trial court should admit "parol evidence to determine the meaning of language used in letters and telegrams which are relied upon as evidencing a contract...." As to indefiniteness the court said: "We think that we should construe 'mutual satisfaction' as reasonable satisfaction and thus uphold the contract." If the parties can't agree as to the terms of Conroy's employment the court can look to current terms of Conroy's employment, terms customary in other businesses and "prior practices at Anchor" (defendants' business.) "Thus, the contract, if established, is capable of specific enforcement." The trial court's dismissal of the case was reversed and the cause remanded. Two judges dissented.]

Hunt Foods, Inc. v. Doliner

26 A.D.2d 41, 270 N.Y.S.2d 937

Supreme Court, Appellate Division, First Department, 1966.

STEUER, Justice.

In February 1965 plaintiff corporation undertook negotiations to acquire the assets of Eastern Can Company. The stock of the latter is owned by defendant George M. Doliner and his family to the extent of 73%. The balance is owned by independent interests. At a fairly early stage of the negotiations agreement was reached as to the price to be paid by plaintiff ($5,922,500 if in cash, or $5,730,000 in Hunt stock), but several important items, including the form of the acquisition, were not agreed upon. At this point it was found necessary to recess the negotiations for several weeks. The Hunt negotiators expressed concern over any adjournment and stated that they feared that Doliner would use their offer as a basis for soliciting a higher bid from a third party. To protect themselves they demanded an option to purchase the Doliner stock. Such an option was prepared and signed by George Doliner and the members of his family and at least one other person associated with him who were stockholders. It provides that Hunt has the option to buy all of the Doliner stock at $5.50 per share. The option is to be exercised by giving notice on or before June 1, 1965, and if notice is not given the option is void. If given, Hunt is to pay the price and the Doliners to deliver their stock within seven days thereafter. The agreement calls for Hunt to pay $1,000 for the option, which was paid. To this point there is substantial accord as to what took place.

Defendant claims that when his counsel called attention to the fact that the option was unconditional in its terms, he obtained an understanding that it was only to be used in the event that he solicited an outside offer; and that plaintiff insisted that unless the option was signed in unconditional form negotiations would terminate. Plaintiff contends there was no condition. Concededly, on resumption of negotiations the parties failed to reach agreement and the option was exercised. Defendants declined the tender and refused to deliver the stock.

Plaintiff moved for summary judgment for specific performance. We do not believe that summary judgment lies. Plaintiff's position is that the condition claimed could not be proved under the parol evidence rule and, eliminating that, there is no defense to the action.

The parol evidence rule, at least as that term refers to contracts of sale, is now contained in Section 2-202 of the Uniform Commercial Code, which reads:

'Terms with respect to which the confirmatory memoranda of the parties agree or which are otherwise set forth in a writing intended by the parties as a final expression of their agreement with respect to such terms as are included therein may not be contradicted by evidence of any prior agreement or of a contemporaneous oral agreement but may be explained or supplemented...(b) by evidence of consistent additional terms unless the court finds the writing to have been intended also as a complete and exclusive statement of the terms of the agreement.' [subdivision (a) not quoted by the court reads: "(a) by course of dealing or usage of trade (section 1- 205) or by course of performance (section 2-208)".]

The term (that the option was not to be exercised unless Doliner sought outside bids), admittedly discussed but whose operative effect is disputed, not being set out in the writing, is clearly 'additional' to what is in the writing. So the first question presented is whether that term is 'consistent' with the instrument. In a sense any oral provision which would prevent the ripening of the obligations of a writing is inconsistent with the writing. But that obviously is not the sense in which the word is used. To be inconsistent the term must contradict or negate a term of the writing. A term or condition which has a lesser effect is provable.

The Official Comment prepared by the drafters of the Code contains this statement: 'If the additional terms are such that, if agreed upon, they would certainly have been included in the document in the view of the court, then evidence of their alleged making must be kept from the trier of fact.' (McKinney's Uniform Commercial Code, Part 1, p. 158)

Special Term interpreted this language as not only calling for an adjudication by the court in all instances where proof of an 'additional oral term' is offered, but making that determination exclusively the function of the court. We believe the proffered evidence to be inadmissible only where the writing contradicts the existence of the claimed additional term. The conversations in this case, some of which are not disputed, and the expectation of all the parties for further negotiations, suggest that the alleged oral condition precedent cannot be precluded as a matter of law or as factually impossible. It is not sufficient that the existence of the condition is implausible. It must be impossible.

The order should be reversed on the law and the motion for summary judgment denied with costs and disbursements to abide the event.

Order and judgment (one paper) unanimously reversed, on the law, with $50 costs and disbursements to abide the event, and plaintiff's motion for summary judgment denied. All concur.

Questions

1. What if this case were decided in Utah? Is the standard for admission/exclusion different? See *Hall, supra*.

Although *Hunt* concerned the sale of stock, the court held that the U.C.C. would be applied by analogy under the holding of a previous case.

The following case involves more than just a term to be added or explained. It concerns what amounts to a whole separate agreement—the tearing down of an ice house.

Mitchill v. Lath

247 N.Y. 377, 160 N.E. 646
Court of Appeals of New York, 1928.

ANDREWS, J.

In the fall of 1923 the Laths owned a farm. This they wished to sell. Across the road, on land belonging to Lieutenant Governor Lunn, they had an icehouse which they might remove. Mrs. Mitchill looked over the land with a view to its purchase. She found the icehouse objectionable. Thereupon 'the defendants orally promised and agreed, for and in consideration of the purchase of their farm by the plaintiff, to remove the said icehouse in the spring of 1924.' Relying upon this promise, she made a written contract to buy the property for $8,400, for cash and mortgage and containing various provisions usual in such papers. Later receiving a deed, she entered into possession, and has spent considerable sums in improving the property for use as a summer residence. The defendants have not fulfilled their promise as to the icehouse, and do not intend to do so. We are not dealing, however, with their moral delinquencies. The question before us is whether their oral agreement may be enforced in a court of equity.

This requires a discussion of the parol evidence rule—a rule of law which defines the limits of the contract to be construed. It applies, however, to attempts to modify such a contract by parol. It does not affect a parol collateral contract distinct from and independent of the written agreement. It is, at times, troublesome to draw the line. Williston, in his work on Contracts (§637) points out the difficulty. 'Two entirely distinct contracts,' he says, 'each for a separate consideration, may be made at the same time, and will be distinct legally. Where, however, one agreement is entered into wholly or partly in consideration of the simultaneous agreement to enter into another, the transactions are necessarily bound together....Then if one of the agreements is oral and the other in writing, the problem arises whether the bond is sufficiently close to prevent proof of the oral agreement.' That is the situation here. It is claimed that the defendants are called upon to do more than is required by their written contract in connection with the sale as to which it deals.

The principle may be clear, but it can be given effect by no mechanical rule. As so often happens it is a matter of degree, for, as Prof. Williston also says, where a contract contains several promises on each side it is not difficult to put any one of them in the form of a collateral agreement. If this were enough, written contracts might always be modified by parol. Not from, but substance, is the test.

In applying this test, the policy of our courts is to be considered. We have believed that the purpose behind the rule was a wise one, not easily to be abandoned. Notwithstanding injustice here and there, on the whole it works for good. Old precedents and principles are not to be lightly cast aside, unless it is certain that they are an obstruction under present conditions. New York has been less open to arguments that would modify this particular rule, than some jurisdictions elsewhere. Thus in Eighmie v. Taylor, 98 N. Y. 288, it was held that a parol warranty might not be shown, although no warranties were contained in the writing.

Under our decisions before such an oral agreement as the present is received to vary the written contract, at least three conditions must exist: (1) The agreement must in form be a collateral one; (2) it must not contradict express or implied provisions of the written contract; (3) it must be one that parties would not ordinarily be expected to embody in the writing, or, put in another way, an inspection of the written contract, read in the light of surrounding circumstances, must not indicate that the writing appears 'to contain the engagements of the parties, and to define the object and measure the extent of such engagement.' Or, again, it must not be so clearly connected with the principal transaction as to be part and parcel of it.

The respondent does not satisfy the third of these requirements. It may be, not the second. We have a written contract for the purchase and sale of land. The buyer is to pay $8,400 in the way described. She is also to pay her portion of any rents, interest on mortgages, insurance premiums, and water meter charges. She may have a survey made of the premises. On their part, the sellers are to give a full covenant deed of the premises as described, or as they may be described by the surveyor, if the survey is had, executed, and acknowledged at their own expense; they sell the personal property on the farm and represent they own it; they agree that all amounts paid them on the contract and the expense of examining the title shall be a lien on the property; they assume the risk of loss or damage by fire until the deed is delivered; and they agree to pay the broker his commissions. Are they to do more? Or is such a claim inconsistent with these precise provisions? It could not be shown that the plaintiff was to pay $500 additional. Is it also implied that the defendants are not to do anything unexpressed in the writing?

That we need not decide. At least, however, an inspection of this contract shows a full and complete agreement, setting forth in detail the obligations of each party. On reading it, one would conclude that the reciprocal obligations of the parties were fully detailed. Nor would his opinion alter if he knew the surrounding circumstances. The presence of the icehouse, even the knowledge that Mrs. Mitchill thought it objectionable, would not lead to the belief that a separate agreement existed with regard to it. Were such an agreement made it would seem most natural that the inquirer should find it in the contract. Collateral in form it is found to be, but it is closely related to the subject dealt with in the written agreement—so closely that we hold it may not be proved.

Where the line between the competent and the incompetent is narrow the citation of authorities is of slight use. Each represents the judgment of the court on the precise facts before it. How closely bound to the contract is the supposed collateral agreement is the decisive factor in each case.

It is argued that what we have said is not applicable to the case as presented. The collateral agreement was made with the plaintiff. The contract of sale was with her husband, and no assignment of it from him appears. Yet the deed was given to her. It is evident that here was a transaction in which she was the principal from beginning to end. We must treat the contract as if in form, as it was in fact, made by her.

Our conclusion is that the judgment of the Appellate Division and that of the Special Term should be reversed and the complaint dismissed, with costs in all courts.

LEHMAN, J. (dissenting).

I accept the general rule as formulated by Judge ANDREWS. I differ with him only as to its application to the facts shown in the record. The plaintiff contracted to purchase land from the defendants for an agreed price. A formal written agreement was made between the sellers and the plaintiff's husband. It is on its face a complete contract for the conveyance of the land. It describes the property to be conveyed. It sets forth the purchase price to be paid. All the conditions and terms of the conveyance to be made are clearly stated. I concede at the outset that parol evidence to show additional conditions and terms of the conveyance would be inadmissible. There is a conclusive presumption that the parties intended to integrate in that written contract every agreement relating to the nature or extent of the property to be conveyed, the contents of the deed to be delivered, the consideration to be paid as a condition precedent to the delivery of the deeds, and indeed all the rights of the parties in connection with the land. The conveyance of that land was the subject-matter of the written contract, and the contract completely covers that subject.

The parol agreement which the court below found the parties had made was collateral to, yet connected with, the agreement of purchase and sale. It has been found that the defendants induced the plaintiff to agree to purchase the land by a promise to remove an icehouse from land not covered by the agreement of purchase and sale. No independent consideration passed to the defendants for the parol promise. To that extent the written contract and the alleged oral contract are bound together. The same bond usually exists wherever attempt is made to prove a parol agreement which is collateral to a written agreement. Hence 'the problem arises whether the bond is sufficiently close to prevent proof of the oral agreement.' See Judge ANDREWS' citation from Williston on Contracts, § 637.

Judge ANDREWS has formulated a standard to measure the closeness of the bond. Three conditions, at least, must exist before an oral agreement may be proven to increase the obligation imposed by the written agreement. I think we agree that the first condition that the agreement 'must in form be a collateral one' is met by the evidence. I concede that this condition is met in most cases where the courts have nevertheless excluded evidence of the collateral oral agreement. The difficulty here, as in most cases, arises in connection with the two other conditions.

The second condition is that the 'parol agreement must not contradict express or implied provisions of the written contract.' Judge ANDREWS voices doubt whether this condition is satisfied. The written contract has been carried out. The purchase price has been paid; conveyance has been made; title has passed in accordance with the terms of the written contract. The mutual obligations expressed in the written contract are left unchanged by the alleged oral contract. When performance was required of the written contract, the obligations of the parties were measured solely by its terms. By the oral agreement the plaintiff seeks to hold the defendants to other obligations to be performed by them thereafter upon land which was not conveyed to the plaintiff. The assertion of such further obligation is not inconsistent with the written contract, unless the written contract contains a provision, express or implied, that the defendants are not to do anything not expressed in the writing. Concededly there is no such express provision in the contract, and such a provision may be implied, if at all, only if the asserted additional obligation is 'so clearly connected with the principal transaction as to be part and parcel of it,' and is not 'one that the parties would not ordinarily be expected to embody in the writing.' The hypothesis so formulated for a conclusion that the asserted additional obligation is inconsistent with an implied term of the contract is that the alleged oral agreement does not comply with the third condition as formulated by Judge ANDREWS. In this case, therefore, the problem reduces itself to the one question whether or not the oral agreement meets the third condition.

I have conceded that upon inspection the contract is complete. 'It appears to contain the engagements of the parties, and to define the object and measure the extent of such engagement;' it constitutes the contract between them, and is presumed to contain the whole of that contract. Eighmie v. Taylor, 98 N. Y. 288. That engagement was on the one side to convey land; on the other to pay the price. The plaintiff asserts further agreement based on the same consideration to be performed by the defendants after the conveyance was complete, and directly affecting only other land. It is true, as Judge ANDREWS points out, that 'the presence of the icehouse, even the knowledge that Mrs. Mitchill though it objectionable, would not lead to the belief that a separate agreement existed with regard to it'; but the question we must decide is whether or not, assuming an agreement was made for the removal of an unsightly icehouse from one parcel of land as an inducement for the purchase of another parcel, the parties would ordinarily or naturally be expected to embody the agreement for the removal of the icehouse from one parcel in the written agreement to convey the other parcel. Exclusion of proof of the oral agreement on the ground that it varies the contract embodied in the writing may be based only upon a finding or presumption that the written contract was intended to cover the oral negotiations for the removal of the icehouse which lead up to the contract of purchase and sale. To determine what the writing was intended to cover, 'the document alone will not suffice. What it was intended to cover cannot be known till we know what there was to cover. The question being whether certain subjects of negotiation were intended to be covered, we must compare the writing and the negotiations before we can determine whether they were in fact covered.' Wigmore on Evidence (2d Ed.) § 2430.

The subject-matter of the written contract was the conveyance of land. The contract was so complete on its face that the conclusion is inevitable that the parties intended to embody in the writing all the negotiations covering at least the conveyance. The promise by the defendants to remove the icehouse from other land was not connected with their obligation to convey except that one agreement would not have been made unless the other was also made. The plaintiff's assertion of a parol agreement by the defendants to remove the icehouse was completely established by the great weight of evidence. It must prevail unless that agreement was part of the agreement to convey and the entire agreement was embodied in the writing.

The fact that in this case the parol agreement is established by the overwhelming weight of evidence is, of course, not a factor which may be considered in determining the competency or legal effect of the evidence. Hardship in the particular case would not justify the court in disregarding or emasculating the general rule. It merely accentuates the outlines of our problem. The assumption that the parol agreement was made is no longer obscured by any doubts. The problem, then, is clearly whether the parties are presumed to have intended to render that parol agreement legally ineffective and nonexistent by failure to embody it in the writing. Though we are driven to say that nothing in the written contract which fixed the terms and conditions of the stipulated conveyance suggests the existence of any further parol agreement, an inspection of the contract, though it is complete on its face in regard to the subject of the conveyance, does not, I think, show that it was intended to embody negotiations or agreements, if any, in regard to a matter so loosely bound to the conveyance as the removal of an icehouse from land not conveyed.

The rule of integration undoubtedly frequently prevents the assertion of fraudulent claims. Parties who take the precaution of embodying their oral agreements in a writing should be protected against the assertion that other terms of the same agreement were not integrated in the writing. The limits of the integration are determined by the writing, read in the light of the surrounding circumstances. A written contract, however complete, yet covers only a limited field. I do not think that in the written contract for the conveyance of land here under consideration we can find an intention to cover a field so broad as to include prior agreements, if any such were made, to do other acts on other property after the stipulated conveyance was made.

In each case where such a problem is presented, varying factors enter into its solution. Citation of authority in this or other jurisdictions is useless, at least without minute analysis of the facts. The analysis I have made of the decisions in this state leads me to the view that the decision of the courts below is in accordance with our own authorities and should be affirmed.

[One other judge joined Judge Lehman's dissent.]

Questions

1. Note that the court found in essence that the promise to remove the ice house would have been included in the writing if the promise existed. Does this mean that the plaintiffs cannot now seek a remedy in promissory estoppel for defendant's promise?

2. Why could not plaintiffs have simply sought to prove a separate contract for the removal of the ice house?

Closing Note—Parol Evidence

The Uniform Commercial Code is probably the most advanced (or destructive depending on your viewpoint) expression of the parol evidence rule. Section 2-202 quoted in several of the cases does not require ambiguity before trade usage, course of dealing, course of performance and additional terms can be introduced to explain or supplement a writing. Unless the writing is found to be the complete and exclusive expression of the parties' intent they are always admissible. Where the writing is a complete and exclusive expression additional terms are not admissible but trade usage, course of dealing and course of performance are. Although section 2-202 only applies to sales of goods it has had a great impact on many areas of the law where its approach has been employed by the courts. Similarly, Corbin's view that anything and everything requires explanation has made a writing intended to embody a contract less of a defining source to discover the intent of the parties and more of a guide to finding it.

Although the cases in this section represent only a small sampling of courts' struggles with the rule, several guiding principles should always be kept in mind. First, the rule only applies to contemporaneous or prior agreements. Section 2-202 says that the writing intended to express the parties' intent may not be contradicted by prior agreements or by contemporaneous oral agreements leaving the door open to contradiction by contemporaneous written agreements. In all its versions, the parol evidence rule does not apply to later agreements, written or oral. These fall within the area of modifications, the subject of the next section.

Second, the rule in all its manifestations is intended to keep out terms that contradict the writing intended to embody the agreement and then only to the extent of the terms in the writing. In other words, the writing may not embody the complete agreement but, if it is found to be a final expression of the parties, to the extent that it covers the agreement it cannot be contradicted. If the writing is found to be the complete and exclusive expression of the agreement, nothing can be added to it.

Third, the writing can be explained. The older view says it can be explained only if it is ambiguous (the plain meaning rule). The newer view says that it can always be explained.

Finally, the initial step, before trying to determine what it said, is to determine if the writing is intended to be a final expression of anything. This is where fraud, duress, mutual mistake, joke, condition precedent come in. Because the writing has no value by itself but only to the extent that it expresses the will of the parties, their intent to be bound, it can always be challenged. The problem is that the writing itself is the starting point. If it says that no representations other than those in the writing have been made, you can always nullify its legal force by proving that you signed because someone had a gun at your head, *i.e.* you had no intent to be bound but only an intent to save your life. But what if it says, there are no conditions precedent and you want to prove that the contract would only be effective when the stock market hit 8,000? Your term would contradict a term of the writing which on its face appears to be effective on signing. Could you say that's a mistake? As we will see in Part V a unilateral mistake will rarely nullify a contract, and hence the writing that embodies it. What if you didn't read it or didn't understand it? Here is where objective manifestation conflicts with subjective intent. You signed it. If you carelessly say something "Get your men out you'll be alright" (*Embry*) you can be held to a contract no matter what your subjective intention. If you sign something that objectively manifests your intent to be bound, should you be any less obligated? We will consider the problem of the standardized contract which one party drafts and the other rarely reads in Part D. Basically, your objective manifestation will bind you. In some states, recognizing that people do not read and/or understand what they sign, state legislatures put limits on what some contracts can say and on how they say it. Many states have mandatory provisions for auto insurance contracts and also require plain language in the writings. Some have laws which allow consumers to avoid contracts signed in their homes for up to three days after signing and require that at signing they receive a copy of the contract and further require that this right of avoidance be in large print above their signatures. If, however, you are a knowledgeable, competent person, the presumption will be that if the writing taken by itself indicates that a contract was entered, the court will presume it was. The signer, unless he/she can prove fraud etc., is then left with an attempt to either explain or add to the writing. As the cases indicate, this is becoming easier but the writing still has a force of its own.

C. Modification

In this section we look not to writings or oral statements that preceded or were contemporaneous with a writing intended to integrate the agreement of the parties but rather with writings or statements coming after such a writing. As with the initial contract itself a modification at common law required consideration and this still remains the rule for many modifications. Under the U.C.C. Article 2 for sales of goods no consideration is necessary to modify a contract. The standard is whether the modification is made in good faith. As we will see in the next case if one party appears to take advantage of another's distress to obtain a modification that is not based on some need that has arisen but only to obtain more or better compensation, the courts will look closely at the modification. Lack of good faith is related to duress and unconscionability which we will examine more closely in Part V. Waiver and estoppel are closely related to modification and in the U.C.C. all are addressed in one section, 2-209. The difference between them is that a modification relates to a change in the parties duties. One party may take on an additional obligation and/or another may have an obligation lessened. Waiver only relates to surrendering a right, not taking on an additional obligation. For example, if I tell you that, although under an installment contract where I am shipping goods to you or performing a series of services for you over a period of time you are to pay for each shipment or service in cash on receipt or performance, you may pay by check, I have probably waived my right to cash. I have given up a right. I must do this knowingly and intentionally for the waiver to be upheld. Once the right is given up at common law I could not revive it, *i.e.* change my mind and tell you I want cash. With estoppel if you started paying by check and I didn't object, I could not claim you were in breach and refuse a check after I had accepted several but I could demand cash in the future, *i.e.* withdraw your right. Under section 2-209 I could withdraw your right to pay cash under either waiver or estoppel but only to the extent that your reliance on them would not cause you harm. Estoppel can also relate to an increased obligation, although this is less common and is likely to be viewed as a modification by performance (see *e.g.* section 2-208 of the U.C.C.). If the contract above called for goods to be delivered to your place of business but I delivered them to your home without objection by you, it could be said that you were estopped to claim your right under the contract to have them delivered to your home. It could also be said that by our actions we had by conduct modified the contract. The difference is that a modification cannot be disregarded by one of the parties whereas an estoppel, and under 2-209 a waiver, can be with notice withdrawn, no longer followed unless the other party has so relied as to create a burden on her.

The key point is that modification goes to a change in duties that is intended to be continued as part of the contract, not a change that is temporary. It also relates to changes after the contract is created, not to terms allegedly entered into contemporaneously or prior to the contract.

Problem on Modification

Jones signs a contract with Smith for the purchase of Blackacre, a 100 acre farm. Jones agrees to pay Smith $100,000 per year for 10 years, without interest, the first payment to be made when the sale closes and the deed is handed to Jones. The contract describes the land, its location, the consideration to be paid for it and the date of closing. It states that "this writing constitutes the complete and exclusive agreement by which Smith agrees to sell Jones Blackacre." Jones later insists that to induce him to buy the land, and as part of the deal, Smith agreed to work on the land for six months and to level a portion of it.

Jones also says that after the contract was signed, Smith agreed to leave his tractor and garden tools so that Jones could begin cultivating the land. Jones says that Smith and he agreed to modify the land contract to include this.

(1) Assess Jones' likelihood of winning on either assertion if litigation arises.

(2) Would it matter if either claim were reflected in a writing signed by both parties?

Austin Instrument, Inc., v. Loral Corporation
29 N.Y.2d 124, 272 N.E.2d 533, 324 N.Y.S.2d 22
Court of Appeals of New York, 1971.

FULD, Chief Judge.

The defendant, Loral Corporation, seeks to recover payment for goods delivered under a contract which it had with the plaintiff Austin Instrument, Inc., on the ground that the evidence establishes, as a matter of law, that it was forced to agree to an increase in price on the items in question under circumstances amounting to economic duress.

In July of 1965, Loral was awarded a $6,000,000 contract by the Navy for the production of radar sets. The contract contained a schedule of deliveries, a liquidated damages clause applying to late deliveries and a cancellation clause in case of default by Loral. The latter thereupon solicited bids for some 40 precision gear components needed to produce the radar sets, and awarded Austin a subcontract to supply 23 such parts. That party commenced delivery in early 1966.

In May, 1966, Loral was awarded a second Navy contract for the production of more radar sets and again went about soliciting bids. Austin bid on all 40 gear components but, on July 15, a representative from Loral informed Austin's president, Mr. Krauss, that his company would be awarded the subcontract only for those items on which it was low bidder. The Austin officer refused to accept an order for less than all 40 of the gear parts and on the next day he told Loral that Austin would cease deliveries of the parts due under the existing subcontract unless Loral consented to substantial increases in the prices provided for by that agreement—both retroactively for parts already delivered and prospectively on those not yet shipped—and placed with Austin the order for all 40 parts needed under Loral's second Navy contract. Shortly thereafter, Austin did, indeed, stop delivery. After contacting 10 manufacturers of precision gears and finding none who could produce the parts in time to meet its commitments to the Navy, Loral acceded to Austin's demands; in a letter dated July 22, Loral wrote to Austin that "We have feverishly surveyed other sources of supply and find that because of the prevailing military exigencies, were they to start from scratch as would have to be the case, they could not even remotely begin to deliver on time to meet the delivery requirements established by the Government.... Accordingly, we are left with no choice or alternative but to meet your conditions."

Loral thereupon consented to the price increases insisted upon by Austin under the first subcontract and the latter was awarded a second subcontract making it the supplier of all 40 gear parts for Loral's second contract with the Navy. Although Austin was granted until September to resume deliveries, Loral did, in fact, receive parts in August and was able to produce the radar sets in time to meet its commitments to the Navy on both contracts. After Austin's last delivery under the second subcontract in July, 1967, Loral notified it of its intention to seek recovery of the price increases.

On September 15, 1967, Austin instituted this action against Loral to recover an amount in excess of $17,750 which was still due on the second subcontract. On the same day, Loral commenced an action against Austin claiming damages of some $22,250—the aggregate of the price increases under the first subcontract—on the ground of economic duress. The two actions were consolidated and, following a trial, Austin was awarded the sum it requested and Loral's complaint against Austin was dismissed on the ground that it was not shown that 'it could not have obtained the items in question from other sources in time to meet its commitment to the Navy under the first contract.' A closely divided Appellate Division affirmed (35 A.D.2d 387, 316 N.Y.S.2d 528, 532). There was no material disagreement concerning the facts; as Justice Steuer stated in the course of his dissent below, '(t)he facts are virtually undisputed, nor is there any serious question of law. The difficulty lies in the application of the law to these facts.' (35 A.D.2d 392, 316 N.Y.S.2d 534.)

The applicable law is clear and, indeed, is not disputed by the parties. A contract is voidable on the ground of duress when it is established that the party making the claim was forced to agree to it by means of a wrongful threat precluding the exercise of his free will. The existence of economic duress or business compulsion is demonstrated by proof that 'immediate possession of needful goods is threatened' or, more particularly, in cases such as the one before us, by proof that one party to a contract has threatened to breach the agreement by withholding goods unless the other party agrees to some further demand. However, a mere threat by one party to breach the contract by not delivering the required items, though wrongful, does not in itself constitute economic duress. It must also appear that the threatened party could not obtain the goods from another source of supply and that the ordinary remedy of an action for breach of contract would not be adequate.

We find without any support in the record the conclusion reached by the courts below that Loral failed to establish that it was the victim of economic duress. On the contrary, the evidence makes out a classic case, as a matter of law, of such duress.

It is manifest that Austin's threat—to stop deliveries unless the prices were increased—deprived Loral of its free will. As bearing on this, Loral's relationship with the Government is most significant. As mentioned above, its contract called for staggered monthly deliveries of the radar sets, with clauses calling for liquidated damages and possible cancellation on default. Because of its production schedule, Loral was, in July, 1966, concerned with meeting its delivery requirements in September, October and November, and it was for the sets to be delivered in those months that the withheld gears were needed. Loral had to plan ahead, and the substantial liquidated damages for which it would be liable, plus the threat of default, were genuine possibilities. Moreover, Loral did a substantial portion of its business with the Government, and it feared that a failure to deliver as agreed upon would jeopardize its chances for future contracts. These genuine concerns do not merit the label "self-imposed, undisclosed and subjective" which the Appellate Division majority placed upon them. It was perfectly reasonable for Loral, or any other party similarly placed, to consider itself in an emergency, duress situation.

Austin, however, claims that the fact that Loral extended its time to resume deliveries until September negates its alleged dire need for the parts. A Loral official testified on this point that Austin's president told him he could deliver some parts in August and that the extension of deliveries was a formality. In any event, the parts necessary for production of the radar sets to be delivered in September were delivered to Loral on September 1, and the parts needed for the October schedule were delivered in late August and early September. Even so, Loral had to 'work...around the clock' to meet its commitments. Considering that the best offer Loral received from the other vendors it contacted was commencement of delivery sometime in October, which, as the record shows, would have made it late in its deliveries to the Navy in both September and October, Loral's claim that it had no choice but to accede to Austin's demands is conclusively demonstrated.

We find unconvincing Austin's contention that Loral, in order to meet its burden, should have contacted the Government and asked for an extension of its delivery dates so as to enable it to purchase the parts from another vendor. Aside from the consideration that Loral was anxious to perform well in the Government's eyes, it could not be sure when it would obtain enough parts from a substitute vendor to meet its commitments. The only promise which it received from the companies it contacted was for commencement of deliveries, not full supply, and, with vendor delay common in this field, it would have been nearly impossible to know the length of the extension it should request. It must be remembered that Loral was producing a needed item of military hardware. Moreover, there is authority for Loral's position that nonperformance by a subcontractor is not an excuse for default in the main contract. (See, e.g., McBride & Wachtel, Government Contracts, § 35.10, (11).) In light of all this, Loral's claim should not be held insufficiently supported because it did not request an extension from the Government.

Loral, as indicated above, also had the burden of demonstrating that it could not obtain the parts elsewhere within a reasonable time, and there can be no doubt that it met this burden. The 10 manufacturers whom Loral contacted comprised its entire list of 'approved vendors' for precision gears, and none was able to commence delivery soon enough. As Loral was producing a highly sophisticated item of military machinery requiring parts made to the strictest engineering standards, it would be unreasonable to hold that Loral should have gone to other vendors, with whom it was either unfamiliar or dissatisfied, to procure the needed parts. As Justice Steuer noted in his dissent, Loral 'contacted all the manufacturers whom it believed capable of making these parts' (35 A.D.2d at p. 393, 316 N.Y.S.2d at p. 534), and this was all the law requires.

It is hardly necessary to add that Loral's normal legal remedy of accepting Austin's breach of the contract and then suing for damages would have been inadequate under the circumstances, as Loral would still have had to obtain the gears elsewhere with all the concomitant consequences mentioned above. In other words, Loral actually had no choice, when the prices were raised by Austin, except to take the gears at the 'coerced' prices and then sue to get the excess back.

Austin's final argument is that Loral, Even if it did enter into the contract under duress, lost any rights it had to a refund of money by waiting until July, 1967, long after the termination date of the contract, to disaffirm it. It is true that one who would recover moneys allegedly paid under duress must act promptly to make his claim known. In this case, Loral delayed making its demand for a refund until three days after Austin's last delivery on the second subcontract. Loral's reason—for waiting until that time—is that it feared another stoppage of deliveries which would again put it in an untenable situation. Considering Austin's conduct in the past, this was perfectly reasonable, as the possibility of an application by Austin of further business compulsion still existed until all of the parts were delivered.

In sum, the record before us demonstrates that Loral agreed to the price increases in consequence of the economic duress employed by Austin. Accordingly, the matter should be remanded to the trial court for a computation of its damages.

The order appealed from should be modified, with costs, by reversing so much thereof as affirms the dismissal of defendant Loral Corporation's claim and, except as so modified, affirmed.

[The decision was 4-3 with the dissenters asserting that the availability of alternatives to Austin was a highly controverted issue of fact which should not be overturned on appeal.]

Detroit Police Officers Association, v. City of Detroit
452 Mich. 339, 551 N.W.2d 349
Supreme Court of Michigan, 1996.

MICHAEL F. CAVANAGH, Justice.

The issue presented by this case is whether the parties' past practice is so widely acknowledged and mutually accepted that it amends the contradictory and unambiguous contract language in the collective bargaining agreement. Applying the majority's analysis and holding in the recently decided Port Huron Ed. Ass'n v. Port Huron School Dist., 452 Mich. 309, 550 N.W.2d 228 (1996), we hold that the association has shown that the parties had a meeting of the minds with respect to the new terms or conditions and that the past practice was so prevalent and widely accepted that there was an agreement to modify the contract. Thus, the board of trustees committed an unfair labor practice when it unilaterally changed a mandatory subject of bargaining.

I. Facts and Procedural History

The charter of the City of Detroit created a pension system that provides retirement and death benefits for its firefighters and police officers. The charter also contains provisions regarding the award of benefits as a result of duty- or nonduty-related incapacity. It provides that the board of trustees, which manages the retirement system, decides whether an applicant's disability is duty related: "If a member shall become totally incapacitated for duty by reason of injury, illness or disease resulting from performance of duty and if the Board of Trustees shall find such injury, illness or disease to have resulted from the performance of duty, ... such member shall be retired...." Additionally, the charter provides that the medical director shall certify to the board of trustees that the person is totally incapacitated. If a dispute arises over the medical director's finding, then the board of trustees is to "refer the matter in dispute to a Medical Board of Review consisting of three physicians or surgeons, of whom one shall be named by the Board of Trustees, one by the affected member, beneficiary, or other person claiming benefits, and the third by the two so named...." Detroit Charter, tit. IX, ch. VI, art. III, § 12(c). The medical findings of this medical board of review are binding on the board of trustees.

However, at some point, perhaps as early as 1941, the actual practice arose of having the medical director determine duty relatedness, as well as physical incapacity, with any dispute going to the medical board of review. Further, under the past practice, the medical board's decision was binding on the board of trustees, even with regard to duty relatedness.

In an attempt to recapture the duty-relatedness decision making, the board of trustees passed a resolution on December 6, 1990, stating in pertinent part: [F]indings made by Medical Boards of Review shall be strictly limited to "medical findings"…. The board of trustees further stated that it was the one responsible for deciding whether the "underlying event or events that gave rise to the disability occurred while in the performance of duty…." The police and firefighter unions responded to this resolution by filing an unfair labor practice charge with the MERC [Michigan Employment Relations Commission.]

The MERC found that an unfair labor practice had been committed and reversed the hearing referee's decision and recommended order of dismissal. The hearing referee had found that the resolution was consistent with the wording of the charter, and that there was no apparent reason for adoption of the resolution other than to emphasize the board of trustees' already clearly delineated authority to determine whether an injury or illness is duty related. He further found that any alleged past practice that resulted in the delegation of the decision making on the issue of duty relatedness from the board of trustees to the medical board of review would be an improper amendment of the charter.

In reversing, the MERC emphasized its understanding that over the years the parties had actually acquiesced in the medical director's determination with regard to duty relatedness, with binding review by the medical board of review. The MERC stated: "Contrary to the holding of the [hearing referee], we find in favor of the Charging Party. Past practice, the opinions of Corporate Counsel, the opinion of legal counsel for the Board of Trustees, and a Circuit Court decision all establish that the Medical Board of Review is the final arbiter of whether an injury/illness is duty related. Pensions and the significant provisions of a pension plan are mandatory subjects of bargaining. We find in the case before us that the board which determines eligibility for a duty-related pension is a significant provision in the Detroit pension plan and is a mandatory subject of bargaining. The unilateral change of that mandatory subject effectuated by the December 6, 1990, resolution is an unfair labor practice." [1993 MERC Lab. Op. 424, 432.] The MERC ordered the board of trustees to rescind the December resolution, and it directed the city and the board of trustees to stop this unilateral changing of the authority of the board of trustees regarding disability pensions.

The parties appealed, and the board of trustees sought a stay of the MERC order. The Court of Appeals granted the stay and affirmed the MERC in every respect. 212 Mich.App. 383, 538 N.W.2d 37 (1995). This Court granted the applications for leave to appeal of the city and the board of trustees.

III. Application

There are a number of facts in the record that indicate that the parties' acceptance of and adherence to the past practice at issue modified the parties' contract language to the contrary.

Before the MERC, the association argued that since 1941, when the charter was adopted, the medical director made the initial determination whether the disability was duty related. If a dispute arose on that issue, it was reviewed by a medical board of review. That was the procedure that was in effect under the charter before the public employment relations act was enacted. M.C.L. § 423.201 et seq.; M.S.A. § 17.455(1) et seq. To establish that this past practice existed, the association introduced into evidence minutes of the board of trustees from 1984 to 1990, in which over one hundred decisions of the medical board of review regarding the issue of duty relatedness were accepted as final and binding by the board of trustees.

As further proof that the past practice existed, the association also introduced evidence that in the city attorney's opening statement before the MERC, she admitted "that there has been a history with the [board of trustees] that the duty-relatedness decision, which is involved in determining whether or not an individual [is] entitled to a duty disability, has been made in the past by the Medical Board of Review." Additionally, the board of trustees' own attorney disapproved of the December resolution, stating, "It is the current and well established practice for the Medical Director to render his opinions, conclusions and recommendations and make findings as to whether the applicant is totally incapacitated for the performance of his/her duties and whether such disability is duty or non-duty related." This is also consistent with the testimony of a member of the board of trustees who testified that from at least 1983, the date the witness became a member of the board of trustees, to 1990 the decisions of the medical board of review regarding both disability and causation were considered binding on the board of trustees. In hundreds of cases, the board of trustees unwaveringly acknowledged and accepted the medical board's determinations regarding whether an individual's disability occurred during the performance of a job-related duty.

In addition, the association entered into evidence several forms developed by the board of trustees for use by the medical board. These forms ask the medical board of review to make a duty-connectedness finding. Specifically, one form states: "It is the duty of the medical director to determine whether or not there is a disability present and whether or not the disability is causally related to the performance of the applicant's duties" as a police officer or firefighter. The form then emphasizes that the medical board of review's findings are final and binding on all parties.

These facts in the record establish not only that a past practice existed, but also indicate that the parties had a meeting of the minds with respect to the new terms or conditions of the past practice. The past practice of the medical board rendering a final and binding decision on the duty-relatedness issue was so prevalent and widely accepted that even the city attorney and the board of trustees' attorney admitted it existed. Thus, the parties' actions in conformity with the past practice indicates that there was an agreement to modify the contract language to the contrary.

The parties' agreement to modify the contract can further be deduced from their course of conduct. The evidence indicates that over a period of several years, the board of trustees unequivocally and intentionally agreed to be bound by the medical board of review's determination on the duty-relatedness issue. An overwhelming indication of this was the forms introduced, which were prepared by the board of trustees, that instructed the medical board of review to make a finding on the duty-relatedness issue and that that decision would be final and binding. The fact that the board of trustees prepared the forms shows not only that it acquiesced in the medical board of review's binding decision on the duty-relatedness issue, but also that it intended that to be the practice. Thus, the evidence in the record supports a finding that the board of trustees intentionally chose to reject the negotiated contract and knowingly acted in accordance with the past practice.

IV. Conclusion

On other grounds, we affirm the decision of the Court of Appeals, which upheld the MERC's finding that the board of trustees had committed an unfair labor practice when it made a unilateral change in a mandatory subject of collective bargaining. The association has shown that the parties had a meeting of the minds with respect to the new terms or conditions and that the past practice was so prevalent and widely accepted that there was an agreement to modify the contract.

Marine Midland Bank, v. Midstate Lumber Co., Inc.
79 A.D.2d 783, 435 N.Y.S.2d 78
Supreme Court, Appellate Division, Third Department, 1980.

MEMORANDUM DECISION.

Appeal from an order of the County Court of Rensselaer County, entered September 27, 1979, which denied plaintiff's motion for summary judgment.

On October 1, 1974 the defendant, Midstate Lumber Co., Inc. (Midstate) entered into a rental agreement with Intertel Communications Corporation (Intertel), whereby Midstate agreed to lease telephone equipment from Intertel for a period of eight years at a monthly rental of $68.90. The rental agreement provided, inter alia, that no oral agreements or modifications would be binding and that the lessee was to make all repairs necessary to maintain the equipment. On November 6, 1974 Intertel assigned the lease to the plaintiff, Marine Midland Bank.

The defendant made all necessary rental payments until October 10, 1977. In March, 1978, Marine Midland, the assignee, commenced the instant action for recovery of overdue rental payments allegedly amounting to $3,281.75. The defendant's answer denied the alleged default, requested dismissal of the complaint and counterclaimed for $5,734.60.

Defendant contends that for two years prior to October, 1977, the leased equipment did not function properly and plaintiff voluntarily performed maintenance services. Moreover, defendant alleges that, in late August, 1977, the plaintiff's agents informed defendant that the equipment was inoperable; that, in October, 1977, the plaintiff agreed to remove the equipment; and that the plaintiff agreed orally to terminate the lease. Defendant also asserts that plaintiff's course of performance was referable to the oral modification. Consequently, defendant contends that there are triable issues of fact on the questions of estoppel, waiver and modification of the rental agreement and, therefore, summary judgment was properly denied by Special Term.

We agree. Summary judgment is not appropriate in this case. Although the rental agreement contained a clause prohibiting oral modification, there are ample examples found in case law permitting oral modification of agreements containing merger clauses. Section 15-301 (subd. 1) of the General Obligations Law, which prohibits oral modification where there is an agreement containing a provision against such oral modification, can be excused or waived by an executed oral modification or by estoppel.

Accepting as true the allegations of defendant's affidavits, it is arguable that there exists triable issues of fact as to whether plaintiff's course of performance constituted a modification of the agreement regarding the respective obligations of the parties to maintain the telephone equipment, as well as whether the parties agreed to waive certain provisions of the rental agreement or terminate it altogether. Accordingly, there are issues of fact requiring resolution by trial.

Order affirmed, with costs.

Note on "Merger Clauses"

In *Marine* the court refers to a "merger clause" which, as related by the court, does not merely refer to oral agreements but also to oral modifications. What is the difference between the following two clauses? "The parties agree that this writing constitutes the complete and exclusive agreement and that there are no other agreements oral or written and no conditions or obligations except as stated in this writing and further that no representations or promises or statements of fact on which either party has relied for any reason have been made except as stated in this writing and further that there are no conditions precedent to its coming into effect or subsequent to terminate it except as may be stated in the writing." "The parties agree that there will be no modification of this contract except by written agreement signed by both parties and that both parties explicitly agree that neither shall waive or claim any waiver of rights or obligations or claim any estoppel of rights and obligations except as shall be agreed by both parties in writing."

Why would you want both types of clauses in your writing?

Which of them was involved in the litigation in *Marine*?

U.C.C. 2-209 (2) states that a clause prohibiting modification or rescission except by a signed writing will be upheld except that if one party is a merchant and the other is not and the merchant supplies the writing with the clause the non-merchant party must separately sign it. Sub (3) states that if a contract is modified so as to bring it within the Statutes of Frauds there must be a writing. Sub (4) states that attempts to modify which fail under subs (2) and (3) may still operate as waivers.

D. Standardized Contracts

Mundy, v. Lumberman's Mutual Casualty Co.

783 F.2d 21
United States Court of Appeals, 1st Cir., 1985.

BREYER, Circuit Judge.

Thomas Mundy, an assistant district attorney of Suffolk County, Massachusetts, and his wife, Madelon, have sued their insurer in an effort to recover the actual value of some silver that was stolen from their home. Since the policy in effect at the time of the burglary limited recovery for loss of silverware to $1000, the company refused to pay them any more. The Mundys noted, however, that an earlier policy had not contained such a limit. They argued that the company did not give them adequate notice of the change when it sent them the policy renewal. And, this failure, in their view, entitles them to recovery under state law theories of contract, tort or unfair trade practice.

The district court granted the company's motion for summary judgment, for the court believed that the record showed—beyond genuine dispute—that the company's notice was adequate. The Mundys now appeal that decision.

The Mundys say in their brief that the "declarations page" of the policy (which they received) said nothing about the change, though "apparently...there was buried in the fine print of the policy a limitation of $1,000.00 with respect to a loss of silverware." The policy itself, however, tells a rather different story.

Mundy testified that Exhibit 4 was the very policy he received "in the form in which [he]...received it." On the jacket (apparently the inside cover) is a table of contents. The page also contains five short sentences in capital letters at its bottom. Four of those sentences read as follows: THIS IS A NEW EASY TO READ POLICY. PLEASE READ YOUR POLICY. THERE ARE SOME COVERAGE CHANGES. IF THERE ARE ANY QUESTIONS, CALL YOUR AGENT OR THE COMPANY RIGHT AWAY. There follows a declarations page containing the cost of premiums for coverages in effect. The declarations page is followed by two slips of paper (about half the ordinary page size) each with one or two sentences (about inflation protection and nonresidential theft). Then, there is a one-page summary of the changes made. Each change noted in the summary is in a separate paragraph, set off from the others by added space and black dots. The relevant paragraph says: "Theft of silverware and guns is now limited to $1,000. Should you wish more coverage for such items, contact your agent." The remainder of the booklet consists of the twelve-page policy itself. On page 2, the policy says: "Special Limits of Liability...7. $1000 for loss by theft of silverware, silverplated ware, goldware, gold-plated ware and pewterware." The whole policy is written in readable English in good-sized print with certain words, such as "Special Limits of Liability," set off in boldface type.

We find nothing in the record that fairly can be read as disputing these facts. Mundy at one point said that the summary of changes was stapled "somewhere" in the policy; but the word "somewhere" is consistent with his concession that Exhibit 4 presents the pages in the proper order. As the district court noted, these facts bring this case well within the scope of Epstein v. Northwestern National

Insurance Co., 267 Mass. 571, 166 N.E. 749 (1929), which binds an insured by the terms of a renewal insurance policy as long as he receives it.

The Mundys argue that Epstein is now out of date and a minority position. As Mundy recognized, these are not adequate reasons for disregarding Massachusetts case law. Nor do we believe the question should be certified to the Massachusetts Supreme Judicial Court, for, in any event, the Mundys cannot prevail. The facts here make this case very similar to GEICO v. United States, 400 F.2d 172, 175 (10th Cir.1968), where even "a casual reading of the mailed material" would have given the plaintiffs adequate notice. And, we find nothing in the cases they cite from other jurisdictions that would require a different result.

The judgment of the district court is

Affirmed.

Allied Van Lines, Inc., v. McKnab and Bratton
351 So.2d 344
Supreme Court of Florida, 1977.

HATCHETT, Justice.

May an interstate shipper avoid the legal consequences of a limitation of liability provision contained in a Bill of Lading issued by a carrier and signed by the shipper, on the ground that the shipper did not read the document and therefore did not assent to its provisions? The Fourth District Court of Appeal (Allied Van Lines, Inc. v. Bratton, 330 So.2d 521 (Fla. 4th DCA 1976)) and the Second District Court of Appeal (Allied Van Lines, Inc. v. McKnab, 331 So.2d 319 (Fla. 2d DCA 1976)) answered this question in the affirmative. Conflict is asserted with Atlantic Coast Line Railroad Company v. Dexter, 50 Fla. 180, 39 So. 634 (1905).

Mrs. Bratton, the "shipper," hired Allied Van Lines, Inc., to transport her household goods from Ohio to Florida. At the time the goods were picked up, Mrs. Bratton signed a Bill of Lading, presented to her by agents of the carrier, which contained a provision limiting carrier's liability to $4,500.00, $1.25 per pound. The shipment was destroyed in transit and respondent sued to recover the full value of her goods. Liability was conceded. The sole issue to be determined was the proper amount of damages. It was Allied's contention that its liability was limited by the provision contained in the Bill of Lading. Mrs. Bratton argued that since she did not read the document and was unaware of any provision affecting carrier's liability, she was not bound thereby. The question was submitted to the jury on respondent's assertions of "mistake" and "lack of assent" and a verdict was entered in favor of Mrs. Bratton in the amount of $10,630.00. The Fourth District Court of Appeal affirmed per curiam.

In accordance with I.C.C. Approved Tariff No. 144-C, immediately above respondent's signature on the Bill of Lading in red letters and boldface type, there appeared the following: UNLESS THE SHIPPER EXPRESSLY RELEASES THE SHIPMENT TO A VALUE OF 60 CENTS PER POUND PER ARTICLE, THE CARRIER'S MAXIMUM LIABILITY FOR LOSS AND DAMAGE SHALL BE EITHER THE LUMP SUM VALUE DECLARED BY THE SHIPPER OR AN AMOUNT EQUAL TO $1.25 FOR EACH POUND OF WEIGHT IN THE

SHIPMENT, WHICHEVER IS GREATER. THE SHIPMENT WILL MOVE SUBJECT TO THE RULES AND CONDITIONS OF THE CARRIER'S TARIFF. SHIPPER HEREBY RELEASES THE ENTIRE SHIPMENT TO A VALUE NOT EXCEEDING

(to be completed by the person signing below) NOTICE, THE SHIPPER SIGNING THIS CONTRACT MUST INSERT IN THE SPACE ABOVE, IN HIS OWN HANDWRITING, EITHER HIS DECLARATION OF THE ACTUAL VALUE OF THE SHIPMENT, OR THE WORDS "60 CENTS PER POUND PER ARTICLE." OTHERWISE, THE SHIPMENT WILL BE DEEMED RELEASED TO A MAXIMUM VALUE EQUAL TO $1.25 TIMES THE WEIGHT OF THE SHIPMENT IN POUNDS. The space providing for the declaration of "actual value" or "60 cents per pound, per article" was left blank by respondent.

Mrs. Bratton testified that at the time she signed the Bill of Lading she realized that she was signing a contract. She also acknowledged that although she did not read the Bill of Lading, no agent of the shipper prevented her from doing so. In addition, several weeks prior to the move, respondent was personally handed an informational booklet entitled "Summary of Information for Shippers of Household Goods, Form BOP 103." This booklet was an I.C.C. publication and contained a thorough description of all aspects of the move, including the Bill of Lading and the carrier's liability. Respondent signed a receipt for the booklet, which receipt was admitted into evidence.

In the companion case, the "shipper," Mrs. McKnab, contracted with Allied for an interstate move of household goods from California to Florida. When the goods were picked up, Mrs. McKnab explained to the carrier's agent that she wanted all available insurance. The agent affirmatively stated that $1.25 per pound was the maximum possible. The agent not Mrs. McKnab, completed the space providing for selection of coverage, by typing in: "$1.25 per pound per order for service."

The goods were destroyed by a fire while in the possession of the carrier and respondent sued. Again, the carrier admitted liability but maintained that liability was limited to $1.25 per pound ($9,300.00) as provided in the Bill of Lading. Mrs. McKnab contended that she was not bound by the provision contained in the Bill of Lading because she was not given "a reasonable and fair opportunity to value her goods." Judgment was entered in favor of Mrs. McKnab in the sum of $33,315. The Second District Court of Appeal affirmed in part and reversed in part, remanding for new trial on the issue of damages. That court found sufficient competent evidence to support a finding of misrepresentation on the part of Allied but stated that "in measuring plaintiff's (Mrs. McKnab) damages, the proper measure of damages for loss of personal property is its market value on the date of the loss." Allied Van Lines, Inc. v. McKnab, supra, at p. 320.

It has long been held in Florida that one is bound by his contract. Unless one can show facts and circumstances to demonstrate that he was prevented from reading the contract, or that he was induced by statements of the other party to refrain from reading the contract, it is binding. No party to a written contract in this state can defend against its enforcement on the sole ground that he signed it without reading it.

As to the validity of a limitation clause contained in a Bill of Lading, this Court, more than 70 years ago, put the issue to rest. In Atlantic Coast Line Railroad Company v. Dexter, supra, 50 Fla. 180, 39 So. at page 635, this Court stated: "The rule is quite generally settled in the United States that an acceptance by a shipper or his agent of a receipt or Bill of Lading containing a limitation of the carrier's liability is binding upon him, when the limitation is not illegal or unreasonable; that it is not essential to the validity of such a limitation that it be shown that the shipper was aware of it, or that he had read it, or that it had been explained to him, or his attention called to it, provided the carrier made use of no improper means to prevent his noticing or objecting to it; and that every shipper is conclusively presumed, in such a case, to have read and assented to the provisions of the receipt or bill of lading given him, whether he in fact assented or not.... Under these circumstances it made no difference whether the plaintiffs ever expressly assented to the contract or not, or even read or knew of its terms and conditions. They are fully bound thereby, and are estopped from gainsaying or repudiating it."

Accordingly, we hold that the shipper's liability in the Bratton case is limited under the liability provision contained in the Bill of Lading to $4,500.00, and the opinion of the Fourth District Court of Appeal is quashed and the case remanded for action consistent with this opinion; the opinion of the Second District Court of Appeal in the McKnab case is affirmed.

It is so ordered.

Beauchamp, v. Great West Life Assurance Company

918 F.Supp. 1091
United States District Court, E.D. Michigan, 1996.

GADOLA, District Judge.

Plaintiff brought this ADEA and Title VII suit, alleging that defendants had discriminatorily fired her because of her age and gender. Defendants now bring the present motion to compel arbitration and/or to dismiss. Pursuant to Local Rule 7.1(e)(2), the court has dispensed with oral argument and will decide the present motion based on the written submissions of the parties. For the reasons stated below, this court will grant the defendants' motion to compel arbitration.

I. Factual Background

Plaintiff began working for the defendants as an insurance salesperson on May 17, 1976. In 1984, plaintiff signed a Uniform Application for Securities Industry Registration (hereinafter "U-4 form"), which states: "THE FOLLOWING SHOULD BE READ VERY CAREFULLY BY THE APPLICANT

. . . . .

5. I agree to arbitrate any dispute, claim, or controversy that may arise between me and my firm, or a customer, or any other person, that is required to be arbitrated under the rules, constitutions, or by-laws of the organizations with which I register...." Plaintiff registered with the National Association of Securities Dealers (hereinafter "NASD"). Part I of the NASD Code of Arbitration Procedure states that the code was created "for the arbitration of any dispute, claim, or

controversy arising out of or in connection with the business of any member of the Association...." This code mandates arbitration of: any dispute, claim, or controversy eligible for submission under Part I of this Code between or among members and/or associated persons, and/or certain others, arising in connection with the business of such member(s) or in connection with the activities of such associated person(s),... at the instance of: (1) a member against another member; (2) a member against a person associated with a member or a person associated with a member against a member; and, (3) a person associated with a member against a person associated with a member.

Plaintiff asserts that she was informed that she had to sign the U-4 form to keep her employment and that she does not remember reading the previously quoted language from the U-4 form. The completed U-4 form was not kept in plaintiff's personnel file in Michigan, but rather at defendants' headquarters in Denver, which oversees compliance with licensing requirements.

Plaintiff alleges in her complaint that she was repeatedly passed over for promotion because of her gender and age. She resigned on January 5, 1995, allegedly the result of a constructive discharge by the defendants. She then brought a complaint before the EEOC and subsequently filed the present lawsuit in September, 1995.

II. Analysis

Defendants argue that plaintiff is compelled to arbitrate this action pursuant to the Federal Arbitration Act and the NASD Code of Arbitration Procedure. The Federal Arbitration Act states, in part: "[A] contract evidencing a transaction involving commerce to settle by arbitration a controversy thereafter arising out of such contract or transaction... shall be valid, irrevocable, and enforceable, save upon the grounds as exist at law or in equity for the revocation of any contract." 9 U.S.C. § 2. Section four of the FAA allows the court to compel arbitration when one party fails to comply with an arbitration agreement. Defendants mainly rely on Gilmer v. Interstate/Johnson Lane Corp., 500 U.S. 20, 111 S.Ct. 1647, 114 L.Ed.2d 26 (1991), and Willis v. Dean Witter Reynolds, Inc., 948 F.2d 305 (6th Cir.1991) in arguing that the FAA and the NASD arbitration agreement apply to plaintiff's ADEA and Title VII claims.

In Gilmer, the Supreme Court held that an ADEA claim could be sent to arbitration when the plaintiff agreed to arbitration under a "Uniform Application for Securities Industry Registration or Transfer," containing the same language regarding arbitration as the U-4 form in the present case. The Court noted that the FAA "provisions manifest a 'liberal federal policy favoring arbitration agreements.'" Gilmer, 500 U.S. at 25, 111 S.Ct. at 1651 (quoting Moses H. Cone Memorial Hospital v. Mercury Construction Corp., 460 U.S. 1, 24, 103 S.Ct. 927, 941, 74 L.Ed.2d 765 (1983)). The Court then stated: "[b]y agreeing to arbitrate a statutory claim, a party does not forego the substantive rights afforded by the statute; it only submits to their resolution in an arbitral, rather than a judicial, forum. Although all statutory claims may not be appropriate for arbitration, '[h]aving made the bargain to arbitrate, the party should be held to it unless Congress itself has evinced an intention to preclude a waiver of judicial remedies for the statutory rights at issue....' If such an intention exists, it will be discoverable in the text of the ADEA, its legislative history, or an 'inherent conflict' between arbitration and the ADEA's underlying purposes." Id. at 26, 111 S.Ct. at 1652 (citations omitted). The Court then examined the text, history, and underlying policies of the ADEA and concluded that there was no inherent conflict between the enforcement of the ADEA and the enforcement of agreements to arbitrate age discrimination claims.

In Willis, the Sixth Circuit extended the holding of Gilmer to Title VII actions: "The Supreme Court [in Gilmer]...held that nothing in the ADEA or its legislative history suggested that the arbitration clause in the Securities Registration Form should not be enforced under the FAA. We find that the Court's analysis and conclusions in Gilmer compels the conclusion that the FAA and arbitration provisions of the Securities Registration Form apply equally to...Title VII claims...." Id. at 307.

Defendants argue that these two cases demonstrate that the arbitration provision in the present case, being identical to the provisions at issue in Gilmer and Willis, applies to the plaintiff's claims and is enforceable under the FAA. Plaintiff disagrees, citing four reasons: (1) plaintiff did not knowingly agree to arbitrate because she was not aware of the arbitration clause and its application to Title VII and ADEA claims when she signed the U-4 form; (2) the contract is an adhesion contract under Michigan law and cannot be enforced; (3) defendants, under M.C.L. 423.502 have waived their right to enforce the arbitration clause because they did not keep the uniform application in plaintiff's personnel file; and (4) defendants have waived their right to enforce the arbitration clause because they did not do so in at least one other, similar case. These arguments will be addressed in turn.

A. Requirement of Actual Knowledge of Arbitration Clause

Plaintiff argues that in order for the arbitration clause to be enforceable, she must have known about the arbitration clause and its application to her claims in the present action. She claims not to have been informed about the arbitration clause and therefore asserts that she did not knowingly relinquish her rights to a judicial forum for employment discrimination claims when she signed the U-4 form.

Plaintiff relies on the Ninth Circuit case of Prudential Ins. Co. v. Lai, 42 F.3d 1299 (9th Cir.1994), which held that a plaintiff who signed a U-4 form to register with the NASD could only be held to the arbitration clause contained therein if he knowingly agreed to arbitrate his particular employment discrimination claims. The Ninth Circuit held that "Congress intended there to be at least a knowing agreement to arbitrate employment disputes before an employee may be deemed to have waived the comprehensive statutory rights, remedies, and procedural protections prescribed in Title VII...." Id. at 1304.

In reaching this conclusion, the Prudential court relied in part on one of the House Reports to the Civil Rights Act of 1991 that stated: "Section 216 [of the 1991 Act] encourages the use of alternative dispute resolution...where appropriate and to the extent authorized by law.... The committee emphasizes...that the use of alternative dispute resolution mechanisms is intended to supplement, not supplant, the remedies provided by Title VII. Thus, for example, the committee believes that any agreement to submit disputed issues to arbitration, whether in the context of a collective bargaining agreement or in an employment contract, does not preclude the affected person from seeking relief under the enforcement provisions of Title VII. This view is consistent with the Supreme Court's interpretation of Title VII in Alexander v. Gardner-Denver Co., 415 U.S. 36 [94 S.Ct. 1011, 39 L.Ed.2d 147]... (1974). The committee does not intend for the inclusion of this section to be used to preclude rights and remedies that would otherwise be available." Id. at 1304 (quoting HR Rep.No. 40(I) 102nd Cong. 1st Sess., reprinted in U.S.C.C.A.N. 549, 635). The court also noted statements made by Senator Dole that the arbitration provision of the Civil Rights Act of 1991 encourages arbitration "where the parties knowingly and voluntarily elect to use these methods." Id. at 1305 (quoting 137 Cong.Rec.S. 15472, S. 15478 (Daily Ed. October 30, 1991)). The Prudential court heavily cited to Alexander v. Gardner-Denver, 415 U.S. 36, 94 S.Ct. 1011, 39 L.Ed.2d 147 (1974), and its progeny. In particular, the Ninth Circuit quoted, in part, the following language from Alexander:

"[L]egislative enactments in this area have long evinced a general intent to accord parallel or overlapping remedies against discrimination.... Consistent with this view, Title VII provides for consideration of employment- discrimination claims in several forums. And, in general, submission of a forum does not preclude a later submission to another. Moreover, the legislative history of Title VII manifests a congressional intent to allow an individual to pursue independently his rights under both Title VII and other applicable state and federal statutes. The clear inference is that Title VII was designed to supplement, rather than supplant, existing laws and institutions relating to employment discrimination. In sum, Title VII's purpose and procedures strongly suggest that an individual does not forfeit his private cause of action if he first pursues his grievance to final arbitration under the nondiscrimination clause of a collective bargaining agreement." Alexander, 415 U.S. at 49-50, 94 S.Ct. at 1019-20.

In reviewing the facts of its case, which are similar to the facts of the present case, the Prudential court refused to enforce the arbitration clause in the U-4 form because the plaintiffs did not knowingly waive their right to a judicial forum; even if the plaintiffs were aware of the clause, the clause did not notify the plaintiffs that employment discrimination claims would fall within the scope of the clause.

Fortunately, Prudential is not binding precedent because this court is not persuaded by its reasoning. The portions of the legislative history relied upon by the Ninth Circuit are slender reeds upon which to rest the weighty and novel conclusion that an arbitration clause is only binding when the claimant has actual knowledge that his particular employment discrimination claims will be covered by the agreement. This conclusion flies in the face of the language of the Civil Rights Act of 1991, the Supreme Court's opinion in Gilmer, and fundamental principles of contract law.

To begin with, the House Report quoted in Prudential merely states that an agreement to arbitrate found in an employment contract or in a collective bargaining agreement will not preclude a Title VII action. The House Report essentially restates the holding in Alexander, a case that was distinguished in Gilmer. As is evident from the above-quoted language in Alexander, the Alexander opinion held that agreeing to arbitrate the issue of employment discrimination allegedly in violation of an antidiscrimination clause in a collective bargaining agreement does not preclude a later Title VII suit in federal court. This is because Title VII was meant to work in combination with other prohibitions of discrimination, whether they be collective bargaining agreements, federal administrative regulations, or state laws. Use of those other authorities will not preclude later use of Title VII. Alexander does not speak to the issue of when a plaintiff may contractually agree to forego a judicial forum for her Title VII claim. This was made clear in Gilmer: "There are several important distinctions between the Gardner-Denver line of cases and the case before us. First, those cases did not involve the issue of the enforceability of an agreement to arbitrate statutory claims. Rather, they involved the quite different issue whether arbitration of contract-based claims precluded subsequent judicial resolution of statutory claims. Since the employees there had not agreed to arbitrate their statutory claims, and the labor arbitrators were not authorized to resolve such claims, the arbitration in those cases understandably was held not to preclude subsequent statutory actions. Second, because the arbitration in those cases occurred in the context of a collective-bargaining agreement, the claimants there were represented by their unions in the arbitration proceedings. An important concern therefore was the tension between collective representation and individual statutory rights, a concern not applicable to the present case. Finally, those cases were not decided under the FAA, which, as discussed above, reflects a 'liberal federal policy favoring arbitration agreements.' Mitsubishi Motors Corp. v. Soler Chrysler-Plymouth, Inc., 473 U.S. 614, 625 [105 S.Ct. 3346, 3353, 87 L.Ed.2d 444] (1985). Therefore, those cases provide no basis for refusing to enforce Gilmer's agreement to arbitrate his ADEA claim." Gilmer, 500 U.S. at 35, 111 S.Ct. at 1657.

Additionally, the Prudential court unjustly attacks the validity of the procedures of the arbitral forum by stating that "[a]lthough the Supreme Court has pointed out that plaintiffs who arbitrate their statutory claims do not 'forego the substantive rights afforded by the statute,' Mitsubishi Motors, 473 U.S. at 628, 105 S.Ct. at 3354-55, the remedies and procedural protections available in the arbitral forum can differ significantly from those contemplated by the legislature." Prudential, 42 F.3d at 1305. The Ninth Circuit then concluded that the lack of a civil jury and the lack of a rule precluding the admission of plaintiff's sexual history (a California rule of evidence) "may be particularly significant" in the sexual harassment context. Id. at 1305 & n. 4. Apparently, the Ninth Circuit believed that Congress was so concerned with these potentially "significant" differences in procedure, that it meant for arbitration agreements to be enforced in employment discrimination cases only when it could be shown that the plaintiff had actual knowledge of the scope of the arbitration agreement to which he was agreeing.

The court fails to explain, in the total absence of Congressional reference to the California rule of evidence, why it believes Congress contemplated the use, in federal Title VII actions, of a California rule of evidence barring the admission of past sexual history. Even if Congress did contemplate the use of such a rule, there is no evidence that Congress felt that the absence of such a rule in an arbitral forum was so critical as to override Congress's express statements in favor of arbitration in the FAA and the Civil Rights Act of 1991.[1]

---

1. The Prudential court recognizes that Congress expressly stated, in the notes to 42 U.S.C. § 1981, that "'Where appropriate and to the extent authorized by law, the use of alternative means of dispute resolutions including,... arbitration, is encouraged to resolve disputes arising under the Acts or provisions of Federal law amended by this title.' § 118 of Pub. L. 102-166, set forth in the notes following 42 U.S.C. § 1981 (Supp.1994)."

Similarly, the court fails to explain why it believes Congress has a preference for trying Title VII actions before a civil jury, rather than an arbitral panel. This, too, is contrary to language in the FAA and the Civil Rights Act of 1991. This assumption also ignores the following statement by the Supreme Court in Gilmer: "[G]eneralized attacks on arbitration 'res[t] on suspicion of arbitration as a method of weakening the protections afforded in the substantive law to would-be complainants,' and as such, they are 'far out of step with our current strong endorsement of the federal statutes favoring this method of resolving disputes.'" Gilmer, 500 U.S. at 30, 111 S.Ct. at 1654 (quoting Rodriguez de Quijas v. Shearson/American Express, Inc., 490 U.S. 477, 481, 109 S.Ct. 1917, 1920, 104 L.Ed.2d 526 (1989)).

"Lastly, the Ninth Circuit's opinion fails to consider that Congress would be unlikely to turn a venerable rule of contract law on its ear without an express statement that it was doing so. It is well settled that the failure of a party to obtain an explanation of a contract is ordinary negligence. Accordingly, this estops the party from avoiding the contract on the ground that the party was ignorant of the contract provisions.... The stability of written instruments demands that a person who executes one shall know its contents or be chargeable with such knowledge...in the absence of circumstances fairly excusing his failure to inform himself." Scholz v. Montgomery Ward & Co., 437 Mich. 83, 92, 468 N.W.2d 845 (1991). See, e.g., 17A Am.Jur.2d Contracts § 224 (1991), and cases cited therein. The Ninth Circuit's rule that a party to an arbitration agreement is not chargeable with knowledge concerning the existence and scope of that agreement with respect to Title VII claims is directly contrary to this well-settled rule of contract law.

Lastly, other courts have chosen not to treat Prudential as persuasive. See Maye v. Smith Barney Inc., 897 F.Supp. 100, 107 (S.D.N.Y.1995), and cases cited therein.

[A] party is generally chargeable with knowledge of the existence and scope of an arbitration clause within a document signed by that party, in the absence of fraud, deception, or other misconduct that would excuse the lack of such knowledge.

Plaintiff argues that the U-4 form was an unreasonable contract of adhesion and, thus, may not be enforced against her. Plaintiff claims that the contract is unenforceable because it was drafted by one party and presented to the other party under circumstances in which there is no realistic opportunity to negotiate. Plaintiff alleges that she had to sign the U-4 form as a condition of her employment although there was no need for her to register with the NASD to properly perform her job.

Gilmer recognized that "fraud or overwhelming economic power" could provide grounds for the revocation of an agreement to arbitrate and that such issues should be "left for resolution in specific cases." Gilmer, 500 U.S. at 33, 111 S.Ct. at 1656. Under Michigan contract law, "[c]ontracts of adhesion are characterized by standardized forms prepared by one party which are offered for rejection or acceptance without opportunity for bargaining and under the circumstances that the second party cannot obtain the desired product or service except by acquiescing in the form agreement." Morris v. Metriyakool, 418 Mich. 423, 440, 344 N.W.2d 736 (1984). However, "even if a contract is one of adhesion…, a challenged provision remains enforceable if it is substantially reasonable and not oppressive or unconscionable." Paulsen v. Bureau of State Lottery, 167 Mich.App. 328, 336, 421 N.W.2d 678 (1988)

First, this court is not convinced that the U-4 form was a contract of adhesion. The form was not prepared by the defendants, it is a standard form used across the country for anyone who wishes to register with a securities organization. Further, there is no evidence that the plaintiff could not have worked as an insurance salesperson without signing such a form. Even if she couldn't have worked for defendants, she very well may have been able to work elsewhere. Under plaintiff's theory, practically every condition of employment would be an "adhesion contract" which could not be enforced because it would have been presented to the employee by the employer in a situation of unequal bargaining power on a "take it or leave it" basis. See Gilmer, 500 U.S. at 33, 111 S.Ct. at 1655 ("there often will be unequal bargaining power between employers and employees. Mere inequality of bargaining power, however, is not a sufficient reason to hold that arbitration agreements are never enforceable in the employment context.")

Second, the U-4 form is substantially reasonable and not oppressive or unconscionable. The Gilmer court has held that plaintiff is not giving up substantive statutory rights through arbitration of her Title VII claim. Gilmer, 500 U.S. at 26, 111 S.Ct. at 1652. Thus, her agreement to arbitrate is not substantively unconscionable. Nor is the language of the U-4 form unconscionable in that it misrepresents the existence or scope of the arbitration clause. The U-4 form clearly states that the applicant should read its provisions very carefully and that any claim between plaintiff and her firm would be arbitrated if required by the arbitration code of the organization with which she registered. Plaintiff does not say that she did not read this language, merely that she does not remember reading this language. In sum, there is no evidence of any fraud or deception concerning the existence or scope of the arbitration clause in the U-4 form that would excuse the plaintiff from enforcement of that clause. If plaintiff did not make herself aware of the existence or scope of that clause, she did so at her own peril.

Questions

1. How does the court deal with plaintiff's ignorance of contract provisions?

2. What is a contract of adhesion? Was this a contract of adhesion? If it was, would that have helped plaintiff?)(See *Wallace* and note following it.)

3. What is the relationship between standardized contracts and the parol evidence rule? For example, how would the court in the above case determine that the signed writing integrated the agreement, the contract of the parties?

Wallace v. National Bank of Commerce

938 S.W.2d 684
Supreme Court of Tennessee, 1996.

REID, Justice.

This case presents for review the decision of the Court of Appeals affirming the trial court's award of summary judgment for the defendants. The trial court found that the record shows, as a matter of law, that the defendant banks did not breach the duty of good faith in imposing fees for returned checks drawn on accounts with insufficient funds. This Court concurs in the decision made by the trial court and the Court of Appeals.

The Case

Forty named plaintiffs filed suit against nine banks doing business in Shelby County asserting six separate causes of action, all based on the allegation that the banks charged "excessive" fees for checks drawn on accounts with insufficient funds ("NSF checks") and for third party checks deposited and returned unpaid ("DIR checks"). The plaintiffs seek compensatory damages, punitive damages, and treble damages. The trial court sustained the defendants' motions to dismiss the suit for failure to state a claim on which relief can be granted. The Court of Appeals, on the first appeal, affirmed the dismissal of all claims except the allegation that the banks breached a common law duty of good faith in the performance of their contractual obligations to their customers. On remand, the defendants' motions for summary judgment, based on the pleadings, affidavits, and stipulations, were granted by the trial court and the Court of Appeals affirmed.

Analysis

The plaintiffs do not contend that there are disputed issues of material fact. They contend instead that the court erred in holding as a matter of law that the defendants did not breach the duty of good faith in the performance of their obligations pursuant to the contracts between the banks and their customers.

The essential facts shown by the record are: each plaintiff had a checking account with at least one of the defendant banks; each account was opened upon the execution of a deposit agreement prepared by the bank and signed by the customer; the agreements provide that the customer agrees to the terms stated in the agreement, including service charges for NSF and DIR checks; each customer was informed, upon the execution of the deposit agreement, of the amount of the NSF and DIR fees; each customer also was informed that the fees were subject to change upon notice to the banks' customers; each customer was given notice prior to the effective date of the increase in fees; and each plaintiff was charged at least one service charge for an NSF or DIR check.

The plaintiffs' allegations raise two further questions—whether the deposit agreements are contracts of adhesion and, if they are contracts of adhesion, are the terms enforceable. This Court recently approved the following statement defining and setting forth the essential characteristics of an adhesion contract: An adhesion contract has been defined as "a standardized contract form offered to consumers of goods and services on essentially a 'take it or leave it' basis, without affording the consumer a realistic opportunity to bargain and under such conditions that the consumer cannot obtain the desired product or service except by acquiescing to the form of the contract." Professor Henderson has observed that "the essence of an adhesion contract is that bargaining positions and leverage enable one party 'to select and control risks assumed under the contract.'" Courts generally agree that "[t]he distinctive feature of a contract of adhesion is that the weaker party has no realistic choice as to its terms." Buraczynski v. Eyring, 919 S.W.2d 314, 320 (Tenn.1996) (citations omitted).

The record in this case does not support the plaintiffs' claim that the agreements between the banks and their customers are adhesion contracts. Some of the characteristics of an adhesion contract are present, the deposit agreements are standardized forms, and, undoubtedly, the opportunity to open an account with a particular bank was presented on a take-it-or-leave-it basis. However, these factors standing alone are not sufficient. The record shows that the banks provided checking accounts which were exempt from overdraft charges. The record does not include a schedule of the charges, and, perhaps most significantly, there is no showing in the record that the customers had no realistic choice but to acquiesce in the imposition of the banks' charges. There is no showing that the fees were the same at all the defendant banks or that banking services could not be obtained from other institutions. It is common knowledge that the banking industry is very competitive. For example, different banks may charge lower fees for some services and higher fees for other services, and they also may charge lower interest rates on loans but higher fees for services, thus providing choices which may appeal to various prospective customers. In the absence of a showing that there was no effective competition in the providing of services among the banks in the area served by the defendants, there is no basis for concluding that the appellants had no realistic choice regarding the terms for obtaining banking services.

And, further, not all adhesion contracts are unenforceable. Even if a contract is found to be adhesive, it is enforceable unless it is unduly oppressive or unconscionable. The Court discussed this issue in Buraczynski v. Eyring: "Our conclusion that the contracts were contracts of adhesion is not... determinative of the contract's enforceability. Enforceability generally depends upon whether the terms of the contract are beyond the reasonable expectations of an ordinary person, or oppressive or unconscionable. Courts will not enforce adhesion contracts which are oppressive to the weaker party or which serve to limit the obligations and liability of the stronger party." Buraczynski, 919 S.W.2d at 320 (citations omitted). The California Supreme Court discussed this rule in Graham v. Scissor-Tail, Inc., 28 Cal.3d 807, 171 Cal.Rptr. 604, 623 P.2d 165 (1981): "Generally speaking, there are two judicially imposed limitations on the enforcement of adhesion contracts or provisions thereof. The first is that such a contract or provision which does not fall within the reasonable expectations of the weaker or 'adhering' party will not be enforced against him. The second—a principle of equity applicable to all contracts generally— is that a contract or provision, even if consistent with the reasonable expectations of the parties, will be denied enforcement if, considered in its context, it is unduly oppressive or 'unconscionable.'" Id. at 172-173 (citations omitted).

As previously discussed, the reasonable expectations of the appellants were that fees would be imposed pursuant to the terms of the agreements. Further, based on the record before the Court, the provisions in the agreements regarding NSF and DIR fees were not oppressive or unconscionable.

The determination that, on the facts shown by the record, the defendants, as a matter of law, have not breached the common law duty of good faith in the performance of the contracts with their checking account customers resolves the issue presented in this case. The defendants' assertion that unconscionable and oppressive provisions of a contract cannot constitute the basis for a cause of action, but only can be pleaded in defense to an action for breach of contract, need not be considered.

The judgment of the Court of Appeals sustaining summary judgment for the defendants and dismissing the suit is affirmed.

Costs will be taxed to the plaintiffs.

Questions

1. Was the court construing or interpreting the language of the contract?

2. Fees are subject to change with notice. Why does this provision not make the contract lacking in consideration?

3. How does an adhesion contract differ from an unenforceable adhesion contract?

4. Which, if any of the following facts, or what combination of them might make the bank's contracts with its customers unenforceable contracts of adhesion? The contracts are all on the same standardized form and customers cannot bargain for changes on the form. All banks in the area use the same standardized bank form. Banks in the area all charge the same fees for the same type of banking services. The charges are not beyond the reasonable expectations of the bank's customers. Charges are beyond the reasonable expectations of bank's customers. Bank's contract states that it reserves the right to change fees without notice.

5. Would any of the provisions in #4 be unconscionable or oppressive?

Note on Adhesion Contracts

In *Beauchamp* and in *Wallace* we have seen plaintiffs endeavoring to use the concept of the "adhesion" contract to bolster their cases. In part their problem stems from common law rules in a non-common law setting. The key to the Common Law of Contracts was negotiation. The problem was (a) determining when negotiation ended and a binding commitment began (in contracts under the U.C.C. the "when" has been, implicitly, replaced by "if" — see § 2-204(2) which states that a contract may be found "even though the moment of its making is undetermined"; under the Code if there is a contract is still important); (b) what that binding commitment was. Where standardized contracts are involved, where one person drafts all the terms and presents them to another on a take or leave basis, the basic substructure of Common Law Contracts is not only eroded but swept away.

As can be seen in the last case, and as seen in the parol evidence cases, a writing is presumed to embody the terms to which a person agreed. If in Part B the basic problem was disputing the meaning of words, in Part D the basic problem is people not knowing what words are in the writing and if they know not understanding them. Courts try to alleviate some of the hardship by requiring provisions in contracts of adhesion to be "substantially reasonable and not oppressive or unconscionable" as the court put it in the principal case. The farther the courts go down this road the more obvious the question becomes "Who is doing the contracting?" Does it matter? Should there be a double standard: one for businesspersons, lawyers, professors, law students, etc. and the other for presumably less savvy members of the public? Is this fair to the second group? Will there be a hesitation to contract with them if they can simply avoid a contract? Probably no—the cost of avoidance will simply be spread over the rest of those in the second group with whom contracts are made.

In Part V we will examine the many ways to escape liability. Keep this Part III in mind as we do that. No Part is separate from the others. Note how they interrelate.

In Part IV we look to conditions—principally those that must occur before a person is obliged to perform an obligation existing under a contract.

Before we do that, let us return to the problem at the start of this Part.

Part IV

Conditions

Introduction

The word condition denotes two different types of events that have an effect on contract law. In one of its uses, it brings a contract into effect. For example, a written contract may have a condition that says: "The parties agree that this contract shall have no effect and shall not come into existence as an exchange of enforceable obligations until the Dow Jones Industrial Average next reaches 12,000." The contract may be for anything, for example for the provision of services: "The Happiness Group of Investment Advisers hereby agrees to provide services, hereinafter enumerated, to John Jones in exchange for Mr. Jones' promise to pay a fee of $5,000 per year plus 1/10 of 1% of the 'net value of the assets managed by us during each year that the contract is in effect' as hereinafter defined, this contract to have a duration of two years from the time it goes into effect. John Jones hereby promises to pay the aforestated consideration at the times hereinafter stated in exchange for the services aforestated. The parties agree that this contract shall not come into existence as an exchange of enforceable obligations until the Dow Jones Industrial Average shall rise to 12,000 or higher." Under this condition Happiness' obligation to provide services to Jones, and Jones promise to pay Happiness, becomes enforceable only when the Dow hits 12,000.

If the condition is not stated in the writing, a parol evidence question might arise. Using the concepts and rules from Part III how might it be resolved? According to Pavel v. Johnson, *supra* Part II-B, either party can withdraw from a contract until the condition occurs. Until the act is performed there is no binding obligation. Not all courts agree on this. Some courts say it depends on whether the condition is within the control of one of the parties. If it is, then that party has made no enforceable promise, because she has control over whether the condition occurs. In this event the party controlling the condition is not bound to anything, and the other party also is not bound. Occasionally, courts will require the party in whose control the happening of the condition rests to act in good faith to make the condition occur. For example, Jones agrees to wash Smith's car if it doesn't rain. That condition (short of Jones or Smith being a rainmaker) is out of their control. If, however, Jones agrees to wash Smith's car if the water company turns on the water before 3:00 P.M. that afternoon, a court might imply a good faith requirement that Jones (or Smith, depending on circumstances) try to get the water company to turn on the water before 3:00 P.M. Other concerns would be how long the condition has force. In the Happiness example above, if the Dow doesn't hit 12,000 for another two years, would the contract then come into effect, or would the force of the condition have expired? As with all things, this would turn on intent. To forestall such problems, good draftspersons put in clauses to cover such contingencies.

The key point is that the purpose of the condition is to bring the contract into being. Until the condition is satisfied no enforceable obligations exist, although there is a writing that looks very much like a contract. This type of condition will be explored in Part A.

The second, and more common use of the term condition is to denote an event either starting or terminating a person's obligation to *perform* a contractual obligation. Unlike the first use of conditions, here the parties *are* bound to an enforceable contract. Conditions in this sense are triggering events. An easy example is the condition most often stated in an insurance policy. The policy promises to pay a sum of money on the happening of an event. For example, Live-Long Life Insurance Co. promises to pay $100,000 to the estate of Jim James on the event of his death. James promises to pay a sum of money, a premium, each month or year until his death. The condition which must be fulfilled before Live-Long's obligation must be performed is that James must die. James' obligation to pay the premium ends on his death. Interesting issues will arise if, for example, James disappears on a solo flight across the Arctic Circle. Assuming that there is not a further condition that states the company has no obligation to pay under these circumstances (and most will have one) the question arises as to whether or not James has actually died. This is the reason that policies are so long. Proof of death will be a further condition etc. In one case a man left home and was reported missing by his family. His car was found in a parking lot at Niagara Falls where it had apparently been for some time. There was no trace of him nor was there a suicide note or other indication that he had committed suicide. Although he had suffered severe business reverses, no one suspected that he was suicidal. No body was found. Had he died or just disappeared? However involved a contract, insurance or otherwise, might be, a condition means that the obligations stated in it do not ripen into duties of performance until an event occurs. These conditions are called conditions precedent. An event must occur before an obligation must be performed.

Besides conditions precedent there are also conditions subsequent, often called forfeitures today. It is often difficult to distinguish between the two. A contract may call for repeated performances by two persons, the obligation of either or both to continue until an occurrence of an event ends them. X Construction Co. agrees to excavate land for the construction of a building by Y Contractors, X's obligation to continue the excavation being conditioned upon Y making regular monthly payments to X and subject to no underground rivers, lakes, or unusually hard rock or debris being found on the site. If an underground lake is found, X's obligation ends. This could also be framed as a condition precedent. "X's obligation to excavate is conditioned on no lake being found." For the most part, we will deal with conditions precedent. The key point is that an obligation under a contract does not become owing as a performance until a condition occurs.

Sometimes, a condition will look much like the consideration for the contract, and in fact, courts sometimes refer to the performance requested under a unilateral contract as a condition. "If you shoe my horse, I will pay you 10 shillings." It is a condition to the duty to pay the 10 shillings that the horse be shoed. More likely, there will be a separate consideration for the promise. This issue is discussed in *Clark v. West, infra* subpart G, where a famous author was promised by the publisher $2.00 per page for a treatise he was writing [this was in 1908] with an additional promise of $4.00 per page more if he did not drink any alcoholic beverages while writing the book. The court pointed out that this was not a contract seeking both a promise to write the book (which the author had given) for $2.00 per page and an additional sum in exchange for his giving up the right to drink while writing it, the additional sum to also be measured by the number of pages written. Rather it amounted to a promise of $6.00 per page for the book, with $4.00 of the $6.00 conditioned on not drinking. In other words, the motivation for the promise of a total of $6.00 was to get the book. The publishers were not trying to reform the writer. Even here, you can see the problems. Clearly, they did not want him to drink but there were not two separate contracts, one for a book and one for abstinence. The conceptual blurring of consideration and condition can be seen here. What might the result have been if they had written the contract to promise $6.00 per page and the author had promised to write the book but they had said: "We promise to pay $6.00 per page for the book and for your not drinking; the consideration for our promise of $6.00 per page is twofold: (1) your promise to write the book and (2) your actual performance of not drinking during the time you are writing it"? He drinks and writes the book. Can they get the book for nothing? He doesn't write the book. Can they sue him for breach? Is he receiving any consideration for his promise?

This last case opens the door to a concept running throughout the later cases in this Part: forfeiture. The law hates forfeitures. Contract reads: "We promise to convey Blackacre to you upon your making the 25 installments of $1,000 called for by our contract on time. If any installment is late, our duty to convey the land terminates and all installments are forfeit by you." Or it might read: "Our duty to convey Blackacre to you is expressly conditioned on your first making the 25 installments on or before the date each is due; in the event such installments are not paid on time, our duty to convey terminates as does your duty to make further installments, all installments made being nonrefundable." See *Porter v. Harrington, [infra,* subpart G]. A policy against forfeitures, and the doctrines of waiver, estoppel, excuse, divisibility of performances, and substantial performance all work against the harsh results that the enforcement of conditions could cause.

Besides express conditions, stated as such in contracts, there are also implied conditions. These most often arise in connection with the promises made by the parties. For example, I promise to sell Blackacre to you for $100,000 and you promise to buy it for that price. Must you first pay me the money or must I first convey Blackacre to you; are our promises to be performed simultaneously, or are they separate promises? At earliest Common Law, they were presumed to be separately performable. If, for example, 10:00 A.M. January 3, 2001 at the county records office were the date and place set for performance and I was not ready to convey Blackacre to you, you nevertheless had a duty to pay me $100,000. If you did not pay the money on that date I could sue you for the

$100,000 but would not first have to be ready to convey the land. You would be in breach of your promise to pay the money. I would also be in breach of my promise to convey the land and you could sue me in specific performance to obtain title and possession of it. In other words, we would both be in breach and the breach by one person did not bar the action by the other. There would be two separate actions. The promises would support each other as consideration: my promise of Blackacre being consideration for your promise of $100,000 but a failure by one person (A) to perform her promise did not bar her suit against the other if she (A) had not performed. These were termed *independent promises*. They are very rare today but still exist where no time is set for performance. This can occur where it is doubtful when each can perform and each has undertaken a duty to perform as soon as he or she can. More likely today, the conditions stated in our example would be *concurrent*. On January 3rd, each one of us would have the duty to tender his/her performance to the other. Your duty to pay the money would be conditioned on my conveying Blackacre and my duty to convey Blackacre would be conditioned on your duty to pay the money. On January 3rd we would both have a duty to meet at the county records office and tender our performances simultaneously to each other. If one (X) of us failed to do so a condition was not fulfilled and the other (Y) *without being in breach* could refuse to perform. The one who was not in breach (*i.e.* was ready to perform) (Y) could sue the person who was in breach (X) even though Y had not yet performed. If both failed to tender then both are in breach and neither could sue the other. Each performance was conditioned on the other's readiness to perform. The *condition precedent* can also exist in connection with a promise.

Jones and Smith agree to buy and sell land pursuant to a contract containing the following statement: "Jones agrees to buy the land subject to the express conditions precedent that (1) Smith tenders to Jones at least 30 days prior to closing a plot plan, as hereinafter described, approved by the planning and zoning boards of the town of Happiness, and (2) Jones obtains financing from First National Bank for the purchase." Because that second express condition appears to be within Jones' sole control and might affect whether or not there is consideration (*i.e.* could Jones simply not get financing and thus has no obligation) with the result that Smith could claim there was no enforceable contract, both Jones and Smith might want a clause that states: "Jones has a good faith obligation to obtain such financing." They might even want a letter from the bank stating that the bank will give financing if such a plot plan is received. How would you want to make the bank's promise to do so binding, if the bank would agree to make it binding? Here we have promises, implied conditions and express conditions. The promise is to buy and sell. The implied concurrent conditions are that Smith will tender the deed and Jones the price on closing day. The express conditions precedent are that the plot plan and financing will take place before Jones and Smith have a duty to close.

Consider the following problem and then the cases.

Problem to Part IV

You are asked to draft a contract which will have as express conditions the following: (1) Every duty of the other party must be on time; (2) the other party must pay on time; (3) every payment and duty of the other party must be performed prior to your having to perform; (4) All work must be done exactly to specification with you determining whether or not the specifications have been met; (5) a failure of the other party to live up to any of the conditions will allow you to keep whatever services, goods or payments have been provided or made, without any duty on your part to give the corresponding performance, payment etc. if it has not already been made.

Look for examples of these clauses in the cases that follow. (You may not find all five.)

A. Conditions Creating the Contract

Gould, v. Artisoft, Incorporated
1 F.3d 544
United States Court of Appeals, 7th Cir., 1993.

ILANA DIAMOND ROVNER, Circuit Judge.

In this diversity action, John Gould alleges that Artisoft, Incorporated ("Artisoft") breached his employment contract. The district court dismissed Gould's complaint, concluding that he had failed to satisfy a condition precedent and, alternatively, that the contract failed for lack of consideration. Because we find that Gould sufficiently alleged the formation of a valid contract supported by adequate consideration, we reverse and remand for further proceedings.

I. FACTS

Artisoft, which distributes computer hardware and software products, hired John Gould in January 1991 to assemble and coordinate its nationwide sales force. In July of that year, Artisoft's Vice President of Sales and Marketing, David Hallmen, sent Gould a written offer to be Artisoft's Director of Sales. After making handwritten changes to Artisoft's offer, Gould signed the agreement on July 15, 1991, and Artisoft accepted Gould's proposed modifications in the last week of July. Under the terms of the agreement, Gould was to assume his new position on or before July 29, 1991, but until then, he was to remain in his previous position.

As a condition of his employment, the contract required Gould to execute "the enclosed nondisclosure and noncompetition agreement." (Gould App. Ex. F, at 6.) But no such agreement accompanied the written offer, nor did Artisoft tender such an agreement for Gould's signature prior to his termination. The contract provided for a three-month probationary period during which Artisoft would evaluate Gould's performance in his new position. At the end of the probationary period, either Gould or Artisoft could terminate the agreement if it became apparent that the arrangement was not mutually beneficial. The contract also contemplated that Gould would relocate to Tucson, Arizona, that Artisoft would pay the cost of his relocation, and that Artisoft would extend a bridge loan to facilitate Gould's purchase of a home in Tucson. If Gould were to resign from Artisoft within one year, however, he would be required to reimburse Artisoft for his relocation expenses. The contract further provided that in addition to his annual salary, Gould was to receive fifty shares of Artisoft stock.

When the parties executed the contract, Artisoft was a privately-held Arizona corporation. Plans were in the works, however, to make an initial public offering of Artisoft stock, and in anticipation of that offering, Artisoft was reincorporated in Delaware. On July 26, 1991, the fifty shares of stock referenced in the agreement were canceled and converted to 10,000 shares of the reincorporated Delaware corporation.

Artisoft terminated Gould's employment on August 7, 1991, less than two weeks after he assumed his new position with the company. The record does not reveal the reason, if any, for Gould's termination. Gould alleges that by the time he was terminated he already had begun "making the necessary arrangements to move and reside in Tucson, Arizona."

After his termination, Gould sued Artisoft in the Circuit Court of Cook County, seeking specific performance of Artisoft's promise to provide fifty shares of stock. Gould asserted that he became entitled to the stock upon acceptance of Artisoft's offer and that his right to the stock was unaffected by his termination. Gould also sought a preliminary injunction barring the public offering of Artisoft stock, which he claimed would diminish the value of his shares.

Artisoft removed the action to federal court, and Gould responded with an emergency motion to remand, which the district court denied. The court found that the $50,000 amount in controversy requirement for diversity jurisdiction had been satisfied because the value of the disputed stock in either a public or private sale was likely to exceed the jurisdictional amount.

After the district court denied Gould's motion for injunctive relief, Artisoft moved to dismiss the complaint, arguing that a condition precedent to the employment contract—execution of the noncompetition agreement—had not been satisfied and that the contract lacked consideration. The district court granted Artisoft's motion in an oral opinion, and Gould appeals.

II. DISCUSSION

1. Condition Precedent

Although the parties' agreement provides that "[a]s a condition of employment, [Gould] will be required to sign the enclosed nondisclosure and noncompetition agreement," (Gould App. Ex. F, at 6), Artisoft never provided a noncompetition agreement for Gould's signature.[1] The district court determined that without the signed noncompetition agreement, no contract had been formed. The court found that Artisoft's failure to tender the agreement did not excuse satisfaction of the condition because it was "at least theoretically possible that Gould could have on his own tendered to the defendant a written promise not to disclose what he learned and not to compete." (Id. at 7.) But this "theoretical possibility" is inconsistent with the plain language of the parties' contract. By failing to tender a noncompetition agreement for Gould's signature, Artisoft waived the condition that Gould execute such an agreement.

---

1. Artisoft's counsel told us at oral argument that his client had prepared the noncompetition agreement and was in the process of submitting the agreement for Gould's signature but that Gould's employment was terminated before that occurred.

Under Illinois law, "[a] condition precedent is some act that must be performed or event that must occur before a contract becomes effective or before one party to an existing contract is obligated to perform." Hardin, Rodriguez & Boivin Anesthesiologists, Ltd. v. Paradigm Ins. Co., 962 F.2d 628, 633 (7th Cir.1992). If the condition is not satisfied, then any obligations of the parties under their agreement are at an end. However, "[c]onditions precedent may be waived when a party to a contract intentionally relinquishes a known right either expressly or by conduct indicating that strict compliance with the conditions is not required." Hardin, Rodriguez & Boivin, 962 F.2d at 633. For example, where satisfaction of the condition is within the sole control of one party, that party may not prevent satisfaction of the condition in order to escape its contractual obligations.

The contract here plainly states that Gould was required to sign the "enclosed nondisclosure and noncompetition agreement." Use of the word "enclosed" placed the obligation on Artisoft to provide such an agreement for Gould's signature, either with the contract or perhaps shortly thereafter. Yet, Artisoft did not provide a noncompetition agreement prior to Gould's termination, and we do not believe that Gould was required to draft and execute his own agreement in light of the express contractual language. Artisoft thus waived satisfaction of the condition, and it may not rely on the failure of the condition precedent to escape its obligations.

III. CONCLUSION

Because Gould alleged facts suggesting that Artisoft had waived the condition precedent and that the contract was supported by adequate consideration, the district court's judgment dismissing Gould's complaint is reversed, and the case is remanded to the district court for further proceedings.

REVERSED AND REMANDED.

Questions

1. Is this a case of defendant claiming that before a contract came into existence a condition had to be fulfilled, or is it a case of defendant claiming that a contract came into existence but defendant need not perform its obligations under it because a condition precedent to its performance was not fulfilled?

2. Why did the defendant lose the case?

3. What is the significance of footnote 1?

B. Express Conditions and Implied Conditions Found in the Mutual Promises of the Parties

K & G Construction Company v. Harris
223 Md. 305, 164 A.2d 451
Court of Appeals of Maryland, 1960.

PRESCOTT, Judge.

Feeling aggrieved by the action of the trial judge of the Circuit Court for Prince George's County, sitting without a jury, in finding a judgment against it in favor of a subcontractor[1], the appellant, the general contractor on a construction project, appealed.

The principal question presented is: Does a contractor, damaged by a sub-contractor's failure to perform a portion of his work in a workmanlike manner, have a right, under the circumstances of this case, to withhold, in partial satisfaction of said damages, an installment payment, which, under the terms of the contract, was due the subcontractor, unless the negligent performance of his work excused its payment?

...K & G Construction Company, Inc. (hereinafter called Contractor), plaintiff and counter-defendant in the Circuit Court and appellant herein, was owner and general contractor of a housing subdivision project being constructed (herein called Project). Harris and Brooks (hereinafter called Subcontractor), defendants and counter-plaintiffs in the Circuit Court and appellees herein, entered into a contract with Contractor to do excavating and earth-moving work on the Project. Pertinent parts of the contract are set forth below: 'Section 3. The Subcontractor agrees to complete the several portions and the whole of the work herein sublet by the time or times following: (a) Without delay, as called for by the Contractor. (b) It is expressly agreed that time is of the essence of this contract, and that the Contractor will have the right to terminate this contract and employ a substitute to perform the work in the event of delay on the part of Subcontractor, and Subcontractor agrees to indemnify the Contractor for any loss sustained thereby, provided, however, that nothing in this paragraph shall be construed to deprive Contractor of any rights or remedies it would otherwise have as to damage for delay. Section 4. (b) Progress payments will be made each month during the performance of the work. Subcontractor will submit to Contractor, by the 25th of each month, a requisition for work performed during the preceding month. Contractor will pay these requisitions, less a retainer equal to ten per cent (10%), by the 10th of the months in which such requisitions are received..Section 5. The Contractor agrees—(1) That no claim for services rendered or materials furnished by the Contractor to the Subcontractor shall be valid unless written notice thereof is given by the Contractor to the Subcontractor during the first ten days of the calendar month following that in which the claim originated. Section 8. All work shall be performed in a workmanlike manner, and in accordance with the best practices. Section 9. Subcontractor agrees to carry, during the progress of the work,...liability insurance against...property damage, in such amounts and with such companies as may be satisfactory to Contractor and shall provide Contractor with certificates showing the same to be in force.'

While in the course of his employment by the Subcontractor on the Project, a bulldozer operator drove his machine too close to Contractor's house while grading the yard, causing the immediate collapse of a wall and other damage to the house. The resulting damage to contractor's house was $3,400.00. Subcontractor had complied with the insurance provision (Sec. 9) of the aforesaid contract. Subcontractor reported said damages to their liability insurance carrier. The Sub-

---

1. There are two appellees; the statement of the case refers to them as 'subcontractor.' We shall do likewise.

contractor and its insurance carrier refused to repair damage or compensate Contractor for damage to the house, claiming that there was no liability on the part of the Subcontractor. Contractor gave no written notice to Subcontractor for any services rendered or materials furnished by the Contractor to the Subcontractor.

Contractor was generally satisfied with Subcontractor's work and progress as required under Sections 3 and 8 of the contract until September 12, 1958, with the exception of the bulldozer accident of August 9, 1958. Subcontractor performed work under the contract during July, 1958, for which it submitted a requisition by the 25th of July, as required by the contract, for work done prior to the 25th of July, payable under the terms of the contract by Contractor on or before August 10, 1958. Contractor was current as to payments due under all preceding monthly requisitions from Subcontractor. The aforesaid bulldozer accident damaging Contractor's house occurred on August 9, 1958. Contractor refused to pay Subcontractor's requisition due on August 10, 1958, because the bulldozer damage to Contractor's house had not been repaired or paid for. Subcontractor continued to work on the project until the 12th of September, 1958, at which time they discontinued working on the project because of Contractor's refusal to pay the said work requisition and notified Contractor by registered letters of their position and willingness to return to the job, but only upon payment. At that time, September 12, 1958, the value of the work completed by Subcontractor on the project for which they had not been paid was $1,484.50.

Contractor later requested Subcontractor to return and complete work on the Project which Subcontractor refused to do because of nonpayment of work requisitions of July 25 and thereafter. Contractor's house was not repaired by Subcontractor nor compensation paid for the damage.

It was stipulated that Subcontractor had completed work on the Project under the contract for which they had not been paid in the amount of $1,484.50 and that if they had completed the remaining work to be done under the contract, they would have made a profit of $1,340.00 on the remaining uncompleted portion of the contract. It was further stipulated that it cost the Contractor $450.00 above the contract price to have another excavating contractor complete the remaining work required under the contract. It was the opinion of the [trial] Court that if judgment were in favor of the Subcontractor, it should be for the total amount of $2,824.50.

Contractor filed suit against the Subcontractor in two counts: (1), for the aforesaid bulldozer damage to Contractor's house, alleging negligence of the Subcontractor's bulldozer operator, and (2) for the $450.00 costs above the contract price in having another excavating subcontractor complete the uncompleted work in the contract. Subcontractor filed a counter-claim for recovery of work of the value of $1,484.50 for which they had not received payment and for loss of anticipated profits on uncompleted portion of work in the amount of $1,340.00.

By agreement of the parties, the first count of Contractor's claim, i. e., for aforesaid bulldozer damage to Contractor's house, was submitted to jury who found in favor of Contractor in the amount of $3,400.00. Following the finding by the jury, the second count of the Contractor's claim and the counter-claims of the Subcontractor, by agreement of the parties, were submitted to the Court for determination, without jury. All of the facts recited herein above were stipulated to by the parties to the Court. Circuit Court Judge Fletcher found for counter-plaintiff Subcontractor in the amount of $2,824.50 from which Contractor has entered this appeal.

The $3.400 judgment has been paid.

It is immediately apparent that our decision turns upon the respective rights and liabilities of the parties under that portion of their contract whereby the sub-contractor agreed to do the excavating and earth-moving work in 'a workman-like manner, and in accordance with the best practices,' with time being of the essence of the contract, and the contractor agreed to make progress payments therefor on the 10th day of the months following the performance of the work by the subcontractor.2

The subcontractor contends, of course, that when the contractor failed to make the payment due on August 10, 1958, he breached his contract and thereby released him (the subcontractor) from any further obligation to perform.

The contractor, on the other hand, argues that the failure of the subcontractor to perform his work in a workmanlike manner constituted a material breach of the contract, which justified his refusal to make the August 10 payment; and, as there was no breach on his part, the subcontractor had no right to cease performance on September 12, and his refusal to continue work on the project constituted another breach, which rendered him liable to the contractor for damages. The vital question, more tersely stated, remains: Did the contractor have a right, under the circumstances, to refuse to make the progress payment due on August 10, 1958?

The answer involves interesting and important principles of contract law. Promises and counter-promises made by the respective parties to a contract have certain relations to one another, which determine many of the rights and liabilities of the parties. Broadly speaking, they are (1) independent of each other, or (2) mutually dependent, one upon the other. They are independent of each other if the parties intend that *performance* by each of them is in no way conditioned upon *performance* by the other. 5 Page, The Law of Contracts, P 2971. In other words, the parties exchange promises for promises, not the *performance* of promises for the *performance* of promises. 3 Williston, Contracts (Rev. Ed.), P813, n. 6. A failure to perform an independent promise does not excuse non-performance on the part of the adversary party, but each is required to perform his promise, and, if one does not perform, he is liable to the adversary party for such non-performance. (Of course, if litigation ensues questions of set-off or re-coupment frequently arise.) Promises are mutually dependent if the parties intend *performance* by one to be conditioned upon *performance* by the other, and, if they be mutually dependent, they may be (a) precedent, i. e., a promise that is to be performed before a corresponding promise on the part of the adversary party is to be performed, (b) subsequent, i. e., a corresponding promise that is not to be performed until the other party to the contract has performed a precedent covenant, or (c) concurrent, i. e., promises that are to be performed at the same time by each of the parties, who are respectively bound to perform each.

---

2. The statement of the case does not show the exact terms concerning the remuneration to be paid the subcontractor. It does not disclose whether he was to be paid a total lump sum, by the cubic yard, by the day, or in some other manner. It does state that the excavation finally cost the contractor $450 more than the 'contract price.'

Professor Page, op. cit., P2971, says there are three classes of independent promises left: (1) those in which the acts to be performed by the respective parties are, by the terms of the contract, to be performed at fixed times or on the happening of certain events which do not bear any relation to one another; (2) those in which the covenant in question is independent because it does not form the entire consideration for the covenants on the part of the adversary party, and ordinarily forms but a minor part of such consideration; and (3) those in which the contract shows that the parties intended performance of their respective promises without regard to performance on the part of the adversary, thus relying upon the promises and not the performances.

In the early days, it was settled law that covenants and mutual promises in a contract were prima facie independent, and that they were to be so construed in the absence of language in the contract clearly showing that they were intended to be dependent. Williston, op. cit., P816; Page, op. cit., PP2944, 2945. In the case of Kingston v. Preston, 2 Doug. 689, decided in 1774, Lord Mansfield, contrary to three centuries of opposing precedents, changed the rule, and decided that performance of one covenant might be dependent on prior performance of another, although the contract contained no express condition to that effect. Page, op. cit., P2946; Williston, op. cit., P817. The modern rule, which seems to be of almost universal application, is that there is a presumption that mutual promises in a contract are dependent and are to be so regarded, whenever possible. Restatement, Contracts, P 266. Cf. Williston, op. cit., P812.

While the courts assume, in deciding the relation of one or more promises in a contract to one or more counter-promises, that the promises are dependent rather than independent, the *intention* of the parties, as shown by the entire contract as *construed* in the light of the circumstances of the case, the *nature* of the contract, the *relation* of the parties thereto, and the other evidence which is admissible to assist the court in determining the intention of the parties, is the controlling factor in deciding whether the promises and counter-promises are dependent or independent..

Considering the presumption that promises and counter-promises are dependent and the statement of the case, we have no hesitation in holding that the promise and counter-promise under consideration here were mutually dependent, that is to say, the parties intended performance by one to be conditioned on performance by the other; and the subcontractor's promise was, by the explicit wording of the contract, precedent to the promise of payment, monthly, by the contractor. In Shapiro Engineering Corp. v. Francis O. Day Co., 215 Md. 373, 380, 137 A.2d 695, we stated that it is the general rule that where a total price for work is fixed by a contract, the work is not rendered divisible by progress payments. It would, indeed present an unusual situation if we were to hold that a building contractor, who has obtained someone to do work for him and has agreed to pay each month for the work performed in the previous month, has to continue the monthly payments, irrespective of the degree of skill and care displayed in the performance of work, and his only recourse is by way of suit for ill-performance. If this were the law, it is conceivable, in fact, probable, that many contractors would become insolvent before they were able to complete their contracts. As was stated by the Court in Measures Brothers Ltd. v. Measures, 2 Ch. 248: 'Covenants are to be construed as dependent or independent according to the intention of the parties and the good sense of the case.'

We hold that when the subcontractor's employee negligently damaged the contractor's wall, this constituted a breach of the subcontractor's promise to perform his work in a 'workmanlike manner, and in accordance with the best practices.'. And there can be little doubt that the breach was material: the damage to the wall amounted to more than double the payment due on August 10. 3A Corbin, Contracts, § 708, says: 'The failure of a contractor's [in our case, the subcontractor's] performance to constitute 'substantial' performance may justify the owner [in our case, the contractor] in refusing to make a progress payment.... If the refusal to pay an installment is justified on the owner's [contractor's] part, the contractor [subcontractor] is not justified in abandoning work by reason of that refusal. His abandonment of the work will itself be a wrongful repudiation that goes to the essence, even if the defects in performance did not.'. Professor Corbin, in § 954, states further: 'The unexcused failure of a contractor to render a promised performance when it is due is always a breach of contract.... Such failure may be of such great importance as to constitute what has been called herein a 'total' breach. .... For a failure of performance constituting such a 'total' breach, an action for remedies that are appropriate thereto is at once maintainable. Yet the injured party is not required to bring such action. He has the option of treating the non-performance as a 'partial' breach only....'

In permitting the subcontractor to proceed with work on the project after August 9, the contractor, obviously, treated the breach by the subcontractor as a partial one. As the promises were mutually dependent and the subcontractor had made a material breach in his performance, this justified the contractor in refusing to make the August 10 payment; hence, as the contractor was not in default, the subcontractor again breached the contract when he, on September 12, discontinued work on the project, which rendered him liable (by the express terms of the contract) to the contractor for his increased cost in having the excavating done—a stipulated amount of $450. Cf. Keystone Engineering Corp. v. Sutter, 196 Md. 620, 628, 78 A.2d 191.

The appellees suggest two minor points that may be disposed of rather summarily. They argue that the contractor 'gave no written notice to subcontractor for any services rendered or materials furnished by the contractor to the subcontractor,' in accordance with the terms of the contract. It is apparent that the contractor's claim against the subcontractor for ill-performance did not involve, in any way, 'services rendered or materials furnished' by the contractor; hence, the argument has no substance. They also contend that the contractor had no right to refuse the August 10 payment, because the subcontractor had furnished the insurance against property damage, as called for in the contract. There is little, or no, merit in this suggestion. The subcontractor and his insurance company denied liability. The furnishing of the insurance by him did not constitute a license to perform his work in a careless, negligence, or unworkmanlike manner; and its acceptance by the contractor did not preclude his assertion of a claim for unworkmanlike performance directly against the subcontractor.

Judgment against the appellant reversed; and judgment entered in favor of the appellant against the appellees for $450, the appellees to pay the costs.

Questions

1. What are the implied conditions in the contract?

2. What are the express conditions?

In *Ziehen v. Smith, 42 N.E. 1080 (N.Y.,* 1896), vendee successfully sued vendor for damages for breach of contract to convey real estate. Vendee did not offer to perform his part of the contract on the day set for closing or on any other day. "It is, no doubt, the general rule that, in order to entitle a party to recover damages for the breach of an executory contract of this character, he must show performance, or tender of performance, on his part....But a tender of performance on the part of the vendee is dispensed with in a case where it appears that the vendor has disabled himself from performance or that he is...unable to perform." Unknown to either party a mortgage created by a prior owner existed on the land at the time of contracting. This, from the point of view of the lower court, constituted a defect in the title which made it impossible for vendor to convey a satisfactory title and gave vendee the right to sue vendor without first tendering his own performance. Held *reversed.* Vendor could have cleared title sufficient to make a satisfactory tender had vendee not refused to go forward with the contract. While vendee would not have been required to perform an unnecessary act, making his own tender knowing vendor could not tender, this was not so certain here. Because neither party had fulfilled the concurrent condition necessary to enable either to bring a suit (vendor was not ready to convey; vendee was not ready to pay), judgment for vendee is reversed.

In *Cohen v. Krantz, 238 N.Y.S.2d 928* (N.Y., 1963) , buyer refused to go through with a purchase of real estate because "the present structure of the premises is not legal." This was the only notice given to seller. Buyer demanded the return of a 10% down payment. Judgment in the trial court for Buyer unanimously *reversed* in the Appellate Division which granted seller $1,500 on the counterclaim for damages based on a lower resale price to another buyer when plaintiff buyer refused to perform. Appellate Division was unanimously *affirmed* in the Court of Appeals. Buyer's failure to specify the nature of the faults and the fact that the faults were curable by closing day or within a reasonable time thereafter meant that buyer was in default for refusing to perform the contract. One concerned a "certificate of occupancy" for a swimming pool which seller obtained prior to sale to a third person; a fence projection was also found to be readily curable. Because seller did not waive buyer's tender of the price and because buyer by rejecting the title prior to the closing day was in default, buyer could not recover the down payment. The only way buyer could have recovered without a tender would be if seller's title defects were incurable defective, which the court defined as not curable "within a reasonable time." Where vendor's title defects are curable, vendee must put vendor in default by demanding a good title. On the question of seller recovering on the counterclaim seller must show that she "has performed all conditions precedent and concurrent unless excused." "In the case of the purchase of real estate [by a buyer], this would be a showing of tender and demand [by the buyer] or, if that be unnecessary, an idle gesture, because of the incurable nature of the title defect, then at least a showing at the trial that the plaintiff vendee was in a position to perform had the vendor been willing and able to perform his part. *Likewise, a vendor,* such as the defendants here must show a basic ability to perform even if actual tender and demand is unnecessary. However, while it cannot be denied that defendants did not have a title conformable to the contract at law date, an applicable corollary of the above rule excuses even inability to perform conditions precedent or concurrent where such inability is caused by advance notice from the other party that he will not perform his part. Not only did buyer's unjustified attempt to cancel the contract and recover her deposit before the adjourned law date render unnecessary and wasteful any attempt by defendants to cure the minor defects before that date, but the failure to specify the objections rendered it impossible. The finding of the Appellate Division, supported by the weight of the evidence, that the defects were curable, means that defendants were basically able to perform and whatever technical inability existed in this regard on the law date was caused by plaintiff and is excused fully as much as the lack of formal tender."

Questions

1. In *Cohen* and *Ziehen* what are the express and/or implied conditions (if any) in the contracts?

C. Express Conditions that Are Not Promises

Koch, v. Construction Technology, Inc.

924 S.W.2d 68

Supreme Court of Tennessee, 1996.

DROWOTA, Justice.

This case involves a contract dispute between Mark Koch (d/b/a Commercial Painting Company, Inc.) and Construction Technology, Inc., (CTI), the former a painting subcontractor and the latter the general contractor on a construction project owned by the Memphis Housing Authority (MHA). The issues for our determination are as follows: (1) whether the Court of Appeals erred in construing the "pay when paid" clause in the subcontract as a condition precedent, thereby making Koch's right to payment dependent upon CTI's receipt of payment from MHA. For the following reasons, we hold that the Court of Appeals erred; therefore, we reverse the judgment of that court and remand the cause for further proceedings.

FACTS AND PROCEDURAL HISTORY

On March 17, 1988, CTI and the MHA entered into a contract in which CTI agreed to make improvements to the Dixie Homes Housing Development in Memphis. On March 30, 1988, CTI subcontracted the painting portion of the project to Koch; CTI also provided a performance and payment bond to him through FDCM. The subcontract included a "payment" clause, which provides in pertinent part, that:

"Partial payments subject to all applicable provisions of the Contract shall be made when and as payments are received by the Contractor. The Subcontractor may be required as a condition precedent to any payment to furnish evidence satisfactory to the Contractor that all payrolls, material bills, and other indebtedness applicable to the work have been paid."

A. Construction of the Payment Clause

The first issue for our determination is whether the payment clause in the subcontract establishes MHA's payment to CTI as a condition precedent to CTI's obligation to pay Koch. Koch argues that the lower courts erred in so construing the clause. Although conceding that the Hussey court construed similar language as a conditional promise, he argues that an overwhelming majority of jurisdictions reject that position, and instead hold that such language establishes an absolute promise to pay on the part of the general contractor, but simply affords it a reasonable amount of time to make the payments. This majority position is sound public policy, Koch contends, because it is inequitable to make the subcontractor's right to payment dependent upon the owner's performance, which might not be forthcoming for any number of reasons out of the subcontractor's control. Because Hussey is at odds with the compelling majority position, Koch concludes, it should be overruled and the majority rule adopted in its place.

CTI responds that the law of other jurisdictions is of no consequence, and that Hussey—the only reported Tennessee decision addressing the issue— controls this case. Therefore, it concludes, the lower courts' construction of the payment clause should be affirmed.

Because the parties and the lower courts relied so heavily upon Hussey, we must first examine it in some detail. In that case, the general contractor, Crass, agreed with the owner to build a section of railroad; and Crass subcontracted the trestle work to Hussey. The subcontract provided that Hussey was to take out "estimates" on or about the 1st of each month, and that "90 per cent of said estimate was to be paid about the 15th of the following month, or as soon thereafter as the railroad company should pay or cause to be paid J.T. Crass therefor..." Hussey, 53 S.W. at 986 (emphasis added). While the work was in progress, the railroad company became insolvent. Because of that development, Crass was only able to obtain 10% of the money due under his contract, despite extensive negotiating with the railroad company during its impending failure; and he paid his subcontractors on that pro rata basis.

Hussey then brought an action against Crass for breach of contract. The general contractor defended by asserting that the "pay when paid" clause was a condition precedent and that, furthermore, Hussey had agreed during the negotiations with the railroad that his claim was dependent upon Crass's obtaining a settlement with that entity. The chancellor ruled in Crass's favor, and Hussey appealed.

On appeal, the Chancery Court of Appeals affirmed the ruling. After setting forth the factual background, the court stated: "We think there can be no doubt that the understanding between the parties was that the money that Mr. Crass expected to pay to his subcontractors was to be realized from the railroad company, and that he would not be liable to the subcontractors, and complainant among the number, unless he could make collection from the railroad company. We think this is the true construction of the contract itself on its face, so far as concerns complainant's claim." Hussey, 53 S.W. at 988.

After making that statement, the Court proceeded to quote extensively from correspondence between the parties during Crass's negotiations with the railroad: this lengthy recitation was undertaken for the purpose of illustrating Hussey's willingness to accept whatever settlement Crass could negotiate with the financially declining railroad. The Court concluded by stating: "From this correspondence, taken in connection with the statement in the contract that the complainant was to be paid when Crass was paid by the railroad company, we have no doubt that the expectation of both parties was that the liability of Mr. Crass depended upon his receiving money from the railroad company. The correspondence above mentioned is unintelligible otherwise." Id. at 988-89.

We believe that the parties attach too much importance to Hussey for purposes of this case. While the Court did state in a single sentence that the language in the contract was a condition precedent to the subcontractor's right to payment, that conclusory statement was supported by no analysis. Indeed, the court spent almost no time on the contractual language, but was primarily concerned with the overwhelming evidence that tended to show that Hussy had agreed, after the railroad company began to show signs of financial collapse, to accept whatever payment Crass could obtain from it. Because of the Court's almost complete reliance on parol evidence, and because of the manifest lack of such evidence here, we cannot agree that Hussey requires that the contractual language at issue here be construed as a condition precedent.

Having concluded that Hussey is not determinative, we must now decide the proper construction of that language. Although we have never specifically addressed the issue, there are a number of settled propositions of law to guide us. First, it is well-established that condition precedents are not favored in contract law, and will not be upheld unless there is clear language to support them. Furthermore, this general rule applies with particular force in the context of "pay when paid" clauses, for the plaintiff is correct that an overwhelming majority of jurisdictions do not construe such clauses so as to release the general contractor from all obligation to make payment to the subcontractor in case of nonperformance by the owner. Rather, these clauses are most often construed as simply affecting the timing of payments that the general contractor is required to make to the subcontractor, regardless of whether the owner performs or not. These courts refuse to shift the risk of the owner's nonperformance from the general contractor to the subcontractor unless the language clearly indicates that the parties intended to do so. A good example of this reasoning is contained in the seminal case of Thos. J. Dyer Co. v. Bishop International Engineering Co., 303 F.2d 655 (6th Cir.1962), wherein the Court was called upon to construe a clause which provided that "no part of [the subcontract price] shall be due until five days after Owner shall have paid Contractor therefor..." Dyer, 303 F.2d at 656. In holding that the clause was not a condition precedent, the Dyer court explained: "It is, of course, basic in the construction business for the general contractor on a construction project of any magnitude to expect to be paid in full by the owner for the labor and material he puts into the project. He would not remain in business for long unless such was his intention and such intention was accomplished. That is a fundamental concept of doing business with another. The solvency of the owner is a credit risk necessarily incurred by the general contractor, but various legal and contractual provisions, such as mechanic's liens and installment payments, are used to reduce this to a minimum. These evidence the intention of the parties that the contractor be paid even though the owner may ultimately become insolvent. This expectation and intention of being paid is even more pronounced in the case of a subcontractor whose contract is with the general contractor, not with the owner. In addition to his mechanic's lien, he is primarily interested in the solvency of the general contractor with whom he has contracted. He looks to him for payment. Normally and legally, the insolvency of the owner will not defeat the claim of the subcontractor against the general contractor. Accordingly, in order to transfer this normal credit risk incurred by the general contractor from the general contractor to the subcontractor, the contract between the general contractor and the subcontractor should contain an express condition clearly showing that to be the intention of the parties. In the case before us we see no reason why the usual credit risk of the owner's insolvency assumed by the general contractor should be transferred from the general contractor to the subcontractor. It seems clear to us under the facts of this case that it was the intention of the parties that the subcontractor would be paid by the general contractor for the labor and materials put into the project. We believe that to be the normal relationship between the parties. If such was not the intention of the parties it could have been expressed in unequivocal terms dealing with the possible insolvency of the owner...." Dyer, 303 F.2d at 660-61 (citations omitted).

With these rules in mind, we conclude that the language here does not evidence the parties' intention to shift the risk of the owner's nonperformance from the general contractor to the subcontractor with sufficient clarity to qualify as a condition precedent. The first sentence—"payments...shall be made when and as they are received by the contractor"—could be interpreted as a timing provision; it is not necessarily indicative of the parties' intent to make CTI's obligation to pay Koch dependent upon CTI's first being paid by MHA. This is particularly so in light of the following sentence in the clause, which provides: "[t]he subcontractor may be required as a condition precedent to any payment to furnish evidence satisfactory to the contractor that all payrolls, material bills, and other indebtedness applicable to the work have been paid." This sentence illustrates that the parties certainly knew how to create a condition precedent if they so desired. That they did not use such unambiguous language in the first sentence prevents us from construing that sentence as a condition precedent to Koch's right to payment.

In *Galloway Corp. v. S. B. Constr. Co., 464 S.E.2d 349, (Va., 1995)* the 'pay when paid' defense by the general against a subcontractor was again raised. When the owner failed to pay the general, the general refused to pay the subs. The following clauses were in the contract. "The Contractor shall promptly pay each subcontractor, upon receipt of payment from the Owner, out of the amount paid to the Contractor on account of such Subcontractor's Work, the amount to which said Subcontractor is entitled....The Contractor shall pay the Subcontractor each progress payment within three working days after the Contractor receives payment from the Owner." On the issue of pay only when paid the court said:

"THE 'PAY WHEN PAID' DEFENSE

This appeal presents our first opportunity to consider the use of "pay when paid" (sometimes rendered as 'paid when paid') clauses in construction contracts. The use of such clauses rose significantly in the 1980s because economic conditions made successful completion of private construction projects more difficult and engendered a cautious attitude throughout the construction industry.

The leading case to address the enforceability of 'pay when paid' clauses is Thos. J. Dyer Co. v. Bishop International Engineering Co., 303 F.2d 655 (6th Cir.1962). In Dyer, the contract provided that 'no part of [the price to be paid to the subcontractor] shall be due until five (5) days after Owner shall have paid Contractor therefor.' Id. at 656. Following the insolvency of the owner, a subcontractor sought to enforce its contract with the general contractor. The Sixth Circuit rejected the general contractor's argument that the language of the contract constituted a condition precedent giving it a defense to the breach of contract claim. The court explained its rationale in the following language: 'In the case before us we see no reason why the usual credit risk of the owner's insolvency assumed by the general contractor should be transferred from the general contractor to the subcontractor. It seems clear to us under the facts of this case that it was the intention of the parties that the subcontractor would be paid by the general contractor for the labor and materials put into the project. We believe that to be the normal construction of the relationship between the parties. If such was not the intention of the parties it could have been so expressed in unequivocal terms dealing with the possible insolvency of the owner. Paragraph 3 of the subcontract does not refer to the possible insolvency of the owner. On the other hand, it deals with the amount, time, and method of payment, which are essential provisions in every construction contract, without regard to possible insolvency. In our opinion, paragraph 3 of the subcontract is a reasonable provision designed to postpone payment for a reasonable period of time after the work was completed, during which the general contractor would be afforded the opportunity of procuring from the owner the funds necessary to pay the subcontractor. To construe it as requiring the subcontractor to wait to be paid for an indefinite period of time until the general contractor has been paid by the owner, which may never occur, is to give to it an unreasonable construction which the parties did not intend at the time the subcontract was entered into.' Id. at 661.

The contract in Dyer further provided that 90 percent of the payment was due in any case 35 days after completion of the work. Id. at 656. The court construed this provision of the contract together with the term relied on by the general contractor as merely postponing the time of payment to the subcontractor on an unconditional promise to pay until payment by the owner, "or for a reasonable period of time if it develops that such event does not take place." Id. at 659. The court premised its result on the fact that it is the general contractor who contracts with the owner. Id. at 660. The court further held that the credit risk inherent in the general contractor's undertaking may be shifted to the subcontractor, but in order to do so, 'the contract between the general contractor and subcontractor should contain an express condition clearly showing that to be the intention of the parties.' Id. at 661.

Since the Dyer decision, the majority of jurisdictions which have considered the 'pay when paid' defense have adopted the reasoning of the Sixth Circuit. See Mootz, Enforceability, 64 Conn.B.J. at 263 and cases cited therein at n. 17; see also Gilbane Building Co. v. Brisk Waterproofing Co., Inc., 86 Md.App. 21, 585 A.2d 248, 250 (1991) (holding that use of term 'condition precedent' in 'pay when paid' clause clearly establishes intent of parties to shift credit risk of owner's insolvency to subcontractor). A minority of jurisdictions as a matter of policy do not allow the risk of owner insolvency to be shifted from the general contractor to the subcontractors. See, e.g., N.C.Gen.Stat. § 22C-2 (1994).

We find the reasoning of the Dyer decision to be sound and in concert with traditional notions of the freedom to contract. However, that reasoning is applicable only where the language of the contract in question is clear on its face. If, as in Dyer, a contract on its face reasonably contemplates eventual payment by the general contractor to the subcontractor, or, as in Gilbane, the parties clearly intend there to be a condition precedent fulfilled before payment comes due, the contract will be construed as written and will not be reformed by the court through the introduction of parol and other extrinsic evidence of a contrary intent. Accordingly, we must consider whether the contracts sub judice are clear on their face as to the parties' intent."

The court then found that the written expressions of the contracts were ambiguous and allowed parol evidence as to the parties intents. In all cases but one it found that the subcontractors had contemplated such a defense when signed contracts with the general contractor and accordingly could not successfully sue it.

Questions

1. How would you draft a "pay when paid" clause to have it stand up as a condition precedent? What would you avoid putting into the writing? What would you want in the writing?

2. What is the essential unfairness with having a "pay when paid" clause as a condition precedent?

D. Substantial Performance

Oppenheimer & Co., Inc., v. Oppenheim, Appel, Dixon & Co.

86 N.Y.2d 685, 660 N.E.2d 415, 636 N.Y.S.2d 734
Court of Appeals of New York, 1995.

CIPARICK, Justice.

The parties entered into a letter agreement setting forth certain conditions precedent to the formation and existence of a sublease between them. The agreement provided that there would be no sublease between the parties "unless and until" plaintiff delivered to defendant the prime landlord's written consent to certain "tenant work" on or before a specified deadline. If this condition did not occur, the sublease was to be deemed "null and void." Plaintiff provided only oral notice on the specified date. The issue presented is whether the doctrine of substantial performance applies to the facts of this case. We conclude it does not for the reasons that follow.

I.

In 1986, plaintiff Oppenheimer & Co. moved to the World Financial Center in Manhattan, a building constructed by Olympia & York Company (O & Y). At the time of its move, plaintiff had three years remaining on its existing lease for the 33rd floor of the building known as One New York Plaza. As an incentive to induce plaintiff's move, O & Y agreed to make the rental payments due under plaintiff's rental agreement in the event plaintiff was unable to sublease its prior space in One New York Plaza.

In December 1986, the parties to this action entered into a conditional letter agreement to sublease the 33rd floor. Defendant already leased space on the 29th floor of One New York Plaza and was seeking to expand its operations. The proposed sublease between the parties was attached to the letter agreement. The letter agreement provided that the proposed sublease would be executed only upon the satisfaction of certain conditions. Pursuant to paragraph 1(a) of the agreement, plaintiff was required to obtain "the Prime Landlord's written notice of confirmation, substantially to the effect that [defendant] is a subtenant of the Premises reasonably acceptable to Prime Landlord." If such written notice of confirmation were not obtained "on or before December 30, 1986, then this letter agreement and the Sublease *   *   * shall be deemed null and void and of no further force and effect and neither party shall have any rights against nor obligations to the other."

Assuming satisfaction of the condition set forth in paragraph 1(a), defendant was required to submit to plaintiff, on or before January 2, 1987, its plans for "tenant work" involving construction of a telephone communication linkage system between the 29th and 33rd floors. Paragraph 4(c) of the letter agreement then obligated plaintiff to obtain the prime landlord's "written consent" to the proposed "tenant work" and deliver such consent to defendant on or before January 30, 1987. Furthermore, if defendant had not received the prime landlord's written consent by the agreed date, both the agreement and the sublease were to be deemed "null and void and of no further force and effect," and neither party was to have "any rights against nor obligations to the other." Paragraph 4(d) additionally provided that, notwithstanding satisfaction of the condition set forth in paragraph 1(a), the parties "agree not to execute and exchange the Sublease unless and until...the conditions set forth in paragraph (c) above are timely satisfied."

The parties extended the letter agreement's deadlines in writing and plaintiff timely satisfied the first condition set forth in paragraph 1(a) pursuant to the modified deadline. However, plaintiff never delivered the prime landlord's written consent to the proposed tenant work on or before the modified final deadline of February 25, 1987. Rather, plaintiff's attorney telephoned defendant's attorney on February 25 and informed defendant that the prime landlord's consent had been secured. On February 26, defendant, through its attorney, informed plaintiff's attorney that the letter agreement and sublease were invalid for failure to timely deliver the prime landlord's written consent and that it would not agree to an extension of the deadline. The document embodying the prime landlord's written consent was eventually received by plaintiff on March 20, 1987, 23 days after expiration of paragraph 4(c)'s modified final deadline.

Plaintiff commenced this action for breach of contract, asserting that defendant waived and/or was estopped by virtue of its conduct from insisting on physical delivery of the prime landlord's written consent by the February 25 deadline. Plaintiff further alleged in its complaint that it had substantially performed the conditions set forth in the letter agreement.

At the outset of trial, the court issued an order in limine barring any reference to substantial performance of the terms of the letter agreement. Nonetheless, during the course of trial, the court permitted the jury to consider the theory of substantial performance, and additionally charged the jury concerning substantial performance. Special interrogatories were submitted. The jury found that defendant had properly complied with the terms of the letter agreement, and answered in the negative the questions whether defendant failed to perform its obligations under the letter agreement concerning submission of plans for tenant work, whether defendant by its conduct waived the February 25 deadline for delivery by plaintiff of the landlord's written consent to tenant work, and whether defendant by its conduct was equitably estopped from requiring plaintiff's strict adherence to the February 25 deadline. Nonetheless, the jury answered in the affirmative the question, "Did plaintiff substantially perform the conditions set forth in the Letter Agreement?," and awarded plaintiff damages of $1.2 million.

Defendant moved for judgment notwithstanding the verdict. Supreme Court granted the motion, ruling as a matter of law that "the doctrine of substantial performance has no application to this dispute, where the Letter Agreement is free of all ambiguity in setting the deadline that plaintiff concededly did not honor." The Appellate Division reversed the judgment on the law and facts, and reinstated the jury verdict. The Court concluded that the question of substantial compliance was properly submitted to the jury and that the verdict should be reinstated because plaintiff's failure to deliver the prime landlord's written consent was inconsequential.

This Court granted defendant's motion for leave to appeal and we now reverse.

II.

Defendant argues that no sublease or contractual relationship ever arose here because plaintiff failed to satisfy the condition set forth in paragraph 4(c) of the letter agreement. Defendant contends that the doctrine of substantial performance is not applicable to excuse plaintiff's failure to deliver the prime landlord's written consent to defendant on or before the date specified in the letter agreement and that the Appellate Division erred in holding to the contrary. Before addressing defendant's arguments and the decision of the court below, an understanding of certain relevant principles is helpful.

A condition precedent is "an act or event, other than a lapse of time, which, unless the condition is excused, must occur before a duty to perform a promise in the agreement arises" (Calamari and Perillo, Contracts § 11-2, at 438 [3d ed.]; see, Restatement [Second] of Contracts § 224. Most conditions precedent describe acts or events which must occur before a party is obliged to perform a promise made pursuant to an existing contract, a situation to be distinguished conceptually from a condition precedent to the formation or existence of the contract itself (see, M.K. Metals v. Container Recovery Corp., 645 F.2d 583). In the latter situation, no contract arises "unless and until the condition occurs" (Calamari and Perillo, Contracts § 11-5, at 440 [3d ed]).

Conditions can be express or implied. Express conditions are those agreed to and imposed by the parties themselves. Implied or constructive conditions are those "imposed by law to do justice" (Calamari and Perillo, Contracts § 11-8, at 444 [3d ed]). Express conditions must be literally performed, whereas constructive conditions, which ordinarily arise from language of promise, are subject to the precept that substantial compliance is sufficient. The importance of the distinction has been explained by Professor Williston: "Since an express condition...depends for its validity on the manifested intention of the parties, it has the same sanctity as the promise itself. Though the court may regret the harshness of such a condition, as it may regret the harshness of a promise, it must, nevertheless, generally enforce the will of the parties unless to do so will violate public policy. Where, however, the law itself has imposed the condition, in absence of or irrespective of the manifested intention of the parties, it can deal with its creation as it pleases, shaping the boundaries of the constructive condition in such a way as to do justice and avoid hardship". (5 Williston, Contracts § 669, at 154 [3d ed].)

In determining whether a particular agreement makes an event a condition courts will interpret doubtful language as embodying a promise or constructive condition rather than an express condition. This interpretive preference is especially strong when a finding of express condition would increase the risk of forfeiture by the obligee (see, Restatement [Second] of Contracts § 227 [1]).

Interpretation as a means of reducing the risk of forfeiture cannot be employed if "the occurrence of the event as a condition is expressed in unmistakable language" (Restatement [Second] of Contracts § 229, comment a, at 185; see, § 227, comment b [where language is clear, "(t)he policy favoring freedom of contract requires that, within broad limits, the agreement of the parties should be honored even though forfeiture results"]). Nonetheless, the nonoccurrence of the condition may yet be excused by waiver, breach or forfeiture. The Restatement posits that "[t]o the extent that the non- occurrence of a condition would cause disproportionate forfeiture, a court may excuse the non-occurrence of that condition unless its occurrence was a material part of the agreed exchange" (Restatement [Second] of Contracts § 229).

Turning to the case at bar, it is undisputed that the critical language of paragraph 4(c) of the letter agreement unambiguously establishes an express condition precedent rather than a promise, as the parties employed the unmistakable language of condition ("if," "unless and until"). There is no doubt of the parties' intent and no occasion for interpreting the terms of the letter agreement other than as written.

Furthermore, plaintiff has never argued, and does not now contend, that the nonoccurrence of the condition set forth in paragraph 4(c) should be excused on the ground of forfeiture. Rather, plaintiff's primary argument from the inception of this litigation has been that defendant waived or was equitably estopped from invoking paragraph 4(c). Plaintiff argued secondarily that it substantially complied with the express condition of delivery of written notice on or before February 25th in that it gave defendant oral notice of consent on the 25th.

Contrary to the decision of the Court below, we perceive no justifiable basis for applying the doctrine of substantial performance to the facts of this case. The flexible concept of substantial compliance "stands in sharp contrast to the requirement of strict compliance that protects a party that has taken the precaution of making its duty expressly conditional" (2 Farnsworth, Contracts § 8.12, at 415 [2d ed 1990]). If the parties "have made an event a condition of their agreement, there is no mitigating standard of materiality or substantiality applicable to the non-occurrence of that event" (Restatement [Second] of Contracts § 237, comment d, at 220). Substantial performance in this context is not sufficient, "and if relief is to be had under the contract, it must be through excuse of the non-occurrence of the condition to avoid forfeiture" (id.)

Here, it is undisputed that plaintiff has not suffered a forfeiture or conferred a benefit upon defendant. Plaintiff alludes to a $1 million licensing fee it allegedly paid to the prime landlord for the purpose of securing the latter's consent to the subleasing of the premises. At no point, however, does plaintiff claim that this sum was forfeited or that it was expended for the purpose of accomplishing the sublease with defendant. It is further undisputed that O & Y, as an inducement to effect plaintiff's move to the World Financial Center, promised to indemnify plaintiff for damages resulting from failure to sublease the 33rd floor of One New York Plaza. Consequently, because the critical concern of forfeiture or unjust enrichment is simply not present in this case, we are not presented with an occasion to consider whether the doctrine of substantial performance is applicable, that is, whether the courts should intervene to excuse the nonoccurrence of a condition precedent to the formation of a contract.

The essence of the Appellate Division's holding is that the substantial performance doctrine is universally applicable to all categories of breach of contract, including the nonoccurrence of an express condition precedent. However, as discussed, substantial performance is ordinarily not applicable to excuse the nonoccurrence of an express condition precedent.

Our precedents are consistent with this general principle. In Maxton Bldrs. v. Lo Galbo, 68 N.Y.2d 373, 509 N.Y.S.2d 507, 502 N.E.2d 184, the defendants contracted on August 3 to buy a house, but included in the contract the condition that if real estate taxes were found to be above $3,500 they would have the right to cancel the contract upon written notice to the seller within three days. On August 4 the defendants learned that real estate taxes would indeed exceed $3,500. The buyers' attorney called the seller's attorney and notified him that the defendants were exercising their option to cancel. A certified letter was sent notifying the seller's attorney of that decision on August 5 but was not received by the seller's attorney until August 9. We held the cancellation ineffective and rejected defendants' argument that reasonable notice was all that was required, stating: "It is settled ... that when a contract requires that written notice be given within a specified time, the notice is ineffective unless the writing is actually received within the time prescribed" (id., at 378, 509 N.Y.S.2d 507, 502 N.E.2d 184). We so held despite the fact that timely oral notice was given and the contract did not provide that time was of the essence.

In Jungmann & Co. v. Atterbury Bros., 249 N.Y. 119, 163 N.E. 123, the parties entered into a written contract for the sale of 30 tons of casein. The contract contained the following clause: "Shipment: May-June from Europe. Advice of shipment to be made by cable immediately goods are dispatched" (id.). Plaintiff shipped the first 15 tons but gave no notice to the defendant, who rejected the shipment. Plaintiff thereafter shipped the remaining 15 tons to defendant, but again failed to provide notice by cable and instead sent two letters. Defendant rejected the remaining 15 tons. This Court was not persuaded by the argument that the defendant had received notice of shipment by other means and thus suffered no harm. "Even if that be true," we stated, "the fact remains that the plaintiff was obligated under its contract to see that defendant obtained advice of shipment by cable" (id., at 121, 163 N.E. 123). Plaintiff's failure to "perform[ ] all conditions precedent required of it," and "to give notice according to the terms of the contract" barred it from recovery (id., at 122, 163 N.E. 123).

Plaintiff's reliance on the well-known case of Jacob & Youngs v. Kent, 230 N.Y. 239, 129 N.E. 889, is misplaced. There, a contractor built a summer residence and the buyer refused to pay the remaining balance of the contract price on the ground that the contractor used a different type of pipe than was specified in the contract. The buyer sought to enforce the contract as written. This would have involved the demolition of large parts of the structure at great expense and loss to the seller. This Court, in an opinion by then-Judge Cardozo, ruled for the contractor on the ground that "an omission, both trivial and innocent, will sometimes be atoned for by allowance of the resulting damage, and will not always be the breach of a condition to be followed by a forfeiture" (230 N.Y., at 241, 129 N.E. 889). But Judge Cardozo was careful to note that the situation would be different in the case of an express condition: "This is not to say that the parties are not free by apt and certain words to effectuate a purpose that performance of every term shall be a condition of recovery. That question is not here. This is merely to say that the law will be slow to impute the purpose, in the silence of the parties, where the significance of the default is grievously out of proportion to the oppression of the forfeiture" (id., at 243-244, 129 N.E. 889).

The quoted language contradicts the Appellate Division's proposition that the substantial performance doctrine applies universally, including when the language of the agreement leaves no doubt that an express condition precedent was intended (see, 205 A.D.2d, at 414, 613 N.Y.S.2d 622). More importantly, Jacob & Youngs lacks determinative significance here on the additional ground that plaintiff conferred no benefit upon defendant. The avoidance-of-forfeiture rationale which engendered the rule of Jacob & Youngs is simply not present here, and the case therefore "should not be extended by analogy where the reason for the rule fails" (Van Iderstine Co. v. Barnet Leather Co., 242 N.Y. 425, 434, 152 N.E. 250).

The lease renewal and insurance cases relied upon by plaintiff are clearly distinguishable and explicable on the basis of the risk of forfeiture existing therein. For example, in Sy Jack Realty Co. v. Pergament Syosset Corp., 27 N.Y.2d 449, 452, 318 N.Y.S.2d 720, 267 N.E.2d 462, this Court gave effect to a late notice of lease renewal. Importantly, while we reaffirmed the general rule "that notice, when required to be 'given' by a certain date, is insufficient and ineffectual if not received within the time specified," we held that the prior courts properly invoked the rule that equity "relieves against * * * forfeitures of valuable lease terms when default in notice has not prejudiced the landlord" (id., quoting Jones v. Gianferante, 305 N.Y. 135, 138, 111 N.E.2d 419; see also J.N.A. Realty Corp. v. Cross Bay Chelsea, 42 N.Y.2d 392, 397, 397 N.Y.S.2d 958, 366 N.E.2d 1313 ["when a tenant in possession under an existing lease has neglected to…renew, he might suffer a forfeiture if he has made valuable improvements on the property"]). We stated: "Since a long-standing location for a retail business is an important part of the good will of that enterprise, the tenant stands to lose a substantial and valuable asset" (id., 27 N.Y.2d, at 453, 318 N.Y.S.2d 720, 267 N.E.2d 462).

III.

In sum, the letter agreement provides in the clearest language that the parties did not intend to form a contract "unless and until" defendant received written notice of the prime landlord's consent on or before February 25, 1987. Defendant would lease the 33rd floor from plaintiff only on the condition that the landlord consent in writing to a telephone communication linkage system between the 29th and 33rd floors and to defendant's plans for construction effectuating that linkage. This matter was sufficiently important to defendant that it would not enter into the sublease "unless and until" the condition was satisfied. Inasmuch as we are not dealing here with a situation where plaintiff stands to suffer some forfeiture or undue hardship, we perceive no justification for engaging in a "materiality-of-the-nonoccurrence" analysis. To do so would simply frustrate the clearly expressed intention of the parties. Freedom of contract prevails in an arm's length transaction between sophisticated parties such as these, and in the absence of countervailing public policy concerns there is no reason to relieve them of the consequences of their bargain. If they are dissatisfied with the consequences of their agreement, "the time to say so [was] at the bargaining table" (Maxton, supra, at 382, 509 N.Y.S.2d 507, 502 N.E.2d 184).

Finally, the issue of substantial performance was not for the jury to resolve in this case. A determination whether there has been substantial performance is to be answered, "if the inferences are certain, by the judges of the law" (Jacob & Youngs v. Kent, 230 N.Y. 239, 243, 129 N.E. 889 supra).

Accordingly, the order of the Appellate Division should be reversed, with costs, and the complaint dismissed.

Order reversed, etc

Questions

1. In part three of the case the court refers to "arm's length transaction between sophisticated parties." When you read the materials in Part V consider the possible difference in result if these parties had not been sophisticated.

2. Review briefly the materials in Part III D (Standardized Contracts). What if such a clause had appeared in an adhesion contract?

3. Is the question of whether there has been substantial performance a question of law or fact?

4. Why is the question of substantial performance not relevant in this case?

In *Jacob & Youngs, Inc., v. Kent, 230 N.Y. 239, 129 N.E. 889 (N.Y., 1921)* Judge Cardozo refused to enforce a specification for a particular type of pipe which was encased in the walls of a house by the time the action was brought. The contractor was suing the owner for the last payment due on the construction of a house and the owner was resisting because of the wrong pipe being used. The majority of the court found that the pipe used was equivalent to that specified in the contract. Among other things he said:

"Substitution of equivalents may not have the same significance in fields of art on the one side and in those of mere utility on the other. Nowhere will change be tolerated, however, if it is so dominant or pervasive as in any real or substantial measure to frustrate the purpose of the contract. There is no general license to install whatever, in the builder's judgment, may be regarded as 'just as good.'. The question is one of degree, to be answered, if there is doubt, by the triers of the facts and, if the inferences are certain, by the judges of the law. We must weigh the purpose to be served, the desire to be gratified, the excuse for deviation from the letter, the cruelty of enforced adherence. Then only can we tell whether literal fulfillment is to be implied by law as a condition. This is not to say that the parties are not free by apt and certain words to effectuate a purpose that performance of every term shall be a condition of recovery. That question is not here. This is merely to say that the law will be slow to impute the purpose, in the silence of the parties, where the significance of the default is grievously out of proportion to the oppression of the forfeiture. The willful transgressor must accept the penalty of his transgression. For him there is no occasion to mitigate the rigor of implied conditions. The transgressor whose default is unintentional and trivial may hope for mercy if he will offer atonement for his wrong."

Questions

1. Is Judge Cardozo offering theological or legal advice here? Is there some blend of morality and law to which Holmes in his *Path of the Law* might object? Are we being "snowed" by a blizzard of fine words?

2. Is there "cruelty," to use his phrase, in saying that parties are free to effectuate a purpose that every term shall be a condition, especially where the writing does not always reflect the intent but is presumed to, almost conclusively presumed to? Has the law outgrown this position? Is the Court of Appeals in *Oppenheimer*, a 1995 case, behind the times in enforcing forfeitures just because words express them?

3. What possible policy reason exists for enforcing forfeitures in 1995? The purpose of law is to make people whole, to provide damages to compensate or specific performance to give the innocent party the bargain she made. Is not Oppenheimer a "punishment case?"

4. *Jacob & Youngs* was a 4–3 decision. Here is a sample of Judge McLaughlin's dissent:

   "I am of the opinion the trial court was right in directing a verdict for the defendant. The plaintiff agreed that all the pipe used should be of the Reading Manufacturing Company. Only about two-fifths of it, so far as appears, was of that kind. If more were used, then the burden of proving that fact was upon the plaintiff, which it could easily have done, since it knew where the pipe was obtained. The question of substantial performance of a contract of the character of the one under consideration depends in no small degree upon the good faith of the contractor. If the plaintiff had intended to, and had, complied with the terms of the contract except as to minor omissions, due to inadvertence, then he might be allowed to recover the contract price, less the amount necessary to fully compensate the defendant for damages caused by such omissions. Woodward v. Fuller, 80 N. Y. 312; Nolan v. Whitney, 88 N. Y. 648. But that is not this case. It installed between 2,000 and 2,500 feet of pipe, of which only 1,000 feet at most complied with the contract. No explanation was given why pipe called for by the contract was not used, nor that any effort made to show what it would cost to remove the pipe of other manufacturers and install that of the Reading Manufacturing Company. The defendant had a right to contract for what he wanted. He had a right before making payment to get what the contract called for."

   Now, with whom do you agree?

In *ADC-I Ltd. v. Pan American Fuels, 525 N.W.2d 190 (Neb., 1994)* ADC, a limited partnership, had solicited bids because it was required to sell some of its property by the Federal Savings and Loan Invest Corp., the conservator of ADC's general partner a savings and loan association. [The case apparently grew out of the savings and loan scandals in the 1980 when many banks were forced to sell assets because of their unsatisfactory financial structure.] [A limited partnership is usually made up of a group of investors who have little or no say in the operation of the partnership and who have limited liability should it fail—usually not more than their investment. The general partner in such a limited partnership has full liability and also the power and responsibility for operating the partnership. The limited partners are investors seeking profit not management power.] In this case a bid by Pan American [PA]was accepted. PA, however, failed to live up to specified "conditions precedent" to completing the sale, including failure to post a letter of credit. ADC sued to "quiet title" to its property. PA counterclaimed for damages. The court said in part:

"Pan American contends that the district court erred in dismissing its claim for damages. This case began as an action to quiet title in ADC. A suit to quiet title is equitable in nature, and an appellate court reviews the record in such a case de novo and reaches an independent conclusion without reference to findings of the trial court. However, when credible evidence is in conflict, the appellate court may give weight to the fact that the trial court observed the witnesses and accepted one version of the facts over another.

The gravamen in this appeal is whether Pan American could bring this action for damages due to ADC's alleged breach. To successfully bring an action on a contract, a claimant first must establish that the contract has been substantially performed on the claimant's part. A contract has been substantially performed if the claimant proves all three of the following elements: (1) It made an honest endeavor in good faith to perform its part of the contract, (2) the results of its endeavor are beneficial to the other party, and (3) the other party retained those benefits. Lange Bldg. & Farm Supply, supra. If the claimant fails to establish any one of these elements, then the contract has not been substantially performed, and the claimant cannot maintain an action on the contract. Id.

In the case at bar, the evidence shows that the claimant, Pan American, failed to establish all three elements. First, Pan American failed to show that it made an honest endeavor in good faith to perform its part of the contract. The evidence is in fact to the contrary. The evidence shows that Pan American continually failed to attempt to meet its obligation under § 2.3.1 to post a $165,000 letter of credit and enforceability opinion, and when it did, Pan American first attempted to post a bogus letter of credit, drawn on itself. Subsequently, when ADC imposed a firm deadline for compliance, Pan American posted only a $27,500 letter of credit and no enforceability opinion. Only after ADC rescinded the contract did Pan American comply with § 2.3.1's requirements. This continual failure to timely satisfy the contractual requirements of § 2.3.1 for posting a letter of credit and enforceability opinion shows that Pan American did not make an honest endeavor to perform its part of the contract in good faith. Pan American therefore has failed to establish the first element.

Second, because Pan American failed to perform at all, ADC did not derive any benefit. Although ADC would have benefited if Pan American had performed, the record contains no evidence that ADC benefited because no act occurred from which ADC could possibly have benefited. Pan American therefore has also failed to establish the second element.

Third, Pan American failed to show that ADC had retained a benefit from its actions. In fact, not only did ADC not retain any benefit from the contract, ADC also lost approximately $6 million due to Pan American's nonperformance. ADC, which had contracted with Pan American to sell its ethanol manufacturing plant to Pan American for more than $16.5 million, eventually sold it for only $10 million. Pan American therefore has also failed to establish the third element.

Because Pan American failed to establish that it had substantially performed under the contract, it cannot maintain an action on that contract against ADC. The district court therefore properly dismissed Pan American's action for damages.

On appeal, Pan American assigns seven additional errors. However, because Pan American failed to substantially perform under the contract and because that issue is dispositive, we do not reach Pan American's seven other assigned errors. We affirm the district court's decision, dismissing Pan American's claim for damages.

AFFIRMED."

In *Ervin Constr. Co. v. Van Orden, 874 P.2d 549 (Idaho Ct. App., 1992)* the court had to determine whether a contract to build a log home had been substantially performed and what measure of damages to apply. In pertinent part the court said:

"The contract expressly guaranteed the home would be built 'in a workmanlike manner.' The Van Ordens moved into the home in the fall of 1986, where they resided at the time of trial. the court found that some of Ervin's work was defective and substandard. Accordingly, the court held that Ervin had breached its express and implied duties under the contract, in that certain parts of the home had not been constructed in a workmanlike manner. The court further held, however, that Ervin's breach was not substantial, and hence, the Van Ordens' refusal to pay the monthly billings for March and April was unjustified and constituted a breach of the contract.

The law of contracts recognizes that a material failure of performance, including defective performance as well as an absence of performance, operates as the nonoccurrence of a condition. See RESTATEMENT (SECOND) OF CONTRACTS § 237 (1981). A party's material failure of performance has the effect of preventing the other's duty from becoming due, at least temporarily, and of discharging that duty when the condition can no longer occur. RESTATEMENT, supra, § 237 comment a. The following Restatement comment and illustration are consistent with Idaho law and pertinent to our resolution of the issue at hand:

d. Substantial Performance. In an important category of disputes over failure of performance, one party asserts the right to payment on the ground that he has completed his performance, while the other party refuses to pay on the ground that there has been an uncured material failure of performance. A typical example is that of the building contractor who claims from the owner payment of the unpaid balance under a construction contract. In such cases it is common to state the issue, not in terms of whether there has been an uncured material failure by the contractor, but in terms of whether there has been substantial performance by him.... If there has been substantial although not full performance, the building contractor has a claim for the unpaid balance and the owner has a claim only for damages. If there has not been substantial performance, the building contractor has no claim for the unpaid balance, although he may have a claim in restitution. Illustration 11. A contracts to build a house for B, for which B promises to pay $50,000 in monthly progress payments equal to 85% of the value of the work with the balance to be paid on completion. When A completes construction, B refuses to pay the $7,500 balance claiming that there are defects that amount to an uncured material breach. If the breach is material, A's performance is not substantial and he has no claim under the contract against B, although he may have a claim in restitution. If the breach is not material, A's performance is said to be substantial, he has a claim under the contract against B for $7,500, and B has a claim against A for damages because of defects. RESTATEMENT, supra, § 237, at 220-21.

The pivotal question here is whether Ervin substantially performed under the contract. 'Substantial performance' is performance which, despite deviation or omission, provides the important and essential benefits of the contract to the promisee. Gilbert v. City of Caldwell, 112 Idaho 386, 394, 732 P.2d 355, 363 (Ct.App.1987). Whether a contractor's performance is substantial, and the defects minor or insubstantial, is a question of degree involving a factual determination. This determination turns upon circumstances such as the particular structure involved, its intended purposes, and the nature and relative expense of the repairs, as well as equitable considerations. In the instant case, the court recognized that while the rustic nature of a log home permits some gaps, cracks, warping and rough finish, some of the construction imperfections present in the Van Ordens' home were excessive. However, the court found that Ervin's breach of its express and implied warranties to build the home in a workmanlike manner was 'not substantial,' that is, not material.

We next consider whether the court applied an appropriate measure of damages. Where, as here, a breach results in defective construction, the injured party may recover damages based on either (1) the diminution in the market price of the property caused by the breach, or (2) the reasonable cost of remedying the defects, if that cost is not clearly disproportionate to the probable loss in value to him. RESTATEMENT, supra, § 348. The 'diminution in the market price' is measured as the difference between the market price that the property would have had without the defects and the market price of the property with the defects. RESTATEMENT, supra, § 348 comment c. The injured party must prove the diminution in value *caused by the other's* breach with reasonable certainty, or damages are not recoverable.

As explained above, Ervin's substantial performance under the contract entitled it to recover the unpaid balance for the work completed, *less any damages caused by its defective performance.*"

Ujdur v. Thompson, 878 P.2d 180 (Idaho Ct. App., 1994)

"This appeal involves the performance of a written agreement entered to settle disputed rights between joint purchasers of real property. The agreement essentially provided for one purchaser to buy out the interest of the other within a specific period of time. The question presented for our review is whether the timely tender of an insufficient payment amount, followed by an untimely tender of the full payment amount, constituted substantial performance under the agreement. Because we conclude that it did not, we affirm the decision of the district court.

Thompson argues that his tender on July 8 of nearly ninety-percent of the required payment constituted substantial performance under the agreement, and that Ujdur was therefore required to accept the payment and deliver the quitclaim deed. We disagree.

'Substantial performance' is performance which, despite deviation or omission, provides the important and essential benefits of the contract. Substantial performance is the antithesis of material breach. Thus, there can be no 'substantial performance' where the part unperformed touches the fundamental purpose of the contract and defeats the object of the parties entering into the contract. See Ervin Construction Co. v. Van Orden, 125 Idaho 695, 699, 874 P.2d 506, 510 (1993). Although the doctrine of substantial performance most often applies to construction contracts, it is not necessarily limited to that context and may apply to any contract. 3A CORBIN ON CONTRACTS § 701 (1960) (Supp.1992); see Weed v. Idaho Copper Co., 51 Idaho 737, 10 P.2d 613 (1932) (doctrine applied to contract for purely personal services). Whether a particular tender of performance is 'substantial' will depend on the facts of the case. However, it has long been recognized that where the line is to be drawn between the important and the trivial cannot be settled by a formula. In the nature of the case, precise boundaries are impossible. The same omission may take on one aspect or another according to its setting.... The question is one of degree, to be answered, if there is doubt, by the triers of fact, and, if the inferences are certain, by the judges of the law. Jacob & Youngs v. Kent, 230 N.Y. 239, 129 N.E. 889, 891 (1921) (Cardozo, J.).

Returning to the facts of the case at hand, we note again that Thompson's offer of payment on July 8, 1992, was $5,719.79 less than the amount required by the settlement agreement. This deficiency in performance, although innocent, was not minor. There can be no question that full payment was a fundamental condition of Ujdur's duty to quitclaim his interest to Thompson and dismiss the underlying lawsuit against him. Payment of less than the agreed amount was a defect going to the very heart of the parties' agreement. Consequently, Ujdur was under no obligation to accept the tendered performance or to deliver his quitclaim deed to Thompson. To the contrary, because he had not paid Ujdur within the time permitted, Thompson was required under paragraph 4 of the agreement to deliver his quitclaim deed to Ujdur.

In *R.J. Berke & Co., Inc., v. J.P. Griffin, Inc., 367 A.2d 583 (N.H., 1976)* a subcontractor sued a general contractor in quantum meruit. Both parties had substantially breached the contract and had no actions under it. The contractor maintained that Berke also had no action in quantum meruit.

"Griffin's argument in contesting the recovery in quantum meruit is twofold. It argues that as a matter of law such recovery is not allowed (1) where substantial performance has not been rendered and (2) where the defaulting party's breach has been willful.

In support of its first contention, Griffin relies on Albre Marble & Tile Co. v. Goverman, 353 Mass. 546, 233 N.E.2d 533 (1968), wherein it was held that substantial performance of the contract was a prerequisite to quantum meruit recovery. This position apparently is attributable to the strict view which Massachusetts generally takes towards quantum meruit recovery. See 3A A. Corbin, Contracts § 707, at 330-31 (1960).

Quantum meruit is a restitutionary remedy intended for use by contracting parties who are in material breach and thus unable to sue 'on contract.' See J. Calamari & J. Perillo, Contracts § 159 (1970); 5A A. Corbin, Contracts § 1124 (1964). It follows that the defaulting party recovering in quantum meruit will generally not have rendered substantial performance. We have permitted recovery to plaintiffs who have failed to substantially perform. See Francoeur v. Stephen, 97 N.H. 80, 81 A.2d 308 (1951); Britton v. Turner, 6 N.H. 481 (1834). There is no compelling reason to adopt a contrary position in this case.

As to the defendants' second argument it is true that generally quantum meruit recovery will not be awarded where the conduct has been 'wilful.' Corbin notes that the term is not easily defined, and that a breach is not ordinarily considered willful if there is involved an honest dispute as to contract obligation. See 5A A. Corbin, Contracts § 1123 (1964). It has been suggested that the quality of the breach bears no logical relationship to the theory of quantum meruit recovery, and that the willful defaulter should thus not be denied relief. Nordstrom & Woodland, Recovery by Building Contractor in Default, 20 Ohio St.L.J. 193, 211-14 (1959). In Britton v. Turner, Supra at 492, the court emphasized the principle that 'where the party receives value-takes and uses the materials, or has advantage from the labor, he is liable to pay the reasonable worth of what he has received.'

We have spoken with approval of recovery for the plaintiff who 'by his voluntary failure to fully perform the work he agreed to do' has conferred a net benefit on the defendant. Anderson v. Shattuck, 76 N.H. 240, 242-43, 81 A. 781, 782 (1911) (emphasis added). And in Stanley v. Kinball, 80 N.H. 431, 436, 118 A. 636, 638 (1922), we held unjust enrichment 'a sufficient foundation' for permitting recovery. We have denied recovery to one whose conduct was 'willful' where the plaintiff through a fraudulent scheme had 'bamboozled' the defendant out of a substantial sum of money. Welch v. Coleman, 95 N.H. 399, 64 A.2d 691 (1949).

The finding here that the plaintiff had been 'sincere in wishing not to fail...to complete a job he had agreed to do' does not support Griffin's charge of bad faith."

E. Substantial Performance or Excuse?

Grenier v. Compratt Construction Company
189 Conn. 144, 454 A.2d 1289
Supreme Court of Connecticut, 1982

PETERS, Associate Justice.

This case concerns the effect of a provision in a construction contract that conditions payment upon a municipal official's certificate of performance. The plaintiffs, Frank Grenier, John Grenier and Eugene Grenier, brought an action against the defendant, Compratt Construction Company, to recover $25,500 which the defendant had agreed to pay for blasting work performed in the construction of certain roads. The defendants responded with an answer and a counterclaim seeking to enforce a liquidated damages clause in the contract. After a trial to the court, judgment was rendered for the plaintiffs in the amount of $23,000 together with interest and costs. The defendant has appealed.

The trial court's memorandum of decision establishes the following facts, which are not contested on this appeal. After disputes had arisen concerning performance under a subdivision contract negotiated on May 26, 1977, the parties entered into a settlement agreement on May 23, 1978. That settlement agreement, which is the subject matter of this lawsuit, entitled the plaintiffs to $25,500 upon the completion of certain subdivision roads by June 30, 1978. The agreement defined "completion" of the roads as "any ... work necessary, so far as the subdivision roads are concerned, so that a certificate of occupancy can be obtained on any lot in the subdivision as of 5:00 p.m. on June 30, 1978, and the providing to Compratt of a letter signed by the City Engineer of the City of Danbury, certifying that a certificate of occupancy can be obtained on any lot owned by Compratt Construction Company in the subdivision." Although the roads were in fact satisfactorily completed, the plaintiffs were unable to provide the stipulated letter from the city engineer because the city engineer did not ordinarily write such letters. Instead, the assistant city attorney, by letter of July 10, 1978, authorized the building inspector to issue certificates of occupancy for the roads in question. Appropriate certificates of occupancy were thereafter issuable and issued.

The contract of May 23, 1978, contained a liquidated damages clause. That clause provided for cumulative weekly penalties to be paid by the plaintiffs to the defendant for failure to complete the roads by 5:00 p.m. on June 30, 1978. The designated amounts were: $1500 at the end of the first week (July 7); an additional $2000 at the end of the second week (July 14); an additional $2500 at the end of the third week (July 21); and an additional $3000 (or daily per diem portion) for each additional week or part thereof. The defendant conceded that accrual of these damages would terminate upon the sworn testimony of the city engineer on September 7, 1978 that the roads in question were approved for the issuance of certificates of occupancy. The amount so cumulated is, according to the defendant's calculations, $26,571.42.

The trial court concluded, on these facts, that the plaintiffs had failed to complete the roads in question on June 30, 1978, but found that the city attorney's letter of July 10, 1978, constituted compliance with the contract as of that date. Although the court recognized that the parties had seriously bargained for a letter from the city engineer, the court held that the parties' major concern was not the letter itself but what it represented, to wit, whether the roads were acceptable so that certificates of occupancy could be issued. On this basis, the city attorney's letter constituted adequate compliance with the terms of the contract. Because of the delay between the contract's date of performance, June 30, and the city attorney's letter, July 10, the court found that the defendant had been damaged to some extent, and that such damages were difficult to ascertain. Although the court found the contract's liquidated damages clause as a whole to be invalid as a penalty clause violative of public policy, the court nonetheless awarded the defendant liquidated damages for a delay of one and one-half weeks in accordance with the contractual liquidated damages clause. Accordingly, the court rendered judgment for the plaintiffs in the amount of $25,500 minus $2500, or $23,000 with interest from July 10, 1978. Only the defendant has appealed.

The defendant has essentially pursued three claims of error. It argues that the trial court erred: (1) in applying a substantial performance test to the settlement agreement; (2) in concluding that the settlement agreement had been substantially performed; (3) in failing to enforce fully the settlement agreement's provision for liquidated damages. Since the first two claims both arise out of the contractual provision requiring a letter from the city engineer, we will consider these claims jointly before we turn to the legality of the liquidated damages clause. With respect to all of the defendant's claims, we find no error.

The defendant's principal claim of error is that the trial court failed to give full effect to the provision in the settlement agreement that made the defendant's obligation to pay conditional upon a letter from the city engineer certifying that the defendant could obtain needed certificates of occupancy for its property. Drawing upon cases involving architects' or engineers' certificates, the defendant argues that the city engineer's failure to give a written certification precludes recovery by the plaintiffs. The defendant claims that the court erroneously applied a substantial performance test to the defendant's conditional contract obligation. We disagree with the defendant's analysis of the relevant cases and of the trial court's memorandum of decision.

It is of course well established that contracting parties are free to impose conditions upon contractual liability. Frequently, building contracts provide that a third party, an architect or an engineer, acting in good faith and in the exercise of his best judgment, shall decide when one of the contracting parties has fulfilled the requirements of the contract. In such circumstances, if the architect or engineer withholds certification, and his decision is not arbitrary or made in bad faith, a court is not authorized to substitute its judgment for that of the designated expert.

The regular enforcement of conditions is, however, subject to the competing but equally well established principle that the occurrence of a condition may be excused in the event of impracticability "if the occurrence of the condition is not a material part of the agreed exchange and forfeiture would otherwise result." 2 Restatement (Second), Contracts § 271; 6 Corbin, Contracts § 1362 (1962); 5 Williston, Contracts (3d Ed.1961) § 793. Excuse of the condition, in such circumstances, is based upon the presumption that insistence on an impracticable condition was not in the contemplation of the parties when they entered into their contract. 6 Corbin, supra, 499; 5 Williston, supra, 783. A prime example of an excused condition, in the context of building contracts, arises upon the death or insanity of the architect or engineer who was to have certified performance. If the work has been properly done, presentation of the unavailable architect's or engineer's certificate is excused. See Hebert v. Dewey, 191 Mass. 403, 410- 11, 77 N.E. 822 (1906); 6 Corbin, supra, 503-504; 5 Williston, supra, § 796. Although this court has not had the occasion to adjudicate a case involving an engineer's death or insanity, we have recognized that enforcement of a condition depends upon a finding of the intent of the parties as evidenced by their agreement; and that an agreement for personal services is normally subject to the condition that the person who is to render the services must be able to perform at the appointed time. Wasserman Theatrical Enterprise, Inc. v. Harris, 137 Conn. 371, 374, 77 A.2d 329 (1950). These cases indicate that Connecticut law is consistent with the statement of the law in § 271 of the Restatement.

The facts of the present case fall somewhere between the usual deference to express conditions and the usual inference of excuse for impracticability. The contracting parties have stipulated for the certification of performance by a city engineer who was not obligated, either by contract or by his employment, to furnish such certification. In contradistinction to the ordinary case where a certificate has not been produced, the engineer has not exercised any judgment that the plaintiffs' performance was wanting. Although physically able to produce the desired certification, he has refused to do so. Given these facts, the trial court was warranted in inquiring whether the failure to produce the engineer's certificate was a material part of the agreed exchange in the contract. The court found that it was not, because the defendant's major concern was not the letter itself but what it represented, "to wit, whether the road was acceptable so that a certificate of occupancy could be issued." In making this finding, the trial court did not, as the defendant alleges, apply a substantial performance test. Instead, the court correctly found that the parties' inability to procure the city engineer's certification entirely excused the plaintiffs from their duty to produce it. This case is therefore similar to Clover Mfg. Co. v. Austin Co., supra, 101 Conn. 214, 125 A. 646, where we held that "[t]he parties bargain for some reasonable degree of expert knowledge of the facts and the contract, and an engineer who fails to give the parties what they bargained for...may justly be said to have acted in 'bad faith' as regards the performance of his contractual obligations." If an engineer's certificate is excused where, by his actions, he fails to give the parties "what they bargained for," it must be equally excused where the engineer refuses entirely to exercise any written judgment at all.

The court also found that, except for the delay between June 30 and July 10, the plaintiffs had fully performed the material part of the bargained-for exchange, because the roads were then sufficiently completed so that the city engineer in fact gave his approval and the defendant thereafter was able to obtain its certificates of occupancy. Although the defendant complains about the quality of the plaintiffs' roadwork, it has not challenged this specific factual finding. It is clear that enforcement of the condition would forfeit the plaintiffs' right to the payment which the trial court found it had earned. This case therefore falls within the principles of § 271 of the Restatement. The plaintiffs may recover, not because there has been substantial performance of the contract, but because there has been full performance, the limiting condition having been excused.

The trial court dealt separately with the effect of the delay between the stipulated date of performance, June 30, and the actual date of the letter of the city attorney, July 10. As to this delay, the court awarded the defendant an offset, finding the delay not so substantial as to warrant a finding of breach of the contract as a whole. The fact that a contract states a date for performance does not necessarily make time of the essence. Kakalik v. Bernardo, 184 Conn. (42 CLJ 50, pp. 4, 5-6) 439 A.2d 1016 (1981). See Ravitch v. Stollman Poultry Farms, Inc., 165 Conn. 135, 148, 328 A.2d 711 (1973). The defendant has made no factual showing of how it was injured by the ten-day delay and relies on its liquidated damages clause to defeat the plaintiffs' recovery. Whatever the validity of the liquidated damages clause, however, that clause cannot in and of itself convert a minor delay into so substantial a breach of contract as totally to foreclose the plaintiffs' recovery. The trial court was not in error in affirming the plaintiffs' ability to recover some sum on the contract despite their delay.

The only issue which remains to be addressed is the validity of the liquidated damages clause and the extent of the offset to which the defendant was entitled because of the plaintiffs' partial breach. We agree with the defendant that a contractual provision for liquidated damages is not illegal simply because the clause uses language of "penal" or "penalty." Berger v. Shanahan, 142 Conn. 726, 731-32, 118 A.2d 311 (1955); 5 Williston, Contracts § 778, pp. 694-95. Nor is such a clause necessarily violative of public policy simply because the amount of damages escalates with the period of delay. To the extent that the trial court ruled to the contrary, it was mistaken. The defendant was not, however, injured by the trial court's mistaken disapproval of the liquidated damages clause, because the trial court awarded the defendant an offset that adopted the formula provided by the liquidated damages clauses. The trial court found that the plaintiffs' performance was delayed for ten days and awarded one and one-half weeks of damages according to the contract's provision for the first two weeks' delay. Having found full performance by July 10, the court could not appropriately have awarded greater damages under the liquidated damages clause even had it found that clause fully enforceable.

There is no error.

In this opinion the other Judges concurred.

F. Excuse and Estoppel

Royal-Globe Insurance Company v. Craven

411 Mass. 629, 585 N.E.2d 315
Supreme Judicial Court of Massachusetts, 1991.

ABRAMS, Justice.

At issue is the liability under an uninsured motorist policy of Royal- Globe Insurance Company (Royal-Globe) to its insured, Theresa M. Craven (Craven), for personal injuries suffered by Craven in a hit and run accident. Royal-Globe sought a declaratory judgment that it was not liable to Craven because Craven's notice to Royal-Globe was not timely. Further, Royal-Globe asked for a declaration that the applicable statute of limitations was three years pursuant to G.L. c. 260, § 2A (1990 ed.), and hence the complaint, which was filed more than three years after the accident, was barred by the statute of limitations. On cross-motions for summary judgment, the Superior Court judge entered a summary judgment for Craven, denied Royal-Globe's motion for summary judgment, and ordered that the matter proceed to arbitration. Royal-Globe appealed. We transferred the appeal to this court on our own motion. We reverse and order that a judgment be entered declaring that Royal-Globe is not liable to Craven because Craven's notice to Royal-Globe was not timely.

The facts are as follows. In the early morning of September 19, 1979, Craven was injured in a hit and run automobile accident. According to Craven, an unidentified motor vehicle forced her automobile off the road and into a wall barrier. Craven was taken by ambulance to a hospital, where she was treated for a number of serious injuries. She remained in intensive care for several days and was released from the hospital twenty-three days after the accident.

Craven gave Royal-Globe formal notice of her claim on January 23, 1980. Royal-Globe denied her claim for recovery under her uninsured motorist policy on April 6, 1981. On December 12, 1984, Craven filed a demand for arbitration of her uninsured motorist claim. On March 11, 1985, Royal-Globe filed a complaint in Superior Court seeking a declaration that it had no obligation to submit to arbitration as it was not liable under the policy.

1. Timely notice. Royal-Globe asks us to reverse the summary judgment for Craven on the ground that Craven did not comply with her contractual obligation to give timely notice of her claim.[1] Craven asserts that whether her notice to Royal-Globe was sufficiently prompt in the circumstances is a question of fact. Craven further maintains that therefore this court may only reverse if the allowance of summary judgment constitutes an abuse of discretion or clearly is erroneous.

"The standard of review of a grant of summary judgment is whether, viewing the evidence in the light most favorable to the nonmoving party, all material facts have been established and the moving party is entitled to a judgment as a matter of law." What constitutes timely notice under the insurance policy is a matter of contract interpretation and is therefore "a matter of law for the court." The judge correctly determined that, in these circumstances, the policy required prompt notice. Because the facts here are undisputed, whether Craven's notice was prompt also is a question of law. Powell v. Fireman's Fund Ins. Co., 26 Mass.App.Ct. 508, 513, 529 N.E.2d 1228 (1988), quoting Segal v. Aetna Casualty & Sur. Co., 337 Mass. 185, 188, 148 N.E.2d 659 (1958) ("What is a reasonable time is a question of fact, but where the basic facts are undisputed it becomes a question of law"). We turn to the language of the policy.

The uninsured motorist policy in effect at the time of the accident requires notice to both the police and the insurer "[w]ithin [twenty- four] hours ... if [the insured has] ... been involved in a hit and run accident." The judge concluded, however, that Craven "was in the intensive care unit during the first twenty-four hours [after the accident]" and could not be expected to notify the police and her insurance company within twenty- four hours. The judge ruled that Craven therefore was excused from the twenty- four hour notice requirement.

Royal-Globe maintains that the judge's ruling on excuse was error because someone hired an attorney to represent Craven the morning of the accident. If Craven or someone acting on her behalf was able within twenty-four hours to engage a lawyer to represent her, Royal-Globe argues, it was error for the judge to conclude that Craven was excused from the twenty-four hour notice requirement. It is undisputed that Craven remained in intensive care for several days after the accident. The judge determined that to expect Craven to give notice

---

1. [The standard Massachusetts automobile insurance policy requires that the insured notify both the police and the insurance company within twenty-four hours if the insured has "been involved in a hit and run accident." The policy further requires that, in all events, the insurance company "must be notified promptly of the accident or loss."]

while she was in intensive care would be "unreasonable." There was no error in that determination.

Royal-Globe next maintains that even if twenty-four hour notice was excused because of disability, the requirement should be reimposed once the disability is removed. Under this interpretation of the policy, disability tolls the running of the twenty-four hour period but does not dispense with it. The judge concluded that in the event that twenty-four hour notice is excused initially by disability, as was the case here, the policy requires prompt notice but not necessarily twenty-four hour notice. We agree. The language of the policy puts a time pressure on the insured to notify the company immediately after the disability is removed.

Royal-Globe contends that based on the undisputed facts in this record, Craven's notification, given more than four months after the accident and more than three months after her release from the hospital, was not prompt. We agree. Royal-Globe argues, and Craven does not dispute, that Craven was released from the hospital twenty-three days after the accident and that she stopped using medication one week after leaving the hospital. While at home, Craven was able to leave her home to visit doctors and dine out with her family. While she was at home, Craven also communicated with her office. Craven returned to work roughly three months after the accident; she did not give notice to Royal-Globe for another month. On this record, we cannot tell precisely when Craven's disability was removed, but it is clear that she did not notify Royal-Globe immediately thereafter.[2]

The burden of proving that she gave her notice promptly was on Craven. Regardless of when her disability is determined to have disappeared, Craven's notice to Royal-Globe was not "performed readily or immediately[; nor was it] given without delay or hesitation." Webster's Third New Int'l Dictionary 1816 (1961). Giving "prompt" its fair meaning, Craven did not notify Royal-Globe promptly as a matter of law. [3]

---

2. The judge reasoned that, where there is an ambiguous provision in an insurance policy, the court must construe it strictly against the insurer. There was, however, no ambiguity in the policy's use of the term "promptly." In any event, the rule of strict construction against the insurer would not apply to this case. This is "because the policy language is controlled by the Commissioner of Insurance and not the insurer." Moore v. Metropolitan Property & Liab. Ins. Co., 401 Mass. 1010, 1011, 519 N.E.2d 265 (1988), citing Bilodeau v. Lumbermens Mut. Casualty Co., 392 Mass. 537, 541, 467 N.E.2d 137 (1984). See Cardin v. Royal Ins. Co., 394 Mass. 450, 453, 476 N.E.2d 200 (1985). See also Manning v. Fireman's Fund Am. Ins. Cos., 397 Mass. 38, 40, 489 N.E.2d 700 (1986).

3. We have said, albeit in dicta, that an insured "did not act with reasonable promptness" when it waited forty-six days after learning of a claim before notifying its insurer. Depot Cafe, Inc. v. Century Indem. Co., 321 Mass. 220, 225, 72 N.E.2d 533 (1947). Similarly, an injured plaintiff who did not notify his insurer of his claim on the policy for two months and six days did not act "with reasonable promptness" and thereby violated the policy's requirement of immediate notice. Wainer v. Weiner, 288 Mass. 250, 252, 192 N.E. 497 (1934). In construing analogous notice provisions, we have held that similar, and even shorter, delays in notifying insurers barred recovery. Cf., e.g., Brackman v. American Employers' Ins. Co., 349 Mass. 767, 208 N.E.2d 225 (1965) (forty days not "as soon as practicable"); Segal v. Aetna Casualty & Sur. Co., supra at 188-189, 148 N.E.2d 659 (four months and four days [approximately same as present case] not "as soon as practicable"); Phillips v. Stone, 297 Mass. 341, 342, 8 N.E.2d 890 (1937) (judge's determination that no-

Craven contends that Royal-Globe is estopped from raising her failure of notice as a basis to deny liability. Craven maintains that from the time she notified Royal-Globe of her claim, the company investigated the claim, communicated with her counsel about the status of the claim, and even informed her counsel of the possibility that liability might be denied because of a failure of proof—all without ever reserving the right to deny the claim based on late notice. The absence of such a reservation of rights, Craven argues, estops the company from denying liability because of her late notice. [4]

"In order to work an estoppel it must appear that one has been induced by the conduct of another to do something different from what otherwise would have been done and which has resulted to his harm...." DiMarzo v. American Mut. Ins. Co., 389 Mass. 85, 112, 449 N.E.2d 1189 (1983), quoting Lunt v. Aetna Life Ins. Co., 261 Mass. 469, 471, 159 N.E. 461 (1928). As we have previously noted, "where the denial of liability takes place after the expiration of the period for...[giving prompt notice], it cannot be said that the insured has been induced to forego steps to prevent a default under the policy, for the default has already occurred. Consequently, there is no basis for an estoppel." Milton Ice Co., Inc. v. Travelers Indem. Co., 320 Mass. 719N8], 722, 71 N.E.2d 232 (1947), citing Salonen v. Paananen, 320 Mass. 568, 573, 71 N.E.2d 227 (1947). See Powell v. Fireman's Fund Ins. Co., supra at 512, 529 N.E.2d 1228.

Moreover, "[t]he mere statement of one ground for denying liability without explanatory words or circumstances does not warrant the inference of an intention to relinquish other defences." Sheehan v. Commercial Travelers' Mut. Accident Ass'n., 283 Mass. 543, 552, 186 N.E. 627 (1933). See New England Structures, Inc. v. Loranger, 354 Mass. 62, 66, 234 N.E.2d 888 (1968) ("While of course one cannot fail in good faith in presenting his reasons as to his conduct touching a controversy, he is not prevented from relying upon one good defence among others urged simply because he has not always put it forward, when it does not appear that he has acted dishonestly or that the other party has been misled to his harm, or that he is estopped on any other ground," quoting Bates v. Cashman, 230 Mass. 167, 168-169, 119 N.E. 663 [1918]).

Because Craven's notice was not prompt, and because Royal-Globe was not estopped from defending against liability on the basis of Craven's late notice, a judgment declaring that Royal-Glove is not liable to Craven because the notice was not timely should be entered.

---

tice given twenty days after accident not "as soon as practicable" was "warranted, if not required [as matter of law]"). The Appeals Court has similarly held. Cf., e.g., Morse v. Employers Liab. Assurance Corp., Ltd., 3 Mass.App.Ct. 712, 323 N.E.2d 769 (1975) (three months and two weeks not "as soon as practicable"); Powell v. Fireman's Fund Ins. Co., supra at 509, 529 N.E.2d 1228 (more than four months not "as soon as practicable").

4. Craven also argues that Royal-Globe's payment of her personal injury protection, medical benefits, and collision benefits claims is inconsistent with its denial of benefits under the uninsured motorist policy. Royal- Globe replies, however, that these benefits are recoverable in a one-car accident. Timely notice of these claims is thus not as crucial to the insurance company. Generally in a one-car accident, fault is not an issue. Craven's argument would require litigation as to claims in which there is no controversy, if there are some claims in dispute. We decline to adopt such a rule.

In *Gilbert v. Globe & Rutgers Fire Ins. Co of the State of New York, 174 P. 1161 (Ore., 1918)* a plaintiff unsuccessfully used an estoppel theory to avoid a twelve month limitation period for bringing suit against defendant in a fire insurance policy. Plaintiff insisted that defendant company's agent made representations that the policy sum for a fire loss would be paid. The twelve months passed. No action was filed. The court was sympathetic to plaintiff but said, in part, "The testimony shows that the plaintiff read over and knew the terms and conditions of the policy at the time of its receipt and it expressly provides that any action must be brought within 12 months next after the fire. The fire occurred on October 2, 1912. This action was commenced on June 29, 1916. The authorities are uniform in holding that a time limitation in which such an action shall be brought is valid, if the time is reasonable, and that a 12 months' limitation is reasonable."

The court then noted that about a year after the fire the company made clear that it would contest his claim. The court said: "Assuming that the defendant was estopped to plead the time limitation, the estoppel was removed when the plaintiff was notified that the defendant denied liability and would contest his claim, and upon receipt of such notice the plaintiff then had a reasonable time within which to commence his action. The action was commenced on June 29, 1916, and under the facts disclosed by the record we hold as a matter of law that it was not commenced within a reasonable time after the defendant notified the plaintiff that it would contest his claim and deny liability, and for such reason the court should have directed the jury to return a verdict for the defendant." The court laid little stress on plaintiff's further statements that after the year had expired "the adjuster told him that he did not have any right to bring action, that he had lost his right if he ever had one." Is this the real heart of plaintiff's complaint? Not just that defendant made a statement on which plaintiff relied, but that plaintiff believed defendant and so did not try to bring suit? What would a judge likely tell plaintiff if he said, "hey, my friend the adjuster, who misled me, told me I didn't have a right to sue"?

G. Waiver and Forfeiture

In *Porter v. Harrington, 159 N.E. 530 (Mass., 1928)* plaintiff made payments on a contract to purchase land. The contract said in part that prompt performance was of the essence of the contract and that if plaintiff failed to perform "at the option of [defendants (sellers)] all...interest of [plaintiff] shall...cease... without any notice to [plaintiff] and all moneys paid...shall be...the absolute property of the [defendants.]" Plaintiff was routinely late making payments. Without making any objection or giving plaintiff any notice defendants exercised the option. The court said in part:

"Parties have a right to make a stated time for performance the essence of a contract. Such an agreement, when not waived either by words or conduct, is binding and will be given effect by courts of equity as well as of law. The contract in the case at bar was of that nature.

No principle of law or equity prevents the waiver by parties of such terms of a contract, however explicit may be its phraseology. Waiver may be manifested by acts as well as by words. The defendants, by a course of conduct covering nearly if not quite three years, accepted from the plaintiff payments long overdue. As a consequence, they have taken from him more than one fourth of the entire amount due under the contract. In addition, he has paid some of the taxes on the land, which accrued to the benefit of the defendants. All this the defendants claim as a forfeiture or, to use the words of the contract, as 'liquidated damages.' There is no finding that the failure of the plaintiff promptly to make payments was intentional or willful or in any way offensive, or that it has caused any loss to the defendants for which full compensation cannot be made by payment of interest. There are no facts in the case at bar on which the principle of Finkovitch v. Cline, 236 Mass. 196, 128 N. E. 12, can be applied, to the effect that the conduct of the party seeking relief in equity must not have been contumacious, willful, or contrary to good conscience. When a party without objection has accepted overdue payments not made in accordance with the strict terms of the contract, an order of business has been established inconsistent with rigid insistence upon a clause of the contract which in effect is a forfeiture or the enforcement of a penalty. The finding of the trial judge in substance was that the conduct of the defendants was such as to lull the plaintiff into a justifiable assumption that, notwithstanding the terms of the contract, he would be given indulgence in making his payments, and that the conduct of the defendants amounted to a waiver of their right to elect to close out all rights of the plaintiff without notice and without giving him a reasonable opportunity to save his payments already made by paying the balance due on his contract, and that the conduct of the defendants was harsh, oppressive and vindictive. It is usually a question of fact whether there has been a waiver of stipulations of a contract. Although that finding is not made in categorical terms in the case at bar, it is the necessary effect of all the findings of the trial judge. Such a finding cannot be pronounced without sufficient support in the evidence. Such a finding is not affected by the words of the contract concerning waiver by the plaintiff of the right to such notice. It is difficult to frame a contract so as to foreclose the operation in equity of the doctrine of waiver in order to prevent an injustice. The terms of the present contract did not go far enough to prevent jurisdiction in equity to relieve against a result which does violence to the sense of fairness and good conscience of a court of equity. It would be unconscionable to permit the defendants, in view of their conduct, without notice or warning to insist upon strict performance of the contract and to forfeit all rights of the plaintiff."

In *Clark v. West, 86 N.E. 1 (N.Y., 1908)* the plaintiff agreed to write a book for defendant. The contract provided for payment of $2.00 per page and an additional $4.00 per page if plaintiff did not drink intoxicants during the time he was writing the book. This was stated as a condition as well as a promise: "the first party [plaintiff] agrees to totally abstain from the use of intoxicating liquors during the continuance of this contract, and that the payment to him in accordance with the terms of this contract of any money in excess of $2 per page is dependent on the faithful performance of this as well as the other conditions of this contract." Plaintiff drank. In a suit by plaintiff defendant demurred to the complaint. The Court of Appeals *reversed*.

Plaintiff alleged completion of the book, the sale of many copies.

The court said in part.

"Briefly stated, the defendant's position is that the stipulation as to plaintiff's total abstinence is the consideration for the payment of the difference between $2 and $6 per page, and therefore could not be waived except by a new agreement to that effect based upon a good consideration; that the so-called waiver alleged by the plaintiff is not a waiver, but a modification of the contract in respect of its consideration. The plaintiff, on the other hand, argues that the stipulation for his total abstinence was merely a condition precedent, intended to work a forfeiture of the additional compensation in case of a breach, and that it could be waived without any formal agreement to that effect based upon a new consideration.

"The subject-matter of the contract was the writing of books by the plaintiff for the defendant. The duration of the contract was the time necessary to complete them all. The work was to be done to the satisfaction of the defendant, and the plaintiff was not to write any other books except those covered by the contract, unless requested so to do by the defendant, in which latter event he was to be paid for that particular work by the year. The compensation for the work specified in the contract was to be $6 per page, unless the plaintiff failed to totally abstain from the use of intoxicating liquors during the continuance of the contract, in which event he was to receive only $2 per page. That is the obvious import of the contract construed in the light of the purpose for which it was made, and in accordance with the ordinary meaning of plain language. It is not a contract to write books in order that the plaintiff shall keep sober, but a contract containing a stipulation that he shall keep sober so that he may write satisfactory books. When we view the contract from this standpoint, it will readily be perceived that the particular stipulation is not the consideration for the contract, but simply one of its conditions which fits in with those relating to time and method of delivery of manuscript, revision of proof, citation of cases, assignment of copyrights, keeping track of new cases and citations for new editions, and other details which might be waived by the defendant, if he saw fit to do so. This is made clear, it seems to us, by the provision that, 'in consideration of the above promises,' the defendant agrees to pay the plaintiff $2 per page on each book prepared by him, and if he 'abstains from the use of intoxicating liquor and otherwise fulfills his agreements as hereinbefore set forth, he shall be paid an additional $4 per page in manner hereinbefore stated.' The compensation of $2 per page, not to exceed $250 per month, was an advance or partial payment of the whole price of $6 per page, and the payment of the two-thirds, which was to be withheld pending the performance of the contract, was simply made contingent upon the plaintiff's total abstention from the use of intoxicants during the life of the contract. It is possible, of course, by segregating that clause of the contract from the context, to give it a wider meaning and a different aspect than it has when read in conjunction with other stipulations; but this is also true of other paragraphs of the contract. The paragraph, for instance, which provides that after the publication of any of the books written by the plaintiff he is to receive an amount equal to one-sixth of the net receipts from the combined sales of all the books which shall have been published by the defendant under the contract, less any and all payments previously made, 'until the amount of $6 per page of each book shall have been paid, after which the first party (plaintiff) shall have no right, title, or interest in said books or the receipts from the sales thereof.' That section of the contract, standing alone, would indicate that the plaintiff was to be entitled, in any event, to the $6 per page to be paid out of the net receipts of the copies of the book sold. The contract, read as a whole, however, shows that it is modified by the preceding provisions, making the compensation in excess of the $2 per page dependent upon the plaintiff's total abstinence, and upon the performance by him of the other conditions of the contract. It is obvious that the parties thought that the plaintiff's normal work was worth $6 per page. That was the sum to be paid for the work done by the plaintiff, and not for total abstinence. If the plaintiff did not keep to the condition as to total abstinence, he was to lose part of that sum. Precisely the same situation would have risen if the plaintiff had disregarded any of the other essential conditions of the contract. The fact that the particular stipulation was emphasized did not change its character. It was still a condition which the defendant could have insisted upon, as he has apparently done in regard to some others, and one which he could waive just as he might have waived those relating to the amount of the advance payments, or the number of pages to be written each month. A breach of any of the substantial conditions of the contract would have entailed a loss or forfeiture similar to that consequent upon a breach of the one relating to total abstinence, in case of the defendant's insistence upon his right to take advantage of them. This, we think, is the fair interpretation of the contract, and it follows that the stipulation as to the plaintiff's total abstinence was nothing more nor less than a condition precedent. If that conclusion is well founded, there can be no escape from the corollary that this condition could be waived; and, if it was waived, the defendant is clearly not in a position to insist upon the forfeiture which his waiver was intended to annihilate. The forfeiture must stand or fall with the condition. If the latter was waived, the former is no longer a part of the contract. Defendant still has the right to counterclaim for any damages which he may have sustained in consequence of the plaintiff's breach, but he cannot insist upon strict performance. Dunn v. Steubing, 120 N. Y. 232, 24 N. E. 315; Parke v. Franco-American Trading Co., 120 N. Y. 51, 56, 23 N. E. 996; Brady v. Cassidy, 145 N. Y. 171, 39 N. E. 814.

"This whole discussion is predicated, of course, upon the theory of an express waiver. We assume that no waiver could be implied from the defendant's mere acceptance of the books and his payment of the sum of $2 per page without objection. It was the defendant's duty to pay that amount in any event after acceptance of the work. The plaintiff must stand upon his allegation of an express waiver, and if he fails to establish that he cannot maintain his action.

"The theory upon which the defendant's attitude seems to be based is that, even if he has represented to the plaintiff that he would not insist upon the condition that the latter should observe total abstinence from intoxicants, he can still refuse to pay the full contract price for his work. The inequity of this position becomes apparent when we consider that this contract was to run for a period of years, during a large portion of which the plaintiff was to be entitled only to the advance payment of $2 per page; the balance being contingent, among other things, upon publication of the books and returns from sales. Upon this theory the defendant might have waived the condition while the first book was in process of production, and yet, when the whole work was completed, he would still be in a position to insist upon the forfeiture because there had not been strict performance. Such a situation is possible in a case where the subject of the waiver is the very consideration of a contract (Organ v. Stewart, 60 N. Y. 413,

420), but not where the waiver relates to something that can be waived. In the case at bar, as we have seen, the *waiver is not of the consideration or subject-matter, but of an incident to the method of performance.* [Emphasis added.] The consideration remains the same. The defendant has had the work he bargained for, and it is alleged that he has waived one of the conditions as to the manner in which it was to have been done. He might have insisted upon literal performance, and then he could have stood upon the letter of his contract. If, however, he has waived that incidental condition, he has created a situation to which the doctrine of waiver very precisely applies.

"The cases which present the most familiar phases of the doctrine of waiver are those which have arisen out of litigation over insurance policies where the defendants have claimed a forfeiture because of the breach of some condition in the contract but it is a doctrine of general application which is confined to no particular class of cases. A 'waiver' has been defined to be the intentional relinquishment of a known right. It is voluntary and implies an election to dispense with something of value, or forego some advantage which the party waiving it might at its option have demanded or insisted upon and this definition is supported by many cases in this and other states. In the recent case of Draper v. Oswego Co. Fire R. Ass'n, 190 N. Y. 12, 16, 82 N. E. 755, Chief Judge Cullen, in speaking for the court upon this subject, said: 'While that doctrine and the doctrine of equitable estoppel are often confused in insurance litigation, there is a clear distinction between the two. A "waiver" is the voluntary abandonment or relinquishment by a party of some right or advantage. As said by my Brother Vann in the Kiernan Case, 150 N. Y. 190, 44 N. E. 698: "The law of waiver seems to be a technical doctrine, introduced and applied by the court for the purpose of defeating forfeitures.... While the principle may not be easily classified, it is well established that, if the words and acts of the insurer reasonably justify the conclusion that with full knowledge of all the facts it intended to abandon or not to insist upon the particular defense afterwards relied upon, a verdict or finding to that effect establishes a waiver, which, if it once exists, can never be revoked." The doctrine of equitable estoppel, or estoppel in pais, is that a party may be precluded by his acts and conduct from asserting a right to the detriment of another party who, entitled to rely on such conduct, has acted upon it.... As already said, the doctrine of waiver is to relieve against forfeiture. It requires no consideration for a waiver, nor any prejudice or injury to the other party.' To the same effect, see Knarston v. Manhattan Life Ins. Co., 140 Cal. 57, 73 Pac. 740.

"It remains to be determined whether the plaintiff has alleged facts which, if proven, will be sufficient to establish his claim of an express waiver by the defendant of the plaintiff's breach of the condition to observe total abstinence. In the 12th paragraph of the complaint, the plaintiff alleges facts and circumstances which we think, if established, would prove defendant's waiver of plaintiff's performance of that contract stipulation. These facts and circumstances are that, long before the plaintiff had completed the manuscript of the first book undertaken under the contract, the defendant had full knowledge of the plaintiff's nonobservance of that stipulation, and that with such knowledge he not only accepted the completed manuscript without objection, but 'repeatedly avowed and represented to the plaintiff that he was entitled to and would receive said royalty payments (i. e., the additional $4 per page), and plaintiff believed and relied upon such representations,... and at all times during the writing of said treatise on Corporations, and after as well as before publication thereof as aforesaid, it was mutually understood, agreed, and intended by the parties hereto that, notwithstanding plaintiff's said use of intoxicating liquors, he was nevertheless entitled to receive and would receive said royalty as the same accrued under said contract.' The demurrer not only admits the truth of these allegations, but also all that can by reasonable and fair intendment be implied therefrom. [W]e think it cannot be doubted that the allegations contained in the twelfth paragraph of the complaint, if proved upon the trial, would be sufficient to establish an express waiver by the defendant of the stipulation in regard to plaintiff's total abstinence."

Question

1. What is the relationship between condition and consideration?

H. Divisibility of Performances

Cherwell-Ralli, Inc. v. Rytman Grain Company, Inc.
433 A.2d 984
Supreme Court of Connecticut, 1980

PETERS, Justice.

This case involves a dispute about which of the parties to an oral instalment contract was the first to be in breach. The plaintiff, Cherwell-Ralli, Inc., sued the defendant, Rytman Grain Co., Inc., for the nonpayment of moneys due and owing for accepted deliveries of products known as Cherco Meal and C-R-T Meal. The defendant, conceding its indebtedness, counterclaimed for damages arising out of the plaintiff's refusal to deliver remaining instalments under the contract. The trial court, Bordon, J., trial referee, having found all issues for the plaintiff, rendered judgment accordingly, and the defendant appealed.

The trial court's unchallenged finding of fact establishes the following: The parties, on July 26, 1974, entered into an instalment contract for the sale of Cherco Meal and C-R-T Meal on the basis of a memorandum executed by the Getkin Brokerage House. As modified, the contract called for shipments according to weekly instructions from the buyer, with payments to be made within ten days after delivery. Almost immediately the buyer was behind in its payments, and these arrearages were often quite substantial. The seller repeatedly called these arrearages to the buyer's attention but continued to make all shipments as requested by the buyer from July 29, 1974 to April 23, 1975.

By April 15, 1975, the buyer had become concerned that the seller might not complete performance of the contract, because the seller's plant might close and because the market price of the goods had come significantly to exceed the contract price. In a telephonic conversation between the buyer's president and the seller's president on that day, the buyer was assured by the seller that deliveries would continue if the buyer would make the payments for which it was obligated. Thereupon, the buyer sent the seller a check in the amount of $9825.60 to cover shipments through March 31, 1975.

Several days later, on April 23, 1975, the buyer stopped payment on this check because he was told by a truck driver, not employed by the seller, that this shipment would be his last load. The trial court found that this was not a valid reason for stoppage of payment. Upon inquiry by the seller, the buyer restated his earlier concerns about future deliveries. Two letters, both dated April 28, 1975, describe the impasse between the parties: the seller again demanded payment, and the buyer, for the first time in writing, demanded adequate assurance of further deliveries. The buyer's demand for assurance was reiterated in its direct reply to the seller's demand for payment. The buyer, however, made no further payments, either to replace the stopped check or otherwise to pay for the nineteen accepted shipments for which balances were outstanding. The seller made no further deliveries after April 23, 1975, when it heard about the stopped check; the buyer never made specific requests for shipments after that date. Inability to deliver the goods forced the seller to close its plant, on May 2, 1975, because of stockpiling of excess material.

The trial court concluded, on the basis of these facts, that the party in breach was the buyer and not the seller. The court concluded that the seller was entitled to recover the final balance of $21,013.60, which both parties agreed to be due and owing. It concluded that the buyer could not prevail on its counterclaim because it had no reasonable grounds to doubt performance from the seller and had in fact received reasonable assurances. Further, the buyer had presented no reasonably accurate evidence to establish the damages it might have sustained because of the seller's failure to deliver.

The buyer on this appeal challenges first the conclusion that the buyer's failure to pay "substantially impaired the value of the whole contract," so as to constitute "a breach of the whole contract," as is required by the applicable law governing instalment contracts. General Statutes § 42a-2-612(3)[1]. What constitutes impairment of the value of the whole contract is a question of fact; The record below amply sustains the trial court's conclusion in this regard, particularly in light of the undenied and uncured stoppage of a check given to comply with the buyer's promise to reduce significantly the amount of its outstanding arrearages.

The buyer argues that the seller in an instalment contract may never terminate a contract, despite repeated default in payment by the buyer, without first invoking the insecurity methodology of General Statutes § 42a-2-609.[2] That is

---

1. General Statutes § 42a-2-612(3) provides: "Whenever nonconformity or default... impairs the value of the whole contract there is a breach of the whole. But the aggrieved party reinstates the contract if he accepts a non-conforming instalment without seasonably notifying of cancellation or if he brings an action with respect only to past instalments or demands performance as to future instalments."

2. General Statutes § 42a-2-609 provides: "Right to Adequate Assurance of Performance. (1) A contract for sale imposes an obligation on each party that the other's expectation of receiving due performance will not be impaired. When reasonable grounds for insecurity arise with respect to the performance of either party the other may in writing demand adequate assurance of due performance and until he receives such assurance may if commercially reasonable suspend any performance for which he has not already received the agreed return. (2) Between merchants the reasonableness of grounds for insecurity and the adequacy of any assurance offered shall be determined according to commercial standards. (3) Acceptance of any improper delivery or payment does not prejudice the aggrieved party's right to demand adequate assurance of future performance. (4) After receipt of a justified demand failure to provide within a reasonable time not exceeding thirty days such assurance

not the law. If there is reasonable doubt about whether the buyer's default is substantial, the seller may be well advised to temporize by suspending further performance until it can ascertain whether the buyer is able to offer adequate assurance of future payments. Kunian v. Development Corporation of America, 165 Conn. 300, 312, 334 A.2d 427 (1973); Dangerfield v. Markel, 252 N.W.2d 184, 192-93 (N.D.1977). But if the buyer's conduct is sufficiently egregious, such conduct will, in and of itself, constitute substantial impairment of the value of the whole contract and a present breach of the contract as a whole. An aggrieved seller is expressly permitted, by General Statutes § 42a-2-703(f)[3], upon breach of a contract as a whole, to cancel the remainder of the contract "with respect to the whole undelivered balance." Nor is the seller's remedy to cancel waived, as the buyer argues, by a law suit seeking recovery for payments due. While § 42a-2-612(3) states that a contract is reinstated if the seller "brings an action with respect only to past instalments" it is clear in this case that the seller intended, as the buyer well knew, to bring this contract to an end because of the buyer's breach.

The buyer's attack on the court's conclusions with respect to its counterclaim is equally unavailing. The buyer's principal argument is that the seller was obligated, on pain of default, to provide assurance of its further performance. The right to such assurance is premised on reasonable grounds for insecurity. Whether a buyer has reasonable grounds to be insecure is a question of fact. AMF, Inc. v. McDonald's Corporation, 536 F.2d 1167, 1170 (7th Cir. 1976). The trial court concluded that in this case the buyer's insecurity was not reasonable and we agree. A party to a sales contract may not suspend performance of its own for which it has "already received the agreed return." At all times, the buyer had received all of the goods which it had ordered. The buyer could not rely on its own nonpayments as a basis for its own insecurity. The presidents of the parties had exchanged adequate verbal assurances only eight days before the buyer itself again delayed its own performance on the basis of information that was facially unreliable. Contrary to the buyer's argument, subsequent events proved the buyer's fears to be incorrect, since the seller's plant closed due to a surplus rather than due to a shortage of materials. Finally, it is fatal to the buyer's appeal that neither its oral argument nor its brief addressed its failure to substantiate, with probative evidence, the damages it alleged to be attributable to the seller's nondeliveries.

There is no error.

In this opinion the other Judges concurred.

---

of due performance as is adequate under the circumstances of the particular case is a repudiation of the contract."

3. General Statutes § 42a-2-703 provides: "Seller's Remedies in General. Where the buyer wrongfully rejects or revokes acceptance of goods or fails to make a payment due on or before delivery or repudiates with respect to a part or the whole, then with respect to any goods directly affected and, if the breach is of the whole contract as provided in section 42a-2-612, then also with respect to the whole undelivered balance, the aggrieved seller may (a) withhold delivery of such goods; (b) stop delivery by any bailee as provided in section 42a-2-705; (c) proceed under the next section respecting goods still unidentified to the contract; (d) resell and recover damages as hereafter provided in section 42a-2-706; (e) recover damages for non-acceptance as provided in section 42a-2-708 or in a proper case the price as provided in section 42a-2-709; (f) cancel."

Aiello Construction, Inc. v. Nationwide Tractor Trailer and Placement Corp

413 A.2d 85
Supreme Court of Rhode Island, 1980

WEISBERGER, Justice.

This case comes before us on appeal from a judgment of the Superior Court which awarded damages to the plaintiffs for a breach of contract allegedly committed by the defendant when it failed to make certain installment payments required by the contract. The case was tried by a justice sitting without the intervention of a jury. The facts as found in his decision are as follows.

The plaintiffs, Aiello Construction, Inc., and Smithfield Peat Co., Inc., as joint venturers, entered into a written contract with defendant in March of 1973. The contract required plaintiffs to haul fill and perform grading work in order to bring a large area owned by defendant to an approximately level condition. The contract further provided that plaintiffs would remove ledge on a portion of the premises, grade eight inches of bank run gravel over the entire yard, grade two inches of crushed run gravel over the entire yard, and finally apply penetration and seal coats of oil topped by application of peastone. The surface was then to be rolled. The defendant was in the trucking business and also engaged in the training and instruction of tractor- trailer operators. The yard area was to be used in the operation of this training enterprise.

In payment for the work to be performed and the material to be furnished, defendant agreed to pay $33,000 in five monthly installments of $6,600 each. The installments were to become due on April 15, May 15, June 15, July 15, and August 15, all during the year 1973. The contract provided that any amount not paid would bear a service charge of 11/2 percent per month.

The plaintiffs began work in late March 1973 and continued the work until on or about May 10, 1973, at which time all of the preliminary work had been done save applying and grading the two inches of crushed run gravel, which was a prerequisite to the performance of the oiling. The plaintiffs then stopped work to allow the ground to settle. Meanwhile, defendant paid the monthly installment that was due on April 15. Thereafter, defendant did not pay the May installment, although over a period from June to August of 1973 it did make partial payments which, when added to the April installment, aggregated $10,500. No further payments were made, and the president of the defendant company indicated that funds were not available to make the payments that were due. As a result of the failure to make payments, plaintiffs did not resume work. The plaintiffs brought the instant action for breach of contract. The defendant filed a counterclaim which alleged that plaintiffs were in breach of the agreement between the parties because they did not complete the work for which they had received payment. The defendant's counterclaim also contained a count which sounded in negligence.

The trial justice found as a fact that defendant was in breach of the contract and that this breach relieved plaintiffs of the obligation to perform any further work under the contract. He further found that defendant was not entitled to recover on its negligence claim. The trial justice awarded damages for the breach of contract by calculating the costs which plaintiffs had incurred in the performance of the work up to the time they withdrew from the project as a result of the breach. He found that the costs amounted to $21,500. To this sum he added $3,000 which he determined from the testimony to be the profit which plaintiffs would have made had the contract been completely performed by both parties. From the sum of $24,500 the trial justice deducted the payments made by defendant in the amount of $10,500. He ordered judgment to enter for plaintiffs in the amount of $14,000 together with interest at the rate of 8 percent per annum from the time of filing of the complaint to the date of judgment. He found the theories underlying defendant's counterclaim difficult to perceive and determined that defendant was entitled to no compensation or diminution of the award of damages. Thus judgment was entered for the plaintiffs for $16,800. This appeal ensued.

The defendant raises a number of points in support of its appeal. It first argues that the trial justice erred as a matter of fact and law in finding that defendant had breached the contract in such a way as to excuse plaintiffs for not completing the work. In regard to the findings of fact, this case involved conflicting testimony offered by witnesses presented by both parties. The trial justice found plaintiffs' witnesses more credible and in some instances found the testimony of defendant's witnesses of little or no probative value. It is well settled that we cannot disturb the finding of a trial justice unless the adverse party is able to show that in resolving testimonial conflicts the trial justice misconceived or overlooked material evidence or was otherwise clearly wrong. In respect to the challenge to the legal validity of the trial justice's holding that failure to pay installments on a construction contract is a breach that would excuse further performance, our holding in Salo Landscape & Construction Co. v. Liberty Electric Co., R.I., 376 A.2d 1379 (1977), is dispositive. There we observed that in the event an owner fails to pay an installment due on a construction contract, such owner "is guilty of a breach that goes to the essence of the contract and that entitles the injured party to bring an action." 376 A.2d at 1382. A similar holding may be found in Pelletier v. Masse, 49 R.I. 408, 410-11, 143 A. 609, 610 (1928), wherein the court noted that nonpayment of an installment due may justify the contractor in refusing to continue the work and in bringing an action on the contract for damages for its breach or quantum meruit for reasonable compensation for what the contractor has done. Under such circumstances, the court suggested, an action on the contract for the amount of the installment due would be inappropriate. Id. at 411, 143 A. at 610. See also 3A Corbin on Contracts § 692 (1960); Restatement Contracts § 346 (1932). Thus, the determination by the trial justice that defendant was solely responsible for the breach of the contract was amply supported by the evidence in the case and by the applicable law.

The defendant next contends that ambiguities in the contract should be resolved against plaintiffs. However meritorious this principle may be, the trial justice found no ambiguities in the contract, and neither do we. Hence, this argument is unavailing.

The defendant further argues that the contract was indivisible and that failure to pay an installment would not excuse the refusal on the part of plaintiffs to complete the work. Our holding in respect to the first argument is also dispositive of this contention. Since the breach by defendant went to the essence of the contract, plaintiffs were excused from further performance.

The defendant argues that the trial justice did not correctly assess damages. He cites in support of his argument George v. George F. Berkander, Inc., 92 R.I. 426, 169 A.2d 370 (1961). In that case the rule of damages for breach of contract was stated to be such "as will serve to put the injured party as close as is reasonably possible to the position he would have been in had the contract been fully performed." Id. at 430, 169 A.2d at 372. It is precisely this rule that the trial justice attempted to apply. Although the measure of damages may be variously stated under the principle of our holding in Berkander, certain alternatives are well set forth in Restatement Contracts § 346(2) as follows: "For a breach by one who has promised to pay for construction, if it is a partial breach the builder can get judgment for the instalment due, with interest; and if it is a total breach he can get judgment, with interest so far as permitted by the rules stated in § 337, for either "(a) the entire contract price and compensation for unavoidable special harm that the defendant had reason to foresee when the contract was made, less instalments already paid and the cost of completion that the builder can reasonably save by not completing the work; or "(b) the amount of his expenditure in part (pe)rformance of the contract, subject to the limitations stated in § 333."[1]

The general rules set forth in the Restatement are further elucidated by the commentary. A portion of the comment on subsection (2) of Restatement § 346 reads as follows: "h. Another common form of stating the measure of recovery is as follows: Damages, measured by the builder's actual expenditure to date of breach less the value of materials on hand, plus the profit that he can prove with reasonable certainty would have been realized from full performance.... The builder has a right to his expenditures as well as his profits, because payment of the full price would have reimbursed those expenditures in full and given him his profit in addition...." An examination of the record in this case discloses that the trial justice scrupulously followed this method of assessment of damages, that his findings of fact were amply supported by the evidence, and that he did not overlook or misconceive the evidence in arriving at his conclusion. Although we approved of a quantum meruit action in Salo Landscape & Construction Co. v. Liberty Electric Co., 376 A.2d at 1382, we recognized alternative remedies in Pelletier v. Masse, 49 R.I. at 410-11, 143 A. at 610. In applying these alternatives, a court must select the most appropriate remedy depending upon the factual posture of the case and the election of remedy by the plaintiff. The remedy selected by the trial justice in this case was appropriately relevant to the factual posture and the remedy sought by plaintiffs. Therefore, the trial justice cannot be faulted for his assessment of damages either in regard to the law or to the facts.

The defendant argues that the trial justice erred in determining that certain evidentiary offerings in support of its counterclaim were irrelevant. The trial justice obviously considered many elements of defendant's counterclaim to be frivolous. Some of the claims relating to damage to defendant's business and property

---

1. Restatement Contracts § 333 (1932) reads in part as follows: "(a) Such expenditures are not recoverable in excess of the full contract price promised by the defendant. "(b) Expenditures in preparation are not recoverable unless they can fairly be regarded as part of the cost of performance in estimating profit and loss. "(c) Instalments of the contract price already received and the value of materials on hand that would have been consumed in completion must be deducted. "(d) If full performance would have resulted in a net loss to the plaintiff, the amount of this loss must be deducted, the burden of proof being on the defendant."

caused by plaintiffs' negligence and the removal of a chain-link fence were considered to be "ridiculous" by the trial justice in light of the totality of evidence in the case. It was the task of the trial justice to consider relevance of evidence relating to damages in the light of his determination that defendant was at fault for breach of this contract and in the light of the failure of defendant to lay a foundation which established liability of plaintiffs for such damages. Such determinations of relevance normally are considered to be within the discretion of the trial justice. In the absence of abuse of discretion, such evidentiary rulings will not constitute a basis for reversal. Gaglione v. Cardi, R.I., 388 A.2d 361, 363 (1978). We have noted that it is the burden of the party opposing such evidentiary rulings to establish that the proposed evidence was material and that its exclusion had a prejudicial influence on the decision of the court. Atlantic Paint & Coatings, Inc. v. Conti, R.I., 381 A.2d 1034, 1036 (1977); Mercurio v. Fascitelli, 116 R.I. 237, 244, 354 A.2d 736, 740 (1976). We believe that defendant in the case at bar has failed to sustain such a burden.

Finally, the defendant contends that the trial justice was in error in awarding interest to the plaintiffs at 8 percent per annum from the date of the filing of the complaint. The defendant argues that G.L.1956 (1969 Reenactment) § 9-21-10[2] is inapplicable since the contract provided for interest at the rate of 1 1/2 percent per month on any installments due and unpaid. The trial justice held that the interest rate contained in the contract was inapplicable since the plaintiffs did not bring suit on the contract, but for breach thereof. We believe this holding to be correct since the trial justice found that the plaintiffs had not sufficiently performed under the contract so as to be entitled to the full contract price. The applicable statute in force at the time of the rendition of this judgment could well be argued to have required interest to be computed from the time of accrual of the action. The statute as it read up until three days prior to rendition of judgment did provide for "interest at the rate of eight per cent (8%) per annum thereon from the date of commencement of the action which shall be included in the judgment entered therein." The interest provided in the contract, if applicable, would have been at the rate of 18 percent per annum. Thus, if the trial justice was in error in assessing interest in accordance with the statute that had previously been in force as opposed to the statute as it had been amended just prior to entry of judgment, or if he was in error in assessing statutory interest rather than the interest set forth in the contract, this error could scarcely be prejudicial to the defendant. Indeed, the trial justice's assessment of interest was the least onerous to the defendant of all available computations. Although the plaintiffs agree that the trial justice erred in the computation of interest inasmuch as the plaintiffs would now prefer either the 18 percent as provided in the contract or 8 percent interest from the date of accrual of the cause of action, since the plain-

---

2. General Laws 1956 (1969 Reenactment) § 9-21-10, as amended by P.L.1976, ch. 146, § 1, and further amended by P.L.1977, ch. 10, § 1 (which became effective March 21, 1977, three days prior to the date of entry of judgment in this case), reads as follows: "In any civil action in which a verdict is rendered or a decision made for pecuniary damages, there shall be added by the clerk of the court to the amount of damages, interest at the rate of eight per cent (8%) per annum thereon from the date the cause of action accrued which shall be included in the judgment entered therein. This section shall not apply until entry of judgment or to any (contractual) obligation where interest is already provided or as to any condemnation action."

tiffs have not appealed in this case they have no standing to challenge the interest awarded. Thus we hold that the trial justice committed no prejudicial error in his award of interest on the judgment.

For the reasons stated, the defendant's appeal is denied and dismissed, the judgment of the Superior Court is affirmed, and the case is remitted to the Superior Court.

Part V

Escaping Liability Under a Seemingly Enforceable Contract

Introduction

Up to this point we have studied the components and formation of a legally binding contract between two parties. We have considered intent, reasons for enforcement of promises (consideration, seal, reliance), offer and acceptance, parol evidence, modification, standardized contracts, and conditions.

Part Five concerns whether, given a seemingly enforceable contract, one party can escape performance of his/her contractual obligations. It is an area which concerns defenses, where a party must raise a particular defense unrelated to the objective bargaining, the offer and acceptance, the terms of the agreement, because on its face, according to the facts, a contract appears to have come into being. In most instances, the party seeking to escape the contract is not disputing that in ordinary circumstances an enforceable agreement would appear to exist. Rather the party is saying—there is some special fact, not necessarily related to the bargain itself which makes this apparent obligation, this apparent contract, unenforceable.

It is important to note that Part V consists of numerous concepts for escaping apparent contractual liability. No one escape is necessarily linked to another. Always be alert to asserting multiple defenses, and when reading the cases pay attention to what the parties were trying to prove as well as what the court accepted.

Part V is broken into two subparts. The first involves looking at the person. The idea behind this section is that by looking at the person entering into the supposed contract we may find some reason to doubt whether the contract should be enforced. For example, in an earlier case under the modification section [*Austin Instrument v. Loral, supra* Part III C] two lower courts found that a modification had occurred in a contract. The state's highest court instead found duress. A party was deprived of his free will to make a choice and was forced to do something against his/her will. The same would be true if someone held a gun to someone's head and said "agree or else."

Another example of a way to escape contractual obligations is if someone is mentally incompetent or underage. Here, while the "contract" may appear to be enforceable, it is not, because someone mentally incompetent or underage may not be able to employ sound judgment in making a choice. The contract is not unenforceable because something is wrong with the contract itself; it is unenforceable because the person entering into it is incapable of exercising intent to enter into a contract. In a sense, this section is a triumph of the subjective over the objective. It is not what appears to the reasonable person that matters (as it does with expressions of offer and acceptance). If McKittrick said to Embry "You're OK get you men out" but McKittrick was having a mental breakdown that prevented him from exercising his free will (and hence form an intent) or if Embry held a gun to McKittrick's head and made him say this, one could either say the contract is unenforceable or, perhaps more accurately, no contract was ever formed. For this reason the title to the section states: "Seemingly Enforceable Contract" rather than just contract. In a very real sense all of the elements are there except the actual intent of one of the parties to be bound; somehow one of them lacked the free will to enter or refuse to enter the contract.

The second portion of this Part examines the actual alleged contract itself. This is not a situation where the parties lack the capacity to form a contract but rather where some error or fault in contract formation or some event which neither party anticipated allows a party to escape liability. Parties to these contracts are presumed to be of sound mind. Thus, the defense to a suit is not that the party sued was under duress, underage, mentally incapable, or in some other fashion a person unable to contract because of some element in that particular person's mental and/or psychological makeup that prevented the person from exercising free will and hence intent to either enter or not enter into a contractual obligation. Relevant issues here revolve around whether the parties have failed to reduce the contract to a signed writing; or was a mistake made as to what was being contracted for (have the parties contracted based on an assumption that did not exist at the time of contracting or that changed after contracting); have the parties discovered that performance, as anticipated by both parties, was impossible or impracticable or no longer desired because the purpose for which it was sought no longer exists; or has one party made a misrepresentation, either expressly or impliedly, to the other. All of these may be reasons for escaping contractual liability.

Whether the defense goes to the person or to the contract itself, the key point is that even if there appears to be a fully enforceable contract with an offer and acceptance, consideration, fulfillment of conditions, no parol evidence problems, there may be a defense to escape it. It is your job to anticipate this and if, unfortunately, it arises to deal with it.

In this part we see the difference between an agreement and a contract, *i.e.* between the bargain reached, or the apparent bargain reached, and whether the courts will enforce it. Courts look for the intent of the parties and most often will phrase their judgments in terms of finding or not finding intent. In some instances, however, they simply do not feel a contract is fair and hence refuse to enforce it. See *Williams v. Walker-Thomas, infra.* In a sense the court is construing not interpreting, it is finding a lack of fairness and refusing to enforce the parties' bargain. Thus, it is not interpreting, unless you would say that by finding an incapacity to contract or a basic error in assumptions, the court is determining that what one party intended was not a true recognizable legal intent. Whatever the rationale not every bargain is enforced. This Part makes that clearer.

Remember, depending on the particular facts, defenses from both areas can be asserted. In the same way do not overlook other defenses that may exist — lack of consideration, definiteness, lack of intent to contract, etc. It is not good to simply throw in defenses like dust in the air. It can annoy courts and jurors. But a good defense or series of defenses, well prepared, can carry the day. Think through the following cases and problems with care.

Read the following problem, then the two cases following. How would you resolve the problem?

Problem to Part V

Billy Bradford (Bradford) is a brilliant, if eccentric, computer and software programmer. Bradford's credentials include university degrees and certificates from business training institutes. Bradford also has occasions when he becomes irrational. On these occasions he cannot distinguish simple problems and their solutions from complex ones, make simple additions or even perform normal functions, such as driving an automobile. Fortunately Bradford has medication to assist him and because of the medication and his doctor's instructions can tell when he is coming toward an irrational period. On these occasions he either checks into a hospital or goes to his parents' home. For the most part, people cannot tell when he is having one of these occurrences unless they ask him to do a problem or perform a task or give an explanation or opinion. His speech is not slurred nor are his ideas totally incomprehensible. It is just that he cannot reason and does foolish things. Further, he has only a very blurred memory of them.

On a weekend two months ago Bradford felt one of these occurrences coming on. He was out of town and could not reach either his parents or his physician. He apparently went to a used car lot and bought an automobile from the salesman for over twice its book value. When Bradford asked the price of the car the salesman quoted the high price because as he said "people always feel better if you let them bring you down a lot and sometimes you get lucky and sell it near the top." To the salesman's surprise Bradford said OK and signed the necessary contract for the car. Bradford cannot remember any of this nor how he eventually returned to his home city. However, two weeks ago he received a notice from a finance company that he had not made any payments on his car and a notice from the used car lot that because he had not picked up his car they were charging him a storage fee of $10 per day.

Bradford wrote the finance company and used car lot and told them he knew nothing about the transaction. They responded with copies of the writings he had signed indicating a contract for the purchase of a car. Bradford wrote again explaining his condition and requesting to be released from contractual liability. Using the cases in this section answer the following questions.

1. Bradford comes to you for advice. Is he liable?

2. In the alternative, the finance company refers this matter to you for collection. Is there an enforceable contract?

A. Looking at the Person

This section examines when a party can escape contractual obligation because something is wrong with the person which prevents the contract from becoming legally binding against that party, and results in the recission of the contract. Recission can be the product of one party's incapacity to contract, or the forced consent to the contract through duress, undue influence or unconscionability.

1. Competency

Section 12 of the Restatement states for a person to be bound by contract they must have legal capacity to incur at least voidable contractual duties. A person is presumed to have full legal capacity to enter into contractual relationships unless (s)he is: (1) under guardianship, (2) an infant, (3) mentally ill or defective, or (4) intoxicated. Infancy is presumed to last up to a person's eighteenth birthday. (see Restatement § 14).

a. Mental Illness

A key idea with regard to mental illness is that the person either lacks the capacity to understand what is happening or that he/she understands but cannot control his/her actions. In the first situation the person is said to lack cognitive capacity. In the second he/she is said to be under a compulsion to act. In either instance the person is unable to make a reasoned choice or decision. From an older viewpoint a contract could not be made because it took a meeting of the minds (plural) and if someone were mentally disabled there was only one functioning mind.

Thus, a person who cannot understand or control his actions lacks mental capacity to enter into a contract. This is the first threshold.

The second concerns timing and subject matter. A person may have delusional episodes in an otherwise clear understanding and self-control or, by contrast, may have clear episodes in a generally delusional state. The key issue here is did the person allegedly enter into a contractual relationship while in a delusional or clear headed state? A subset of this question is subject matter. Some people are remarkably clear headed on all but one or two subjects where they become irrational. When I was a law student as part of a Law and Psychiatry seminar the psychiatrist who conducted the seminar jointly with a law professor took a group of us to a mental hospital. I recall two patients who seemed very normal except when, in one case, you discussed television and in the other "Indians." The first patient held long discussions with people on the television screen and had to dress appropriately for these interviews depending on who was appearing. They told the patient what to wear. The second person seemed very normal but had been creating a problem by calling the police periodically (and with increasing frequency) because the "Indians" were invading the patient's apartment. This latter patient discussed in some detail how these invasions occurred. In each case a seemingly normal person was set off by one situation. Unless a person is totally incapacitated mentally, (s)he can enter into contractual obligations during lucid periods. The problem is discovering when these lucid periods are.

The third threshold is the knowledge or reason to know of the disabled person's mental disability. If the person dealing with the mentally disabled person does not know and has no reason to know of the disability, that can often be a ground for holding the disabled person to the contract *if* the terms are fair.

Fairness is the fourth threshold. Are the terms fair? If they are then it is far more likely that the contract will be upheld than if they are not.

Assuming someone lacks capacity to understand what he is doing, that this disability occurred when he allegedly entered into a contract, that the person with whom he was dealing knew or had reason to know of the disability or did not know or have reason to know of it but the terms of the alleged contract were unfair, the contract will probably be avoided.

Mental disability is a serious problem in the law of contracts. The two cases below barely scratch the surface. How are they different? How are they the same? How do they help solve the problem?

Shoals Ford, Inc. v. Clardy

588 So.2d 879
Supreme Court of Alabama, 1991.

HOUSTON, Justice.

Shoals Ford, Inc., appeals from a judgment based on a jury verdict in favor of Maxine Clardy, as conservator for Bobby Joe Clardy. We affirm.

Ms. Clardy sued Shoals Ford, seeking to have a transaction entered into between Shoals Ford and her husband Bobby Joe for the purchase of a 1989 Ford pickup truck set aside and to recover the monies paid by Bobby Joe to Shoals Ford, alleging that Bobby Joe suffered from a manic-depressive disorder and was in a manic state when he transacted with Shoals Ford to purchase the truck and also alleging that Shoals Ford was negligent, wanton, and willful in dealing with Bobby Joe. She sought compensatory damages, punitive damages, and rescission of the contract.

Shoals Ford answered, asserting that it had acted without notice of Bobby Joe's incompetency, that the conservatorship proceeding was not instituted until nearly a month after Bobby Joe had purchased the truck, that the family members had been contributorily negligent in assisting Bobby Joe in purchasing the truck, and that there had been an accord and satisfaction. It amended its answer, adding the affirmative defense of estoppel and pleading "that there was no failure of consideration or undue influence taken of" Bobby Joe in his purchase of the truck and that Ms. Clardy failed to mitigate damages.

Both Shoals Ford and Ms. Clardy filed motions for summary judgment, which the trial court denied. Both Shoals Ford and Ms. Clardy moved for a directed verdict, which the trial court denied. The jury returned a verdict in favor of Ms. Clardy in the amount of $6,715.02 in compensatory damages and $18,000 in punitive damages. Shoals Ford filed a motion for new trial or, in the alternative, for judgment notwithstanding the verdict, which the trial court denied.

Shoals Ford appeals.

Shoals Ford contends that the evidence was insufficient to sustain the jury's verdict, because, it argues, Ms. Clardy failed to establish the elements necessary for recovery in this case, specifically those elements relating to the incapacity of Bobby Joe at the time he consummated the transaction and took possession of the truck. It contends that the contract was completed, that the truck was delivered, and that Bobby Joe took possession of the truck, all on April 3, 1989, when all of the paperwork was finalized, and that, on that date, Bobby Joe was not incompetent.

Ms. Clardy contends that the evidence establishes that Bobby Joe completed the transaction on April 5, 1989, when he took actual possession of the truck, i.e., when he drove the truck off the lot, and that, on that date, he was incompetent to handle his affairs.

The well-settled law in Alabama is that contracts of insane persons are wholly and completely void. In McAlister v. Deatherage, 523 So.2d 387, 388 (Ala.1988), this Court explained the cognitive (understanding) test that Alabama adopted in order to determine whether a contract can be avoided because of insanity: " '[To] avoid a contract on the ground of insanity, it must be satisfactorily shown that the party was incapable of transacting the particular business in question. It is not enough that he was the subject of delusions not affecting the subject-matter of the transaction, nor that he was, in other respects, mentally weak. A party cannot avoid a contract, free from fraud or undue influence, on the ground of mental incapacity, unless it can be shown that his insanity . . . was of such character that he had no reasonable perception or understanding of the nature and terms of the contract.' "

Viewing the tendencies of the evidence most favorably to the prevailing party and indulging all reasonable inferences that the jury was free to draw, as required under our applicable standard of review, see Warren v. Ousley, 440 So.2d 1034 (Ala.1983), we find the following:

On April 1, 1989, Bobby Joe talked to Kelly Cole of Shoals Ford concerning the purchase of a truck; on that day he filled out the initial papers. By April 3, 1989, all the necessary paperwork had been completed and Bobby Joe had signed the necessary documents, but when he went to pick up the truck, he was advised that because of his poor credit rating, Shoals Ford would require a $10,500 down payment instead of the $5,000 down payment previously discussed. On April 5, 1989, Bobby Joe returned to Shoals Ford with the down payment and, at that time, picked up the truck.

According to Ms. Clardy, Bobby Joe had suffered from a manic-depressive disorder for 15 years and was taking lithium to control his condition. She said that she observed in mid-March 1989 that Bobby Joe was becoming manic, but she said that because he was not violent and had not endangered himself or anyone else at that time, she could not involuntarily commit him for treatment. On April 5, 1989, Ms. Clardy received a telephone call from Leslie Clardy Daniel, Ms. Clardy and Bobby Joe's daughter ("the daughter"), concerning Bobby Joe's condition. The daughter told Ms. Clardy that Bobby Joe had threatened her and had obtained $500 from her to make the down payment on a truck he was going to buy from Shoals Ford. Subsequently, Ms. Clardy drove to Shoals Ford and noticed that the truck Bobby Joe had previously looked at, in her presence, was still on the lot. At that time she spoke with a salesperson, and she later telephoned a sales representative with Shoals Ford, concerning Bobby Joe's incompetency and asked that they not allow Bobby Joe to take the truck—that is, she told them that Bobby Joe was not working, that he was ill and would be committed, and that the truck could not be insured. Thereafter, on April 5, 1989, Shoals Ford gave Bobby Joe possession of the truck after he gave it $10,000 as the down payment. Ford Motor Credit Company eventually repossessed and sold the truck and mailed Ms. Clardy a check for $3,284.98, which left a balance of $6,715.02 of the $10,000 down payment unrecovered by Ms. Clardy.

According to the daughter, when Bobby Joe visited her around April 1, 1989, she tried to get him to resume taking his medicine. He became agitated and went out of control, threw his medicine into a burning pile of leaves, and then left. Around 5 A.M. on April 5, 1989, Bobby Joe returned to the daughter's house, banged on the doors and windows until he awakened the household, threatened their lives, and forced the daughter to write him a check for $500. When he left, the daughter telephoned 911 to report the incident and, as soon as the probate office opened, she telephoned the probate judge to inform him of the situation. She then went to her attorney's office, explained the situation to him, and asked that he prepare a petition to have Bobby Joe involuntarily committed for treatment. While in her attorney's office, she notified the bank to stop payment on the $500 check she had written to Bobby Joe and then called to notify Shoals Ford of Bobby Joe's mental condition, telling a representative that Bobby Joe would be coming in to purchase a truck, specifically describing the particular truck; telling the representative that Bobby Joe was not healthy; and telling the representative that she had filed a petition to have Bobby Joe involuntarily committed. She also asked Shoals Ford to call the Lauderdale County sheriff, a family member, her attorney, Riverbend Center for Mental Health, or the probate office for verification in the event Bobby Joe did appear at the dealership. She further explained to the representative that "buying sprees" was a symptom of Bobby Joe's illness, that he would not be able to make the payments, and that he was not insurable. When she notified Shoals Ford of the situation, it merely stated that if Bobby Joe had the money to purchase the truck, it was "none of her concern." Around 10 A.M. on April 5, 1989, she drove by Shoals Ford and, noticing that the truck was still there, she once again telephoned "to plead" with Shoals Ford to notify her when Bobby Joe arrived. At this time, the representative told her that "it was really not of concern to Shoals Ford."

According to Dr. Joseph W. Glaister, a local psychiatrist who had treated Bobby Joe since 1984, Bobby Joe suffered from a manic depressive illness, manic type, recurrent. Dr. Glaister testified that Bobby Joe's illness was episodic, that his competency could come and go, and that there were stages of the illness when, on mere observation, one might think that Bobby Joe was a slightly excessive, overly friendly individual. He further testified that Bobby Joe had been admitted to the hospital after regular working hours on April 5, 1989, and that when he saw Bobby Joe on April 6, 1989, Bobby Joe was incompetent. Furthermore, according to the testimony of Dr. Glaister, he could not visualize Bobby Joe being otherwise on April 5, 1989.

The daughter's attorney testified that he remembered the events of April 5, 1989, when the daughter contacted him, when he obtained a history of the events of the day, and when he prepared the commitment petition and other documents that were filed with the probate court on that morning. He stated that he did not prepare and file the petition to appoint Ms. Clardy as conservator and limited guardian for Bobby Joe until a month after the petition to commit, because Bobby Joe was hospitalized during that period of time and, in the attorney's opinion, had no opportunity to dissipate his estate.

Based on the foregoing, we hold that there was sufficient evidence to support the jury's verdict that during the period in question—from April 1, 1989 (when Bobby Joe began negotiations to purchase the truck), to April 3, 1989 (when Shoals Ford alleges the transaction was completed), to April 5, 1989 (when Ms. Clardy alleges the transaction was completed)—Bobby Joe was incompetent; that during that period of time, he was incapable of understanding and appreciating the nature, terms, and effect of the contract.

[AFFIRMED.]

Questions

1. The court speaks about Bobby Joe's "manic- depressive disorder for 15 years". Does that mean that any contract Bobby Joe entered into during this time is void?

2. Should the same result have been reached if Bobby Joe was taking his medicine as prescribed by his doctor?

3. What is the standard by which Bobby Joe should be measured against to see if he is competent to contract?

4. Was Bobby Joe's illness one of cognition or compulsion?

5. What was the significance of Ms. Clardy's contact with Shoals Ford? What if she had not contacted them? Different result?

6. What if Shoals Ford had listened to Ms. Clardy, telephoned the sheriff, the mental health center and others and learned that Bobby Joe had periodic bouts with manic-depression but was not always ill and could make judgments when not? They then sell him the truck and say "he looked and sounded OK when we saw and talked with him."

7. What significance would it have if the price that the truck was sold for was a fair one, *i.e.* in line with similar prices for similar vehicles in the area?

Note Cognitive vs. Compulsion

As the next case points out, cognitive tests are more established than compulsion tests. This is because a person who does not know who he is, or where he is clearly seems to be incapable of contracting, whereas a person who claims he was under a compulsion is more difficult to verify. A fast moving businesswoman who buys and sells real estate on a hunch may be a genius or a manic-depressive; it may not be easy to tell. If, however, she believes that she is Marie Antionette, Queen of France in 1789, dresses the part, requires all to bow before her and thinks that she is buying a new building on the outskirts of Versailles to augment the palace when in fact she is buying the Waldorf Towers in New York, it is probably easier for most people to tell that she is having a cognitive problem. Even here, what is the borderline between eccentricity and insanity? The law is not clear. The rules vary. The next case opens a door a little wider in New York.

Ortelere v. Teachers' Retirement Board of New York, 303 N.Y.S.2d 362, (N.Y., 1969.)

BREITEL, Judge.

This appeal involves the revocability of an election of benefits under a public employees' retirement system and suggests the need for a renewed examination of the kinds of mental incompetency which may render voidable the exercise of contractual rights. The particular issue arises on the evidently unwise and foolhardy selection of benefits by a 60-year-old teacher, on leave for mental illness and suffering from cerebral arteriosclerosis, after service as a public school-teacher and participation in a public retirement system for over 40 years. The teacher died a little less than two months after making her election of maximum benefits, payable to her during her life, thus causing the entire reserve to fall in. She left surviving her husband of 38 years of marriage and two grown children.

There is no doubt that any retirement system depends for its soundness on an actuarial experience based on the purely prospective selections of benefits and mortality rates among the covered group, and that retrospective or adverse selection after the fact would be destructive of a sound system. It is also true that members of retirement systems are free to make choices which to others may seem unwise or foolhardy. The issue here is narrower than any suggested by these basic principles. It is whether an otherwise irrevocable election may be avoided for incapacity because of known mental illness which resulted in the election when, except in the barest actuarial sense, the system would sustain no unfavorable consequences.

The husband and executor of Grace W. Ortelere, the deceased New York City schoolteacher, sues to set aside her application for retirement without option, in the event of her death. It is alleged that Mrs. Ortelere, on February 11, 1965, two months before her death from natural causes, was not mentally competent to execute a retirement application. By this application, effective the next day, she elected the maximum retirement allowance. She thus revoked her earlier election of benefits under which she named her husband a beneficiary of the un-exhausted reserve upon her death. Selection of the maximum allowance extinguished all interests upon her death.

Following a nonjury trial in Supreme Court, it was held that Grace Ortelere had been mentally incompetent at the time of her February 11 application, thus rendering it 'null and void and of no legal effect'. The Appellate Division, by a divided court, reversed the judgment of the Supreme Court and held that, as a matter of law, there was insufficient proof of mental incompetency as to this transaction.

Mrs. Ortelere's mental illness, indeed, psychosis, is undisputed. It is not seriously disputable, however, that she had complete cognitive judgment or awareness when she made her selection. A modern understanding of mental illness, however, suggests that incapacity to contract or exercise contractual rights may exist, because of volitional and affective impediments or disruptions in the personality, despite the intellectual or cognitive ability to understand. It will be recognized as the civil law parallel to the question of criminal responsibility which has been the recent concern of so many and has resulted in statutory and decisional changes in the criminal law.

Mrs. Ortelere, an elementary schoolteacher since 1924, suffered a 'nervous breakdown' in March, 1964 and went on a leave of absence expiring February 5, 1965. She was then 60 years old and had been happily married for 38 years. On July 1, 1964 she came under the care of Dr. D'Angelo, a psychiatrist, who diagnosed her breakdown as involutional psychosis, melancholia type. Dr. D'Angelo prescribed, and for about six weeks decedent underwent, tranquilizer and shock therapy. Although moderately successful, the therapy was not continued since it was suspected that she also suffered from cerebral arteriosclerosis, an ailment later confirmed. However, the psychiatrist continued to see her at monthly intervals until March, 1965. On March 28, 1965 she was hospitalized after collapsing at home from an aneurysm. She died ten days later; the cause of death was 'Cerebral thrombosis due to H(ypertensive) H(eart) D(isease).'

As a teacher she had been a member of the Teachers' Retirement System of the City of New York. This entitled her to certain annuity and pension rights, preretirement death benefits, and empowered her to exercise various options concerning the payment of her retirement allowance.

Some years before, on June 28, 1958, she had executed a 'Selection of Benefits under Option One' naming her husband as beneficiary of the unexhausted reserve. Under this option upon retirement her allowance would be less by way of periodic retirement allowances, but if she died before receipt of her full reserve the balance of the reserve would be payable to her husband. On June 16, 1960, two years later, she had designated her husband as beneficiary of her service death benefits in the event of her death prior to retirement.

Then on February 11, 1965, when her leave of absence had just expired and she was still under treatment, she executed a retirement application, the one here involved, selecting the maximum retirement allowance payable during her lifetime with nothing payable on or after death. She also, at this time, borrowed from the system the maximum cash withdrawal permitted, namely, $8,760. Three days earlier she had written the board, stating that she intended to retire on February 12 or 15 or as soon as she received 'the information I need in order to decide whether to take an option or maximum allowance.' She then listed eight specific questions, reflecting great understanding of the retirement system, concerning the various alternatives available. An extremely detailed reply was sent, by letter of February 15, 1965, although by that date it was technically impossible for her to change her selection. However, the board's chief clerk, before whom Mrs. Ortelere executed the application, testified that the questions were 'answered verbally by me on February 11th.' Her retirement reserve totaled $62,165 (after deducting the $8,760 withdrawal), and the difference between electing the maximum retirement allowance (no option) and the allowance under 'option one' was $901 per year or $75 per month. That is, had the teacher selected 'option one' she would have received an annual allowance of $4,494 or $375 per month, while if no option had been selected she would have received an annual allowance of $5,395 or $450 per month. [*Author's note: this $75 is a 20% increase in benefits. In today's economy, with the dollar's significantly reduced buying power since 1965 it would be the difference between receiving about $2,500 and receiving $3,000 per month. Could there be a valid reason why she might take out $50,000 (again today's buying power) and increase a monthly benefit by $500 when she was so ill? Consider the additional facts infra.*] Had she not withdrawn the cash the annual figures would be $5,247 and $6,148 respectively.

Following her taking a leave of absence for her condition, Mrs. Ortelere had become very depressed and was unable to care for herself. As a result her husband gave up his electrician's job, in which he earned $222 per week, to stay home and take care of her on a full-time basis. She left their home only when he accompanied her. Although he took her to the Retirement Board on February 11, 1965, he did not know why she went, and did not question her for fear 'she'd start crying hysterically that I was scolding her. That's the way she was. And I wouldn't upset her.'

The Orteleres were in quite modest circumstances. They owned their own home, valued at $20,000, and had $8,000 in a savings account. They also owned some farm land worth about $5,000. Under these circumstances, as revealed in this record, retirement for both of the Orteleres or the survivor of them had to be provided, as a practical matter, largely out of Mrs. Ortelere's retirement benefits.

According to Dr. D'Angelo, the psychiatrist who treated her, Mrs. Ortelere never improved enough to 'warrant my sending her back (to teaching).' A physician for the Board of Education examined her on February 2, 1965 to determine her fitness to return to teaching. Although not a psychiatrist but rather a specialist in internal medicine, this physician 'judged that she had apparently recovered from the depression' and that she appeared rational. However, before allowing her to return to teaching, a report was requested from Dr. D'Angelo concerning her condition. It is notable that the Medical Division of the Board of Education on February 24, 1965 requested that Mrs. Ortelere report to the board's 'panel psychiatrist' on March 11, 1965.

Dr. D'Angelo stated '(a)t no time since she was under my care was she ever mentally competent'; that '(m)entally she couldn't make a decision of any kind, actually, of any kind, small or large.' He also described how involutional melancholia affects the judgment process: 'They can't think rationally, no matter what the situation is. They will even tell you, 'I used to be able to think of anything and make any decision. Now,' they say, 'even getting up, I don't know whether I should get up or whether I should stay in bed.' Or, 'I don't even know how to make a slice of toast any more.' Everything is impossible to decide, and everything is too great an effort to even think of doing. They just don't have the effort, actually, because their nervous breakdown drains them of all their physical energies.'

While the psychiatrist used terms referring to 'rationality', it is quite evident that Mrs. Ortelere's psychopathology did not lend itself to a classification under the legal test of irrationality. It is undoubtedly, for this reason, that the Appellate Division was unable to accept his testimony and the trial court's finding of irrationality in the light of the prevailing rules as they have been formulated.

The well-established rule is that contracts of a mentally incompetent person who has not been adjudicated insane are voidable. Even where the contract has been partly or fully performed it will still be avoided upon restoration of the Status quo.

Traditionally, in this State and elsewhere, contractual mental capacity has been measured by what is largely a cognitive test. Under this standard the 'inquiry' is whether the mind was 'so affected as to render him wholly and absolutely incompetent to comprehend and understand the nature of the transaction'. A requirement that the party also be able to make a rational judgment concerning the particular transaction qualified the cognitive test. Conversely, it is also well recognized that contractual ability would be affected by insane delusions intimately related to the particular transaction.

These traditional standards governing competency to contract were formulated when psychiatric knowledge was quite primitive. They fail to account for one who by reason of mental illness is unable to control his conduct even though his cognitive ability seems unimpaired. When these standards were evolving it was thought that all the mental faculties were simultaneously affected by mental illness. This is no longer the prevailing view.

Of course, the greatest movement in revamping legal notions of mental responsibility has occurred in the criminal law. The nineteenth century cognitive test embraced in the M'Naghten rules has long been criticized and changed by statute and decision in many jurisdictions.

While the policy considerations for the criminal law and the civil law are different, both share in common the premise that policy considerations must be based on a sound understanding of the human mind and, therefore, its illnesses. Hence, because the cognitive rules are, for the most part, too restrictive and rest on a false factual basis they must be re-examined. Once it is understood that, accepting plaintiff's proof, Mrs. Ortelere was psychotic and because of that psychosis could have been incapable of making a voluntary selection of her retirement system benefits, there is an issue that a modern jurisprudence should not exclude, merely because her mind could pass a 'cognition' test based on nineteenth century psychology.

There has also been some movement on the civil law side to achieve a modern posture. For the most part, the movement has been glacial and has been disguised under traditional formulations. Various devices have been used to avoid unacceptable results under the old rules by finding unfairness or overreaching in order to avoid transactions.

In this State there has been at least one candid approach. In Faber v. Sweet Style Mfg. Corp., 40 Misc.2d 212, at p. 216, 242 N.Y.S.2d 763, at p. 768, Mr. Justice MEYER wrote: '(i)ncompetence to contract also exists when a contract is entered into under the compulsion of a mental disease or disorder but for which the contract would not have been made' (noted in 39 N.Y.U.L.Rev. 356). This is the first known time a court has recognized that the traditional standards of incompetency for contractual capacity are inadequate in light of contemporary psychiatric learning and applied modern standards. Prior to this, courts applied the cognitive standard giving great weight to objective evidence of rationality.

It is quite significant that Restatement, 2d, Contracts, states the modern rule on competency to contract. This is in evident recognition, and the Reporter's Notes support this inference, that, regardless of how the cases formulated their reasoning, the old cognitive test no longer explains the results. Thus, the new Restatement section reads: '(1) A person incurs only voidable contractual duties by entering into a transaction if by reason of mental illness or defect...(b) he is unable to act in a reasonable manner in relation to the transaction and the other party has reason to know of his condition.'

The avoidance of duties under an agreement entered into by those who have done so by reason of mental illness, but who have understanding, depends on balancing competing policy considerations. There must be stability in contractual relations and protection of the expectations of parties who bargain in good faith. On the other hand, it is also desirable to protect persons who may understand the nature of the transaction but who, due to mental illness, cannot control their conduct. Hence, there should be relief only if the other party knew or was put on notice as to the contractor's mental illness. Thus, the Restatement provision for avoidance contemplates that 'the other party has reason to know' of the mental illness (Id.).

When, however, the other party is without knowledge of the contractor's mental illness and the agreement is made on fair terms, the proposed Restatement rule is: 'The power of avoidance under subsection (1) terminates to the extent that the contract has been so performed in whole or in part or the circumstances have so changed that avoidance would be inequitable. In such a case a court may grant relief on such equitable terms as the situation requires.' (Restatement, 2d, Contracts, Supra, § 18C, subd. (2).)

The system was, or should have been, fully aware of Mrs. Ortelere's condition. They, or the Board of Education, knew of her leave of absence for medical reasons and the resort to staff psychiatrists by the Board of Education. Hence, the other of the conditions for avoidance is satisfied.

Lastly, there are no significant changes of position by the system other than those that flow from the barest actuarial consequences of benefit selection.

Nor should one ignore that in the relationship between retirement system and member, and especially in a public system, there is not involved a commercial, let alone an ordinary commercial, transaction. Instead the nature of the system and its announced goal is the protection of its members and those in whom its members have an interest. It is not a sound scheme which would permit 40 years of contribution and participation in the system to be nullified by a one-instant act committed by one known to be mentally ill. This is especially true if there would be no substantial harm to the system if the act were avoided. On the record none may gainsay that her selection of a 'no option' retirement while under psychiatric care, ill with cerebral arteriosclerosis, aged 60, and with a family in which she had always manifested concern, was so unwise and foolhardy that a factfinder might conclude that it was explainable only as a product of psychosis.

On this analysis it is not difficult to see that plaintiff's evidence was sufficient to sustain a finding that, when she acted as she did on February 11, 1965, she did so solely as a result of serious mental illness, namely, psychosis. Of course, nothing less serious than medically classified psychosis should suffice or else few contracts would be invulnerable to some kind of psychological attack. Mrs. Ortelere's psychiatrist testified quite flatly that as an involutional melancholiac in depression she was incapable of making a voluntary 'rational' decision. Of course, as noted earlier, the trial court's finding and perhaps some of the testimony attempted to fit into the rubrics of the traditional rules. For that reason rather than reinstatement of the judgment at Trial Term there should be a new trial under the proper standards frankly considered and applied.

Accordingly, the order of the Appellate Division should be reversed, without costs, and the action remanded to Special Term for a new trial.

JASEN, Judge [dissents on the facts].

1. Is there much doubt about which way the Court of Appeals wants this case to come out after the new trial?

2. What significance is there to her detailed inquiries when she wrote to the retirement board?

3. Why might she want an extra $75 per week for as long as she lived? Is there any indication that her husband was disabled or retiring from work permanently? Why might he not be working now but be able to work later? What was his trade?

4. You are the administrator for a retirement system and someone who has had a nervous breakdown and who has decided to retire comes in with a request to change his/her benefit payout schedule. Can you reasonably say to someone "You don't look so good to me. I think you shouldn't take the benefits without the option—your family needs the money more than you do"? Or could you say "We'll be glad to change your benefit schedule but we want a letter from your psychiatrist first saying you're competent to make decisions"? Might you be in breach of contract to do this?

Note on Coming of Age in America—or Liability Until You Do

Minority in most states is presumed until a person reaches the age of 18. Further, until that age the minor is not liable for most contractual obligations unless they are "necessaries." In some states the minor has a duty to restore the benefits received under the contract to the best of his/her ability before the contract can be avoided. In other states this is not required. Further, if a person is "emancipated" prior to his/her 18th birthday, the person can be held liable for all contractual obligations. Emancipation usually means being on your own, not living with parents or older siblings or relatives but supporting yourself. It is a complex doctrine and again varies from state to state. Marriage contracts which we will not explore in this course can be entered into at different ages in different states. One of the surest ways to obtain emancipation from parents is marriage.

Webster Street Partnership, Ltd., v. Sheridan, 220 Neb. 9, 368 N.W.2d 439 (Neb., 1985). Webster Street, a Nebraska based real estate company, entered into a written lease with two minors, Matthew Sheridan and Pat Wilwerding. At the time of execution of the lease both tenants were minors and, Webster Street "knew that fact." Webster Street commenced this suit after the tenants were unable to pay rent.

KRIVOSHA, Chief Justice.

As a general rule, an infant does not have the capacity to bind himself absolutely by contract. The right of the infant to avoid his contract is one conferred by law for his protection against his own improvidence and the designs of others. The policy of the law is to discourage adults from contracting with an infant; they cannot complain if, as a consequence of violating that rule, they are unable to enforce their contracts. As stated in Curtice Co. v. Kent, 89 Neb. 496, 500, 131 N.W. 944, 945 (1911): "The result seems hardly just to the [adult], but persons dealing with infants do so at their peril. The law is plain as to their disability to contract, and safety lies in refusing to transact business with them."

However, the privilege of infancy will not enable an infant to escape liability in all cases and under all circumstances. For example, it is well established that an infant is liable for the value of necessaries furnished him. An infant's liability for necessaries is based not upon his actual contract to pay for them but upon a contract implied by law, or, in other words, a quasi-contract.

Just what are necessaries, however, has no exact definition. The term is flexible and varies according to the facts of each individual case. In Cobbey v. Buchanan, 48 Neb. 391, 397, 67 N.W. 176, 178 (1896), we said: " 'The meaning of the term "necessaries" cannot be defined by a general rule applicable to all cases; the question is a mixed one of law and fact, to be determined in each case from the particular facts and circumstances in such case.' " A number of factors must be considered before a court can conclude whether a particular product or service is a necessary. As stated in Schoenung v. Gallet, 206 Wis. 52, 54, 238 N.W. 852, 853 (1931): "The term 'necessaries,' as used in the law relating to the liability of infants therefor, is a relative term, somewhat flexible, except when applied to such things as are obviously requisite for the maintenance of existence, and depends on the social position and situation in life of the infant, as well as upon his own fortune and that of his parents. The particular infant must have an actual need for the articles furnished; not for mere ornament or pleasure. The articles must be useful and suitable, but they are not necessaries merely because useful or beneficial. Concerning the general character of the things furnished, to be necessaries the articles must supply the infant's personal needs, either those of his body or those of his mind. However, the term 'necessaries' is not confined to merely such things as are required for a bare subsistence. There is no positive rule by means of which it may be determined what are or what are not necessaries, for what may be considered necessary for one infant may not be necessaries for another infant whose state is different as to rank, social position, fortune, health, or other circumstances, the question being one to be determined from the particular facts and circumstances of each case." (Citation omitted.) This appears to be the law as it is generally followed throughout the country.

In 42 Am.Jur.2d Infants § 67 at 68-69 (1969), the author notes: "Thus, articles are not necessaries for an infant if he has a parent or guardian who is able and willing to supply them, and an infant residing with and being supported by his parent according to his station in life is not absolutely liable for things which under other circumstances would be considered necessaries."

The undisputed testimony is that both tenants were living away from home, apparently with the understanding that they could return home at any time. It would therefore appear that in the present case neither Sheridan nor Wilwerding was in need of shelter but, rather, had chosen to voluntarily leave home, with the understanding that they could return whenever they desired. One may at first blush believe that such a rule is unfair. Yet, on further consideration, the wisdom of the rule is apparent. If, indeed, landlords may not contract with minors, except at their peril, they may refuse to do so. In that event, minors who voluntarily leave home but who are free to return will be compelled to return to their parents' home—a result which is desirable. We therefore find that both the municipal court and the district court erred in finding that the apartment, under the facts in this case, was a necessary.

Because the rental of the apartment was not a necessary, the minors had the right to avoid the contract, either during their minority or within a reasonable time after reaching their majority. Disaffirmance by an infant completely puts an end to the contract's existence, both as to him and as to the adult with whom he contracted. Because the parties then stand as if no contract had ever existed, the infant can recover payments made to the adult, and the adult is entitled to the return of whatever was received by the infant.

REVERSED AND REMANDED WITH DIRECTIONS.

Problems on Competency to Contract

1. Bobby Young is sixteen years old and contracts to lease a car from the We-Rent-Wrecks auto dealership for 5 years at $50 per month. After four months, Bobby decides that his bicycle is adequate and tells the dealership that he will not pay any more money. When We-Rent-Wrecks sues Bobby, will Bobby be able to escape liability? What about the $200 Bobby already paid?

2. Assume the same facts as #1, but Bobby is fully emancipated from home. Any difference?

3. Assume the same facts as #2 and Bobby told the dealership that he planned to use the car as his primary vehicle in his delivery service. Any difference?

4. Using the concept of implied contracts and necessity, can you think of any situations where a court would be likely to find a child (or infant) bound to a contract? See *Statler v Dodson 466 S.E.2d 497, (W. Va., 1995)*, which held the court can imply a contract for legal services with an infant if the "services are determined to be reasonably necessary to protect the infant's interest." In what other situations might a court want to imply a contract between an otherwise incompetent person and another party?

2. Duress, Undue Influence and Unconscionability

Note on Duress

According to Section 174 of the Restatement duress resulting from physical pressure will prevent the formation of a contract if the conduct appearing to be manifestation of assent was unintended by the party and physically compelled. Example X tells Y to say sign here. When Y refuses X kicks Y. Y then signs to avoid being kicked. Here, the writing shows a manifestation of assent, but Y's assent was compelled through the pressure of further physical harm by X.

If a party's manifestation of assent was induced by an improper threat of physical harm whereby the victim had no reasonable alternative to assenting, the contract can be voided by the victim. See Section 175 of the Restatement. A points gun at B and says "sign or else I will shoot."

Note on Undue Influence

According to Section 177 of the Restatement a party exercises undue influence when one party is under the domination of the other, or is of a relationship with the other party that the victim is justified in assuming that the party would not act against his welfare. If one party's manifestation of assent is induced by undue influence that contract can be voided by the victim.

Tidwell v. Crtiz, 282 S.E.2d 104, (Geo., 1981). The next case involves a supposed partnership between two doctors which went bad. Tidwell responded to an advertisement Critz placed in the American Medical Association Journal for the position as a radiotherapist. On December 10, 1979, the two signed a hand-written document ("Agreement") for a "medical association." In January 1980, after the two started working together, Critz presented Tidwell with a second detailed writing "Second Agreement" which created an employee-employer relationship between the parties and contained vastly different terms and conditions from the first Agreement. Under the Second Agreement either party could terminate the association by giving 30 days notice. The Second Agreement also contained an integration clause in paragraph 18. "This Agreement contains the entire understanding between the parties hereto, and supersedes any previous agreement or understanding between such parties."

Tidwell objected to the Second Agreement and claims Critz told him it was "temporary," and did not contradict the first signed Agreement. Tidwell finally signed the Second Agreement in late March 1980 because "Critz threatened to end his association with Tidwell and to have Tidwell's privileges to practice at Georgia Baptist and DeKalb General revoked if the latter did not sign the agreement." It is undisputed that Tidwell consulted his attorney prior to signing the Second Agreement.

Critz ended his association with Tidwell in October, 1980 citing poor work performance by Tidwell and his inability to cooperate with other hospital employees. Tidwell proceeded with this suit against Crtiz claiming the Second Agreement was invalid and should be canceled because he signed it "under duress and the undue influence of Critz." Critz moved for summary judgment on the grounds that Tidwell had freely signed the second agreement after consulting with his attorney, that the Second Agreement superseded the first.

The trial court granted summary judgment to Critz on the issue of duress, finding "that Tidwell's allegations were insufficient, as a matter of law, to constitute duress, but that even if they were sufficient, Tidwell had waived any claim 'by acceptance of benefits and performance under' the second contract." Tidwell appeals.

GREGORY, Justice.

Code Ann. § 20-503 provides: "The free assent of the parties being essential to a valid contract, duress either of imprisonment or by threats or other acts, by which the free will of the party is restrained and his consent induced will render the contract voidable at the instance of the injured party. Legal imprisonment, if not used for illegal purposes, is not duress." "Duress is considered a species of fraud in which compulsion in some form takes the place of deception in accomplishing an injury, and, like fraud, constitutes a meritorious ground to set aside a contract executed as a result thereof." King v. Lewis, 188 Ga. 594, 597, 4 S.E.2d 464 (1939). "Duress which will avoid a contract must consist of threats of bodily or other harm, or other means amounting to coercion, or tending to coerce the will of another, and actually inducing him to do an act contrary to his free will." Russell v. McCarty, 45 Ga. 197, 198 (1872). The threats must be sufficient to overcome the mind and will of a person of ordinary firmness." King v. Lewis, supra, at 597, 4 S.E.2d 464.

Tidwell alleges that each of Critz's threats meets the tests for duress set out above. First, he argues that Critz threatened to end his business association with Tidwell to induce him to sign the March 1980 employment agreement, "contrary to his free will." However, the threat of losing a job or fear of such loss is not duress which will void a contract.

Tidwell argues that this failure to act in concert with Critz's threats to have Tidwell's privileges to practice at DeKalb General and Georgia Baptist Hospitals revoked, "overcame" Tidwell's "will to reject the (March 1980) contract." Tidwell insists he "simply had no choice but to sign the second contract." At oral argument counsel for Tidwell stated that Tidwell was forced to sign the contract "out of sheer practicality." In determining that these alleged threats and acts by Critz, even if true, do not amount to a claim for duress which will render the second employment contract voidable, we take into account the fact that Tidwell, a highly educated professional, waited for nearly three months after being presented with the second employment contract before signing it. During this time Tidwell discussed the contract with an attorney of his own choosing. We cannot accept Tidwell's argument that "no amount of consultation with lawyers could alleviate the duress imposed by Critz." See Yearwood v. National Bank of Athens, 222 Ga. 709, 152 S.E.2d 360 (1966).

While we are not unsympathetic to Tidwell's difficult bargaining position, we cannot say that Critz's conduct or threats were such to induce Tidwell to act contrary to his free will or to coerce Tidwell "to pursue a different course from that which his own judgment at that time dictated as the best for his own interests." Candler v. Byfield, 160 Ga. 732, 738, 129 S.E. 57 (1925).

One may "not void a contract on grounds of duress merely because he entered into it with reluctance, the contract is very disadvantageous to him, the bargaining power of the parties was unequal or there was some unfairness in the negotiations preceding the agreement." 17 C.J.S. 944, § 168.

Giving Tidwell "the benefit of all reasonable doubts and all favorable inferences that may be drawn from the evidence." We conclude that there is no genuine issue as to any material fact and that Critz is entitled to a judgment on the issue of duress as a matter of law. The trial court did not err in granting Critz's motion for summary judgment on this issue.

Critz avers that the trial court erred in denying his motion for summary judgment on the issue of an accounting. He argues that the handwritten agreement between the parties, executed on December 10, 1979, was not to become effective until February, 1980; that while Tidwell waited until late March of 1980 to sign the second employment agreement, the agreement clearly states that it is "effective as of January 16, 1980"; that, therefore, even if the first agreement was valid, it never took effect. Critz further argues that even if Tidwell had signed the second agreement under duress or undue influence, he ratified the contract by accepting benefits under it. Consequently since an employer-employee relationship existed between the parties at all times, Tidwell is not entitled to an accounting under the "partnership" agreement of December 10, 1979.

We note at the outset that Code Ann. § 20-503, supra, does not render an otherwise valid contract made under duress void, but merely "voidable at the instance of the injured party." "Where the execution of a contract is procured by duress, the person executing it may, after the removal of duress, waive the duress and ratify the contract." Monk v. Holden, 186 Ga. 549, 555, 198 S.E. 697 (1938). For example, admission of liability under a contract, after removal of the duress, amounts to a ratification of the contract. The courts of this state have also recognized that accepting and retaining benefits arising from a contract executed under duress after removal of the duress, will result in a ratification of the contract. It must, however, be shown under each of these circumstances that the party intended to ratify the contract.

Once the complaining party is relieved from the operation of the duress he is "in a position either to disaffirm (his contract) or to allow it to stand undisturbed as the free and formal disposition of (his) rights. If (his) choice (is) to disaffirm, it might (be) evidenced by suit timely brought or by another action disclosing (his) purpose to those who would be affected." Barnette v. Wells Fargo National Bank, 270 U.S. 438, 444, 46 S.Ct. 326, 328, 70 L.Ed. 669 (1925).

Although Tidwell contends that he could not have ratified the contract because the duress was never removed, we cannot agree. Tidwell [does not] allege that Critz, at any time after the execution of the March 1980 agreement, threatened to end their association or to have Tidwell's privileges to practice medicine revoked if Tidwell did not continue to abide by the agreement. What the record does show is that Tidwell accepted compensation and bonus sums as provided under the second agreement, without apparent complaint, until the termination of his employment in October, 1980 when he filed this lawsuit. Thus while we find that Tidwell was not induced to sign the March 1980 agreement under duress, we conclude that since Tidwell took no action to disaffirm the March 1980 contract until after his employment was terminated, he waived any claim of duress. We further find that Tidwell ratified this agreement by accepting and retaining benefits under it. As the March, 1980 agreement states that it "supersedes any previous agreement" and as it is clear that the parties intended for this agreement to be effective on January 16, 1980, prior to the date when the "partnership" created by the December 10, 1979 agreement was to take effect, we agree with Critz that a partnership never existed between the parties.

Tidwell also alleged in his complaint that he had signed the March 1980 contract because of the "undue influence" of Critz. Critz denied the allegation and moved for summary judgment on this issue. Both parties complain that the trial court did not rule on this issue in its order granting partial summary judgment to Critz. "Where one party is under the domination of another, or by virtue of the relation between them is justified in assuming that the other party will not act in a manner inconsistent with his welfare, a transaction induced by unfair persuasion of the latter is induced by undue influence and is voidable." Restatement of Contracts, Vol. II, § 497.

"Undue influence which overturns an otherwise legal contract is the exercise of sufficient control over the person, the validity of whose act is brought into question, to destroy his free agency and constrain him to do what he would not have done if such control had not been exercised." Burroughs v. Reed, 150 Ga. 724, 725, 105 S.E. 290 (1920). To be "undue" the influence must be such to deprive a party "of his free agency by substituting for his will that of another." Scurry v. Cook, 206 Ga. 876, 878, 59 S.E.2d 371 (1950). In determining whether undue influence has been exerted, the courts will closely scrutinize confidential relationships or facts which show that the defendant "created the relationship of dominance" over the plaintiff. However, not all influence can be said to be undue "since a person is not prohibited from exercising proper influence to obtain a benefit to himself." Id. As with contracts made under duress, a contract made under undue influence is not ordinarily void, but merely voidable, and may be ratified once the undue influence has been removed.

As noted, the trial court correctly found, as a matter of law, that Tidwell waived his claim of duress when he ratified the March 1980 contract by accepting benefits and performing under it. We interpret this ruling to include a finding that Tidwell waived any claim of undue influence when he ratified the agreement.

We conclude that the trial court erred in not granting Critz's motion for summary judgment in its entirety.

Judgment affirmed.

Questions

1. What elements in the above relationship might constitute undue influence?

2. What is the difference between undue influence and duress?

3. The court notes that by taking benefits under the contract allegedly entered into because of duress or undue influence Tidwell waived his claims under those theories of disaffirmance. What types of situations might arise where the claimant could both take the benefit and still retain his/her claims?

Note on Confidential Relationships

Confidential relationships are recognized in law where the particular relationship between the parties creates an element of trust so that one party will believe he/she can rely on the other to act in his/her best interests. Examples are doctor/patient, lawyer/client, clergyperson/parishioner, husband/wife, parent/child. Often, however, particular facts will show such a relationship to exist between close friends. It is most often found where the relationship creates an aura of dependence of one person on another for advice, counsel, support. In some such relationships conversations between the parties are privileged and one party cannot be made to testify against another (lawyer, doctor, clergy, spouse.) Undue influence can arise because the dependent party can be taken advantage of by the dominant party. It is for this reason that contracts between lawyer and client where the lawyer is buying something from the client are often subject to strict scrutiny by the courts if the client claims he/she was taken advantage of. In some cases undue influence crosses over into a type of mental incapacity or disadvantage because the dependent person's will is bent by the dominant party. As with all of these cases the question boils down to whether the dependent party was capable of exercising free will or whether because of the circumstances he/she was influenced to such an extent that a choice was not possible.

Note on Void vs. Voidable

If something is void it has no legal effect. It is without legal effect *ab initio*, from the very beginning. An agreement to pay a gambling debt in many states has no legal effect. It cannot be sued upon by either party. Once the nature of the agreement comes to the court's attention, the suit will be dismissed. A voidable agreement, on the other hand, is effective as a contract until a party seeks to have it avoided. The agreements which we examine in Part V are voidable. In essence the difference is that the party seeking to avoid the contract must establish the grounds for avoidance, infancy, mental incapacity, duress. If the party does not seek avoidance on these grounds, the other party may enforce it.

Myers v. United States, 943 F.Supp. 815, (Mich., 1996).

[Mary Myers (plaintiff) and Matthew Myers (third party defendant) are married. On September 4, 1986, Mr. Myers was indicted on drug conspiracy charges, possession with intent to distribute and the distribution of marijuana, and operating a continuing criminal enterprise and faced a possible life sentence if convicted on all charges. The government also maintained that because Mr. Myers' assets were the result of a "continuing criminal conspiracy" they were all subject to forfeiture pursuant to the 18 U.S.C. § 1963. On May 16, 1987, two days before his scheduled trial Mr. Myers struck a plea bargain with the Government. He agreed to surrender all of his property with the exception of his estate on which there would be a lien to insure the payment of apparently past due taxes. Both Mr. and Mrs. Myers signed the plea bargain agreement. No one from the government ever discussed the terms of the agreement with Mrs. Myers or the fact that her signature was required to effect the forfeiture and lien. Mr. Myers spent approximately four years in prison, while Mrs. Myers remained on the residential estate. He then joined her there (on the estate.)

In 1994, Mary Myers brought this action to quiet title, asking this Court to find that the government has no interest in her alleged undivided one-half interest in the residential estate. The government filed a counterclaim seeking enforcement of the plea agreement signed by the Myers.]

BENJAMIN F. GIBSON, District Judge.

The parties agree that Michigan contract law should be used to determine the validity of the plea agreement as it relates to Mrs. Myers. Plaintiff claims that the plea agreement is void because...(2) plaintiff was under duress at the time she signed the agreement, (3) plaintiff did not understand the ramifications of the contract....

Plaintiff argues that the agreement is voidable because she was under duress at the time she signed the agreement. " 'The question as to what constitutes duress is a matter of law, but whether duress exists in a particular case is a question of fact.' " Norton v. Michigan State Highway Dept., 315 Mich. 313, 24 N.W.2d 132, 135 (1946) (quoting Clement v. Buckley Mercantile Co., 172 Mich. 243, 137 N.W. 657 (1912)).

The Norton court adopted the definition of duress and coercion established in Hackley v. Headley, 45 Mich. 569, 8 N.W. 511, 512 (1881), which held: "Duress exists when one by the unlawful acts of another is induced to make a contract or perform some act under circumstances which deprive him of the exercise of free will." Norton, 24 N.W.2d at 135 (quoting Hackley, supra). In Apfelblat v. National Bank Wyandotte-Taylor, 158 Mich.App. 258, 404 N.W.2d 725, 728 (1987), the court held that "[d]uress requires compulsion or coercion by which one is illegally forced to act by fear of serious injury to person, reputation or fortune." The court explained that "[f]ear of financial ruin alone is insufficient to establish economic duress; it must also be established that the person applying the coercion acted unlawfully." Id.

This Court finds from the testimony of every witness, including Mrs. Myers, that no one representing the government ever spoke with Mrs. Myers about the plea agreement. Therefore, this Court finds, as a matter of law, that Mrs. Myers did not sign the agreement under duress.

Next, plaintiff argues that the contract is voidable because her emotional state prevented her from understanding the details of the agreement, and the government failed to explain them to her. Mrs. Myers testified that she was distraught the day she signed the agreement and was not thinking about her property. Instead, she claims she was focusing on her husband and his possible jail sentence. She explained that, in this emotional state, she was unable to understand the contents of the agreement even though she read it. She further explained that at that time in her life she lacked assertiveness and always did whatever others asked her to do. She said that she would never have refused to sign an agreement her husband asked her to sign.

In Horn v. Cooke, 118 Mich.App. 740, 325 N.W.2d 558, 561 (1982), the plaintiff challenged the validity of an agreement because "she was unable to understand the nature and consequences of the arbitration agreement due to her limited ability to read and her fears regarding the surgery, as well as defendants failure to explain the agreement to her." The court upheld the agreement, finding that plaintiff knowingly waived her right to trial. In doing so, the court quoted from Sponseller v. Kimball, 246 Mich. 255, 260, 224 N.W. 359 (1929), which held: "The stability of written instruments demands that a person who executes one shall know its contents or be chargeable with such knowledge. If he cannot read, he should have a reliable person read it to him. His failure to do so is negligence which estops him from voiding the instrument on the ground that he was ignorant of its contents, in the absence of circumstances fairly excusing his failure to inform himself." Id. 325 N.W.2d at 561-62.

The Court finds that if Mrs. Myers could not understand the plea agreement for any reason, except mental incapacity, she had the duty to request an explanation. Her failure to do so estops her from claiming the contract is void because she did not understand its provisions.

In addition, being in a state of emotional distress is not a sufficient reason to void a contract. In Van Wagoner v. Van Wagoner, 131 Mich.App. 204, 346 N.W.2d 77, 82 (1983) (citing Star Realty Inc. v. Bower, 17 Mich.App. 248, 258, 169 N.W.2d 194 (1969)), the court held that "emotional disorders, alone, will not invalidate a contract." Instead, a person must show that he or she lacked the mental capacity to understand the contract. The court in Star Realty explained the test for mental capacity as follows: The well-settled test of mental capacity to contract...is whether the person in question possesses sufficient mind to understand, in a reasonable manner, the nature and effect of the act in which he is engaged. However, to avoid a contract it must appear not only that the person was of unsound mind or insane when it was made, but that the unsoundness or insanity was of such a character that he had no reasonable perception of the nature or terms of the contract.

There has been no testimony to suggest that Mrs. Myers was mentally incapable, as the law defines those terms, of entering into the plea agreement on May 16, 1987. Accordingly, the Court finds that Mary Myers was competent to enter into an agreement with the government.

[Judgment for the government].

Question

1. Mrs. Myers tried to argue the plea bargain was obtained under duress, or in the alternative she signed it while under severe emotional stress? Which one would give her legal relief? What facts would she need to prove?

DuFort v. Aetna Life Insurance Co., 818 F.Supp 578 (S.D.N.Y., 1993). [In 1986 Henry DuFort filed for a claim for total disability benefits under his policy with Aenta Life Insurance Company, due to a back condition which prevented him from working. Aetna stopped payments in January 1987, when a doctor acting on Aetna's behalf determined DuFort "was not totally disabled within the meaning of the policy." The two parties disputed these issues until a March 3, 1989, conversation between Dufort and Feury, an Aetna agent. DuFort alleges that Feury offered him $102,000 on a "take it or leave it basis," and Feury threatened him that "we are going to make this thing drag...and if you go to court, it will take years to be resolved, and from what I understand, from where you live and what I know about you, you will become homeless and hungry." Feury denies these statements and claims that DuFort proposed the $102,000 settlement. Both sides agree, however, that as a result of the March 3, 1989 discussion, Aetna and DuFort agreed to settle DuFort's claim for a lump sum payment of $102,000.

As part of the settlement, DuFort signed a general release prohibiting him and his heirs from ever bringing any action against Aetna. However, within a week of signing the release, DuFort allegedly called Aetna's office to try to cancel the agreement. After Aetna refused his request, DuFort picked up and spent the settlement funds.

Since February 1989, DuFort has been receiving treatment from a psychiatrist, Dr. Martin Hurwitz . Hurwitz diagnosed DuFort as a psychotic depressive which prevents him from exercising reasoned judgment in business matters, although there are periods of time where his judgment and comprehension fluctuate markedly. Hurwitz further testified that the day DuFort signed the release he was "[u]nstable, agitated, disheveled" and suicidal. Although DuFort claims to have been mentally incompetent throughout his relationship with Aetna, he concedes that he never specifically informed Aetna of that condition. Rather, during their March 1989 conversation, DuFort merely told Feury in that he was "very, very sick."

Defendants move for summary judgment on the grounds that DuFort's claims are precluded by the March 1989. DuFort claims that the release is not binding because he signed it while under economic duress and while mentally incompetent.]

FREEH, District Judge.

It is well established in New York that " 'a valid release which is clear and unambiguous on its face and which is knowingly and voluntarily entered into will be enforced as a private agreement between parties.' " Skluth v. United Merchants & Manufacturers, Inc., 163 A.D.2d 104, 559 N.Y.S.2d 280, 282 (1st Dept.1990). Thus, a release will be binding on the parties absent a showing of fraud, duress, undue influence, or some other valid legal defense.

1. Economic Duress

DuFort claims that the March 1989 release is not binding because he signed that release as a result of economic duress. While claims of economic duress frequently involve factual issues which cannot be resolved by summary judgment, DuFort has failed to raise any question of fact as to an essential element of this defense. Accordingly, defendants are entitled to judgment as a matter of law on that claim.

In order to make out a claim for economic duress, DuFort must establish that the release was obtained "(1) by means of a wrongful threat precluding the exercise of free will; (2) under the press of financial circumstances; (3) where circumstances permitted no other alternative." Austin Instrument, Inc. v. Loral Corporation, 29 N.Y.2d 124, 324 N.Y.S.2d 22, 272 N.E.2d 533 (1971).

New York courts have interpreted the first of these elements, a wrongful threat precluding the exercise of free will, fairly strictly, and have held that "[a] threat to do that which one has the right to do does not constitute duress." Gerstein v. 532 Broad Hollow Road Co., 75 A.D.2d 292, 429 N.Y.S.2d 195, 199 (1st Dept.1980). The party seeking to avoid an otherwise valid contract on duress grounds cannot simply claim that the other party threatened to breach their agreement. See Orix Credit Alliance, Inc. v. Hanover, 182 A.D.2d 419,582 N.Y.S.2d 153, 154 (1st Dept.1992) ("A mere threat by one party to a contract to breach it by not delivering required items, indeed, financial or business pressure of all kinds, even if exerted in the context of unequal bargaining power, does not constitute economic duress."); Weinraub v. International Banknote Co., 422 F.Supp. 856, 859 (S.D.N.Y.1976) ("[m]ere hard bargaining positions, if lawful, and the press of financial circumstances, not caused by the defendant, will not be deemed duress").

A party raising duress must also do more than merely claim that the other party knew about and used his or her poor financial condition to obtain an advantage in contract negotiations. Rather, in order to prevail on a duress claim, the plaintiff must show that the defendant's actions "deprived [him] of [his] free will," and that "the ordinary remedy of an action for a breach of contract would not be adequate." Austin, 324 N.Y.S.2d at 26, 272 N.E.2d 533.

DuFort cannot do so here. Even assuming, as the Court must, that DuFort's account of his March 3, 1989 conversation with Feury is true, Feury's statements amount to no more than a threat to defend vigorously Aetna's position that it had no liability under the disability policy. DuFort had been examined by a licensed physician who declared that he was not "totally disabled" within the meaning of Aetna's policy. Thus, Aetna had no clear legal obligation to make any payment to DuFort. While Aetna may have lost had DuFort sued for breach of the policy, under the circumstances, a legitimate dispute existed as to DuFort's disability and Aetna made no "wrongful threat" by defending its position in that dispute.

In the Court's view, Feury's statement that DuFort "[would] become homeless and hungry" if he did not settle with Aetna was unnecessarily harsh. However, the legal question is whether that statement constituted a "wrongful threat" as a matter of law. It is undisputed that Aetna was not the cause of DuFort's financial problems. Thus, Feury's statement amounts to no more than a prediction or dramatization of DuFort's hardship, not a threat to impose such a hardship.

DuFort [also] alleges mental incapacity as well as economic duress. If DuFort was mentally incompetent at the time he spoke with Feury in March 1989, he could have perceived Feury's statements as threats rather than hard bargaining tactics. However, DuFort has not cited—and the Court has not located—any New York case holding that the existence of a wrongful threat is determined by the alleged incompetent's subjective perceptions. To the contrary, it appears that the existence of a wrongful threat must be evaluated under an objective standard. See Harrison, 790 F.Supp. at 455 (analyzing alleged duress under objective standard, even where plaintiff had alleged mental incompetence). As a result, DuFort cannot rely on his alleged mental incompetence to support his duress claims.

2. Mental Incompetence

DuFort contends that the release is voidable because at the time he signed that agreement, he was mentally incompetent to do so. In New York, capacity to contract is presumed. The party asserting incompetence must prove that status "at the time of the disputed transaction,... an extremely heavy [burden]." Harrison, 790 F.Supp. at 447 (citing Feiden v. Feiden, 151 A.D.2d 889, 542 N.Y.S.2d 860, 862 (3d Dept.1989)). DuFort must also show that Aetna knew or should have known of his condition.

The parties dispute whether DuFort was in fact incompetent to contract at the time he signed the release on March 16, 1989. It is undisputed, however, that Aetna did not know and had no reason to know about DuFort's alleged mental condition. In fact, at his deposition, DuFort conceded that he never told Feury or any other Aetna employee that he was depressed or otherwise mentally incapacitated. According to DuFort, he merely told Feury that he was "very, very sick" and not feeling well, statements that were consistent with his claim of total physical disability. Nothing in the record suggests that, by his conduct or statements, DuFort put Aetna on notice of a potential mental incapacity. As a result, the Court finds that Aetna did not know and should not have known of DuFort's alleged mental condition.

In Ortelere [see *supra*,], however, the New York Court of Appeals recognized that, under certain limited circumstances, a contract may be voided even if one party had no reason to know of the other's mental incompetence. Quoting the Restatement 2d of Contracts, the Court stated that "[w]hen...the other party is without knowledge of the contractor's mental illness and the agreement is made on fair terms...[t]he power of avoidance...terminates to the extent that the contract has been so performed in whole or in part or the circumstances have so changed that avoidance would be inequitable. In such a case a court may grant relief on such equitable terms as the situation requires." 303 N.Y.S.2d at 369-70, 250 N.E.2d 460. See, e.g., Pentinen v. New York State Employees' Retirement System, 60 A.D.2d 366, 401 N.Y.S.2d 587, 588 (3d Dept.1978) (noting that in retirement system cases, courts have allowed rescission of contracts despite lack of knowledge regarding mental incompetency where "there was proof that the [defendant] would not be prejudiced or that avoidance would not be inequitable").

DuFort argues that this Court should exercise its equitable powers to set aside the 1989 release despite Aetna's lack of knowledge regarding his condition and despite the fact that the contract has been fully performed.

However, given the factual dispute regarding DuFort's actual mental condition at the time the release was signed and DuFort's heavy burden on this issue, the Court cannot do so at this time.[1] A hearing will therefore be held on April 22, 1993 at 10:00 a.m. regarding DuFort's mental condition on March 16, 1989. If appropriate, defendants may renew their motion for summary judgment following that hearing.

For the foregoing reasons, defendants' motion is granted in part and denied in part.

Question

1. The court cites *Austin v. Loral, supra* Part III-C. How does the *Dufort* case differ on the duress issue?

Note on Unconscionability

Unconscionability differs from bad faith in that unconscionability most often goes to the contract formation stage whereas bad faith goes to the manner in which a person performs his/her duties under the already formed contract. This distinction, however, is not always recognized by the courts.

As with infancy, mental incapacity, duress and undue influence, the question is whether the person seeking to disaffirm the contract was able to make a reasoned choice. In some way was his free will overcome. Was he forced to do something. The force, however, is not so much overt physical or psychological force as a more subtle influencing of the will. Furthermore, no element of confidentiality is needed. Unconscionability is more akin to fraud or trickery than it is to pressure although elements of pressure are often present. It is in many ways a catch-all basis for asserting the unfairness and hence unenforceability of a contract. Duress in its most basic form is the use of force or the threat of force. Undue influence is akin to this but not so blatant. Unconscionability is taking advantage of someone's naiveté or unease. There is a fine line between driving a hard bargain and acting in an unconscionable way. It is a very fact specific remedy.

The cases below illustrate various situations where it arises. The more educated, intelligent, worldly-wise a person is, the less likely he or she will be able to find a remedy here. Unconscionability does not imply force. It implies manipulation. The line between being a good salesperson and being unconscionable often depends on the person with whom you are dealing.

Unconscionability often is divided into two subparts—substantive unconscionability and procedural unconscionability. The two often blend together. Substantive unconscionability relates to the substance of the bargain; procedural unconscionability relates to how it was made. Many state statutes have their source and foundation in this doctrine. The Uniform Consumer Credit Code

---

1. DuFort's psychiatrist did testify during his deposition that DuFort suffers from a mental condition which prevented him from exercising reasoned judgment or understanding the "nature of a surrender of an insurance policy." (Friedman Aff.Ex. 8 at 52). That doctor also indicated DuFort's condition went beyond mere depression into psychosis. However, the record does not clearly indicate whether DuFort was psychotic or suffering some other condition at the time he signed the release on March 19, 1989. Given DuFort's heavy burden on this issue, the Court cannot find that DuFort was mentally incompetent as a matter of law, and cannot rely on that incompetence to set aside the release.

(U.C.C.C.) and the Uniform Consumer Sales Practices Act (U.C.S.P.A.) are two such acts. Although the UCCC has been enacted in more states, both set up certain objective standards which make a bargain unenforceable. For example, finance charges are limited in amount and in the manner in which they can be calculated in the UCCC. While the act does not state that a higher charge or a different manner of calculation is unconscionable but merely makes them unenforceable and sets penalties for violators, in essence the basis for the limitations is fairness, conscionability. The UCSPA is more specific. For example, a higher charge for goods than is customary in a given area is a form of substantive unconscionability and the contract can be voided; to sell goods which are not needed to people with limited education or language skills, even if they are fairly priced, is procedurally unconscionable and the contract is voidable.

One common example of an objective, specific right available to any buyer is the right in many states for anyone to avoid a contract within a specific period of time after it was entered into (often 72 hours) if the contract was signed in the person's home. Oddly enough, people are most vulnerable to sales manipulation in their own homes. Courtesy or hospitality to the nice young man or woman making the oh, so friendly pitch causes many people to agree to obligations which on reflection they later regret. They find it hard to say no and just tell the salesperson to go. To make certain that people know of this right, statutes require home sales contracts to have the legend in capital letters immediately above where people sign telling them of their 72 hour right of cancellation and their right to a copy of the writing they sign immediately upon signing. Failure to follow these requirements voids the contract at the buyer's option.

Many years ago, before these statutes were ever drafted, I learned from a district attorney that sales teams gear their pitches to the neighborhoods and populations they are working. In some, they will tell the customer that he or she is helping the salesperson go to school, or seek treatment for an illness. In others, they use attractive women or personable young men to distract the mark. The goods are often of fine quality. It is just that the buyers don't often really want or need them but for whatever reason find it hard to say no. Magazines, encyclopedias, aluminum siding, roofing, home heating—there is no limit. The line between selling and deceiving is often a thin one. The deception is often not as to what the person is receiving but to how much is being charged or how the deal is closed.

The statutes grew out of case law and public awareness of the problem.

Our first case is a classic. So much so that it is cited in the comments to Uniform Commercial Code section 2-302 as an early example from which the statute was drawn. Under the U.C.C. the key elements are surprise and oppression. It is not fraud and it is not duress. It is a first cousin to both.

Campbell Soup Co. v. Wentz

172 F.2d 80
United States Court of Appeals, Third Circuit, 1948.

[The plaintiff Campbell Soup Co. sought a decree of specific performance from the lower court to compel defendant, a carrot farmer, to deliver the crop of Chantenay carrots which plaintiff had contracted for at $30 per ton and which were selling for up to $90 per ton on the open market. Equitable relief was being sought because carrots were "virtually unobtainable" on the open market and therefore plaintiff maintained it had no adequate remedy at law in damages. The lower court denied equitable relief on the ground that plaintiff had not established the need for the carrots in its business.]

GOODRICH, Circuit Judge.

These are appeals from judgments of the District Court denying equitable relief to the buyer under a contract for the sale of carrots. . . .

A party may have specific performance of a contract for the sale of chattels if the legal remedy is inadequate. Inadequacy of the legal remedy is necessarily a matter to be determined by an examination of the facts in each particular instance.

We think that on the question of adequacy of the legal remedy the case is one appropriate for specific performance. It was expressly found that at the time of the trial it was 'virtually impossible to obtain Chantenay carrots in the open market.'

The trial court concluded that the plaintiff had failed to establish that the carrots, 'judged by objective standards,' are unique goods. This we think is not a pure fact conclusion like a finding that Chantenay carrots are of uniform color. It is either a conclusion of law or of mixed fact and law and we are bound to exercise our independent judgment upon it. That the test for specific performance is not necessarily 'objective' is shown by the many cases in which equity has given it to enforce contracts for articles- family heirlooms and the like- the value of which was personal to the plaintiff.

Judged by the general standards applicable to determining the adequacy of the legal remedy we think that on this point the case is a proper one for equitable relief. There is considerable authority, old and new, showing liberality in the granting of an equitable remedy. We see no reason why a court should be reluctant to grant specific relief when it can be given without supervision of the court or other time-consuming processes against one who has deliberately broken his agreement. Here the goods of the special type contracted for were unavailable on the open market, the plaintiff had contracted for them long ahead in anticipation of its needs, and had built up a general reputation for its products as part of which reputation uniform appearance was important. We think if this were all that was involved in the case specific performance should have been granted.

The reason that we shall affirm instead of reversing with an order for specific performance is found in the contract itself. We think it is too hard a bargain and too one-sided an agreement to entitle the plaintiff to relief in a court of conscience. For each individual grower the agreement is made by filling in names and quantity and price on a printed form furnished by the buyer. This form has quite obviously been drawn by skillful draftsmen with the buyer's interests in mind.

Paragraph 2 provides for the manner of delivery. Carrots are to have their stalks cut off and be in clean sanitary bags or other containers approved by Campbell. This paragraph concludes with a statement that Campbell's determination of conformance with specifications shall be conclusive.

The defendants attack this provision as unconscionable. We do not think that it is, standing by itself. We think that the provision is comparable to the promise to perform to the satisfaction of another and that Campbell would be held liable if it refused carrots which did in fact conform to the specifications.

The next paragraph allows Campbell to refuse carrots in excess of twelve tons to the acre. The next contains a covenant by the grower that he will not sell carrots to anyone else except the carrots rejected by Campbell nor will he permit anyone else to grow carrots on his land. Paragraph 10 provides liquidated damages to the extent of $50 per acre for any breach by the grower. There is no provision for liquidated or any other damages for breach of contract by Campbell.

The provision of the contract which we think is the hardest is paragraph 9, set out in the margin.[1] It will be noted that Campbell is excused from accepting carrots under certain circumstances. But even under such circumstances the grower, while he cannot say Campbell is liable for failure to take the carrots, is not permitted to sell them elsewhere unless Campbell agrees. This is the kind of provision which the late Francis H. Bohlen would call 'carrying a good joke too far.' What the grower may do with his product under the circumstances set out is not clear. He has covenanted not to store it anywhere except on his own farm and also not to sell to anybody else.

We are not suggesting that the contract is illegal. Nor are we suggesting any excuse for the grower in this case who has deliberately broken an agreement entered into with Campbell. We do think, however, that a party who has offered and succeeded in getting an agreement as tough as this one is, should not come to a chancellor and ask court help in the enforcement of its terms. That equity does not enforce unconscionable bargains is too well established to require elaborate citation.

The plaintiff argues that the provisions of the contract are separable. We agree that they are, but do not think that decisions separating out certain provisions from illegal contracts are in point here. As already said, we do not suggest that this contract is illegal. All we say is that the sum total of its provisions drives too hard a bargain for a court of conscience to assist.

The judgments will be affirmed.

Questions

1. The parties reached a legally binding and effective contract, yet the farmers were excused from performing. Why? Specifically, what makes this contract unconscionable?

2. Why is Campbell suing for specific performance? The court states it could have awarded Campbell specific performance but did not. Why? Do you agree with the court?

---

1. 'Grower shall not be obligated to deliver any Carrots which he is unable to harvest or deliver, nor shall Campbell be obligated to receive or pay for any Carrots which it is unable to inspect, grade, receive, handle, use or pack at or ship in processed form from its plants in Camden (1) because of any circumstance beyond the control of Grower or Campbell, as the case may be, or (2) because of any labor disturbance, work stoppage, slowdown, or strike involving any of Campbell's employees. Campbell shall not be liable for any delay in receiving Carrots due to any of the above contingencies. During periods when Campbell is unable to receive Grower's Carrots, Grower may with Campbell's written consent, dispose of his Carrots elsewhere. Grower may not, however, sell or otherwise dispose of any Carrots which he is unable to deliver to Campbell.'

3. What result should be reached if Campbell and the farmers entered into the same contract but without the clause under footnote 1? See *Campbell Soup Co. v. Diehm, 111 F.Supp 211 (Penn., 1952).*

Wollums v. Horsley
20 S.W. 781
Court Of Appeals Of Kentucky, 1892

HOLT, C.J.

In August, 1887, the appellant, John Wollums, was living upon his mountain farm of about 200 acres in Bell county. He was then about 60 years old, uneducated, afflicted with disease disabling him from work, owned no other land, and but very little personal property. He knew but little of what was going on in the business world, owing to his situation and circumstances in life. He moved in a small circle. At this time the appellee, J.W. Horsley. who was then a man of large and varied experience in business, who was then buying mineral rights in that locality by the thousands of acres, and who was evidently familiar with all that was then going on and near at hand in the way of business and development in that section, through his agent entered into a contract with the appellant, which was signed by the latter only, by which he sold to Horsley all the oils, gases, and minerals in his land, with customary mining privileges, for 40 cents per acre, and obligated himself to convey the same by general warranty deed free of dower claim or other encumbrance when the money was paid, to wit, one half in three months, and the balance in four months from the first payment, or as soon as the deed should be made; three dollars of it, however, being then paid.

It is suggestive upon the question of the then value of the purchase, and as regarded by Horsley, that his agent, who made me it, was to get $80 for his pay, or as much as Wollums was to receive for all he sold, and also that this agent does not testify in the case.... In December, 1888, this suit was brought for a specific performance of the contract. The main defense is that it was procured through undue advantage, and under such circumstances that in equity its performance should not be decreed.... The specific execution of the contract was ordered. Considering all the circumstances, and the rule applicable in such a case, the judgment should not be upheld. There is a distinction between the case of a plaintiff asking a specific performance of a contract in equity and that of a defendant resisting such a performance. Its specific performance is not a matter of absolute right in the party, but of the sound discretion in the court. It requires less strength of case on the side of the defendant to resist the bill than it does upon the part of the plaintiff to enforce it. *If the court refuses to enforce specifically, the party is left to his remedy at law.* [Emphasis supplied] Thus a hard or unconscionable bargain will not be specifically enforced, nor, if the decree will produce injustice, or under all the circumstances be inequitable, will it be rendered. In other words, a court of equity will not exercise its power in this direction to enforce a claim which is not, under all the circumstances, just as between the parties, and it will allow a defendant to resist a decree where the plaintiff will not always be allowed relief upon the same evidence. A contract ought not to be carried into specific performance unless it be just and fair in all respects. When this relief is sought, ethics are considered, and a court of equity will sometimes refuse to set aside a contract, and yet refuse its specific performance. Story says:

"Courts of equity will not proceed to decree a specific performance where the contract is founded in fraud, imposition, mistake, undue advantage, or gross misapprehension, or where, from a change of circumstances or otherwise, it would be unconscientious to enforce it." 2 Story, Eq. Jur. § 750a. Kent also says: "It is a rule in equity that all the material facts must be known to both parties to render the agreement fair and just in all its parts; and it is against all the principles of equity that one party, knowing a material ingredient in an agreement, should be permitted to suppress it, and still call for a specific performance." 2 Kent, Comm. p. 491. It was held in Patterson v. Bloomer, 95 Amer. Dec. 218, and the same rule has been announced in other cases, that an application for specific performance is addressed to the court's sound discretion, and will not be granted unless the contract is made according to legal requirements, is certain, reasonable, equitable, mutual, on sufficient consideration, consistent with public policy, and is free from gross misapprehension, fraud, surprise, or mistake. The appellee testifies that he did not know anything as to the mineral value of this land when the contract was made, but it is evident he had a thorough knowledge of the value in this respect of lands generally in that section, and of the developments then in progres or near at hand. All this was unknown to the appellant. It is evident his land was valuable almost altogether in a mineral point of view. While it is not shown what it was worth at the date of the contract, yet it is proven to have been worth in April, 1889, $15 an acre, and that this value arises almost altogether from its mineral worth; and yet the appellee is asking the enforcement of a contract by means of which he seeks to obtain all the oil, gas, and minerals, and the virtual control of the land, at 40 cents an acre. The interest he claims under the contract is substantially the value of the land. Equity should not help such a harsh bargain. The appellee shows pretty plainly by his own testimony that when the contract was made he was advised of the probability of the building of a railroad in that locality in the near future. His agent, when the trade was made, assured the appellant that he would never be bothered by the contract during his lifetime. He was lulled in the belief that the Rip Van Winkle sleep of that locality in former days was to continue, and the grossly inadequate price of this purchase can only be accounted for upon the ground that the appellant was misled and acted under gross misapprehension. The contract was not equitable or reasonable, or grounded upon sufficient consideration, and no interest has arisen in any third party. A court of equity should therefore refuse its specific enforcement, but the appellant should have what was in fact paid, with its interest, and, when this is done, his petition should be dismissed. Judgment reversed, and cause remanded for proceedings consistent with this opinion.

Questions

1. If the land was worth $15 at the time of contracting what would appellee's damages be if appellee pursued his remedy at law?

2. Why might appellee hesitate to pursue his remedy at law in rural Kentucky in the 1890's?

3. Why refuse an equitable remedy while allowing appellee to pursue a legal remedy?

4. Whatever happened to the rule that courts will not consider the adequacy of consideration but only its sufficiency?

5. Is there any way that Horsley could have made a contract with Wollums and had it enforceable in equity?

Note on Law vs. Equity

In the last two cases the courts refused an equitable remedy. This result is possible because at early English Common Law the chancellors in equity would act only when a remedy at law was not possible. The King's law courts operated on the basis of writs. If your case did not fit into the terms of a writ, you could not gain access to the courts. Disappointed would-be litigants then turned to the King's Chancellor who was often a churchman, a bishop or other high office holder. The Chancellor would act if he thought the case had merit and the plaintiff was acting fairly and honestly. The chancellor would not act if the plaintiff did not have "clean hands." The chancellor's court became know as a court of conscience or equity. Instead of fixed rules of law, the chancellor would apply more broadly based principles developed often from theology. Ideas of fairness and evenhandedness developed here less in terms of fixed rules and more in terms of flexible ideas. A principle role of the chancellor was to refuse to act even if the litigant had no remedy in the King's courts unless the litigant could show the worthiness of his cause. Although law and equity are united in one court system in almost all states today, the principles of equity jurisdiction and action remain.

Unconscionability was rooted in equity, therefore, because equity was a court of conscience. Today, the doctrine exists at law also. Courts are more hesitant to apply it in law proceedings. The line between a hard bargain and an unconscionable one is not easy.

More Problems on Looking at the Person

Consider the following four situations. Which of them, if any, illustrates any of the following invalidating causes: infancy, mental incompetence, duress, undue influence, unconscionability.

1. Seventeen year old high school graduate, married and a member of the armed forces, signs a contract to buy a computer for $5,000 three days before being sent to a war zone. Her husband is a laborer with a 6th grade education who does not know what a computer is. She cannot take the computer with her. She signed the contract for it because the computer salesman, her first cousin, said "What's the matter, afraid you're not coming back or are you just cheap?" She admits she was angry and signed the contract just to "show up" her cousin. She also admits she is a little superstitious and had earlier confided to her cousin that she was afraid she might not return from her assignment. She thought it might be "bad luck" to not buy it. The computer is a model which is soon to be outdated by a newer model. A number of stores were selling it for $1,500 at the time she bought it.

2. Student comes to friend in hallway and says: "Have you got a quarter? I need to make a phone call about a job. It's ten to five and I just heard about it. If I don't call right away I may not get it. Friend says "You can have a quarter if you promise to pay $20 for it." Student agrees.

3. Jones makes a contract with Smith to buy Blackacre for $100,000. Smith is 85 years old, retired but mentally alert. Smith reads the newspapers and

watches television news and listens to public service radio every day. Smith, however, suffers from periodic episodes of irrationality when he thinks he is the reincarnated King Henry VIII. During one of these episodes Smith sold Blackacre to Jones. Blackacre is worth at least $175,000. Smith refuses to convey and Jones sues for specific performance.

4. **Student** needs casebook for course. "Friend" tells him he can get the book and will sell it at the going rate of $40 if student still wants it. Friend gets book. Student says great I want it. Friend says that the price has gone up to $90. Student needs book for class the next day when he is scheduled to be called on. Student pays $90 for book and later sues to recover $50 of this amount.

Compare the next two cases.

Smith, v. Price's Creameries

98 N.M. 541, 650 P.2d 825
Supreme Court of New Mexico, 1982.

[Plaintiff, Smith, lost on a summary judgment motion made by defendant Price's Creameries. Smith appeals. Smith and Price's Creameries had entered a written contract on June 14, 1979 authorizing Smith to distribute Price's dairy products. The agreement contained the following clause, "Either party, upon thirty (30) days written notice to the other shall be entitled to terminate this AGREEMENT for any reason, but without prejudice to any rights of either party to monies due or to become due under this AGREEMENT." Smith alleges that during the negotiation for the agreement Price's representative told them "as long as they performed satisfactorily, the distributorship would continue indefinitely." The agreement also contained a clause forbidding Smith from competing with Price "for a period of two years within the distributorship area." The Smith's invested a total of over $100,000 in the distributorship, including purchasing "the distributorship and equipment" from the former distributor and obtaining working capital. On January 7, 1980, just over seven months after they entered into the written contract, Price elected to exercise the 30 day notice for termination due to "unsatisfactory performance" by Smith. Smith disputes the allegation and sued Price for breach of contract and wrongful misrepresentation as to the circumstances under which the contract could be terminated.]

DONNELLY, Judge.

I. Unconscionability of Termination Clause.

Smiths contend that the termination provision contained in the written agreement of the parties was unconscionable and void as a matter of law. The Smiths also assert surprise in ascertaining the specific language and far reaching consequences of the provisions of the termination clause, and that the contract between the parties unreasonably imposed a disproportionate allocation of risks upon them when balanced by the mere corresponding inconvenience which could be vested upon Price's in the event of any termination by the Smiths.

The evidence is undisputed that appellants were not rushed into signing the agreement, nor deprived of an opportunity to fully examine the terms of the contract prior to its execution, or to have an attorney selected by them to go over each of the contract's provisions. Appellant elected not to hire an attorney to advise them concerning the transaction, and there were no negotiations or attempts by appellants to change any of the provisions in the agreement prior to its execution.

At the time of the formulation of the agreement between the parties, Mr. Smith was approximately 28 years of age, had a working knowledge of the duties of a route man for a dairy products distributor, and had previous experience working with a finance company, and additionally he had worked both as an insurance salesman and as a police officer. Mr. Smith also had three and one-half years of college education. Under the circumstances no material disputed factual issue has been shown to exist concerning lack of adequate opportunity to fairly review the contract, inability to understand the provisions of the document, or lack of opportunity to seek independent professional advice regarding the terms and provisions of the agreement.

The Smiths although conceding that they were aware of both the existence and language of the termination clause, argue that they were assured prior to the execution of the agreement that the contract would continue to remain in effect as long as they performed satisfactorily under the distributorship. Even assuming the truth of this assertion, in the face of the clear wording of the rights of the parties under the termination clause, the oral statement of Price's made prior to execution of the agreement cannot be deemed to constitute fraud or misrepresentation.

The termination clause specifically set forth the right of either party to terminate the agreement upon the giving of proper notice. Generally, a party who executes and enters into a written contract with another is presumed to know the terms of the agreement, and to have agreed to each of its provisions in the absence of fraud, misrepresentation or other wrongful act of the contracting party. Each party to a contract has a duty to read and familiarize himself with its contents before he signs and delivers it, and if the contract is plain and unequivocal in its terms, each is ordinarily bound thereby.

The plain language of the termination clause indicates that either party was free to terminate the contract "for any reason." Although a contract may be declared void where it is unconscionable and oppressive in its terms, nevertheless, the fact that some of the terms of the agreement resulted in a hard bargain or subjected a party to exposure of substantial risk, does not render a contract unconscionable where it was negotiated at arm's length, and absent an affirmative showing of mistake, fraud or illegality.

Section 55-2-302, N.M.S.A.1978, is declarative of the duties of the court when a contract is determined to be unconscionable in whole or in part. This statute provides: (1) If the court as a matter of law finds the contract or any clause of the contract to have been unconscionable at the time it was made the court may refuse to enforce the contract, or it may enforce the remainder of the contract without the unconscionable clause, or it may so limit the application of any unconscionable clause as to avoid any unconscionable result. (2) When it is claimed or appears to the court that the contract or any clause thereof may be unconscionable the parties shall be afforded a reasonable opportunity to present evidence as to its commercial setting, purpose and effect to aid the court in making the determination.

Whether a contract or any of its terms are unconscionable is an issue of law to be determined by the court. Viewing the agreement as a whole, in light of each of Smith's contentions, we agree with the trial court, that the contract is not contrary to substantive fairness nor unconscionable in its terms.

The evidence is undisputed that the contract was freely entered into between the parties. Under these circumstances it is not the province of the courts to alter or amend a contract made by the parties for themselves. The courts cannot change or modify the language of a contract, otherwise legal, for the benefit of one party and to the detriment of another.

The terms of the agreement arrived at between the parties were not unconscionable or oppressive and the trial court properly determined this issue as a matter of law.

II. Obligation of Good Faith

The Smiths also charge that Price's breached its obligation of dealing in good faith and in seeking to terminate the agreement. Smiths argue that under [U.C.C § 1-203] every contract validly entered into between parties imposes an obligation of good faith in its performance, and that summary judgment was inappropriate because a question of fact existed as to whether Price's action in declaring the contract to be terminated was made in good faith.

The parties to a contract may agree to terminate an agreement upon any terms that are fair and just, and either at the option of one or both of the participants. Contractual provisions relating to termination or cancellation of an agreement not arrived at by fraud, or unconscionable conduct, will be enforced by law. Where a contract provides for a manner by which termination can be effected, those provisions must ordinarily be enforced as written.

Appellant's argument as to whether Price's action in terminating the contract was done in good faith is not material to the issues herein. The parties were at liberty to include in the contract executed by them, a provision permitting the contract to be terminated upon the option of either party. Davies v. Boyd, supra; compare McKay v. Farmers & Stockmens Bank of Clayton, 92 N.M. 181, 585 P.2d 325 (Ct.App.1978).

Smiths' argument concerning the necessity of inquiry into Price's motives in seeking to terminate the contract, would, if followed by us, result in a construction of the termination clause contrary to the plain wording of the agreement. Instead of interpreting the clause to permit cancellation "for any reason," Smiths seek to modify this to require that termination be restricted only to instances supported by a showing of good cause.

As set out in Phillips Machinery Co. v. LeBlond, Inc., 494 F.Supp. 318 (N.D.Okl.1980), cancellation of a distributorship is proper if undertaken in accordance with the terms of the agreement and where there is no showing of a material disputed issue of fact concerning the good faith of a party initially entering into the agreement. The motivation of a party in canceling a contract which by its terms is terminable at will by either party, is immaterial. In the instant case, similar to the facts of Phillips, appellants have not alleged or made any showing that Price's lacked good faith at the time of the formulation and execution of the contract between the parties. Smiths' claims of bad faith are focused solely upon defendant's basis or lack thereof in seeking to end the contract. In Phillips, supra, the court held in applicable part: "It is true in this case that a fact issue remains as to the good faith of defendant in terminating the distributor agreement. The fact issue, however, is not material...Unconscionability is a question of law for the Court. Since the clause involved in this case is not unconscionable as a matter of law, the question of good faith of defendant is immaterial, since it cannot affect the outcome of the litigation. Even if defendant terminated the contract in bad faith, plaintiff cannot recover...." (Id. at 325).

The trial court correctly granted summary judgment in favor of Price's. No material disputed issue of fact existed for determination by the trier of fact.

The judgment of the trial court is affirmed. Appellee is awarded its costs incident to this appeal.

IT IS SO ORDERED.

Questions

1. Would the court in *Hunt v. Dolimer, supra* Part III-B, have come out differently on the issue of whether the oral statement concerning termination could be admitted? This court appears to exclude the "satisfactory performance" statement because it conflicts with the writing. It cannot even come in on a fraud issue because the writing is clear. Is plaintiff trying to add or to explain here? Would a Corbin court let the statement in?

2. Was the court right on the good faith issue? Obviously, it is right in New Mexico where it is the highest court. But, if a court in another state that had not yet determined this issue were considering following this case, what might be said against it?

3. Article two of the U.C.C. includes a definition of good faith that includes "reasonable commercial standards of fair dealing in the trade" as well as "honesty in fact." [See § 2-103(1)(b).] Assuming that this contract has sale of goods at its core [the sale of Price's dairy products] and that Article two applies, might this provision have helped the plaintiff? Does it seem likely that the court would have been influenced by it?

4. Distinguish good faith from unconscionability.

Note on Good Faith

Good faith is another doctrine that has its source in equity although it has been so fully adopted by the courts in all actions as to make this history almost irrelevant. Although it defies definition, and is sometimes said to be the absence of bad faith, the Uniform Commercial Code attempts to give the term a positive meaning. In section 1-201(19) it is defined as "honesty in fact in the conduct or transaction involved." This Article 1 definition applies in all articles of the Code unless a particular Article has a different definition. For example, Article 2, as noted above, adds to Article 1's "subjective" honesty an "objective" requirement of "reasonable commercial standards of fair dealing in the trade;" Article 3, which governs Negotiable Instruments (checks, promissory notes, drafts) § 3-103(a)(4) follows the Article 2 definition without the words "in the trade;" Article 4 on Bank Collections (rules concerning, principally, collecting payment on checks) and Article 4A on electronic Funds Transfers apply Article 3's definition; Article 5 on letters of credit applies the Article 1 definition.

Article 1 is different from Article 2 in that Article 1 is subjective. Article 1 looks for the "honesty" of the person involved. Article 2 includes an objective component: fair dealing according to trade standards.

Neither standard is easy to define or apply. But at least they open a door to relief from hard bargains — at least some of the time.

Williams v. Walker-Thomas Furniture Company

350 F.2d 445, 121 U.S.App.D.C. 315
United States Court of Appeals District of Columbia Circuit, 1965.

J. SKELLY WRIGHT, Circuit Judge:

Appellee, Walker-Thomas Furniture Company, operates a retail furniture store in the District of Columbia. During the period from 1957 to 1962 each appellant in these cases purchased a number of household items from Walker-Thomas, for which payment was to be made in installments. The terms of each purchase were contained in a printed form contract which set forth the value of the purchased item and purported to lease the item to appellant for a stipulated monthly rent payment. The contract then provided, in substance, that title would remain in Walker-Thomas until the total of all the monthly payments made equaled the stated value of the item, at which time appellants could take title. In the event of a default in the payment of any monthly installment, Walker-Thomas could repossess the item.

The contract further provided that 'the amount of each periodical installment payment to be made by (purchaser) to the Company under this present lease shall be inclusive of and not in addition to the amount of each installment payment to be made by (purchaser) under such prior leases, bills or accounts; and all payments now and hereafter made by (purchaser) shall be credited pro rata on all outstanding leases, bills and accounts due the Company by (purchaser) at the time each such payment is made.' The effect of this rather obscure provision was to keep a balance due on every item purchased until the balance due on all items, whenever purchased, was liquidated. As a result, the debt incurred at the time of purchase of each item was secured by the right to repossess all the items previously purchased by the same purchaser, and each new item purchased automatically became subject to a security interest arising out of the previous dealings.

On May 12, 1962, appellant Thorne purchased an item described as a Daveno, three tables, and two lamps, having total stated value of $391.10. Shortly thereafter, he defaulted on his monthly payments and appellee sought to replevy all the items purchased since the first transaction in 1958. Similarly, on April 17, 1962, appellant Williams bought a stereo set of stated value of $514.95.[1] She too defaulted shortly thereafter, and appellee sought to replevy all the items purchased since December, 1957. The Court of General Sessions granted judgment for appellee. The District of Columbia Court of Appeals affirmed, and we granted appellants' motion for leave to appeal to this court.

---

1. At the time of this purchase her account showed a balance of $164 still owing from her prior purchases. The total of all the purchases made over the years in question came to $1,800. The total payments amounted to $1,400.

Appellants' principal contention, rejected by both the trial and the appellate courts below, is that these contracts, or at least some of them, are unconscionable and, hence, not enforceable. In its opinion in Williams v. Walker-Thomas Furniture Company, 198 A.2d 914, 916 (1964), the District of Columbia Court of Appeals explained its rejection of this contention as follows:

'Appellant's second argument presents a more serious question. The record reveals that prior to the last purchase appellant had reduced the balance in her account to $164. The last purchase, a stereo set, raised the balance due to $678. Significantly, at the time of this and the preceding purchases, appellee was aware of appellant's financial position. The reverse side of the stereo contract listed the name of appellant's social worker and her $218 monthly stipend from the government. Nevertheless, with full knowledge that appellant had to feed, clothe and support both herself and seven children on this amount, appellee sold her a $514 stereo set.

'We cannot condemn too strongly appellee's conduct. It raises serious questions of sharp practice and irresponsible business dealings. A review of the legislation in the District of Columbia affecting retail sales and the pertinent decisions of the highest court in this jurisdiction disclose, however, no ground upon which this court can declare the contracts in question contrary to public policy. We note that were the Maryland Retail Installment Sales Act, Art. 83 §§ 128-153, or its equivalent, in force in the District of Columbia, we could grant appellant appropriate relief. We think Congress should consider corrective legislation to protect the public from such exploitive contracts as were utilized in the case at bar.'

We do not agree that the court lacked the power to refuse enforcement to contracts found to be unconscionable. In other jurisdictions, it has been held as a matter of common law that unconscionable contracts are not enforceable. While no decision of this court so holding has been found, the notion that an unconscionable bargain should not be given full enforcement is by no means novel. In Scott v. United States, 79 U.S. (12 Wall.) 443, 445, 20 L.Ed. 438 (1870), the Supreme Court stated:

'... If a contract be unreasonable and unconscionable, but not void for fraud, a court of law will give to the party who sues for its breach damages, not according to its letter, but only such as he is equitably entitled to....'

Since we have never adopted or rejected such a rule, the question here presented is actually one of first impression.

Congress has recently enacted the Uniform Commercial Code, which specifically provides that the Court may refuse to enforce a contract which it fails to be unconscionable at the time it was made. 28 D.C.CODE s. 2-302 (Supp. IV 1965). The enactment of this section, which occurred subsequent to the contracts here in suit, does not mean that the common law of the District of Columbia was otherwise at the time of enactment, nor does it preclude the court from adopting a similar rule in the exercise of its powers to develop the common law for the District of Columbia. In fact, in view of the absence of prior authority on the point, we consider the congressional adoption of s. 2-302 persuasive authority for following the rationale of the cases from which the section is explicitly derived. Accordingly, we hold that where the element of unconscionability is present at the time a contract is made, the contract should not be enforced.

Unconscionability has generally been recognized to include an absence of meaningful choice on part of one of the parties together with contract terms which are unreasonably favorable to the other party. Whether a meaningful choice is present in a particular case can only be determined by consideration of all the circumstances surrounding the transaction. In many cases the meaningfulness of the choice is negated by a gross inequality of bargaining power. The manner in which the contract was entered is also relevant to this consideration. Did each party to the contract, considering his obvious education or lack of it, have a reasonable opportunity t understand the terms of the contract, or were the important terms hidden in a maze of fine print and minimized by deceptive sales practices? Ordinarily, one who signs an agreement without full knowledge of its terms might be held to assume the risk that he has entered a one-sided bargain. But when a party of little bargaining power, and hence little real choice signs a commercially unreasonable contract with little or no knowledge of its terms, it is hardly likely that his consent, or even an objective manifestation of his consent, was ever given to all the terms. In such a case the usual rule that the terms of the agreement are not to be questioned should be abandoned and the court should consider whether the terms of the contract are so unfair that enforcement should be withheld.

In determining reasonableness or fairness, the primary concern must be with the terms of the contract considered in light of the circumstances existing when the contract was made. The test is not simple, nor can it be mechanically applied. The terms are to be considered 'in the light Corbin suggests the test as being whether the terms are 'so extreme as to appear unconscionable according to the mores and business practices of the time and place." 1 CORBIN, op. Cit. Supra Note 2.[2] We think this formulation correctly states the test to be applied in those cases where no meaningful choice was exercised upon entering the contract.

Because the trial court and the appellate court did not feel that enforcement could be refused, no findings were made on the possible unconscionability of the contracts in these cases. Since the record is not sufficient for our deciding the issue as a matter of law, the cases must be remanded to the trial court for further proceedings.

So ordered.

Note on Free Will and the Right to Contract

Do the above four cases mean that if you are ignorant, uninformed, poor, populous, and moving in small circles, someone will look out for you? Observe that as with infancy and irrationality, the contracts are voidable not void and are, generally speaking, voidable by the disadvantaged party. Is there a basic difference between a minor, a mentally incapacitated person, someone under duress and someone "suffering from" unconscionability. Is there any indication in the last four cases that the people involved were disabled, prevented from reading what they were signing, unable to obtain needed goods or services from alternate sources? Is there an element of paternalism or maternalism here, of Big Brother

---

2. The traditional test as stated in Greer v. Tweed, supra Note 3, 13 Abb.Pr.,N.S., at 429, is 'such as no man in his senses and not under delusion would make on the one hand, and as no honest or fair man would accept, on the other.'

knows best and will keep you from making a bad deal? Were farmers stuck selling to Campbell, and only Campbell, for $30 or were they just "sore" when the price went up and they weren't going to get the higher amount? What is contract if not a desire to make agreements on which you can rely in the future? Mr. Wollums sounds like a difficult case but in reality he might have sat on that land forever and never been offered anything for it. Is it any of his business that the agent got as much as he did? Eighty dollars in hand is worth more than nothing. Did Horsley owe Wollums a duty to say: "By the way, Wollums, there's a railroad probably coming through here soon" or "you know, these minerals are probably worth $15 an acre on the market"? If Wollums weren't so lazy sitting under a tree, probably with jug in hand or close by, he might know what was going on. On the other hand, he might not care. Then there's Smith. He is almost too good to be true. He had 3 and 1/2 years of college, worked for an insurance company and a finance company, was a police officer and is so starry eyed that he believes what he is told and doesn't get it in writing; or maybe he wasn't told that at all. Finally we have Mrs. Williams. If you had seven kids running around the house I bet you'd want a stereo too, a loud one. Who is Judge Wright to tell her that just because she's on welfare she can't spend her money the way she wants?

It is a long way from the Godfather's pleasant invitation, "you can either put your name on the contract or we'll put your brains on it," to the Wentz, Wollums, Smith, Williams whine for justice. Nonetheless, there is a lesson in the cases. A hard bargain may not be a good one. The old American sense of "caveat emptor" may be gone. For the educated, privileged person there is an obvious warning. Be wary when you are dealing with someone who is disadvantaged. Bend over backwards to make the deal fair. If you don't, you may have no deal at all.

The next case makes a good summary both for unconscionability and for this whole section on defenses based on the person contracting as opposed to the contract itself. Note that in this last case the action is brought by the State Attorney General. Remember that federal agencies (especially the Federal Trade Commission) as well as state officials stand ready to assist the consumer if a violation of a statute or regulation has taken place. Sometimes the mere threat of bringing in state or federal officials will make a person who has engaged in sharp practice back off. For this reason, a study of consumer legislation can be of great value to anyone whose practice of law will include remedying individual wrongs or enforcing individual rights.

State of New York, v. AVCO Financial Service of New York Inc.

50 N.Y.2d 383, 406 N.E.2d 1075, 429 N.Y.S.2d 181
Court of Appeals of New York, 1980.

FUCHSBERG, Judge.

The Attorney-General, acting on a consumer complaint, instituted this special proceeding under subdivision 12 of section 63 of the Executive Law to enjoin respondent Avco's use of a security clause in a loan agreement form.[1] The

---

1. [Author's note—This provision states: "Whenever any person shall engage in repeated fraudulent or illegal acts or otherwise demonstrate persistent fraud or illegality in the

petition alleged that the clause was illegal and void as against public policy on the theory that it constituted an impermissible waiver of the personal property exemption afforded a judgment debtor under CPLR 5205 (subd. (a)). Special Term summarily declared the clause invalid for this reason. Although the Appellate Division, over a single dissent, affirmed the order and judgment, it did so on the ground that the provision was unconscionable. We now reverse, holding that it is not illegal and that the determination of unconscionability was improperly made without any opportunity for an evidentiary presentation as to the commercial and bargaining context in which the clause appears.

The clause at issue is one regularly inserted by Avco, a finance company, in its loan agreements. Its terms unmistakably provide: "This loan is secured by...all household goods, furniture, appliances, and consumer goods of every kind and description owned at the time of the loan secured hereby, or at the time of any refinance or renewal thereof, or cash advanced under the loan agreement secured hereby, and located about the premises at the Debtor's residence (unless otherwise stated) or at any other location to which the goods may be moved."

It is not denied that this language must be understood to create a security interest in items of personal property which include the ones made exempt from the reach of a judgment creditor by CPLR 5205 (subd. (a)).[2] From its inception, this statute along with its venerable antecedents has embodied the humanitarian policy that the law should not permit the enforcement of judgments to such a point that debtors and their families are left in a state of abject deprivation.

It is well recognized, however, that simply because the law exempts such property from levy and sale upon execution by a judgment creditor does not mean that the exemption statute was intended to serve the far more paternalistic function of restricting the freedom of debtors to dispose of these possessions as they wish. No statute precludes exempt property from being sold; nor is there

---

carrying on, conducting or transaction of business, the attorney general may apply...to the...court...for an order enjoining the continuance of such business activity or of any fraudulent or illegal acts....The word 'fraud' or 'fraudulent' as used herein shall include any device, scheme or artifice to defraud and any deception, misrepresentation, concealment, suppression, false pretense, false promise or *unconscionable* contractual provisions. The term 'persistent fraud' or 'illegality' as used herein shall include continuance or carrying on of any fraudulent or illegal act or conduct." [Emphasis added.]

2. CPLR 5205 (subd. (a)) provides in pertinent part, as follows: "(a) Exemption for personal property. The following personal property when owned by any person is exempt from application to the satisfaction of a money judgment except where the judgment is for the purchase price of the exempt property or was recovered by a domestic, laboring person or mechanic for work performed by that person in such capacity: "1. all stoves kept for use in the judgment debtor's dwelling house and necessary fuel therefor for sixty days; one sewing machine with its appurtenances; "2. the family bible, family pictures, and school books used by the judgment debtor or in the family; and other books, not exceeding fifty dollars in value, kept and used as part of the family or judgment debtor's library; "5. all wearing apparel, household furniture, one mechanical, gas or electric refrigerator, one radio receiver, one television set, crockery, tableware and cooking utensils necessary for the judgment debtor and the family; "6. a wedding ring; a watch not exceeding thirty-five dollars in value; and "7. necessary working tools and implements, including those of a mechanic, farm machinery, team, professional instruments, furniture and library, not exceeding six hundred dollars in value, together with the necessary food for the team for sixty days, provided, however, that the articles specified in this paragraph are necessary to the carrying on of the judgment debtor's profession or calling."

any which expressly interdicts the less drastic step of encumbering such property. So, for example, while contractual waivers of a debtor's statutory exemptions are usually held to be void, the law has not forbidden a debtor to execute a mortgage upon the property so protected and thus create a lien which may be foreclosed despite the property's exempt status[3]. The clause here permits no more and, hence, cannot be said to contravene the exemption statute.

The Attorney-General nevertheless argues that the clause should be invalidated under the doctrine of unconscionability. The contention, as accepted by the majority of the Appellate Division, is that "the inequality of bargaining position and the granting to the creditor of enforcement rights greater than those which the law confers upon a judgment creditor armed with execution, lead inevitably to the conclusion that the absence of choice on the part of the debtor left him with no recourse but to grant to his creditor rights which, in good conscience, the law should not enforce" (70 A.D.2d 859, 860, 418 N.Y.S.2d 52). The clause is also alleged to be unconscionable in that its broad terms create security interests even in items not sold or financed by Avco and function mainly as an in terrorem device to spur repayment.

In this connection, we note initially that the statute under which this proceeding was brought lists "unconscionable contractual provisions" as a type of "fraudulent" conduct against which the Attorney-General is authorized to move. Furthermore, an application for injunctive or other relief under this provision is one which may properly look to the exercise of a sound judicial discretion. But the petition here provided no opportunity for the operation of such discretion on the issue of unconscionability since it alleged only that the clause per se was "illegal" and "void as against public policy and contrary to law", theories which, as we have seen, are not consonant with established law. Indeed, the only ground presented to nisi prius was that the clause violated CPLR 5205 (subd. (a)); the petitioner never raised an unconscionability argument until it arrived at the Appellate Division.

As a general proposition, unconscionability, a flexible doctrine with roots in equity, requires some showing of "an absence of meaningful choice on the part of one of the parties together with contract terms which are unreasonably favorable to the other party" (Williams v. Walker-Thomas Furniture Co., D.C.Cir., 350 F.2d 445, 449). The concept, at least as defined in the Uniform Commercial Code which both parties seem to agree governs the transactions at issue here is not aimed at "disturbance of allocation of risks because of superior bargaining power" but, instead, at "the prevention of oppression and unfair surprise." To that extent at least it hailed a further retreat of caveat emptor.

By its nature, a test so broadly stated is not a simple one, nor can it be mechanically applied. So, no doubt precisely because the legal concept of unconscionability is intended to be sensitive to the realities and nuances of the bargaining process, the Uniform Commercial Code goes on to provide: "When it is claimed or appears to the court that the contract or any clause thereof may be unconscionable the parties shall be afforded a reasonable opportunity to present

---

3. Bankruptcy Code § 522(f)(1)(B) now makes such liens void, unless taken by the seller or a lender on the property sold by the seller or financed by the lender to secure payment of the purchase price of the property.

evidence as to its commercial setting, purpose and effect to aid the court in making the determination" (Uniform Commercial Code, § 2-302, subd. 2).

That such evidence may be crucial is made plain too by the drafters' own explication of unconscionability as "whether…the clauses involved are so one-sided as to be unconscionable under the circumstances existing at the time of the making of the contract" (Uniform Commercial Code, § 2-302, Official Comment 1). And, in the light of this dependency upon the particular circumstances surrounding a transaction, courts and commentators have consistently construed subdivision 2 of section 2-302 to mandate at least the opportunity for an evidentiary hearing.

But as indicated, here a case on unconscionability was not presented to Special Term either in form or substance. Nor was that issue available when raised on appeal for the first time. Specifically, at no point did the Attorney-General by affidavits from borrowers or otherwise make any factual showing as to such matters as, for instance, deception of borrowers as to the clause's content or existence, or the presence of language difficulties or illiteracy affecting its execution, or any other reasons that would have made it unlikely that consent was freely and knowingly given, all within the embrace of what is sometimes referred to as "procedural unconscionability". Nor, for that matter, in light of the limited scope of its petition, was there occasion to delve into, much less attempt to prove, the now belated assertion of so-called "substantive unconscionability".

Accordingly, the order of the Appellate Division should be reversed and the petition should be dismissed, without costs, with leave to the petitioner to commence a new proceeding, if it be so advised.

Question.

1. How does the court distinguish substantive from procedural unconscionability in the second last paragraph of the opinion?

Closing Note

There is no easy standard for unconscionability. Duress implies force. Undue influence implies trickery over someone who has a reason to trust or rely on you. Unconscionability simply means unfairness. But, unless society is fully regulated, people will always be paying too much and getting too little. We have all been victims and may be again. To some it is the price of freedom. You learn not to rely on what you are told, to read what you sign and to not hurry after the deal that is too good to be true (and often is just that.) In short, you become savvy. You have to.

Nonetheless there is the new category of those protected. It is a fact specific protection. It depends on the person, on the circumstances. If there is a principle, it seems to be: is the other person trying to dominate to gain an unfair advantage or does the contract contain clauses that if known to the person signing would cause surprise and probably dismay.

For you, law students and lawyers to be, there is no unconscionability. You presumably know how to read and do not walk in such small circles that you cannot say no. In short, you are or should be too savvy at this point to need the protection of an unconscionability statute.

B. Looking at the Contract

This section will examine escaping contractual liability based on defenses of: (1)Statute of Frauds, (2) mistake, (3) reasons for nonperformance including frustration of purpose, impossibility of performance and impracticability of performance, and (4) misrepresentation. Just as in Part A do not treat each defense as existing alone. Often many can and are raised within the same case.

1. Statute of Frauds

Note on Statute of Frauds

We have been introduced to the Statute of Frauds previously. (see *supra* Part I-B). The Statute of Frauds dates back to the England of 1677. It is, as its title suggests an act whose purpose is the prevention of fraud. Then as now people lie. Schoolchildren lie, courtroom experts lie, all sorts and conditions of people lie for all kinds of reasons. It is not a pleasant topic but it is a fact. When I was a law student a young instructor told us that at least 80% of all testimony, and probably more, in one of the lower courts (city court) was perjured. As he put it, the average witness there wanted the lawyer to tell him/her what to say. It didn't matter what happened. People also lie about obligations, contractual obligations.[1]

For this reason we have a Statute of Frauds. Presumably, people will be less inclined to forge a paper, especially someone else's signature, than they will be to lie. After all, memory fades and plays tricks—caught in a lie a person can often say, I guess I made a mistake. It is sometimes very hard to prove whether the person is telling the truth and is just forgetful or is lying. It is, however, much harder to say I guess I made a mistake and wrote all this out and *signed* the other party's name to it. Somehow, it just doesn't sound quite right.

Here is a reprint of the New York Statute of Frauds (NY GEN OBLIG § 5-701). It is representative of a modern American Statute. You are not required to memorize it but rather to use it to refresh your recollection of what we have so far learned: to charge someone on a contract for personal services that will take more that one year, on a land contract, or on a sale of goods for over $500 there must be a writing that reflects the likelihood of such a contract, signed by the party to be charged with liability.

General Obligations Law § 5-701. Agreements required to be in writing.

a. Every agreement, promise or undertaking is void, unless it or some note or memorandum thereof be in writing, and subscribed by the party to be charged therewith, or by his lawful agent, if such agreement, promise or undertaking:

1. By its terms is not to be performed within one year from the making thereof or the performance of which is not to be completed before the end of a lifetime;

---

1. [A caveat for lawyers and law students. There was a time when the bar looked the other way when lawyers let clients tell whoppers. Now, more and more, the lawyer is being held to at least investigate the truth of what the client is going to say.]

2. Is a special promise to answer for the debt, default or miscarriage of another person;

3. Is made in consideration of marriage, except mutual promises to marry;

[4. Repealed]

5. Is a subsequent or new promise to pay a debt discharged in bankruptcy;[1]

6. Notwithstanding section 2-201 of the uniform commercial code, if the goods be sold at public auction, and the auctioneer at the time of the sale, enters in a sale book, a memorandum specifying the nature and price of the property sold, the terms of the sale, the name of the purchaser, and the name of the person on whose account the sale was made, such memorandum is equivalent in effect to a note of the contract or sale, subscribed by the party to be charged therewith;

[7, 8. Repealed]

9. Is a contract to assign or an assignment, with or without consideration to the promisor, of a life or health or accident insurance policy, or a promise, with or without consideration to the promisor, to name a beneficiary of any such policy. This provision shall not apply to a policy of industrial life or health or accident insurance.

10. Is a contract to pay compensation for services rendered in negotiating a loan, or in negotiating the purchase, sale, exchange, renting or leasing of any real estate or interest therein, or of a business opportunity, business, its good will, inventory, fixtures or an interest therein, including a majority of the voting stock interest in a corporation and including the creating of a partnership interest. "Negotiating" includes procuring an introduction to a party to the transaction or assisting in the negotiation or consummation of the transaction. This provision shall apply to a contract implied in fact or in law to pay reasonable compensation but shall not apply to a contract to pay compensation to an auctioneer, an attorney at law, or a duly licensed real estate broker or real estate salesman.

b. Notwithstanding paragraph one of subdivision a of this section:

1. An agreement, promise, undertaking or contract, which is valid in other respects and is otherwise enforceable, is not void for lack of a note, memorandum or other writing and is enforceable by way of action or defense provided that such agreement, promise, undertaking or contract is a qualified financial contract as defined in paragraph two of this subdivision and (a) there is, as provided in paragraph three of this subdivision, sufficient evidence to indicate that a contract has been made, or (b) the parties thereto, by means of a prior or subsequent written contract, have agreed to be bound by the terms of such qualified financial contract from the time they reach agreement (by telephone, by exchange of electronic messages, or otherwise) on those terms.

2. For purposes of this subdivision, a "qualified financial contract" means an agreement as to which each party thereto is other than a natural person and which is:

(a) for the purchase and sale of foreign exchange, foreign currency, bullion, coin or precious metals on a forward, spot, next-day value or other basis;

---

1. [Author's Note: federal law, the Bankruptcy Code, governs this and makes this state provision irrelevant.]

(b) a contract (other than a contract for the purchase and sale of a commodity for future deliver[y] on, or subject to the rules of, a contract market or board of trade) for the purchase, sale or transfer of any commodity or any similar good, article, service, right, or interest which is presently or in the future becomes the subject of dealing in the forward contract trade, or any product or byproduct thereof, with a maturity date more than two days after the date the contract is entered into;

(c) for the purchase and sale of currency, or interbank deposits denominated in United States dollars;

(d) for a currency option, currency swap or cross-currency rate swap;

(e) for a commodity swap or a commodity option (other than an option contract traded on, or subject to the rules of a contract market or board of trade);

(f) for a rate swap, basis swap, forward rate transaction, or an interest rate option;

(g) for a security-index swap or option or a security (or securities) price swap or option;

(h) an agreement which involves any other similar transaction relating to a price or index (including, without limitation, any transaction or agreement involving any combination of the foregoing, any cap, floor, collar or similar transaction with respect to a rate, commodity price, commodity index, security (or securities) price, security-index or other price index); or

(i) an option with respect to any of the foregoing.

3. There is sufficient evidence that a contract has been made if:

(a) There is evidence of electronic communication (including, without limitation, the recording of a telephone call or the tangible written text produced by computer retrieval), admissible in evidence under the laws of this state, sufficient to indicate that in such communication a contract was made between the parties;

(b) A confirmation in writing sufficient to indicate that a contract has been made between the parties and sufficient against the sender is received by the party against whom enforcement is sought no later than the fifth business day after such contract is made (or such other period of time as the parties may agree in writing) and the sender does not receive, on or before the third business day after such receipt (or such other period of time as the parties may agree in writing), written objection to a material term of the confirmation; for purposes of this subparagraph, a confirmation or an objection thereto is received at the time there has been actual receipt by an individual responsible for the transaction or, if earlier, at the time there has been constructive receipt which is the time actual receipt by such an individual would have occurred if the receiving party, as an organization, has exercised reasonable diligence; and a "business day" for the purposes of this subparagraph is a day on which both parties are open and transacting business of the kind involved in that qualified financial contract which is the subject of the confirmation;

(c) The party against whom enforcement is sought admits in its pleading, testimony or otherwise in court that a contract was made; or

(d) There is a note, memorandum or other writing sufficient to indicate that a contract has been made, signed by the party against whom enforcement is sought or by its authorized agent or broker. For purposes of this paragraph evidence of an electronic communication indicating the making therein of a contract or a confirmation, admission, note, memorandum or writing is not insufficient because it omits or incorrectly states one or more material terms agreed upon, so long as such evidence provides a reasonable basis for concluding that a contract was made.

4. For purposes of this subdivision, the tangible written text produced by telex, telefacsimile, computer retrieval or other process by which electronic signals are transmitted by telephone or otherwise shall constitute a writing and any symbol executed or adopted by a party with the present intention to authenticate a writing shall constitute a signing. The confirmation and notice of objection referred to in subparagraph (b) of paragraph three of this subdivision may be communicated by means of telex, telefacsimile, computer or other similar process by which electronic signals are transmitted by telephone or otherwise, provided that a party claiming to have communicated in such a manner shall, unless the parties have otherwise agreed in writing, have the burden of establishing actual or constructive receipt by the other party as set forth in subparagraph (b) of paragraph three of this subdivision.

Comment on New York Statute of Frauds

Note subsections 3(b) and (c). These are common provisions in statutes of frauds. They provide a substitute for a person's signature on a writing. Like the seal, the Statute of Frauds in often overlooked. Do not do so. It can provide a means of relief from a bad bargain as surely as a claim of duress or unconscionability. Sometimes, it is even more effective.

Also, do not mix up the parol evidence rule with the Statute of Frauds. The parol evidence rule does not require a writing. It merely states that if there is a writing certain things may not be added to it etc. The Statute of Frauds on the other hand requires a writing in certain circumstances but does not tell what can or cannot be added to it.

McIntire, dba Hillside Machine v. Woodall, 666 A.2d 934, (N.H., 1995).

Woodall (the defendant) approached McIntire with an offer to bring him business in exchange for a commission of 10% of the resulting sales. In July, 1987 McIntire was awarded a contract with Varion Extrion, a Massachusetts company which Woodall provided. In April 1989 McIntire told Woodall that unless she brought him more business he intended to break off contractual relations with her. Additionally, McIntire informed Woodall that they were reducing the commission to 8% on the Varion contract. In May 1989 payments pursuant to the Varian contract stopped. McIntire ultimately filed a petition for declaratory judgment, seeking the court to rule "that the agreement between the parties was governed by New Hampshire law and that the plaintiff lawfully terminated his relationship with the defendant." Woodall counterclaimed requesting her full ten percent commission for the life of the Varian account. McIntire responded by asserting the statute of frauds, as a defense to the enforcement of any agreement between the parties.

THAYER, Justice.

[New Hampshire's Statute of Frauds] provides that "[n]o action shall be brought…upon any agreement…that is not to be performed within one year from the time of making it, unless such promise or agreement…is in writing and signed by the party to be charged." It is uncontested that the agreement in this case was oral and therefore would be subject to the statute of frauds unless it falls within some exception to the rule. The trial court ruled that the agreement was not subject to the statute of frauds because (1) the defendant had fully performed her obligations under the contract, and (2) it was a contract that could be performed within one year without breach by either party.

The plaintiff argues that the trial court erred in applying the "full performance" exception to the statute of frauds because that exception is not recognized under New Hampshire law. The plaintiff correctly notes that we have previously stated that "the execution of the agreement upon one side, whether partial or complete, does not take it out of the statute, but that a note or memorandum is necessary if any part of the agreement is not to be performed within a year." Emery v. Smith, 46 N.H. 151, 155 (1865). However, we also have case law that arguably adopts the rule of full performance. If an "agreement can be fully performed by either of the parties within the year, and it is so performed, the agreement of the other party is not within the statute, though it may be impossible to perform it within a year." Blanding, 33 N.H. at 246 (emphasis added). If, however, neither party fully performs within the one-year period, even though he or she may fully perform at some later time, the contract is within the statute. Emery, 46 N.H. at 155. This rule serves the goals of the statute of frauds, which include promoting certainty and protecting against fraud and perjury, while preventing the harsh and inequitable results that could result from rigid enforcement of the statute.

The defendant fully performed her obligations under the contract when she provided the plaintiff with plans from Varian, which resulted in a contract for the plaintiff. The trial court, therefore, did not err in ruling that enforcement of the agreement was not barred by the statute of frauds. The judgment of the trial court is affirmed.

Affirmed.

Questions

1. Why does this agreement not fit within New Hampshire's Statute of Frauds?

2. Would the result change at all if New Hampshire did not recognize a full performance exception to the statute of frauds? If so, what would the result have been?

2. Mistake

Note on Mistake

Mistakes are of two kinds—unilateral and bilateral. Unilateral mistakes, a mistake by one of the parties about what was being contracted for, will not usually avoid a contract in the absence of special circumstances. One such special circumstance is constructive fraud. For example, if a mother or father who had little business experience and little opportunity to gain it asked the advice of their son regarding the value of something they were going to sell and the son said he would buy it from them, in a later dispute the court would most likely view the contract with some scrutiny. Because the son is in a confidential relationship with his parents they would look at it for fairness. Assume that it is a piece of land that the parents inherited but never explored. The son has been over the land many times and has knowledge that there is valuable timber on it. Son offers a price 1/10 the value of the land, a price that would be fair if it had no timber. The mistake as to what is being bought and sold is unilateral—the son knows, the parents do not. It is a one-sided mistake. Normally, a one-sided mistake will not be grounds for voiding a contract. Here, because parents presumably relied on son to look out for their best interests it can be voided. See *Jackson v. Seymour,* 193 Va. 735, 71 S.E. 2d 181 (1952) for a case with similar facts.

The fact that one person thinks what he is selling is worth far less than it is or has some essential quality basically different from what it really is will not void the contract. If both parties make a mistake at the time of contracting as to something basic to the bargain, the contract is voidable by the party adversely affected. For example, in the illustration in the above paragraph assume an arm's length sale of the land. The buyer believes that it has valuable timber or minerals on it; the seller does not. The contract is valid. Both parties believe that the land is valueless except for pasture when in fact it has valuable timber or minerals. There is a mutual mistake. For several reasons in this instance even though there is a mutual mistake there may be no avoidance. For one thing, a court may put the risk on the seller to know what he is selling. Second, it may say that the essence of the contract is the land itself and the minerals and/or timber are only incidental to the contract. In other words there was no mistake going to the essence of the contract. Third, as a matter of policy, the court may refuse to apply mutual mistake to land contracts. See *Hoffman v. Chapman, infra.* What if both parties believed that there was a building on the land suitable for habitation. Unbeknownst to either of them it is infested with termites. If the building goes to the essence of the contract and both are mistaken as to its condition, the contract may be avoided.

The key principle in mutual mistake concerns what the minds of the parties have met on, the thing which is at the heart or core of the contract. Both thought that they were contracting for one thing and in point of fact that very thing did not exist. It is not a case of subjective vs. objective intent. Objectively A expresses a wish to sell and B expresses a wish to buy Blackacre, or a painting or a warehouse full of goods. Both know that B intends to use Blackacre as a housing subdivision and neither knows that it is unsuitable for this because it was once a toxic waste dump; or both believe the painting is merely a copy of a Rembrandt and it turns out to be the real thing; or the warehouse is believed to be full of goods but at the time of contracting without knowledge of A or B thieves have stolen them. The point is that while their minds and the expressions they use to express their mental intent are on the same thing, that thing in point of fact does not exist. There is a mutual mistake as to some essential fact going to the essence of the bargain.

A subset of this, which is likely to cause more problems today, is when the writing which both parties intend to reflect their agreement contains some basic error. In other words, the writing does not state what they agreed. A agrees to sell and B agrees to buy Whiteacre, a parcel of land which is 200 acres in extent. Both A and B agree to have C draw up the document which is to reflect this agreement. C makes a mistake and describes Whiteacre as a 100 acre parcel and describes it in metes and bounds that include only 100 acres. Both A and B sign this paper. B discovers the error and draws it to A's attention. A refuses to convey the 100 acres left out of the writing. Can B obtain relief in a court? Yes. A problem could arise if C were not the agent of both parties. The question then would be whether the mistake was in fact mutual or only unilateral. The mistake would be unilateral as to the actual creation of the writing; it would be mutual in that both parties adopted the writing thinking that it contained something other than it did. The remedy in the first case, and possibly the second, would be reformation, *i.e.* reform the writing to reflect the real intent of the parties. Note that just as duress and fraud may be used to avoid the application of the parol evidence rule, so may mutual mistake. Further, the Parol Evidence Rule does not bar reformation where there is a mutual mistake. The net result of this is that a writing may be shown to not embody the intent of the parties—the threshold issue regarding parol evidence—on yet another ground. This does not mean that the court will reform the writing to reflect 200 acres without a trial if A now states that the contract was in fact only for 100. It does mean that B's evidence that it was a contract for 200 acres will not be barred.

Just as parol evidence concerns prior or contemporaneous negotiations or agreements and modification goes to changes after the contract was entered, so also mutual mistake goes only to facts at the *time of contracting*. If, for example, A agreed to sell Blackacre to B, both parties intending that a housing subdivision would be built on it and selling and buying only for that purpose, and a toxic waste dump that was in existence on the land at the time of contracting is found after the contract is entered, the issue would be mutual mistake. Assume that the dump is cleaned up and that B takes the land and contracts with C to build the subdivision. The town of Happiness in which Blackacre lays passes an ordinance which prohibits the construction. This is not a mutual mistake. The ordinance did not exist at the time the contract was entered. Rather this would come under impossibility/impracticability/frustration of purpose, *infra* this Part.

The next case illustrates a mutual mistake in the written expression; the one following it a mistake in the contract itself.

Hoffman v. Chapman
182 Md. 208, 34 A.2d 438
Court of Appeals of Maryland, 1943.

DELAPLAINE, Judge.

This appeal was brought by Joseph Stanley Hoffman and wife from a decree of the Circuit Court for Montgomery County reforming their deed for a house and lot in a suburban real estate development at Kensington.

On August 18, 1941, William A. Chapman and wife, of Gaithersburg, through a real estate agent, agreed to sell to appellants part of lot 4 in the section known as Homewood on Edgewood Road, the size to be 96 by 150 feet. The purchase price of this part, improved by a bungalow, was $3,600. Before the parcel was surveyed, appellants were given immediate possession. After the survey was made, the real estate agent sent the plat to the Suburban Title and Investment Corporation with instructions to examine the title and arrange for settlement. On October 20, 1941, when appellants made final payment in the office of the title company, they clearly understood that they were receiving only a part of lot 4 containing one dwelling; but the deed actually conveyed the entire lot, which was improved by other dwelling property. When the mistake was discovered some time afterwards, they were requested to deed back the unsold part, but they refused to reconvey. The grantors thereupon entered suit in equity to reform the deed on the ground of mistake.

It is a settled principle that a court of equity will reform a written instrument to make it conform to the real intention of the parties, when the evidence is so clear, strong and convincing as to leave no reasonable doubt that a mutual mistake was made in the instrument contrary to their agreement. It is a general rule of the common law that parol evidence is inadmissible to vary or contradict the terms of a written instrument. But equity refuses to enforce this rule whenever it is alleged that fraud, accident or mistake occurred in the making of the instrument, and will admit parol evidence to reform the instrument, even though it is within the Statute of Frauds. 'A court of equity would be of little value,' Justice Story said, 'if it could suppress only positive frauds, and leave mutual mistakes, innocently made, to work intolerable mischiefs contrary to the intention of parties. It would be to allow an act, originating in innocence, to operate ultimately as a fraud by enabling the party, who receives the benefit of the mistake, to resist the claims of justice under the shelter of a rule framed to promote it.... We must, therefore, treat the cases in which equity affords relief, and allows parol evidence to vary and reform written contracts and instruments, upon the ground of accident and mistake, as properly forming, like cases of fraud, exceptions to the general rule which excludes parol evidence, and as standing upon the same policy as the rule itself.' 1 Story, Equity Jurisprudence, 12th Ed., secs. 155, 156.

It was urged by appellants that there was no meeting of the minds as to the exact location of the parcel sold, and therefore the contract of sale is void. This Court cannot agree with that contention. If an agreement is so vague and indefinite that the court finds it impossible to gather from it the full intention of the parties, it must be held void, for the court cannot make an agreement for the parties. Yet the law does not favor, but leans against, the annulment of contracts on the ground of uncertainty. If the intent of the parties can be ascertained from the express terms of the contract or by fair implication, the contract should be sustained by the court. Of course, if the parties to a contract of sale did not understand each other as to the identity of the property, they cannot invoke the aid of equity, for in such a case there was no meeting of the minds. However, where there is no mistake as to the identity of the property, but merely an incorrect description, whether in conveying too much property or too little, or referring to property entirely different from that intended to be conveyed, the court will correct the description, except as against bona fide purchasers for value without notice.

Equity reforms an instrument not for the purpose of relieving against a hard or oppressive bargain, but simply to enforce the actual agreement of the parties to prevent an injustice which would ensue if this were not done. Chief Judge Alvey warned: 'The court will never, by assuming to rectify an instrument, add to it a term or provision which had not been agreed upon, though it may afterwards appear very expedient or proper that it should have been incorporated.' Stiles v. Willis, 66 Md. 552, 556, 8 A. 353, 354. Nevertheless, where the description in a deed is not complete, but the contract of sale specified the amount of land to be conveyed, and thereafter a plat was prepared from a survey, extrinsic evidence may be admitted to show the real intention of the parties, and thereupon the court has power to make the description more definite under the maxim, 'Id certum est, quod certum reddi potest.' Nolen v. Henry, 190 Ala. 540, 67 So. 500, 501, Ann.Cas.1917B, 792. In the present case there could not be any doubt about the identity of the dwelling which appellants agreed to buy, because they lived in it about two months before they made their final payment on the purchase price. It was understood and agreed by the parties that the parcel should have a frontage of 96 feet on the north side of Edgewood Road, and its depth should be 150 feet. Shortly thereafter the surveyor found that a part of the road ran across the southwest corner of the lot, and he suggested that the County Engineer might be induced to shift the road slightly so as to enable the owners to convey a parcel exactly 150 feet in depth. But when the real estate agent gave assurance that the owners would be willing to convey a few more feet on account of the curve in the road, the surveyor made a revised plat allowing a depth of 150 feet on the east side and 161.24 feet on the west side. Therefore, since the decree of the chancellor, based upon the revised survey, allows dimensions slightly larger than those stipulated in the contract, appellants certainly have no reason to complain.

Appellants insisted that the mistake in the deed was not due to their fault, but to culpable negligence of the grantors and their agents, and that no relief can be granted because the mistake was unilateral. It is axiomatic that equity aids the vigilant, and will not grant relief to a litigant who has failed to exercise reasonable diligence. In Boyle v. Rider, 136 Md. 286, 191, 100 A. 524, it was stated that people cannot sign papers carelessly and then expect a court to excuse them from their negligence, especially when their action has misled others. But mere inadvertence, or negligence not amounting to a violation of a positive legal duty, does not bar a complainant from relief, especially if the defendant has not been prejudiced thereby. Hence, it is not necessary for the complainant in a suit for reformation to prove that he exercised diligence to ascertain what the instrument contained at the time he signed it. The term 'mistake' conveys the idea of fault, and the mere fact that a mistake was made in the phraseology of an instrument does not establish such negligence as to preclude the right of reformation; for if it did, a court of equity could never grant relief in such a case.

The general rule is accepted in Maryland that a mistake of law in the making of an agreement is not a ground for reformation, and where a mistake, either of law or of fact, is unilateral, equity will not afford relief except by rescinding the agreement on the ground of fraud, duress or other inequitable conduct. The mistake in this case was not unilateral. Here the draftsman of the deed was acting as the agent of the parties. His mistake in the description of the real estate became the mistake of all the parties. The Court of Appeals recognized in Boulden v. Wood, 96 Md. 332, 337, 53 A. 911, that a court of equity may correct an instrument wherein a provision was inserted by mistake of an attorney. Where a deed is intended to carry into execution a written or oral agreement, but fails to express the manifest intention of the parties on account of a mistake of the drafts-man, whether from carelessness, forgetfulness or lack of skill, equity will rectify the mistake to make the deed express the real intention of the parties.

As it is beyond doubt that a mutual mistake was made in the description of the property in this case, the decree of the chancellor reforming the deed will be affirmed.

Sherwood v. Walker, 33 N.W. 919, (Mich., 1887).

This landmark case involves the forever famous "Rose 2d of Aberlone." Sherwood, the plaintiff, contracted with Walker, a cattle raiser, and agreed to pay "five and one-half cents per pound, live weight" for a polled Angus cow. Sher-wood never received Rose because Walker refused delivery when it was discov-ered Rose was a breeding cow, and not the barren meat cow both parties be-lieved. Sherwood brought this action seeking delivery of the cow.

"It appears from the record that both parties supposed this cow was barren and would not breed, and she was sold by the pound for an insignificant sum as compared with her real value if a breeder. She was evidently sold and purchased on the relation of her value for beef, unless the plaintiff had learned of her true condition, and concealed such knowledge from the defendants. Before the plain-tiff secured the possession of the animal, the defendants learned that she was with calf, and therefore of great value, and undertook to rescind the sale by re-fusing to deliver her. The question arises whether they had a right to do so. The circuit judge ruled that this fact did not avoid the sale and it made no difference whether she was barren or not. I am of the opinion that the court erred in this holding. I know that this is a close question, and the dividing line between the adjudicated cases is not easily discerned. But it must be considered as well settled that a party who has given an apparent consent to a contract of sale may refuse to execute it, or he may avoid it after it has been completed, if the assent was founded, or the contract made, upon the mistake of a material fact,—such as the subject-matter of the sale, the price, or some collateral fact materially inducing the agreement; and this can be done when the mistake is mutual.

If there is a difference or misapprehension as to the substance of the thing bargained for; if the thing actually delivered or received is different in substance from the thing bargained for, and intended to be sold,—then there is no contract; but if it be only a difference in some quality or accident, even though the mistake may have been the actuating motive to the purchaser or seller, or both of them, yet the contract remains binding. 'The difficulty in every case is to determine whether the mistake or misapprehension is as to the substance of the whole con-tract, going, as it were, to the root of the matter, or only to some point, even though a material point, an error as to which does not affect the substance of the whole consideration.' Kennedy v. Panama, 2 Q.B. 580, 587. It has been held, in accordance with the principles above stated, that where a horse is bought under the belief that he is sound, and both vendor and vendee honestly believe him to be sound, the purchaser must stand by his bargain, and pay the full price, unless there was a warranty.

It seems to me, however, in the case made by this record, that the mistake or misapprehension of the parties went to the whole substance of the agreement. If the cow was a breeder, she was worth at least $750; if barren, she was worth not over $80. The parties would not have made the contract of sale except upon the understanding and belief that she was incapable of breeding, and of no use as a cow. It is true she is now the identical animal that they thought her to be when the contract was made; there is no mistake as to the identity of the creature. Yet the mistake was not of the mere quality of the animal, but went to the very nature of the thing. A barren cow is substantially a different creature than a breeding one. There is as much difference between them for all purposes of use as there is between an ox and a cow that is capable of breeding and giving milk. If the mutual mistake had simply related to the fact whether she was with calf or not for one season, then it might have been a good sale, but the mistake affected the character of the animal for all time, and for its present and ultimate use. She was not in fact the animal, or the kind of animal, the defendants intended to sell or the plaintiff to buy. She was not a barren cow, and, if this fact had been known, there would have been no contract. The mistake affected the substance of the whole consideration, and it must be considered that there was no contract to sell or sale of the cow as she actually was. The thing sold and bought had in fact no existence. She was sold as a beef creature would be sold; she is in fact a breeding cow, and a valuable one. The court should have instructed the jury that if they found that the cow was sold, or contracted to be sold, upon the understanding of both parties that she was barren, and useless for the purpose of breeding, and that in fact she was not barren, but capable of breeding, then the defendants had a right to rescind, and to refuse to deliver, and the verdict should be in their favor.

The judgment of the court below must be reversed, and a new trial granted, with costs of this court to defendants."

3. Mutual Mistake vs. Implied Warranty

Hinson v. Jefferson
287 N.C. 422, 215 S.E.2d 102
Supreme Court of North Carolina, 1975.

[Plaintiff sues defendant to try to rescind a conveyance of land sold solely for, and restricted in the deed to use solely for, residential purposes. After the contract was entered and the land conveyed the County Health Department certified the lot of land "would not support a septic tank or on-site sewage disposal system.' The deed did not contain a warranty or covenant that the land could be used for residential purposes. Because of a high water table and severe drainage problems which were for all practical purposes insoluble, and because a septic system was needed to make the land suitable for residential use, the plaintiff in effect had a piece of land which she could not use but merely view.]

COPELAND, Justice.

Based on these uncontroverted facts, the Court of Appeals held that plaintiff was entitled to rescind the contract on the grounds of 'mutual mistake of material fact' coupled with a 'total failure of consideration.' 24 N.C.App. at 238—39, 210 S.E.2d at 502—03. Assuming, arguendo, that the Court of Appeals was correct, and that this is a true mistake case, then it is one that must necessarily involve a mistaken assumption of the parties in the formation of the contract of purchase. In these mistaken assumption cases, unlike other kinds of mistake cases, the parties communicate their desires to each other perfectly; they intend to complete a sale, or a contract of sale, and their objective acts are in accord with their intent. Difficulties subsequently arise because at least one of the parties has, either consciously or unconsciously, mistaken beliefs concerning facts that make the sale appear more attractive to him than it actually is.

In attempting to determine whether the aggrieved party is entitled to some kind of relief in these mistaken assumption cases, courts and commentators have suggested a number of factors as relevant. E.g., was the mistake bilateral or unilateral; was it palpable or impalpable; was one of the parties unjustly enriched; was the other party unjustly impoverished; was the risk assumed by one of the parties (i.e., subjective ignorance); was the mistake fundamental or collateral; was the mistake related to present facts or to future expectations; etc.

Our research has failed to disclose a prior North Carolina case applying the doctrine of mutual mistake pertaining to a physical condition of real property as a ground for rescission. However, we have found a few cases from other jurisdictions.

In Blythe v. Coney, 228 Ark. 824, 310 S.W.2d 485 (1958), the court allowed rescission where the vendor and purchaser of a residence were mistaken as to the adequacy of water pressure. The court declared that a contract may be rescinded for a mutual mistake regarding a material fact and that the mistaken assumption of the parties could be characterized as such a mistake in view of the evidence that the water meter in the home was unconnected at the time it was shown to the purchasers so that neither party was aware of the water shortage until after the sale.

Likewise, in Davey v. Brownson, 3 Wash.App. 820, 478 P.2d 258 (1970), cert. denied, 78 Wash.2d 997 (1971), the court relied on the doctrine of mutual mistake of a material fact in rescinding the sale of, inter alia, a 26-unit motel that, unknown to either party at the time of signing the contract, was infested with termites, a condition that could only be corrected by substantial structural repair. The court, quoting from Lindeberg v. Murray, 117 Wash. 483, 495, 201 P. 759, 763 (1921), stated: 'We think it is elementary that, where there is a clear bona fide mistake regarding material facts, without culpable negligence on the part of the person complaining, the contract may be avoided, and equity will decree a rescission. We take it that the true test in cases involving mutual mistake of fact is whether the contract would have been entered into had there been no mistake....' Id. at 824, 478 P.2d at 260.

One court has held that there were sufficient grounds for rescission of a sale of realty where both the vendor and the vendee were mistaken as to the suitability of the soil or the terrain for agricultural purposes.

The closest mistaken assumption case we have found to our fact situation is A & M Land Development Co. v. Miller, 354 Mich. 681, 94 N.W.2d 197 (1959). In that case, the court held that the trial judge was correct in refusing to rescind the sale of 42 building lots slated for subdivision and development, because of mutual mistake regarding the poor absorptive qualities of the soil that resulted in a tentative refusal of septic tank permits to the subdivider. The court concluded that assuming there was a mutual mistake, to grant rescission would be improper since the purchaser received the property for which he contracted, notwithstanding that it was less attractive and less valuable to him than he had anticipated.

There are, however, several important distinguishing factors between the Miller case and our case. First, the purchaser in Miller was a developer-speculator; in our case the purchaser is a consumer-widow. Second, the property in Miller was not rendered valueless for its intended use, but only rendered less valuable because it could not be developed as densely as originally anticipated; in our case the property was rendered totally valueless for the intended use.

In our view, the difficulty with the above listed factors and with the decisions we have examined is that in any given case several factors are likely to be present, and each may point toward a different result. For example, in A & M Land Development Co. v. Miller, Supra, the mistake appears to have been mutual and it also appears to have been induced by misrepresentations of the vendor (i.e., vendor furnished reports of privately engaged engineers and local public sanitation officials indicating that the character of the soil was suitable for the use of individual septic tank systems). Yet, the court held that rescission would be improper since the purchaser received the property for which he had contracted. Perhaps the court felt that since the vendee was a developer-speculator he assumed the risk of soil defects. In short, the relation of one factor to another is not clear. In any event, because of the uncertainty surrounding the law of mistake we are extremely hesitant to apply this theory to a case involving the completed sale and transfer of real property. Its application to this type of factual situation might well create an unwarranted instability with respect to North Carolina real estate transactions and lead to the filing of many nonmeritorious actions. Hence, we expressly reject this theory as a basis for plaintiff's rescission.

Is plaintiff therefore without a remedy? Did plaintiff buy this property 'at the end of the halter' (an expression of horse traders)? At this moment, plaintiff has naked legal title to a tract of real estate whose use to her is limited by the restrictive covenants and by the facts as stipulated to what she calls 'the dubious pleasure of viewing the same.' On the other hand, defendants have $3,500 of plaintiff's money. There can be no question but that the parties to this transaction never contemplated this particular use of the subject property. In fact, the deed, by its very terms, makes it clear that the intended use was for the construction of a single-family residence, strictly limited as to costs and as to design. The stipulation further indicates that both prior to and at the time of the conveyance neither defendants nor plaintiff knew that the property would not support a septic tank or on-site sewage disposal system.

In the face of these uncontroverted facts, defendants rely upon the doctrine of Caveat emptor as a legal defense to plaintiff's action for rescission.

The common law doctrine of caveat emptor historically applied to sales of both real and personal property. Its application to personal property sales, however, has been restricted by the Uniform Commercial Code. See G.S. § 25—2—314 et seq. [ed. note: U.C.C. § 2-314 et seq. Section 2-314 provides for an implied warranty of merchantability. Briefly summarized, a merchant, someone who deals in goods of the kind sold, warrants when she sells the goods that they will be of at least fair, average quality, sufficient to pass in the trade; in other words, generally as good as other goods of like kind.] Over the years, as to real property, the number of cases that strictly apply the rule of caveat emptor appears to be diminishing, while there is a distinct tendency to depart therefrom, either by way of interpretation, or exception, or by simply refusing to adhere to the rule where it would work injustice. [ed. note: Caveat emptor — "let the buyer beware" — does not exist where § 2-314 applies because the seller is saying: "I guarantee that these goods are at least as good as other goods of this kind sold by other people and if they are not you may sue me for damages."]

In recent years the rule of caveat emptor has suffered severe inroads in sales of houses to be built or in the course of construction. Today, it appears that a majority of the states imply some form of warranty in the purchase of a new home by a first purchaser from a builder/vendor.

During the course of this litigation, and subsequent to the oral arguments of this case in the Court of Appeals, this Court decided the case of *Hartley v. Ballou*, 286 N.C. 51, 209 S.E.2d 776 (1974) [Emphasis added]. In that case, this Court, in an opinion by Chief Justice Bobbitt, approved the 'relaxation of the rule of Caveat emptor' in respect of defects of which the purchaser of a recently completed or partially completed dwelling was unaware and could not discover by a reasonable inspection, and substituted therefore, for the first time in this State, an implied warranty defined as follows:

'(I)n every contract for the sale of a recently completed dwelling, and in every contract for the sale of a dwelling then under construction, the vendor, if he be in the business of building such dwellings, shall be held to impliedly warrant to the initial vendee that, at the time of the passing of the deed or the taking of possession by the initial vendee (whichever first occurs), the dwelling, together with all its fixtures, is sufficiently free from major structural defects, and is constructed in a workmanlike manner, so as to meet the standard of workmanlike quality then prevailing at the time and place of construction; and that this implied warranty in the contract of sale survives the passing of the deed or the taking of possession by the initial vendee.' Id. at 62, 209 S.E.2d at 783. At the same time, Hartley made it clear that such implied warranty falls short of 'an absolute guarantee.' 'An implied warranty cannot be held to extend to defects which are visible or should be visible to a reasonable man....' Id. at 61, 209 S.E.2d at 782.

We believe many of the mutual mistake cases [cites omitted above] were in fact embryo *implied warranty* cases. [Emphasis added.] For example in Davey v. Brownson, Supra, the purchaser obtained rescission because of termites on the ground of mutual mistake. Although the court denied its decision was based on implied warranty, it is difficult to understand the application of the mutual mistake doctrine. In this context, Hartley could easily be classified as a mutual mistake case, i.e., both parties assumed that the basement wall was sufficiently free from structural defects so as to prevent any water leakage. But, in Hartley we recognized the implied warranty as a limited exception to the general rule of Caveat emptor; if we had elected to totally abolish the doctrine, then perhaps application of the mutual mistake theory would have been appropriate. Hartley is not an abrogation of the doctrine of Caveat emptor; on the contrary it is only a well-reasoned exception.

Concededly, this is not the Hartley fact situation. Hartley involved a builder-vendor of new homes and a consumervendee. Nonetheless, we believe that Hartley provides the legal precedent for deciding this case. The basic and underlying principle of Hartley is a recognition that in some situations the rigid common law maxim of Caveat emptor is inequitable. We believe this is one of those situations. As a result, we hold that where a grantor conveys land subject to restrictive covenants that limit its use to the construction of a single-family dwelling, and, due to subsequent disclosures, both unknown to and not reasonably discoverable by the grantee before or at the time of conveyance, the property cannot be used by the grantee, or by any subsequent grantees through mesne conveyances, for the specific purpose to which its use is limited by the restrictive covenants, the grantor breaches an implied warranty arising out of said restrictive covenants.

Defendant contends that if plaintiff is permitted to rescind, then any contract or conveyance can be set aside under a set of circumstances rendering the land no longer attractive to a purchaser. If we applied the mutual mistake doctrine, then there might be some merit to this argument. But, under the rule we have announced, a purchaser is bound by patent defects or by facts a reasonable investigation would normally disclose. In the instant case, it is clear that a reasonable inspection by the grantee either before or at the time of conveyance would not have disclosed that the property could not support a septic tank or on-site sewage disposal system.

Therefore, under the facts of this case, we hold that defendant grantors have breached the implied warranty, as set out above, and that plaintiff, by timely notice of the defect, once it was discovered, is entitled to full restitution of the purchase price; provided that she execute and deliver a deed reconveying the subject lot to defendants. The judgment of the Court of Appeals, as modified herein, is thus affirmed.

Modified and affirmed.

Questions

1. Why did the court not simply apply *Hartley v. Ballou?*

2. How does implied warranty, as defined by the court, differ from mutual mistake?

3. Note that the deed did not contain a warranty that the land could be used for residential purposes.

    a. Would it be reasonable to assume that, where the land is sold solely for residential purposes but the deed contains no warranty or covenant that it be so used, it is the intent of the parties that the suitability of the land be at the risk of the purchaser?

    b. Note that in paragraph eight of the opinion the purchaser is described as a "consumer-widow." Do you think this had a bearing? There is no evidence of fraud or misrepresentation here. Nor is it claimed that the writing did not reflect what they agreed—the purchase and sale of land. Is this a hidden unconscionability case?

Note on Implied Warranty

The court in *Hinson* says a warranty is not a guarantee because the warrantee (she who receives the warranty) cannot use it to overcome her responsibility for observing patent defects. This is fair enough and under the U.C.C. this is the rule [see § 2-316.] A warranty does not cover defects which the warrantor has disclaimed [see *Stormont, infra*] or which by a reasonable inspection the buyer could discover. In *Hinson* the water table was allegedly undiscoverable. Is this true? What about the shoreline eroding along the Eastern seaboard? How hard is it to discover this? Note, however, that as applied in *Hartley* the rule makes sense —it applies to new construction. How can you tell how well the electrical circuits have been installed when the wires are behind the plaster. In my town, there was once a contractor whom we can call Jones, "One nail Jones." He got this name because he never used two nails if one would do. After some years the house might sag but without dismantling it when you bought it there was no way to tell.

Why might mutual mistake going to the essence of the contract make a better rule for land and implied warranty for new construction? A person who is a builder should know how good his/her work is. Land, however, is what it is—no one except God made it; no one can be sure what is under it without exploration.

Why didn't the court in *Hinson* want to apply the doctrine of mutual mistake to land?

4. Assuming the Risk — Losing the Benefit of Mutual Mistake, Implied Warranty and Frustration of Purpose

Note on Frustration of Purpose

Frustration of Purpose is a doctrine which we will examine in greater depth later in this Part. It is left in here because of the attempt of plaintiff to use it to overcome the problem that he faced of assuming the risk

Note on Disclaiming Warranties

In the next case plaintiff signed a lease and purchase option which described the property as being leased/sold "as is." Those words mean what they say. You take it as it is—you can't complain and claim an implied warranty. It can also be difficult to claim mutual mistake or anything else. "As is" means that the buyer once again is the one who should beware. In essence, "as is" is the modern "Caveat emptor." At early Common Law everything was presumed to be "Caveat emptor." Today everything is presumed to have some implied warranty —at least if it is sale of goods. "As is" restores by a specific term what all contracts contained at Common Law—a warning that the buyer is assuming the risk.

Problem

Jones goes to an art gallery and admires a painting. It is signed "Raoul Dufy," an artist whose works are valuable. Without inquiring further from the gallery as to its authenticity, Jones inquires as to its price and buys it. The painting turns out to be a fake painted by Ralph Duffy in a loft in New York. Neither the art gallery nor Jones realized that the painting was a fake. The art gallery bought the painting at an estate sale. The decedent had purchased the painting from a small art shop in lower New York and had always thought he had a find. In fact, decedent had originally planned to give the painting to a gallery in order to get a tax deduction but died before he could do so. The shop where decedent had bought the painting is now a pizza parlor and the proprietor of the defunct art shop is both unknown and unlocatable. Duffy also cannot be found. What if any are Jones' remedies?

Would it matter if instead of a painting Jones had bought the land and buildings in which the decedent had lived with the intent to subdivide them and sell individual houses only to learn that a zoning ordinance prevented this? Would it make a difference if unbeknownst to either the seller or buyer an underground stream had recently changed course and made subdevelopment impossible?

Would it matter if the sale to Jones was "as is"? What if the words "as is" were not mentioned but as Jones gave the gallery a check it gave him a certificate showing that he had that day purchased from the gallery "a work purported to be by Raoul Dufy which is sold to the buyer 'as is.'" What if prior to giving the check and receiving the painting and certificate, buyer had said to seller: "is this really a Raoul Dufy" and seller had said: "It is. We stand behind all our paintings." Would it matter if the "as is" clause was on the back of the certificate in small type?

Stormont, v. Astoria Limited
889 P.2d 1059
Supreme Court of Alaska, 1995.

RABINOWITZ, Justice.

In April 1992 Michael Stormont signed a lease and an option to purchase real property, including an eleven-unit apartment complex and house (the property), from Astoria Limited (Astoria). These documents repeatedly reiterate that Stormont accepts the property "as is." In May, a city inspection determined that the building was a "dangerous and substandard building," and in June a building inspector sent Stormont notice that the property would have to be vacated and demolished. Stormont sought rescission of the lease and option on the basis of mistake [and] frustration. He also sought reliance damages, averring that he had expended considerable time and money renovating the property. Astoria counterclaimed for past due payments under the lease. The superior court granted summary judgment in favor of Astoria, and Stormont appealed. We affirm.

A. Mutual Mistake

Stormont's discussion of the mistake issue apparently embodies three allegations of mistake: (1) a belief that the structure would not be demolished; (2) a belief that the apartments were in better condition at the time of the agreement than they in fact were; and (3) a belief that there had not been a condemnation order.

When the parties to an agreement share a mistaken belief about a material fact, the agreement may be voidable. See Restatement (Second) of Contracts § 152 (1981). The Restatement sets forth three requirements for a successful mistake argument. The party seeking to void the contract must prove that (1) the mistake relates to a "basic assumption on which the contract was made," (2) the mistake has a material effect on the agreed exchange of performances, and (3) the party seeking relief does not bear the risk of the mistake. Restatement (Second) of Contracts § 152 cmt. a (1981).

The first mistake Stormont alleges is that at the time of the signing neither party anticipated the imminent demolition order which was sent on June 2, 1992. The order was a result of an inspection by the Fairbanks Building Department on May 29, 1992. However, this error does not qualify as a mistake justifying rescission because it concerns a future event. See Beals v. Tri- B Assocs., 644 P.2d 78, 80 (Colo.App.1982) ("If the parties harbor only mistaken expectations as to the course of future events and their assumptions as to facts existing at the time of the contract are correct, rescission is not proper.")

Stormont also alleges that the parties did not know how severe the building's problems were at the time they signed the agreements. The first question is whether this acknowledged mistake relates to a fundamental assumption underlying the contracts. The property was listed as "income property," and Stormont was interested in it for its rental value. Thus, assumptions about the building's suitability for commercial leasing (i.e. its habitability) went to the heart of the contracts.

The second requirement is that the mistake must have a material effect on the agreed-upon exchange. Stormont has not satisfied this requirement because he has not alleged that he received something fundamentally different from what the parties believed he would. Thus, the mistake could not have had a material effect on the agreed exchange of performances.

The third requirement also fails as all the evidence offered suggests that Stormont bore the risk of a mistake as to the condition of the building.[1] Astoria sold the property "as is." As Astoria notes, "this is not a case of a single 'as is' clause buried in the middle of fine print." Moreover, the parties discussed the condition of the building, and Stormont had opportunities to inspect it. By signing the contracts, Stormont treated his knowledge of the building's condition as adequate. He does not allege that Astoria concealed significant information from him. Nor does he assert that the defects were hidden. Additionally, the fact that he was an experienced contractor at the time weighs against him. We hold that Stormont has not made out a case for relief based upon mistake.

B. Frustration

Stormont argues that he is entitled to judgment as a matter of law based on the doctrine of frustration of purpose, or that at a minimum there is a genuine issue of material fact that precludes summary judgment in favor of Astoria on this issue. Frustration is an affirmative defense, and Stormont bears the burden of proof.

---

1. As to bearing the risk of the mistake, the Restatement (Second) § 154 (1981), states as follows: A party bears the risk of a mistake when (a) the risk is allocated to him by agreement of the parties, or (b) he is aware, at the time the contract is made, that he has only limited knowledge with respect to the facts to which the mistake relates but treats his limited knowledge as sufficient, or (c) the risk is allocated to him by the court on the ground that it is reasonable in the circumstances to do so.

Allocation of risks is an important consideration when a party pleads frustration.[2] That factor weighs against Stormont. The agreements did not explicitly mention demolition or condemnation. However, under the agreements, Stormont assumed the risk that the building would not be suitable for his purposes due to unknown or undiscovered defects. Thus, we conclude that Stormont has not met his burden of proving frustration.

The superior court's grant of summary judgment in favor of Astoria is AFFIRMED.

Questions

1. Did those two words, "as is," take away all rights of the lessee/buyer?
2. What is frustration of purpose? How is it different from mutual mistake or warranty?

5. Impossibility (and Its First Cousin Impracticability) and Frustration of Purpose. Events Occurring After the Contract is Entered Which Relieve a Party from the Obligation of Performance

Note

What if something changes after the contract has been entered and what you thought was the substance of your contract no longer exists? For example, you agree to rent space on the side of a building to advertise your law practice. Your agreement with the lessor says nothing about what happens if the building burns down. After you and the building owner sign the agreement the building is destroyed by fire. It is impossible for the owner to let you put up the sign. There is no building. Assume that instead of a fire destroying the building, the fire leaves the one wall standing on which your sign was to go. However, it is impracticable for the owner to not remove that wall and either rebuild or sell the lot to someone else. It is not impossible to put up your sign; it is, however, not practical to use the land for just one sign or to try to build around it. Assume that the city puts a new ramp in for access to a freeway. The ramp is so constructed that it blocks anyone from seeing the wall on which you are to put your sign. Your purpose in making the contract is frustrated.

---

2. Under the Restatement (Second) of Contracts § 265, "Where, after a contract is made, a party's principal purpose is substantially frustrated without his fault by the occurrence of an event the non-occurrence of which was a basic assumption on which the contract was made, his remaining duties to render performance are discharged, unless the language or the circumstances indicate the contrary." Comment A notes three requirements implicit in this statement: "First, the purpose that is frustrated must have been a principal purpose of that party in making the contract.... Second, the frustration must be substantial.... The frustration must be so severe that it is not fairly to be regarded as within the risks that he assumed under the contract. Third, the non-occurrence of the frustrating event must have been a basic assumption on which the contract was made." The Comment further notes that foreseeability is an important component of the third factor. We have adopted the Restatement's test for frustration. See U.S. Smelting, Ref. & Mining Co. v. Wigger, 684 P.2d 850, 857 (Alaska 1984).

As summarized above, the rule sounds and is easy. Applying it is not so easy. As with mutual mistake, the doctrines of impossibility, impracticability and frustration of purpose go to the substance of the contract. If some peripheral, non-basic, right is affected, they will most probably not apply.

The key to their application is that the parties both entered the contract with certain presumptions that go to the heart of the contract as to what will happen in the future. When these do not turn out, the avoidance of liability follows the same general path as that employed by mutual mistake—both parties are relieved from liability.

7200 Scottsdale Road General Parnters, v. Kuhn Farm Machinery, Inc.

184 Ariz. 341, 909 P.2d 408
Court of Appeals of Arizona, 1995.

TOCI, Judge.

Kuhn Farm Machinery, Inc. ("Kuhn") contracted with 7200 Scottsdale Road General Partners dba Scottsdale Plaza Resort (the "resort"), to use the resort's facilities for a convention at which Kuhn's European personnel were to present new products to Kuhn's dealers and employees. In this appeal from the granting of a summary judgment for Kuhn, we consider the following issue: did the risk to air travel to Scottsdale, Arizona, posed by the Gulf War and Saddam Hussein's threats of worldwide terrorism, substantially frustrate the purpose of the contract?

Reversing the trial court's grant of summary judgment for Kuhn, we hold as follows. First, the resort did not contract with the understanding that Kuhn's European personnel were crucial to the success of Kuhn's convention. Thus, even if the attendance of the Europeans at the Scottsdale convention was thwarted by the threat to international air travel, their nonattendance did not excuse Kuhn's performance under the contract. Neither did the risk to domestic air travel posed by the Gulf War entitle Kuhn to relief. Although that risk may have rendered the convention uneconomical for Kuhn, the threat to domestic air travel did not rise to the level of "substantial frustration." Finally, Kuhn's cancellation based on the perceived risk of terrorism was not an objectively reasonable response to an extraordinary and specific threat. Consequently, Kuhn is not entitled to relief on the theory of "apprehension of impossibility."

I. FACTS AND PROCEDURAL HISTORY

A. Background

On February 9, 1990, the resort and Kuhn signed a letter agreement providing that Kuhn would hold its North American dealers' convention at the resort. The agreement required the resort to reserve, at group rates, a block of 190 guest rooms and banquet and meeting rooms for the period from March 26, 1991, to March 30, 1991. Kuhn, in turn, guaranteed rental of a minimum number of guest rooms and food and beverage revenue of at least $8,000 from the use of the meeting and banquet rooms.

The agreement contained remedies protecting the resort if Kuhn canceled the meeting. Kuhn was required to pay liquidated damages for any decrease after January 25, 1991, of ten percent or more in the reserved room block. Additionally, the resort agreed to accept individual room cancellations up to seventy-two hours prior to arrival without penalty so long as total attrition did not exceed five percent. The agreement also provided that, because the loss of food and beverage revenues and of room rentals resulting from cancellation were incapable of estimation, cancellation would result in assessment of liquidated damages.

Because Kuhn refused to hold its dealers' meeting at the resort at the time specified in the agreement, the resort sued for breach of contract, seeking the liquidated damages provided for in the agreement. The resort then moved for partial summary judgment to obtain a ruling in its favor on the issue of liability. Kuhn filed a cross motion for summary judgment, alleging that its performance was discharged or suspended pursuant to the doctrines of impracticability of performance and frustration of purpose.

B. Additional Facts Established by Kuhn's Motion

In support of its motion for summary judgment, Kuhn offered the following facts. Kuhn S.A., the parent of Kuhn, is headquartered in France, where it manufactures farm machinery. Both companies engage in international sales of farm machinery manufactured by Kuhn S.A. They sell their products through direct sales by their employees and through independent dealerships.

Kuhn and Kuhn S.A. planned to use the North American dealers' convention to introduce new products to Kuhn's sales people and dealers, stimulate enthusiasm for the new products, and provide its sales people and dealers with information to effectively market and sell the products. To accomplish these goals, Kuhn invited its top 200 independent dealers from the United States and Canada ("North Americans"), as well as some of its overseas suppliers, to attend the meeting. Approximately twenty-five Kuhn and Kuhn S.A. employees and suppliers from the United States, Europe, and Australia were to host the convention and present the new products.

Kuhn considered the overseas personnel ("Europeans") crucial to the presentation and success of the dealers' meeting. Of all of Kuhn's personnel, they were the most familiar with the design, manufacture, and production of the new products. Kuhn intended the Europeans to play the primary role in presenting the products and leading the discussions at the convention.

On August 2, 1990, Iraq invaded Kuwait. A few days later, the United States began sending troops to the Middle East. On January 16, 1991, the United States and allied forces, in Operation Desert Storm, engaged in war with Iraq. As a result, Saddam Hussein and other high-ranking Iraqi officials threatened terrorist acts against the countries that sought to prevent Iraq's takeover of Kuwait. Hussein stated, "hundreds of thousands of volunteers... [would become] missile[s] to be thrown against the enemy..." and "the theater of operations would [include] every freedom fighter who can reach out to harm the aggressors in the whole world...."

Because many newspapers reported a likelihood of terrorism, Kuhn became concerned about the safety of those planning to attend the convention. Kuhn was particularly concerned about international travel, but Kuhn also perceived a risk of terrorism within the United States.

Kuhn discovered that, apparently because of the war, convention attendance would not meet expectations. Many of Kuhn's employees who were to attend the meeting were concerned about the safety of air travel. Timothy Harman, general sales manager of Kuhn, personally spoke with several dealers who voiced their apprehension about traveling during the war. Because tentative registration was lower than Kuhn had anticipated when it signed the agreement, in late January—two months prior to the date of the planned convention—Kuhn reduced the reserved room block by more than twenty-five percent.

Interest in the proposed convention continued to wane. From February 4 to February 14, 1991, several of Kuhn's top dealerships who had won all-expense-paid trips to the convention canceled their plans to attend. By mid-February, eleven of the top fifty dealerships with expense-paid trips had either canceled their plans to send people to the convention or failed to sign up.

Kuhn S.A. wrote to the resort on February 14, 1991, requesting cooperation in rescheduling the meeting for a later date. Among other things, the letter stated that Kuhn was concerned with the safety of its people, that the dealers were reluctant to travel, and that attendance had decreased to a level making it uneconomical to hold the convention.

Without waiting for the resort's response, Kuhn decided to postpone the scheduled meeting. On February 18, 1991, Kuhn notified all potential convention participants that the dealers' meeting had been postponed. Although Kuhn and the resort did attempt to reschedule the meeting for the following year, the rescheduling negotiations broke down. The convention was never held at the resort.

C. The Resort's Response To Kuhn's Motion

The resort did not dispute Kuhn's description of the planned convention; rather, the resort contested the extent of the threat to air travel. Specifically, the resort noted that the articles cited by Kuhn indicated either that there was little risk or that the risk was primarily to overseas locations.

The resort also contested the inferences to be drawn from the facts presented by each party. The resort asserted that the facts did not establish that the threat of terrorism frustrated the ability of Kuhn associates to fly to Scottsdale. Although conceding that several dealers canceled because of fear of terrorism, the resort emphasized that nearly all of the approximately 150 dealers registered for the meeting signed up after the Operation Desert Storm attack on Iraq. In the resort's view, Kuhn's January 29, 1991, request for a reduction in the room block to 140 rooms impliedly reconfirmed the convention after the commencement of the war. The resort argued that these facts, taken with all others that had been presented, demonstrated as a matter of law that the defenses of *impracticability of performance* and *frustration of purpose* were inapplicable. [Emphasis added.]

The trial court granted summary judgment to Kuhn, ruling that Kuhn proved both of its defenses. Before formal judgment was entered, the resort filed a motion for reconsideration, asking the trial court to consider certain new evidence it had obtained through discovery. The trial court denied the motion. The resort appeals from the summary judgment ruling, from the denial of its motion for reconsideration, and from the denial of a request it made to strike certain evidence that Kuhn had presented.

II. IMPRACTICABILITY DISTINGUISHED FROM FRUSTRATION OF PURPOSE

The trial court held that the contract was discharged under the doctrines of impracticability of performance and frustration of purpose. These are similar but distinct doctrines. See Restatement (Second) of Contracts ("Restatement") § 265 cmt. a (1981) (discussing the differences between impracticability of performance and frustration of purpose). Impracticability of performance is, according to the Restatement, utilized when certain events occurring after a contract is made constitute an impediment to performance by either party. See Restatement § 261. Traditionally, the doctrine has been applied to three categories of supervening events: death or incapacity of a person necessary for performance, destruction of a specific thing necessary for performance, and prohibition or prevention by law. Id. cmt. a.

On the other hand, frustration of purpose deals with "the problem that arises when a change in circumstances makes one party's performance virtually worthless to the other...." Restatement § 265 cmt. a. "Performance remains possible but the expected value of performance to the party seeking to be excused has been destroyed by a fortuitous event, which supervenes to cause an actual but not literal failure of consideration." Lloyd v. Murphy, 25 Cal.2d 48, 153 P.2d 47, 50 (1944). While the impact on the party adversely affected is the same regardless of which doctrine is applied, frustration of purpose, unlike the doctrine of impracticability, involves no true failure of performance by either party.

Notwithstanding, some cases speak of a contract as "frustrated" when performance has become impossible or impracticable. This usage is inaccurate. "[F]rustration is not a form of impossibility even under the modern definition of that term, which includes not only cases of physical impossibility but also cases of extreme impracticability of performance." Lloyd, 153 P.2d at 50.

Turning to the contract between Kuhn and the resort, Kuhn clearly has no claim for impossibility or impracticability. The contract required the resort to reserve and provide guest rooms, meeting rooms, and food and services. In return, Kuhn was required to pay the monies specified in the contract. Kuhn does not allege that it was impossible or impracticable to perform its contractual duty to make payment for the reserved facilities. Rather, it contends that the value of the resort's counter-performance—the furnishing of convention facilities—was rendered worthless because of the Gulf War's effect on convention attendance. This is a claim of frustration of purpose.

III. FRUSTRATION OF PURPOSE

A. Krell v. Henry

The doctrine of frustration of purpose traces its roots to Krell v. Henry, [1903] 2 K.B. 740. There, the owner of a London apartment advertised it for rent to observe the King's coronation parade. Responding to the advertisement, the renter paid a deposit and agreed to rent the apartment for two days. When the coronation parade was postponed, the renter refused to pay the balance of the rent. The court held that the contract to rent the apartment was premised on an implied condition—the occurrence of the King's coronation parade. Accordingly, when the parade was canceled, the renter's duty to perform was discharged by the frustration of his purpose in entering the contract.

Several aspects of Krell are worth noting. First, the owner of the apartment was prepared to render the entire performance promised by him; the postponement of the coronation procession did not diminish the value of the contract to the owner. Second, the renter could have performed by simply paying the rental fee for the apartment. In other words, there was no impediment to the renter's performance of the contract. The renter's sole grievance was that his intended benefit from the contract had not been realized.

The complaint that a contracting party did not realize the benefit he intended to realize from the contract has been described as "frustration-in-fact." Frustration-in-fact results when, because of events subsequent to formation of a contract, the desirability of the performance for which a party contracted diminishes. The issue then becomes: should legal consequences flow from a contracting party's failure to realize the expected benefit from a contract?

B. Frustration of Purpose and The Equitable Doctrine of Lloyd

Significantly, the very courts that created the doctrine of frustration of purpose have questioned its soundness. Lloyd, 153 P.2d at 49. In this country, some commentators have asserted that the doctrine rests on a tenuous rationale for shifting the burdens of unexpected events from the promisor to the promisee.

Despite this criticism, many authorities, including the courts of Arizona, extend limited relief for frustration-in-fact through an extraordinary legal remedy closely resembling relief in equity. As Justice Traynor pointed out in his frequently cited opinion in Lloyd:

"The question in cases involving frustration is whether the equities of the case, considered in the light of sound public policy, require placing the risk of a disruption or complete destruction of the contract equilibrium on defendant or plaintiff under the circumstances of a given case, and the answer depends on whether an unanticipated circumstance, the risk of which should not be fairly thrown on the promisor, has made performance vitally different from what was reasonably to be expected." 153 P.2d at 50 (citations omitted). Virtually all Arizona cases applying the doctrine have approved of this approach.

C. The Restatement Approach to Frustration of Purpose

Although the modern doctrine of frustration of purpose appears in Restatement § 265 and the comments, past Arizona cases applying the doctrine of frustration of purpose have relied on Lloyd rather than on the Restatement. Applying Lloyd 's rationale that the "purpose of a contract is to place the risks of performance upon the promisor," 153 P.2d at 50, Arizona courts have stated that " '[t]he doctrine of frustration has been severely limited to cases of extreme hardship so as not to diminish the power of parties to contract....' " Matheny, 147 Ariz. at 360, 710 P.2d at 470 (quoting Garner, 18 Ariz.App. at 183, 501 P.2d at 24).

Nevertheless, neither Lloyd nor the Arizona cases that have relied upon it are inconsistent with Restatement section 265. The reporter's note to Restatement section 265 cites Lloyd as authority for illustration 6 of that section. Furthermore, in line with the Arizona cases of Matheny and Garner, the requirements for the doctrine of frustration of purpose stated in comment a provide adequate protection for the power to contract. Consequently, we follow Restatement section 265, particularly comment a, in this case.

IV. RESOLUTION OF THIS CASE

A. Requirements for Relief

Restatement section 265 comment a lists four requirements that must exist before relief may be granted for frustration of purpose. First, "the purpose that is frustrated must have been a principal purpose of that party" and must have been so to the understanding of both parties. Restatement § 265 cmt. a. Second, "the frustration must be substantial...; [it] must be so severe that it is not to be regarded as within the risks assumed...under the contract." Id. Third, "the non-occurrence of the frustrating event must have been a basic assumption...." Id.; see Restatement § 261, cmt. b. Finally, relief will not be granted if it may be inferred from either the language of the contract or the circumstances that the risk of the frustrating occurrence, or the loss caused thereby, should properly be placed on the party seeking relief. Restatement § 265 cmt. b; see Restatement § 261 cmt. c.

Kuhn contends that the Gulf War with its attendant threats of terrorism was an "event the non-occurrence of which was a basic assumption" of the contract. The resort, on the other hand argues that these events were merely normal incidents of life in the modern world. We conclude, however, that under Restatement section 265 comment a, the parties "basic assumption" is only relevant if the other requirements listed in comment a are satisfied. Here, because we find no substantial frustration of a principal purpose entitling Kuhn to relief, we need not decide if the nonoccurrence of the Gulf war and Saddam Hussein's threats of terrorism was a basic assumption of the parties.

B. Principal Purpose

1. A Forum For European Personnel

Kuhn contends that its principal purpose in scheduling the convention was to provide a forum for its European personnel to introduce new and innovative products to its North American dealers. The resort acknowledged that the primary threat of terrorist activity was to the United States' international interests rather than domestic targets. Even if we take this as an implied concession by the resort that it was too dangerous for Kuhn's European personnel to fly to Scottsdale, Kuhn is not entitled to relief for frustration of purpose on this ground.

For Kuhn to obtain relief based on the frustration of its plans for its European employees to introduce new products, those plans must have been understood by the resort as Kuhn's "principal purpose" in entering the contract. As the court noted in Krell, to establish that "the object of the contract was frustrated," it must be shown that the frustrated purpose was "the subject of the contract... and was so to the knowledge of both parties." [1903] 2 K.B. at 754 (emphasis added). It is not enough that the promisor "had in mind some specific object without which he would not have made the contract." Restatement § 265 cmt. a. "The object must be so completely the basis of the contract that, as both parties understand, without it the transaction would make little sense." Id. (emphasis added). In Krell, for example, the "coronation procession and the relative position of the rooms [was] the basis of the contract as much for the lessor as the hirer." [1903] 2 K.B. at 751.

Here, Kuhn never established that both parties had a common understanding that Kuhn's principal purpose in entering the contract was a convention at which the European personnel would be present. First, the contract itself makes no mention of any particular purpose for the convention. Second, neither the deposition and affidavit of Timothy Harman—Kuhn's general sales manager responsible for scheduling the convention—nor the deposition of William Kilburg—the resort's vice president—raised any factual inference that the resort knew of Kuhn's plans concerning the European personnel. Harman's affidavit only related Kuhn's understanding of the purpose of the convention. The only other reference in the record to the purpose of the convention is Harman's deposition testimony that his role was to find a venue for a North American dealers' meeting.

In sum, although Kuhn thought that attendance of the Europeans was crucial to the success of the convention, the record is devoid of any evidence that the resort contracted with that understanding. Neither does the record establish any reasonable inference that, when the parties contracted, the resort knew or had reason to know that its counter-performance—the furnishing of resort facilities—would make little sense without the presence of the Europeans. We conclude, therefore, that Kuhn's principal purpose—the attendance of the European personnel—was not so completely the basis of the contract, as understood by the resort, that without such attendance the transaction was meaningless. Accordingly, Kuhn is not entitled to relief on that theory.

2. Attendance Of Most Invited Personnel

Nevertheless, Kuhn argues that the parties contracted with the idea that "all or *most*" of Kuhn's employees and dealers would come to Scottsdale for the meeting. We agree that this was a principal purpose of Kuhn's contract with the resort. Nevertheless, nothing in this record establishes that the resort contracted with the understanding that all or most of Kuhn's dealers and employees would attend the convention. Kuhn's degree of success was not of primary concern to the resort. To the contrary, the resort clearly contemplated that the convention might not meet Kuhn's expectations. Not only does the contract include a provision for attrition in attendance and outright cancellation, it assigns the risk of such events to Kuhn. Thus, as with the attendance of the European employees, the attendance of all or most of Kuhn's dealers and employees was not so completely the *basis of the contract*, as understood by the resort, that without such attendance the transaction would make little sense. [Emphasis added.]

Kuhn did establish, however, that the resort contracted with knowledge that a principal purpose of Kuhn was a convention at which some of Kuhn's employees and dealers would attend. If that purpose was substantially frustrated by the Gulf War, Kuhn is entitled to relief. Consequently, we next consider whether the Gulf War and Saddam Hussein's threats of terrorism substantially frustrated a convention for some of Kuhn's employees and dealers.

C. Substantial Frustration

Kuhn argues that its purpose was effectively frustrated because air travel was unexpectedly rendered unreasonably dangerous. The resort, on the other hand, while essentially conceding that Kuhn's decision to cancel was made in good faith, contends that the general threat of terrorism was not sufficient to justify Kuhn's cancellation of the convention. We agree with the resort.

Preliminary, as discussed above, Kuhn cannot rely on the absence of the Europeans as a basis for canceling the contract. Kuhn never established that both parties had a common understanding that Kuhn's principal purpose in entering the contract was a convention at which the European personnel would be present. Thus, in resolving this issue, we do not consider the threat posed to the European employees traveling internationally by air.

On the other hand, the threat to domestic air travel is a relevant consideration. Most of those invited to the convention resided in the United States and in Canada. Furthermore, the resort did not controvert Kuhn's assertion in its statement of facts that "the parties assumed that Kuhn personnel could and would travel to Scottsdale." Consequently, if the Gulf War effectively precluded domestic air travel, Kuhn could not have hosted a convention attended by even some of its dealers and employees. Under such circumstances, the resort's furnishing of its facilities would have been rendered valueless to Kuhn. We could then say that Kuhn's purpose in entering the contract was substantially frustrated. We conclude, however, that the contrary is true.

We begin our analysis on this point with the proposition that substantial frustration means frustration "so severe that it is not fairly to be regarded as within the risks...assumed under the contract." Restatement § 265 cmt. a. Furthermore, "*it is not enough that the transaction has become less profitable* for the affected party or even that he will sustain a loss." Id. [Emphasis added.] The value of the counter-performance to be rendered by the promisee must be "totally or nearly totally destroyed" by the occurrence of the event. Lloyd, 153 P.2d at 50.

Here, the conduct of Kuhn and its dealers clearly demonstrates that the value of the resort's counter-performance—the furnishing of its facilities for Kuhn's convention—was not totally or nearly totally destroyed by terrorist threats. In late January, after the United States attacked Iraq and when the threat of terrorism was at its highest level, Kuhn implicitly confirmed the convention date by reducing the reserved room block from 190 to 140. Furthermore, although several dealers canceled in early February, the uncontroverted record demonstrates that over one hundred dealers registered for the convention after the commencement of Operation Desert Storm on January 16, 1991. Thus, the frustration was not so severe that it cannot fairly be regarded as one of the *risks assumed* by Kuhn under the contract. [Emphasis added.]

Kuhn argues, however, that even if the jointly understood purpose in holding the convention was not substantially frustrated by the actual risk of terrorism, it was entitled to cancel the convention because of its perception of a serious risk to air travel. For this proposition, Kuhn relies primarily on the wartime shipping cases.

These cases, however, are not frustration of purpose cases. The wartime shipping cases are the source of the rules governing impossibility or impracticability of performance in the original Restatement of Contracts ("First Restatement") section 465 (1932). This doctrine, referred to by the First Restatement as "apprehension of impossibility" was subsequently incorporated into comment d of Restatement section 261.

The wartime shipping cases essentially held that a ship captain is entitled to take reasonable precautions, including abandoning the voyage, in the face of a reasonable apprehension of danger. Read together, they establish that the promisor's decision not to perform must be an objectively reasonable response to an extraordinary, specific, and identifiable threat. See Kronprinzessin Cecilie, 244 U.S. at 20-24, 37 S.Ct. at 490-492 (German passenger ship justified in turning back from voyage to England on the day the German Emperor declared war (World War I)); The Wildwood, 133 F.2d at 768 ("reasonable apprehension" of "actual and substantial" danger of running a World War II naval blockade justified cancellation of ship's voyage in light of the seizure of a ship carrying identical cargo to the same destination).[1] The degree of danger is judged in light of the facts available at the time, First Restatement section 465 comment b, but "[m]ere good faith... will not excuse" cancellation of performance. The Styria, 186 U.S. at 10, 22 S.Ct. at 734.

Assuming solely for the purposes of argument that the above authorities cited by Kuhn are applicable to frustration of purpose, they do not help Kuhn. Even though Kuhn canceled the convention in good faith, under the cited authorities Kuhn's cancellation did not excuse its performance of the contract with the resort. Press reports in circulation at the time Kuhn canceled the convention indicated that the risk to domestic air travel was slight. Moreover, the United States government announced that it was taking measures to insure the safety of domestic air travel and that travelers should not be put off by the threat of terrorist activity.

Furthermore, the record establishes that by the time Kuhn canceled the convention, the risk of terrorism, if any, was diminishing. First, the danger, publicized since October 1990, had failed to materialize. Second, Kuhn itself recognized that even its French employees could possibly travel as early as April. Finally, even after the commencement of Operation Desert Storm, more than 100 of Kuhn's dealers expressed their willingness to travel to Scottsdale.

We conclude that Kuhn's cancellation of the convention because of the perceived threat of terrorism was not an objectively reasonable response to an extraordinary and specific threat. The slight risk to domestic air travel by vague threats of terrorism does not equate with the actual and substantial danger of running a naval blockade in time of war. Consequently, Kuhn gains nothing by recasting its frustration of purpose argument as one of "apprehension of impossibility."

Finally, we consider whether Kuhn is entitled to relief on the ground that fear of terrorist activities resulted in less than expected attendance, which in turn made the convention uneconomical. Although economic return may be characterized as the "principal purpose" of virtually all commercial contracts, mere economic impracticality is no defense to performance of a contract. See Restatement § 265 cmt. a. ("it is not enough that transaction has become less profitable for affected party or even that he will sustain a loss"); Thus, although the Gulf

---

1. Our conclusion that the proper standard is an objective one is supported by the First Restatement section 465, cited by Kuhn: "In determining whether a promisor's failure to [perform] is reasonable...consideration is given to...the degree of probability, apparent from what he knows or has reason to know,...of physical or pecuniary harm or loss to himself or to others...." See also First Restatement § 465 cmts. b, c.

War's effect on the expected level of attendance may have rendered the convention uneconomical, Kuhn was not on this ground relieved of its contractual obligation.

VI. CONCLUSION

We conclude that Kuhn is not entitled to relief from the contract under either the doctrine of impracticability of performance or the doctrine of frustration of purpose. Accordingly, we reverse the judgment in favor of Kuhn, order that partial summary judgment on the issue of liability be entered in favor of the resort, and remand for further proceedings consistent with this decision.

Questions

1. If the convention was scheduled to be held in London is there any frustration of purpose? What if in Baghdad?

2. Impossibility (or impracticability) vs. frustration of purpose—define the difference.

   a. The convention is to be held at the Baghdad Hilton. During the war the hotel is

       1) destroyed by bombs.

       2) occupied by Iraqi troops.

       3) open for business and awaiting the conventioneers.

           In each of these cases if the convention did not go there would their best defense be impossibility, impracticability or frustration of purpose?

   b. The court speaks of "risks assumed" by the plaintiff and links this to the specific provisions in the writing regarding the number and timing of cancellations etc. What is the relationship between the risk and those facts?

3. If you represented the hotel, what would you want in the contract to make certain that the convention will pay for the space whether they come or not?

4. If you represented the convention, what would you want in the contract to make certain that if enough people didn't come you could cancel without being liable for breach?   .

Kel Kim Corporation, v. Central Markets, Inc.

70 N.Y.2d 900, 519 N.E.2d 295, 524 N.Y.S.2d 384
Court of Appeals of New York, 1987.

MEMORANDUM.

The order of the Appellate Division, 131 A.D.2d 947, 516 N.Y.S.2d 806, should be affirmed, with costs.

In early 1980, plaintiff Kel Kim Corporation leased a vacant supermarket in Clifton Park, New York, from defendants. The lease was for an initial term of 10 years with two 5-year renewal options. The understanding of both parties was that plaintiff would use the property as a roller skating rink open to the general public, although the lease did not limit use of the premises to a roller rink.

The lease required Kel Kim to "procure and maintain in full force and effect a public liability insurance policy or policies in a solvent and responsible company or companies...of not less than Five Hundred Thousand Dollars...to any single person and in the aggregate of not less than One Million Dollars...on account of any single accident". Kel Kim obtained the required insurance coverage and for six years operated the facility without incident. In November 1985 its insurance carrier gave notice that the policy would expire on January 6, 1986 and would not be renewed due to uncertainty about the financial condition of the reinsurer, which was then under the management of a court-appointed administrator. Kel Kim transmitted this information to defendants and, it asserts, thereafter made every effort to procure the requisite insurance elsewhere but was unable to do so on account of the liability insurance crisis. Plaintiff ultimately succeeded in obtaining a policy in the aggregate amount of $500,000 effective March 1, 1986 and contends that no insurer would write a policy in excess of that amount on any roller skating rink. As of August 1987, plaintiff procured the requisite coverage.

On January 7, 1986, when plaintiff's initial policy expired and it remained uninsured, defendants sent a notice of default, directing that it cure within 30 days or vacate the premises. Kel Kim and the individual guarantors of the lease then began this declaratory judgment action, urging that they should be excused from compliance with the insurance provision either because performance was impossible or because the inability to procure insurance was within the lease's force majeure clause.[1] Special Term granted defendants' motion for summary judgment, nullified the lease, and directed Kel Kim to vacate the premises. A divided Appellate Division affirmed.

Generally, once a party to a contract has made a promise, that party must perform or respond in damages for its failure, even when unforeseen circumstances make performance burdensome; until the late nineteenth century even impossibility of performance ordinarily did not provide a defense. While such defenses have been recognized in the common law, they have been applied narrowly, due in part to judicial recognition that the purpose of contract law is to allocate the risks that might affect performance and that performance should be excused only in extreme circumstances. Impossibility excuses a party's performance only when the destruction of the subject matter of the contract or the means of performance makes performance objectively impossible. Moreover, the impossibility must be produced by an unanticipated event that could not have been foreseen or guarded against in the contract.

Applying these principles, we conclude that plaintiff's predicament is not within the embrace of the doctrine of impossibility. Kel Kim's inability to procure and maintain requisite coverage could have been foreseen and guarded against when it specifically undertook that obligation in the lease, and therefore the obligation cannot be excused on this basis.

For much the same underlying reason, contractual force majeure clauses—or clauses excusing nonperformance due to circumstances beyond the control of the

---

1. The clause reads: "If either party to this Lease shall be delayed or prevented from the performance of any obligation through no fault of their own by reason of labor disputes, inability to procure materials, failure of utility service, restrictive governmental laws or regulations, riots, insurrection, war, adverse weather, Acts of God, or other similar causes beyond the control of such party, the performance of such obligation shall be excused for the period of the delay."

parties—under the common law provide a similarly narrow defense. Ordinarily, only if the force majeure clause specifically includes the event that actually prevents a party's performance will that party be excused. Here, of course, the contractual provision does not specifically include plaintiff's inability to procure and maintain insurance. Nor does this inability fall within the catchall "or other similar causes beyond the control of such party." The principle of interpretation applicable to such clauses is that the general words are not to be given expansive meaning; they are confined to things of the same kind or nature as the particular matters mentioned.

We agree with the conclusion reached by the majority below that the events listed in the force majeure clause here are different in kind and nature from Kel Kim's inability to procure and maintain public liability insurance. The recited events pertain to a party's ability to conduct day-to-day commercial operations on the premises. While Kel Kim urges that the same may be said of a failure to procure and maintain insurance, such an event is materially different. The requirement that specified amounts of public liability insurance at all times be maintained goes not to frustrated expectations in day-to-day commercial operations on the premises—such as interruptions in the availability of labor, materials and utility services—but to the bargained-for protection of the landlord's unrelated economic interests where the tenant chooses to continue operating a public roller skating rink on the premises.

[Affirmed]

Note — Foreseeability

Foreseeability is a component of many contract rights. In assessing damages for breach a court will inquire as to whether the particular harm caused by the breaching party was foreseeable to it at the time it entered into the contract. In the principal case, the promisor was told that it could have foreseen the problem of insurance not being available and therefore took on the responsibility for the unconditional nature of its promise. Does this mean that in drafting a contract, the draftspersons had better put in every contingency they can think of—"I promise to get $1,000,000 insurance so long as it is available on the market at reasonable terms, reasonable being defined in this sentence as no higher in cost than it is now adjusted for cost of living increases in accordance with the following index [fill in name] and if it not available at reasonable terms I promise to obtain whatever coverage is available at reasonable terms [etc. etc. etc.]"? Probably yes. In other words, the basis of the bargain, the nature of the promise is not only what the parties actually foresaw and intended but what they could have foreseen. If you can foresee it it's not unforeseen, and if it's not unforeseen you cannot use the event to relieve you from an otherwise unconditional obligation.

This leads to the question of what is presumed by language. If you make what seems to be an unconditional promise to do something you will be held to it unless you can prove that something you didn't foresee and couldn't foresee and which would have changed the nature of the promise occurred. An unconditional promise in form is presumed to be unconditional. To escape from it, proof of some far out event is necessary. Would the court in *Hunt Foods v. Doliner, supra* Part III-B, be more inclined to let in evidence showing that the apparently unconditional promise was not really meant to be so absolute? How might parol evidence issues blend with frustration of purpose issues?

Mishara Construction Company v. Transit-Mixed Concrete Corp., 310 N.E.2d 363, (Mass., 1974.)

[Transit-Mixed Concrete Corp. agreed to deliver concrete ordered by Mishara Construction Comp. at $13.25 per cubic yard. The agreement was for any time and any amount that Mishara requested. However, a labor dispute erupted which disturbed work. Transit was unable to deliver Mishara's requests for concrete, forcing Mishara to look elsewhere to fulfill its needs for concrete. Mishara sued for damages of the cost incurred by the higher replacement of concrete. Transit assert the defense of impossibility.]

REARDON, Justice.

Objection was made [by Mishara] to the introduction of all evidence regarding the existence of a picket line at the job site and the difficulty which Transit did encounter or might have encountered in attempting to make deliveries through that picket line. Furthermore, Mishara requested an instruction that Transit 'was required to comply with the contract regardless of picket lines, strikes or labor difficulties.' As a result Mishara would have completely withdrawn the question of impossibility resulting from the picket line from the jury. We are asked to decide as matter of law and without reference to individual facts and circumstances that 'picket lines, strikes or labor difficulties' provide no excuse for nonperformance by way of impossibility. This is too sweeping a statement of the law and we decline to adopt it.

The excuse of impossibility in contracts for the sale of goods is controlled by the appropriate section of the Uniform Commercial Code, G.L. c. 106, § 2—615.[1] That section sets up two requirements before performance may be excused. First, the performance must have become 'impracticable.' Second, the impracticability must have been caused 'by the occurrence of a contingency the non-occurrence of which was a basic assumption on which the contract was made.' This section of the Uniform Commercial Code has not yet been interpreted by this court. Therefore it is appropriate to discuss briefly the significance of these two criteria.

With respect to the requirement that performance must have been impracticable, the official Code comment to the section stresses that the reference is to 'commercial impracticability' as opposed to strict impossibility. This is not a radical departure from the common law of contracts as interpreted by this court. Although a strict rule was originally followed denying any excuse for accident or 'inevitable necessity,' it has long been assumed that circumstances drastically increasing the difficulty and expense of the contemplated performance may be

---

1. 'Excuse of Failure of Presupposed Conditions. 'Except so far as a seller may have assumed a greater obligation and subject to the preceding section on substituted performance '(a) Delay in delivery or non-delivery in whole or in part by a seller who complies with paragraphs (b) and (c) is not a breach of his duty under a contract for sale if performance as agreed has been made impracticable by the occurrence of a contingency the nonoccurrence of which was a basic assumption on which the contract was made or by compliance in good faith with any applicable foreign or domestic governmental regulation or order whether or not it later proves to be invalid.'

within the compass of 'IMPOSSIBILITY.' By adopting the term 'impracticability' rather than 'impossibility' the drafters of the Code appear to be in accord with Professor Williston who stated that 'the essence of the modern defense of impossibility is that the promised performance was at the making of the contract, or thereafter became, impracticable owing to some extreme or unreasonable difficulty, expense, injury, or loss involved, rather than that it is scientifically or actually impossible.'

The second criterion of the excuse, that the intervening circumstance be one which the parties assumed would not occur, is also familiar to the law of Massachusetts. The rule is essentially aimed at the distribution of certain kinds of risks in the contractual relationship. By directing the inquiry to the time when the contract was first made, we really seek to determine whether the risk of the intervening circumstance was one which the parties may be taken to have assigned between themselves. It is, or course, the very essence of contract that it is directed at the elimination of some risks for each party in exchange for others. Each receives the certainty of price, quantity, and time, and assumes the risk of changing market prices, superior opportunity, or added costs. It is implicit in the doctrine of impossibility (and the companion rule of 'frustration of purpose') that certain risks are so unusual and have such severe consequences that they must have been beyond the scope of the assignment of risks inherent in the contract, that is, beyond the agreement made by the parties. To require performance in that case would be to grant the promisee an advantage for which he could not be said to have bargained in making the contract. 'The important question is whether an unanticipated circumstance has made performance of the promise vitally different from what should reasonably have been within the contemplation of both parties when they entered into the contract. If so, the risk should not fairly be thrown upon the promisor.' Williston, Contracts (Rev. ed.) § 1931 (1938). The emphasis in contracts governed by the Uniform Commercial Code is on the commercial context in which the agreement was made. The question is, given the commercial circumstances in which the parties dealt: Was the contingency which developed one which the parties could reasonably be thought to have foreseen as a real possibility which could affect performance? Was it one of that variety of risks which the parties were tacitly assigning to the promisor by their failure to provide for it explicitly? If it were, performance will be required. If it could not be so considered, performance is excused. The contract cannot be reasonably thought to govern in these circumstances, and the parties are both thrown upon the resources of the open market without the benefit of their contract.

With this backdrop, we consider Mishara's contention that a labor dispute which makes performance more difficult never constitutes an excuse for nonperformance. We think it is evident that in some situations a labor dispute would not meet the requirements for impossibility discussed above. A picket line might constitute a mere inconvenience and hardly make performance 'impracticable.' Likewise, in certain industries with a long record of labor difficulties, the nonoccurrence of strikes and picket lines could not fairly be said to be a basic assumption of the agreement. Certainly, in general, labor disputes cannot be considered extraordinary in the course of modern commerce. Admitting this, however, we are still far from the proposition implicit in the plaintiff's requests. Much must depend on the facts known to the parties at the time of contracting with respect to the history of and prospects for labor difficulties during the period of performance of the contract, as well as the likely severity of the effect of such disputes on the ability to perform. From these facts it is possible to draw an inference as to whether or not the parties intended performance to be carried out even in the face of the labor difficulty. Where the probability of a labor dispute appears to be practically nil, and where the occurrence of such a dispute provides unusual difficulty, the excuse of impracticability might well be applicable. Thus in discussing the defense of impossibility, then Chief Judge Cardozo noted an excuse would be provided 'conceivably in some circumstances by unavoidable strikes.' Canadian Industrial Alcohol Co. Ltd. v. Dunbar Molasses Co., 258 N.Y. 194, 198, 179 N.E. 383, 384 (1932). The many variables which may bear on the question in individual cases were canvassed by Professor Williston in Williston, Contracts (Rev. ed.) § 1951A (1938), and he concluded that the trend of the law is toward recognizing strikes as excuses for nonperformance. We agree with the statement of the judge in Badhwar v. Colorado Fuel & Iron Corp., 138 F.Supp. 595, 607 (S.D.N.Y.1955), affd. 245 F.2d 903 (2d Cir. 1957), on the same question: 'Rather than mechanically apply any fixed rule of law, where the parties themselves have not allocated responsibility, justice is better served by appraising all of the circumstances, the part the various parties played, and thereon determining liability.' Since the instructions requested by the plaintiff and the exclusion of the evidence objected to would have precluded such a factual determination, the requests were more properly refused, and the evidence was properly admitted.

Exceptions overruled.

Questions

1. What is the relationship between "foreseeability" of an event and the second prong of § 2-615, that the event be one the "non-occurrence of which was a basic assumption on which the contract was made"?

2. What is the relationship between "foreseeability" and "assumptions" and the concept of allocating risk to a particular party?

3. Why is the determination of impracticability so fact specific, or do you believe it is?

Sagittarius Broadcasting Corp. v. Evergreen Media Corp., 641 N.Y.S.2d 267,(A.D.1996).

Sagittarius granted Evergreen an exclusive license to broadcast "The Howard Stern Show" on the Chicago radio station WLUP-AM for a three year period ending in October 1995. Evergreen refused to perform the agreement after finding out "plans by the FCC to pursue an unprecedented escalation of fines and other regulatory actions against shows that broadcast materials that the FCC found indecent, as well as an allegedly undisclosed FCC inquiry against plaintiff Sagittarius and its affiliates, WYSP-FM in Philadelphia and WJFK-FM in Washington, D.C., relating to broadcasts of the Howard Stern Show."

Sagittarius' motions for summary judgment on breach of contract and action for recovery based on an indemnification provision were denied. Sagittarius' motion to strike Evergreen's impossibility defense were likewise denied, "since conflicting affidavits of the parties raise triable issues of fact as to whether defendant Evergreen was excused from performing under the agreement by the doctrine of impossibility, because of the asserted unforeseeability of the FCC actions (see,

Kel Kim Corp. v. Central Mkts., 70 N.Y.2d 900, 902, 524 N.Y.S.2d 384, 519 N.E.2d 295)."

J.J. Cassone Bakery, Inc. v. Consolidated Edison Co., 638 N.Y.S.2d 898, (Sup.Ct., 1996).

In 1990 Consolidated Edison (Con Ed) started a cost saving program called, "Curtailable Electric Service—Summer Savings Program" (CES). Customers would receive credit for electricity if they reduced usage in peak summer months. The CES was established by an approved tariff by the Public Service Committee (PSC) was set at $15 per kilowatt where the customer would comply on a thirty minute notification. The CES guaranteed stable rates for a five year period, but contained the clauses "All terms and conditions of this Special Provision E, including the levels of credit and penalty and number and duration of curtailments are subject to change and may differ during the period in which this Special Provision is in effect... Con Edison will supply CES service only under PSC-approved tariffs."

J.J Cassone executed its application in May 1991. In the same month Con Ed entered hearings with the PSC, which culminated in the April 1992 decision to cut the CES credit to $12 per kilowat in 1993 and $9 thereafter. J.J. brings this suit for damages in fraud and for breach of contract, claiming damages of $39,208.50 as the per kilowatt differential credit denied it and $250,000 for the purchase and installation of generators in reliance upon the savings it believed it would receive under the original CES program. J.J also requests punitive damages.

LEFKOWITZ, Justice.

The arguments being advanced with respect to whether plaintiff has a viable claim relate to the doctrine of impossibility of performance by supervening events; in this case, a change in the tariff, rate or credit under the CES program, as required by the PSC. Plaintiff contends that the doctrine is not applicable as Con Ed contributed to the situation by asking for a rate increase and then agreeing to reduce the CES credit. Con Ed submits that it was not precluded from requesting a rate increase and acted in good faith at all times.

Every commercial contract carries an obligation that the parties shall act in good faith with respect to the promises to be performed.

Impossibility of performance caused by a superseding judicial, executive or administrative order is a recognized defense to a claim under a contract affected by such order.

A supervening event excuses a promisor's duty if the event is not caused by the actions of the promisor. Restatement 2d, Contracts, § 265; Uniform Commercial Code § 2-615(a). To excuse the promisor's performance by reason of a supervening act, it is generally understood that such act was unforeseeable when the contract was created, the events causing the result were fortuitous and beyond the control of either party to the contract and the event, when it occurred, was vigorously challenged by diligent efforts of the promisor to avoid the consequences of impossibility.

A party is not necessarily at fault, within the meaning of the principle that excuses performance by reason of impossibility, where it does an act which is lawful, although such act ultimately frustrates the purpose of a contract and renders performance impossible.

It was seemingly innocuous for Con Ed to seek a rate increase and presumably it was not barred by the CES agreement with the plaintiff from going forward with its request even when the PSC suggested that CES credits be reduced. Indeed, it may be forcefully argued that the plaintiff assumed the risk of an adverse change in the CES credits by reason of the language set forth in the application and pamphlet. However, plaintiff certainly did not assume the risk that Con Ed would violate its good faith obligation to provide the called-for performance under the agreement by bargaining away plaintiff's benefits under the program by way of a settled rate increase with the PSC.

At bar, therefore, the Court concludes that a viable claim is presented at this time regarding the conduct of Con Ed's involvement with settlement of its rate increase application as its "performance should be excused only in extreme circumstances".

[Motion to dismiss is denied.]

American Trading and Production Co. v. Shell International Marine LTD., 453 F.2d 939 (2d Cir., 1972).

Shell International hired a vessel from American Trading to transport cargo from Texas to India. The agreement provided, "that the freight rate would be in accordance with the then prevailing American Tanker Rate Schedule (ATRS), $14.25 per long ton of cargo, plus seventy-five percent (75%), and in addition there was a charge of $.85 per long ton for passage through the Suez Canal." However, the Suez Canal was closed when the transport reached it because of the Suez Canal Crisis, which necessitated that the vessel proceed to India via the Cape of Good Hope. The result of that diversion was American Trading's suit for $131,978.44 which it desired as extra compensation for the nearly double mileage.

The court stated: "The owner argues that transit of the Suez Canal was the agreed specific means of performance of the voyage charter and that the supervening destruction of this means rendered the contract legally impossible to perform and therefore discharged the owner's unperformed obligation (Restatement of Contracts § 460 (1932)). Consequently, when the WASHINGTON TRADER eventually delivered the oil after journeying around the Cape of Good Hope, a benefit was conferred upon the charterer for which it should respond in quantum meruit. The validity of this proposition depends upon a finding that the parties contemplated or agreed that the Suez passage was to be the exclusive method of performance, and indeed it was so argued on appeal. We cannot construe the agreement in such a fashion. The parties contracted for the shipment of the cargo from Texas to India at an agreed rate and the charter party makes absolutely no reference to any fixed route. It is urged that the Suez passage was a condition of performance because the ATRS rate was based on a Suez Canal passage, the invoice contained a specific Suez Canal toll charge and the vessel actually did proceed to a point 84 miles northwest of Port Said. In our view all that this establishes is that both parties contemplated that the Canal would be the probable route. It was the cheapest and shortest, and therefore it was in the interest of both that it be utilized. However, this is not at all equivalent to an agreement that it be the exclusive method of performance. The charter party does not so provide and it seems to have been well understood in the shipping industry that the Cape route is an acceptable alternative in voyages of this character.... We hold that all that the ATRS rate establishes is that the parties obviously expected a Suez passage but there is no indication at all in the instrument or dehors that it was a condition of performance."

American Trading also unsuccessfully tried to argue it was excused from performance because of commercial impracticability. "There is no extreme or unreasonable difficulty apparent here. The alternate route taken was well recognized, and there is no claim that the vessel or the crew or the nature of the cargo made the route actually taken unreasonably difficult, dangerous or onerous. The owner's case here essentially rests upon the element of the additional expense involved — $131,978.44. This represents an increase of less than one third over the agreed upon $417,327.36. We find that this increase in expense is not sufficient to constitute commercial impracticability under either American or English authority.... Mere increase in cost alone is not a sufficient excuse for non- performance. It must be an "extreme and unreasonable expense.[1]"

6. Fraud and the Like

In the next case, *Neves v. Wright,* the defendants sold land to which they did not have legal title at the time of the contract for sale. They did not disclose this to plaintiffs. Plaintiffs sued. The difference between active misstatement and simply nondisclosing a fact becomes apparent in this case. No one asked if the sellers had title, probably because they assumed that the old Jay Gould (a 19th century entrepreneur — *i.e.* robber baron) rule — "He who sells what isn't his'n must buy it back or go to pris'n" — held true in real estate contracts as much as it did in stock deals. [Gould was referring to the practice — still popular — of selling stock "short" (that is, without actually owning it) in the expectation that the price would fall and you could buy whatever you needed to cover your sale contract more cheaply than you sold it for before the time came to deliver it to your buyer.] The court, however, in essence ruled that even if the seller did not have title so long as seller could and did get title there was no breach.

In *Brewer v. Brothers, infra,* an "as is" clause fails to overcome a direct fraudulent misrepresentation. Furthermore, a failure to disclose known defects may in some circumstances be the equivalent of a positive misstatement. But many other elements must be proved before recovery is possible: the misrepresentation must be material, made with knowledge of its falsity or with reckless disregard for the truth, with an intent to mislead another into relying on it and with the result that it was reasonably relied on to the injury of the person relying. Ask yourself whether the contract and the addendum should have prevented plaintiff's suit? It is easy to say 'the trial court found that a misrepresentation was made' but that after all is just a judge or jury listening to evidence and saying yes

---

"1. The Restatement gives some examples of what is "extreme and unreasonable"-Restatement of Contracts § 460, Illus. 2 (tenfold increase in costs) and Illus. 3 (costs multiplied fifty times) (1932); compare § 467, Illus. 3. See generally G. Grismore, Principles of the Law of Contracts § 179 (rev. ed. J. E. Murray 1965)."

it's more likely than not that the seller said whatever it is the buyer said was said. The seller tries to protect himself/herself from this result by having a writing. What would you recommend to sellers to avoid the problem in the *Brewer* case?

In *Bowman v. Meadow Ridge, Inc., infra*, a clause specifically addressed the fraud that buyers were claiming. From buyers' point of view is there any advantage to claiming "We never read it so it shouldn't apply"? The court also noted that reliance, an essential element, was not reasonable because buyers could have checked prices, the alleged misrepresentation, themselves.

In *Nationwide Insurance Co. v. Patterson, infra*, a "mere expression of opinion" was found to be actionable where the two contracting parties were not on equal ground. In this "constructive fraud" case, there was no confidential relationship and apparently no intent to deceive, merely negligence, yet the court found the defendant liable. The Company by its own written information informed the insured to seek answers to questions from the agent who supplied the misinformation. It did not behoove the Company well to say that the insured could have found out the truth for himself in this circumstance.

In all of these cases there is a struggle involving a standardized written contract, an undertone of one person in an advantageous position (usually the seller) and another not, the strictures of the parol evidence rule, and the allegation of a misrepresentation which fouled or at least soured the deal. Note the interrelationship of these areas as you proceed through the cases.

Problem

Buyer negotiates with seller for the purchase of Whiteacre, a 250 acre tract of land. The land is in Arkansas to which state buyer recently moved after retiring as a building contractor in New York. Buyer intends to use the land to build a retirement home for himself on 25 acres and to use 25 additional acres for a golf course, hiking trails and picnic areas, and to build 50 retirement homes on the remaining 200 acres. Buyer asks seller if there will be any trouble with zoning for these varied uses, to which seller responds: "This is Arkansas, friend. You won't find any restrictions here." Buyer also asks seller if there would be any difficulty with septic systems as a result of water tables etc. Seller said it was out of his line but he had never heard of anyone having that kind of trouble in the area. Buyer also asked about drilling for water and wells and was told by seller: "Sweetest water in all Arkansas, maybe the whole mid-South, right here. That's one thing you needn't worry about."

Buyer buys the land. The water is brackish, the zoning boards of several townships in which the land fell created time consuming barriers to building, the local health departments have opposed building more than 20 homes on the whole area because of the fear of sewage runoff into streams and underground water supplies, the deed for the land, prepared by seller's agent as well as the land description in the sales contract, left off over 40 acres of the most scenic land and added in close to 90 acres of swamp for a total of 160 usuable acres. Buyer failed to detect this in the contract or deed because he didn't understand the description and only realized the error when he tried to go on the scenic land that was left out of the contract and deed and found it fenced with no trespassing signs.

Buyer claims in the alternative: actual and constructive fraud, mutual mistake, unilateral mistake, breach of warranty implied in the contract of sale, impossibility of performance, impracticability and frustration of purpose.

Seller moves for summary judgment on all claims of buyer.

You are the judge. Based on the above facts rule on the claims. What other facts might you want established and how would this affect the summary judgment motion?

Neves v. Wright

638 P.2d 1195
Supreme Court of Utah, 1981.

STEWART, Justice:

Plaintiffs entered into a uniform real estate contract on April 19, 1977, to purchase from defendants a residence situated in Fillmore, Utah. On May 31, 1977, the parties executed a corrected contract and an escrow agreement. The defendants executed a warranty deed which was deposited with the contract in escrow. According to the escrow agreement, the warranty deed was to be delivered to plaintiffs upon payment of the purchase price plus interest.

Eight days prior to the execution of the first contract, on April 11, 1977, the defendants conveyed by a quitclaim deed their interest in the premises to the parents of defendant, Bruce Earl Wright. The deed was recorded the same day. Bruce Earl Wright testified he had been engaged in litigation with Western General Dairies in April 1977. Although Western General Dairies had no security interest in the property, its counsel wrote Mr. Wright two letters threatening to attach the property to satisfy any judgment that might be rendered in its favor. According to Wright, defendants conveyed the property to his parents with the oral understanding that when the lawsuit with Western General was resolved, they would reconvey the property. In June of 1978 the Western General Dairies lawsuit was dismissed, and the property was reconveyed in December, 1978. Wilford Neves testified that had he known the facts, he would not have entered into the contract to purchase.

In February 1978, plaintiffs discovered the prior conveyance and sent a letter to defendants renouncing the sale as fraudulent and void. Plaintiffs notified defendants they were vacating the premises, tendered back the property, and demanded the return of their payments. Later, plaintiffs filed this action seeking rescission on grounds of fraud and breach of contract.

On appeal, defendants contend that the trial court erred in ruling that plaintiffs could rescind the contract on the ground that the defendants did not have title to the property at the time the contract was executed. Defendants maintain that a seller under a uniform real estate contract need not have marketable title until final payment is made or tendered.

As early as 1909, this Court established the fundamental rule that a seller need not have legal title during the entire executory period of a real estate contract.

This Court reiterated the basic principle in Leavitt v. Blohm, 11 Utah 2d 220, 223, 357 P.2d 190, 192-93 (1960): In considering the soundness of the judgment, we acknowledge our accord with the rule relied upon by the plaintiffs that the vendor in a real estate contract is generally not obliged to have full and clear marketable title at all times during the pendency of his contract of sale because, ordinarily, title need not be conveyed until the final payment is made or tendered; and we further agree that the purchaser cannot use a claimed deficiency in title as an excuse for refusing to keep a commitment to purchase property, as was attempted in the case of Woodard v. Allen. (1 Utah 2d 220, 265 P.2d 398 (1953).)

The rule that a seller of real estate need not have title at all times during the executory period of a contract, is not designed to favor sellers over buyers; rather, the purpose is to enhance the alienability of real estate by providing necessary flexibility in real estate transactions. Nevertheless, it is essential that in every case there be a close scrutiny of the facts, and the rule must be carefully applied to avoid unfairness, sharp practice, and outright dishonesty. Accordingly, the rule is not without limitation. If it plainly appears that a seller has lost or encumbered his ownership so that he will not be able to fulfill his contract, he cannot insist that a buyer continue to make payments.

The basic test in determining whether a buyer can rescind is whether the defect, by its nature, is one that can be removed, as a practical matter, as distinguished from defects which, by their nature, cannot be removed by the seller as a practical matter. A defect which, by its nature cannot be removed by the seller as a practical matter is one "of such a nature that the vendor neither has title 'nor in a practical sense any prospect of acquiring it.'" Davis v. Dean Vincent Inc., 255 Or. 233, 465 P.2d 702 (1970).

In the instant case, the value of the buyer's bargain was not impaired. The sellers were able to obtain clear title to the property, and at the time of trial had done so. *Nor is there evidence that the sellers actively misrepresented their interest in the property.*[1] Although the buyers argue, and the trial court found, that the sellers had represented they had clear title, *the record only establishes that the sellers failed to disclose that Mr. Wright's parents were the record owners. There is nothing in the language of the real estate contract to the contrary.* [Emphasis added.]

The buyers' reliance on the warranty deed in support of the claim of misrepresentation, is also without merit. The defect in the record title at the time the warranty deed was placed in escrow is of no consequence. A warranty deed placed in escrow creates no warranties until the conditions of the escrow are met and the deed delivered. The deed does not therefore constitute a representation as to the status of the title. In Foxley v. Rich, 35 Utah 162, 99 P. 666 (1909) the Court stated: (E)ven in the absence of any stipulation, the placing of the deed in escrow left it, so far as the passing of title is concerned, precisely as if no deed

---

1. We express no opinion as to what the result should be if a vendor actively misrepresents the state of the title. In Hall v. Hickey, 156 Cal.App.2d 94, 319 P.2d 33 (1957), the court recognized the well-settled rule that one may make a valid contract to sell property to which he has no legal title and that the purchaser may not rescind or recover money paid unless the seller, when the time comes to convey title, is unable or unwilling to do so. Even though the seller in that case falsely represented that he had clear title, the court found that the seller contracted to sell the property at a fair price, that he was able and willing to deliver the title as agreed, and that the misrepresentation that he owned the property gained him no advantage. Indeed, the seller did secure title to the property and sold it to the buyer in accordance with the terms of the contract.

had been executed. A deed placed in escrow does not become effective until the conditions upon which it is executed have been fully performed, and taking possession of the property by the purchaser, and part performance, ordinarily do not change this rule.

Although the parents of Mr. Wright appeared as record title holders at the time of the sale, they, nevertheless, intended to reconvey the property to the sellers and at no time asserted an interest, legal or equitable, in the property. The deed to the parents was recorded prior to the purchase, and a preliminary title report or an abstract of title would have disclosed the conveyance. Furthermore, upon discovering the prior conveyance, the buyers made no inquiry as to the rights of the seller or the ability of the sellers to acquire the title in fulfillment of their contractual obligations.

Under these circumstances, the sellers are not guilty of misrepresentation or breach of contract.

Reversed and remanded for consideration of defendants' counterclaim. Costs to appellants.

Brewer v. Brothers

82 Ohio App.3d 148, 611 N.E.2d 492
Court of Appeals of Ohio, 1992.

KOEHLER, Presiding Judge.

Plaintiff-appellant, Blake O. Brewer, appeals a decision of the Warren County Court of Common Pleas in favor of defendants-appellees, Paul A. and Barbara Brothers ("the Brotherses").

On September 20, 1990, Brewer filed a complaint against the Brotherses alleging breach of contract, fraudulent misrepresentation and negligent construction in connection with the Brotherses' sale of a residence to Brewer. Specifically, Brewer complained that the Brotherses had failed to replace windows as required by the contract and had misrepresented the quality of the electrical system, which was defective.

The case was tried to the court on September 12, 1991. The evidence showed that the parties entered into a contract on January 23, 1990 for the sale of real estate located at 143 Maple Street, Harveysburg, Ohio. The contract stated that "Purchaser has examined the Property and, except as otherwise provided in the Contract, is purchasing it 'as is' in its present condition, relying upon such examination as to the condition, character, size, utility and zoning of the Property." The parties also signed an "inspection addendum" stating that Brewer had the right to have various inspections done on the residence during a specified time period. The addendum stated that "[f]ailure to notify seller of any defects before expiration of the inspection period, shall constitute a waiver of such defects and purchasers shall take the property 'as is' with respect to such defects."

The deed to the property was in Barbara Brothers' name. The Brotherses lived in the residence for several years prior to the sale. Paul Brothers is a builder who did extensive work on the house prior to offering it for sale, including rewiring the electrical system.

The Brotherses showed the house to Brewer on two occasions. On each of these occasions, Brewer was accompanied by Keith Cowden, a real estate agent. Brewer and Cowden both testified that Paul Brothers made extensive references to the quality of the work he had done throughout the house. Cowden testified that when Paul Brothers was specifically asked about the electrical work, he stated, "You have nothing to worry about." Brewer testified that he specifically relied upon Paul Brothers' representations regarding the electrical system in choosing not to have an electrical inspection done. Brewer had other inspections done because there were evident defects.

After the sale, Brewer discovered extensive problems with the electrical work. Two electricians testified that the electrical system was defective, that it was a fire hazard, and that it violated numerous provisions of the Warren County Electrical Code and the National Electrical Code. They also testified that these defects would not be evident to a lay person. Brewer had the electrical system fixed at a cost of $2,102.49.

Paul Brothers denied making any representations to Brewer regarding the quality of the work done. He claimed to have obtained an electrical permit for the work done, although Brewer presented testimony the permit was only a "certificate of occupancy." Paul Brothers conceded that the agreement was breached in regard to the windows and agreed to pay damages to Brewer on that issue.

The trial court dismissed the negligent construction claim, concluding that there was no evidence to show that the Brotherses had a duty of ordinary care towards Brewer or that they breached that duty. The court awarded Brewer $1,269.01 for the breach of contract claim with regard to the windows. With regard to the fraudulent misrepresentation claim, the court found in favor of the Brotherses, stating:

> "As to the electrical system, the Court finds that at the time of the instant transaction the electrical system in this residence was defective. We further find that the Defendant Paul A. Brothers misrepresented the condition of the electrical system to the Plaintiff. However, in light of the 'Inspection Addendum' to the Contract to Purchase, the Court cannot find that the Plaintiff relied upon any misrepresentations by the Defendants. The Plaintiff had the opportunity to have the electrical system thoroughly inspected by a qualified inspector, but did not so [sic] so. Consequently, under the terms of the Addendum, the defect is waived.
>
> "Further, there is complete absence of any evidence to show the extent, in money, of any damage suffered by the Plaintiff as the result of said defect."

This appeal followed.

Brewer presents three assignments of error for review. In his first assignment of error, he states that the trial court erred "in finding that a *standard* 'inspection addendum' to a contract to purchase real estate precluded recovery when the sellers engaged in fraud." [Emphasis added.] He argues that an "as is" clause does not bar a claim for fraudulent misrepresentation. We find this assignment of error to be well taken.

In Ohio, a seller may be liable for nondisclosure of a latent defect where the seller is under a duty to disclose facts and fails to do so. An "as is" clause in a real estate contract places the risk upon the purchaser as to the existence of defects. It relieves the seller of any duty to disclose. However, an "as is" clause does not bar a claim for "positive" fraud, a fraud of commission rather than omission. An "as is" clause cannot be relied upon to bar a claim for fraudulent misrepresentation or fraudulent concealment.

In Mancini, *supra*, Eugene and Roberta Mancini purchased a residence from William and Margaret Gorick, who resided in the home. William Gorick informed the Mancinis that he was the architect and general contractor of the house. Later, the Mancinis discovered that the roof had structural defects. They filed a complaint against the Goricks, alleging among other things that the Goricks committed fraud by failing to disclose the roof's defects. The trial court granted summary judgment in favor of the Goricks. On appeal, the Summit County Court of Appeals reversed the trial court, rejecting the Goricks' argument that an inspection addendum, similar to the one in the present case, barred the Mancinis' claim. The court stated:

"Although a claim of nondisclosure will not overcome an 'as is' clause, a claim of fraudulent concealment will.... Nondisclosure will become the equivalent of fraudulent concealment when it becomes the duty of a person to speak in order that the party with whom he is dealing may be placed on an equal footing with him.... The duty to speak does not necessarily depend on the existence of a fiduciary relationship....' ...It may arise in any situation where one party imposes confidence in the other because of that person's position, and the other party knows of this confidence....' ...In the instant case, William Gorick told Eugene Mancini that he was an architectural engineer and had personally designed and built the house. Mancini claimed that he did not have the house inspected because he relied on Gorick's professional expertise in believing the house to have been constructed in a workmanlike manner, free of latent defects." (Citations omitted.) Id., 41 Ohio App.3d at 374-375, 536 N.E.2d at 9-10.

In a similar vein, courts have concluded that the buyer's duty to inspect the premises to discover defects terminates when representations are made with respect to a material fact in response to a buyer's direct inquiry.

In the present case, the trial court concluded that Paul Brothers misrepresented the condition of the electrical system. Brewer had a right to rely upon Paul Brothers' representation since Brothers had superior knowledge regarding the electrical system. At the time the representation was made, Brewer's duty to inspect terminated and the Brotherses cannot now hide behind an "as is" clause or an inspection addendum to avoid liability for a fraudulent misrepresentation. Accordingly, we hold that the trial court erred in finding that the defect was waived due to the inspection addendum to the contract.

An action for fraudulent misrepresentation requires proof of (1) a representation, (2) which is material to the transaction at hand, (3) made falsely, with knowledge of its falsity, or with such utter disregard and recklessness as to whether it is true or false that knowledge may be inferred, (4) with the intent of misleading another into relying upon it, (5) justifiable reliance upon the representation or concealment, and (6) a resulting injury proximately caused by the reliance. In the present case, the trial court concluded that there was a misrepresentation. However, it made no specific findings on the other elements of fraudulent misrepresentation because it determined that the inspection addendum controlled the case. Therefore, we sustain Brewer's first assignment of error and remand the case for the trial court to make findings of fact on Brewer's claim for fraudulent misrepresentation.

In his second assignment of error, Brewer states that the trial court erred in finding that no evidence of his damages was presented at trial. He argues that he presented prima facie evidence of damages he sustained due to the Brotherses' misrepresentation by demonstrating the amount he paid to have the necessary repairs done to the electrical system. He argues that the cost of repair is a proper measure of damages. We find this assignment of error to be well taken.

A person injured by fraud is entitled to recover damages naturally and proximately resulting from the fraud. The fundamental rule is that the owner must be compensated for the loss sustained. Where there is fraud inducing the purchase or exchange of real estate, Ohio courts have held that the proper measure of damages is the difference between the value of the property as it was represented to be and its actual value at the time of purchase or exchange. This is known as the "benefit of the bargain" rule. Courts have also held that the cost of repair or replacement is a fair representation of damages under the benefit of the bargain rule and is a proper method for measuring damages. Given the practical difficulties of establishing the value of the property with and without the defects in these types of cases, we accept the proposition that repair or replacement cost is an adequate measure of damages, particularly given that the goal is to compensate the owner for the loss sustained.

Brewer presented evidence that it cost him approximately $2,000 to have the defects in the electrical system repaired. The trial court concluded that Brewer failed to present any evidence of damages. We disagree. Where pecuniary damage does exist, evidence of the exact amount of the difference in value is not necessarily required. Where the existence of damage is established, the evidence need only tend to show the basis for the computation of damages to a fair degree of probability. In the present case, Brewer showed that the electrical system failed to meet the requirements of the local electrical code in many respects, that the defects constituted a fire hazard and that he incurred substantial expense to have the defects repaired. His damages were not predicated on "mere speculation,... hypothesis, conjecture or whim." It was therefore incumbent upon the Brotherses to present evidence to rebut Brewer's evidence of damages. Accordingly, we hold that the trial court erred in concluding that Brewer did not present any evidence of damages. Brewer's second assignment of error is sustained.

Judgment reversed and cause remanded.

In *Bowman v. Meadow Ridge, Inc., 615 A.2d 755 (Penn., 1992)*, buyers claimed that sellers "intentionally and fraudulently misrepresented to them that they were purchasing the premises [a house] for the lowest price" for that model when in point of fact the same house had previously sold for $3,000 [or about 2%] less. The written contract contained the following integration clause:

"ENTIRE AGREEMENT: This is the entire Agreement between the parties, and there are no other terms, obligations, covenants, representations, statements or conditions, oral or otherwise, of any kind whatsoever which are not herein referred to or incorporated. In entering into this Agreement, Buyer has not relied upon any representation, claim, advertising, promotional activity, brochure or plan of any kind made by Seller or Seller's agents of employees unless expressly incorporated or stated in this Agreement. All amendments, supplements or riders hereto, if any, shall be in writing and executed by both parties."

Among other things buyers questioned: "Did the lower court err by not finding that the fraud of [seller] vitiated the integration clause?" The court responded, in part:

"[A]bsent reliance upon the alleged misrepresentation, there can be no action sounding in fraud against the maker of the statement or anyone else."

"[W]e find that the parol evidence rule bars admission of evidence of the alleged misrepresentation to vary, modify or supersede the integration clause of the written sales agreement. Appellants specifically represented in the contract that they did not rely upon any "representation" or "promotional activity" of the seller's agents. Whether [seller's] representation concerning the price of the house was true was readily ascertainable before the purchase was completed. All appellants needed to do was check the public record as to the prices for which the same model homes had sold.[1]

"This is not a case where the misrepresentation concerned the physical condition of the home and could not have been discovered by an inspection of the premises. Rather, appellants not only could have easily ascertained the truth but also expressly stated in the contract that they did not rely upon the promotional representations of appellees.

Having determined that the parol evidence rule bars evidence of the alleged misrepresentations, we find that the lower court properly dismissed appellants' complaint."

[Affirmed.]

Question

1. Is *Bowman* a case where the court found no reliance, no reasonable reliance, no reasonable reliance because of the clause in the agreement or something else?

In *Nationwide Ins. Co. v. Patterson, 331 S.E.2d 490 (Va., 1985)* an insurance agent explained to an insured changes that the company made in a medical policy, and in doing so made misrepresentations, to wit, he told the insured that 100% of expenses would be covered whereas the policy stated "100% of all eligible expenses." The company tried to state that the insured did not rely on the agent's statements and that the statements should not bind the company. Having failed, it then proposed that "Huffman's statement was not actionable because it was a mere expression of opinion."

The court stated: "Nationwide relies on a letter written by Huffman after the fact in which he stated that his description of the policy to Patterson was merely

---

1. While we recognize that there is no obligation on the part of a purchaser to check the public record prior to the purchase, LaCourse v. Kiesel, 366 Pa. 385, 389, 77 A.2d 877, 880 (1951), we also note that a purchaser is "required to use his senses, and cannot recover if he blindly relies upon a misrepresentation the falsity of which would be patent to him if he had utilized his opportunity to make a cursory examination or investigation." Restatement (Second) of Torts, § 541 comment a.

his interpretation of the policy. At trial, Patterson said he never heard Huffman use the word 'interpretation' during the conversation in which the misrepresentation was made. The trial court believed Patterson.

"Moreover, where the parties are on unequal terms even an opinion can be actionable. In Cerriglio v. Pettit, we quoted Grim v. Byrd, 73 Va. (32 Gratt.) 293, 301-02 (1879), as follows: 'Even a matter of opinion may amount to an affirmation, and be an inducement to a contract, especially where the parties are not dealing upon equal terms, and one of them has, or is presumed to have, means of information not equally open to the other.' 113 Va. at 541, 75 S.E. at 307. Here, Huffman was an insurance professional, a longtime Nationwide agent, while Patterson, his customer, was a layman. On this record, Huffman must be presumed to have means of information about the policy not equally available to Patterson.

"With regard to the second main issue, Nationwide argues that it is an innocent principal and cannot be held responsible for Huffman's misrepresentation. We cannot accept this contention. Nationwide argues that only by its direct participation can it be held liable for its agents' conduct. We have long adhered to the rule that 'a principal is bound by representations of his agent, made either in the scope of his employment or in furtherance of the object for which he is employed.' Cerriglio v. Pettit, 113 Va. at 542, 75 S.E. at 307. In Jefferson Stand. Ins. Co., we explained that the rule is one of public policy and convenience; we said that 'in no other way could there be any safety to third persons in their dealings, either directly with the principal, or indirectly with him through instrumentality of agents. In every such case, the principal holds out his agent, as competent, and fit to be trusted; and thereby, in effect, he warrants his fidelity and good conduct in all matters within the scope of the agency.' 181 Va. at 834, 27 S.E.2d at 202

"In this case, Huffman was held out as Nationwide's agent. He was so listed in the local telephone directory. He used Nationwide's letterhead. He was sent to Patterson's business by Nationwide to explain the new policy to Patterson. He was acting within the scope of his employment in representing to Patterson the extent of the coverage provided by the policy.

"For all the foregoing reasons, the judgment appealed from will be affirmed."

Question

1. Why might an insurance agent be held to a misrepresentation where a used car salesman might not? What is the nature of reliance in the following relationships: spouse, parent/child, clergy, lawyer, medical doctor, long term friend, insurance agent, real estate agent, used car seller, salesman/woman in clothing store? Could an insurance agent, although not on a level with a spouse or lawyer nevertheless be somewhat above a used car or clothing salesperson in terms of reasonable reliance? Why?

Closing Note

As you can see from this part, escaping contractual liability is not easy. The obvious ways of infancy, mental incompetence, duress, fraud—where because of someone's act or someone's mental state or maturity minds cannot be said to have met objectively or subjectively there is no contract—are neither available to all nor easy to prove. Unconscionability opens a few more doors, warranty can extend mutual mistake, and the Statute of Frauds is always there. Above and in-volved in all, however, is the ever present writing with its ever present integration clauses and language specifically stating that the signatories have relied on noth-ing that is not in the writing.

An individual might escape the impact of this where a standardized contract is used but those who employ them are ever alert to the law's nuances and have learned that once people want something they are likely to not pay much atten-tion to anything you say or anything written and will sign and initial as directed.

In the 1970's a movement began to break through the barrier created by the writing to reach the real intent of the parties and to impose fairness from without —*i.e.* not by interpreting what the parties intended from the printed words no one had read or understood but by asking the courts to construe what was fair and what was not. For a while a double standard developed—for business and for others. To some degree it still exists in F.T.C. (Federal Trade Commission) regulations and in statutes like the Uniform Consumer Credit Code and the Uni-form Consumer Sales Practices Act. In short, the consumer gets a break, that is if the consumer knows enough to demand his/her rights and/or can afford an attor-ney to pursue them or is politically savvy enough to seek out federal and state of-ficials to help.

It is possible to escape liability. It is not easy.

As you review Part V keep in mind conditions in Part IV, parol evidence in Part III and the joke cases in Part I. All the parts interact.

In our last part, Part VI, we will examine third parties, specifically third party beneficiaries to contracts, assignees of contract rights and the liability of a third party who interferes with another's contract. This last area, tortious inter-ference, created a stir when one of America's largest companies, Texaco, was forced to enter Chapter 11 bankruptcy because of an adverse 11 *billion* dollar ($11,000,000,000) judgment because Texaco interfered with the contractual rights of the Pennzoil Company with the Getty Co. Texaco's argument that the Pennzoil/Getty arrangement was not yet a contract because nothing had been signed was swept away by a Texas jury that was told again and again by Pennzoil's lawyer that in Texas a handshake was enough for a contract. There is a lesson here. Don't skip Part VI.

Part VI

Third Parties

Introduction

In this final part of the materials we will consider persons who were not parties to the original contract but who either derive benefit or assume obligation from it or who incur liability because of their interference with it.

This Part is broken into two subparts. In subpart A we consider both third party beneficiaries and third party assignees. In subpart B we consider tortious interference.

In the third party beneficiary scenario, the question is whether a particular person, or group of people, was intended by the original contracting parties to derive a benefit from the contract. If the third party was intended to derive a benefit, then she can sue on the contract if the benefit is not performed, the same as if she were a party to the contract. The problem is often in determining if the particular person was intended to receive the benefit or was merely incidentally benefited from the contract. There is no hard and fast rule for determining this. But there are guidelines. It is these that we will consider.

The second scenario in subpart A is the assignee. This is a person to whom is assigned the rights and often the obligations of one of the original parties to the contract. The difficulty at Common Law with courts enforcing assignments, as well as third party beneficiary contracts, was the Common Law doctrine of privity. Privity meant direct contact or involvement. The third party beneficiary was not in privity because by definition (s)he is not one of the two parties whose agreement created the legally enforceable obligation—the contract. The assignee was not in privity because again (s)he was not a party to the original obligation—only later did one of the original parties assign an obligation to her.

The problem with third party beneficiary contracts usually revolves around the right of the third party to sue on the contract to which (s)he was not a party. Sometimes, however, one of the original parties wishes to ignore the rights of the third party beneficiary and sue on the original contract.

The problems with assignees are more involved,. Can the assignee sue? Can the assignee be sued? Did the assignee intend to accept duties as well as rights when (s)he accepted an assignment of rights to her?

These and other problems we examine in Part A.

A. Creating Rights in Persons Not Party (Privy) to the Original Contract.

1. Third Party Beneficiaries

Problem #1

John Jones owes money to Sam Smith. Al Able owes money to John Jones. Jones goes to Able and says to him: "Instead of paying to me the money that you owe me, please pay it to Sam Smith for me. I owe him money." Able does not pay the money to Smith. Can Smith sue Able on the contract between Jones and Able? Is Smith a third party beneficiary of the contract between Jones and Able?

The basis for this problem is an 1859 New York case[1] which is considered by many to be the seminal third party beneficiary case. The objections to Smith suing Able are two fold: (1) first and most important, Smith was not a party to the contract between Able and Jones. Contract in the 19th century and before was intensely personal and, as we have already seen, subjective. What a person subjectively intended determined whether he was bound and to whom he was bound. The only way to be bound was to make a promise to someone and receive for that promise a valuable consideration. The notion that a person could sue someone on a promise that was never made to the person suing ran afoul of the personal nature of contract. As a dissenting judge put it: "The plaintiff had nothing to do with the promise on which he brought this action. It was not made to him nor did the consideration proceed from him. If he can maintain the suit, it is because an anomaly has found its way into the law of contracts. In general, there must be privity of contract." The majority sidestepped this issue and held the promise enforceable. Two concurring judges "were of the opinion that the promise was to be regarded as being made to the plaintiff through the medium of his agent, whose action he could ratify when it came to his knowledge, though taken without his being privy thereto." Do you see a problem with this theory? Who is who's agent here?

(2) The second objection is that Able received no consideration for his promise to pay Smith. In the original case, Able did not owe Jones money. Rather, Jones gave Able the money and Able promised to pay it to Smith the next day. The court found consideration. Do you see how? In our problem is there consideration for Able's promise to pay Smith? Why is consideration needed? Is it needed?

The type of contract in Problem #1 came to be known as a creditor beneficiary contract. Having boldly stepped forth into a new area of the law, the New York courts retreated. The doctrine grew slowly. Where Y owed money to Z and X promised Y to pay Y's debt to Z the courts, following *Lawrence v. Fox* had little difficulty enforcing the promise. The legal right which Z had to sue X was based on the obligation which Y had to Z. While the agency theory of the concurrence in *Lawrence v. Fox* was not generally relied upon (that X had made a promise to Z through Z's agent Y), the presence of a debt and the 19th century

---

1. *Lawrence v. Fox*, 20 N.Y. 268 (1859).

emphasis on trade, commerce and the movement of money to facilitate commence (among other things this was the great age of the development of negotiable instruments, checks, notes and drafts, which enabled merchants to pay debts without the risk of carrying or transporting large amounts of gold or silver)[2] made the enforcement of promises for the payment of debts attractive even where the promises were not made to the person to be paid.

Soon thereafter there arose what came to be known as the enforcement of "donee" beneficiary contracts. This is where two persons would make a contract not so that one could pay off the debt of the other to a third person, Problem # 1 above, but to confer a benefit on someone to whom no legal obligation was owed. These contracts were generally enforced where the object of the benefit was a spouse, child, or near relative.[3]

From here, the doctrine carried forward to anyone "intended" to be benefited by a contract. In the Restatement of Contracts, First, a creditor beneficiary was someone to whom one of the parties to a contract owed money. The creditor beneficiary was presumed to be intended to be benefited by the parties and could enforce the contract. Any other third party beneficiary who was intended to be benefited was termed a donee beneficiary under the First Restatement. The terms of the promise and the circumstances surrounding it determined whether the parties intended to confer a benefit on the third party and thus whether the promise would be enforceable as a third party donee beneficiary promise.

---

2. The development of paper to represent money - which up to the Great Depression when gold was withdrawn from circulation and the early 1970's when silver was taken from the coinage consisted only of gold and silver - is matched in importance today only by the use of computers to move billions of dollars daily in what are known as wire transfers where no "money" and no paper changes hands. The use of the promissory note in which a person by using the words "to the order of" or "bearer" could make a promise on a piece of paper which could then be enforced by some remote taker of the paper was already in common use among traders, especially merchants involved in international trade, in 1859. If Y sold goods to X, X might give Y a 'promissory note' in which X promised to pay the price of what was sold to Y "or his order" which meant that Y could transfer, "negotiate" the note to someone else (Z) who could then demand payment from X. X's promise to Y was thus enforceable by Z who might never have seen or had anything to do with X. If the note was made by X to "bearer" then X was promising to pay anyone who presented the note for payment.

The "draft" was another instrument in which someone in essence agreed to pay a stranger. Y sells goods to X. Z owes money to X. X and Z agree that X can give drafts to persons who will then present the drafts to Z for payment. X draws a draft (which meant an order) on Z in which X orders Z to pay the price of the goods to Y "or his order." Or X could give Y a draft drawn on Z made out to "bearer." Your ordinary bank check is a demand draft drawn on a bank.

The point of this is that a promise (or order) which was made to one person and which would be enforced by another was not uncommon in 1859. Such promises (or orders) were, however, limited to written promises which contained the words "bearer" or "to the order of" and were in the strict form (not fully described in this note) which the law required for negotiable instruments.

The courts were hesitant to move the rules of negotiable instruments, which derived from what is known as the Law Merchant (the customs of merchants) in England, into the mainstream of the Common Law. At the same time the courts would be more willing to allow strangers to enforce promises if the promises were based on debts owed than if they were simple promises of gifts.

3. See *Seaver v. Ransom*, 224 N.Y. 233, 120 N.E. 139 (1918).

Problem #2

a. Wife says to her brother, "I'm worried about John"(her husband). "Promise me you'll take care of him when I'm gone." Brother says: "I promise."

b. Wife says to her brother, "I'm worried about John" (her husband). If you promise me you'll take care of him when I'm gone, I'll leave Whiteacre to you in my will." Brother says: "I promise."

c. Wife says to her brother, "I'm worried about John" (her husband). "If you promise to take care of him when I'm gone, I'll convey Blackacre to you right now. I want you to take him into your house and make sure he has a good place to live and food and medical and other care just like you would for me." Brother says: "I promise." Wife conveys Blackacre to Brother.

Questions

1. Which of the above promises, if any, are enforceable by husband?

2. Husband learns of Wife's arrangements and says: "I wouldn't live with your brother if he was the last person on earth." Should Wife be able to recover Blackacre from brother? Would Wife be liable to brother for Whiteacre? What problems are inherent here?

In *Lawrence v. Fox* the court wondered what would happen if the original parties discharged the bargain without paying the beneficiary. Jones gave Able money and Able promised to pay Smith. Assume that Jones had said to Able, "I've changed my mind. I'll take the money back. Forget Smith." Could Smith sue Able on Able's promise to Jones or could Jones in effect cancel the promise if Able agreed?

The Restatement 2nd, § 311, would allow Jones to cancel, unless the original contract makes such changes ineffective, or the beneficiary changes position in reliance on the promise before being told of the change.

This raises more problems. Once a third party beneficiary appears to exist, better inquire of him/her if they have relied before trying to cancel. Of course, once you inquire you have given the person ideas and (s)he may decide that reliance has occurred. Better still to say in the contract that there is no intent to confer any benefit on any third parties by the provisions of this contract, that there is no intent to confer any rights to sue on any person other than the immediate signatories to it, that the provisions of the contract are meant to benefit only the immediate signatories, and name who they are.

As time went on, third party beneficiary contracts, and suits by people alleging to be the beneficiaries of them, became more commonplace. One of the most common, and most troublesome, would be contracts between public bodies, such as municipalities, and private agencies for services to the municipalities. In early cases members of the public were not permitted to sue on contracts made by their cities and towns for such things as water service.[4] Later cases found liability

---

4. See *Moch Co. v. Rensselaer Water Co.*, 228 N.Y., 159 N.E. 896 (1928). As the Chief Judge, Benjamin Cardozo, wrote for the court: "[A] member of the public may not maintain an action under Lawrence v. Fox against one contracting with the city to furnish water at the hydrants, unless an intention appears that the promisor is to be answerable to individual

owing to third party beneficiaries.[5] Third party beneficiaries of commercial contracts also sued.[6]

The Restatement 2nd, § 302, divided beneficiaries into intended and incidental. Intended included the old categories of creditor and donee beneficiary, the promisor will satisfy a monitory obligation of the promisee to the beneficiary, or circumstances show that the promisee intended the beneficiary to receive the benefit of the promise. An incidental beneficiary was any other beneficiary. Intended beneficiaries could sue on the promise. Incidental beneficiaries could not. The difficulty was determining the difference.

If a person was named in the contract, this provided some but not conclusive evidence of an intent to benefit the person. For example, if A promises B to pay money to B's niece (N), to pay a debt B owes to C and to pay $500,000 to the Sunshine Benefit Life Insurance Company (S) which is to take out an annuity payable to B during his life, the Restatement would probably consider N and C intended and S an incidental beneficiary. The rationale seems to be that C fits within creditor categories, while N falls into the circumstances (close family relative) categories, but annuity[7] could be paid to B by any number of companies and hence although S is named, S is not intended. To me this is a specious division. Nonetheless there is a rationale here.

Another Restatement 2d example concerns Builder (B) who is to build a house for owner (A). B's contract with A requires B to obtain a surety bond to

---

members of the public as well as to the city for any loss ensuing from the failure to fulfill its promise.... [T]o give a right of action to a member of the public *not formally a party* [t]he benefit...must be one that is not incidental and secondary.... It must be primary and immediate in such a sense and to such a degree as to bespeak the assumption of a duty to make reparation directly to the individual members of the public if the benefit is lost.... By the vast preponderance of authority, a contract between a city and a water company to furnish water at the city hydrants has in view a benefit to the public that is incidental rather than immediate, an assumption of duty to the city and not its inhabitants." [emphasis supplied.]

5. See *Doyle v. South Pittsburgh Water Co.*, 414 Pa 199, 199 A2d 875 (1964). Individuals were allowed to sue the water company for negligence in letting water freeze in the hydrants. The defense that the individuals were not owed a duty under the contract between the city and the water company was discarded as a relic of the past where courts felt obliged to protect those providing essential services. "[W]ater companies...must accept adult responsibility as all other public utilities are required to shoulder it." The court found that where a harm was foreseeable from breach of a duty to a party to the contract and that the harm would extend to non-contracting parties, the duty is owed to all.

6. See *Vikingstadt v. Baggott*, 46 Wash. 2d 494, 282 P.2d 824 (1955). Purchaser (P1) made down payment on real estate to Real Estate Broker (B). Later, P1 became uncertain about whether she wanted the property. A second purchaser (P2) indicated an interest in it if B would promise to return the downpayment to P1. B promised. The money was never returned. P1 sued B on B's promise to P2. P1 prevailed even though the motive for P2 obtaining a promise from B was to make certain she would get a clear title to the land without any claim or cloud by P1. The court said in part (adopting language from an ALR report): "'If the terms of the contract *necessarily require the promisor to confer a benefit upon a third person*, then the contract, and hence the parties thereto, *contemplate a benefit to the third person*...; and this should be sufficient to enable the latter to enforce the contract, although it worked to the advantage of the immediate parties thereto[,]...and although the actual purpose motivating the parties...was the purely selfish one of benefiting or protecting themselves.'"

7. An annuity is like a life insurance policy, except it pays money to the beneficiary during his life, without someone necessarily dying to trigger payment.

insure that all subcontractors and laborers on the house are paid. B contracts with surety company (S) which pursuant to a payment bond to A promises A to pay all of B's debts owing to subcontractors and laborers. Electrician (E) and carpenter (C) work on house and are not paid by B. E and C sue S as third party intended beneficiaries of S's promise to A. E and C will win. Although they are not named specifically, the intent of the promisee (A) is to have these parties benefit from S's promise.

Notice the element of selfishness running through these examples. In the first example B wants to pay money to his niece (not a stranger) and to pay a debt. These things benefit B (although the first would not be a legal obligation even if the promise were made by B to the niece, unless under promissory estoppel.) To pay a debt is to relieve oneself of a liability. However, paying money to S does not relieve B of either a moral or a legal obligation. It will bring B a benefit, but other companies can do the same.

In the second example, E and C could probably get mechanic's liens on the house and even if they could not might be able to sue A in quasi contract for a benefit received, possibly in quantum meruit if B is seen as A's agent. It is in A's best interest to make sure they are paid. Hence, allow them (E and C) to sue S directly on S's promise to A. Even though B contracted with S to get S to promise, so that the consideration to S does not even move from A, the purpose of B's contract with S is to fulfill his own contract obligation with A and A's purpose is to get a house with no clouds on it. However remote A may be from S in terms of legal obligation to S, the whole purpose of S's promise is to benefit A and the only way that can happen is if the unnamed beneficiaries can sue S.

Problem #3

Building contains several condominium units. One of these Units is owned by Y, another by Z. Y and Z operate businesses in the building. The other units are owned by B who by agreement with Y and Z has the right to manage and improve the building. Y and Z pay a condominium charge to B for his management and improvement costs. This charge is based on the amount of space they own in the building and on the cost of maintenance and improvement of the building. B enters contract with construction contractor (C) for building renovations. The contract is to renovate parts of Y's and Z's areas and also the common areas and the units still owned by B. The contract between B and C states in part "C agrees to conduct renovations in such a way that the business of Y and Z will not be disrupted in any way." Y and Z are not mentioned anywhere else in the contract. The contract also states that "C agrees to do all work for B in a thoroughly satisfactory and workmanlike fashion." Although B is satisfied with C's work, Y and Z are not. Y and Z sue C on his promise to B. They claim defects in the work done in their areas. They do not claim defects in the work done in common areas or for disruption of their business while the work was being done. Are they intended beneficiaries? See *F.O. Bailey v. Ledgewood, Inc.*, 603 A.2d 466 (Me 1992). What if they had sued for poor work on common areas? For disruption of their business?

Third party beneficiary contracts are relatively new to the law of contract. For almost a century and a half the law has struggled with the problem. The main point is cautionary. It is probably best today to put a clause in a contract saying that no third party beneficiaries are intended to be created by the contract, unless of course you do intend to create them. Many third party beneficiary contracts are governed, some strictly governed, by statute. Auto insurance. Can the injured person (IP) sue the insurance company (IC) which promised the insured (IN) to pay for damages caused to IP by IN or must IP sue IN? Direct action statutes allowing suit by IP against IC are common. Life insurance. Can the beneficiary of the policy sue the company. If (s)he can't who can once the insured is dead? The insured's estate? Collective bargaining. To what extent can the individual members of the union sue a company for alleged breaches of agreement made between the company and the union?

These and many other third party problems will face you as new technology and new relationships based on it come to fulfillment.

2. Assignment

Like third party beneficiary contracts, assignments concern persons who were not parties to the original contract. Assignment is not a situation where the original parties create rights in a third party as a part of the original contract. Rather, it is a situation where some or all of the rights of one of the original parties are transferred to someone who was not a party. Today, assignment of rights is an essential part of commercial finance. Governed by Article 9 of the Uniform Commercial Code, rights to the payment of money for goods sold or services rendered can be easily transferred, assigned, to third persons either as security for debt or as an outright sale. In a sense the debtor's right to pay her creditor is destroyed. The creditor can assign the right to receive the debtor's payment to anyone and the debtor can be required to pay that person. Under the U.C.C. [9-318] the debtor can demand proof that the person claiming the right to the debtor's payment has in fact been assigned that right by the creditor, and until the proof is forthcoming the debtor may continue to pay the creditor.[8] Such rights are known as accounts. If the rights are embodied in a negotiable instrument (a note, check, draft), then the rules of negotiable instruments apply. If the rights described above are not so embodied they called accounts. The person buying the account, the right to payment, has no greater rights to enforce the account than the assignor, the original creditor.

---

8. A caveat: if the debt is embodied in a negotiable instrument [see footnote 2] the debtor should not pay the creditor without seeing the note and having the amount of the payment recorded on the face of it. Debts embodied in promissory notes and checks have the greatest degree of assignability. Without notice to anyone the creditor can negotiate [*i.e.* transfer possession of] the note to a third person. The third person can demand payment of the debt and if the debtor has paid the creditor without the payments being recorded on the note the debtor will have to pay the third person again. For the third person to have this power, she must be known as a holder in due course—have taken the note for value, in good faith and without notice of any claim or defense. If the payments are on the face of the note, that would be notice, the taker would not be a holder in due course and the debtor would not have to pay twice. As footnote 2 points out the key language which shows whether a note, draft, check is in fact negotiable is the word "bearer" or the words "to the order of." If you see these words you are dealing with negotiable paper, the fastest way to transfer rights prior to the wire transfer. The 1990 Revision provides that checks are negotiable without these words; § 3-104(c).

Rights not governed by the U.C.C. are mortgage rights. To buy a house, a buyer (the mortgagor) will usually give a mortgage to a bank (the mortgagee). The mortgage is a lien on the house and if the buyer does not pay, the bank will foreclose the lien and sell the house to pay the debt. The buyer will also sign a contract, often in the form of a negotiable promissory note, indicating how much and when the buyer will pay off the debt. Often a state statute will take away the principal aspect of negotiability where the note is taken in connection with a mortgage. The problems in paying the creditor who has taken a note which are described in footnote 8 do not apply in many states where the note is part of a mortgage transaction. Specifically, until the debtor is notified that the mortgage and the debt it secures have been transferred, the debtor may go on paying the mortgagee without fear of having to pay twice. But, the mortgage can be transferred.

Privity is not a problem where all the creditor is assigning is rights to payment of money. The right is universally upheld. The problem for the debtor is that he thinks he is dealing with someone locally, *e.g.* a local bank, and the bank has the right to assign its right to payment to a bank somewhere across the country. The debtor can no longer stroll down to the friendly neighborhood bank to explain a late payment or discuss refinancing. If a payment is missed he can expect a late notice, a fee charge, a demand and possibly a threat of foreclosure from that far-away creditor.

The right to assign a right to payment exists even if the contract between the original parties agrees that assignment is prohibited. The assigning party may be (and probably would be) in breach of contract where such a clause exists but the validity of the assignment would not be impaired.

In a very real sense *contract becomes property* at this point where the person to person rights created by two people become transformed into a transferable asset which can be used to secure loans or can be sold outright.

What about delegating obligations to perform? Section 2-210 governs the delegating of the duty to deliver goods. For example, A agrees to sell 1,000 widgets to B for $1 per widget. From our previous paragraphs we know that A can assign her right to the payment of the $1,000 to C and may choose to do so if B is not obliged to pay for the widgets immediately. C may buy A's right to payment for $900 "up front" and take the risk of B not paying and in any event waiting for the time when B's payment comes due. (A clause in the contract between C and A may, however, say that A agrees to buy back uncollectable amounts on the A/B contract thus shifting the risk back to A.) [It is for this reason that you *read* contracts, however dull and uninspiring their language may be.]

Can A delegate to D his obligation to ship 1,000 widgets to B. Under § 2-210, yes. Unless widgets are a special item, or A has special skill, A can delegate to D and B must accept D's performance. If, however, D breaches the contract by shipping the wrong widgets, below quality standard widgets, or too few widgets, A can be held liable for D's breach. Unlike assignment of rights, a contract can provide that duties are not delegable and such clauses will generally be upheld. [Do you see why the courts treat them differently?]

If A were to paint B's portrait, a court would be less likely to allow A to delegate his performance to D. But if A agreed to change the oil in B's car it would probably be a delegable task.

One thing to watch closely is that if an assignor assigns "all my rights under the contract" or "the contract" or some similar general statement, the courts generally construe this as an assignment of rights and a delegation of duties. The assignee by accepting the rights impliedly promises to perform the duties and this promise is enforceable either by the promisee/assignor/delegator or by the person to whom the performance is owing.[9] Example: A agrees to sell widgets to B. A assigns "the contract" to D. D accepts the assignment. D has now accepted the right to be paid by B and the duty to deliver the widgets to B. Restatement § 328 contains the caveat that the rule that assignment of the contract or all rights includes delegating duties may not apply to the purchaser of land who assigns "all her rights under the land purchase" to someone else. This is because a famous New York case, *Langel v. Betz*[10] held that the assignee of a purchaser's right to buy land could not be held subject to the land seller's action in specific performance unless the assignee had specifically bound himself to perform the assignor's duties.

As can be seen, the words "assign all my rights" really mean delegate all my duties. Once again, common usage, or Common Law usage of terms trumps mere logic.

Problem #4

George Jones, a race car driver, agrees with Philip Pots to drive Pots' racing car in the Indianapolis 500 race for $100,000, to be paid after the race. Can Jones assign his right to the $100,000? Can he delegate his duties to drive the car?

Jones hires mechanics (m), tire changers (t) and lubricating assistants (l) to maintain the car during the race at pit stops. May m, t and l assign their rights under their contracts with Jones? May they delegate their duties?

Problem #5

A sells his car to B, the contract stating that B is to pay the price in 10 monthly installments. A assigns his right to payment to C. After paying 1 installment, B refuses to pay more because the engine in the car burned out. A had warranted that the engine would last for at least 25,000 miles. B had driven the car less than 2,000 miles when the engine burned out. C sues B for payment .

1. Would B have a good defense against paying A if A sued B for payment?

2. If B had a good defense against A would the defense be good against C?

---

9. See U.C.C. § 2-210(4) and Restatement of Contracts, 2nd § 328.

10. 250 N.Y. 159, 164 N.E. 890 (1928). In cases for breach of a contract to sell land the buyer, as noted earlier, has an action for specific performance on the theory that land is unique and damages will not make the buyer whole. At earliest Common Law there soon grew up the doctrine of "mutuality of remedy" which said in essence if one party had a right to a particular remedy if the other breached then the other had the same remedy. If buyer could sue for specific performance if seller breached, then seller could sue for specific performance if buyer breached.

Problem #6

A sells his car and his library to B. B gives A a promissory note in the amount of $2,500 payable in 10 monthly installments to the "order of A" in exchange for the car. B signs a contract with A for the library in which B says: "In exchange for A's library, which A is to deliver to me in no less than one week from the time of signing this contract, I, B, promise to pay A $1,500 in 10 installments of $150 each month until this debt is paid." A negotiates the $2,500 note to C and assigns her right to the $1,500 to C. B refuses to pay either the note or the library debt because B claims that A never delivered the library and the car burned out. As part of the car transaction, A had warranted the car's engine for 12 months or 12,000 miles. Less than one month and 1,000 miles had passed. C sues B on the note and contract. Will C prevail on either, both, neither? What other facts, if any, do you need to know?

At Common Law rights were not assignable because they were intangible. We today are so accustomed to disembodied rights that we take no special note of them. To the Common Lawyer, intangible rights were attached to a person—they could not be separated from the person. Tangibles, such as land and chattels, could be separated from the person who owned them. Thus, if A sold a plow to B, A's rights to the plow were able to be separated from it. However, A's right to be paid by B, unlike the plow, was not embodied in anything you could see or touch—it was an intangible and to the Common Law was personal to A and could not be separated from A. This notion was reinforced by privity. A chose to deal with B and B with A. B did not choose to pay C or anybody else to whom A might want to assign her right to payment. These ideas prevailed through the 19th century and into the 20th. It was not until 1978 that the Bankruptcy Code recognized that all rights of a debtor in bankruptcy, tangible and intangible, became part of the bankruptcy estate. Prior to 1978, only property which the debtor could transfer or on which a creditor could get a lien came into the estate. In many states intangibles could not be transferred and creditors could not get liens on them.

In 1970 a professor named Grant Gilmore gave a series of lectures on the death of contract. These later became a short book.[11] Although Gilmore greatly exaggerated the demise of the field, it is fair to say that in the last 30 years certain revolutionary ideas have taken root. Promissory estoppel has moved further into the field. Parol evidence bars fewer contemporaneous and earlier negotiations. An acceptance need no longer mirror an offer to create a contract. Modifications, at least where sale of goods is concerned, do not require consideration. Third party beneficiary contracts and assignment of rights are no longer strange anomalies. On a deeper lever the law is struggling to deal with intangibles in a world in which computerization and world wide communication make intangibles perhaps the most valuable form of property. In the Uniform Commercial Code, Article 2A has been enacted in most states to deal with leases of goods (just as Article 2 deals with sales.) A uniform statute on licensing is being drafted. The *ProCD*[12] and *Hill*[13] cases show the problems of offer and acceptance

---

11. See Gilmore, Grant, *The Death of Contract* (Ohio State University Press 1974, 1995).
12. *Supra* part II-G.
13. *Supra* part II-G.

in an age when the seller is seeking to limit the use of the information contained in his product or to be assured of a particular remedy and the buyer is unaware of the particular terms until she opens the package.

The world of contract is far from dead. In the 1980's a publication to which I became privy noted that the 10 highest monetary awards in litigation for several years running were in contract not tort. Where contract stands now I do not know. But it is likely that the field will expand. People will always make agreements and will want them enforced. Courts will need counsel to figure out to what they agreed. The subject matter and even the manner of becoming obligated may differ; the field will remain.

B. Tortious Interference

In *Texaco, Inc., v. Pennzoil Co.,*[14] one of the largest, if not the largest, jury awards for tortious interference with contractual rights was upheld by an appellate court. The court cut punitive damages from three billion to one billion dollars, but left standing an award of just over seven and one half billion in compensatory damages. Even by Texas standards, this was quite a verdict. Eventually, Texaco filed for protection under Chapter 11 of the Bankruptcy Code (seen by many as a delaying tactic) and following negotiations with Pennzoil ultimately agreed to pay three billion dollars.[15]

What was the essence of the action by Pennzoil against Texaco? Condensing the opinion from its 122 pages is not so difficult as it might seem. Other issues besides contract were before the court, including whether the trial judge had been fair and whether under New York law (which the court determined applied here) three billion in punitive damages was excessive (as mentioned above, it was.) Pennzoil alleged that it had a contract with holders of Getty Oil stock to buy up their large blocs of Getty stock. Texaco, according to the allegation, knowing of the contract between Getty and Pennzoil induced the Getty holders to breach their contracts with Pennzoil by offering them more money. According to Pennzoil, and later a jury and a Texas appellate court, Texaco succeeded and thereby opened itself up to a multi-billion dollar lawsuit. Texaco's defense that there was no contract between Pennzoil and the Getty holders of stock was not accepted by the jury. The case is reminiscent of *Empro, supra* part I-A. When do contract negotiations ripen into a contract and when are they only negotiations? When is something still for sale and when has a sale occurred? In Texas a handshake was good enough for a multi-billion dollar deal. In New York, no one could believe it but they believed it there and that is where the trial was held. The judge made it clear to the jury that they were to find whether Pennzoil and each of the Getty entities intended to be bound. In New York they basically thought you had to have it on paper for it to be binding. It was a multi-billion dollar mistake.

---

14. 729 S.W.2d 768 (Court of Appeals of Texas 1987).

15. See Delaney, Kevin J., *Strategic Bankruptcy* (University of California Press 1992), Chapter 5.

Many aspects of the case were criticized including the manner in which damages were assessed. In theory Pennzoil received damages to compensate it for the loss of the Getty Oil reserves which it would have controlled. Pennzoil was reported to have had a poor record for finding oil and the question was asked if their below par ability to find oil should be compensated. In other words, if Pennzoil had a great record for discovering oil it wouldn't cost that much more finding it than buying Getty's proven reserves. By having a bad record it received higher damages. Nevertheless, the idea behind damages is compensation. What would it cost Pennzoil to make up the loss of the contract benefit it would have received if Texaco had not interfered with its rights to the Getty Oil stock? Pennzoil's inability to find oil easily was Texaco's bad luck. Such harm was presumably foreseeable to Texaco.

Today, where contract is known by experts, *i.e.* lawyers, *i.e.* you to be formable without the various embellishments of the Common Law, the existence of a contract can be more easily found by a jury. While knowledge of its existence by the breaching party must also be proved, that is not so hard as might be thought. The court allowed the jury to rely on press releases and to infer that the Texaco representatives had read them even when some swore they did not and no evidence was produced to prove they had. It was sufficient to establish that the releases appeared in newspapers which oil executives or their employees would be expected to read. Once again, don't overlook evidence in your studies. It's not who's right or wrong. It's who can prove someone is right or wrong. Knowing how to do this is essential.

We have come full circle. We began with intent and we end with it. There has been much in between. There is much more that you will learn in the course of your careers. I hope that these last months have been a good foundation for you.

GOOD LUCK!

Index